HUMAN STRESS AND COGNITION IN ORGANIZATIONS

Wiley Series On
ORGANIZATIONAL ASSESSMENT AND CHANGE

Series Editors:
**Edward E. Lawler III and
Stanley E. Seashore**

HUMAN STRESS AND COGNITION IN ORGANIZATIONS

An Integrated Perspective

Edited by
TERRY A. BEEHR
Department of Psychology
Central Michigan University

RABI S. BHAGAT
School of Management
University of Texas at Dallas

A WILEY-INTERSCIENCE PUBLICATION

JOHN WILEY & SONS

New York · Chichester · Brisbane · Toronto · Singapore

Library of Congress Cataloging in Publication Data:

Main entry under title:
  Human stress and cognition in organizations.

  (Wiley series on organizational assessment and change)
  Includes indexes.
  1. Job stress—Addresses, essays, lectures.
2. Stress (Psychology)—Addresses, essays, lectures.
3. Organizational behavior—Addresses, essays, lectures.
I. Beehr, Terry A. II. Bhagat, Rabi S. III. Series.
HF5548.85.H86 1985 158.7 84-20868
ISBN 0-471-86954-6

Printed in the United States of America

10 9 8 7 6 5 4 3 2

Contributors

TERRY A. BEEHR
Department of Psychology
Central Michigan University

RABI S. BHAGAT
School of Management
University of Texas at Dallas

GEORGE V. COELHO
National Institute of Mental Health
Rockville, Maryland

CARY L. COOPER
Department of Management Sciences
University of Manchester Institute
  of Science and Technology

DAVID L. FORD, JR.
School of Management
University of Texas at Dallas

NINA GUPTA
Department of Management
University of Arkansas

G. DOUGLAS JENKINS, JR.
Department of Management
University of Arkansas

TODD D. JICK
The Faculty of Administrative
  Studies
York University

RALPH KATZ
Human Resource Management
  Department
Northeastern University

ANN E. MCGOLDRICK
Department of Management
  Sciences
University of Manchester Institute
  of Science and Technology

RANDALL S. SCHULER
Graduate School of Business
New York University

JAMES C. SEGOVIS
Federal Home Loan Bank System
Dallas, Texas

JAMES R. TERBORG
Department of Management
University of Oregon

R. VAN HARRISON
Institute for Social Research
The University of Michigan

Foreword

It is difficult to keep a clear, sharp focus, and it is even more difficult to find a good perspective. One can easily lose sight of salient features of the "world" that is the object of research.

Take stress research. New research findings have been appearing at an increasing rate. They seem to present more questions than answers. Uncertainties abound: How should major constructs be defined conceptually? How should these constructs be interrelated theoretically? How can we demonstrate the validity of the operational measures of these constructs? How can threats to the validity of laboratory and field research designs be minimized? What units of analysis (organization, group, person, episode) and sampling plans (number and nature of units, duration and frequency of observation) should be used? How can conflicting findings be reconciled? What viewpoints (micro or macro, physical or psychological, economic or sociological, illness or wellness, etc.) will be helpful?

Here is a book that offers an integrated, multidisciplinary perspective on stress and cognition. This work is an advanced research-based book for researchers and doctoral students which focuses on conceptual and empirical foundations. The authors examine the current state of knowledge in human stress and cognition where *Organizational Stress: Studies in Role Conflict and Ambiguity* by Kahn, Wolfe, Quinn, Snoek and Rosenthal (1964) leaves off.

Beehr and Bhagat begin by offering a theoretical model that interrelates stress and cognition, specifically duration, uncertainty, and importance in decision-making situations. The model is based on the conceptual work of McGrath (1976), Beehr and Newman (1978), Schuler (1980), and others.

All contributing authors use elements of the model in developing their chapters. The authors provide a more complete view of how work-related and other stresses affect individuals at work, and how individuals and organizations learn to cope with stress by using social support and other mechanisms.

Finally, Bhagat and Beehr examine knowledge utilization, surely the issue which provides the impetus for all the rest. Stress research carries its own special burden in this regard because research participants have hopes and expectations concerning ameliorative findings.

Application provides the long-term perspective needed to keep research and theory from getting lost in aimless intellectual meandering. It motivates this work, and its success provides the ultimate criterion. It is a difficult test, and its attainment makes tolerable the stress of lengthy episodes of making decisions about important outcomes.

There are many yet-to-be-resolved theoretical and methodological issues in stress reseach, and it is difficult to keep a clear, sharp focus. The prospect for useful application provides a good perspective, the perspective of this book.

MILTON D. HAKEL

Columbus, Ohio
January 1985

Series Preface

The ORGANIZATIONAL ASSESSMENT AND CHANGE SERIES is concerned with informing and furthering contemporary debate on the effectiveness of work organizations and the quality of life they provide for their members. Of particular relevance is the adaptation of work organizations to changing social aspirations and economic constraints. There has been a phenomenal growth of interest in the quality of work life and productivity in recent years. Issues that not long ago were the quiet concern of a few academics and a few leaders in unions and management have become issues of broader public interest. They have intruded upon broadcast media prime time, lead newspaper and magazine columns, the houses of Congress, and the board rooms of both firms and unions.

A thorough discussion of what organizations should be like and how they be improved must comprehend many issues. Some are concerned with basic moral and ethical questions—What is the responsibility of an organization to its employees?—What, after all, is a "good job"? —How should it be decided that some might benefit from and others pay for gains in the quality of work life? —Should there be a public policy on the matter? Yet others are concerned with the strategies and tactics of bringing about changes in organizational life, the advocates of alternative approaches being numerous, vocal, and controversial; and still others are concerned with the task of measurement and assessment on grounds that the choices to be made by leaders, the assessment of consequences, and the bargaining of equities must be informed by reliable, comprehensive, and relevant information of kinds not now readily available.

The WILEY SERIES ON ORGANIZATIONAL ASSESSMENT AND CHANGE is concerned with all aspects of the debate on how organizations should be managed, changed, and controlled. It includes books organizational effectiveness, and the study of organizational changes that represent new approaches to organization design and process. The volumes in the series have in common a concern with work organizations, a focus on change and the dynamics of change, an assumption that diverse social and personal interests need to be taken into account in discussions of organizational effectiveness, and a view that concrete cases and quantitative data are essential ingredients in a lucid debate. As such, these books consider a broad but integrated set of issues and ideas. They are intended to be read by managers, union officials, researchers, consultants, policy makers, students, and others seriously concerned with organizational assessment and change.

EDWARD E. LAWLER, III
STANLEY E. SEASHORE

Ann Arbor, Michigan
January 1985

Preface

This book presents sixteen original chapters in the growing field of human stress and cognition in organizations. Our objective is to advance theoretical perspectives on various topics in which major research programs have been or could be initiated. Some of the topics discussed have had a significant influence on thinking about how stress might originate within organizations and how it might affect human responses in organizational settings. Issues concerning $P-E$ fit, job characteristics, social support, cognitive appraisal, and coping, for example, have always been very important in shaping theory in the area of human stress and cognition in organizations, and we present chapters by researchers in these areas. In addition, a number of fresh or "new perspectives" in related domains are presented. For example, issues concerning how women and minorities such as blacks and ethnic groups might experience various sources of stress in work organizations and how their stressful experiences might differ from the "mainstream" experiences are discussed. We as editors of this book believe that a careful evaluation of the "mainstream" perspectives—with an appreciation of neglected issues—is necessary for developing new directions for research in this growing area of inquiry. Since the early 1960s there has been a significant increase in the number of research papers, monographs, and books on organizational stress. The publication of *Organizational Stress: Studies in Role Conflict and Ambiguity* by Robert L. Kahn and associates in 1964, marked the beginning of the growing importance of stress, coping, social support, and other related topics in the organizational sciences. Many researchers interested in the psychological processes concerning how people think, relate to each other, and perform in their work roles in organizations have almost by necessity focused on the causes and consequences of human stress in such social systems. We hope this book helps to advance this worthwhile endeavor.

Two growing concerns led to the book's development: a need to provide a definition of the concept of stress which not only relies on earlier major perspectives but goes beyond these perspectives to capture the essence of the concept more fully, and a need to integrate the various topics within a meaningful framework. Chapter One is our attempt to address these two issues.

We discussed the idea of organizing these thoughts in the form of an edited book during a symposium entitled "Effects of Stress on Behavior within Organizations: A Broadened Perspective" in the annual meetings of the Academy of Management in 1980 and again at the Academy meeting in 1981. We realized that we had to identify prospective authors whose current research programs would fit the framework we were planning to develop. Several prospective authors were initially contacted. We were pleased to note that our prospective contributors shared our concern about the state of the field, and they welcomed the idea of a book that attempted to integrate the various topical areas. In each chapter, contributors were asked to develop their theoretical perspectives by attempting to focus on some of the elements of the definition of stress that are presented in Chapter One, to summarize the major findings that have emerged in that particular topical area, and to discuss the directions and implications of their work for future research in human stress and cognition in organizations.

Each chapter was then read by both editors, and the chapters were revised to follow the aims of the book closely: to integrate the knowledge in the area and to help broaden future research perspectives based on a common grounding of the concept of stress in work organizations. The cooperation of the contributors in revising their chapters has been essential to the mission of the book. The contributors had a task more difficult than writing a chapter of the typical edited book, since they were asked to write chapters using a framework that was not of their own creation. They responded to the challenge admirably, as the quality of each chapter attests.

The preparation, editing, and revision of the original chapters by many busy people represented a major effort. We were fortunate to work with a group of enthusiastic authors whose cooperation with this project was particularly crucial to complete the task within a reasonable length of time.

Series editors Edward E. Lawler III and Stanley E. Seashore and Wiley-Interscience editor John B. Mahaney provided encouragement throughout the endeavor. We are particularly indebted to John Mahaney for his helpful advice at various stages of the project. Milton D. Hakel, editor of *Personnel Psychology*, and Harry C. Triandis also provided much appreciated encouragement. Several doctoral students at The University of Texas at Dallas, in particular James C. Segovis, read several chapters and provided useful feedback. Appreciation is also expressed for Barbara Dastoor for her efforts in preparation of the indices of the book. Finally, we are thankful to our families, especially our wives, Karen and Ebha, for their continued support throughout this undertaking. The editorial work for this book was shared equally by us and we are thankful for the cooperation and friendship that this book has generated between us.

TERRY A. BEEHR
RABI S. BHAGAT

Mt. Pleasant, Michigan
Richardson, Texas
January 1985

Contents

HUMAN STRESS AND COGNITION IN ORGANIZATIONS

INTRODUCTION

Part One of this book sets the stage for all chapters that follow by proposing a model of the process experienced by people as their jobs become stressful. The model derives from a great deal of previous research and modeling by a number of people, but probably most directly from Beehr and Schuler (1982), Kahn et al. (1964), and McGrath (1976). It is proposed that many stressful situations related to the work role are experienced by employees as special types of uncertainty and that the effects of stress are dependent upon the duration of the uncertainty and the importance with which the person views probable outcomes related to the uncertainty. Examples are provided in Chapter 1, and subsequent parts of the book integrate several organizational science topics with the model presented in Part One.

CHAPTER ONE

Introduction to Human Stress and Cognition in Organizations

TERRY A. BEEHR AND RABI S. BHAGAT

Writers on stress in organizations and other topics with labels designating similar content areas (e.g., occupational stress, managerial stress, job decision-latitude, staff burnout, and industrial mental health) have created a large and rapidly expanding international literature. This literature focuses both on the policy implications for the effects of stress on employee performance and health and on social science research on the theoretical underpinning of the phenomenon of stress. It is difficult, however, to combine some of the existing concepts into a single theoretical framework. Furthermore, the need for policy-oriented research and the scientific investigation of stress transcend the domain of several social and biological science disciplines, making it very difficult to understand organizationally relevant stress. Stress may be due in part to characteristics of the work, of the nonwork environment, or to characteristics of the person, such as age, sex, and ethnic or cultural origin.

An aim of this book is to provide both a greater awareness of these issues and to combine the conceptual issues within an integrated model of human stress and cognition. Toward this end, the following questions are addressed

What are the common underlying cognitive processes that accompany the selective and differential perception and resolution of stress for different individuals—even while working under identical environments?

How can the stresses from various life domains be viewed in an integrated framework so as to understand the cumulative effects of various types of stress operating on the individual at any given point of time?

How can the individual and the organization be helped to develop coping strategies that allow them to realize the full range of their capabilities and interests within a useful framework?

This book provides a range of perspectives for addressing these issues. It is not, of course, the first attempt to deal with these concerns. During the past three decades a number of theoretical frameworks (e.g., the Kahn–Wolfe–Quinn–Snoek–Rosenthal concept of organizational stress focusing on role ambiguity and conflict, 1964; the French–Rogers–Cobb model of person-environment fit, 1974; the McGrath model of job stress, 1976; the Beehr–Newman facet analysis, review and model linking job stress to organizational effectiveness, 1978; and recently the Schuler conceptualization of stress in organizations, 1980) have been proposed within the stress field. However, the reports on occupational stress are scattered through many published and unpublished documents, both in theoretical as well as applied fields of inquiry, and this results in a relatively rich but unorganized and nonsystematic body of literature. As a consequence, the knowledge that is accumulating in this area is largely unavailable to those who might learn from it and design organizations to minimize any deleterious effects of various stressors with their control.

This introductory chapter discusses the nature of stress within a historical perspective—what it is and why it is important—and examines the pervasiveness of stress in various domains of life in contemporary society. A theoretical cognitive framework for the study of stress is then proposed as a guideline for integrating the themes discussed in later sections of the book. The chapter concludes with an overview of the importance of the framework and with a discussion of some of the themes and assumptions that are presented in subsequent chapters.

AN HISTORICAL PERSPECTIVE

In an examination of the use of stress terminology in today's literature, Selye (1980) noted that stress is a scientific concept which, as with the concept of relativity in physics, has suffered from the fate of being widely used and little understood in scientific circles. Since people are constantly exposed to various kinds of stressors in their daily lives, and because the responses to these stressors often determine the quality of people's lives and their performance in various situations, more knowledge about the causes and effects of stress would help to minimize its harmful effects.

In fact, this general orientation has governed much of the research on stress since its early conception by Hans Selye, who is often called the father of stress research. Although Cannon used the term stress in medicine and psychology as early as 1914 (cf. Mason, 1975), it was Hans Seyle (1956) who revolutionized the medical field with his proposal of nonspecific bodily reactions to many types of demands made upon it. Many of his early examples of "demands" tended to be physical rather than psychological or social demands (e.g., disease-producing agents involved in scarlet fever or flu), perhaps because of his observations as a young student that many such agents seemed to produce the same *general* syndrome. In addition to the unique consequences of these demands, Selye was able to recognize a similar syndrome in response to damage of *any* kind to the body. This syndrome eventually came to be known as the General Adaptation Syndrome (GAS), with its three distinct stages of alarm reaction, resistance, and exhaustion. Alarm is usually described as a generalized call to arms of all of the defenses of the body, resistance is the replenishing of the body's defensive capacities that were somewhat depleted in the alarm stage, and exhaustion is the premature aging and breakdown of the body due to excessive demands which the body is having difficulty meeting.

The initial description by Selye, based upon the observation of physical stressors or demands, have subsequently been enlarged to include psychological demands such as the type of work an employee does and the lifestyle of an individual (Selye, 1974). Whereas the initial, biological stressors seemed clearly to be demands upon the *body*, most of the psychosocial types of stressors appear to be more directly making demands upon the person's behaviors, thoughts, or attitudes. Still, Selye has maintained that these stressors have physical effects just as the physical stressors do, and Mason (1975) has observed that the overwhelming bulk of interest and effort in the field today is concerned with this type of psychological stress rather than with the physical stressors. Most of this more recent research and practice regarding the psychological stressors or demands have followed Selye's theory and propositions only very loosely. Instead, this research has been relatively atheoretical, seeking only to find linkages between psychological demands or states and mental or physical dysfunction.

An historically important set of studies that were among the first post-Selye efforts to uncover such linkages were the Executive Monkey studies (Brady, 1958), in which a monkey that was forced to make "decisions" (with punishments for being incorrect) developed ulcers, while another monkey (which received the same punishments but made no decisions) did not develop ulcers. It was generally concluded, therefore, that the decision-making situation can be stressful if there are important consequences attached to one's decisions.

It is important to note that Selye has always had critics within the medical research professions (Mason, 1975) and that some physiological psychologists' results are contrary to Brady's results (e.g., Weiss, 1968). Nevertheless, the general concept of stress as a real phenomenon is widely accepted; the biggest controversies concern specific definitions, theories, and models offered to explain the causes and effects that are included by various experts in this field.

IMPORTANCE OF STRESS IN TODAY'S WORLD

Stress at work affects employee behavior in adverse ways. Some of the effects associated with stress are neuroses, coronary heart disease, alimentary conditions such as dyspepsia and ulcers, cancer, asthma, hypertension, backaches, and the use of alcohol and drugs (Beehr and Schuler, 1980). It is believed that stress can cause these problems or at least make them more severe. The list offered here is quite broad and diverse, and that fits with Selye's description of stress as having nonspecific results on the individual. It is in part this very generality of effects that leads to the conclusion that stress is indeed important in our everyday lives.

In terms of its effect on the economy of the nation, stress at work seems to play a very important role. Nationally, for example, the results of stress might be seen in overuse of medical and mental health facilities, or from reduced Gross National Product due to increased illnesses. It has been estimated that the economic cost of peptic ulcers and cardiovascular disease, to name but two potential effects of stress, is around $45 billion annually in the United States (Putt, 1970; Moser, 1977), and Greenwood (1978) has estimated that the cost of executive stress alone is in the billions of dollars. Most such estimates are based upon the direct costs of illnesses. In addition, it is probable that there is some additional cost due to decreased organizational effectiveness of employees who show up for work but who are operating at reduced levels of effectiveness.

Another indication of the importance placed upon stress is that some worker compensation laws now make an employing organization liable for employees' mental as well as physical illnesses if they are due to or made more severe by any aspect of employment. Thus, the legal machinery of the nation may force even those organizations that would rather ignore the problem to see it as important.

FRAMEWORK FOR UNDERSTANDING HUMAN STRESS AND COGNITION IN WORK ORGANIZATIONS

As indicated earlier, this book offers an integrated model for understanding the role of stress and cognition in today's organizational contexts. Stress is defined as a cognitive state in which an individual confronts a decision-making or problem-solving situation characterized by high levels of *uncertainty*, associated with obtaining *important* (i.e., positively valent) outcomes and, in which existence of such uncertainties are long in their *duration*.

This definition of stress incorporates several important aspects of stress definitions and stress research from both the health and organizational sciences. Stress is viewed here as a multiplicative function of uncertainty, importance, and duration. Figure1-1 depicts this graphically and in mathematical form: $S = (U_c \times I \times D)$. This multiplicative function suggests that there would be no stress in a situation where the individual (1) has no *important set* of outcomes to obtain, (2) has no *uncertainties* associated with obtaining the rewards or outcomes, or (3) experiences these conditions for virtually no length of time (*duration* is close to zero).

It should be noted that the term *decision-making* is used broadly here, so that it encompasses McGrath's (1976) notion of "response selection" in his four-stage cycle of job stress. Anyone who is performing any action has made a decision in the sense that he or she has chosen one course of action from among many potential courses. Although many such response selections do not involve complex decisions, they are decisions nonetheless, and they become more stressful as the uncertainty of important outcomes attached to those actions increases. Thus, making a telephone call, going to work on time, and firing an unproductive subordinate are all activities that result from decisions according to this view, although each decision may not take equal amounts of time and thought to make.

It is also proposed in Figure 1-1 (second example) that stress will be a function of the perceived demands on the individual and the perceived resources and coping strength of the individual, multiplied by the perceived importance of meeting the demands and the duration of the situation. The exact nature of the combination of environmental demands and individual resources is unspecified in Figure 1-1, because while there are several stress theories incorporating these two concepts, the way in which the concepts are combined vary from theory to theory. The function is unspecified, therefore, in order to be consistent with more than one theory of stress.

One such theory comes from part of the Person-Environment (*P-E*) fit approach, in which the absolute difference between organizational demands and employee abilities is related to the experience of stress (Van Harrison, in his chapter, refers to this difference in his discussion of stress that leads to strain for the organization rather than for the individual; his focus in explaining stress on the individual employee, however, describes a *P-E* fit between two different dimensions). McGrath (1976) alternatively proposes that this absolute difference be subtracted from a constant in order to predict stress outcomes. In effect, this would have the opposite meaning: Smaller differences between the two elements would result in more stress. Two of the better-known approaches, therefore, have some agreement on the elements within brackets in the second example of Figure 1-1 but are almost directly contradictory in their explanations regarding the means of combining the elements.

1. *In Problem—Solving and Decision—Making Situations.*

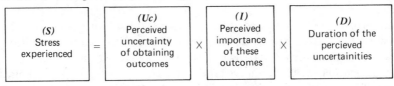

2. *In Other Situations Which Do Not Involve Decision—Making and Problem Solving.*

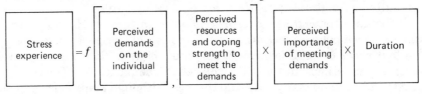

3. *Additivity Feature of the Present Conceptualization.*

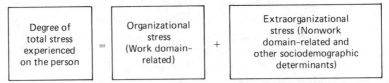

Figure 1-1   A framework for understanding components of human stress and cognition in organizations.

It can be noted that if the elements in brackets in the figure were replaced by the concept of uncertainty, the second example would be remarkably similar to the first example in the figure. It should be no surprise, therefore, that we propose that the particular combination of the two elements in brackets will lead to stress primarily if it results in uncertainty for the individual. Consistent with this, McGrath's (1976) formula was based on his logic that this particular combination of the elements would result in uncertainty, but there is little strong evidence available to support or refute this logic. Furthermore, it is possible that more than one combination could result in uncertainty. More research is needed before reaching a conclusion on this issue.

Explanation of the Components of the Present Conceptualization of Stress Importance

The concept of importance does not imply only positive importance of outcomes. An outcome can be very important because it is extremely negative or aversive to the individual; for example, the possibility of losing one's job or of losing one's life due to terminal illness. An outcome can be important either because it is very attractive or because it is very repulsive to the individual. It is, however, the individual's own perception of the attractiveness or repulsiveness of the outcome that is the issue here. What other people think about the outcome is irrelevant except insofar as those opinions of others influence the individuals's own opinions.

This concept of importance is related to the concept of valence in expectancy theory of motivation (e.g., Mitchell and Biglan, 1970; Lawler, 1973; Vroom,1964). Valence is often measured by researchers on a single scale, although it actually has two dimensions. The dimensions are direction and strength. An outcome may be attractive or repulsive (positive or negative direction of valence), and attractiveness or repulsiveness may vary in strength from very strong to very weak. The concept of importance in the present framework is analogous to the *strength* dimension of valence. The model is not formally concerned with the *direction* of valence, but instead focuses on the strength with which the outcome is attractive or repulsive. When that strength nears zero, there is likely to be little stress, and when the strength increases, the stress will also increase (if $Uc > 0$ and $D > 0$).

The origin of the importance an individual places upon a given outcome is presumably based, in part, in his or her past life experiences. In a given culture there may be some shared norms among people in how they value various objects and events, but there is also some variation from person to person within the same culture. This is because people within the same culture share many common experiences in their development from infancy to old age, and yet they still have some experiences that are different from the majority's experiences. Thus, for example, many Americans are likely to value a promotion in their work positively, but some will value it more positively than others. In addition, some Americans even value a promotion negatively. The strength (rather than the direction) of the importance is proposed to be the primary concern in the stress framework offered here, and it is of some concern to this discussion that there is variation among people in the strength of the importance they attach to such outcomes. To the extent that such variation exists, then, the same demand characteristics would result in varying degrees of stress among individuals. The framework handles this concept with its recognition that importance can vary.

Uncertainty

The uncertainty in the framework can also be linked to expectancy theory, but it is linked to the expectancies rather than to the valences in this theory. Expectancy theory usually is used to predict motivation to perform some activity or to strive for some goal; expectancies are the individual's subjective probability that (1) his or her effort will result in the desired level of performance behaviors ($E \rightarrow P$) or that (2) his or her performance behaviors will result in obtaining various outcomes ($P \rightarrow O$). In work, the meaning of performance is obvious. In nonwork situations, its meaning is any *behavior* that one's friends, family, and other important associates expect of him or her. For example, in moving from one geographic location to another (a potential life stress), there might be a conflict between one's own desire to move and one's spouse's desire to remain. This geographic move is a *behavior*, and there may be conflicting demands upon the person regarding this behavior.

In typical versions of expectancy theory, motivation is predicted to be based upon a combination (usually multiplicative) of the valences and the *level* of these expectancies. In the stress framework the clarity or *certainty* of these expectancies, rather than their level, is addressed. It is proposed that, in stressful circumstances, individuals are actually uncertain regarding the level of their own expectancies. They do not know whether the probability of obtaining outcomes based upon their own performance or the probability of their own performance being related to their effort is high, low, or somewhere between.

Table 1-1 outlines the propositions regarding the effects of three examples of demand characteristics (ambiguity, overload, and underutilization) that are popularly offered as stressors in the literature (e.g., Kahn et al., 1964; French and Caplan, 1973; Beehr and Newman, 1978). Uncertainty may appear in the $E \rightarrow P$, $P \rightarrow O$, or both expectancies. The three stressors in Table 1-1 were chosen to illustrate each type of uncertainty.

In the first column the perceived demands refer to any felt demand or request upon an individual to do something; for example, to perform at a high level in one's work. Although it is easiest to think of these demands as emanating from others in one's environment (e.g., one's supervisor or one's spouse), the demands may also originate within the person—people can place demands upon themselves that cause uncertainty!

Reviewing this table briefly, when the demands themselves are ambiguous—for example, when people are not sending clear messages re-

Table 1-1 An Expectancy Framework for Understanding the Uncertainty Inherent in Stress

Stressors: Perceived Demand Characteristics (Examples of Stressors)	Uncertainty Regarding an Expectancy	
	Effort-to-Performance Expectancy ($E \rightarrow P$)	Performance-to-Outcome Expectancy ($P \rightarrow O$)
Ambiguity	Uncertainty	Uncertainty
Overload	Uncertainty	
Underutilization of skills		Uncertainty

garding what they expect of an individual—it is proposed that the individual may become uncertain regarding the level of both types of expectancies. He or she may not be certain how to direct his or her own efforts if there is ambiguity regarding the performance that is demanded (resulting in an uncertain $E \to P$), and people also sometimes send ambiguous messages regarding the outcomes that will accrue based upon "successful" or "unsuccessful" performance (resulting in an uncertain $P \to O$). Both of these kinds of uncertainties have been included in measures of stressful ambiguities in the literature.

In Table 1-1, overload is predicted to create uncertainty in the $E \to P$ expectancy. This stressful demand characteristic represents the situation in which individuals are uncertain of meeting the required levels of performance, even though it may be clear to them what the definition of good performance is. Rather than lack of clarity regarding the definition of good performance, the problem inherent in these demand characteristics is that the individuals may not be able to perform at the required levels, due to lack of time or ability. The uncertainty is whether they can perform well even if they try hard (effort). They may still be certain that they would receive the outcomes if they were able to perform the required behavior $(P \to O)$.

Underutilization of skill, the third stressor in the table, is represented by the situation in which people have some special abilities and skills that they would like to use but are prevented from using in a given situation. A work-related example might be a job which is too menial for the employee; a nonwork example might be a marital conflict in which one spouse is habitually given only menial family tasks (e.g., washing the dishes), while the other engages in the more complex and challenging tasks (e.g., the family's financial planning). As the first spouse does the menial tasks, he or she may be very certain the effort (e.g., at washing the dishes) will lead to performance, but a particular kind of $P \to O$ expectancy would be uncertain. This particular type of $P \to O$ expectancy is the type in which the outcome is intrinsic rather than extrinsic. For many people an intrinsic outcome such as a sense of worthwhile accomplishment is an uncertain outcome from the performance of menial tasks, because the task is so simple that it could be done by almost anyone without using one's valued high-level skills. This is true of either employment or in not-for-pay tasks. Why should the individual feel a sense of worthwhile accomplishment in performing a task requiring little effort or skill?

It is appropriate to comment here on the fact that the demands, expectancies, and their uncertainty in the framework are *perceptions*. In Table 1-1, the overload, ambiguity, and underutilization job characteristics refer to perceived overload, ambiguity, and underutilization of skills. The experience of stress from each of these is due to uncertainty that comes from perceiving such characteristics in one's life roles. Similarly, the expectancies and the uncertainty itself are perceptions of the individual in the potentially stressful situation. Two people in the same objective situation may not experience equal amounts of stress, therefore, since their perceptions of that situation may differ somewhat.

All of the perceptions involved in the framework come, in part, from the objective situation of the individual; that is, in part, the person perceives his or her environment accurately. One is more likely, for example, to perceive a situation of overload when one has many things demanded of him or her than when fewer things are demanded. Thus, an adult who has recently lost a spouse through death or divorce, and who must care for five children and also work for a living, is likely to feel more overloaded than before the loss of the spouse.

The expectancies are subjective (perceived) probabilities of the extent to which two events are related (E and P or P and O). These come in part from the present objective situation and in part from the past objective situations the individual has experienced. In work situations, for example, if an employee has a contract that specifies that pay will be based upon performance (e.g., a piece-rate incentive system), the employee is likely to have a relatively strong $P \to O$ expectancy (for the one O, pay). An example of past situations influencing present expectancies might be the expectancy of being able to obtain a mortgage on a new house. If one had obtained mortgages on houses previously, one might expect that effort to obtain the mortgage this time would also have a high probability of success (an $E \to P$ expectancy). This may be an example of lack of congruence between objective and subjective situations, however, if the amount of mortgage money in the economy has declined since one's last application for a mortgage. Thus, experiences in similar situations in the past can be used as a cue for current expectancies.

Objective past or present situations only explain part of the present perceptions of any individual, however. To some extent these perceptions also are idiosyncratic and due to distortion of the objective environment by the person. It seems likely, for example, that people with strong intolerance of ambiguity would tend to reduce the ambiguity in any way possible. One such way may be to perceive the environment incorrectly; that is in this case to perceive demands or expectancies clearly when there is little objective reason for doing so. Here it is argued that such people might seldom experience ambiguity in demands; even if they were receiving demands that most people would perceive as ambiguous, they would interpret them in some way to make them clear. It is proposed, therefore, that the perceived demands, expectancies, and uncertainties are partly due to the accurate perception of the objective environment (past or present), and partly due to inaccurate perception of this environment.

Duration

The concept of duration is an important one in the stress framework. It helps in distinguishing between coping and adaptive skills that demand mobilization of new resources when confronted with an acute, situationally determined stressful event versus coping and adaptive skills that require continuous monitoring of various kinds of resources when confronted with a gradually developing stressful event. In the field of medicine, as progress has been made to conquer or control acute illness, the focus has begun to shift to finding cures for chronic diseases of long-lasting duration. However, in the field of organizational sciences, research on stressful events of long-term durations have been relatively rare. Kasl's work (1979) on job loss and plant shutdown and some recent work in the area of job transfer (reviewed in Brett, 1980) are examples of work that involve looking at stressful events that require longer periods of time if they are to be resolved fully or coped with adequately.

The concept of duration provides a theoretical argument for analyzing human stress for the following reasons:

1. The cognitive processes (i.e., learned helplessness, feelings of depression, etc.) pertaining to resolution of "stress" and "distress" in long-term phenomena are different from those involved in short-term phenomena (Weick, 1969; Doob, 1971).

2. As mentioned earlier, coping and adaptive resources vary, depending on whether one is coping with a long-term event or a short-term event.

The Abramson et al. (1978) theory about learned helplessness can be tied with our notion of duration associated with some stressful events. Stressful events requiring long-term and repeated coping and adaptive resources may induce the person to experience lack of control over the event and his or her environment, and such lack of control over important outcomes could lead to depression (Abramson et al., 1978). Therefore, duration is an important element in the formulation of stress.

Types of Outcomes: Intrinsic versus Extrinsic Sources of Stress

The expectancy theory framework for stress applies to both intrinsic and extrinsic outcomes, as can be noted from the preceding discussion. The intrinsic/extrinsic dichotomy is not as simple as it may appear, since some outcomes seem to contain elements of both. The receipt of extrinsic outcomes may be a type of feedback to the individual indicating successful performance, and this feedback may trigger the intrinsic rewards such as sense of worthwhile accomplishment. Thus, the two may often appear simultaneously, making their distinction practically difficult even if theoretically easy.

Apparently the theoretical distinction between intrinsic and extrinsic outcomes is not so clear either, however, as a study by Dyer and Parker (1975) illustrates. Industrial/organizational psychologists, professionals who use the intrinsic/extrinsic terminology frequently in their work, were asked in different ways to define and give examples of intrinsic and extrinsic outcomes. The conclusion was that the results supported the "confusion" hypothesis. There was not good agreement among these professionals regarding the conceptualization of this dichotomy. These professionals did not agree in their definitions of intrinsic and extrinsic outcomes.

The distinction is not especially crucial for the stress framework proposed here, but readers should be forewarned that outcomes that might be used as examples in this book may seem widely divergent and strange if only one type were inferred from reading the word *outcome*. The authors prefer to consider outcomes that are typically awarded to the individual directly by others (family, friends, the organization or its agents, etc.) as extrinsic, and outcomes that are given directly to the individual only by himself or herself as intrinsic (feelings of pride, accomplishment, achievement, etc.). This is consistent with most other general definitions, although a complete listing of the specifics in each category might conflict with the specifics offered by others with the same general definition.

ADDITIVITY OF STRESS FROM VARIOUS LIFE DOMAINS

The overall amount of stress experienced by a person is represented as follows:

$$\text{Stress} = \left[\sum_{i=1}^{n} (I_i \times Uc_i \times D_i) \right] \text{Work Domain}$$

$$+ \left[\sum_{j=1}^{m} (I_j \times Uc_j \times D_j) \right] \text{Nonwork Domain}$$

As indicated in Figure 1-1, it is proposed that the total stress an individual experiences is a combination of the stresses from both work and nonwork domains.

This additivity proposal is offered as a starting point for future research. Since there is little empirical evidence regarding the manner in which work- and nonwork-related stress combine to affect the total human being, the simplest combination is recommended here. Research may eventually lead to the discarding of this proposition in favor of an interactive approach in which specific types of work- and nonwork-related stress may add to, dampen, or exacerbate the effects of each other.

The stressful life events scales in the literature (e.g., the scales from Holmes and Rahe, 1967; Sarason et al., 1978) are constructed and scored in a manner that is generally consistent with the additivity hypothesis, since they contain both work- and nonwork-related items and the person's score is obtained via a (weighted) sum across all items. On the other hand, many intuitive combinations of work- and nonwork-related stressors impinging upon dual career couples may have interactive effects (e.g., see Chapter Six).

COMMENTS ABOUT SOME OF THE THEORETICAL FORMULATIONS USED IN THE BOOK

In editing this volume, an attempt has been made to provide a thematic overview and a general conceptual framework for understanding human stress and cognition in organizations. An attempt will now be made to focus on some specific points of departure suggested in this book.

Level of Specificity as Suggested in This Framework

The expectancy framework for understanding the uncertainty inherent in stress is, in some ways, more specific than many of the previous approaches to stress. In work-related stress, for example, one popular approach is to compare and even rank-order occupations along a stress continuum to indicate which jobs are most stressful. When this comparison is completed, one has some idea regarding the relative degree of stress that is typically inherent in several jobs (often by comparing "illness" rates of the workers), but it is still unknown *why* those jobs are stressful. The proposed framework allows an analysis of the demand characteristics of the various jobs, in terms of three components, to help understand *why* those jobs are stressful. Another popular approach to work-related stress is to analyze the jobs in terms of some of the demand characteristics, such as those in Table 1-1, and to find statistical associations between them and employee health and welfare (e.g., Kahn et al., 1964; Beehr, 1976). The proposed framework represents an attempt to integrate the findings of many such studies into a single overall conceptual scheme involving *importance*, *uncertainty*, and *duration*.

This framework is also more specific than the popular approach to life stress mentioned previously, namely the procedure of relating life events to the incidence of illness (e.g., Holmes and Rahe, 1967; Sarason et al., 1978). The framework can be used for analyzing stressful life events in order to determine why they are stressful; that is, what is uncertain, how important it is, and how long its duration would be within each such event. Thus, for example, it might be asked, what are the particular uncertainties involved in losing one's job or in other stressful life events?

In some ways the framework is also *less* specific than it might be. One might hypothesize, for example, that uncertainty of $E \rightarrow P$ is more deleterious in its effects upon the person's well-being than the uncertainty of $P \rightarrow O$ is, or vice-versa. In addition, it might be hypothesized that uncertainty regarding $P \rightarrow O$ varies systematically according to whether the O in question is an intrinsic or an extrinsic outcome. Each of these hypotheses is an intriguing question and is worthy of thought and research, but the present framework stopped short of making such proposals because there is little evidence upon which to base such specific hypotheses. Instead, the authors chose to take a more conservative (and parsimonious) approach by taking only the first step in the direction of integrating such disparate research findings as now exist.

Person-Environment (*P-E*) Transaction as a Central Feature of the Present Conceptualization

The present formulation focuses on the dynamic processes of *P-E* transactions as important elements in the determination of stress. Cognitive processes involving *P-E* exchanges are not simply static *cognitions* but rather are viewed as stages of phenomenological activities linking the person to environment. It is suggested that reactions to stress and coping resources brought to bear in each situation are products of cognitions that construe the basis of how a person appraises his or her transactions with the environment. Thus, the theme of cognitive appraisal (e.g., due to Coyne and Lazarus, 1980) becomes an extremely important one in the present formulation. The role of these evaluative cognitions is to help determine the person's stress reactions, emotional outcomes, and coping strategies.

Interdisciplinary Approach for Studying Stress

In line with our earlier observations, this topic of stress needs to be considered in a comprehensive fashion. Since stress transcends narrowly defined micro and macro disciplinary areas within the behavioral sciences, we have included contributions that reflect this healthy trend. For example, the study of stress in nonwork situations is an important element in the overall scheme of how an employee might define and adapt to his or her overall pattern of stress reactions. Topics traditionally not discussed in organizational literature have been given their due recognition if they help to broaden the knowledge of how stress and cognition interact within organizational settings.

STRUCTURE OF THE REMAINDER OF THE BOOK

The remainder of the book carries the stress model developed here through an exploration of several points of organizational life thought to be stressful for the individuals involved.

In Part Two typical sources of stress in modern-day organizations are addressed, using the stress model. Two of the most common ways of thinking about organizational stress are explored in the chapters on person-environment fit and the job characteristics approaches to stress, and the stressful effects of the current and recurrent economic recessions are addressed in a special chapter on the relationship of budget cuts to stress.

While Part Two investigates general approaches to job stress within organizations, Part Three examines stress at the interface between organizations and their environments. The three chapters of this section focus on stress evolving from the individual's initial contacts with the organization, on an increasingly common stressful state of people during the middle and all phases of organizational membership (dual careers), and on stress encountered when the individual prepares to and does leave the organization through retirement.

Parts Four and Five carry this work-nonwork interface theme further by presenting an explication of the stresses that become apparent when organization members' extraorganizational lives are recognized as important for understanding members' actions and reactions both at work and off the job. Thus, personal lives and demographic-cultural characteristics of employees are parts of the individual that cannot be ignored if one is to understand the topic.

In Part Six a model of the coping process is presented, and one of the best-known and widely accepted ways of alleviating the negative effects of stress (the use of social support) is investigated with respect to the stress model presented in the first chapter.

Finally, Part Seven concludes the book with discussions of potential applications and recommendations for future research regarding the model of job stress presented here.

Focus on Relevance of the Book for Coping with Stress and Organizational Practice

An attempt has been made to make this book helpful for organizational practice. The editors and the contributors are acutely aware that unless the theoretical work on stress focuses on the real-life problems of the work organization, the book will serve only as an academic exercise with little use for practitioners who are constantly engaged in search for better theoretical frameworks for understanding and managing stress. The editors truly believe, as has often been attributed to Kurt Lewin, that there is nothing more practical than a good theory.

REFERENCES

Abramson, L. Y., Seligman, M. E. P., and Teasdale, J. D. Learned helplessness in humans: Critique and reformulation. *Journal of Abnormal Psychology*, 1978, **87**, 49–74.

Beehr, T. A. Perceived situational moderators of the relationship between subjective role ambiguity and role strain. *Journal of Applied Psychology*, 1976, **61**, 35–40.

Beehr, T. A. and Newman, J. E. Job stress, employee health, and organizational effectiveness: A facet analysis, model, and literature review. *Personnel Psychology*, 1978, **31**, 665–699.

Beehr, T. A. and Schuler, R. S. Current and future perspectives on stress in organizations. In K. M. Rowland and G. R. Ferris (Eds.), *Personnel management: New perspectives*. Boston: Allyn and Bacon, 1982.

Brady, J. V. Ulcers in "executive monkeys." *Scientific American*, 1958, **199**, 95–100.

Brett, J. Effects of job transfer on employees and their families. In C. L. Cooper and Roy Payne (Eds.), *Current concerns in occupational stress*. New York: Wiley, 1980, 99–136.

Coyne, J. C. and Lazarus, R. S. Cognitive style, stress perceptions, and coping. In I. Kutash and L. Schlesinger (Eds.), *The handbook on stress and anxiety*. San Francisco: Jossey-Bass, 1980, 144–158.

Doob, L. *Patterning of time*. New Haven: Yale University Press, 1971.

Dyer, L. and Parker D. F. Classifying outcomes in work motivation research: An examination of the intrinsic-extrinsic dichotomy. *Journal of Applied Psychology*, 1975, **60**, 455–458.

French, J. R. P., Jr. and Caplan, R. D. Organizational stress and individual strain. In A. J. Marrow (Ed.), *The failure of success*. New York: AMACOM, 1973.

French, J. R. P., Jr., Rogers, W., and Cobb, S. Adjustment as person-environment fit. In G. V. Coelho, D. A. Hamburg, and J. E. Adams (Eds.), *Coping and adaptation*. New York: Basic Books, 1974.

Greenwood, J. W. Management stressors. In *Reducing occupational stress*. Cincinnati: NIOSH Research Report, 1978.

Holmes, T. H. and Rahe, R. H. The Social Readjustment Rating Scale. *Journal of Psychosomatic Research*,1967, **11**, 213–218.

Kahn, R. L., Wolfe, D. M., Quinn, R. P., Snoek, J. D., and Rosenthal, R. A. *Organizational stress: Studies in role conflict and ambiguity*. New York: Wiley, 1964.

Kasl, S. The Impact of retirement. In C. L. Cooper and R. Payne (Eds.), *Current concerns in occupational stress*, New York: Wiley, 1980, 137–186.

Lawler, E. E. III. *Motivation in work organizations*, Monterey, Calif.: Brooks-Cole, 1973.

Mason, J. W. A historical view of the stress field. *Journal of Human Stress*, 1975, **1**, pt. 1, March, 6–12, pt. 2, June, 22–35.

McGrath, J. E. Stress and behavior in organizations. In M. Dunnette (Ed.), *Handbook of industrial and organizational psychology*. Chicago: Rand McNally, 1976.

Mitchell, T. and Bigland, A. Instrumentality theory: Current uses in psychology. *Psychological Bulletin*, 1971, **76**, 432–456.

Moser, M. Hypertension: A major controllable public health problem—industry can help. *Occupational Health Nursing*, 1977, August, 19–26.

Putt, A. M. One experiment in nursing adults with peptic ulcers. *Nursing Research*, 1970, **19**, 484–494.

Sarason, I. G., Johnson, J. H., and Siegel, J. M. Assessing the impact of life changes: Development of the Life Experiences Survey. *Journal of Consulting and Clinical Psychology*, 1978, **46**, 932–946.

Schuler, R. S. Definition and conceptualization of stress in organizations. *Organizational Behavior and Human Performance*, 1980, **24**, 184–215.

Selye, H. In I. Kutash and L. Schlesinger (Eds.), *The handbook of stress and anxiety*. San Francisco: Jossey-Bass, 1980, 127–143.

Selye, H. *The stress of life*. New York: McGraw-Hill, 1956.

Selye, H. *Stress without distress*. Philadelphia: Lippincott, 1974.

Vroom, V. H. *Work and motivation.* New York: Wiley, 1964.

Weick, K. *Social psychology of organizations,* (2nd ed.). Reading, Mass.: Addison-Wesley, 1979.

Weiss, J. M. Effects of coping responses on stress. *Journal of Comparative and Psysiological Psychology,* 1968, **65**, 251–260.

CAUSES AND CONSEQUENCES OF ORGANIZATIONAL STRESS

Part Two focuses on the nature of stress in organizational life. Chapter 2 describes one of the more advanced theories of occupational stress, the person-environment (*P-E*) fit theory. That chapter notes that the role of uncertainty in occupational stress may be explained as either a *P-E* fit (or lack of fit) on the dimension of environmental uncertainty in the present or in the anticipated future. Combinations of fit on uncertainty and fit on other environmental dimensions (e.g., work load) are examined, and hypotheses are proposed for these combinations.

Chapter 3 examines the dimensions of uncertainty, importance, and duration in employing organizations, describing and proposing differentiation between the concepts of role ambiguity and uncertainty. Relationships between characteristics of jobs thought to be stressful and a variety of types of work-related effectiveness are proposed.

Finally, Chapter 4 describes the nature of an increasingly common source of stress in organizations: budget cuts. It is proposed that one source of employee stress is the uncertainty resulting from budget cutting or from anticipated budget cutting, and the duration of the effects of those cuts.

CHAPTER TWO

The Person-Environment Fit Model and the Study of Job Stress

R. VAN HARRISON

What is the ultimate source of job stress? Some researchers have focused on the demands of the job, such as work overload, uncertainty, and alienating technologies. In their extreme form these situations will be stressful for most individuals. Other researchers have focused on characteristics of the worker, such as aptitudes, Type A behavior, rigidity in dealing with problems, and achievement motivation. Individuals falling at either extreme on any of these characteristics would probably find many typical occupations to be stressful. Clearly, characteristics of both the job and the individual can make important contributions to stress.

How can the contributions of the job and the person be systematically analyzed and integrated in the study of job stress? At first glance this question seems simple. However, the problems in integrating the effects of the person and the environment are as complex as people and as occupations. For several years researchers at the Institute for Social Research and elsewhere have been systematically developing a theory of the fit between the person and the environment and its relationship to job stress. While a great many issues are not yet resolved, the theory has been sufficiently developed and tested to indicate that it holds much promise in providing a systematic approach to the conceptualization, assessment, and reduction of job stress.

This chapter has been organized into five sections. The first section presents the basic theory of person-environment fit and its relationship to strain. The second section notes results of some of the previous research concerning the theory and its unique aspects. The third section applies this conceptual approach to better define the problem of uncertainty as an element of job stress. In the fourth section the focus shifts to organizational problems resulting from poor fit between the person and the job. The final section reviews some methods for reducing individual and organizational stress that are suggested by the theory.

PERSON-ENVIRONMENT FIT THEORY

One model of stress introduced in the first chapter of this book indicates that stress is a function of both the person and the environment. *P-E* fit theory offers a more detailed conceptualization of the relationship between the person and the environment that reflects stress. This theory been elaborated over a number of years, principally by French and Kahn (1962), French, Rogers, and Cobb (1974), Caplan, Cobb, French, Harrison, and Pinneau (1980), Harrison (1978), French, Caplan, and Harrison (1982), and Caplan (1983). However, the importance of the interface between the individual and the job has generally been recognized, for example, by Pervin (1968), Hulin and Blood (1968), Lofquist and Dawis (1969), Hackman and Lawler (1971), Argyris (1973), and Feather (1975). This theory is based on the descriptions of motivational processes by Lewin (1951) and Murray (1938).

Two types of fit between the individual and the environment are specified. One type of fit is the extent to which the job provides rewards and supplies to meet the individual's needs and preferences. Misfit of this type reflects stress for the individual. For example, the job may provide too little security, pay, or achievement opportunity for the needs of the individual, resulting in dissatisfaction, anxiety, or psychosomatic complaints. The other type of fit is the extent to which the individual's skills and abilities meet the demands and requirements of the job. Misfit of this type reflects strain for the organization. For example, the individual may not have the managerial skills or technical competence to perform the designated work role, resulting in poor coordination and lowered productivity within the organization.

The two types of fit are often—but not always—related. For example, an individual's security and advancement often depends on successfully meeting the demands of the job. Poor fit between job demands and individual abilities usually results in poor fit between the individual's needs and the rewards provided by the job. However, the rewards may not be contingent upon job performance. For example, in a seniority or tenure system misfit on the dimensions most relevant to the organization's needs may not affect fit with regard to the individual's needs. The relationship between poor fit and organizational stress will be discussed further in later sections of this chapter. In the present section we will focus on the effects of both types of misfit on individual stress.

Basic Model of *P-E* Fit

A model of the relationship between person-environment fit and individual strain is presented in Figure 2-1. A basic distinction is made between the person and the surrounding environment. Another basic distinction is made between objects and events as they exist independently and objects and events as they are perceived by the person. These two basic distinctions are used to identify four components of the model: the objective environment, the subjective environment, the objective person, and the subjective person.

The *objective environment* exists independently from a person's perception of it. The *subjective environment* consists of the person's perceptions—the cognitive construction of the world in which the person lives—including the perceived demands, opportunities, and rewards. Similarly, the *objective person* refers to the actual characteristics of the person, identifiable by unbiased, replicable observations. The *subjective person* represents the individual's perception of himself or herself, including perceived needs, values, and abilities.

French et al. (1974) indicate that these four concepts can be used to define four additional concepts which are represented in circles in Figure

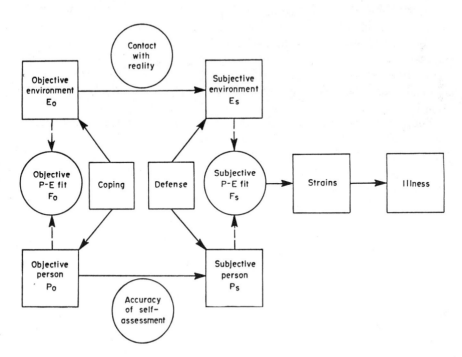

Figure 2-1   A model describing the effects of psychosocial stress in terms of fit between the person and the environment. Concepts within circles are discrepancies between the two adjoining concepts. Solid lines indicate causal effects. Broken lines indicate contributions to interaction effects (Harrison, 1978).

2-1. Two of the concepts represent the accuracy of the individual's perceptions. *Contact with reality* is the extent to which the subjective environment of the person matches the objective environment. *Accuracy of self-assessment* is the extent to which the individual's subjective perceptions of himself or herself match the objective person. The other two concepts describe the compatibility or fit between the characteristics of the environment and those of the individual. *Objective P-E fit* is the extent to which the demands and supplies in the objective environment match the needs and abilities of the person. Similarly, *subjective P-E fit* is the match between the subjective environment and the subjective person.

The four types of discrepancy can be measured only if the objective environment, the subjective environment, the objective person, and the subjective person are measured on the same conceptual dimensions. For example, production rate can be used as a dimension. An inspector on an assembly line may be capable of inspecting 15 units in an hour (objective person), but may believe that he can inspect 20 units per hour (subjective person). The pacing of the assembly line may be planned for the inspection of 22 units per hour (objective environment), while the individual thinks he is expected to inspect 18 units per hour (subjective environment). The inspector's contact with reality, accessibility to self, objective *P-E* fit, and subjective *P-E* fit can all be determined with respect to work pace.

Job stress is not pictured in Figure 2-1. This general concept is given a fairly specific definition using *P-E* fit theory. A job (or any environment) is stressful to the extent that it does not provide supplies to meet the individual's motives and also to the extent that the abilities of the individual fall below those demands of the job that are prerequisite to receiving supplies.

Poor fit can lead to several types of *strain* or deviation from normal responses in the person. The individual's psychological, behavioral, and physiological problems result from the individual's perceptions of poor fit (see Figure 2-1). Psychological strains include job dissatisfaction, anxiety, and lowered self-esteem. Behavioral symptoms of strain include increased smoking or absenteeism. Physiological strains include high blood pressure and elevated serum cholesterol.

As strains continue over time, their effects can culminate in various kinds of clinical *illness* (see Figure 2-1). These illnesses can include psychological illness (e.g., acute or chronic clinical depression) and physical illness (e.g., heart disease, peptic ulcer). It should also be noted that good fit can enhance the well-being of the individual. For example, Morse (1975) suggests that the continued experience of good fit enhances the individual's sense of competence and self-worth.

Several more relationships could be represented in the model. For simplicity, only two relationships with coping and defense have been presented in Figure 2-1. *Coping* referes to those activities of the individual aimed at improving the fit between the objective environment and the objective person. For example, the inspector on the assembly line would have improved objective fit on work pace by either having the speed of the assembly line slowed or by developing a more efficient routine for inspecting units. *Defenses* are perceptual distortions of the objective world that affect only the subjective fit between the environment and the person. For example, the inspector can perceive the work pace to be lower than it is, or his speed in inspecting units to be faster than it is. Coping and defensive activities can also be focused on strains. For example, the individual may actively plan breaks away from work demands or may deny the experience of strain. Another relationship not represented in Figure 2-1 is the potential effect of strain on the person and the environment. For example, depression or psychosomatic complaints may reduce the individual's ability to perform the work, leading to increasingly poorer *P-E* fit and even higher levels of strain.

Relationships between *P-E* Fit and Strain

The mechanism at the core of most theories of psychosocial stress is the concept of sustained motive arousal (cf. Mason, 1975). Motivational theories typically identify goals or states that the individual strives to attain. The goals include the things and situations to meet basic needs as well as objectives that the individual has through socialization learned to value. To the extent important goals of the individual are not attained, the well-being of the individual are not attained, the well-being of the individual is impaired or threatened. The notion of the congruence between the person and the environment is implicit in the concepts relating the motivational forces within the individual to environmental factors facilitating or constraining the attainment of the goals.

An ongoing problem in the study of motives and their goals is the identification of specific motives. A number of motives have been conceptualized by various authors; for example, a need for security, an achievement motive, and a need for consistency in one's cognitive view of the world (cf. Lawler, 1973).

Identifying a universal list of goals that individuals are trying to achieve is difficult because individuals' goals are shaped and modified as those individuals are socialized. An example of this process occurring on the job is the acquisition of the job demands as valued goals. As noted earlier, meeting the demands of the job is usually extrinsically motivated because supplies (e.g., pay, esteem of others) are contingent on meeting the demands. The individual may also come to find that meeting many job demands is intrinsically rewarding. In these circumstances the individual has come to view the norms for work role behavior as values that he or she should seek to exemplify. In meeting the job demands, the individual's self-esteem and sense of self-identity are enhanced. This process can blur the distinction between work demands and individual motives. The work demands may be translated as goals that are intrinsically motivating for an individual. In such instances poor fit between the individual and the job demands can affect several motives. For example, an administrator who cannot keep up with his heavy work load is faced with the loss of job security and with the loss of his self-image as a competent executive.

P-E fit theory attempts to conceptualize the forces acting on the individual by identifying dimensions of common situations and roles where several motives and abilities can interact or conflict. *P-E* fit theory does not identify specific motives or job demands to be studied. Investigators select motives or job demands that appear to be most relevant to the situation being studied. *P-E* fit is then measured on those dimensions. In the terms used by Campbell et al. (1970), it is a "mechanical or process" theory. The basic process is that *strain should increase as P-E fit dimensions reflect increased insufficiency of supplies for motives.* To predict the type of strain that will occur, the investigator usually considers additional factors such as the motive(s) that are not being met and the genetic and social background of the individual.

French et al. (1974) used the potential relationship between *P-E* fit and strains to specify three differently shaped relationships that may occur between a measure of *P-E* fit and a strain. These relationships are presented in Figure 2-2. The vertical axis represents any strain that may result from sustained motive arousal. The horizontal axis is a scale of *P-E* fit. The numbers on the scale are discrepancies between person scores and environment scores on a dimension. The zero represents perfect fit where the person score and the environment score are equal. The negative scores indicate the person score is increasingly larger than the environment score. The positive scores indicate the environment score is increasingly larger than the person score.

To illustrate the three shapes, we will assume that the *P-E* fit dimension reflects the fit between an individual's motive and environmental supplies for the motive. The solid line in Figure 2-2 illustrates the decrease in strain that occurs as environmental supplies increase to the point of matching motive levels. This relationship applies to all dimensions where supplies do not meet motive levels; for example, food, money, love, or opportunities for achievement.

The relationship between *P-E* fit and strain is more complicated when the supplies exceed the motive level. House (1972) points out that excess supplies should have no further effect on strain so long as the excess does not affect supplies for other motives. This relationship is described by line *A* in Figure 2-2. For example, a hungry person eats until he or she is full. Having additional food available at that time will not reduce strain further.

The level of strain will continue to decrease when excess supplies can be preserved or exchanged for supplies for other motives. This relationship is represented by line *B* in Figure 2-2. For example, excess pay or unexpected

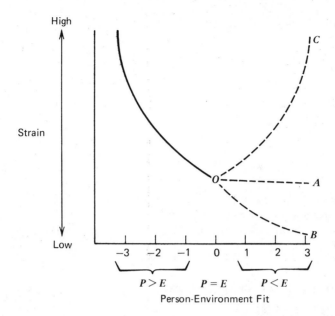

High

Strain

Low

-3   -2   -1   0   1   2   3

P > E   P = E   P < E

Person-Environment Fit

Figure 2-2 Three hypothetical shapes of the relationship between P-E fit and strain. The curves can also be drawn as their mirror images to depict functions that are their respective reverse opposites.

bonuses can be used to purchase comforts beyond those normally sought. Saving the money can increase future security. Either activity would reduce strain below its level at perfect fit on income.

The final relationship between *P-E* fit and strain has the U-shape illustrated by curve *C* in Figure 2-2. French and others (1974) suggest that excess supplies for one motive may be associated with insufficient supplies for another motive. For example, insufficient opportunities to interact with other people can be stressful, with the isolation resulting in strains such as depression. As interactions with others are increased, the level of strain decreases. However, when the number of interactions increases beyond the desired level, the individual's needs for privacy are threatened. More interactions with others are likely to result in increases in strains such as anger. Such trade-offs can occur frequently because a number of motives can conflict with or counterbalance each other.

A somewhat lengthier discussion of the three relationships and a parallel illustration of the three relationships on a dimension reflecting fit between demands of the job and abilities of the individual is presented in Harrison (1978).

This section has introduced *P-E* fit theory. Various aspects of the theory have been elaborated elsewhere (e.g., French et al., 1974; Caplan et al., 1980; Harrison, 1978; French et al., 1982; Caplan, 1983). Lewin (1951) noted that there is nothing as practical as a good theory. In what ways is this theory practical? It should predict outcomes, particularly outcomes that have not been predicted by other theories. Also, good theory should provide an explanation of the causal path leading to the outcomes. The model of relationships can then be used to deduce other relationships that are likely to occur. It can also be used to direct efforts to intervene in the causal process and change outcomes. This section has introduced the causal processes and predictions of relationships between *P-E* fit and strain. In the remaining sections of the chapter evidence of the practicality of the theory will be presented. The next section reviews some of the empirical tests of the predicted relationships between *P-E* fit and strain. The following sections present elaborations of the theoretical model, seeking to provide a better conceptualization of the effects of uncertainty, the interface between individual stress and organizational stress, and ways to reduce job strain.

TESTS OF THE RELATIONSHIPS BETWEEN *P-E* FIT AND STRAIN

The unique prediction of *P-E* fit theory is that the characteristics of the job and the person can interact in specific patterns to produce strain. A turning point in the relationship between *P-E* fit and strain may occur at the point of a perfect fit. Therefore, strain can be a function of the environment and the person relative to each other, not just a function of the level of either separately or added together.

Curvilinear Relationships between *P-E* Fit and Strain

Several studies have used commensurate measures of the person and the environment to test the relationship between *P-E* fit and strain. One of the first studies was performed by Pervin (1967a, b), testing the relationships between fit and structuredness in educational approach and the strains of school dissatisfaction and dropping out of school. Another test of the theory in the educational setting was performed by Kulka and his associates (Kulka, 1975, 1979; Kulka, Mann, and Klingel, 1980; Kulka, Klingel, and Mann, 1980). Kahana, Liang, and Felton (1980) studied the fit of elderly persons with their environments. However, the majority of the studies of *P-E* fit have examined fit between the individual and the job. Although Locke (1969) was not testing the *P-E* fit theory, the data he reports concerning university students and their summer jobs are relevant to it. House (1972) collected relevant data from workers in the community of Tecumseh. Tannenbaum and Kuleck (1976) collected *P-E* fit data from workers in 52 industrial plants in five countries. Caplan (1972) examined *P-E* fit data of employees at a base of the National Aeronautics and Space Administration. Probably the most systematic examination of relationships between *P-E* fit and strain was performed by Harrison, French, Caplan and their colleagues (Harrison, 1976; Caplan et al., 1980; French et al., 1982) on a sample of 2010 workers in 23 occupations.

All of these studies have found nonlinear relationships similar to the shapes in Figure 2-2 between some dimensions of *P-E* fit and some strain. An illustrative finding from Caplan et al. (1980) is reproduced in Figures 2-3 and 2-4. The worker's rating of the complexity of his job (Job

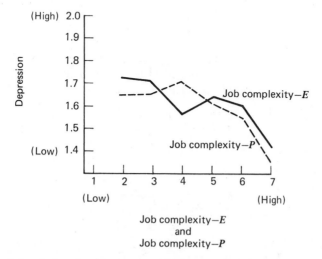

Figure 2-3   Relationships between scores on depression and scores on job complexity—*E* and job complexity—P. R = 0.14 (NS) and 0.19 (NS), respectively. *N* = 318 men from 23 occupations. (From Caplan et al., 1980, p. 90.)

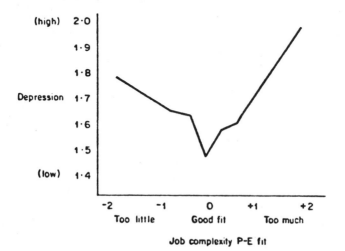

Figure 2-4   Relationship between complexity *P-E* fit and depression. R = 0.26 (*p* < .002). *N* = 318 men from 23 occupations. (From Caplan et al., 1980, p. 91.)

Complexity—E) and preferences concerning job complexity (Job Complexity—P) were obtained along with a measure of depression. As is indicated in Figure 2-3, neither the environment measure nor the person measure were significantly related to depression. However, when P-E fit scores were calculated as discrepancies between the individual's environment score and preferred score, a significant U-shaped relationship was found between P-E fit on complexity and depression (see Figure 2-4).

A more complete graphical representation of these relationships is presented in Figure 2-5 for the item concerning the lack of specification of job procedures from the job complexity index. The cells at the base of the figure represent various combinations of job and preference scores on the extent to which job procedures are not specified. The average level of depression in each cell is represented by the height of its column. The "valley" on the upper surface is the U-shaped curve between P-E fit and

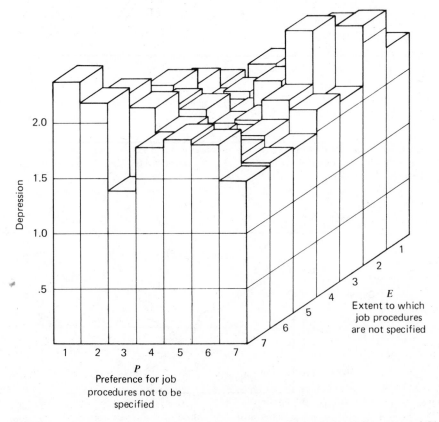

Figure 2-5   An isometric representation of Depression scores grouped by cell in a person (P) by environment (E) matrix of scores on "lack of specification of job procedures." Data are from the study Job Demands and Worker Health (Caplan et al., 1980; French et al., 1982). $N = 2010$ individuals.

strain with the lowest level of depression occurring along the diagonal where the environment scores match the person scores.

Before we conclude the discussion of curvilinear relationships between P-E fit and strain, interactions predicted by P-E fit theory should be distinguished from other interactions between the person and the environment. An "interaction" occurs when the relationship between a predictor and an outcome differs depending on the level of a second predictor. As has been noted earlier, P-E fit theory is concerned with interactions reflecting how well or poorly the environment and the person match each other, with a potential turning point in their relationship with strain found along the diagonal of perfect fit in Figure 2-5.

Other types of interactions occur when measures of the environment and the person have different relationships to strain. For example, individuals scoring high on measures of Type A (coronary heart disease prone) behavior appear to be hyperresponsive to environmental demands, experiencing disproportionately high levels of strain when compared with individuals who are low on Type A behavior and under the same environmental demands (cf. Dembroski, MacDougall, Herd, and Shields, 1979; Dembroski, MacDougall, Shields, Pettito, and Lushene, 1978). This interaction reflects a causal mechanism that operates independently of P-E fit. The person and the environment measures are not conceptualized or measured on commensurate dimensions and there is no conceptual matching of scores for the environment and the person. P-E fit refers to only a group of the many possible causal mechanisms and patterns of relationships reflected in interactions between the environment and the person. Joyce, Slocum, and Von Glinow (1982) discuss some additional models of interactions between the person and the environment.

The failure to distinguish between P-E fit and other types of interactions between the person and the environment can lead to unnecessary conceptual confusion and difficulties in interpreting results and formulating recommendations. For an example of this confusion, see the attempt by Ivancevich, Matteson, and Preston (1982) to discuss the interaction between Type A behavior and occupational stress as though it represented a P-E fit relationship.

Some Theoretical and Methodological Limitations

Of course, many relationships between P-E fit and strain are not curvilinear or even significant. Do such results discredit P-E fit theory? No, because both theoretical and methodological requirements underlying the prediction are often not met. The theory applies to situations where (1) misfit on a P-E fit dimension reflects insufficient supplies for the individual's motives, and (2) the strain is one that occurs when those particular motives are not met.

Harrison (1978) presents data underscoring the importance of the assumptions about motives reflected by *P-E* fit dimensions. On the dimension of work load, too much work (i.e., the environment level greater than the individual's preferred level) was related to increased job dissatisfaction for both administrators and assembly line workers. Presumably excessive work loads threaten supplies for a number of motives such as job security and opportunities to interact with family and friends, resulting in dissatisfaction with the job. Interestingly, too little work to do (individual's preferences greater than the environmental level) was related to increasing levels of job dissatisfaction for administrators, but had no effect on the job dissatisfaction of assembly line workers. These findings suggest that too little work reflects insufficient supplies for the professional values and identity of the administrators, while the assembly line workers do not share these motives to the same extent. This example illustrates the importance of selecting *P-E* fit dimensions relevant to the situation and individuals being studied. The theory assumes that *P-E* fit dimensions reflecting potential misfit on important motives have been selected.

As was noted above, the theory also assumes that strains relevant to the *P-E* fit dimension have been studied. For example, the measure of *P-E* fit on job complexity presented in Figure 2-4 has no linear or curvilinear relationship to obesity, only too little complexity is related to boredom, and only too much complexity is related to irritation (French et al., 1982).

Even when appropriate dimensions of *P-E* fit and strain are selected, methodological problems may affect the relationships observed between them. Several methodological issues have been discussed by Harrison (1976, 1978), Kulka (1975), and Caplan (1983). If the sample contains individuals with scores on a *P-E* fit dimension representing only an environmental excess or only an environmental deficiency, one cannot test for the predicted curvilinear relationships with strain. The observed *P-E* fit scores fall only on one side of the potential turning point of perfect fit. For example, French et al. (1982) found that virtually no one reported preferring less income than they were receiving. These one-sided distributions are typical in studies examining discrepancies between ideal and actual levels on various dimensions directly measuring motives and supplies for them (e.g., Evans, 1969; Porter, 1961; Wall and Payne, 1973; Wanous and Lawler, 1972). Distributions on both sides of perfect fit have been found more often for dimensions reflecting job demands and preferences concerning them (e.g., French et al., 1982; Kulka, 1975; Locke, 1969).

Another important methodological problem is the *contamination* of the measures of the environment and the person. Virtually all studies of *P-E* fit using commensurate dimensions have been performed with interviews and questionnaires. The individual's perception of the environment may be affected by his or her preferences, and his or her reports concerning preferences may be affected by his or her perception of the environment. Such biases may result in reports concerning the environment or the person reflecting to some extent the fit between the person and the environment. The "contamination" can enhance the relationship of measures of the person and the environment to strains, and will reduce the relationship of the calculated measure of P-E fit and strains (cf. French et al., 1974; Harrison, 1976).

Other Findings Relevant to P-E Fit Theory

Two additional sets of findings are relevant to assessing the predictive utility of P-E fit theory. Most of the studies formally testing P-E fit theory have computed the variance in strains accounted for by the measures of the environment and the person and their linear combination, and then computed the additional variance in strain accounted for by the curvilinear relationships predicted by the theory. When curvilinear relationships are found, they typically account for an additional 1 to 5 percent of the variance in the strain. While this amount may not be very impressive in absolute terms, it is often equal to the variance in the strain associated with the measures of the environment and the person on the dimension.

French et al. (1982) report a specific set of analyses that attempts to test the causal path suggested by P-E fit theory. As illustrated in Figure 2-1 environmental and individual characteristics should affect strains via subjective P-E fit. The analysis used more than 50 predictors, including measures of environmental characteristics, personal characteristics, and P-E fit dimensions. These predictors were included in a series of stepwise multiple regressions for each of 18 strains. Overall, P-E fit measures tended to be significant, independent predictors of strains, a result that supports their hypothesized position in the model as the immediate precursor of strains.

Importance of Measures of the Environment and the Person

The results supporting P-E fit theory do not mean that the independent contributions of measures of the person and the environment should be ignored. Results from various studies show that they are often related to strains and that this relationship may be independent of relationships between P-E fit and strains. Such relationships can occur because of contamination between measures of the environment and person, confounding with other variables, or additional substantive causal pathways.

The effects of the contamination of measures of the environment and person with each other were noted earlier. To the extent that our present methods are affected by this bias, we must examine the measures of the environment and person for indications that they reflect misfit rather than describe the person or the environment.

Main effects of measures of the environment and person must also be examined to determine whether they are confounded with other variables and reflect the effects of these variables. For example, jobs that are highly complex typically provide higher income, status, and other rewards than jobs that are routine. A main effect between complexity of the job and strain may simply reflect the effects of correlated factors that are causing the strain.

Finally, measures of the person or the environment may reflect interactive causal mechanisms that operate independently of P-E fit. The interaction between Type A behavior and environmental demands in producing strain was noted earlier. Whenever measures of the person or the environment are expected to interact in a nonmatching pattern, separate scores on the person and the environment measures are needed to examine that relationship to strains.

Someday it may be possible to interpret many, if not all, of the main effects and nonmatching interactions of measures of the environment and the person in terms of P-E fit theory. This would require the identification of all relevant dimensions in terms of P-E fit. Their relationships to each other would also have to be identified, including confounding among the dimensions and conflicts between dimensions where good fit on one dimension means poor fit on another.

It will certainly be a long time before that extent of theory about the content of dimensions of P-E fit is added to the present theory about the potential processes. Meanwhile, it is useful to examine all of the information available concerning strain and measures of the environment, the person, and P-E fit on dimensions thought to be relevant to the specific situation being investigated.

Conclusions about Tests of P-E Fit Theory

The evidence indicates that the processes predicted by P-E fit theory do take place, that the curvilinear relationships predicted by the theory can meaningfully increase the predicted variance in strain, and that factors in the subjective environment and the subjective person tend to affect strain via subjective P-E fit. The results also highlight several restrictions of the current "process" theory: (1) theories must be developed for dimensions of P-E fit and strains that apply to specific situations; (2) methodological limitations must be overcome for the theory to be most useful; and (3) independent effects of the environment and the person cannot be ignored. Even with these restrictions, the results show that P-E fit theory as it is currently elaborated makes a useful contribution to the empirical prediction of strain.

STRESS, UNCERTAINTY, AND ANTICIPATED P-E FIT

The preceding two sections have elaborated components of the model in Chapter 1 in terms of an employee's current P-E fit. A second important concept is the potential for stress resulting from uncertainty about future events. In this section the implications of *P-E* fit theory for stress due to future uncertainty will be considered. The two additional components in the model in Chapter 1—duration and importance—will also be discussed.

Several authors (e.g., Feather, 1975; Lazarus, 1966, 1972) note that the expectation of inadequate supplies for motives can result in motive arousal. Cognitive abilities are central to this process. One aspect of stress is the sustained tension that occurs when the environment threatens not to provide the supplies that the individual seeks. The basic model presented in the introductory chapter concerning this process indicates that this type of stress is a function of (1) the perceived *uncertainty* of obtaining outcomes, (2) the perceived *importance* of these outcomes, and (3) the perceived *duration* of the uncertaintly. *P-E* fit theory suggests conceptual refinement for each of these factors.

Uncertainty and Duration

Uncertainty about the future has been related to strains such as anxiety (e.g., Archer, 1979). Perhaps the most obvious elaboration of the model concerning the stress of uncertain outcomes comes from the recognition that stress associated with uncertainty may be a function of *P-E* fit on uncertainty rather than of the absolute level of uncertainty. A number of studies have demonstrated that individuals differ in tolerance for role ambiguity and that these individual differences interact with the actual level of role ambiguity on the job in producing strain (e.g., Kahn et al., 1967; Beehr, 1974). Indeed, uncertainty is necessary for some types of motives to be satisfied; for example, the need for achievement (Atkinson and Feather, 1969) and the need for a sense of mastery (deCharms, 1968). Individuals differ in the level of these motives, suggesting that the conceptualization and measurement of uncertainty in terms of *P-E* fit would be an appropriate refinement of the model.

It is reasonable to expect that an individual's preference for uncertainty will vary with the implications and importance of the outcome being considered. For example, preferences for the uncertainty of making a sale may be much higher than preferences concerning the uncertainty of the company closing down. The measurement of *P-E* fit on the dimension of uncertainty should probably specify the outcome under consideration. The extent of misfit between person and environment regarding uncertainty concerning that outcome can indicate the level of arousal or "stress" associated with that uncertainty.

The effects of the duration of the uncertainty have not been studied as systematically as uncertainty and related concepts. It is reasonable to suppose that individuals also differ in their preferences and tolerances for the length of time that a given level of uncertainty exists. As with uncertainty, an individual's preferences or tolerances concerning the duration of uncertainty may vary with the outcome being considered. Measures of *P-E* fit on duration may better reflect its relationship to stress than a simple measure of actual duration.

Importance

Importance is included in the model to represent the effect of the consequences of the outcome if it should occur. Importance represents the extent to which the outcome will satisfy (positive direction of valence) or thwart (negative direction of valence) the motives of the individual and the priority of those motives for the individual.

A measure of anticipated P-E fit relevant to the outcome would indicate the extent to which the outcome may satisfy (good fit) or thwart (poor fit) the motives of an individual. For example, aspects of the importance of low sales can be represented on a P-E fit dimension of sales rate. An advantage of conceptualizing uncertainty about the anticipated outcome in terms of P-E fit is that the potential effects of deficiencies and excesses are highlighted. A disadvantage is that the P-E fit conceptualization does not indicate the priority of the relevant motives for the individual. The application of the P-E fit approach assumes that P-E fit dimensions being used in a given situation have been selected because they represent important motives for the situation.

The concepts of P-E fit on several dimensions and the importance of each dimension could be conceptually integrated in a formula that multiplies the discrepancy on each P-E fit dimension by the importance of that dimension. However, the operationalization of such measures may prove difficult. Quinn and Mangione (1972) tested a similar model that predicted overall job satisfaction, using the sum of the products of the satisfaction with a specific facet of the job multiplied by the importance of that facet. They found that weighting each facet by importance did not improve the prediction of overall job dissatisfaction. The failure of the weighting by importance to improve predictions could be due to several problems in operationalizing and testing such models. The individual's response in indicating the degree of satisfaction (or of misfit) may be contaminated by the importance of the facet (or P-E fit dimension). Such contamination could result in the same amount of objective misfit being subjectively perceived as greater by individuals for whom the dimension is important than by individuals for whom the dimension is less important, building an importance rating into the initial score. Even if undistorted ratings were available, the ratings typically used do not have the ratio scale properties typically assumed in applying multiplicative models.

Future methodological developments may allow the operationalization and testing of more complex formulations involving both P-E fit measures and ratings of their importance. Until these more complex formulations have been shown to be worthwhile, it is simplest to choose either the P-E fit approach or the importance approach, depending on the problem at hand.

For example, the concept of importance may be useful when more than one potential outcome is being considered. The concept of anticipated *P-E* fit may be useful when the potential effects of anticipated good fit or poor fit on a dimension are being compared.

Stress as a Function of *P-E* Fit on Present Uncertainty and of Anticipated *P-E* Fit

P-E fit theory predicts that at least three relationships may exist between a measure of *P-E* fit and strain. When the simultaneous effects of two or more *P-E* fit dimensions are considered, various combinations of these potential relationships are possible. For the present purpose of exploring implications of *P-E* fit theory for uncertain events, two examples and their underlying assumptions will be used to illustrate some of the additional predictions generated by *P-E* fit theory. The joint effects of the anticipated level of fit and present fit regarding the uncertainty of the anticipated level will be considered. To simplify the discussion, *P-E* fit the dimension of duration will not be considered. The potential effects of *P-E* fit on duration should parallel the potential effects of *P-E* fit on uncertainty. Also, to simplify the discussion, distinctions will not be made between the different types of strain that may result from deficiencies or excesses on *P-E* fit dimensions. The discussion will focus on the overall level of strain that is experienced.

Work load will be used as an illustrative dimension of anticipated fit. Uncertainty concerning the level of work can be low, moderate, or high. The left side of Table 2-1 shows the various patterns of anticipated fit scores that can occur at a particular level of uncertainty. The first three rows indicate that uncertainty is low, but in each row a different level of *P-E* fit on work load is anticipated (too little work [$P > E$], good fit on work load [$P = E$], and too much work [$P < E$], respectively). In the fourth through sixth rows a moderate level of uncertainty is represented, with a different combination of two levels of *P-E* fit on work load anticipated on each line, including an anticipation of "feast or famine" in the sixth line. The last line indicates total uncertainty where all levels of *P-E* fit on work load are equally likely.

What levels of strain might be anticipated in these various circumstances? Such predictions require hypotheses about the relationships between the *P-E* fit dimensions and strains. For an initial hypothetical example, assume that the individual's preference is for low levels of uncertainty. Strain associated with *P-E* fit on uncertainty would then be lowest at low levels of uncertainty and highest at high levels of uncertainty. (See the first column under the heading "Example 1" in Table 2-1.)

For the relationship between anticipated fit on work load and strain, a curvilinear relationship, similar to that found between fit on work load and job dissatisfaction for administrators, will be assumed. Strain should

Table 2-1 A Hypothetical Model of the Level of Strain as a Function of Anticipated Fit on Work Load and of Fit on Uncertainty about the Work Load

Level of Uncertainty About Work Load (E)	Anticipated P-E Fit on Work Load[a]			Example 1[b] Level of Strain:		Example 2[c] Level of Strain:	
	P>E	P=E	P<E	Due to Fit on Uncertainty	Due to Anticipated Fit on Work Load	Due to Fit on Uncertainty	Due to Anticipated Fit on Work Load
Low		XXXX		low	low	moderate	low
Low	XXXX			low	moderate	modertae	low
Low			XXXX	low	high	moderate	high
Moderate	XXXXXXXXXX			moderate	low-moderate	low	low
Moderate		XXXXXXXXXX		moderate	moderate	low	moderate
Moderate	XXXXX	XXXXX		moderate	moderate-high	low	moderate
High	XXXXXXXXXXXXXXX			high	moderate	high	low-moderate

[a] The X's indicate the range of P-E fit scores that are anticipated.

[b] Assumptions about P-E fit on uncertainty: (1) preferred level of uncertainty is low: (2) low uncertainty produces low strain; moderate uncertainty produces moderate strain; (4) high uncertainty produces high strain. Assumptions about anticipated fit and level of strain: (1) P>E produces moderate strain; (2) P=E produces low strain: (3) P<E produces low strain; (4) and the strain produced when more than one level of fit is anticipated is the average of the anticipated strain levels.

[c] Assumptions about P-E fit on uncertainty: (1) preferred level of uncertainty is moderate; (2) low uncertainty produces moderate strain; (3) moderate uncertainty produces low strain; (4) high uncertainty produces high strain. Assumptions about anticipated fit and level of strain: (1) P>E produces low strain; (2) P=E produces low strain; (3) P<E produces high strain: and (4) the strain produced when more than one level of fit is anticipated is the average of the anticipated levels of strain.

be lowest when a good fit is anticipated between the future level of work and the individual's ability to handle it. A moderate level of strain occurs when the work load is less than that preferred by the individual. A high level of strain occurs when the work load is greater than the individual can handle. In Table 2-1 it is assumed that the level of strain produced when more than one level of fit is anticipated is the average of the strain associated with each anticipated level. (See the second column under the heading "Example 1" in Table 2-1.)

What is the total level of strain experienced in the various conditions in this example? Computation of the total level of strain requires assumptions about the combined effects of misfit across dimensions. If the dimensions are considered to be independent, it is reasonable to hypothesize that their effects on strain are independent and additive. If the dimensions are considered to be interactive, their effects on strain can be multiplicative.

As a comparison, a second example has been included in Table 2-1. In this example the individual is assumed to prefer moderate levels of uncertainty, with too little uncertainty producing moderate levels of strain and too much uncertainty producing high levels of strain. Also, anticipated fit on work load is assumed to follow the relationship observed between fit on work load and job dissatisfaction for assembly line workers—low strain is associated with both good fit on work and too little work, and high strain occurs with too much work. When these assumptions are used, the pattern of strain varies somewhat from that in the initial example.

What do these possible relationships between uncertainty, anticipated fit, and strain indicate? P-E fit theory suggests that strain due to expectations concerning future events may be produced by fairly complex cognitive processes. Better predictions of the level and type of strains experienced may be developed by considering the dimension(s) of fit that are involved, the anticipated level of fit, P-E fit with regard to the uncertainty and the duration of the uncertainty, and the implications of misfit on the dimensions for the motives of the individual.

This conceptual approach is not in conflict with the simpler approach using the concepts of uncertainty, importance, and duration. In fact, both approaches have roots in the work of Kurt Lewin. The approach presented in this section represents a conceptual elaboration of the simpler model. This elaboration takes into account both individual and environmental differences on the three basic concepts and the possibility of curvilinear as well as linear relationships with strains.

An additional advantage of the more differentiated framework for studying anticipated events is the opportunity to integrate theories covering more limited domains within the framework. For example, individuals faced with an undesirable situation that is thought to be unalterable in the future are likely to become depressed and may come to behave in a pattern of "learned helplessness" (e.g., Abramson et al., 1978). Caplan (1983) discusses this issue, the possible effects of perceived control, and some additional issues that may characterize or modify the relationship of anticipated fit and strain.

P-E FIT THEORY, INDIVIDUAL STRESS, AND ORGANIZATIONAL STRESS

P-E fit theory has been almost exclusively applied to the problem of individual stress and strain. It has not been generally recognized that the theory offers a systematic conceptual approach to some aspects of stress and strain within the organization employing the individual. This section introduces the application of the theory to organizational (as opposed to individual) strain at the microorganizational level and the interface between individual stress and organizational stress.

A Parallel Model of Stress within the Organization

When P-E fit theory was introduced in the first section of this chapter, two types of dimensions were indentified: dimensions reflecting fit between motives and supplies, and dimensions reflecting fit between demands and abilities. Individual stress is fundamentally based on insufficient environmental supplies to meet motives. Just as meeting needs and values is fundamental to the continued functioning and existence of the individual, meeting role demands is fundamental to the continued functioning and existence of the organization. The individual seeks in the environment the supplies for motives. Similarly, the organization seeks in its "environment" for individuals to meet role demands.

Although the present terminology is slanted toward the perspective of individual stress, and underlying parallel emerges between individual stress and organizational stress at the microorganizational level. A conceptual model including the parallel processes of organizational stress is presented in Figure 2-6. The basic change between the P-E fit model in Figure 2-1 and the right half of Figure 2-6 is the specification that the focus is one the job environment. The left half of Figure 2-6 introduces parallel concepts for the organization. Within the organizations are perceptions of the job, its role demands, and rewards, as well as perceptions of the person, the person's abilities, and needs.

Within the organization there may be several sets of perceptions of the job and the individual: the perceptions of staff in the personnel office responsible for filling a job, the perceptions of the supervisor over the job, the perceptions of coworkers and others. To simplify the present discussion, it will focus on the perception of the supervisor over the individual in the job. The supervisor's perceptions are most likely to be the basis upon which the individual's performance in meeting job demands is evaluated for the organization, and therefore the basis for the provision of rewards by the organization. By comparing the organization's perceptions (particu-

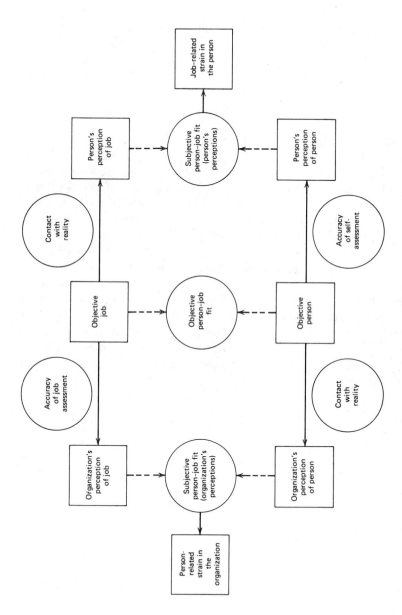

Figure 2-6 A model describing effects of individual stress and microorganizational stress in terms of the fit between the person and the job. Concepts within circles are discrepancies between the two adjoining concepts. Solid lines indicate causal effects. Broken lines indicate contributions to interaction effects. The term *organization's perceptions* can be operationalized as the perceptions of individuals in roles that represent the organization in evaluating and rewarding performance, typically the supervisor of the person under consideration.

larly those of the supervisor), with objective assessments (for example, those of an independent consultant), the organization's accuracy of assessment concerning the job and the organization's contact with reality concerning the person can be defined.

The organization's perceptions of the job and the individual are compared to determine the fit between them. Misfit can result in strains in organizational functioning, such as poor communication, interruptions in work flow, inadequate planning, dissatisfaction of other employees, increased supervisory time, and lowered productivity. To simplify the figure, the effects of coping and defense and the feedback effects of strains are not presented.

The model, as drawn in Figure 2-6, focuses on the organization's perception of misfit and its consequences. The focus on perceived misfit results from the model in Figure 2-6 being drawn in strict parallel to the model for psychosocial stress in Figure 2-1. It is assumed that the effects of psychosocial stressors operate only if the individual is aware of them and responding to them. Of course, aspects of the environment can affect the well-being of the individual even though the individual is not aware of them. For example, toxic chemicals may be present. In the present perspective the presence of a toxic chemical can be represented as a poor fit on an objective biological dimension that affects well-being through a mechanism other than cognitive processes. Similarly, objective misfit that is not recognized by the organization can occur. Recognizing this alternative, the present discussion will focus on those aspects of misfit that are perceived by responsible agents of the organization. This focus will simplify the discussion and highlight misfit that the organization recognizes and can attempt to improve.

Parallels between Processes Producing Strain

The theoretical elaboration of potential relationships between $P\text{-}E$ fit measures and individual strain can also be applied to organizational strain. It was noted earlier that organizational stress should occur whenever the individual's abilities do not meet the role demands. When is organizational stress reflected by misfit on dimensions about individuals' motives and supplies for them on the job? First, misfit on a motive-supply dimension will result in organizational strain when the individual's performance of the role demands is contingent upon the individual's motives being met. An obvious example is failure to pay workers resulting in their stopping work. More subtle processes can occur. For example, a worker who wants challenge and does not have it in his or her job may "fool around" and even perform small acts of sabotage to make the time at work more interesting.

The second type of relationship between organizational strains and motive-supply dimensions occurs when the organization has accepted the responsibility of trying to meet specific individual needs as an organizational goal. Failure to meet this goal automatically indicates some organizational shortcoming for such an organization. This process parallels the individual con :ng to value role demands as worthwhile activities in themselves. While meeting worker's needs may not be an intrinsic goal of many industrial organizations, it may be an important goal of voluntary organizations, such as churches and social organizations.

What shape of relationships can exist between P-E fit dimensions and organizational strain? The three shapes illustrated in Figure 2-2 are possible. When an individual's abilities do not meet the role demands, organizational strain will be high. When the individual's abilities exceed those required by the job, one of three effects on organizational strain is possible. If the excess abilities are not used or are not relevant to the job, organizational stress is not affected. If the excess abilities allow the individual to perform additional activities important to the functioning of the organization, the level of organizational strain can be reduced. For example, a secretary who is a fast typist may finish the normally assigned work and take overflow work from other secretaries. If the excess abilities get in the way of other job demands, the level of organizational strain may increase. For example, a job may require that an individual be able to work well in a competitive setting. The individual may be so competitive that coordination with other members of the organization is disrupted.

Interface between the Person and the Job

P-E fit can be applied to individual stress or aspects of organizational stress because it focuses on the motivational basis of the interface between the job and the person. The motivational aspect of the theory suggests specific steps for organizations to maximize the work performance of individuals and for individuals to maximize rewards from organizations.

Organizations can maximize the likelihood that job demands are met by making rewards contingent on performance. If rewards are not contingent on performance, failure to meet job demands has no consequence for the individual. For example, rewards are less contingent on performance in seniority-and tenure-based reward systems. To maximize the contingency of extrinsically supplied rewards, the role demands and the contingency reward structure must be clearly identified and communicated to the worker. Then performance must be monitored and rewarded appropriately. To maximize the contingency of intrinsically supplied rewards, the organization should try to facilitate the individual's acceptance of role demands as intrinsically worthwhile. One way to do this is to redesign the task so that good performance on it would naturally result in intrinsic reward feelings (e.g., see Hackman and Oldham, 1980).

Individuals can maximize the likelihood that needs and values are met by making job performance contingent on rewards. If performance is not contingent on receiving rewards, the organization's failure to provide rewards and opportunities has no consequence for the organization. To maximize the contingency of performance, the expected rewards and opportunities and the contingent work activities must be clearly identified and communicated to the organization. Then rewards for previous work must be monitored and subsequent work performed accordingly.

The preceding statements are basic premises familiar to anyone who has studied motivation of individuals in organizations or management-labor relations. Their importance here is in highlighting the relationships of *P-E* fit theory of stress and strain to related areas where the underlying motivational assumptions have been applied.

Future Uncertainty, *P-E* Fit, and Organizational Strain

Earlier in this chapter the relationship between uncertainty and individual strain was discussed from a perspective of *P-E* fit. A parallel perspective can be developed for uncertainty and organizational strain. Just as the uncertainty of outcomes can have important consequences for the individual, the uncertainty of outcomes can also have important consequences for organizations. For example, if a supervisor is uncertain that an individual can handle the assigned work, the supervisor may have to tell other departments that work schedules may not be met or may add staff to ensure that the work will be accomplished. Such events can reduce the organization's ability to coordinate its activities and lower productivity per person.

As noted earlier, three key concepts in describing the potential effects of uncertainty are the amount of uncertainty, the duration of uncertainty, and the importance of the outcome. In our discussion of uncertainty, the concept of *P-E* fit was used to point out that individuals vary in their tolerance for uncertainty. Similarly, organizations can differ in the extent to which uncertainty about the performance of an individual will produce strains, particularly depending on the aspects of performance under consideration and the implications of the outcome for the organization. For example, uncertainty on many performance dimensions is anticipated and planned for in the work of individuals in research and development units. However, similar levels of uncertainty concerning the work of individuals on a payroll could be devastating to the organization. Parallel points can be made concerning the duration of uncertainty. The most fundamental effects do not arise from uncertainty and its duration as such, but from the fit between the organization and the individual concerning uncertainty and its duration on specific performance dimensions.

As was noted earlier, the concept of importance is not replaced or subsumed by *P-E* fit theory. The theory assumes that the investigator will identify dimensions reflecting important outcomes for the organization, will check both the uncertainty of the individual's performance on that dimension and the organization's tolerance for uncertainty on that dimension, and will consider the possible effects on the organization of both too much and too little uncertainty concerning the individual performance.

Some conjectures can be made concerning likely relationships between the importance of the outcome and the organization's tolerance for uncertainty. In general, the organization is likely to have a low tolerance for uncertainty on *P-E* fit dimensions that reflect important outcomes for the organization. This expectation is particularly likely to apply to organizations that produce goods and specific services. Organizations such as educational institutions and religious groups, with additional types of primary goals, may have more tolerance for uncertainty on many dimensions of fit between the organization and the individual that have important consequences for the organization.

Summary

This section has continued the demonstration of the ability of *P-E* fit to provide a framework for conceptualizing process and developing hypotheses. *P-E* fit theory underscores the importance of the individual and the job for aspects of organizational strain as well as individual strain. The theory focuses on the interface between the person and the job and the processes that result in strain. The theory specifies three shapes of relationships that can occur between measures of *P-E* fit and strain in either the individual or the organization.

Little previous attention has been paid to elaborating or testing the theory as it applies to organizational strain. The potential fruitfulness of the theory is demonstrated by its ability to conceptualize processes and develop hypotheses in this area, particularly in applying a fit perspective to the conceptualizations of uncertainty concerning individual performance and its effects on the organization.

P-E FIT THEORY AND THE REDUCTION OF STRESS

For a theory to be useful, it must not only predict strain and conceptualize the underlying processes, but the findings and conceptualizations must also indicate appropriate methods for reducing stress. Implications of *P-E* fit theory for reducing job stress have been discussed in Caplan et al. (1980), Harrison (1978), French et al. (1982), and Caplan (1983). Some of the suggestions from those publications are summarized below and have been incorporated with some observations about implications of *P-E* fit theory for the reduction of organizational stress.

Parameters to be Changed

More general models of occupational stress identify two basic targets for interventions to reduce stress: the person and the job (Newman and

Beehr, 1979). Within these two target categories, however, *P-E* fit theory directs the intervention strategy toward specific characteristics of the person or the job that have the most promise for reducing the stress. If the focus of change is on the person, effort may be directed toward changing the person's abilities or the person's needs and values. If the focus of change is on the organization, effort may be directed toward changing the demands of the job or the rewards associated with the job. The appropriate focus of the change effort must be determined in light of the particular problem: the type of misfit, the extent to which the relevant motives, abilities, demands, or supplies are alterable, and ethical considerations concerning the objective of the change.

The example of the inspector on the assembly line that was used earlier in the chapter can be used to illustrate each of these changes. In this example it is assumed that pay is contingent on performing at the standard rate, and that the performance at a rate below that expected can produce both individual stress and organizational stress. One method to reduce misfit would be to lower the standard rate, that is, the role demands. Another method would be to provide training that would bring the worker's abilities to the standard level. Another method would be to attempt to reduce the worker's needs and values about money so the worker can adjust to living on an income proportionately below the standard rate. Another method would be to assure the worker of the standard rate of pay by paying him or her by the hour rather than by piecework. Many additional interventions are possible, including redesigning the work task, firing the worker, or the worker quitting the job. All of these interventions affect one or more of the demands and rewards of the job and the motives and abilities of the person. Some of the implications of these changes for the organization and for the individual are discussed below.

An additional set of parameters introduced by the model is objective fit and subjective fit. The changes in the above example are all focused on changing the objective person and the objective environment. It is also possible to improve perceived fit by attempting to change only perceptions. For example, the worker's perception of fit could be improved for a short while if the worker distorted his or her assessment of his or her work rate, or if feedback from the worker's supervisor led him or her to believe he or she was performing at the acceptable rate. The organization's perception of the worker's rate could also be shifted toward better fit if incorrect production figures were provided by either the worker or a supervisor. Some circumstances can be identified where the reduction of strain by distorting perceptions of reality are ultimately acceptable. For example, distortions can be used, particularly when the distortion will produce reductions in excessive stress, to facilitate the implementation of other efforts to produce objective changes. However, the ethical problems typically encountered when only perceptions are changed indicate that change efforts should usually focus on the objective person and the objective environment.

Systematic Attempts to Improve Fit

The initial opportunity to ensure a good fit between the person and the job occurs when a job is created. Attention should be paid to putting together a set of role demands and rewards that are likely to fit prospective employees. In the job seeking and hiring process both the individual and the organization should assess the fit between the individual and the job. The fit between abilities and role demands has received a great deal of attention in the area of personnel selection. The performance demands of many jobs are specified and compared with the individual's job-related ability or previous performance records. A moderate amount of success has been achieved in predicting criteria of relevance to the organization from ability-related measures (Dunnette, 1976; Ghiselli, 1966; Guion, 1965).

Less attention has been paid to developing assessments of individuals' motives and of the corresponding supplies that accompany a job. For example, attempts can be made to assess the need and opportunity to achieve, or the need for and amount of appreciation and respect. The attempts by personnel psychologists to predict criteria based on measures of motives have been fewer in number and less successful than their attempts using measures of abilities (Ghiselli, 1966; Guion, 1965). Measures for appropriate dimensions of fit must still be developed. The maximum use of the data and greatest long-range reductions in organizational and individual strain should occur when the results of assessments are available to both the potential employer and the potential employee.

After the individual is on the job, the fit between the person and the job can be periodically assessed to identify the effects of changes in the job or in the person on fit. The assessments can range from informal observations to structured assessments using quantitative measures of P-E fit. Attempts to reduce stress can involve processes such as counseling, training, job redesign or transfer, and altered reward allocations.

Who should be responsible for monitoring stress and initiating corrective actions? The organization will typically monitor organizational strain and attempt to improve fit to reduce it. The reduction of individual strain typically becomes an issue for the organization only when the individual's strain affects organizational functioning. Similarly, the individual will typically monitor individual strain and attempt to improve fit to reduce it. The reduction of organization strain becomes an issue for the individual only when the organization's strain affects individual well-being. When these biases are recognized, it appears that both the organization and the worker must accept some responsibility for monitoring stress.

An optimal system for the reduction of both individual and organizational stress must include the perspective of both the individual and the organization. On a larger scale, contract negotiations between labor and management and management-worker councils are mechanisms to attempt to improve the fit between individuals and jobs at a gross level. On a smaller scale, the joint consideration of individual and organizational strain occurs when the worker participates in the decisions made concerning the job (Likert, 1961, 1967). This joint participation allows ongoing corrections and improvements to be made in person-environment fit aimed at minimizing both individual strain and organizational strain.

Employee participation has multiple meanings, but many of them would be likely to improve *P-E* fit. Sashkin (1976) has described four types of participation: participation in setting personal goals, in decision making, in problem solving, and in developing and implementing change. Each type of participation may help lead to a better fit between the employee and the job. Segovis and Bhagat (1981) have recently argued that participation should result in reduced stress. Their logic and reasoning is quite consistent with the proposal that the effect of participation on stress is at least in part achieved through the influence of participation on *P-E* fit.

Problems in Improving Fit

The joint participation of workers and organizational representatives in attempts to reduce strain becomes even more important when the potential conflicts are understood. The predisposition of the individual in attempting to reduce job stress is to seek to modify the job to fit better with the person. Such modifications may create serious problems for the organization. In the hypothetical example concerning the assembly line inspector, two options to improve fit by changing the job were to lower the role demands or to make pay not contingent on production rate. Either of these options may have serious implications for the functioning of the organization.

Similarly, the predisposition of the organization in attempting to reduce organizational stress is to seek to modify the person to fit better with the job. In the hypothetical example, two options to improve fit were to attempt to train the person to perform better or to attempt to reduce the person's expectations concerning pay. These options may be incompatible with the person's abilities or values.

Many times the reduction of individual strain will reduce organizational strain, and vice versa. For example, the training program may succeed in improving the inspector's performance, enhancing his self-esteem, and increasing his work efficiency in the organization. Other times, the changes to improve strain in one will not affect strain in the other. For example, an individual may be able to modify the schedule of incoming work to make the demands more even without affecting important work flow to others.

It is likely that many of the most stressful situations will require substantial investments of time and resources to resolve simply because employees and organizations would have already resolved them if a resolution advantageous to both parties were evident. This assumption is not made to dishearten, but to forewarn. Working out innovative compromises between individual goals and organizational goals may take appreciable preparation and ingenuity. For example, consider the attempt to reduce both individual and organizational strain by converting a fixed-pace assembly line to a team-production unit. Not only are role demands and the reward structure of the organization changed, but the control and coordination systems are changed as well. Similarly, the workers must acquire new skills, and their values concerning work roles taken into consideration and possibly modified.

Constraints on organizations and individuals will limit the extent to which the fit between persons can be maximized and stress reduced. However, *P-E* fit theory provides a useful framework for directing improvement efforts. The theory focuses on demands, rewards, motives, and supplies and provides insight into how they can affect the individual and the organization. With these insights individuals can better identify types of changes, and procedures for introducing these changes, that are likely to be optimal for both the individual and the organization.

CONCLUSIONS

The purpose of this chapter was to explain and demonstrate the utility of *P-E* fit theory. Its utility was demonstrated in the empirical support for its predictions, the guidance it offers in conceptualizing stress both as a function of the person and the environment and as a function of future uncertainty, the guidance it offers in conceptualizing the larger issue of the interface between the individual and the organization, and the direction it offers in identifying approaches to reducing individual and organizational stress.

The strength of the theory is its encompassing both the person and the environment. This broad focus encourages the systematic examination of their interrelationship and the processes that underlie it.

The theory also has limitations. It is essentially a "process" theory. Assumptions about particular motives, abilities, role demands, and rewards must be incorporated from "content" theories relevant to the problem under consideration. One direction for future research is to elaborate dimensions that reflect important "content" of individual motives and job demands. For example, no rigorous examination of *P-E* fit on uncertainty has been performed, although suggestive findings are available from the literature on tolerance for role ambiguity. The selection of dimensions to be explored will be guided by the primary characteristics of the job and persons being studied and the outcomes of interest to the researcher. However, many dimensions may be found to be important in a variety of occupational settings.

Probably more systematic emphasis will be placed on exploring the processes highlighted by the theory. The relationship between objective *P-E* fit and subjective *P-E* fit has received little empirical study, and no study has related objective fit to both individual and organizational perceptions of misfit and the associated organizational and individual strains. *P-E* fit theory offers a framework to integrate theories of motivation, perception and cognition, coping and defense, psychosomatic relationships, and organizational functioning. The problems involved with the static operation of these processes are sufficiently complex to hold the attention of most researchers. However, future researchers will also have to examine these processes in the context of changes over time in individuals' motives and organizational needs, the feedback effects of individual and organizational strain on *P-E* fit, and other dynamic processes.

Research concerning methodological issues also needs to be performed. There is now no empirical indication of the extent to which responses to the measures of the environment and the person currently used are contaminated by the respondents' perceived fit on the dimension. Nor are the effects understood for alternative wordings of items (e.g., how much do you: need, want, deserve . . . ; how much: do you have, are you required to, opportunity do you have . . .) and for separate placement or juxtaposition of items concerning the environment and person. The implications of and procedure for the combining scores across several dimensions of *P-E* fit have not been carefully considered. Of particularly interest to the model for the effects of uncertainty discussed in this book would be an examination of the relationship between the importance of an outcome to *P-E* fit on uncertainty concerning the outcome.

The scope of *P-E* fit theory and the systematic approach to its development are no accident. More than 20 years ago French and Kahn (1962) laid out the plan for a program of research to conceptualize and elaborate the relationship of the industrial environment to mental health. Since that time the elaboration and testing of the theory has continued. Its utility in conceptualization, prediction, and intervention assure its continued development and application in the years to come.

ACKNOWLEDGMENT

I would like to thank Terry A. Beehr and John R. P. French, Jr., for their helpful comments concerning this chapter.

REFERENCES

Abramson, L. Y., Seligman, M. E. P., and Teasdale, J. D. Learned helplessness in humans: Critique and reformulation. *Journal of Abnormal Psychology*, 1978, **87**, 49–74.

Archer, R. P. Relationships between locus of control and anxiety. *Journal of Personality Assessment*, 1979, **43**.

Argyris, C. Personality and organization theory revisited. *Administrative Science Quarterly*, 1973, **18**, 141–167.

Atkinson, J. W., and Feather, N. T. *A theory of achievement motivation*. New York: Wiley, 1966.

Beehr, T. A. Role ambiguity as a role stress: Some moderating and intervening variables. Doctoral dissertation, University of Michigan, 1974. *Dissertation Abstracts International*, 1975, **35**, 3631B–3632B. (University Microfilms No. 75-630, 1970)

Campbell, J. P., Dunnette, M. D., Lawler, E. E., III, and Weick, K. E., Jr. *Managerial behavior, performance, and effectiveness*. New York: McGraw-Hil¹ 1970.

Caplan, R. D. Organizational stress and individual strain: a social-psychological study of risk factors in coronary heart disease among administrators, engineers, and scientists. Doctoral dissertation, University of Michigan, 1971. *Dissertation Abstracts International*, 1972, **32**, 6706B-6707B. (University Microfilms No. 72-14822)

Caplan, R. D., Cobb, S., French, J. R. P., Jr., Harrison, R. V. and Pinneau, S. R., Jr. *Job demands and worker health: Main effects and occupational differences*. Ann Arbor, Mich. Institute for Social Research, 1980.

Caplan, R. D. Person-environment fit: Past, present and future. In C. L. Cooper (Ed.), *Stress research: Where do we go from here?* London: Wiley, 1983, 35–77.

De Charms, R. *Personal causation: The internal affective determinants of behavior*. New York; Academic Press, 1968.

Dembroski, T. M., MacDougall, J. M., Herd, J. A., and Shields, J. L. Effects of level of challenge on pressor and heart responses in Type A and B subjects. *Journal of Applied Social Psychology*, 1979, **9**, 209–228.

Dembroski, T. M., MacDougall, J. M., Shields, J. L., Petitto, J., and Lushene, R. Components of the Type A coronary-prone behavior pattern and cardiovascular responses to psychomotor challenge. *Journal of Behavioral Medicine*. 1978, **1**, 159–176.

Dunnette, M. D. Aptitudes, skills, and abilities. In M. D. Dunnette (Ed.), *Handbook of industrial and organizational psychology*. Chicago: Rand McNally, 1976, 473–520.

Evans, M. G. Conceptual and operational problems in the measurement of various aspects of job satisfaction. *Journal of Applied Psychology*, 1969, **53**, 93–101.

Feather, N. T. *Values in education and society*. New York: The Free Press, 1975.

French, J. R. P., Caplan, R. B., and Harrison, R. V. *The mechanisms of job stress and strain*. London: Wiley, 1982.

French, J. R. P. and Kahn, R. L. A programmatic approach to studying the industrial environment and mental health. *Journal of Social Issues*, 1962, **18**, 3, 1–47.

French, J. R. P., Rogers, W., and Cobb, S. A model of person-environment fit. In G. V. Coelho, D. A. Hamburgh, and J. E. Adams (Eds.), *Coping and adaptation*. New York: Basic Books, 1974.

Ghiselli, E. E. *The validity of occupational aptitude tests*. New York: Wiley, 1966.

Guion, R. M. *Personnel testing*. New York: McGraw-Hill, 1963.

Hackman, J. R. and Lawler, E. E., III. Employee reactions to job characteristics. *Journal of Applied Psychology*, 1971, **55**, 259–286.

Hackman, J. R. and Oldham, E. E. III. *Work redesign*. Reading, Mass.: Addison-Wesley, 1980.

Harrison, R. V. Job demands and workers health: Person environment misfit, Doctoral dissertation, University of Michigan, 1976. 320pp. *Dissertation Abstracts International*, 1976. (University Microfilms #76-19, 150)

Harrison, R. V. Person-environment fit and job stress. In C. L. Cooper and R. Payne (Eds.), *Stress at work*. London: Wiley, 1978.

House, J. S. The relationship of intrinsic and extrinsic work motivations to occupational stress and coronary heart disease risk. Doctoral dissertation, University of Michigan, 1972. *Dissertation Abstracts International*, 1972, **33**, 2514A. (University Microfilms No. 72-29094)

Hulin, C. L. and Blood, M. R. Job enlargement, individual differences, and worker response. *Psychological Bulletin*, 1968, **69** 41–55.

Ivancevich, J. M., Matteson, M. T., and Preston, C. Occupational stress, Type A behavior, and physical well-being. *Academy of Management Journal*, 1982, **25**, 373–391.

Joyce, W., Slocum, J. W., Jr., and Von Glinow, M. A. Person-situation interaction: Competing models of fit. *Journal of Occupational Behavior*, 1982, **3**, 265–280.

Kahana, E., Liang, J., and Felton, B. J. Alternative models of person-environment fit: Prediction of morale in three homes for the aged. *Journal of Gerontology*, 1980, **35**, 584–595.

Kahn, R. I., Wolfe, D. M., Quinn, R. P., Snoek, J. D., and Rosenthal, R. A. *Organizational stress: Studies in role conflict and ambiguity*. New York: Wiley, 1964.

Kulka, R. A. Person-environment fit in the high school: A validation study (2 vols.). Doctoral dissertation, University of Michigan, 1975. *Dissertation Abstracts International*, 1976, 36, 5352B (University Microfilms, No. 76-9438)

Kulka, R. A. Interaction as person-environment fit. *New Directions for Methodology of Behavioral Science*, 1979, **2**, 55–71.

Kulka, R. W., Klingel, D. M., and Mann, D. W. School crime and disruption as a function of student school fit: An empirical assessment. *Journal of Youth and Adolescence*, 1980, **9**, 353–370.

Kulka, R. W., Mann, D. W., and Klingel, D. M. A person-environment fit model of school crime and disruption. In K. Baker and R. J. Rubel (Eds.), *Violence and crime in the schools: Theoretical perspectives*. Lexington, Mass.: Heath, 1980.

Lawler, E. E., III. *Motivation in work organizations*. Belmont, Calif.: Wadsworth Publishing Company, 1973.

Lazarus, R. S. *Psychological stress and the coping process*. New York: McGraw-Hill, 1966.

Lazarus, R. S. and Averill, J. R. Emotion and cognition: With special reference to anxiety. In C. D. Spielberger (Ed.), *Anxiety: Current trends in theory and research, Vol. 2*. New York: Academic Press, 1972.

Lewin, K. *Field theory in social science*. New York: Harper, 1951.

Likert, R. *Management by participation*. New York: McGraw-Hill, 1961.

Likert, R. *The human organization*. New York: McGraw-Hill, 1967.

Locke, E. A. What is job satisfaction? *Organizational Behavior and Human Performance*, 1969, **4**, 309–336.

Lofquist, L. H. and Dawis, R. B. *Adjustment to work*. New York: Appleton-Century-Crofts, 1969.

Mason, J. W. A historical view of the stress field Part I. *Journal of Human Stress*, 1975, **1**, 1, 6–12.

Morse, J. J. Person-job congruence and individual adjustment and development. *Human Relations*, 1975, **28**, 841–861.

Murray, H. A. *Explorations in personality*. New York: Oxford University Press, 1938.

Newman, J. and Beehr, T. A. Personal and organizational strategies for handling job stress: A review of research and opinion. *Personnel Psychology*, 1979, **32**, 1–43.

Pervin, L. A. Satisfaction and perceived self-environment similarity: A semantic differential study of student-college interaction. *Journal of Personality*, 1967a, **35**, 623–634.

Pervin, L. A. A twenty-college study of student x college interaction using TAPE (transactional analysis of personality and environment): Rationale, reliability, and validity. *Journal of Educational Psychology*, 1967b, **58**, 290–302.

Pervin, L. A. Performance and satisfaction as a function of individual-environment fit. *Psychological Bulletin*, 1968, **69**, 56–68.

Porter, L. W. A study of perceived need satisfactions in bottom and middle management jobs. *Journal of Applied Psychology*, 1961, **45**, 1–10.

Quinn, R. P. and Mangione, T. W. Evaluating weighted models of measuring job satisfaction: A Cinderella story. *Proceedings of the 80th Annual Convention of the American Psychological Association*, 1972, **7**, 435–436.

Sashkin, M. Changing toward participative management approaches: A model and methods. *Academy of Management Review*, 1976, **1**, 75–86.

Segovis, J. C. and Bhagat, R. S. Participation revisited: Implications for organizational stress and performance. *Small Group Behavior*, 1981, **12**, 299–328.

Tannenbaum, A. S. and Kuleck, W. J., Jr. The effect on organization members of discrepancy between perceived and preferred rewards implicit in work. *Human Relations*, 1978, **31**, 809–822.

Wall, T. D. and Payne, R. Are deficiency scores deficient? *Journal of Applied Psychology*, 1973, **58**, 322–326.

Wanous, J. P. and Lawler, E. E., III. Measurement and meaning of job satisfaction. *Journal of Applied Psychology*, 1972, **56**, 95–105.

CHAPTER THREE

Organizational Stress and Employee Effectiveness
A Job Characteristics Approach

TERRY A. BEEHR

Chapter 2 of this book described the person-environment $(P\text{-}E)$ fit model of job stress, a model in which the individual employee and the employee's environment are given equal emphasis in their contributions to the stress of the employee. In that model (and relevant to the present chapter), stress on individuals is considered to be partly a function of the nonfulfillment of the employee's needs, that is, the resources provided by the job do not match the employee's desires. This lack of fit between the employee and the job results in stress and in the consequences to the individual that are described in Chapter 2.

While the $P\text{-}E$ fit model is particularly adept at describing a situation of certainty, that is, the certainty that the employee will not have his or her needs fulfilled by working in a given job, this chapter describes job stress in a way that places more emphasis upon the characteristics of the employee's work environment (i.e., the employee's job) than on the employee's personal characteristics (e.g.,needs). This approach, which is perhaps more common among some segments of the public, is more adept at describing the *uncertainty* existing in the present stressful situation of the employee. Figure 3-1 illustrates the distinction between these two approaches and places the contents of the present chapter into context.

The dimension defined by the continuum goes from certainty that one's needs (motives) will be fulfilled to certainty that one's needs (motives) will not be fulfilled. The midpoint represents uncertainty regarding need fulfillment or nonfulfillment.

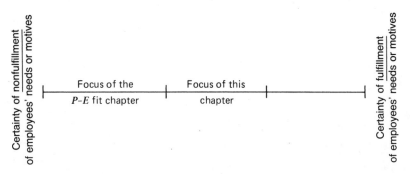

Figure 3-1 Distinction between *P-E* fit approach and this chapter's job characteristics approach.

As can be seen in the figure, the two approaches make different assumptions about the degree of certainty related to stress in the present job situation. In this chapter it is argued that job characteristics cause the employee to be uncertain about his or her need fulfillment on the *present* job. The major uncertainty in the *P-E* fit model is the uncertainty of need fulfillment in the *future*. When the present job allows for little fulfillment of employees' needs, it is argued that they feel less certain about future need fulfillment (or the lack thereof) because they may try to obtain new jobs, try to obtain or be given promotions or lateral transfers within the same company, or even quit their jobs without any concrete prospects for more satisfying work. Any such contemplations resulting from lack of fulfillment in the present job would lead to uncertainty of fulfillment in the future. In a similar manner the job characteristics approach in this chapter would predict an uncertain future for employees in jobs with stressful characteristics, but it additionally describes stressful jobs in which there is uncertainty regarding current need fulfillment.

DEFINITION OF EMPLOYEE EFFECTIVENESS

Choosing the criteria for effective employee performance is not as easy as it may at first appear. The criteria that organizational behavior experts have often considered first include quantity and quality of performance, absenteeism (or attendance), and turnover (or membership). While appearing to be very different, such criteria are also very consistent in that they are from the same value perspective—that of the organization. In organizational behavior, people have traditionally been employed by and done research for organizations or the people responsible for the welfare of the organization. As a result, the value perspective considering the organization's welfare as primary has been dominant.

There are, however, other value perspectives that could be invoked in choosing criteria for employee effectiveness. Among people studying stress, for example, the value perspective of the individual's welfare has been very strong. This is evidenced by the choice of criteria for many researchers and practitioners dealing with stress; they tend to choose employees' physical and psychological health. This approach, therefore, is from the individual's value perspective.

There is at least one other value perspective that could be invoked in examining the outcomes of job stress, namely, the perspective of the welfare of the community or society within which the organization and the individual reside. This value perspective is often ignored by researchers studying job stress, perhaps because it seems so difficult to operationalize. From this perspective one would like to know the effects of job stress on criteria that are valuable to the society as a whole. Examples of such criteria would include the effects of job stress on the nation's short supply of medical and psychological personnel and facilities, on the gross national product, or on the enthusiastic participation of the populace in the process of self-government. It is easy to see why researchers and practitioners alike might be willing to overlook such complex issues. In fact, the issue is even more complicated than this; once it is recognized that effectiveness needs to be considered from the viewpoint of those outside the organization, it becomes obvious that the organization's environment is composed of many discrete entities and is not a single, amorphous mass. Thus, a truly final analysis of effectiveness would deal with many internal and many external constituencies.

While the effectiveness of the individual employee is a micro issue, it has parallels on the macro level in the definition of the effectiveness of entire organizations. Steers (1977) has indicated that there is no one accepted definition or set of criteria for organizational effectiveness. In discussions of the goal approach to organizational effectiveness, early theorizing by Cyert and March (1963) and Thompson (1967) led to the concept of coalitions of various constituencies that determine organizations' goals. For present purposes, it is of interest that there are constituencies or groups of people with similar values or self-interests and that these groups may evaluate the effectiveness of the organization by different criteria. Although such constituencies are most commonly thought to be within the organization, Pennings and Goodman (1977) have noted that there maybe other constituencies that exist in the environment. The idea of a societal perspective, offered here, is the global combination of such environmental constituencies.

Examples of evidence for the grouping of constituencies or of value perspectives include Friedlander and Pickle's (1968) finding of three components of effectiveness of small businesses, namely, an employee perspective, an owner perspective, and a societal perspective. This study used organizations as the unit of analyses, and it was therefore a macrolevel investigation. In parallel to this at the microlevel, Gupta and Beehr (1981), in a factor-analytic study of employees' work and nonwork attitudes and behaviors, found that individuals' work-related activities and their nonwork activities did not load on the same factor. In addition, among the work-related activities, those that can be classified as belonging to the organizational perspective and those that belong to the individual perspective did not load on the same factor. This was replicated for individuals within four different organizations. Thus, at both the macro- and the microlevel, it appears that the three perspectives can be identified. As indicated by the title of this chapter, the primary interest here is in employee effectiveness, or the effects of stress on microlevel behaviors of the employees. These behaviors, however, may have value for the individual, the organization, or society as a whole.

Employee Effectiveness from the Individual Value Perspective

Individual consequences of job stress, often collectively labeled strain, may be categorized as physical, psychological, or behavioral (e.g., Beehr and Newman, 1978; House, 1974; Schuler, 1980). The physical effects of job stress include coronary heart disease and its various symptoms and risk factors (e.g., Friedman et al., 1957; House et al., 1979), and gastrointestinal disorders (e.g., Cobb and Kasl, 1972).

Typical psychological consequences include anxiety, depression, and dissatisfaction with the job (e.g., Beehr, 1976; Beehr et al., 1976; Abdel-Halim, 1981). Behavioral individual consequences are less well documented, but are thought to include drug use and abuse, suicide, and poor interpersonal relations (see review by Newman and Beehr, 1979). These are all consequences that are assumed to be more important to the individual himself or herself than to the organization or the society as a whole.

It is commonly thought that stressful stimuli (e.g., job characteristics) evoke the pituitary-adrenal response to stress, in which the posterior hypothalamus stimulates the adjacent anterior pituitary gland, resulting in chemical "messages" sent by the pituitary to the adrenal glands through the bloodstream. The messages cause the adrenalines to release catecholamines into the bloodstream (Bovard, 1959; Selye, 1976). Animal studies show that one of the eventual effects of stress is that substances (norepinephrine and serotonin) that are responsible for transmitting impulses across synapses between nerve cells are not available in normal amounts (Sweeney, 1981). Thus an interplay between the circulatory and nervous systems is thought to be responsible for some of the physical and/or psychological consequences of stress for the individual.

Employee Effectiveness from the Organizational Perspective

Organizational consequences of job stress are those outcomes that are traditionally defined as employee effectiveness by those who take the welfare of the organization as their primary value. From this perspective any employee behavior that has obvious, immediate consequences for the organization (either costs or benefits) is a measure of employee effectiveness. Three of the most traditional of such criteria that have been linked with job stress have already been noted: Job performance, membership, and attendance have all been linked with job stressors by organizational researchers.

Job Performance.   Of these three organizational criteria for employee effectiveness, the relationship of the last one (job performance) to job stressors has been the least well documented. Although two well-known models predict performance changes due to job stress, there are problems with the evidence supporting both of them.

The first and oldest of these models appears to be a variant of the turn-of-the century Yerkes–Dodson Law and has been especially popular in describing the effects of physical stressors on job performance. The illustration in Figure 3-2, commonly proposed in the job stress literature (e.g., Ivancevich and Matteson, 1980; Levi, 1981; Schuler, 1980) shows the basics of the principle. The use of this model in explaining the performance effects of occupational stress generally assumes that arousal is the key to understanding the performance of people experiencing stress. This idea, promoted earliest and most explicitly in the managerial literature on social psychological variables by Scott (1966) to explain the effects of task design on employees, contends that parts of the brain stem and the person are aroused or made more alert by certain characteristics of or levels of stimulation or changes in stimulation. This alerting or arousing is then linked to job performance, but not in a simple, direct manner. If the horizontal axis of Figure 3-2 were relabeled, "physiological arousal," the inverted U-shaped curve is assumed to represent the relationship between arousal and performance. Accordingly, increased arousal improves performance only up to a certain point (the apex of the curve), after which further increases in arousal are linked with decrements in performance.

Figure 3-2 Yerkes–Dodson law revised with job-stress terminology.

Figure 3-2 goes a step beyond the description offered by arousal theory in that it assumes a direct relationship between certain job characteristics and arousal; the particular job characteristics relevant here are those labeled job stressors—those discussed later in this chapter. The characteristics of jobs that make them stressful cause increases in physiological and neurological arousal and this arousal is related in a curvilinear manner to job performance. This is a very attractive explanation, since it would account for instances in which increasing pressures (stressors) on employees would lead to increased performance, no changes in performance, or decreased performance. Since managers know that motivating employee performance is complex and that what works at one time does not do so well at others, the complexity of the model matches the complexity of organizational life. It is as if pressure leads to performance until the employee reaches his or her "breaking point" and can no longer take the pressure.

This inverted U-shaped curve is commonly thought to represent the relationship between stressors of all sorts (including physical stressors such as heat or noise) and performance, but as noted by Landy and Trumbo (1980), the evidence for it is far from conclusive. One obvious problem with this formulation is that the curvilinearity of the proposed relationship makes it very difficult to refute. Any relationship found in a single study, for example, can be claimed to fit somewhere on the curve. Therefore, although the model has been promoted for many decades, it is not proven and, as noted by Ivancevich and Matteson (1980), it contains nagging "loose ends."

The second model is from McGrath (1976), who has proposed a four-stage stress cycle for analyzing the dynamics of job stress. It focuses on job performance behavior as the primary dependent variable. In his model the employee perceives a situation that would lead to undesirable outcomes for him or her, and the employee chooses a response aimed at improving the expected outcomes. Based upon the perception of the actual outcomes, the employee then chooses further responses, and the cycle begins again. While leaving open the possibility of the old notion of a curvilinear relationship between stressors and performance, McGrath's model and the research on which it is based did not support it.

In McGrath's model, task performance is most directly a function of experienced stress or arousal, the actual task ability of the employee, and actual task difficulty of the job. Experienced stress is determined by the perceived consequences of task performance and by uncertainty of successful task performance. This fits well with the model in Chapter 1, since uncertainty is a prime determinant of stress. McGrath also states that this "uncertainty is at a maximum when perceived difficulty is equal to perceived ability" (p. 1365). In terms proposed in the framework in chapter 1, this is the equivalent of saying that uncertainty is strongest when the $E \rightarrow P$ probability is about .5. This is because $E \rightarrow P$ increases toward $+1.0$ when the perceived difficulty of the task is less than the perceived ability of the person, and the $E \rightarrow P$ probability decreases toward 0 when the perceived task difficulty is greater than the perceived task ability. This approach links uncertainty to actual levels of $E \rightarrow P$. It could alternatively be proposed that uncertainty is somewhat independent of the level of expectancy. This proposition is explored in more detail later in this chapter.

Besides uncertainty, McGrath postuates that the other prime determinant of stress is the level of perceived consequences attached to task performance. Perceived consequences are one of the types of contingencies proposed in the framework in Chapter 1 to be a determinant of importance. Thus, both *uncertainty* and *importance* from the framework are essential parts of McGrath's formulation of stress. In addition to these characteristics, it is proposed here that *duration* of this uncertainty and importance will affect performance.

For the present purposes the biggest problem with McGrath's (1976) model is one recognized by McGrath (1974) himself, namely, it was developed from a study of little league baseball players:

> Now the reader surely must be asking, "What has little league baseball got to do with our topic?" Baseball is not "life," and a little league is only one very special instance of an organization, if it is that (p. 1358).

In spite of the research advantages to studying this sample of people, it must be acknowledged that the best evidence for the model suffers from a severe lack of generalizability to the population of primary concern to organization behavior: adult employees. Little leaguers are developmentally quite different people from adult employees, and the type of performance and task in which they engage is very different from nearly any employee's job. Thus, both in terms of sample and task, the evidence suffers greatly. This is unfortunate, since it is one of the more well developed models explicitly predicting employee job performance, as opposed to other outcomes of job stress.

Turnover. The other two employee effectiveness outcomes from an organizational perspective are more straightforward and better documented. Absenteeism and turnover can both be seen as types of withdrawal behaviors, since in each case the employee is staying away from the workplace. It is almost axiomatic that people try to get away and stay away from unpleasant situations, and it comes as no surprise to learn that employees would withdraw from jobs with unpleasant characteristics. Lyons (1971) has shown that voluntary turnover is linked with job stressors among a sample of nurses, and Gupta and Beehr (1979) found similar relationships among a sample that included a variety of occupations in five different organizations.

Absenteeism. In the same study Gupta and Beehr (1979) have also shown that job stressors are linked with absenteeism. In fact, the prediction of absenteeism from stressor levels was significant even when prediction of absenteeism from typical demographic predictors was held constant. In addition, since the prediction of absenteeism subsequent to the measurement of stressors was significantly greater than the prediction of absenteeism prior to the measurement of stressors, there was tentative support for the idea that the stressors were causing the absenteeism, rather than merely related to it. The support was only tenative because the nonexperimental nature of the study left some results open to alternate interpretations, for example, that the measurement of the stressors heightened employee awareness of job stress, causing them to be more often absent subsequent to the measurement. It can be said, however, that both absenteeism and turnover have been linked with job stressors among adult workers in real employment situations.

Employee Effectiveness from the Societal Perspective

In part, the welfare of society consists of the welfares of the individuals and organizations within it. Therefore, one theme of the societal perspective is that the accumulation of all of the individual and organizational effects of stress, if widespread, have an effect on society as a whole. Thus, it can be argued that when people are not as productive on their jobs as they can be and when they are absent frequently, for example, the nation's GNP does not grow as fast as it might (or it might even decline); that if people are frequently ill, there is a great drain on the national medical and mental health resources; and that taxes of certain types (e.g., unemployment and workers' compensation) increase, taking this money away from more productive uses. Statistics showing the evidence of the tremendous cost of such events exist, but there is little hard evidence that these obviously monumental costs are caused in part by occupational stress. Instead, it must be left to logic and rational argument for people to see that the individual and organizational costs associated with occupational stress have larger, societal implications as well.

An example from the research on occupational stress is a study by Anderson (1976), in which 100 owner-managers of small businesses experiencing floods due to Hurricane Agnes (June of 1972) were studied as they sought to recover. That stress as well as the physical damage caused by the hurricane itself was involved in the economic recovery of the community studied was apparent, since (1) the actual financial loss did not account for performance or recovery differences among businesses although perceived stress did, and (2) the type of coping or problem-solving activities of the owner-managers was related to the amount of stress they perceived. Thus, it can be argued that the experience of stress by the managers was an important factor in the economic recovery of the community.

Another argument for the effect of job stress on the society as a whole is related to a proposal by Kornhauser (1959) that "mass society," that is, a country in which people are not linked together by interlocking memberships in various groups or organizations (e.g., clubs, political parties, volunteer organizations, etc.) are conducive to mobilization by totalitarian leaders. Research is lacking, but if it were found that the societal behaviors of employees described by Gupta and Beehr (1981), (mentioned previously) are affected by job stress, it could be that such a mass society would be created or promoted by stress. Taken to the extreme, it could be argued that the very existence of the political democracy of a country could be endangered by job stress. These seemingly unlikely possibilities, primarily at a macro or sociological level thinking, are not addressed in current job stress research, since the societal perspective is the one most seldom invoked in this area of organizational behavior. This difficult-to-research area is obviously open to speculation and is in need of investigation.

The Beehr-Newman Metamodel of Job Stress

The Beehr-Newman model of job stress (Figure 3-3) is really a metamodel, a model that is intended to encompass many or all others. It is too broad to

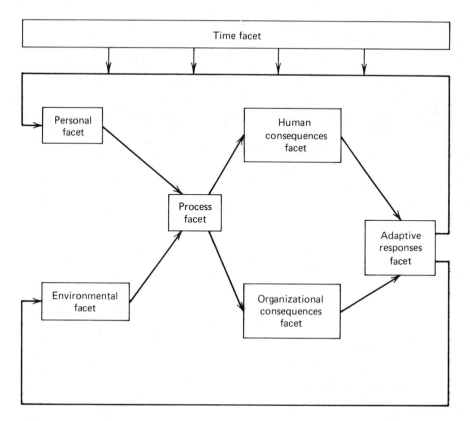

Figure 3-3 The Beehr–Newman metamodel of job stress (Beehr and Newman, 1978).

be explanatory or predictive, but it outlines the categories of interest to job stress researchers and the most typical hypothesized relationships among these categories. In the foregoing discussion of the three perspectives of the definition of effectiveness, the individual value perspective is represented by the human consequences facet and the organizational value perspective is represented by the organizational consequences facet. The societal perspective is not represented in the model, although Beehr and Newman note that adaptive strategies for dealing with job stress can be initiated by parties from outside the organization, and they expand upon this in a subsequent article (Newman and Beehr, 1979).

THE JOB CHARACTERISTICS APPROACH TO JOB STRESS

The job characteristics approach to job stress takes the characteristics of jobs as the primary causal factors in job stress (Beehr, 1980). Hackman and Oldham (1975) have proposed job characteristics as likely causal factors in employee satisfaction and motivation in their Job Description Survey. The job characteristics they outline are, however, not the only characteristics of jobs that have an important influence on employees. The concern here is with other job characteristics, job stressors, that are linked to employee health and effectiveness. It can be argued that Hackman and Oldham's model of intrinsic motivation due to job characteristics places primary emphasis on the job rather than on the individual characteristics, since individual characteristics are described as moderating the relationship between the job characteristics and employee outcomes. Similarly, in the job characteristics approach to job stress, the primary emphasis is on the job, and employees' individual characteristics are seen as moderating variables of secondary importance. Although both the Hackman and Oldham approach to intrinsic motivation and the job characteristics approach to stress acknowledge the role of individual differences, these seem to take a back seat to the job characteristics.

The difference between the job characteristics approach and the P-E fit approach of Chapter 2 is thus one of emphasis. The job characteristics approach would redraw the left side of the Beehr–Newman model as in Figure 3-4, to indicate that the environmental facet (which contains job characteristics) is the primary cause of stress, and the personal facet (which contains individual differences) is "only" a moderating facet. Often the job characteristics approach ignores this personal facet entirely. For this reason, and consistent with this job characteristics approach, the discussions in this chapter give minimal attention to individual differences. Chapter 2 exhibits a more balanced approach between personal and environmental characteristics.

The stressful uncertainty experienced by the individual is in the process facet, and it is assumed to derive directly from the job characteristics in the

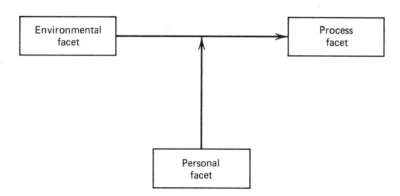

Figure 3-4 The left side of the Beehr–Newman model redrawn to correspond to a job characteristics approach.

environmental facet. Typical job characteristics that are stressors include (objective) role ambiguity, role overload, role conflict, underutilization of skills, job insecurity or actual job loss, and lack of participation in organizational decision making (e.g., Beehr, 1976; Beehr et al., 1976; Caplan et al., 1975; Cobb and Kasl, 1972; French and Caplan, 1973). These have been linked to various forms of employee ill health or well-being, and will shortly be discussed separately in regard to their hypothesized links with stressful uncertainty.

As described in the first chapter, these job characteristics are assumed to result in uncertainty regarding important outcomes, and consistent with Ivancevich and Matteson (1980) it is believed that the duration of this uncertainty is crucial to determining the severity of the stress outcomes.

Chapter 1 indicated that there is more than one type of uncertainty that can plague the employees in stressful job situations. A cognitive theory of motivation, expectancy theory, explains that these uncertainties can take different specific forms, primarily depending upon whether they represent uncertainty in the effort-to-performance expectancy $(E \rightarrow P)$ or the performance-to-outcome expectancy $(P \rightarrow O)$. It was argued there that ambiguity, overload, and underutilization of skill in any facet of one's life are stressful because they cause uncertainty. In job characteristics approaches to job stress, these correspond directly to the stressful job characteristics (stressors) commonly known as role ambiguity, role overload, and underutilization of skills at work. Since these three stressors were mentioned previously in Chapter 1, they will be discussed first, followed by analyses of two other stressful job characteristics, job insecurity and lack of participation.

Role Ambiguity

Role ambiguity is linked with uncertainty in both the $E \rightarrow P$ expectancies and the $P \rightarrow O$ expectancies. Exactly what role ambiguity is and how it ought to be measured is discussed in more detail in the next section of this chapter, but briefly, it is an objective job situation in which there are inadequate or misleading pieces of information regarding how one is supposed to do the job.

People get the message regarding how they are supposed to perform their work in several ways. First, and most directly, new employees may be given instructions by the supervisor or by a trainer or they may be given a set of written rules to read and comprehend. This is common in most jobs in formal organizations. Unfortunately, it is impossible for such "orientations" to cover all contingencies that may arise on a given job or to be sufficient in enough detail to answer all of the questions that may arise after the employee begins working on the job. Katz and Kahn (1978) argue that this incompleteness of information is inherent in organizations and is one of the reasons that leaders are necessary. The leaders must continually clarify the typical work situations and must make decisions regarding the novel situations emerging as time passes.

Second, ambiguity for veteran workers can be affected by rewards or punishments that the supervisors, coworkers, or even subordinates and customers bestow on them in return for certain specific job behaviors. For example, if the supervisor recommends the employee for a pay raise or promotion soon after or explicitly because of the employee's high quantity of performance, the employee may take this as a message indicating that quantity of performance is part of the definition of his or her job. If, on the other hand, the employee received no such rewards after completing an assignment in which he or she had high quality of performance, the employee may assume that this quality is not one of the expectations of his or her job. While more indirect than the role definition messages the employee received in orientation or in direct orders, this type of role message is an important one. Although these examples cite rewards, a complementary process occurs when punishments are given contiguously with or explicitly because of employees' role behaviors. It should also be repeated here that the supervisor is not the only source of role definition in an employee's work life.

When these types of role messages are absent, incomplete, infrequent, or distorted, role ambiguity exists and uncertainties of $E \rightarrow P$ or $P \rightarrow O$ arise.

Role Overload

Role overload is proposed to have its primary effect on uncertainty regarding the $E \rightarrow P$ expectancy. Since overload is in part defined as having too much work to do in the time available (e.g., French and Caplan, 1973), the immediate effect would be on the expectation that one can get enough work done at all, even with great effort. It is this uncertainty that effort will lead to adequate quantity of performance that is the essence of what has been labeled quantitative overload.

There is also a stressful job characteristic called qualitative overload (e.g., French and Caplan, 1973), a situation in which employees are not sure that effort will lead to adequate performance because they are not sure they have the skills required to do the job well. Whereas quantitative overload is related to the amount of time available, qualitative overload is related to the skill level of the employee. This might occur, for example, if an employee is promoted into a job that he or she is not qualified to do. If promotions are used for rewarding employees and not enough attention is given to using promotion as a means of matching people to jobs, this could happen. The Peter Principle is a tongue-in-check description of this type of organizational policy. Peter and Hull (1969) describe the case of Mal D'Mahr, who worked his way from ingot handler to general manager over a 20-year period and soon suffered a series of stress-related illnesses (ulcers and high blood pressure) because he was not qualified to make the decisions necessary to perform his new role. This fictional case captured the essence of qualitative role overload and its effects on the health of employees with this stressful job characteristic.

It is instructive here to note that when a stressful job characteristic results in uncertain $E \rightarrow P$ expectancies, there is also some uncertainty regarding the obtaining of the final outcome, O. Since the employee cannot be certain that good performance (P) will result from his or her efforts, he or she also cannot be sure of receiving an important O that is contingent upon P. It is still plausible, however, that the $E \rightarrow P$ expectancy is the only expectancy that is uncertain, since $P \rightarrow O$ may remain quite certain under such circumstances. This would occur if the employee believes that important outcomes will be forthcoming contingently upon good performance. It is entirely possible for an employee to be unsure that P will follow E and still to be very sure the O will follow P if P occurs. One must be careful not to confuse the uncertainty of receiving an outcome (O) due to an uncertain $E \rightarrow P$ with the uncertainty of $P \rightarrow O$.

Underutilization of Skills

Underutilization of skills is in some ways the converse of role overload. An employee whose skills are being underutilized has too much ability for the job he or she currently has. In the job characteristics approach it is assumed that there are jobs in which most people would be or are underutilized. The characteristics of the job are such that there are unlikely to be enough people who have so few skills that they would fit the job. The stereotypical examples are production jobs that are at the bottom of the organizational hierarchy. If such jobs have been designed via time and motion studies, the typical error is to make them too simple.

Taylor (1911) long ago acknowledged that designing jobs in the one best way in order to make them efficient in their use of time and human energy was only one of the keys to job design from his point of view. Another was to hire employees whose skills exactly matched the jobs that had been designed this way. Unfortunately, this second key point has seldom been followed, for two reasons. The first is that so many jobs have been designed requiring few skills that there are not enough people with such low skill levels available to fill these jobs. Taken to the extreme, it is easy to see that if every job were designed for very unskilled people, there would be a shortage of unskilled people to fill them. Therefore, there would be many employees experiencing underutilization of skills, and it would be primarily a fault of the characteristics of the job. Secondly, many organizations may not want to hire workers who have very limited skills because they want to have the option of promoting employees into more skilled positions. Therefore, they may ignore Taylor's ancient recommendation of hiring workers whose skills exactly fit the job, hiring instead employees who would be able to perform jobs into which they may eventually be promoted. Again, the result is having many employees whose skills are underutilized.

It is proposed that underutilization of skills will have little effect on the uncertainty of the $E \rightarrow P$ expectancy, since highly able employees doing unskilled jobs can be sure that their efforts will lead to good performance. If one has much more ability then the job requires, one can be relatively sure that effort will result in at least adequate performance. Uncertainty may result, however, in the $P \rightarrow O$ expectancy, particularly regarding intrinsic outcomes (O's). Since intrinsic rewards are on the average more possible if the job is more demanding, and since a nondemanding job is usually the cause of underutilization of skills, it follows that there is uncertainty regarding the receipt of intrinsic rewards such as pride in accomplishment or achievement following a job that is well done. Of course, this type of uncertainty would have its greatest impact on those employees who have the strongest needs for such intrinsic rewards. In the language of the model in Chapter 1, these are the employees for whom intrinsic rewards are most important.

There is less reason to believe, on the other hand, that underutilization of skills will be related to uncertain $P \rightarrow O$'s for extrinsic rewards. Even in the situation of underuse of the abilities of employees, employees may still be quite certain that a specific level of performance will result in a specific level of payment. In fact, Taylor's version of scientific management recommended precisely this method of payment. The use of some form of piece rate for production level jobs was intended to make it clear to the employee exactly what levels of payment would be received for what levels of performance.

Role Conflict

In the pioneering work of Kahn et al. (1964) on job stress, two stressful job characteristics were investigated: role ambiguity and role conflict. There are several styles of role conflict, but the essense of each is that there are two or more incompatible expectations made of the employee. In order to comply with one of the expectations, therefore, the employee would have to behave in ways that make compliance with another expectation more difficult.

In role theory a "sender" is someone who sends role messages to or places demands on an employee. The typical styles of role conflict are intersender conflict, intrasender conflict, interrole conflict, and person-role conflict. *Intersender role conflict* is probably the type that comes most easily to mind. It is the situation in which the expectations, pressures, or demands from one member of one's role set (perhaps a supervisor, a coworker, a subordinate, or a customer) are in conflict with the demands of at least one other member of the role set. Different people want the employee to do different things. An example would be a salesperson in pharmaceuticals whose supervisors expect him or her to make a large number of sales and whose customers (M.D.s) expect him or her to inform them of problems with the drugs, such as troublesome side-effects. By conforming to the demands of the M.D.s, the salesperson may make it less likely that the M.D. will prescribe the drug, thus lessening the likelihood of the high volume of sales demanded by the supervisor.

Intrasender role conflict occurs when the *same* member of a role set demands that the employee perform acts that are mutually exclusive or incompatible with each other. An example offered by Kahn et al. (1964) is the situation wherein a subordinate is ordered by the same supervisor to obtain materials that are not available through normal channels and yet is required not to go outside normal channels to acquire materials.

Interrole conflict is the situation in which the expectations and demands of members of the role set at work conflict with the expectations and demands of members of another role set outside of work. All people have multiple roles, and at times two or more of them may come into conflict with each other. Many "dual career" couples, for example, find that there are certain to be instances in which one does not have time to do everything demanded by both one's work role and one's family role. Chapter 6 describes this phenomenon.

Person-role conflict occurs when the demands of the work role set conflict with one's personal values. An example of this is the American executive of a multinational company whose personal value system maintains that it is immoral to bribe or to be bribed, and who finds that as part of dealing with some foreign countries it is customary to offer and to accept personal side payments for services done in the line of one's work role. The conflict here, therefore, is between the demands placed on the person by himself or herself and by the people that expect such "bribery" as a normal part of doing business. In a sense, this type of conflict recognizes that people are role senders in their own role set.

It is proposed here that these types of work-role conflict affect the employee partly by imposing a resulting experience of uncertainty on him or her. When Kahn et al. (1964) first proposed these conflicts as job characteristics that produce stress, they conclude that role overload was often related to them and was a type of conflict. Since then, most researchers have separated conflict and overload to treat them as separate stressors. Still, if they are somewhat related, it might be expected that role conflict would affect uncertainty in much the same manner that role overload does. Consistent with this, it is proposed here that role conflict has its primary impact on uncertainty of the $E \rightarrow P$ expectancy of the employee. Since not every demand can be met when one is in a situation of role conflict (by definition), it is difficult for the employee to know how to direct his or her efforts in order to result in adequate performance.

Job Insecurity or Job Loss

Job security or, at the extreme, even the loss of one's job is intuitively stressful. Job insecurity is a stressful job characteristic, but job loss technically may not quite fit the category of a job characteristic—since it is difficult for one to have any characteristics of a job when one has no job. It is useful, however, to treat these two together, since they are obviously linked. If the concept of "job" were expanded to mean "work," then job loss can be viewed as a "work" characteristic, that is, a factor in one's working life.

It is proposed that the primary uncertainty resulting from job insecurity or job loss is uncertainty about the $P \rightarrow O$ expectancy. In this case the outcome (O) is a secure job. This outcome is important for most employees and also for those who currently have no job. For the currently employed person the uncertainty revolves around the question of what performance (if any) on his or her job will make it more likely that the organization will retain him or her. For the currently unemployed person the meaning of performance is somewhat different. Performance is simply a job-specific term for the more general expectancy theory category, behavior. The question for the unemployed person, therefore, is what behavior will be followed by the acquisition of a new job. Logically, such behaviors might include searching the help-wanted advertisements, walking into personnel offices and completing job applications, asking for help from influential friends, taking job-retraining courses, and so on. The problem for most people is that they are uncertain what the probabilities are that these behaviors (performances) will lead to the outcome of acquring a stable job.

It is acknowledged that, as a result of the uncertain $P \rightarrow O$, the person may not know how to direct his or her efforts (E). The $E \rightarrow P$ probability, however, may still be quite certain if only the correct P were known. Thus, the problem is primarily in the uncertainty of the effort-to-performance end of the model.

Cobb and Kasl (1972) have shown some of the physiological and psychological effects of job insecurity and job loss in a sample of male workers whose jobs were abolished because of a plant shutdown. It is instructive to note that some of the changes in health began to occur when the employees heard that the plant might shut down, that is, during a period of job insecurity or anticipation of job loss. Of course, the effects continued during the period of actual job loss. These effects included high concentrations of uric acid and cholesterol in the bloodstream, high blood pressure, ulcers, and low self-esteem.

Similarly, it should be noted that both Sarason et al. (1978) and Holmes and Rahe (1967) discuss scales of stressful life events that include job loss as one such event, with the Sarason et al. scale also including the threat of job loss. While the relationship between these particular items and illness is unknown, the scale as a whole is related to the incidence of stress-related illnesses.

Lack of Participation

Increased participation in problem solving or decision making has been advocated by some schools of thought (e.g., Likert, 1961, 1967) for the purpose of increasing organizational effectiveness and employee satisfaction. There is also some indication, however, that the job characteristic of participation is related to employee health and welfare. French and Caplan (1973) and Beehr et al. (1976), for example, have found positive relationships between nonparticipation and employees' poor mental health. Since both of these studies also found that participation was positively related to role ambiguity, and since French and Caplan proposed that participation may be causally related to low ambiguity, it is hypothesized here that nonparticipation is related to uncertainty in the identical way that role ambiguity is: Nonparticipation results in uncertainty regarding both the $E \rightarrow P$ and the $P \rightarrow O$ expectancies.

Employees whose jobs allow them to participate in making decisions and solving problems related to their own work are more likely to understand what efforts lead to good performance on their jobs and also to understand what types of performance certain outcomes are likely to follow. This is simply because they are privy to more of the organization's policies and workings.

In summary, it is proposed here that several of the job characteristics (role overload, role ambiguity, role conflict, underutilization of skills, job insecurity or job loss, and lack of participation) that are typically labeled stressors are linked to uncertainty. Specific hypotheses were proposed regarding whether the uncertainty resulting from each is likely to occur in the $E \rightarrow P$ or the $P \rightarrow O$ expectancies in the expectancy theory framework of stress proposed in Chapter 1 of the book.

ROLE AMBIGUITY AS A CENTRAL CONSTRUCT IN THE JOB CHARACTERISTICS APPROACH TO JOB STRESS

Role ambiguity has consistently been one of the stressors investigated by many job stress researchers, probably because it has more intuitive links with the concept of uncertainty than most of the other stressors. It also is a central construct in some other models of organizational behavior in general, indicating that it may be of importance for many areas of organizational life in addition to job stress. House and Rizzo (1972), for example, cite role ambiguity and role conflict as the two major intervening variables in a model encompassing almost all of organizational behavior. They proposed that it is a potential product of many aspects of organizational life and is a causal factor in many outcomes, both personal and organizational. Similarly, Walsh et al. (1980) have developed a path analytic model of job satisfaction in which clarity (low role ambiguity) and challenge are the two crucial variables explaining the relationship between leadership styles, intrinsically motivating job characteristics, and other popular organizational behavior variables and job satisfaction. All in all, the further investigation of role ambiguity therefore seems promising, for many reasons.

Confusion Resulting from Role Ambiguity Scales

Role ambiguity also presents problems, however, for our present purposes, since it may be difficult to distinguish from uncertainty itself. It is important to note that there is a distinction between the subjective experience of uncertainty and the more objective, environmental factors that lead people to experience uncertainty. The former is labeled uncertainty, and the latter, role ambiguity. The distinction is a fine but necessary one. Uncertainty results from any of the stressors, of which role ambiguity is but one. This is a conceptual problem with role ambiguity that must be overcome. This problem can be seen in questionnaire items that ask about feelings of uncertainty regarding what one is supposed to do on one's job and those asking about the clarity of messages the employee receives from others. Conceptually, the references to role messages are face-valid measures of role ambiguity, while the references to feeling of uncertainty are face-valid measures of the resulting uncertainty that the framework of this book proposes as a major element of job stress.

There are corresponding operational problems with the measurement of role ambiguity. Tracy and Johnson (1981) have done some secondary reanalyses of the questionnaire that is most frequently used to operationalize role ambiguity in the organizational behavior literature. The factor analysis of the House and Rizzo (1972) scales can most simply be interpreted as resulting in factors that load items in large part according to the positive or negative wording of the items, rather than according to the intended content of the items (role ambiguity versus role conflict). All of the items chosen from Rizzo et al. (1970) to be included in their final factor-analytically derived scale have this problem: All of the chosen role conflict items are worded negatively (i.e., they describe aversive conditions for the employee), and all of the chosen role ambiguity items are worded positively (i.e., they describe "good" conditions for the employee). This evidence is more compelling than the conclusion from Schuler et al. (1977), based upon their analyses of the scales, that the scales are *valid*. Instead, their analyses can be viewed, in the light of the Tracy and Johnson study, as showing at best that the scales are *reliable*. The most accurate conclusion about the House and Rizzo scales is that their exclusive and unquestioned use is unwarranted. The tendency to settle on these as the most accepted scales is premature and has slowed the attempts to understand role ambiguity more thoroughly.

Regarding the content of the scale items of the House and Rizzo role ambiguity scale, many of the items overlap with the concept of individual uncertainty as well as with the concept of environmental role ambiguity. Items that begin with "I feel certain" or "I know" are face valid items of uncertainty, while items describing the nature of explanations that are given to the employee and the nature of the goals of the job are face-valid measures of the concept of role ambiguity.

There are scales other than the House and Rizzo scales that are worth continued use and development at this early stage of investigation. No doubt any of them would need further psychometric development; the House and Rizzo scales receive special treatment here only because of their heavy and often unquestioned use. Other investigations of role ambiguity scales may help the readers to see problems with and comparabilities among several of them: Abdel-Halim (1978) and Breaugh (1980) have provided two such investigations.

It is obvious from these studies that no one scale is good enough to deserve exclusive use or continued use without further development. Tracy and Johnson also recommended the use of nontraditional methods of measurement such as behavioral and projective measures of role ambiguity. As defined here, role ambiguity is not likely to be measured accurately projectively, but it may be possible to measure it through observation of the behaviors of people *other than* the focal person, namely, the focal person's associates who send messages to him or her. Uncertainty as defined here may be amenable to projective measures or behavioral observation of the focal person, although such measures have yet to be developed. The individual employee's uncertainty regarding his or her $E \rightarrow P$ or $P \rightarrow O$ expectancies would need to be measured. Schuler et al. (1977) came close to this approach when they demonstrated relationships between role ambiguity and expectancy I $(E \rightarrow P)$ in five different organizational sites, but they did not go far enough to test the framework proposed here for two reasons: (1) they measured role ambiguity with the contaminated House and Rizzo scales and (2) they correlated role ambiguity with the *level* of expectancy instead of with the *certainty* regarding the level of expectancy.

Pearce (1981) has recently proposed that role ambiguity is linked to the predictability (uncertainty) of the $E \rightarrow P$ expectancy, although the model offered there seems also to implicate the uncertainty of the $P \rightarrow O$ expectancy as a consequence of role ambiguity. This insightful interpretation also includes the concept of importance and notes of the problems with the contamination of many of the measures of role ambiguity that are currently in use. In the use of the term *role ambiguity*, Pearce is often referring to uncertainty rather than role ambiguity as the terms are used here.

Thus, the uses of the construct role ambiguity have been fraught with problems for understanding occupational stress. Only Pearce has shown clear understanding that the predictability of expectancies is an important element in the study of job stress. As a further aid to the reader's understanding of the distinction between role ambiguity and uncertainty, in the Beehr and Newman (1978) model role ambiguity consists of elements of the environmental facet (of the job or work organization), and uncertainty is placed in the process facet (see Figure 3-3).

Suggested Methods for Developing Separate Measures of Uncertainty and Role Ambiguity

The beginning efforts to develop separate measures of role ambiguity emanating from ambiguous messages and the resulting uncertainty of $E \rightarrow P$ or $P \rightarrow O$ might well take a two-pronged approach. One effort would be to develop the two measures by surveying both as perceptions from a single source, the job incumbent. This, the easier approach, might consist of developing questionnaire (or interview) items with face-valid questions (described earlier) of each construct; administering the items to a large group of workers; and factor- or cluster-analyzing the resulting responses, searching for two factors that match the face-valid, a priori categorizations of the items. After a few iterations of this approach, a face-valid questionnaire with some discriminant validity could probably be developed for further investigation.

The second approach would be more difficult, but it may ultimately have greater benefits. It consists of developing questionnaire (or interview) items of role ambiguity that could be administered to the job incumbent's role senders, to measure the degree of ambiguity in their expectations and role messages. Alternatively, or in addition, more controlled (but probably more artificial) situations could be developed in which observers could be trained to observe and record the degree of role ambiguity inherent in role messages sent to the job incumbent by the role senders. The resulting uncertainty would then be measured with questionnaire (or interview) items administered to the job incumbent.

A truly two-pronged attack on the problem would be best, however. Both of the approaches described above would be executed simultaneously, focused on a single set of job incumbents, and the resulting measures would be examined for their interrelationships. The measures of role ambiguity administered to the role senders or to the observers should be more closely related to the measures of role ambiguity administered to the job incumbents than to the measures of uncertainty administered to the job incumbents. Since it is theorized that role ambiguity partially causes uncertainty, however, it would be expected that all of the measures should be positively correlated.

Once empirically separate measures of the uncertainties and role ambiguity are developed, testing of the cognitive model of stress proposed in this book can begin. Uncertainty, along with importance and duration, would be the central constructs in this model. This chapter devotes considerably more space to uncertainty than to importance or duration, because the understanding and measurement of uncertainty are more problematic.

DIRECTIONS FOR FUTURE RESEARCH

This chapter suggests eight themes for future research. The first three of these are related to the measurement and analyses of the uncertainties presented in the framework in Chapter 1. First, separate measures of role ambiguity and uncertainty need to be developed. The problems noted earlier with the present measures of role ambiguity are a major problem for future research that could test the framework. Some of the current operationalizations measure uncertainty of $P \rightarrow O$ and $E \rightarrow P$, and some do not. Even those that do appear to measure these have combined such items with items that are more truly role ambiguity as described in this chapter. Until role ambiguity is operationally separated from uncertainty, research on the model of job stress offered in this book cannot continue.

Second, and related to the first needed direction for research, measures of uncertainty need to be developed. Current measures of the *levels* of $P \rightarrow O$ and $E \rightarrow P$ expectancies have problems, but no one has even attempted to measure the *uncertainty* of these expectancies. This will no doubt be a difficult undertaking if the difficulty with measuring the levels of $E \rightarrow P$ and $P \rightarrow O$ are any indication.

Third, once the measurement problems have been overcome, the next task will be to determine the extent to which the uncertainties of $E \rightarrow P$ and $P \rightarrow O$ expectancies are related to the various stressors such as role ambiguity, role conflict, role overload, and so on. In this chapter it has been suggested that each of the stressors is related differentially to one or both of these uncertainties, but these suggestions are only hypotheses at this point. When adequate measures of the uncertainties become available, these hypotheses can be tested. At a minimum the stressors would have to be related to one or the other type of uncertainty in order to be consistent with the framework proposed in the first chapter.

The fourth and fifth recommendations for future research concern the Chapter 1 concepts of importance and duration, respectively. The fourth is that the job characteristics approach needs to incorporate the concept of importance more prominently than it has done previously. As can be ascertained from the preceding discussion in this chapter, this would make the approach less rigidly a job characteristics approach, but that is probably necessary to improve the model's fidelity to real-world stress. The manner in which Hackman and Oldham (1975) incorporate needs (importance) into their job characteristics approach to employee motivation is a potential example to follow.

The fifth area for future research is the testing of the effects of the Chapter 1 concept, duration. This would require longitudinal studies in which stressful job characteristics, uncertainty, importance, and employee effectiveness (and/or strain) are measured repeatedly over a period of time. If duration is a key factor, stressful job characteristics that persist over time would result in more extreme effects on uncertainty than would stressful job characteristics that are more fleeting. Similarly, prolonged uncertainty of $E \rightarrow P$ or $P \rightarrow O$ would result in greater effects on employee effectiveness than would brief experiences of uncertainty.

Sixth, absenteeism and turnover have been shown related to stressors, but there is little evidence regarding the reason for this empirical result. The framework proposes to explain the experienced nature of job stress, but can it also help to explain the relationships between the causal elements of stress (stressors) and some of the consequences that are important to organizations? Behavioral intention theories may help to explain the occurrence of such behaviors in combination with the framework. Along with the uncertainties of work-related expectancies in the job stress situation, are other important elements also uncertain, such as the social norms of behavioral intention theory? The field of job stress needs eventually to go beyond the discovery of events and relationships between events to understand and explain the reasons behind the events more fully.

The seventh recommendation is to focus some future research on the potential effect of job stress on the well-being of the society as a whole. As noted earlier in this chapter, community or societal well-being has only rarely been investigated as a consequence of work-related stress. Such studies could borrow theory and concepts from the more sociologically oriented, better established work on the general relationships between work- and nonwork-related attitudes and behaviors of employees (e.g., see Gupta and Beehr, 1979; Kabanoff, 1980; Meisner, 1971, Near et al., 1980; Wilensky, 1960).

Eighth, and finally, validity of the popular assumption that social stressors on the job (Love and Beehr, 1981) have an inverted, U-shaped relationship with job performance needs to be tested systematically. This requires more than post hoc interpretations of confusing empirical results. Large-scale studies in which very large ranges of stressor strength are manipulated or measured are necessary, as are adequate measures of a type of performance that is free to vary according to the activities of the workers. Such studies are difficult to do, but the rewards accruing include the ability to obtain strong evidence regarding this relationship.

REFERENCES

Anderson, C. R. Coping behaviors as intervening mechanisms in the inverted-U-stress-performance relationship. *Journal of Applied Psychology*, 1976, **61**, 30–34.

Abdel-Halim, A. A. Employed affective responses to organizational stress: Moderating effects of job enrichment characteristics. *Personnel Psychology*, 1978, **31**, 561–569.

Abdel-Halim, A. A. Effects of role stress-job design-technology interaction on employee work satisfaction. *Academy of Management Journal*, 1981, **24**, 260–273.

Beehr, T. A. Job stress: A new managerial concern. In K. M. Rowland, M. London, G. R. Ferris, and J. L. Sherman (Eds.), *Current issues in personnel management.* Boston: Allyn & Bacon, 1980.

Beehr, T. A. Perceived situational moderators of the relationship between subjective role ambiguity and role strain. *Journal of Applied Psychology*, 1976, **61**, 35–40.

Beehr, T. A. and Newman, J. E. Job stress, employee health, and organizational effectiveness: A facet analysis, model and literature review. *Personnel Psychology*, 1978, **31**, 665–699.

Beehr, T. A., Walsh, J. T. and Taber, T. D. Relationship of stress to individually and organizationally valued states: Higher order needs as a moderator. *Journal of Applied Psychology*, 1976, **61**, 41–47.

Bovard, E. W. The effects of social stimuli on the response to stress. *The Psychological Review*, 1959, **66**, 267–277.

Breaugh, J. A. A comparative investigation of three measures of role ambiguity. *Journal of Applied Psychology*, 1980, **65**, 584–589.

Caplan, R. D., Cobb, S., French, J. R. P., Jr., Van Harrison, R., and Pinneau, S. R. *Job demands and worker health: Main effects and occupational differences.* Washington, D.C.: U.S. Government Printing Office, 1975.

Cobb, S. and Kasl, S. V. Some medical aspects of unemployment. In G. M. Shatto (Ed.): *Employment of the middle-aged: Papers from industrial gerontology seminars.* Springfield, Ill.: Thomas, 1972, 87–96. Reprinted in *Industrial Gerontology*, Winter 1972, **12**.

Cyert, R. M. and March, J. G. *A behavioral theory of the firm.* Englewood Cliffs, N.J.: Prentice-Hall, 1963.

French, J. R. P., Jr., and Caplan, R. D. Organizational stress and individual strain. In A. J. Marrow (Ed.), *The failure of success.* New York: AMACOM, 1973.

Friedlander, F. and Pickle, H. Components of effectiveness in small organizations. *Administrative Science Quarterly*, 1968, **13**, 289–304.

Friedman, M., Rosenman, R. and Carroll, V. Changes in the serum cholesterol and blood clotting time of men subject to cyclic variation of occupational stress. *Circulation*, 1957, **17**, 852–861.

Gupta, N. and Beehr, T. A. Job stress and employee behaviors. *Organizational Behavior and Human Performance*, 1979, **23**, 373–387.

Gupta, N. and Beehr, T. A. Relationships among employees' work and nonwork responses. *Journal of Occupational Behavior*, 1981, **2**, 203–209.

Hackman, J. R. and Oldham, G. R. Development of the Job Diagnostic Survey. *Journal of Applied Psychology*, 1975, **60**, 159–170.

Holmes, T. H. and Rahe, R. H. The social readjustment rating scale. *Journal of Psychosomatic Medicine*, 1967, **11**, 213–218.

House, J. S. Occupational stress and coronary heart disease: A review and theoretical integration. *Journal of Health and Social Behavior*, 1974, **15**, 12–27.

House, J. S., McMichael, A. J., Wells, J. A., Kaplan, B. H., and Landerman, L. R. Occupational stress and health among factory workers. *Journal of Health and Social Behavior*, 1979, **20**,139–160.

House, R. J. and Rizzo, J. R. Role conflict and ambiguity as critical variables in a model of organizational behavior. *Organizational Behavior and Human Performance*, 1972, **7**, 467–505.

Ivancevich, J. M. and Matteson, M. T. *Stress and work: A managerial perspective.* Glenview, Ill.: Scott, Foresman, 1980.

Kabanoff, B. Work and nonwork: A review of models, methods, and findings. *Psychological Bulletin*, 1980, **88**, 60–77.

Kahn, R. L., Wolfe, D. M., Quinn, R. P., Snoek, J. D., and Rosenthal, R. A. *Organizational stress: Studies in role conflict and ambiguity.* New York: Wiley, 1964.

Katz, D. and Kahn, R. L. *The social psychology of organizations*, 2nd ed. New York: Wiley, 1978.

Kornhauser, W. *The politics of mass society.* New York: The Free Press, 1959.

Landy, F. J. and Trumbo, D. A. *Psychology of work behavior*, rev. ed. Homewood, Ill.: Dorsey Press, 1980.

Levi, L. *Preventing work stress.* Reading, Mass.: Addison-Wesley, 1981.

Likert, R. *New patterns of management.* New York: McGraw-Hill, 1961.

Likert, R. *The human organization: Its management and value.* New York: McGraw-Hill, 1967.

Love, K. G. and Beehr, T. A. Social stressors on the job: Recommendations for a broadened perspective. *Group and Organization Studies*, 1981, **6**, 190–200.

Lyons, T. Role clarity, need for clarity, satisfaction, tension and withdrawal. *Organizational Behavior and Human Performance*, 1971, **6**, 99–110.

McGrath, J. E. Stress and behavior in organizations. In M. D. Dunnette (Ed.), *Handbook of industrial and organizational psychology.* Chicago: Rand McNally, 1976.

Meissner, M. The long arm of the job: A study of work and leisure. *Industrial Relations*, 1971, **10**, 239–260.

Near, J. P., Rice, R. W., and Hunt, R. G. The relationship between work and nonwork domains: A review of empirical literature. *Academy of Management Review*, 1980, **5**, 415–430.

Newman, J. E. and Beehr, T. A. Personal and organizational strategies for handling job stress. A review of research and opinion. *Personnel Psychology*, 1979, **32**, 1–43.

Pearce, J. L. Brining some clarity to role ambiguity research. *The Academy of Management Review*, 1981, **6**, 665–674.

Pennings, J. M. and Goodman, P. S. Toward a framework of organizational effectiveness. In P. S. Goodman and J. M. Pennings (Eds.), *New perspectives on organizational effectiveness.* San Francisco: Jossey-Bass, 1977.

Peter, L. F. and Hull, R. *The Peter principle.* New York: William Merrow, 1969.

Rizzo, J. R., House, R. J., and Lirtzman, S. I. Role conflict and ambiguity in complex organizations. *Administrative Science Quarterly*, 1970, **15**, 150–163.

Sarason, I. G., Johnson, J. H., and Siegel, J. M. Assessing the impact of life changes: Development of the Life Experiences Survey. *Journal of Consulting and Clinical Psychology*, 1978, **46**, 932–946.

Schuler, R. S. Definition and conceptualization of stress in organizations. *Organizational Behavior and Human Performance*, 1980, **25**, 184–215.

Schuler, R. S., Aldag, R. J., and Brief, A. P. Role conflict and ambiguity: A scale analysis. *Organizational Behavior and Human Performance*, 1977, **20**, 111–128.

Scott, W. E. Jr. Activation theory and task design. *Organizational Behavior and Human Performance*, 1966, **1**, 3–30.

Selye, H. *The stress of life*. New York: McGraw-Hill, 1976.

Steers, R. M. *Organizational effectiveness: A behavioral view*. Santa Monica, Calif.: Goodyear, 1977.

Taylor, F. W. *Principles of scientific management*. New York: Harper & Row, 1911.

Thompson, J. D. *Organizations in action*. New York: McGraw-Hill, 1967.

Tracy, L. and Johnson, T. W. What do the role conflict and role ambiguity scales measure? *Journal of Applied Psychology*, 1981, **66**, 464–469.

Walsh, J. T., Taber, T. D., and Beehr, T. A. An integrated model of perceived job characteristics. *Organizational Behavior and Human Performance*, 1980, **25**, 252–267.

Wilensky, H. L. Work, careers, and social integration. *International Social Science Journal*, 1960, **12**, 543–560.

CHAPTER FOUR

As the Ax Falls

Budget Cuts and the Experience of Stress in Organizations

TODD D. JICK

Simply put, it just is not as much fun working and managing in a contracting organization as it is in an expanding one.
                                                    (LEVINE, 1979:80)

I didn't think this [budget crisis] would affect me. I didn't think this would happen to me. I've always been on time and worked hard at my job. It's something I never expected.
                            A BOSTON MUNICIPAL EMPLOYEE ON HIS LAST
                            DAY AT WORK BEFORE BEING LAID OFF
                            (*BOSTON HERALD AMERICAN*, APRIL 1, 1980)

SIGNS OF THE TIMES

Newspaper headlines proclaiming budget cuts, economic slowdown, and layoffs have appeared routinely in Western developing countries during the late 1970s and early 1980s. A spirit of austerity has become an integral part of the political and economic environment within which private and public sector organizations operate. And most predictions indicate that this state of affairs will continue well into the 1980s.

Perhaps most surprising and drastic have been the cutbacks in the public sector. These cutbacks, defined as lower levels of resource consumption and activity (Levine, 1979), are represented by terms such as contraction, retrenchment, streamlining, reductions-in-force, and zero-based budgeting. Among the most commonly cited reasons for the cuts are:

(1) the decline in population growth rates; (2) the high rate of deficit spending by government, which some agree has exacerbated the rate of inflation; (3) a drift to the right in political sentiments advocating a general reduction in the involvement of the state in people's lives; and (4) disillusionment among politicians, the media, and the public in the ability and efficiency of many public-sector organizations.

Symbolized by Proposition 13 in California, Proposition 2½ in Massachusetts, and the piercing knife of Reaganomics, stringent cuts have occurred at all levels of government—municipal, state, and federal. Job openings, public programs, and the scope of governmental involvement have been reduced in many areas. In short, the image of the public sector as a protected bastion of secure jobs and programs has been dramatically eroded. Such expectations have become permanently violated.

The advent of funding cutbacks has produced near chaos in many public agencies and programs. Levine et al. (1980) argue that organizational retrenchment in the public sector is more turbulent, more conflict prone, and more uncertain than in private-sector industries where firms have more control over goal setting and over the means to change direction and structure. Moreover, for those public-sector managers who grew up with the notion that people would only demand more of their organization's services and be willing to pay as much as necessary to get them, managing with less has been particularly trying.

And, as organizations adapt to leaner times, employees have been subject to multiple sources of stress, including (1) the uncertainty and instability of their work lives in the face of constant change and decline, (2) the fear of job loss, (3) the burdens of "doing more with less" as a result of decreased staffing, (4) the pressure to cut costs wherever possible, (5) the increase in paperwork to document all spending and activity, (6) the strain between administrators and staff over the direction and mission of many organizations, and (7) the fear that job performance will be adversely affected. In short, it is a stress situation that is likely to contain many more demands and constraints than opportunities (McGrath, 1976; Payne, 1979). Moreover, it is a situation that individually and organizationally contains many crisislike characteristics in terms of demands and time pressure (Jick and Murray, 1982).

Recent anecdotal evidence abounds on the deleterious consequences for many individuals. For example, federal budget cuts seem to have played a significant role in a recent increase in federal employees' usage of health services. In light of feared reductions of federal workers, almost triple the number of federal employees were treated at the Department of Health and Human Services for stress-related symptoms such as dizziness, stomach cramps, diarrhea, and increased blood pressure (Rosellini, 1981). In Denver, government employees whose staff had been pruned and reorganized were found to be so fearful about their future that productivity suffered (Blundell, 1981). One manager estimated that the atmosphere of "gloom" cost the equivalent of about a month's work per year per employee.

Unfortunately, largely because of the recency of the phenomenon, there has been very little systematic research and conceptual work conducted on the stress of budget cuts—that is *how individuals react to the threat and the reality of budget cuts.* Using related research in areas such as threat, crisis, disasters, and uncertainty, this chapter will develop a conceptual framework on which to base subsequent empirical studies of the effects of funding cutbacks on individuals. The focus will be on how and why individuals perceive cutbacks as they do and how they react to, and are affected by, such situations.

This area of research is important to stress researchers for several reasons:

1. It allows for the study of large samples of individuals "at risk." Recent criticism of stress research has suggested that too many stress studies misguidedly examine relatively stress-free populations (Fletcher and Payne, 1980). It is expected that employees in shrinking organizations will be prone to considerable stress and thus more likely to manifest strain symptoms of interest to stress researchers.

2. It represents a real and relevant problem for individuals, organizations, and society. The effects of "hard-times" stress provides, and will likely continue to provide, opportunities for field study in an area of public concern.

3. Given the likely continuation of cutbacks, this research can investigate through longitudinal study the differences between chronic and acute stress. Research has typically been conducted in situations of acute stress (Payne et al., 1982), but there is increasing interest in the effects of long-term stressors.

4. It is consonant with the recent interest in organizational behavior in the understanding of organizational decline and crisis. (Jick and Murray, 1982; Billings et al., 1980; Whetten, 1980a,b).

5. It is intended to develop conceptual and diagnostic tools for helping managers manage hard times more effectively and humanely. That is, research on the effects of budget cuts should lead to a better understanding of both organizationally and individually based coping strategies.

6. In the context of this book on stress, it is a field of study that can usefully apply a cognitive focus for understanding the psychological reactions to cutbacks. That is, the employees' actual interpretation of the cutbacks and their felt threats (or challenges) will be examined.

We will begin then by presenting an overall conceptual framework for the analysis of the factors affecting the way in which individuals perceive cutbacks and respond to them. The supportive literature and evidence for the framework will follow, as well as various hypotheses suggestive of further research.

CONCEPTUAL REVIEW AND A MODEL

Although stress researchers have not explicitly addressed the context of declining organizations, the stress of "hard times" on individuals and organizations in other contexts has been a prominent topic of interest. For example, some have investigated the overall effects of economic change on mental health (Pearlin et al., 1981; Catalano et al., 1981; Dooley and Catalano, 1980; Brenner, 1973), and the victims of job loss and plant closings (Kaufman, 1982; Jick, 1979; Strange, 1978; Cobb and Kasl, 1977; Slote, 1969), thus recalling Depression studies of the unemployed (Bakke, 1940; Zawadzki and Lazarsfeld, 1935; Eisenberg and Lazarsfeld, 1938) and the aftermath of natural disasters (Turner, 1976; Brouilette and Quarantelli, 1971; Withey, 1962). These studies indirectly address a wide variety of stress responses likely to arise out of conditions bearing some parallels to the impact of cutbacks.*

The growing literature on crisis, decline, and uncertainty (e.g., Nottenburg and Fedor, 1981; Billings et al., 1980; Whetten, 1980a,b; Holsti, 1978; Fink et al., 1971; Hermann, 1963) is still another source of related material. Recent work by Jick and Murray (1982) has explicitly linked this literature with *organizational* reactions to externally imposed funding cuts but not with individual-level stress responses. Similarly, there is a small body of literature that discusses the strategic decision responses of organizations to budget cut mandates (Levine, 1980; Levine, 1978; Glassberg, 1978) as well as the preconditions for making cuts (Levine et al., 1980), but tends to ignore the individual-level behavioral and attitudinal reactions to the organizational stress. One can only infer some of these rections from anecdotal and case material (Levine and Wolohojian, 1980; Levine, 1979; Rubin, 1979; Bozeman and Slusher, 1979; Starbuck et al., 1978; Dunbar and Goldberg, 1978).

This section will attempt to systematically link the organizationally focused literature on budget cuts with the literature on individual-level stress responses. Figure 4-1 presents a broad overview of the stress process, which will serve as a basis for understanding how budget cuts and stress are related. Based upon the model of Beehr and Bhagat in Chapter 1 and some commonly used stress models (McGrath, 1976; Caplan et al., 1975), this framework contains the following components: (1) *environmental demands* (Caplan et al., 1975) or what others have called "environmental stress" (Hall and Mansfield, 1971), "objective crisis" (Jick and

---

* Clearly not all cutback situations will elicit negative stress responses. However, this paper will be directed at understanding the conditions under which such responses are most likely to occur.

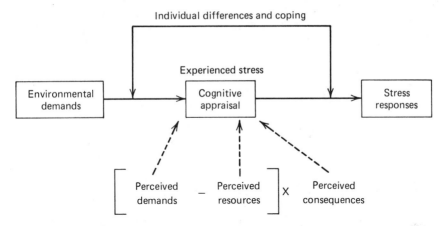

Figure 4-1   An overall framework of stress dynamics.

Murray, 1982), or "environmental threat" (Staw et al., 1981); (2) *cognitive appraisal* (Lazarus, 1966) or subjective stressors (Caplan et al., 1975) as operationalized by the appraisal of perceived demands, perceived resources, and perceived importance or consequences (McGrath, 1976); (3) *individual differences and coping* (Caplan et al., 1975; Ivancevich and Matteson, 1981; Jick and Payne, 1980); and (4) *stress responses* or strain (e.g., Caplan et al., 1975).

According to this framework, stress is portrayed as the result of a transaction between an environmental event (e.g. a budget cut) and the perceptions of the focal person. The objective conditions produce a subjective definition of the situation in the eyes of an individual. It is the *perceived* situation that is the primary determinant of the stress response (Billings et al., 1980; Whetten, 1980a,b; Weick, 1979). Thus objective stressors, as mediated by subjective stressors, are posited to lead to differential response patterns (emotional, behavioral, and physiological outcomes). Moreover, individual differences and coping skills are expected to moderate the relationship between objective conditions and subjective appraisal, as well as between the appraisal and the manifestation of stress symptoms. That is, individual responses to environmental demands and to the subjective appraisal of stress will vary as a result of differences in personality, abilities, and coping skills.

In applying this framework to the case of budget cuts, we will focus particularly on the cognitive components. Our assumption is that individuals differ from one another in the way they respond to events such as budget cuts. That is, Figure 4-2 proposes a model that reflects the sources and dynamic of *experienced stress* for an individual employed by an organization subject to budget cuts. Environmental demands are indicated to evolve from the *threat* of budget cuts to the actual cuts themselves and then

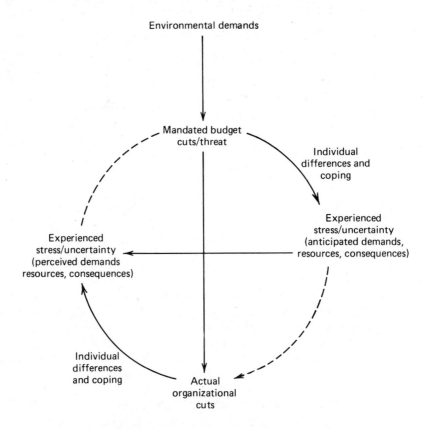

Note: ⟶ = temporal linkage, but not causally related

Figure 4-2   A framework for understanding individual stress reactions to budget cuts.

back to threats for future cuts. Similarly, reactions to these changing demands must be viewed dynamically over time.

Specifically, it can be seen that our framework begins with the mandate to reduce an organization's budget. Typically, after weeks, months, and even years of rumors, employees are officially informed that budget cuts of X percent have been mandated by the funding source, or by the organization's central finance department. This announcement represents what we are calling an "environmental demand," arousing information that serves as the stimulus for a sequence of reactions. The extent of the demand, however, presumably varies—at least in part because of its objective characteristics. That is, the degree of threat is expected to vary as a result of the objective severity and expectedness of the threatened cutbacks. Thus, the first step in the analysis is to assess the degree of *objective* threat.

These objective conditions are in turn hypothesized to influence the subjective definition of the situation, which may differ substantially from that intended by those imposing the cuts or from the interpretations of a group of impartial observers of the objective threat (Billings et al., 1980). Thus we next turn to the perceived situation, or what might be called the "sense-making" process—initially, the interpretation of anticipated demands as a result of the threatened cuts, anticipated resources and coping strength to meet those demands, and anticipated consequences for not meeting the demands (McGrath, 1976). It is the uncertainty, not knowing whether one has sufficient resources and coping strength to meet future demands, which primarily determines the initial level of experienced stress.

The likelihood that the budget cut threats will lead to a state of experienced stress is also shaped by various *individual differences* related to individual vulnerability, preparedness, and coping skills (Burke and Weir, 1980). Thus, for example, individual differences in the number of previous "encounters" with budget cuts, degree of self-perceived power to resist the cuts, coping response repertories, and tolerance levels of felt stress are all likely to moderate the relationship between objective and felt threat and thus affect the degree of experienced uncertainty.

As indicated in Figure 4-2, the individual is likely to be affected next by the organization's choices of whom or what to cut, so-called "internal responses" of the organization (Jick and Murray, 1982). The actual organizational cuts might include changes in work procedures, supervisory practices, personnel policies (e.g., layoffs or a hiring freeze), and/or reductions in services and key resources. The degree of experienced stress caused by these changes and disruptions, however, again must be understood in terms of the degree of uncertainty of outcome (McGrath, 1976). This appraisal process is expected to be shaped, as discussed above, by (1) the actual magnitude and frequency of the cuts and changes, (2) the individual's perception of factors such as work overload, deadline pressures, promotional obstacles, job security, and group relations, and (3) various individual differences related to personality, ability, and coping skills. Figure 4-2 also suggests that stress experienced as a result of actual cuts will be cumulative, such that felt stress from initial threats will have an effect on the felt stress from actual changes.

This portrayal of an individual's experience of felt stress as a result of budget cuts is presented in cyclical form because, often, the budget cuts occur regularly. That is, a second round of budget cuts may very well follow the period of experienced stress from the first round of cuts. The magnitude of the experienced stress during any one cycle will likely vary to the extent that the cuts are more chronic than acute—that is, of longer *duration* in Beehr and Bhagat's framework—although it is not obvious whether, over time, an individual will become more immune, more cynical and resistant, more vulnerable, or none of these in the face of a longer duration of an uncertain future.

This brief exposition of the nature of the conceptual framework introduces the basic approach taken to reviewing and extending existing thinking on individual responses to budget cut threats and changes. The remainder of this chapter will explore in more detail the relationships described above and their implications for further research.

PROPERTIES OF THREATENED OR ACTUAL CUTBACKS: A TYPOLOGY OF BUDGET CUT SITUATIONS

Agency budgets are said to be filled with "fat," "padding," "grease," "pork," "oleaginous substance," "water," "oil," "cushions," "waste tissue," and "soft spots." The action verbs most commonly used are "cut," "carve," "slice," "prune," "whittle," "squeeze," "wring," "trim," "lop off," "chop," "slash," "pare," "shave," "fry," and "whack" . . .

(Fenno, 1966: 105)

Budget cuts, whether threatened, impending, or implemented, may be characterized in terms of certain objective characteristics. Clearly, there are many different conditions under which budgets occur and the very nature of cuts varies widely. At the most obvious level, some cuts are simply larger than others and thus, objectively speaking, likely to produce more stress for organizational members. But there are other factors that may be seen as objective properties of cuts and that would help us discriminate among the range of budget cut situations. This section will review the critical dimensions of cutback situations and develop a typology of situations that would be predicted to be associated with various levels of experienced stress.

Funding cuts in organizations have recently been viewed in terms of their crisislike properties (Jick and Murray, 1982; Rubin, 1979; Starbuck and Hedberg, 1977). Hermann's (1969) definition of crisis, probably the most widely accepted in the literature, states that crisis is a situation that (1) threatens high priority goals, (2) restricts the amount of response time available, and (3) surprises organization members when it occurs. It is furthermore asserted that all three conditions must be present for a crisis to exist. Ford (1980) and Jick and Murray (1982) have collapsed these three conditions into two critical dimensions: severity (or threat) and time pressure. A crisis is thus viewed as a situation of high severity and high time pressure.

The extent to which budget cuts by funding agencies constitute a crisis can vary. The initial large cuts that occurred in many organizations during the 1970s were severe, sudden, and required short response time; hence, they were genuine, full-blown crises. As cuts have continued regularly since that time for many organizations, the element of surprise and lack of preparation time has diminished in significance, while severity has remained high or increased. Thus, the situation may indeed have taken on more importance.

Past research has not yet analyzed and interpreted budget-cut situations in terms of these conceptual distinctions. Intuitively, however, it seems plausible to suggest that the greater the severity and time pressure associated with budget cuts, the greater the likelihood of experienced stress in an organization. As listed in Figure 4-3, severity and time pressure are each a function of multiple factors.

In operationalizing severity, for example, one would investigate: (1) the size of the cuts (see Glassberg, 1978); (b) the threat to high priority goals, programs, and organizational survival (consistent with Hermann's (1969) concept of "threat"); (3) the frequency of cuts (i.e., the rate of occurrence); (4) the extent of organizational slack or alternate funding availability (as cuts become more frequent, it is expected that there will be fewer areas of "fat" and thus less maneuverability around vital areas); (5) the extent of management assurances regarding job security and organizational survival; (6) the extent to which the budget cuts are individually or collectively directed; and (7) the extent to which they are selective or uniform. One could speculate that budget cuts are objectively more stressful if individuals are directly affected (e.g., threatened layoffs) as opposed to indirectly affected through their group or department affiliation (e.g., reduced departmental material resources). Similarly, selective cuts, where "fairness" is likely to be painfully in dispute and uncertainty acute, are likely to be more stressful to everyone than across-the-board

Dimensions	
Severity	Time pressure
• Size of cuts	• Forewarning
• Impact on goals, programs, or survival prospects	• Information clarity
• Frequency of cuts	• Response time/duration
• Organizational slack; availability of alternate funds	
• Extent of management assurances	
• Individually vs. collectively directed	
• Selective vs. across-the-board	

Figure 4-3 Objective dimensions of budget cut situations.

reductions which, while extensive, may be buffered by their symbolically egalitarian mode.

Essentially, as the objective severity of the threatened or actual cuts increases, it might be expected that there would be more uncertainty of knowing how to respond (e.g., uncertain $P \rightarrow O$ relationship described in Chapter 1) and thus more experienced stress. On the basis of the above, one might test the following in cases of threatened or actual cuts:

Hypothesis 3:1   The greater the size of the budget cuts, the higher the likelihood of experienced stress/uncertainty.

Hypothesis 3:2   The greater the extent to which the cuts affect a change in goals, programs, or organizational survival, the higher the likelihood of experienced stress/uncertainty.

Hypothesis 3:3   The higher the frequency of cuts, the higher the likelihood of experienced stress/uncertainty.

Hypothesis 3:4   The less the organizational slack and the fewer the opportunities for alternate funding, the higher the likelihood of experienced stress/uncertainty.

Hypothesis 3:5   The fewer the management assurances (e.g., regarding job security, or department survival), the higher the likelihood of experienced stress/uncertainty.

Hypothesis 3:6   The more the cuts are individually rather than collectively directed, the higher the likelihood of experienced stress/uncertainty.

Hypothesis 3:7   The more the cuts are selective rather than uniform, the higher the likelihood of experienced stress/uncertainty.

The time pressure dimensions may be characterized in terms of four factors: forewarning information, clarity, response time, and duration. What Hermann (1969) called "surprise" can be differentiated into two concepts, information clarity and forewarning. Information clarity refers to the degree of ambiguity in the information available regarding the likelihood of future events. Objective forewarning refers to whether there was a clear indication that the budget cut was coming and how long a period there was between such information being presented and the event itself. Presumably, the less the forewarning and the lower the information clarity, the greater the surprise and then the greater the predicted experienced stress and uncertainty of knowing how to respond. The factor, "response time," refers to the time between the occurrence of the crisis event and the point at which responses and changes are made. A funding reduction may allow several months between the official notification of what the next year's appropriation or grant would be and the time that a firm budget may be announced and related changes made. Finally, some cuts are mandated to last longer than others and it is expected that the more permanent and longer lasting the cuts, the more stress will occur. On the basis of the above, then, one might posit the following:

Hypothesis 3:8   The less forewarning information of impending budget cuts, the higher the likelihood of experienced stress/uncertainty when the cuts finally occur.

Hypothesis 3:9   The lower the information clarity regarding impending budget cuts, the higher the likelihood of experienced stress/uncertainty.

Hypothesis 3:10   The lower the response time available between the mandate to cut and the actual cuts, the higher the likelihood of experienced stress/uncertainty.

Hypothesis 3:11   The longer the mandated duration of the budget cuts, the higher the likelihood of experienced stress/uncertainty.

Together, both dimensions of crisis—severity and time pressure—can clearly vary independently along continua from one extreme to the other and combine to create many different types of individually uncertain situations. At this time there is little evidence to speculate on the relative influence of severity and time pressure in terms of their stress producing effects. But considering only the extremes, one could have a situation such as an unexpected legislated mandate to close down a facility immediately—thus, a highly stressful and uncertain crisis situation due to its high severity, little response time, and little forewarning. Conversely, the reverse situation would occur in the case of a 10 percent increase in institutional telephone rates—likely to be of low severity, with much response time, and usually considerable forewarning and thus what could be called a relatively stress-free, routine situation. Importance and uncertainty would be relatively low.

To simplify somewhat, Jick and Murray (1982) have narrowed down the total range of cutback situations to a relatively few common patterns (See Figure 4-4):

1. *Unanticipated Major Cuts* (The "Big Bomb" Cut). This is a large reduction in funding that is objectively severe, requiring response in a very short time period, and preceded by little clear information, little forewarning, and in the context of a very low rate of prior occurrence. Many state-supported universities, funded on a grant-per-student formula, suffered such cuts when enrollments first took a large decline in the early 1970s after the postwar birth rates began to decline.

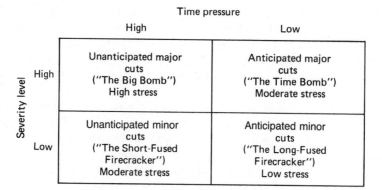

Figure 4-4   A typology of cutback situations.

2. *Anticipated Major Cuts* (The "Time Bomb" Cut).   These cuts also involve a large reduction in funding, but with considerable lead time. Unlike the aforementioned universities, certain funding agencies, in the area of public schooling, for example, were faced with cuts for the first time in years but were provided considerable clear information in the form of demographic forecasts, which allowed ample time to prepare for them. Thus they knew they were sitting figuratively on a time bomb and had some time to prepare for, though not prevent, its detonation.

3. *Unanticipated Minor Cuts* (The "Short-Fused Firecracker" Cut) These reductions are not especially severe but present little forewarning. Governmental bodies that frequently change hands between political parties or leaders of widely divergent philosophies commonly manifest this situation. The little "extras" associated with the old guard are suddenly cut back or dissolved.

4. *Anticipated Minor Cuts* (The "Long-Fused Firecracker" Cut)   This pattern is the same as the preceding one except the cuts are not as severe. Typical are municipally funded services in slowly declining communities, in which they are not able to keep budgets up to the rate of inflation, but conversely, do not have to actually reduce them. The effect is to experience a "slow squeeze" on services.

Based on Ford (1980), each of these situations can be characterized differently. The "Big Bomb" type is clearly most similar to a crisis, high-stress situation, whereas the "Long-Fused Firecracker" cuts tend to be routine (low stress). In between are the "Time Bomb" cuts, which tend to be *Important* but not crisislike, while the "Short-Fused Firecracker" cuts tend to be of more *urgency* than importance (both are likely to be thus moderately stressful). Notably, this typology represents the degree of crisis in only the broadest sense, and in its most objective or factual terms. Thus, one could predict, for example, that a budget reduction of 10 percent with only 2 months' notice is, objectively speaking, a greater crisis than a cut of 5 percent with twelve months to plan for the implementation because the uncertainty is significantly greater. Based on this notion, the following hypotheses are proposed:

Hypothesis 3:12   Under conditions of unanticipated major cuts there is likely to be a large degree of experienced stress/uncertainty.

Hypothesis 3:13   Under conditions of anticipated major cuts there is likely to be a moderate degree of experienced stress/uncertainty.

Hypothesis 3:14   Under conditions of unanticipated minor cuts there is likely to be a moderate degree of experienced stress/uncertainty.

Hypothesis 3:15   Under conditions of anticipated minor cuts there is likely to be a low degree of experienced stress/uncertainty.

Partial support for the hypotheses associated with Figure 4-3 can be found in Blonder (1976). He examined the relationship between the severity of the cutbacks (operationalized in terms of the severity of layoffs) and the degree of impact on employees. Blonder (1976) compared the work-related attitudes, anxiety level, and motivation of employees in organizations that had experienced sporadic or minor layoffs with employees in organizations that had had severe layoffs (i.e., more than 10 percent in a 2-year period). He expected that the more severe the layoffs, the more dysfunctional the consequences on retained employees. Although Blonder's results did not yield consistent support for his hypothesis, he did find that there was more unease and anxiety and less expressed motivation among employees in situations of more severe cutbacks and decline. There was no difference in attitudes found regarding company satisfaction, however.

Thus, this section has suggested that differences in experienced stress and uncertainty due to budget cuts can be understood, in part, on the basis of differences in the objective properties of cutback situations. Severity and time pressure were posited to be the two most critical dimensions worthy of further study. Clearly, however, the response to threatened or actual budget reductions is also shaped by the *perceived* severity and time pressure that ultimately produces the degree of experienced importance and uncertainty, respectively. The next section will examine some of the internal mechanisms by which individuals perceive and respond to budget cut situations.

EXPERIENCED STRESS

While the above typology of cutback situations has intuitive appeal, it is deficient in one important respect for predicting the effects of budget cuts on individuals. Subjective interpretations of budget crises may well differ from their "objective" characteristics (Billings et al., 1980; Whetten, 1980a,b; Ford, 1980). Recent conceptual advances in the study of organizations have stressed the importance of sensemaking (Louis, 1980) and how individuals enact their reality (Weick, 1977). Similarly, models of stress (e.g., Lazarus, 1966), including Chapter 10 (Segovis, Bhagat, and Coelho) in this volume, highlight the critical role of cognitive appraisal in moderating the relationship between environmental stressors and outcomes. Events in organizations then, such as budget cuts, are stressful and meaningful only insofar as they are perceived and acknowledged by individuals in terms of their importance and uncertainty. As a result, the stress experienced in the face of budget cuts tends to have subjective determinants and will not lead to uniform response patterns across all individuals.

Accordingly, the objective severity and suddenness of budget cuts can differ from the interpreted or *perceived* severity, time pressure, and uncertainty (whether valid or not). The subjective assessment of severity and time pressure can be shaped, for example, by feelings of relative, rather than absolute, deprivation (Lerner, 1979). Moreover, the literature on individual and organizational responses to impending disaster is replete with evidence on the failure of victims to notice the signals, prepare for the event, or cope with it constructively once it has occurred (e.g., Dunbar and Goldberg, 1978; Starbuck et al., 1978; Janis and Mann, 1977; Turner, 1976).

Unfortunately, there is no empirical evidence to suggest how various objective cutback situations lead to perceived "crisis" characteristics, which, in turn, affect the nature of individual responses. It is unclear, for example, whether "Big Bomb" cuts are more prone to differential interpretation than "Time Bomb" cuts, or whether the objective time pressure or the objective severity is more critical in determining the subjective interpretations. These issues remain open to further research.

1. *Conceptualization of the Cognitive Appraisal Process.*   What do we know, however, about this appraisal process? What reactions can be expected of employees faced with varying degrees of budget cut situations as described above? Let's use as a starting point the initial announcement or apprehension of impending budget cuts. Figure 4-5 offers a typical letter that might be posted or sent to employees—in this case, announcing plans for a cost-saving consolidation of two hospitals. Based upon McGrath's (1976) conceptualization of cognitive appraisal, and other research pertaining to common reaction patterns to threats or crisis (Withey, 1962; Fink et al., 1971; Cobb and Kasl, 1977; Staw et al., 1981), we will review the nature of the appraisal process in the context of budget cuts.

Following the announcement or perceived expectation of impending budget cuts, an individual is likely to follow a fairly common sequence of cognitive steps to assess the information and level of threat. Withey's (1962) work on individual reactions to uncertain threat provides a useful

To: All Employees

I want to take this opportunity to announce to you that the Department of Mental Hygiene will consolidate X and Y Hospital Centers. This consolidation, which has been under consideration for a number of years, will begin on the first of June and will concentrate on administrative and support activities ...

The consolidation will result in a reduction in force. Normal attrition will account for some of this reduction but the possibility of small target layoffs does exist. Every attempt will be made to provide alternative employment for those who are affected.

I am sure that the merger will raise many questions in your mind. I have asked the Ad Hoc Committee for each facility to collect questions for prompt and specific replies. The days ahead are bound to be difficult. I sincerely believe that this consolidation will prove to be in the best interest of those (patients) served in this area.

Sincerely,

Hospital Director

Figure 4-5 Announcement of cutbacks letter.

starting point. According to Withey, individuals can be expected to go through several stages of cognitive appraisal prior to the adoption of a coping behavior. The proposed sequence is as follows:

1. The presence of information about the threat (internal or external crisis).
2. The perception or awareness of such information.
3. Subjective probability of the impending event occurring.
4. Subjective assessment of the nature of such an event—for example, sequence and consequences.
5. Subjective estimate of the severity to the development.
6. Subjective estimate of means for coping with the threat.
7. Subjective estimate of the probability of the success of these means.
8. Subjective estimate of the cost to the individual of such means.
9. A resolution and decision about behavior.
10. A testing of behavior with success or return to a previous stage.

These stages, although presented sequentially, are likely to become virtually simultaneous at times. Based on Withey's reaction pattern, it can be inferred that budget cut threats will be associated with experienced stress to the extent that the severity of the possible or impending event, its probability of occurrence, and the ability of the person to cope with the eventuality result in various degrees of apprehension, worry, fear, or anxiety—in short, uncertainty of the employee's actions in obtaining important outcomes (uncertain $P \rightarrow O$). McGrath (1976) incorporates similar elements in his conceptual framework of cognitive appraisal and argues that it is not the threat of probable failure to meet the demands, but rather the uncertainty of success in nullifying or combatting the demands, that leads to maximum arousal.

Together, McGrath (1976) and Withey (1962) provide useful tools for understanding the nature of cognitive appraisal under conditions of threat or crisis. Figure 4-6 has integrated these concepts into a causal model portraying the antecedents of subjectively experienced stress. The general model indicates that an individual, once becoming aware of information regarding the threat, will conduct a cognitive calculus involving perceived demands, perceived resources, and perceived importance. Each of the components is operationalized in the model.

Thus, "perceived demands" consists of the two crisis dimensions described earlier in the chapter: (1) perceived severity (e.g., magnitude, frequency, targets); and (2) perceived time pressure (i.e., perceived expectedness and perceived response time). To underscore the point, these perceptions may very well differ from the actual threat or the objective time as indicated by a clock or calendar (Ford, 1980). "Perceived resources and coping strength" is operationalized in terms of three components: (1) perceived means for coping with the threat; (2) the perceived probability of success if such coping techniques were utilized; and (3) the costs to the individual of such means. Finally, an individual perceives the potential consequences or importance of not meeting the demands in terms of both personal and professional stakes—that is, the degree to which he or she will be unable to achieve, obtain, or maintain important values, resources, or objectives (Ford, 1980). That is, if the situation is unattended, and thus unsuccessfully managed, what would be the costs and consequences to the individual's work and nonwork circumstances? What would be the magnitude or value of the potential loss as well as the probability of realizing that loss? The outcome of this assessment will affect the potential for experienced stress (given individual differences, which will be discussed later).

This model is immediately applicable to the case of budget cuts, as Figure 4-6 also shows. Following the announcement of cuts such as that illustrated in Figure 4-5, employees attempt to evaluate the information through a process of sense making (Louis, 1980). The consolidation case can be used to apply the components of the model. For the sake of discussion, a "typical" employee with average seniority, average dedication,

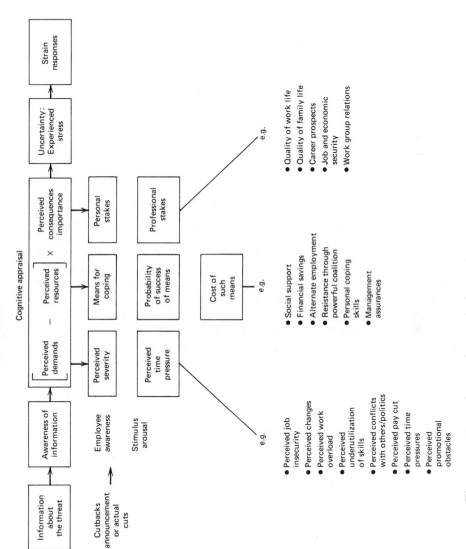

Figure 4-6 Antecedent conditions of subjectively experienced stress and uncertainty.

99

average income, and an average performance record will be considered. First of all, what are the perceived demands? The cuts, in the form of a consolidation, are likely to be perceived as rather demanding because they may involve "small target layoffs" (increasing the job insecurity of the average employee) and because they are imminent (to begin to be implemented in a matter of days after the announcement). In a survey of employees in this situation, Jick (1979a) found that whereas only 3.5 percent reported an extremely high likelihood of being laid off before the cutbacks, 27.3 percent reported such concerns after the letter was circulated. In addition to perceived job insecurity, other perceived demands might include the fear of work overload or impeded performance due to the consolidation of services, changes in work assignments, the prospect of potential conflict and politics with employees over scarce resources, the fear of wage freezes, shrinking promotional opportunities, and insufficient time to implement and absorb the threatened changes.

The magnitude of these demands and the resultant uncertainty, however, depend in part on an employee's capacity to mitigate their impact through various coping strategies. In this case the presence of social support (House, 1981) and personal stress-management skills might immediately reduce an individual's vulnerability if they were to be effective and not too costly. Similarly, financial savings or the confidence that alternate employment was available would cushion the magnitude of the demands. In addition, one might be reassured by management guarantees or by powerful coalitions of employees (e.g., unions) that could lead a campaign to resist or delay the cuts. In the case of this consolidation, however, few of these buffers existed given the absence of clear management reassurances, a weak union, a tight labor market, and an already stretched pocketbook for most employees.

For many individuals experiencing budget cut situations such as the consolidation example, uncertainty of outcomes (McGrath, 1976) then is likely to be intense. In expectancy theory terms, some illustrative uncertainties are indicated in Figure 4-7. For example, individuals may be uncertain whether they can perform well (even if they try hard) when they perceive themselves to be overloaded, under unrealistic deadlines, and/or in chronic conflict with their peers over scarce resources. Similarly, ambiguous messages may exist regarding the outcomes that will accrue based upon successful performance (i.e., the performance-outcome expectancy). When there are threatened or actual cutbacks in jobs, programs, or promotional opportunities, individuals may fear that performing well will not necessarily guarantee job security, may not involve their special abilities and skills, and may not lead to a promotion.

For many employees threatened by such budget cuts, the perceived consequences for not meeting the demands can be perceived as important. That is, unless the situation is altered (either changing the environment or the ability to live with the environmental demands), important areas of employees' personal and professional lives may be adversely affected:

STRESSORS Commonly Associated with Cutbacks	Effort to Performance Expectancy E → P	Performance to Outcome Expectancy P → O
1) Job insecurity	---	Uncertainty
2) Overload/Unrealistic deadlines	Uncertainty	---
3) Underutilization of skills	---	Uncertainty
4) Promotional obstacles	---	Uncertainty
5) Intra-group or inter-group competition	Uncertainty	---

Figure 4-7 An expectancy framework for identifying uncertainties commonly associated with cutbacks.

quality of work life, quality of family life, career prospects, job and economic security, work group relations, personal job standards, and one's performance record.

Given this scenario, it is not surprising that the potential for experienced stress is strong under conditions of "Big Bomb" cuts as described earlier. The specific components of the cognitive appraisal portrayed in Figure 4-6 have not been directly tested in the context of budget cuts. However, there is some evidence that under conditions in which the outcome of the cognitive appraisal calculus can be likened to perceived crisis and uncertainty, commonly recognized stress symptoms emerge. The next section will review the evidence of experienced stress under various crisis or threat conditions.

2. *Strain Response Tendencies.* What are the signs of experienced stress and uncertainty under conditions of high threat and crisis? In a recent review of the effects of threat on individuals, groups, and organizations, Staw et al. (1981) identified some common patterns. The individual-level effects of a threatening stimulus include: (1) restrictions in information from tendencies to rely upon internal hypotheses, prior expectations, and dominant cues; and (2) constriction in control from tendencies to emit dominant, well-learned, or habituated responses in threat situations (e.g., Smart and Vertinsky, 1977). Moreover, as noted earlier, threatened individuals may "freeze up" or fail to heed warnings (Janis and Mann, 1977; Holsti, 1978). In short, as posited by Jick and Murray (1982):

Hypothesis 3:16   The greater the level of internal stress created by cutbacks, the less the span of attention, the greater the cognitive rigidity, and the shorter the time perspective of individuals.

Levine and Wolohojian (1980) developed a 2 by 2 matrix of retrenchment situations as a function of the extent of decline (i.e., severity) and the amount of *uncertainty* about the organizations' long-term prospects (somewhat analogous to the "information clarity" dimension). Based on anecdotal observations, Levine and Wolohojian (1980) predicted different forms of employee responses that essentially reflect the differing degrees of cutback severity. Using the attachment of employees to their organizations as their dependent measure, they suggested the following:

1. Under conditions of low uncertainty and low decline, employees will experience a moderate degree of unease; some will search for another job.
2. Under conditions of low uncertainty and high decline (i.e., in excess of 10 percent in one year or 25 percent over three years), employees will exhibit a protective posture. That is, high seniority employees will attempt to structure layoff rules to protect themselves while low seniority employees and those in low priority programs will leave quietly (while protecting their recall rights).
3. Under conditions of high uncertainty but low decline, the most marketable employees will leave.
4. Under conditions of high uncertainty and high decline, employee behavior will be dominated by caution, withdrawal, anxiety, tentativeness and resistance to change.

A more dynamic model of individual reactions to crisis situations was proposed by Fink et al. (1971). They posited a four-stage sequence of crisis reactions: (1) shock; (2) defensive retreat; (3) acknowledgement; and (4) adaptation and change. In this developmental model the first stage is likened to the initial state of appraisal in which the threat is perceived. Assuming a perception of a full-fledged crisis, in this case, a threat to self-preservation, Fink et al. (1971) identified the following manifestations of anxiety and panic: feelings of confusion, inability to fully grasp what's happening and poor planning of an adequate coping response. In short, an individual under such conditions is expected to experience a state of chaos or disorganization. The second stage, defensive retreat, can be characterized by many of the elements identified by Staw et al. (1981). According to Fink et al. (1971), this phase involves a clinging to the past, reality avoidance or denial, rigid thinking, and resistance to change. The final two phases involve, first, a period of acceptance of the new situation and then eventual adjustment so that the individual no longer experiences a state of crisis.

The first two phases of the Fink et al. (1971) model have received the most attention and have been labelled "the crisis syndrome" (Jick and Murray, 1982). It is during these early phases that experienced stress is most intense. Moreover, given the recurring quality of many cutback conditions, individuals seem more likely to get "stuck" in the early phases and become unable to remove the experienced stress entirely.

While this model has not been empirically tested in the strictest sense, there is some inferential empirical support. For example, Hayes (1976) and Cobb and Kasl (1977) studied the longitudinal effects of job loss on individuals and discovered parallel dynamics to those indicated by Fink et al. (1971). Hayes (1976) found that initial reactions to layoffs were typically those of surprise, shock, fear, and a feeling of injury. This was followed by a period of false hopes and optimism, a sense that life can be "business as usual," denying the need to seek a new status or establish a new pattern of relationships. When it becomes clear that life cannot continue as if nothing has changed, Hayes (1976) found that feelings of depression and withdrawal arise, and, if the unemployment is prolonged, it can lead to more severe depression, divorce, and even suicide. Finally, however, an individual is expected to adapt himself or herself to the new state but with a narrower scope (e.g., reduced aspirations or reduced standards of satisfaction).

Cobb and Kasl (1977) studied the phsyiological and psychological changes in individuals over more than 2 years, beginning 4–7 weeks before a plant closing. Interestingly, there were several stress-related physiological changes during the acutely uncertain period of anticipation (the so-called "shock" phase), although few psychological changes appeared. In the period of unemployment many adverse psychological effects appeared as well as various coronary-prone symptoms. For most, it took several months and a new job before returning to "normal" states.

The strongest empirical evidence of the crisis syndrome as applied to budget cuts per se can be found in Jick (1979a). In a study of a hospital merger and work force reductions, Jick identified several manifestations of the demand stress associated with the early crisis phases of shock and defensive retreat. Threatened jobs and general uncertainty were found to be correlated with increases in voluntary resignations, reduced job satisfaction, weakened loyalty toward the organization, various psychomatic and somatic symptoms, and decreased productivity due to reduced effort on the job. Although most of these reactions were behavioral or attitudinal, there was evidence to suggest the occurrence of cognitive rigidity as well.

Further confirmation of these stress effects was found by Walsh and Tracey (1980) in their study of municipal employees in a large California city. As a result of Proposition 13, the city's departments were reorganized, some department head positions were eliminated, and considerable layoffs occurred. A pay cut was also instituted, although salary levels were restored some months later. Walsh and Tracey (1980) found that initial reactions were typically characterized by shock and extreme anxiety regarding job security and the continued desirability of a career in the public sector. The shock gave way to feelings of powerlessness and submission. Survey data collected before and after the changes showed a significant increase in turnover intentions and a significant decrease in job participation, pay satisfaction, and intrinsic motivation.

To summarize, the models, empirical findings, and anecdotal evidence suggest that the experienced stress created as a result of budget cuts will be manifest in terms of well-recognized behavioral, psychological, and physiological symptoms. However, this literature has not clearly specified which conditions lead to which responses (just as the stress literature has often grouped stressors and strains rather than untangling some of the specific relations, (Fletcher and Payne, 1980).

Moreover, this section should not be understood to suggest that *all* individuals will experience more stress as a result of budget cuts. As noted earlier, the degree of experienced stress will vary in part as a result of the degree of perceived crisis. What remains open to speculation, however, is the relationship between perceived degree of crisis and stress responses. One hypothesis would suggest that the relationship is linear—that is, the more severe the crisis and uncertainty, the more debilitating and negative the stress responses. Thus, perceived moderate cuts would lead to more adverse consequences than routine situations but less than high-crisis conditions. On the other hand, some might argue that the relationship is curvilinear. That is, perceived "moderately demanding" situations are likely to be associated with "eustress" or "opportunity stress," that is stimulating higher performance, stronger motivation, group cohesion, and a generally positive work milieu. Staw and others (1981) posited that threatening situations resulting from common or familiar problems may result in performance increments while threats arising from radical changes may lead to performance decrements.

Whether the effects of moderate threat are positive or negative, it is clear that individuals will differ to the extent that their perceptions of the degree of crisis differ. In addition, given certain individual characteristics, or coping skills, some will experience more, or less, stress even under conditions of equivalently perceived crisis. The next section will examine some of these individual difference characteristics.

INDIVIDUAL DIFFERENCES

Neither the cognitive appraisal of stress nor the common manifestations of experienced stress can be predicted solely from the objective intensity of its sources. Stress research has clearly shown that individuals confront stressful conditions with a variety of behaviors and cognitions that can serve to alter these difficult conditions or mediate their impact (Pearlin et al., 1981). Thus, individual differences, especially coping skills, serve as critical moderators or mediators of experienced stress (Pearlin and

Schooler, 1978; Burke and Weir, 1980; Folkman, 1982). Pearlin et al. (1981) described these mediators as the resources, actions, and perceptions mobilized by individuals as they seek to avoid or minimize distress.

Given the overall framework for this paper, the role of individual differences is critical to the predicted likelihood of experienced stress. To illustrate, let's take the example of a "Time Bomb" type of budget cut situation, such as a 20 percent budget cut to be implemented in 6 month's time. Consider two very different reactions by employees. For one, the perceived threat and experienced stress was minimal while, for another, the anticipated cuts produced a panic reaction and an active search for alternate employment. What would explain these individual differences? What factors would lead one person to perceive the situation as a threat while others view the same circumstances as either unthreatening or challenging?

Empirical support for such individual differences was found by Jick (1979a). Initial reactions to threatened budget cuts varied considerably across individuals. Although retrospective, respondents were asked to reconstruct their reactions to the announcement of a consolidation plan. Not surprisingly, a little more than half the employees (54 percent) recalled being "worried." Interestingly, however, almost 12 percent reported feelings of indifference, while 4 percent were "pleased." Other reported reactions included being puzzled or angry.

While only a few studies (Blonder, 1976; Greenhalgh and Jick, 1982) have examined the source of these differences in the context of budget cuts, one can turn to common moderator variables identified in the literature on stress, threat, and crisis. Variables such as personality, experience, seniority, and occupational level are likely to shape an individual's assessment of the importance of the cuts and the resources for coping with those demands.

1. *Expectations and Previous Experience.* Two related factors that have been predicted to influence the perception of a crisis are cognitive expectations and previous experience. Withey (1962) examined reactions to uncertain threats such as disaster warnings. He posited a series of hypotheses regarding the interpretation of warning signals as a function of people's expectations and previous experience. First, for individuals not expecting disaster, any threat cues will tend to be interpreted as unthreatening until such interpretations can no longer be made (e.g., when the hurricane actually is manifest). However, when an individual is set to expect disaster, an apparent over sensitivity to stress cues develops such that even a *minor* suggestion of possible threat will be capable of stimulating emergency-type reactions.

Jick and Murray (1982) similarly posited that decision makers who have had minimal past experience with budget cuts of a similar nature and extent will be more likely to perceive them as severe crises and thus likely to experience more felt anxiety. Some support for this hypothesis has been found by Dunbar and Goldberg (1978), Starbuck et al. (1978), and Anderson et al. (1977). At the organization level of analysis Nottenburg and Fedor (1981) also note that previous experience can affect the likelihood that scarity information will be perceived, and deemed valid. Specifically, they argue that an organization that has experienced previous periods of scarcity will have information-sensing and processing mechanisms highly sensitized to information that is suggestive of anticipated scarcity. As a result of the expectation, however, this can also lead to a misperception of scarcity.

In the context of a budget cut threat, one might therefore posit the following:

Hypothesis 3:17   If budget cuts are threatened where there have been no previous cuts (either in the focal department or organization, or in similar organizations), the tendency will be to interpret them as unthreatening until such interpretation can no longer be made.

Hypothesis 3:18   Under conditions of recent, but not repeated, cuts individuals will develop an oversensitivity to budget cut threat cues.

Withey (1962) also suggests, however, that under conditions of repeated exposure to threat (e.g., a seasoned combat veteran), there will be a selective sensitivity unlike either of the predicted reactions above. In part, this is related to cognitive expectations but also to the amount of knowledge, training, or experience possessed by individuals in similar situations, real or simulated. That is, a veteran sea captain or airplane pilot is usually superior to a novice in dealing with an emergency in his or her craft as a result of previous experiences with similar situations. Repeated experience with cutback situations, similarly, should lead individuals to interpret new information and warning signals more accurately and direct more attention to political processes. While few managers and employees in public-sector organizations had any prior experience with unwanted and unanticipated decline up until a few years ago, it is expected that seasoned "combat" veterans of multiyear budget crises will become more and more numerous in the future. Thus, one might posit:

Hypothesis 3:19   Under conditions of repeated exposure to and experience with budget cut threats, individuals will develop a selective sensitivity to perceive warning signals and tend to interpret new information more accurately.

2. *Personality Factors: Self-Esteem and Locus of Control.*   Personality moderators have been identified as related to the determinants of crisis perceptions, although few have actually been tested in cases of

budget cuts. In reviewing the literature on the effect of individual differences on key decision makers under crisis conditions, Jick and Murray (1982) posited that personality types of high anxiety, low self-esteem, and Type A will be more likely to perceive budget cuts as severe crises (Billings et al., (1980). In addition, empirical support for the relationship of felt control with perceived threat was found by Anderson et al. (1977) in their study of 90 owner-managers of small businesses that experienced flood damage from a hurricane. Those managers identified as Internals reported significantly less initial perceived threat than individuals identified as Externals (an especially strong relationship, $r = .61, p < .001$). Interestingly, another factor predicted to influence the perception of threat, "personal resources," was not significantly correlated except in the case of high levels of applicable insurance.

In a more directly applicable study Blonder (1976) investigated how self-esteem influenced the relationship between retrenchment stress and individual stress responses. This study examined the impact of layoffs on retained employees in four organizations of white-collar professionals. Blonder predicted that under conditions of severe layoffs, the higher the retained employee's self-esteem, the lower the degree of experienced stress (because such individuals are expected to have more confidence in their fortitude and skill to cope effectively with stress situations).

Blonder (1976) in fact found negative, although modest, correlations between self-esteem and felt anxiety. Blonder reasoned, based upon Weiner (1973), that high self-esteem individuals remain largely unaffected because they either discredit the source of their failure or frustration or blame the environment for the cause of the failure. By doing so, this rationalization or defensive attribution (Nottenburg and Fedor, 1981) allows him or her to maintain previously held expectations of success. Overall, however, Blonder's investigation of other moderator variables (e.g., work-ethic, organizational level) suggested that the impact of moderator variables indeed varies considerably. The most consistent findings in the literature thus far suggest:

Hypothesis 3:20   Under conditions of cutbacks, personalities characterized by low self-esteem, high Type A, and low felt control, will be more likely to perceive the crisis as threatening.

Greenhalgh and Jick (1982) also examined the role of personality differences under similar conditions of objective uncertainty, that is, ambiguity arising from conditions of organizational decline. They expected that some individuals would be better prepared to cope with these ambiguities than others. Specifically, they examined the impact of "tolerance for ambiguity" and "need for security" on experienced stress. They predicted that individuals with high need for security and a low tolerance for ambiguity would manifest more adverse reactions to the uncertain threats.

Surprisingly, however, the results suggested otherwise. A breakdown of the dependent variables (i.e., reported health and felt strain) by ambiguity and the two personality characteristics showed a pattern opposite to what had been predicted. The conditions of ambiguity had *less* effect on individuals who were intolerant of ambiguity and high in need for security. Greenhalgh and Jick (1982) argued, however, that while the moderating effects did not emerge in the predicted direction, other cognitive differences were manifest in the initial "decoding" of the environmental data (i.e., the ambiguous stimulus). Individuals who had a basic aversion to threatening ambiguous situations evidently handled ambiguous stimuli by constructing a reality free of their objective predicament through denial or distortion. These results suggest the use of *cognitive restructuring* as a short-term defense mechanism to reduce the level of experienced stress for those less tolerant of ambiguous situations such as budget cut threats. Some people, as Beehr and Bhagat indicate in Chapter 1, seldom experience ambiguity in demands because of defensive sense-making processes. Such restructuring represents an individual difference in the capacity to absorb and process ambiguous information. Staw et al. (1981) also suggest that one response to threat is to energize a search for additional information to discredit it.

To summarize, a number of individual difference factors have been identified that are likely to moderate the stress experience. Although evidence is sparse, factors such as experience, expectations, self-esteem, cognitive restructuring, and locus of control are all worthy of further research in context of budget cut crises. One could easily point to other personality factors as well. For example, Oshry (1978) identifies individuals as more or less "loose" with resources. It would be expected that individuals who are loose with resources would experience more stress in tight times. Another moderator, social support (discussed in Chapter 14), can also be expected to play the role of a mediating resource (House, 1980; Turner, 1981; Pearlin et al., 1981), but there is as yet no empirical evidence of its impact under conditions of budget cuts. Similarly, one can point to other background variables such as occupational level, age, sex, financial security, and so on (Little, 1976), whose effects need to be carefully researched as well. Finally, there are numerous individual coping mechanisms for minimizing personal overreaction to unexpected change and reducing uncertainty—for example, new psychological strategies, knowing one's self even better, and developing personal checks and balances (McLean, 1979)—whose effectiveness might be examined in the context of budget cuts.

A RESEARCH AGENDA

This chapter has reviewed and explored the dynamics of experienced stress under conditions of fiscal cutbacks. Just as Catalano and Dooley (1981) concluded that individuals who experienced economic changes are at higher risk of exhibiting health problems than those who did not, one can safely conclude that individuals who work in cutback environments are likely to be at higher risk than those who do not. As fiscal cuts are perceived to be "at hand" and, or, ultimately realized, many threatened employees are likely to feel and behave in ways that are detrimental to themselves as well as the functioning of the organization. The frameworks utilized in this chapter provide some conceptual clarity regarding the conditions under which experienced stress and uncertainty are likely to be manifest.

Figure 4-8 is designed to summarize the key concepts and relationships addressed in this chapter, around which a research agenda naturally emerges. It underscores the process by which "demand stress" can lead to predictable strain response patterns. As stated, though, not all individuals will suffer negative stress reactions to budget cuts. One can imagine two individuals hit with the same pattern of cuts, one who ends up limping along wracked with stress, just a hollow shell of his or her former self, desperately seeking to get out if possible; while the other appears to be maintaining all essential activities or even exhibiting new and original activities while exuding confidence, loyalty, and commitment to the organization. What makes for the difference? This review has attempted to specify some of the individual differences that can shape the degree of accurate anticipation and preparedness for crisis events such as funding cutbacks.

The effect of the duration of one or multiple budget cuts is a relatively unexplored research topic. There is the distinct possibility that funding cutbacks will persist with moderate severity for the next decade, especially in specific industries/public-sector organizations. It is unknown how individuals react to crises of prolonged duration. That is, what are the long-term effects of chronically declining organizations on individual well-being and effectiveness? Will the severity of the "crisis syndrome" diminish or increase as cutbacks become more routine? These are apt questions for this proposed research agenda.

And these issues are seemingly more and more applicable to the private sector as well. The economic slowdown has reached crisis proportions in a number of private industries. The widespread elimination of jobs through plant closings or company wide layoffs has plagued employees in auto, steel, airlines, and other sectors. The unprecedented acceptance of wage cuts and concessions by unions is still another signal that the very survival of some industries is at stake. As a result, the future for many private-sector workers appears bleak, and likely to foster many of the stress responses observed among public sector employees. It would be useful to conduct comparative research between public- and private-sector employees subject to similar degrees of fiscally provoked stress conditions. What seems certain is the loss of a sense of invulnerability to unemployment across diverse sectors in the work force as organizations contract.

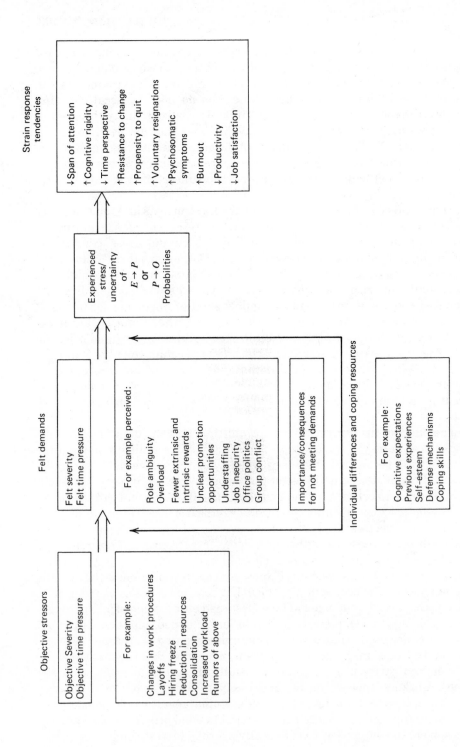

Figure 4-8 Demand stress under hard times in organizations—a summary diagram of key concepts.

Overall this chapter is intended to stimulate some exciting new applications for stress research. The models, hypotheses, and speculations contained in this chapter will need to be tested and refined. Jick (1979b) has described at length the value of a "triangulation" methodology for uncovering complex patterns of experienced stress. It is clear that future research must be able to evaluate the effects of cutbacks on individuals over time, the effects of cutbacks on different types of individuals, and the effects of different cutback situations (i.e., differing degree of threat) on individuals. By doing so, it is expected that our understanding of the following key areas will be sharpened: (1) the stressors most often associated with budget cuts; (2) the relationship between objective stressors and cognitive appraisal; (3) the impact of individual differences and coping skills; and (4) the manifestation of strain responses most likely to emerge under conditions of budget cuts.

This knowledge derived from the "living laboratory" of individuals experiencing stress from budget cuts can then be utilized to help develop individual and organizational strategies for managing the challenging demands of hard times. This chapter has emphasized how hard times caused by budget reductions tend to threaten important individual outcomes and create stress-producing uncertainties in the lives of many. But these perceptions are subject to change and, thus, researchers also face the pragmatic mandate to identify the mechanisms by which individuals and organizations can most effectively adapt to new circumstances.

REFERENCES

Anderson, C. R., Hellriegel, D., and Slocum, J. Managerial response to environmentally induced stress. *Academy of Management Journal*, 1977, **20**(2), 260–272.

Bakke, E. W. *The unemployed worker: A study of the effects of unemployment upon the worker's social relations and practice.* New Haven: Yale University Press, 1940.

Billings, R. S., Millburn, T. M., and Schaalman, M. L. A model of crisis perception: A theoretical and empirical analysis. *Administrative Science Quarterly*, 1980, **25**(2), 300–316.

Blonder, M. D. *Organizational repercussions of personnel cutbacks: Impacts of layoffs on retained employees.* PhD dissertation, City University of New York, 1976.

Blundell, W. E. As the budget axe falls so does productivity of grim U.S. workers. *Wall Street Journal*, August 17, 1978.

Bozeman, B. and Slusher, E. A. Scarcity and environmental stress in public organizations, *Administration and Society*, 1979, **11**, 334–335.

Brenner, M. H. *Mental illness and the economy*, Cambridge, Mass: Harvard University Press, 1973.

Brouillette, J. and Quarantelli, E. L. Types of patterned variations in bureaucratic adaptations to organizational stress. *Sociological Inquiry*, 1979, **41**, 39–45.

Burke, R. J. and Weir, T. Coping with the stress of managerial occupations. In C. Cooper and R. Payne (Eds.), *Current concerns in occupational stress.* New York: Wiley, 1980, 299–336.

Caplan, R., Cobb, S., French, J. R., Harrison, R. V., and Pinneau, S. *Job demands and worker health.* Cincinnati: NIOSH Research Report, 1975.

Catalano, R. and Dooley, D. The health effects of economic instability: A test of the economic stress hypothesis. Unpublished manuscript, Public Policy Research Organization, University of California, Irvine, 1981.

Catalano, R., Dooley, D., and Jackson, R. Economic predictors of admissions to mental health facilities in a nonmetropolitan community. *Journal of Health and Social Behavior,* September 1981, **22**(3), 284–297.

Cobb, S. and Kasl, S. V. *Termination: The consequences of job loss.* Cincinnati: NIOSH Report, June 1977.

Dooley, D. and Catalano, R. Economic change as a cause of behavioral disorder. *Psychological Bulletin,* 1980, **87**(3), 450–468.

Dunbar, R. and Goldberg, W. Crisis development and strategic response in European corporations. In C. F. Smart and W. T. Stanbury (Eds.) *Studies on crisis management.* Toronto: Butterworth, 1978, 135–146.

Eisenberg, P. and Lazarsfeld, R. P. The psychological effects of unemployment. *Psychological Bulletin,* June 1938, **35**, 358–390.

Fenno, R. F., Jr. *The Power of the Purse.* Boston: Little Brown, 1966.

Fink, L., Beak, J., and Taddeo, K. Organizational crisis and change. *Journal of Applied Behavioral Science,* 1971, **47**(1), 15–41.

Fletcher, B., and Payne, R. Stress and work: A review and theoretical framework. *Personnel Review,* 1980.

Folkman, S. An approach to the measurement of coping. *Journal of Occupational Behavior,* 1982, **3**, 95–107.

Ford, J. D. The management of organization crises. Unpublished manuscript, Indiana University, 1980.

Glassberg, A. Organizational responses to municipal budget decreases. *Public Administration Review,* 1978, **38**, 325–349.

Greenhalgh, L. and Jick, T. D. The phenomenology of sense-making in a declining organization: Effects of individual differences. Unpublished manuscript, 1982.

Hall, T., and Mansfield, R. Organizational and individual response to external stress. *Administrative Science Quarterly,* 1971, **16**(3), 533–547.

Hayes, J. Loss of employment. In J. Adams, H. Hayes, and B. Hopson (Eds.). *Transition,* 1976.

Hermann, C. F. Some consequences of crisis which limit the viability of organizations. *Administrative Science Quarterly,* 1963, **8**(1), 61–82.

Hermann, C. F. *Crises in foreign policy: A stimulation analysis.* Indianapolis: Bobbs-Merrill, 1969.

Holsti, R. Limitations of cognitive abilities in the face of crisis. In C. F. Smart and W. T. Stanbury (Eds.). *Studies in crisis management.* Toronto: Butterworth, 1978, 35–52.

House, J. S. *Work stress and social support.* Reading, Mass.: Addison Wesley, 1981.

Ivancevich. J. M. and Matteson, M. T. *Stress and work.* Glenview, Ill.: Scott, Foresman, 1980.

Janis, I. and Mann, L. Emergency decision-making: A theoretical analysis of responses to disaster warnings, *Journal of Human Stress,* June 1977, 35–48.

Jick, T. D. *Process and Impacts of a Merger: Individual and Organizational Perspectives.* Unpublished doctoral dissertation, Cornell University, 1979a.

Jick, T. D. Mixing qualitative and quantitative methods: Triangulation in action. *Administrative Science Quarterly,* 1979b, **24**(4), 602–611.

Jick, T. D. and Murray, V. V. The management of hard times: Budget cutbacks in public sector organizations. *Organization Studies*, 1982, **3**(2), 141–169.

Jick, T. D. and Payne, R. Stress at work. *Exchange: The Organizational Behavior Teaching Journal*, 1980, **5**(3), 50–56.

Kaufman, H. *Professionals in search of work: Coping with the stress of job loss and under-employment*. New York: Wiley-Interscience, 1982.

Lazarus, R. S. *Psychological stress and the coping process*. New York: McGraw-Hill, 1966.

Levine, C. H. (Ed.) *Managing fiscal stress*. Chatham, N. J.: Chatham House, 1980.

Levine, C. H. More on cutback management: Hard questions for hard times. *Public Administration Review*, 1979, **39**(1), 179–182.

Levine, C. H. Organizational decline and cutback management. *Public Administration Review*, 1978, **31**(2), 316–325.

Levine, C. H., Rubin, I. S., and Wolohojian, G. G. Preconditions for managing organizational retrenchment: Deficiencies and adaptations in the public sector. Paper presented at the Annual Meeting of the Academy of Management, Detroit, 1980.

Levine, C. H. and Wolohojian, G. G. Retrenchment, uncertainty, and human resources: Combatting the discount effects of a bleak future. Paper presented at the Annual Conference of the American Society for Public Administration, San Francisco, 1980.

Lerner, S. Behaviour in the crunch. *Alternatives*, 1979, **8**, 5–11.

Little, C. B. Technical-professional unemployment: Middle-class adaptability to personal crisis. *Sociological Quarterly*, 1976, **17**, 262–75.

Louis, M. Surprise and sense-making: What newcomers experience in entering unfamiliar organizational settings. *Administrative Science Quarterly*, 1980, **25**, 226–251.

McGrath, J. Stress and behavior in organizations. In M. D. Dunnette, (Ed.). *Handbook of industrial and organizational psychology*. Chicago: Rand McNally, 1976, 1351–1395.

McLean, A. *Work stress*. Reading, Mass.: Addison-Wesley, 1979.

Nottenburg, G. and Fedor, D. B. Scarcity in the environment: Organizational perceptions, interpretations and responses. Paper presented to the National Academy of Management Meetings, 1982.

Payne, R. L. Demands, supports, constraints, and psychological health. In C. J. McKoy, and T. Cox (Eds.). *Response to stress: Occupational aspects*. London: London International Publishing Corporation, 1979.

Payne, R., Jick, T. D., and Burke, R. J. Whither stress research? An agenda for the 1980's. *Journal of Occupational Behavior*, 1982, **3**, 131–145.

Pearlin, L. I., Lieberman, M. A., Menaghan, E. G., and Mullan, J. T. The stress process. *Journal of Health and Social Behavior*, December 1981, **22**, 337–56.

Pearlin, L. I. and Schooler, C. The structure of coping. *Journal of Health and Social Behavior*, 1978, **19**, 2–21.

Rosellini, L. Federal cuts increasing workers' stress levels. *New York Times,* December 16, 1981.

Rubin, I. S. Retrenchment, loose structure and adaptability in the university. *Sociology of Education*, 1979, **52**, 211–222.

Slote, A. *Termination: The closing at baker plant*. New York: Bobbs-Merrill, 1969.

Smart, C. and Vertinsky, I. Designs for crisis decision units. *Administrative Science Quarterly*, 1977, **22**(4), 640–657.

Starbuck, W. H., Greve, A., and Hedberg, B. Responding to crisis: Theory and the experience of European business. In C. F. Smart and W. T. Stanbury (Eds.), *Studies in crisis management*, Toronto: Butterworth, 1978, 107–134.

Staw, B. M., Sandelands, L. E., and Dutton, J. E. Threat-rigidity effects in organizational behavior: A multilevel analysis. *Administrative Science Quarterly*, Dec. 1981, **26**, 4, 501–524.

Strange, W. Job loss: A psychosocial study of worker reactions to a plant-closing in a company town in southern Appalachia. PhD dissertation, Cornell University, 1978.

Turner, B. The organizational and interorganizational development of disaster. *Administrative Science Quarterly*, 1976, **21**(2), 378–397.

Turner, R. J. Social support as a contingency in psychological well-being. *Journal of Health and Social Behavior*, Dec. 1981, **22**, 357–67.

Walsh, J. T. and Tracy, D. S. Long-term organizational effects of voter-mandated property tax relief. Paper presented at the American Psychological Association Annual Meeting, Montreal, 1980.

Weick, K. E. Enactment processes in organizations. In B. Staw and G. Salancik (Eds.) *New directions in organizational behavior*, Chicago: St. Clair, 1977.

Weick, K. E. *The social psychology of organizing*, 2nd ed. Reading, Mass.: Addison-Wesley, 1979.

Whetten, D. A. Organizational decline: Sources, responses and effects. In J. R. Kimberly, H. Miles, and Associates, *The organizational life cycle*. San Francisco: Jossey-Bass, 1980a.

Whetten, D. A. Organizational decline: A neglected topic in organizational science. *Academy of Management Review*, 1980b **5**(4), 577–588.

Wiener, Y. Task, ego-involvement and self-esteem as moderators of situationally devalued self-esteem. *Journal of Applied Psychology*, 1973, **58**(2), 225–232.

Withey, S. B. Reaction in uncertain threat. In G. W. Baker and D. W. Chapman (Eds.), *Man and society in disaster*. New York: Basic Books, 1962, 93–123.

Zawadzki, B., and Lazarsfeld, P. The psychological consequences of unemployment. *Journal of Social Psychology*, 1935, **6**, 224–251.

CAUSES AND CONSEQUENCES OF STRESS FROM THE INTERFACE OF WORK AND NONWORK DOMAINS

Part Three focuses on stress at the beginning and end of one's career and on an increasingly common form of stress in the middle, the stress experienced by dual-career couples. Chapter 5 explores the stress typically encountered by employees who are usually just beginning their careers—employees who are first entering an organization and who are beginning to experience the organization's socialization process. Hypotheses regarding situations that make the socialization either more or less stressful are proposed.

Chapter 6 describes the experiences of dual-career couples, an increasingly common occurrence accompanied by the development of new problems for individuals and their employing organizations. This phenomenon has become a source of stress for many people during the middle of their careers.

Chapter 7 outlines probable stressors for most older employees, those nearing or at the retirement stage of their working lives. The most likely causes of stress at this career stage are documented, making future research and applications more apparent.

CHAPTER FIVE

Organizational Stress and Early Socialization Experiences

RALPH KATZ

For many individuals their first year of organizational employment is a very frustrating experience, full of stress, anxiety, and disillusionment. Their struggles to become accepted by others and to function as "true" contributing members within their new work settings are sufficiently dissatisfying that many switch companies within the first couple of years. In fact, Schein (1964) estimated that more than 50 percent of the college graduates entering industrial corporations leave their firms within the first four or five years. The end result, of course, is a very high rate of organizational turnover among new groups of employees—a wasteful outcome, not only economically, but also in terms of lost promise and potential (Porter and Steers, 1973; Mirvis and Lawler, 1977).

For other individuals, however, the initial years are a marvelously satisfying experience, full of excitement, achievement, and personal development. Not only are these individuals more likely to remain with their organizations, but it is also likely that they will continue to perform effectively and develop strong commitments to both their job and organizational settings (Berlew and Hall, 1966; Steers, 1977).

Given this range of difference in the individual experiences of organizational newcomers, what is it that takes place during one's initial work years that affects the amount of stress one feels and determines one set of outcomes over the other? As discussed by Hughes (1958), Wanous (1980), and many others, one explanation lies in the perceptual accuracy with which individuals enter their new organizational environments. Generally speaking, the more individuals begin their jobs with unrealistic views and expectations, the more they encounter "reality shock" as they confront the true demands of their everyday task activities. Contrastingly, individuals who assume their new organizational positions with a more realistic understanding and perspective will feel less surprised and disenchanted since they possess, at least initially, more compatible "psychological contracts" with both their supervisors and peers (Argyris, 1960; Levinson, 1962).

Based on this argument, if newcomers are given more accurate information about their prospective jobs, they would be able to undertake their new responsibilities with far less discomfort and frustration. They would be, in a sense, better innoculated against the idealistic hopes and expectations that so many young employees form about their upcoming organizational involvements. More "realistic previews" during recruiting, then, can play an important role in preventing disappointments from emerging and disillusioning newcomers as they begin to carry out their daily job assignments.

Although much can be done to educate and prepare new hires for their new world of work, one should also realize that the concerns, reactions, and accomplishments of new employees are eventually shaped by the structure of events and interactions taking place throughout their entire socialization experience within the organization (Katz, 1980; Schein, 1978). A "sink or swim" type of socialization process, for example, evokes considerably more tension and stress than a socialization process that is highly supportive and well structured, even though the actual task demands may be equivalent in both cases. If our ultimate objective is to learn how to provide newcomers with a better "joining-up" process—one that is not only less stressful but also more meaningful and personally developmental— then we need to understand more fully how individual needs and concerns should be met throughout this important introductory period of organizational careers.

CONTENT OF SOCIALIZATION

During the initial socialization phase, individuals undertaking their first organizational assignments are for the most part very uncertain insofar as organizationally relevant attitudes, behaviors, and procedures are concerned. It is in this early job stage, therefore, that individual newcomers learn not only the specific technical requirements of their jobs but also the socially acceptable attitudes and behaviors necessary for becoming effective organizational members. If new employees hope to direct and orient their own organizational performance in a meaningful and contributive manner, then they must develop a genuine understanding of the events and activities taking place around them. They must build a "situational perspective" within which ideas and assumptions can be tested, interpreted, and interrelated.

As discussed by Katz (1980), Louis (1980), and Schein (1980), creating this perceptual outlook is analogous to building a mental or cognitive map of one's organizational surrounding including its idiosyncratic cast of characters. To come to know a job situation and act within it implies that the newcomer has developed a sufficiently useful scheme for making sense out of the vast array of experiences associated with his or her participation in the new job setting. The newcomer must come to know what others in the organization are about, how they operate, and how he or she should perform on the job relative to these others. In time, these perceptions provide the new employee with a meaningful way of classifying events and organizing the many interrelationships that exist within the workplace.

In developing this local organizational perspective, every newcomer must accomplish at least three important tasks. They must build their own role identities within their new job contexts; they must discover how to deal with peers and other authority figures, especially their boss; and they must decipher the appropriate reward systems and situational norms of acceptable social and task-related behaviors.

1. *Establishing One's Organizational Role Identity.* As new hires start their organizational careers, they are faced with the problem of developing situational identities that will be viable and suitable both from their own perspectives and from the perspectives of other relevant organizational members. Whether one is aware of it or not, each newcomer must find an answer to the question of "Who and what am I to be in this organization?"

This issue exists simply because all of us have a large repertory of possible roles and behavioral styles that can be enacted in any particular situation. The person who is viewed as influential, aggressive, and helpful in one organizational setting, for example, may be seen by others in a different situation as quiet, reserved, and uninvolved. To some extent, therefore, we can be different people in different situations, depending upon the particular sets of perceptions that come to surround and envelop us.

Newcomers are typically hired into their organizations as the result of some valued educational background or some highly specialized training program. But until they are actually working and participating in their specific job contexts, neither they nor their organizations can really be sure how they will fit into their new work environments. The socialization period, therefore, is a time of mutual discovery between the new employee and the employing organization, each learning more and more about the other. With increasing experience and organizational exposure, the new employee gradually acquires enough self-knowledge to develop a clearer image of his or her own strengths and weaknesses, assessing his or her own preferences, values, talents, and abilities. In a similar fashion, other organizational employees also develop their own perceptual views of the individual newcomer. And as these perceptions and expectations become more firmly established, they function to constrain the role behaviors that the individual is allowed to play within the overall work setting. Thus, it is the intersection among many sets of perceptions that eventually defines the specific role or situational identity of each individual employee. During socialization, then, every newcomer is testing his own self-image against the views and reactions of other organizational employees. The greater the fit between these developing perspectives, the less stress experienced by the new individual since the paths through which he is expected to contribute become increasingly well defined and mutually agreeable. Accordingly, the following is hypothesized:

> Stress is inversely related to the level of congruence between how the organization and how the new employee views his or her emerging role within the job setting—the more congruent these perspectives, the lower the level of stress.

It is very possible, of course, that not everyone in the work environment will have the same reaction to or will develop the same impression of the new employee. Some may come to value or respect his particular skills and abilities; others may view his areas of expertise as unnecessary and irrelevant. Coworkers or colleagues might also develop a picture of the new employee that is vastly different from the one constructed by his or her supervisor, the one formulated by his or her subordinates, or even the one held by those professionals, customers, or clients outside the organization. All of these types of discrepancies can be operationalized in many different ways. Nevertheless, in a very general sense, it is extremely difficult for newcomers to break into their new organizations with a well anchored sense of "psychological safety and security" as long as these kinds of differences remain strong or become increasingly diverse and pronounced within the work environment. As many studies have shown (e.g., Katz, 1980; Hall and Nougaim, 1968), as long as basic personal needs remain conflicted and unfulfilled, new employees will continue to feel very anxious and concerned about their situational roles and organizational identities. The following is therefore hypothesized:

> Stress is inversely related to the level of organizational consensus surrounding the situational identity of the new organizational employee—the more intense the disparaties, the greater the level of stress.

To build this new role identity, socialization must take place along both dimensions of interpersonal and task-related activities. The newcomer has a strong need to obtain answers to a number of important underlying interpersonal questions; while only some of these may be conscious, all need to be answered as quickly as possible. Having entered a strange and unfamiliar social arena, newcomers are strongly concerned with inclusion, that is, becoming a necessary and significant part of the overall organization. According to Schein (1971), Graen (1976), and Katz (1978a), to become accepted and recognized as an important contributing member within one's work setting is one of the major obstacles with which new employees must struggle and which they must eventually overcome. To what extent, then, will they be considered worthwhile? Will they be liked, supported, and appreciated? Will they be kept informed, included, and be given opportunities to make meaningful contributions? These are some of the key interpersonal issues preoccupying employees as their new situational identities become progressively established.

From the technical or task-performance point of view, the newcomer must also figure out whether or not he or she can do the job effectively. As discussed by Schein (1964) and others, to prove or test themselves on the job is another very important concern of new employees. Having spent most of their lives in an educational environment, which has kept them at arm's length from the "real," industrial world, young employees need to discover just what sort of persons they are and of what they are really capable. They need to see how they function on actual work tasks where the outcomes make a significant difference. For this reason the testing of one's skills and abilities is of critical importance. Furthermore, new employees are not only concerned with using their present knowledge, they also want opportunities that enable them to continue to learn and grow — to extend their talents and areas of expertise. One of the inevitable results of prolonged professional education is the expectation that one should continue to self-develop and be given the opportunities and freedom to do so. In short, what is really important to young employees during socialization is the opportunity to clearly demonstrate their work competence and future promise by being meaningfully utilized in some critical aspect of the organization's activities.

2. *Learning to Deal With One's Boss and Other Employees.*   A first boss plays a disproportionate role in a young person's career (Webber, 1976). According to the results of many studies, one of the most critical factors influencing the professional and organizational career success of young employees falls within the mentoring domain of one's immediate supervisor (Kanter, 1977; Vicino and Bass, 1978; Graen and Ginsburgh, 1977). Despite the obvious importance of this supervisor-subordinate relationship, very few newcomers are entirely satisfied with their initial boss.

One of the major tasks of socialization, then, is to learn how to deal and get along with this individual. He or she may be too Machiavellian, too unstructured, too busy, too fickle, too competent, or even too incompetent. Nevertheless, young employees must learn to adapt to the reality of being dependent upon their particular supervisors.

The newcomer's immediate boss plays a critical role in linking the new employee to the rest of the organization, in making sure his work priorities are consistent with organizational needs, in securing adequate resources, and in providing the additional information and expertise that is necessary to perform well. While some bosses do an excellent job of caring for their new subordinates in these ways, a more reasonable expectation is that only a modest amount of assistance will be forthcoming. In most instances, therefore, newcomers must assume primary responsibility for their own careers and development and must learn to seek the help and information they need to do their work effectively instead of waiting or wishing for their bosses to provide it.

This is not always an easy undertaking. It is often very stressful simply because of the high "psychological costs" that are involved in seeking help from supervisors who are in evaluative and more powerful positions. As summarized by Allen (1977), much research has shown that individuals tend to use information sources that have the least psychological cost instead of using the most effective or most immediate sources of information. However, as in any negotiation or conflict situation, it becomes somewhat easier to approach the "other party" as one generates more meaningful information about those individuals. In a similar fashion it should become easier and less stressful for newcomers to deal with their boss as they acquire a more comprehensive picture of that individual. The more new employees gain insight into the characteristics and perspectives of their supervisor, the easier it will be for them to interact with him. Such insight typically requires a very good understanding of his goals, expectations, and work-related values; the personal and task-related pressures that confront him; his areas of managerial strength and weakness; his preferences for different work styles, habits, and so on. In general, then, new employees will become less anxious and will have added control and predictability in dealing with their bosses as they generate increasingly more useful information about them. This argument leads to the following hypothesis:

> During socialization, stress is inversely related to the new employee's ability to develop a complete and through understanding of his boss.

In any interpersonal situation, individuals are also more likely to get along and work well together when they are more similar to each other and more compatible in their goals, values, and priority systems. Communication and interaction are always facilitated when individuals have common frames of reference (Rogers and Shoemaker, 1971). As a corollary to the previous hypothesis, then, one would speculate that organizational socialization would be smoother for those new employees who have the most in common with their immediate supervisors. In a recent doctoral dissertation on mentoring, for example, Lindholm (1983) clearly demonstrated that the single most important determinant of a supervisor-subordinate mentoring relationship resided in the nature of their interpersonal relationship and attraction and not in the nature of their task association or performance. Accordingly, the following is proposed:

> Stress is inversely related to the level of homogeneity between a new employee and his immediate boss, including their individual characteristics, value systems, and work-related styles and preferences.

It is also likely that the very idea of having a boss is inherently uncomfortable to young employees who have recently left the autonomy of university student life. New employees, as a result, are likely to experience considerable conflict as they struggle to balance their desire for independence with their more immediate needs for security and dependence (Becker, 1964; Katz, 1978a). Clearly, as socialization progresses and employees come to feel more comfortable and psychologically safe in their jobs, their relative concern for independence will increase significantly. Nonetheless, new hires must first clarify and then learn how to relate to the demands and expectations of their supervisors—how to keep them informed and how to seek their support and approval. At the same time, they must also begin to display an ability to function on their own, to take initiative, to define problems accurately by themselves, and to uncover relevant sources of new and useful information. One of the major accomplishments of socialization, then, in the ability to cope with the creative tension that stems from being dependent, on one hand, yet demonstrating one's independence on the other (Pelz, 1967; Katz, 1982a).

This trade-off between autonomy and control is often one of the major sources of tension between young professionals and their employing work organizations, according to the personal interviews conducted by Bailyn (1982). Quite often, organizations try to create an atmosphere for their young professionals that is very conducive to creative work; one in which professionals are given as much autonomy as possible in choosing problems. This high level of independence, however, is very frustrating to the relatively new professional. In the rapidly changing world of technology, it is not clear to the new employee just what problems or projects are most relevant to the organization's overall goals and objectives. What the young professional really wants is to be placed in a well-defined project that is central to the organization's mission. Having been given this kind of assignment, he then expects to be given resources, independence, and discretion to carry out his assignment. Too often, however, the opposite seems to take place. After giving the young professional the autonomous mandate to "be creative," the organization then places a great deal of control on his everday problem-solving activities. In short, what becomes stressful to young professionals in the early years of work is to be given a very high level of freedom to choose which problems to work on only to be told *how* to work on these problems. In the industrial world of work, young professionals are more likely to welcome the reverse situation; otherwise, they would have remained in university-type settings. Based on these findings, the following is hypothesized:

> During socialization stress is inversely related to the assignment of new-comers to well-defined, important organizational problems equipped with the freedom to be creative in how they pursue their problem-solving and idea-generation activities.

In addition to gaining the acceptance of their boss, newcomers must also learn to deal with other members of the hierarchy and with other peer group members. For those entering with a clear group assignment, the only problem is how to mesh their own needs and abilities with the requirements of the group. For others, however, the problem is to locate the appropriate peer or reference groups with which to align themselves. Much of what goes on in an organization occurs through informal channels and associations that have evolved over time (Allen, 1977; Farris, 1972). Thus, one comes to understand and appreciate the political aspects of different reporting relationships and organizational undertakings primarily through the individual and group contacts of which one has become a part.

The building of relationships within the organization is also important simply because they help us form the coalitions through which we are able to discover new pieces of key information, make important decisions efficiently, and carry out decisions and programs successfully. Very few organizations are completely ruled through omnipotent hierarchies and very few are pure democracies where the majority point of view dominates. Most organizations require the skillful building of interpersonal and political relationships, both formal and informal, in order to function and contribute effectively. All too often, it takes much too long to finally convince newcomers that the organization is composed of many people with whom they must build and cultivate a personal relationship.

3. *Deciphering Reward Systems and Situational Norms.* As new employees learn to relate to other relevant individuals within the work setting, they must also unravel the customary norms of acceptable social and task related behaviors. If one truly hopes to become a viable, function-

ing member of the organization and pursue a long-term relationship, then one is required to learn the many attitudes and behaviors that are appropriate and expected within the new job setting. One must discover, for example, when to ask questions, offer new ideas or suggestions, push for a change, take a vacation, or ask for a pay raise or promotion. Newcomers must also align their own assumptions, values, and behavioral modes of conduct against parallel perspectives that are held by their peer and reference groups. Most likely, as employees are able to adopt the collectively held view of things during their socialization, they will be viewed more positively by the organization and will receive more favorable evaluations (Van Maanen and Katz, 1979).

On the other hand, if the new employee finds it difficult to develop a situational perspective that is consistent with those that already exist within the work environment, a high level of stress is likely to result. This dilemma can come about in at least two ways. First, the new employee may strongly disagree with the collectively held view, operating under a very different set of assumptions, values, or priorities. The new assistant professor, for example, may be very excited about teaching and working with graduate students only to discover that his university colleagues value research output almost exclusively. Or there may be strong disagreement concerning the importance of different areas of research, the value of different research methodologies, or the merits of particular application areas. The specific sources of strain will certainly vary with each particular organizational and occupational setting; nevertheless, the more the individual sees oneself as having a "deviant" perspective within the workplace, the more he or she will experience stress in attempting to gain acceptance and prove oneself as a valuable, contributing member.

A second source of stress can occur simply when there is no collectively held view of things to guide the new employee. This situation can come about when there is little consensus within the environment, either because the individuals disagree among themselves, or because there has been insufficient time or insufficient stability to develop a collective viewpoint. In either case new employees who find themselves in these situations will experience considerably more stress because of the vast amount of uncertainty that still exists both within their own roles and within their relevant work environments. These arguments lead to the following proposition:

Stress is directly related to the failure of new employees to adopt the organization's collective perspective or the absence of a collective perspective to guide their behaviors and activities.

In addition to this general situational perspective, specific beliefs and assumptions about means-end relationships or behavior-outcome contingencies must become clearly defined to help guide and organize the newcomer's eventual participation in the workplace (Staw, 1977). From the individual's perspective, he or she must discover what is really expected and what is really rewarded. To what extent can they trust the official formal statements of reward practices and policies? To what extent can they rely on information provided by older, more experienced employees, especially if the situation happens to be changing? New employees must determine for themselves how reward systems actually function so they can comfortably decide where to put their efforts and commitments.

Surprisingly enough, in most organizational settings, the criteria surrounding advancement and other kinds of rewards are very ambiguous especially to young employees in the midst of socialization. Moreover, different employees usually see very different things as being important in getting ahead, covering the full spectrum of possibilities from pure ability and performance to pure luck and politics. Part of the reason for all this ambiguity is that organizational careers are themselves highly variable in that one can succeed in many different ways. Nevertheless, as pointed out by Beehr and Bhagat in Chapter 1, as long as newcomers remain uncertain about the relative importance of alternative outcomes, they will experience considerable tension and stress as they execute their daily activities.

Much of the uncertainty that surrounds reward systems in today's organizations can be traced to the local-cosmopolitan distinctions originally discussed by Gouldner (1957) and Merton (1957). Having recently been trained in an educational or university-type setting, new employees usually enter their organizations with a relatively strong professional orientation. At the same time, however, they must begin to apply this professional knowledge for the good of the organization; that is, they must develop a parallel orientation in which their professional interests and activities are matched against the current and future demands of their functioning organization. This balancing act can lead to a great deal of tension and frustration, particularly if the young employee is forced to allocate his or her time and efforts between two relatively independent sets of interests and rewards. To what extent should they pursue task activities that will be well recognized and rewarded within their profession or within their organization? Can they, in fact, do both relatively easily? All too often, young employees face job situations in which there is too little overlap between the demands, challenges, and rewards of their profession and those of their actual work environments.

Certainly the distinctions among alternative career paths, orientations, anchors, and the like (cf. Schein, 1978 and Hall, 1976) become increasingly salient and probably more differentiated as employees age and build a work history within their organizations. The young employee, however, is not really ready or properly prepared to deal effectively with these kinds of career and reward distinctions. More than likely, young employees want to experience and test their talents in both their job world and their professional world. Considerable stress, therefore, will probably result if young employees are confronted prematurely by these kinds of role conflicts. As a result, the following is proposed:

> During socialization, stress is inversely related to the congruence between the demands and rewards within the young employees' job settings and those of their profession.

By trying to build an accurate picture of the reward system, the young employee is dealing, of course, with only a part of the overall issue. He or she must also begin to question the likelihood of achieving certain results and desired outcomes. An individual's willingness to carry out an action is greatly influenced by whether one feels he or she can perform the action, by one's beliefs concerning the consequences of doing it, and by the attractiveness of the outcomes associated with doing it. To answer these kinds of questions, a reasonable amount of critical performance feedback from supervisors and peers is required. Such feedback provides the newcomer with a clearer sense of how he or she is being viewed and regarded, helping each to find his or her particular "niche" in the overall scheme of things. Unfortunately, in most organizations this kind of useful feedback from supervisors is a rather rare occurrence. In fact, in my own research surveys on engineering professionals, performance feedback was one of the lowest rated behaviors attributed to engineering supervisors in over ten separate RD&E facilities (Katz and Allen, 1978). New employees, therefore, are faced with the problem of obtaining adequate feedback on their own individual performances which can be particularly difficult if one's work is diffused within a larger group or project effort. What becomes most distressing to new employees, then, is that they have entered the organization with an underlying expectation that they would be learning and improving on their first job, yet their supervisors fail to realize that they should act and feel responsible for teaching and helping the employees to accomplish this objective.

Based on the model put forth by Beehr and Bhagat (see Chapter 1), employees need to determine how effectively they are currently performing, how difficult it might be for them to achieve desired outcomes, and how readily they could obtain or develop the various skills and knowledge, that is, the resources necessary to meet the demands and expectations of the organization. However, as long as these critical concerns remain unmet and uncertain to new employees, the amount of stress they experience will escalate dramatically. Accordingly, for many employees one of the most important, yet most trying, learning experiences during socialization is how to obtain valid feedback in those particular situations in which it does not automatically or effectively take place. And for many young professionals, the ultimate learning experience is to figure out how to become an excellent judge of one's own individual performance. Nevertheless, during socialization, the following are hypothesized:

> Stress is inversely related to the supervisor's ability to: (1) make an accurate assessment of the new employee's performance and give useful and valid feedback on this performance; (2) transmit the right kinds of values and norms to the new employee in terms of the long-run contributions that are expected of him or her; and (3) design the right mix of meaningful, challenging tasks that permit the new employee to utilize and extend his or her professional skills and build his or her new situational identity.

PROCESS OF SOCIALIZATION

Underlying the tasks represented by the socialization stage is the basic idea that individuals are strongly motivated to organize their work lives in a manner that reduces the amount of uncertainty they must face and that is therefore low in stress (Pfeffer, 1981; Katz, 1982b). In the words of Weick (1969), employees seek to "enact" their environments by directing their activities toward the establishment of a workable level of certainty and clarity. As they enter their new job positions, they are primarily concerned with reality construction, building more realistic understandings of their unfamiliar social and task environments and their own situational roles within them. They endeavor, essentially, to structure the world of their experience, trying to unravel and define the many "constitutive rules" that steer the workplace toward social order rather than toward social chaos (Garfinkel, 1967; Katz, 1980).

One of the most obvious, yet most important and often overlooked aspects of new employee socialization is simply that it must take place. By and large, people will not accept uncertainty. They must succeed over time in formulating situational definitions of their workplace with which they can coexist and function comfortably; otherwise, they will feel terribly strained and will seek to leave the given work organization. Until the new employee has created a situational perspective on himself or herself, constructed guidelines regarding what is expected, and built certain situationally-contingent understandings necessary to participate meaningfully within the work setting, the individual cannot act as freely and as fully as he or she would like.

What is very important to recognize here is that stress does not come from the uncertainty itself; it comes from the individual's inability to reduce or lower it. As long as one is making progress in reducing uncertainty, that is, as long as socialization is being facilitated and the individual is making increasing sense out of his or her new work surroundings, stress and anxiety will be lowered and satisfaction will be raised. However, if new employees are somehow prevented from accomplishing any or all of the broad socialization tasks previously discussed, then they are not succeeding in reducing as much of the uncertainty as they need to. This can become highly frustrating and anxiety producing, resulting eventually in higher levels of dissatisfaction and increased levels of organizational turnover. Just as the engineer is highly motivated to reduce technical uncertainty in his or her laboratory activities, the new employee is highly motivated to reduce social and interpersonal uncertainty within his or her new environments. Generally speaking, activity that results in the reduction of uncertainty leads to increasing satisfaction and reduced stress; whereas, activity or change that generates uncertainty creates dissatisfaction and higher stress. Thus, it is not change per se that is resisted, it is the increase in uncertainty that usually accompanies it that is so difficult for individuals to accept. Based on these premises, the following is proposed:

> For organizational newcomers stress is not positively related to high levels of situational uncertainty per se; instead, stress is inversely associated with the rate of change at which a particular content area or dimension of uncertainty is being reduced.

One must also realize that socialization, unlike an orientation program, does not take place over a day or two. It takes a fair amount of time for employees to feel accepted and competent and to accomplish all of the tasks necessary to develop a situational perspective. How long this socialization period lasts is not only influenced by the abilities, needs, and prior experiences of individual workers, but it also differs significantly across occupations (Feldman, 1977; Katz, 1978b). In general, one might posit that the length of one's initial socialization stage varies positively with the level of complexity of one's job and occupational requirements, ranging perhaps from as little as a month or two on very routine, programmed-type jobs to as much as a year or more on very skilled, unprogrammed-type jobs, as in the engineering and scientific professions. It is generally recognized, for example, that a substantial socialization phase is usually required before an engineer can fully contribute within the organization, making use of his or her knowledge and technical specialty. Even though one might have received an excellent university education in mechanical engineering principles, one must still figure out how to become an effective mechanical engineer at Westinghouse, Dupont or General Electric.

Socialization Is a Social Process

Another very important assumption about socialization is that it must take place through interaction—interaction with other key organizational employees and relevant clientele. By and large, new employees can only reduce uncertainty through interpersonal activities and interpersonal feedback processes.

Newcomers' perceptions and responses are not developed in a social vacuum but evolve through successive encounters with their work environments. Their outlooks become formulated as they interact with and act upon different aspects of their job setting. Their development cannot transpire in isolation, for it is the social context that provides the information and cues with which new employees define and interpret their work experiences (Blumer, 1969; Salancik and Pfeffer, 1977).

One of the more important features of socialization is that the information and knowledge previously gathered by employees from their former colleges or other institutional settings are no longer sufficient nor completely appropriate for interpreting and understanding their new organizational domains. As a result, they must depend on individuals within their new situations to help them make sense out of the numerous activities taking place around them. The greater their unfamiliarity, the more they must rely on their new situations to provide the necessary information and interactions by which they can eventually construct their own individual perspectives and situational identities. And it is precisely this situational reliance and social dependence that forces new employees to be more easily influenced during socialization through social interaction (Salancik and Pfeffer, 1978). As a result, the following is hypothesized:

> Stress is inversely related to the transmission of important information through interpersonal contact and communication rather than through impersonal communications such as formal, written media.

Clearly, as employees become increasingly cognizant of their overall job surroundings, they become increasingly capable of relying on their own perceptions for interpreting events and executing their daily task activities. Once they have managed to build a sufficiently robust situational perspective, they are freer to operate more self-sufficiently in that they are now better equipped to determine for themselves the importance and meaning of the various events and information flows surrounding them. On the other hand, as long as new employees have to balance their situational perspectives against the views of significant others within the workplace, frequent interaction with those individuals will be required.

New employees absorb the subtleties of local organizational culture and climate and construct their own definitions of organizational reality—and in particular their own role identities—through symbolic interactions with other individuals, including peers, supervisors, subordinates, and customers (Mead, 1932; Schutz, 1967). A newcomer orients himself or herself to the new world, not by responding directly and instinctively to events themselves, but by responding in terms of his or her own "interpretation" of those events. Since multiple meanings are likely for any particular event, it is the newcomer's active interpretation of the event, strongly influenced by interacting with one's reference group members, that is so important in constructing his personal view of reality. Furthermore, the more individuals with whom the new employee interacts, the more likely he or she is to put together a view that is both comprehensive and realistic, since different individuals will emphasize different aspects of the work setting and will also differ in the way they interpret events. Recent hires, as a result, formulate their concepts and guide their activities around the anticipated reactions and expectations of the many key employees with whom they are connected. Given the critical role of communication in reducing uncertainty, the following are proposed:

(a) Stress is inversely related to the frequency of interpersonal communication that takes place between the new employee and other key individuals within his or her relevant work environment.

(b) Stress is inversely related to the number of key individuals within the work environment with whom the new employee has established ongoing interpersonal communication.

Organizations, of course, differ significantly in how they are structured to carry out their everyday work activities. Some organizations can rely on formal structures and relatively bureaucratic, standardized procedures to operate efficiently within their stable or somewhat mature industrial and economic environments. Other organizations have to rely more and more on informal structures and mechanisms to innovate and meet the demands of their rapidly changing and uncertain environments. Since the more "organic" type of organization requires significantly more integration and more informal communication procedures to function effectively than the more "mechanistic" type of organizational model (e.g., Burns and Stalker, 1961; Lawrence and Lorsch, 1967), the following corollary to the previous hypotheses should be researched:

The relationships between stress and interpersonal communication will be significantly moderated by the characteristics of the work environment; the more organic the work environment, the stronger the inverse relationships between stress and interpersonal contact.

Of all the concepts that each individual newcomer acquires through the plethora of interpersonal contacts that takes place, perhaps the most important is one's self-concept. It has often been argued that one's fellow workers help to define for each newcomer many of the diverse aspects of the new job setting by the way they act and behave toward these aspects, for example, how they deal with absenteeism, budget overruns, schedule slippages, staff reports, or subordinate suggestions. Similarly, fellow employees help newcomers create perspectives on themselves as particular kinds of individuals by the way the fellow employees act and respond toward these organizational newcomers. As a result, a new employee's self-image is largely a social product, significantly affected by the behaviors and attitudes of other employees within his or her organizational neighborhood. In essence the newcomer's situational identity is strongly influenced by the self-concept that is gleaned from the eyes of those significant others whom they come to know and with whom they interact.

If newcomers strive to reduce uncertainty by locating and orienting themselves relative to the views and expectations that emerge from those individuals on whom they are most dependent and with whom they are most interactive, then it should not be surprising that some of the most important and most satisfying experiences for new employees are those which attune them to what is expected of them. There is a strong need for newcomers to identify closely with those colleagues and supervisors who can furnish guidance and reassurance concerning such expectations (Merton, 1957; Graen, 1976). If on the other hand, the individual newcomer is precluded from reducing uncertainty and making increasing sense out of his or her organizational surrounding, then he or she will feel stressed and will be unable to act in a completely responsive and undistracted manner. Many circumstances can arise in any work setting to delay or inhibit a newcomer's socialization, circumstances that invariably prevent the necessary and essential set of interpersonal interactions. Consider, for example, the new employee whose boss is out of town, on vacation, or is simply too busy to help with his or her integration; or the new employee who is assigned to a job location or given an office far away from his or her boss or reference group. Chances are that the reduction of situational uncertainty under these kinds of conditions will be a much prolonged process, perhaps interfering with the newcomer's potential success or even his or her willingness to remain in the organization. Research by Allison (1974) and Lazarsfeld and Theilens (1958) has shown, for example, that when professionals are highly recognized and maintain their strongest links with professionals outside their organization, they are more likely to leave their organizations. In a more recent longitudinal study, Katz and Tushman (1983) found some evidence suggesting that engineers who communicated more often outside than inside their organization were also more likely to leave their organization over the next few years. Based on these arguments and findings, the following proposition is put forth:

> During socialization, stress is directly related to the relative predominance of employee interactions with individuals outside the organization versus those with individuals inside the organization.

Socialization Experiences Are Highly Influential and Long-Lasting

According to the law of primacy expressed by Brown (1963), early social-ization experiences are particularly important because they greatly influ-ence how later experiences will be interpreted. The early images and perspectives that are formed in the first year or two of one's organizational career have a strong and lasting influence on one's future task assign-ments, perceived performance and abilities, and promotional success (Hall, 1976).

More specifically, what has become clear from a large number of studies (e.g., Berlew and Hall, 1966; Bray et al., 1974; Vincino and Bass, 1978) is that the degree to which an employee perceives his or her job as important and challenging by the end of the first year will strongly influence future performance and promotional opportunities. Using overall measures of job challenge, these studies have verified that after one year of employment, young managers who evaluated their jobs more highly or who were viewed more positively by their supervisors were also more likely to have higher performance ratings and higher rates of promotion some five to ten years later. In a similar fashion, Pelz and Andrews (1976) concluded from their cross-sectional study that engineers who were able to utilize more di-verse skills and abilities to accomplish an output that became widely known and recognized were more likely to advance within the organiza-tion than engineers who were frequently rotated from project to project during their early career years. As a final example, career tracking studies at General Electric have discovered that the best predictor of career suc-cess for young professionals at GE was the number of different supervisors who had personal knowledge of the task activities and accomplishments of the young individuals. Given the general consistency in this pattern of findings, it is clear that the newcomer who gets widely known and comes to be seen and sponsored as a valued high performer gains a considerable long-term advantage over the newcomers not so fortunately viewed—the proverbial self-fulfilling prophecy.

In the process of interpreting their early work experiences, young em-ployees begin to observe their colleagues as well as other members who have been labelled as successful or unsuccessful within the organization. They then begin to assess their own careers relative to these individuals. This process of comparison involves many factors, but temporal compari-sons represent some of the most critical. By comparing one's progress against these other individuals, the new employee beings to form an implicit "career benchmark" against which both the individual and the organization can start to determine how well he or she is doing. In his large study of British managers, Sofer (1970) shows just how sensitive organiza-tional members can become to their relative career progress. In another example Dalton et al. (1982) strongly argue from their study of R&D

professionals that organizations have clearly defined expectations about the behaviors and responsibilities of their more successful engineers at well-defined age-related career stages.

These and many other examples all emphasize that soon after beginning work, employees gradually become concerned about how their progress fits within some framework of career benchmarks. Where are they— are they on schedule, ahead of schedule, behind schedule? The pressure from these kinds of comparisons can become extremely acute especially as the relative judgments become increasingly salient and competitive and their timing increasingly fixed and inflexible. Such events seem to occur in at least two different ways. First, the comparisons can become highly intense as employees enter an organization as part of a well-defined, well-bounded cohort but are then forced to compete amongst themselves for the best individual evaluations, as in the case of many law firms, public accounting firms, consulting companies, universities, and so on. The directness and clarity of these comparisons make the implicit aspects of the career benchmarking process more explicit and, in general, place the young employee under a great deal of stress as he or she competes for the next level of advancement.*

For other young employees the occupation or other organization itself can present a fixed timetable for measuring success and career advancement. The tenure process in universities, standardized professional exams (e.g., registered engineer, CPA) or certain apprenticeship periods are all examples of highly structured, well-defined timetables of career progress. These kinds of explicit benchmarks can also place the young employee under severe stress particularly if the employee loses control over the timing of the process or it becomes more like an "up or out" or a "pass/fail" type of system. While the climate that emerges from these more explicit models of career benchmarking may not be very supportive, they may "energize" a great deal of activity and long hours of work on the part of the new employee, at least during his or her early career years. The following is therefore hypothesized:

> Stress is directly related to the extent to which career success benchmarking becomes increasingly explicit either through strong peer comparisons or through fixed thresholds of achievement.

Because the employee's immediate supervisor influences and controls so many aspects of the communication, task, and career benchmarking factors

---

* As discussed by McCain et al. (1981), the existence of a well-defined entering cohort could also lead to a situation in which the cohort develops a strong feeling of group solidarity, competing against the established organization for resources and control. In this instance, however, we are talking about individuals who are more likely to identify with each other than with the joining-up process, perceiving themselves to be distinct from the organization and its members.

during socialization, it becomes clear why so many studies have pinpointed the new employee's first boss as being so critical with respect to his or her successful advancements both organizationally and professionally (Kanter, 1977; Schein, 1978; Henning and Jardim, 1977). While supervisors play a critical role in linking their subordinates to other parts of the organization (Likert, 1967; Tushman and Katz, 1980), they can also assume a broader role within their work groups, becoming actively involved in the training, integration, and socialization of their more recently hired members.

By building close working relationships with young subordinates, supervisors might not only improve their group's performance (Katz and Tushman, 1981), but they might also directly affect the personal growth and development of their young professionals. To the extent that supervisors help their new employees participate and contribute more effectively within their work settings, have clearer working relationships with other key organizational individuals, and communicate more easily with outside customers, clients, or professionals, these young professionals will experience less stress and will be less likely to leave the organization. Graen and Ginsburgh (1977) showed, for example, that organizational newcomers who built strong dyadic relationships with their immediate supervisors and who saw a strong relationship between their work and their professional careers were more likely to remain with the organization.

In a much longer longitudinal study, Katz and Tushman (1983) found that young engineers who had high levels of interaction with their first and second level supervisors were significantly less likely to leave the organization over the next 5 years. These supervisors were seen as technically competent and were viewed as valuable sources of new ideas and information. As a result, they became more interactive simply because they were consulted and listened to more frequently on work related matters. At the same time, this high level of interpersonal activity allowed these supervisors to create close working relationships with their younger engineering subordinates, helping them become established and integrated during their early career years. Thus, it may be this high level of interpersonal contact with technically competent supervisors that not only facilitates socialization but also results in more accurate expectations, perceptions, and understandings about one's role in the job and in the larger organization—all of which are important in decreasing turnover and the anxiety levels of new employees. All of this leads to the following hypothesis:

> During socialization, stress is inversely related to the strength of the connection and the level of interpersonal contact between an employee and his or her supervisor.

It has been argued throughout this paper that becoming an integral part of the organization's communication and information processing networks and learning the organization's customs and norms are critically important for reducing stress and fostering more positive attitudes during the early stages of employees' careers. It has also been argued that supervisors play a very direct role in dealing with the initial concerns of young employees, allowing them to reduce uncertainty by helping them understand and interpret the reality of their new settings. In essence, supervisors operate as effective socializing agents and networks builders for their young employees.

In many cases, however, the supervisor is not the only socializing agent of the new employee. The veteran group as a unit can also affect the attachment of new members to the organization. In line with the findings of Katz (1982b) and McCain et al. (1981), for example, the larger the proportion of group members with the same group tenure and shared work history, the more distinct that cluster of individuals might become from other organizational members, in general, and from new entering members, in particular. Young employees, as a result, might experience a great deal of stress and frustration in trying to integrate themselves into a well-established, older cohort. The following is therefore hypothesized:

> For new employees, stress will be higher when they try to become part of a group in which a very large proportion of the members have entered at the same time.

Additional conflicts and power issues are also likely to result when there are larger gaps between cohorts within the overall work group. If the group has been staffed on a regular basis, then the new employee's integration is more likely to proceed in a smooth fashion since socialization can be nurtured through the existence of closer, linking cohorts (e.g., Ouchi and Jaeger, 1978). If there are large gaps between cohorts, however, then it is likely that perceptions and beliefs will differ more, resulting in considerable communication difficulty and impedance. The existence of well-differentiated cohorts, according to McCain et al. (1981), increases the possibility of different intragroup norms and expectations which can result in a group atmosphere that is characterized by severe intragroup conflict—a very stressful experience for new employees. Accordingly, the following is also proposed:

> For new employees, stress is directly related to the size of the gap between cohorts.

CONCLUSIONS

Perhaps the most important notion in this paper is that individuals undergoing a transition into a new organization are placed in a high anxiety-producing situation. They are motivated, therefore, to reduce this anxiety by learning the functional and social requirements of their new role as quickly as possible. What must be recognized and understood by organizations is that supervisors and group colleagues of new employees have a very special and important role to fulfill in inducting and socializing the new employee. The careful selection of these individuals for young professionals should go a long way toward alleviating many of the problems that usually occur during the "joining-up" process. One must recognize that the problems and concerns of young professionals are real and must be dealt with before these young employees can become effective organizational members. Although organizations might want to develop specific training programs to teach managers how to "break-in" the young professional more effectively, an alternative strategy would be to make sure that young professionals are integrated and socialized into their job environments only through those particular groups and supervisors who appear especially effective in this function. Rather than allowing all supervisors and groups to recruit and hire new employees as additional staffing needs arise, a more centralized policy of rotating or transferring individuals to some areas in order to hire new employees through other key integrating areas might prove more beneficial to the organization as a whole in the long run. The careful assignment of groups and supervisors to new college recruits, combined with some training for these individuals, should go a long way toward utilizing the great potential in most young professionals, thereby reducing the high levels of frustration, stress, and dissatisfaction that so many of them experience during their initial career years.

REFERENCES

Allen, T. J. *Managing the flow of technology.* Cambridge: MIT Press, 1977.

Allison, P. D. Inter-organizational mobility of academic scientists. Paper presented at the meeting of the American Sociology Association, Montreal, 1974.

Argyris, C. *Understanding organizational behavior.* Homewood, Ill.: Dorsey, 1960.

Bailyn, L. Resolving contradictions in technical careers; or, what if I like being an engineer. *Technology Review,* 1982, November-December, 40–47.

Becker, H. Personal changes in adult life. *Sociometry,* 1964, **27**, 40–53.

Berlew, D. and Hall, T. The socialization of managers: Effects of expectations on performance. *Administrative Science Quarterly,* 1966, **11**, 207–223.

Blumer, H. *Symbolic interactionism: Perspective and method.* Englewood Cliffs, N.J.: Prentice-Hall, 1969.

Bray, D. W., Campbell, R. J., and Grant D. L. *Formative years in business: A long-term study of managerial lives.* New York: Wiley, 1974.

Brown, J.A.C. *Techniques of Persuasion.* Baltimore: Penguin Books, 1963.

Burns, T. and Stalker, G. M. *The Management of Innovation.* London: Tavistock, 1961.

Dalton, G. W., Thompson, P. H., and Price, R. L. The four stages of professional careers: A new look at performance by professionals. In R. Katz (Ed.), *Career issues in human resource management.* Englewood Cliffs, N. J.: Prentice-Hall, 1982.

Farris, G. The effect of individual roles on performance in innovative groups." *R&D Management*, 1972, **3**, 23−28.

Feldman, D. The role of initiation activities in socialization. *Human Relations*, 1977, **30**, 977−990.

Garfinkel, H. *Studies in ethnomethodology*. New York: Prentice-Hall, 1967.

Gouldner, A. W. "Cosmopolitans and socials: Towards an analysis of latent social roles," *Administrative Science Quarterly*, 1957, **2**, 446−467.

Graen, G. Role-making processes within complex organizations. In M. D. Dunnette (Ed.), *Handbood of industrial and organizational Psychology*. Chicago: Rand McNally, 1976.

Graen, G. and Ginsburgh, S. Job resignation as a function of role orientation and leader acceptance. *Organizational Behavior and Human Performance*, 1977, **19**, 1−17.

Hall, D. T. *Careers in organizations*. Pacific Palisades, Calif.: Goodyear, 1976.

Hall, D. T., and Nougaim, K. E. An examination of Maslow's need hierarchy in an organizational setting. *Organizational Behavior and Human Performance*, 1968, **3**, 12−35.

Henning, M. and Jardim, A. *The managerial woman*. New York: Doubleday, 1977.

Hughes, E. C. *Men and their work*. Glencoe, Ill: Free Press, 1958.

Kanter, R. M. *Work and family in the United States*. New York: Russell Sage, 1977.

Katz, R. Job longevity as a situational factor in job satisfaction. *Administrative Science Quarterly*, 1978a, **23**, 204−223.

Katz, R. The influence of job longevity on employee reactions to task characteristics. *Human Relations*, 1978b, **31**, 703−725.

Katz, R. Time and work: Toward an integrative perspective. *Research in Organizational Behavior*, 1980, **2**, JAI Press, 81−127.

Katz, R. Managing careers: The influence of job and group longevities. In R. Katz (Ed.), *Career Issues in Human Resource Management*. Englewood Cliffs, N. J.: Prentice-Hall, 1982a, 154−181.

Katz, R. The effects of group longevity on project communication and performance. *Administrative Science Quarterly*, 1982b, **27**, 81−104.

Katz, R. and Allen, T. J. The technical performance of long duration R&D project groups. Technical report to the chief of studies management office, Department of the Army, Grant Number DASG-60-77-C-0147, 1978.

Katz, R. and Allen, T. J. Investigating the not invented here (NIH) syndrome. *R&D Management*, 1982, **12**, 7−19.

Katz, R. and Tushman, M. An investigation into the managerial roles and career paths of gatekeeper and project supervisors in a major R&D facility. *R&D Management*, 1981, **11**, 103−110.

Katz, R. and Tushman, M. A longitudinal study of the effects of boundary spanning supervision on turnover and promotion in research and development, *Academy of Management Journal*, 1983, **26**, 437−456.

Lawrence, P. R. and Lorsch, J. W. *Organizations and environment*. Boston: Harvard Business School, 1967.

Lazarsfeld, P. F., and Theilens, W. *The academic mind*, Glencoe, Ill: The Free Press, 1958.

Levinson, H. *Men, management, and mental health*. Cambridge, Mass.: Harvard University Press, 1962.

Likert, R. *The human organization*. New York: McGraw-Hill, 1967.

Lindholm, J. A study of the mentoring relationship in work organizations. Unpublished MIT Doctoral Dissertation, 1983.

Louis, M. Surprise and sense making: What newcomers experience in entering unfamiliar organizational settings. *Administrative Science Quarterly*, 1980, **25**, 226−251.

McCain, B. R., O'Reilly, C., and Pfeffer, J. The effects of departmental demography on turnover: The case of a university. Working Paper, March 1981.

Mead, G. H. *The philosophy of the present.* Chicago: Open Court, 1932.

Merton, R. K. *Social theory and social structure.* New York: Free Press, 1957.

Mirvis, P. and Lawler, E. E. Measuring the financial impact of employee attitudes. *Journal of Applied Psychology*, 1977, **62**, 1–8.

Ouchi, W. G. and Jaeger, A. M. "Type Z organization: Stability in the midst of mobility." *Academy of Management Review*, 1978, **3**, 305–314.

Pelz, D. C. Creative tension in the research and development climate. *Science*, 1967, **157**, 160–165.

Pelz, D. C. and Andrews, F. M. *Scientists in organizations.* Ann Arbor: University of Michigan, 1976.

Pfeffer, J. Management as symbolic action: The creation and maintenance of organizational paradigms. *Research in Organizational Behavior*, 1981, **3**, JAI Press, 1981.

Porter, L. and Steers, R. Organizational, work, and personal factors in employee turnover and absenteeism. *Psychological Bulletin*, 1973, **80**, 151–176.

Roger, E. M., and Shoemaker, F. F. *Communication of innovations: A cross-cultural approach.* New York: The Free Press, 1971.

Salancik, G. R. and Pfeffer, J. An examination of need satisfaction models of job attitudes. *Administrative Science Quarterly*, 1977, **22**, 427–456.

Salancik, G. R. and Pfeffer, J. A social information processing approach to job attitudes and task design. *Administrative Science Quarterly*, 1978, **28**, 224–253.

Schutz, A. *The phenomenology of the social world.* Evanston, Ill.: Northwestern University Press, 1977.

Schein, E. H. How to break in the college graduate. *Harvard Business Review*, 1964, **42**, 168–76.

Schein, E. H. *Career dynamics*, Reading, Mass.: Addison-Wesley, 1978.

Schein, E. H. *Organizational psychology*, 3rd ed. Englewood Cliffs, N.J.: Prentice-Hall, 1980.

Sofer, C. *Men in mid-career: A study of British managers and technical specialists.* London: Cambridge University Press, 1970.

Staw, B. Motivation in organizations: Toward synthesis and redirection. In B. Staw and G. Salancik (Eds.) *New directions in organizational behavior.* Chicago: St. Clair Press, 1977.

Steers, R. M. Antecedents and outcomes of organizational commitment. *Administrative Science Quarterly*, 1977, **22**, 46–56.

Tushman, M. and Katz, R. External communication and project performance: An investigation into the role of gatekeepers. *Management Science*, 1980, **26**, 1071–1085.

Van Maanen, J. and Katz, R. The cognitive organization of police perceptions of their work environment. *Sociology of Work and Occupations*, 1979, **6**, 31–58.

Vicino, F. L. and Bass, B. M. Lifespace variables and managerial success. *Journal of Applied Psychology*, 1978, **63**, 81–88.

Wanous, J. *Organizational entry.* Reading, Mass.: Addison-Wesley, 1969.

Webber, R. Career problems of young managers. *California Management Review*, 1976, **18**, 19–53.

Weick, K. E., *The social psychology of organizing.* Reading, Mass.: Addison-Wesley, 1969.

CHAPTER SIX

Dual-Career Couples

Stress, Stressors, Strains, and Strategies

NINA GUPTA AND G. DOUGLAS JENKINS, JR.

Most people agree that the number of dual-career couples in this country is on the rise. There is also some recognition that the problems, the issues, and the stress faced by dual-career couples are somewhat different from those encountered by more conventional, single-career families. Despite this recognition, little has been done to identify the special needs of dual-career couples and to detail the action steps that would meet these needs. But the study of dual-career couples is important for many theoretical and practical reasons. A systematic examination of the problems and issues relevant to dual-career couples can be useful in the development of psychological/sociological/organizational theories; it can shed light on many management and personnel issues; it can help local, corporate, and federal decision makers in enunciating policies and procedures that stimulate productivity, growth, and satisfaction. Through such a systematic examination, strategies can be developed for coping with dual-career stress before the number of dual-career couples burgeons still further, and their problems assume alarming proportions.

In this chapter, we propose a framework for understanding the nature, causes, and consequences of stress among dual-career couples and the coping strategies available to handle dual-career stress. Before the theoretical framework is elucidated, however, it is necessary to derive a common definition of terms used throughout the chapter. Therefore, the first section of this chapter is primarily introductory and presents definitions of some key concepts. It also presents the general theoretical framework used in the chapter. The other three major sections are more substantive in nature. In the second section, the specific sources of stress among dual-career couples are outlined, and in the third section the consequences of dual career stress are discussed. The final section is devoted to an examination of the coping strategies that can be useful in the amelioration of dual-career stress.

KEY CONCEPTS AND RELATIONSHIPS

Two major concepts are most central to the focus of this chapter. These concepts are (1) dual-career couples and (2) stress. Each concept is discussed briefly below.

Dual-Career Couples

A few years ago, Rapoport and Rapoport (1978) remarked that the concept of the *dual-career* family was rather imprecise, in that it incorporated a constellation of family types instead of representing a single uniform or homogeneous family type. The observation is still accurate today, since little conceptual or empirical effort has been devoted in the interim to a precise specification of exactly what defines a dual-career family or couple.

In the present context, the term "career" does not refer simply to working for pay outside the home, that is, holding a job. A career involves more planning and progression than does an unrelated series of jobs. Thus, Rapoport and Rapoport (1971) defined the term "career" as designating "those types of jobs which require a high degree of commitment and which have a continuous developmental character" (p. 18). Careers can progress either *within* a single organization or *across* a series of organizations. Regardless of the organizational context, however, the critical factors that distinguish careers from jobs are *commitment* to a work role and a *developmental progression* in that work role.

A conceptual definition of the term "career" is much more easily derived than is an operational distinction between "jobs" and "careers." For instance, it is simple to view doctors, lawyers, and so on as having "careers," and to view janitors and garbage collectors as having "jobs." But the matter becomes more complex when work roles such as those of secondary school teachers and executive secretaries are considered. Are these "jobs" or "careers?" The answer probably varies from one individual to another, since commitment and progression may be different across role occupants, and since these work roles tend to be somewhere between the classifications of "jobs" and "careers" in terms of their levels of commitment and progression. Therefore, it is useful to conceptualize work roles as falling on a continuum that ranges from no commitment/progression at one end to high commitment/progression at the other end. Classification of a particular occupation along this continuum is contingent on the attitude of the individual to his or her work role. Thus, it is possible for a university professor (who views the work role as providing money, and who does little to stimulate progression) to be holding a job, and a school teacher (who is committed and who sees himself or herself as steadily rising in the work role) to be holding a career. The psychological response of an individual to his or her job is critical in distinguishing between jobs and careers, since stress experienced by people in their work roles is largely dependent on the attitudes they hold about their work.

A *couple* is traditionally defined as two marital partners sharing a household. Following Hall and Hall (1979), however, a couple is conceptualized more broadly here to include a variety of coupling arrangements, the most common of which is still the conventional marriage, although stable cohabitation with a person of the same or opposite sex is also a frequent alternative. The legal or moral status of the relationship is irrelevant in the present context. What is relevant is that the partners feel a bond between each other, a commitment to the pursuit of a mutually satisfactory relationship, and hold a relatively long-term perspective on the survival of the relationship.

In short, a dual-career couple can be viewed as "two partners, each of whom feels an emotional commitment to the other partner and to his or her own work role, and whose work roles exhibit developmental sequences." The personal and organizational experiences of people who fit this definition are likely to be markedly different from the experiences of other people.

Stress

The definition of stress used in this chapter is consistent with the remainder of this volume. Stress is viewed here as a cognitive state in which an individual confronts a decision-making and problem-solving situation characterized by high levels of *uncertainty*, associated with obtaining *important* (i.e., valent) outcomes for the person, and in which the existence of such uncertainties is long in its *duration* (see the introductory chapter of this volume for an elaboration of this theoretical perspective). All three elements, uncertainty, importance, and duration must be present at least to a minimum degree for stress to be experienced by an individual.

A further word about the concept of uncertainty is in order. Uncertainty can result from many different sources. For instance, role conflict occurs when an individual is exposed to incompatible expectations, whether within a given role or across different roles; role ambiguity occurs when role expectations are unclear and/ or unpredictable; and role overload occurs when there are too many or too difficult role expectations. Regardless of the specific situation, however, uncertainty is evident about (1) what the individual should do (expectations), (2) how the individual should do it (methods), or (3) what the consequences of the behaviors might be (outcomes). If the uncertainty occurs with respect to matters that are also important and relatively long lasting, the cognitive state of stress is likely to result.

Two further aspects of the concept are particularly relevant to this chapter. First, the cognitive states of two individuals, and not just one individual, are of concern. That is, the cognitions of both partners of a dual-career couple, either separately or taken together, may have a bearing on stress. Second, both the work roles and the family roles of the members of dual-career couples are germane to the present discussion. Instead of focusing exclusively on work or family roles, therefore, the present chapter is also concerned with *interactions* among these roles in determining the stress experiences of members of dual-career couples.

General Theoretical Approach

The general theoretical approach to be used throughout this paper is presented in Figure 6-1. The figure shows interactions of work and family roles within and between the partners of a dual-career couple. Characteristics of each role, as well as interactions among the roles, give rise to uncertainties regarding expectations, methods, and outcomes; these uncertainties often tend to be long lasting and involve matters that are of crucial concern to members of dual-career couples. Because of the presence of the three necessary prerequisites (viz., uncertainty, importance, and duration), members of dual-career couples can experience severe stress.

The stress experienced by dual-career couples has implications for the work and family roles of each partner. Do the members of dual-career couples perform effectively at work? Are they satisfied with their family roles? What effect does dual-career status have on the children of these couples? How does the health of dual-career couples compare with the health of others? These and similar questions regarding the consequences of dual-career stress are discussed in Section 3 of this chapter. Several sets of consequences of dual-career stress are considered relevant in this context: consequences for the work lives of dual-career couples; consequences for the family lives of dual-career couples; health consequences; and consequences for the organizations employing dual-career partners.

The coping strategies that members of dual-career couples can adopt to alleviate the potentially harmful consequences of their stress are discussed in the last section. This section also addresses approaches that employing organizations can adopt to minimize the occurrence of deleterious outcomes of dual-career stress. The chapter concludes with suggestions for the design of research aimed at highlighting the nature, causes, and consequences of stress among dual-career couples.

Summary

This chapter is concerned with the stress experienced by members of dual-career couples, either individually or as a couple, through their

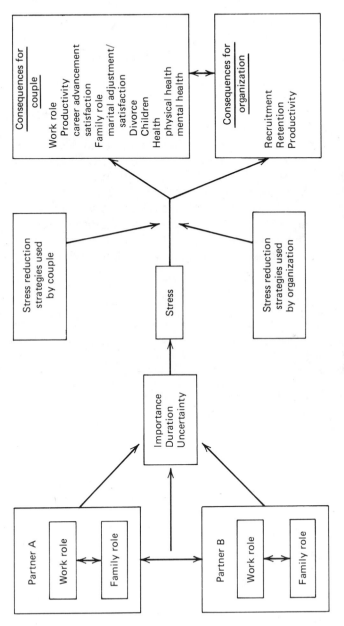

Figure 6-1 Conceptual framework for the examination of dual-career stress.

145

enactment of work and family roles. Because *both* partners in a dual-career situation consider *both* roles to be salient, and are committed to the effective execution of these roles, the probability of occurrence of stress is relatively high for these individuals.

SOURCES OF DUAL-CAREER STRESS

Stressors, the sources of stress, can be present in several life domains of dual-career couples. For instance, each partner can experience stress due to his or her own work role, his or her own family role, or the interactions of these two roles. Dual-career couples can also experience stress due to the interaction of their own roles with those of their partners. These different sources of stress are depicted diagrammatically in Figure 6-2, which also shows the particular stressors that are unique to dual-career couples and those shared by other people as well.

The figure shows six types of stressors that may be experienced by dual-career couples. Three of these stressors stem from each partner's own roles (intraindividual stressors), and the other three stem from the interplay between own roles and partner's roles (interindividual stressors). The

	Work role	Family role	Interrole
From own role(s)	1 Experienced by job/career holders	2 Experienced by couples	3 Experienced by job/career holders
From interaction with partner's role(s)	4 Experienced by two-job/career couples	5 Experienced by couples	6 Experienced by two-job/career couples

Figure 6-2 Sources of dual-career stress.

specific stressors experienced by members of dual-career couples can be labeled as follows:

1. Intraindividual work role stressors.
2. Intraindividual family role stressors.
3. Intraindividual interrole (work versus family role) stressors.
4. Interindividual work role stressors.
5. Interindividual family role stressors.
6. Interindividual interrole (work versus family role) stressors.

Intraindividual work role stressors (Cell 1) stem from characteristics of the work roles of members of dual-career couples and are expected to affect most job/career holders. Members of dual-career couples may also experience stress from their own family roles, that is, from intraindividual family role stressors (Cell 2). These stressors are expected to typify all "coupled" individuals, that is, all individuals holding a relatively stable relationship with a person of the same or opposite sex. The last stressors that a member of a dual-career couple may experience as a function of his or her own roles stem from the impingement of his or her work role on the family role and vice versa, namely, from intraindividual interrole stressors described in Cell 3.

Members of dual-career couples may also experience parallel stressors due to the interplay between their own work/family roles and those of their partners. Thus, Cell 4 depicts interindividual work role stressors, which focus on the interactions of the work roles of the two partners. This stressor is considered unique to dual-job (and, therefore, dual-career) couples. Cell 5, focusing on the interactions between the family roles of the partners (i.e., interindividual family role stressors), is characteristic of most couples. Finally, Cell 6 concerns the interplay among all four roles (i.e., partner A's work and family roles and partner B's work and family roles) in the determination of stress, and is labeled interindividual interrole stressors. These stressors are also unique to dual-job/dual-career couples. This classification of stressors is similar to that proposed by Pleck (1977).

Dual-career couples are likely to experience stress from each of these sources. As mentioned earlier, however, some sources of stress (e.g., intraindividual work role stressors) do not distinguish between members of dual-career couples and others, while other stressors (e.g., interindividual interrole stressors) are shared only by dual-job and dual-career couples. In both cases, dual-career couples are expected to experience some stressors that are different, qualitatively and quantitatively, from those experienced by other people, other couples, or by dual-job couples. For instance, the interindividual work role stressors experienced by dual-career couples, where both partners exhibit strong career commitment, are likely to be somewhat different from those experienced by dual-job couples, where the partners view their work roles as primarily a means of obtaining money. Because of the special stressors dual-career couples experience within each stressor group, and to ensure exhaustive treatment, all six stressors are discussed below, but only the particular problems and issues of dual-career couples are emphasized in each case.

Within each stressor group, it will be remembered that stress is experienced in situations that are uncertain, important, and at the same time long lasting. Uncertainty is particularly likely to occur when characteristics such as conflict, ambiguity, and overload (Kahn, Wolfe, Quinn, Snoek, and Rosenthal, 1964) are present either within a given role or across different roles. When these characteristics occur with respect to situations that are also important and relatively long lasting, the cognitive state of stress tends to occur.

Cell 1: Intraindividual Work Role Stressors

The work role experiences of dual-career partners, taken in isolation, are not significantly different from those of other workers, especially those who view their work roles more as "careers" than as "jobs." Characteristics of tasks, supervisors, and so on are likely to be stressful for dual-career couples just as they are for traditional couples (cf. chapters by Beehr, Harrison, and Jick in this volume; Beehr and Newman, 1978; Cooper and Marshall, 1976, 1978; Gupta, 1981; McGrath, 1976; Schuler, 1980, etc., for elaborations of these characteristics). But other characteristics of the work role are uniquely stressful for dual-career couples, and it is these characteristics that are discussed briefly below.

A common source of stress among people with careers is the *pressure for mobility* (Marshall and Cooper, 1976). A large proportion of managers move every few years (Pahl and Pahl, 1971). Since many members of dual-career couples are in professional or managerial positions, mobility pressures can be severe for them. A similar demand placed on most committed professionals is the expenditure of inordinate amounts of *time* on the work role. The high-demand work environment of dual-career couples has been noted by many authors (e.g., Hall and Hall, 1979; Shaevitz and Shaevitz, 1979). Holmstrom (1973) likewise referred to the career as an all-consuming activity. The demand of the work role in terms of the sheer number of hours tends to cause overload problems; the situation is aggravated by the expectation that professionals will respond to work demands at a moment's notice. *Travel* is a frequent requirement among professional work roles (Hall and Hall, 1979). The extent to which dual-career couples are expected to travel as part of their work roles—in fact, the extent to which traveling can enhance career success in professional work roles—is likely to be related to the pressures experienced by these people.

These and similar work demands can plague many dual-career couples.

A common theme running across the different work stressors (time, travel, mobility, etc.) is the rigidity of organizational norms and expectations. Because rigidity stimulates overload on salient issues among members of dual-career couples, and because these issues pose ongoing concerns for dual-career couples, the likelihood of intrawork role stress is high.

These stressors characterize both the women and the men in dual-career couples. Women are susceptible to some additional stressors, largely because so few of them occupy upper managerial or professional ranks. Stressors affecting professional women are discussed elsewhere in this volume (cf. chapter by Terborg). Suffice it to say here that many women in dual-career situations experience discriminatory managerial attitudes (Rosen et al., 1975) and conflicting work role expectations (Kanter, 1977). The stress is compounded by the fact that women have few role models they can follow (Darley, 1976). For women in dual-career couples, then, overload issues are exacerbated by managerial attitudes and expectations to produce intrawork role stress.

By definition, their careers are important to members of dual-career couples. The same role expectations that create overload and other uncertainties for members of dual-career couples can also define career success for them when satisfactorily fulfilled. For instance, career advancement is often based on the ability of a business executive to "come through" in times of crises. But "coming through" can also be stress producing because the outcomes (i.e., career advancement) are important to members of dual-career couples. Because careers take time to develop, furthermore, work role stressors tend to occur on a continuing basis, that is they are long lasting. All the ingredients necessary for a stress experience are present, therefore, in the work lives of dual-career couples, and are likely to have greater stress potential among women than among men.

Cell 2: Intraindividual Family Role Stressors

Like intra-individual work role stressors, intraindividual family role stressors are common across many people. Figure 6-2 shows that this stressor group is experienced by most couples. For instance, changing social norms and values create ambiguities about role definitions for most people. In a dual-career situation, the problems are worsened because of the strong emphasis given to the family role by the partners.

The family role is usually at least as important as the work role for members of dual-career couples. Dual-career couples tend to be more achievement oriented than their single career or two income counterparts (Martin et al., 1975). They often aspire to achieving complete success in the fulfillment of their family roles. The pressure for outstanding performance is captured in terms such as "super-mom," "super-wife," and "super-dad." The dearth of available role models and the ambiguity of role expectations, however, render uncertainty in this area high for both the male and the female partner.

Hall and Hall (1979) noted that a major life change occurs with the birth of the first child—adjustment problems are also severe when there are two or more preschool children in the family. For dual-career couples with children, then, overload and ambiguity are particularly severe at certain family stages.

In short, uncertainty abounds about role definitions and expectations, the family roles are considered important, and issues persist throughout family stages. Thus, intraindividual family role stressors are common among members of dual-career couples.

Cell 3: Intraindividual Interrole Stressors

Figure 6-2 shows that intraindividual interrole stressors (stemming from interplays between work and family roles) are experienced by most people who have work roles in addition to family roles. With respect to dual-career couples, it has been noted that both the men and the women experience stress due to the coincidence of their work and family roles (Holahan & Gilbert, 1979). But many of the pressures are also different across sexes. Therefore, the intraindividual interrole stressors experienced by women and men in dual-career couples are discussed separately below.

The intraindividual stressors of *women* in dual-career couples have been the subject of much theoretical and empirical work. Taken together with research on working women, working wives, and working mothers (e.g., Amatea and Cross, 1981; Bhagat and Chassie, 1981; Curtis, 1976; Hoffman and Nye, 1975), some insights can be gained about the way women in dual-career couples balance their work and family roles.

Johnson and Johnson (1975), from interviews with 28 dual-career families, concluded that women in these families, particularly women with younger children, experience severe problems due to the proliferation of role demands. The greatest problems occurred with respect to the maternal role, in which many women reported experiencing guilt and anxiety. Similar findings have also been reported by Gilbert et al. (1981). Across roles, as within the family role, women's personal values and norms often conflict with social norms and socialization. Years of conditioning have suggested to them that maternal deprivation may be harmful for the child (Rapoport et al., 1978), and that good parenting necessitates the mother staying at home with children (Working Family Project, 1978). Changing social mores and personal values point out, on the other hand, that the *quality* of time a working mother spends with her child is more important than the sheer *amount* of time (Howell, 1973a,b; Rowe, 1976, 1977). In time, as these social norms stabilize, it is possible that the stresses inherent in the conflict between maternal and career roles will be resolved.

This argument is reinforced by the results of Houseknecht and Macke (1981), who reported that the marital adjustment of working women was higher than that of nonworking women. The work role also affects other aspects of women's family roles. Time constraints often dictate that the woman spends less time on household chores than she would if only the husband had a work role. The woman may also be able to spend less time with her partner than she would like to (Hall and Hall, 1979). In these and similar ways, the work roles of women in dual-career couples impinge on their family lives.

But the family role has an impact on the work role too. Care of a sick child is much more likely to be assigned to the mother than the father among working couples, for instance (Rapoport and Rapoport, 1971), necessitating that she take time off from work. Likewise, Heckman et al. (1977) reported that many work-related problems experienced by women may be attributable to the fact that they are more willing than their working partners to subjugate their career needs to the needs of the family. This secondary emphasis on their careers often entails less career success for women. Because people make inferences about others from behaviors and accomplishments (Darley, 1976), an image of women as marginal employees is fostered. This image, in turn, can cause employers to be less likely to have confidence in working mothers, and to be less predisposed to furthering the advancement of women into upper managerial echelons.

Thus, on the one hand, a woman in a dual-career situation experiences uncertainties in her family role due to the demands of the work role; on the other hand, she is also subject to differential expectations and evaluations at work because her family role may impinge on the work role.

Men also suffer interrole stress from the interaction of their work and family roles, although these stressors have generally been ignored in the past. The traditional expectation of the man being the breadwinner and the woman being the homemaker is obviously inappropriate for dual-career couples. Men must often curtail the extent to which they can devote extra time to their work roles; instead, they must cope with the demands of the family roles. Shaevitz and Shaevitz (1979) pointed out that paternity leave is becoming a common fringe benefit meted out by corporations. In any case, the family roles of men who are part of dual-career couples impinge on their work roles, and necessitate that career demands no longer be considered all-consuming.

Men have traditionally held both work and family roles. The interrole stressors that men may experience when the work role impinges on the family role, therefore, are not significantly different for men in dual-career versus single-career families. These stressors are not addressed specifically in this section for this reason.

In short, men in dual-career couples also experience uncertainties, particularly in their family roles. Like their counterpart women, the men lack adequate role models and reference groups. They must continuously develop new role definitions and new strategies in their different roles— roles, it should be remembered, that are important to them.

To summarize, work and family roles are central to each dual-career partner, and uncertainties within and across roles are ongoing concerns for them. Thus, intraindividual interrole factors can be potent stressors among dual-career couples.

Cell 4: Interindividual Work Role Stressors

Each member of a dual-career couple experiences stressors in his or her own work and family roles. In addition, each partner can also experience stressors through the interaction of his or her own role with that of the partner. Cell 4 in Figure 6-2 concerns the stressors experienced by dual-career couples as a result of the interaction between their work roles. As the figure shows, this stressor group is shared by all two-job and two-career couples, although the stressors at the "job" end of the continuum are somewhat different from those at the "career" end. The latter constitute the focus of the following paragraphs.

In a dual-career couple both members have work roles to which they are committed and in which they want to advance and flourish. In most instances both careers are salient and require high levels of effort and energy for success. Dual-career partners can have careers that are similar to each other (e.g., both are lawyers, both are business executives), or they can have careers that are quite dissimilar (e.g., one is a business executive, the other is a physician). The kinds of stressors experienced by dual-career couples holding similar careers are qualitatively different from those common among dual-career couples pursuing relatively unrelated careers. Hall and Hall (1979) argued that the two careers are more likely to be compatible if both partners are in similar fields. But similar careers can also stimulate unique pressures for dual-career partners. Thus, it is important to examine the specific careers of dual-career couples in the exposition of their interindividual work role stressors.

In an early essay Parsons (1954) argued that "so long as lines of achievement are segregated and not directly comparable, there is less opportunity for jealousy, a sense of inferiority, etc. to develop" (p. 192). According to this argument, a sex-linked division of labor (or at least independent occupational fields) are necessary to prevent feelings of competition between partners. Empirical evidence has indicated otherwise, however. Holmstrom (1973), who interviewed 20 dual-career couples, noted that feelings of competition were relatively rare among these individuals, regardless of whether or not the careers were in the same field. Despite the absence of competitiveness, problems can arise when the partners pursue careers in similar fields. In a study of female lawyers, Epstein (1968, 1971) found that women were expected to hold occupational ranks that were lower than (at best equal to) those of their husbands. In her study five women held higher occupational positions than their husbands, and were quite uneasy about it. Likewise, the husbands are also likely to be uncomfortable with the situation, since their occupational realities are in conflict with personal and societal norms and expectations (Holmstrom, 1973).

Bryson, Bryson, Licht, and Licht (1976), examining 200 psychologist dual-career couples, noted that husbands in these pairs were significantly more productive than were wives, although wives were more productive than other women who were not members of same-occupation dual-career couples. Their data indicated, furthermore, that women in such couples tend to be willing to make greater sacrifices for their husbands' careers than vice versa, and that these wives were less satisfied than were other psychologists. The lower productivity of women in same-occupation dual-career partners, coupled with their willingness to subordinate their careers to those of their husbands, reinforces stereotypic assumptions about the marginal commitment of professional women to their work roles. This, in turn, intensifies institutional constraints against the advancement of women, setting the stage for conflict and stress. The presence of the husband as an objective standard for comparison is unavoidable, and comparisons *are* made, both by the husband and the wife, and also by institutional decision makers. These comparisons also intensify the stressful potential of the work roles held by male and female members of dual-career couples.

Occupationally similar dual-career couples can also encounter problems of another sort. Pingree et al. (1978) surveyed chairpersons of psychology and sociology departments and discovered that many (37%) of them were opposed to hiring professional couples, despite the HEW declaration regarding the discriminatory nature of antinepotism rules. Biases against the hiring of couples often affect the woman's career more strongly than the man's, in that the former accept suboptimal positions as compromises. Even when both partners work for the same employer, antinepotism norms and implicit and explicit prejudices are also likely to affect the career success of one or both partners (Hall and Hall, 1978). Flynn and Litzsinger (1981) noted that, at the upper organizational levels, transfers are often difficult to achieve in tandem. Likewise, for dual-career couples pursuing similar careers, finding suitable jobs in the same geographic location causes problems and often requires the generation of innovative life styles. Among academics, Bryson et al. (1976) reported that negative attitudes were directed by administrators toward wives more than toward husbands.

Dual-career couples in different occupations are subject to strikingly different stressors. Hall and Hall (1979) noted that the likelihood of providing support and understanding is greater if both partners are in the same or similar fields. A fellow physician, according to this argument, is more likely to be sympathetic to late-night emergency calls than a business executive would be, for instance. Thus, the chances of conflicts and ambiguities about each other's careers are much higher for different-occupation than for similar-occupation dual-career couples. In other words, occupationally different dual-career couples may not feel competitiveness toward their partners; they also cannot receive the same levels of support from them.

Furthermore, same-occupation dual-career couples can share support and friendship networks more easily than can different-occupation dual-career couples. Rapoport and Rapoport (1971) argued that dual-career couples tend to generate social networks as "couples" rather than as individuals—partly as a matter of shared ideologies, but also partly to be insulated against the environmental sanctions that accrue to the adoption of an "unconventional" lifestyle. Thus, shared social networks can be a source of emotional support (House, 1981) for dual-career couples; they may also be able to provide other kinds of social support. For instance, instrumental support can be derived in social events where both partners make contacts significant for career development. These and similar forms of social support are much more available to occupationally similar than -different dual-career couples. The importance of social support in organizational and personal experiences has received some recent emphasis (e.g., Chapter 14 in this volume; Cobb, 1976; House, 1981; LaRocco et al., 1980). Lacking such social support, members of occupationally different dual-career couples are likely to suffer stress. Titus (1980) remarked that social comparisons with friends provided a frame of reference for couples that generated more realistic expectations for the marriage.

To recapitulate, stress may result among occupationally similar dual-career couples because of career comparisons, competitiveness, and administrative attitudes and policies. Stress may also result among occupationally dissimilar dual-career couples because the opportunities for social support and understanding are limited. Once again, because the work roles are important to both partners, because these interindividual problems tend to be enduring in character, and because uncertainties are high, dual-career couples can experience severe stress in the realm of interindividual work roles.

Cell 5: Interindividual Family Role Stressors

This stressor group concerns the interplay between the family roles of the partners of dual-career couples. As Figure 6-2 shows, this general stressor group is shared across single-career and dual career couples. The specific stressors within the general category are, however, quite different for them. At least three areas of potential interindividual family stress can be identified for dual-career couples, namely, housework, parenting, and being a spouse (or partner).

Traditionally the responsibility of most day-to-day activities of the family role have been assigned to the woman. In a study of cohabiting and married couples, Stafford et al. (1977) reported that married couples were significantly more traditional than cohabiting couples. Still, women in both groups continued to assume major responsibility for the performance of most household tasks. The results indicated, furthermore, that this traditional division of household labor was neither the outcome of a power struggle nor the differential availability of time. Rather, the subconscious ideologies developed from parental modeling appeared responsible for the preservation of traditional sex roles. Likewise, in a study of 86 male and 52 female university students, Kassner (1981) found that male students preferred traditional (single-career) marriages and female students preferred egalitarian (dual-career) marriages. From her study of 32 professional couples Weingarten (1978) also concluded that couples may negotiate a division of labor between them whereby women can make up for their daytime absence from home by taking on many child-care responsibilities, and the men choose other household work less threatening to their traditional sex-role socialization. Perrucci, Potter, and Rhoads (1978) reported, therefore, that socialization and ideology, more so than relative resources and the availability of time, accounted for the division of household labor among 98 couples.

The division of household work along sex-role lines poses different stressors for women and men members of dual-career couples. Overload, of course, is a common consequence for women (Bhagat and Chassie, 1981; Holmstrom, 1973; Rapoport and Rapoport, 1971). To the extent that it is impossible to fulfill the family role perfectly because of time constraints, furthermore, guilt and resentment of the spouse develop. For the men conflicting role expectations are more likely to be stressors. Traditional sex-role expectations, on the one hand, and equity considerations, on the other, can present difficulties for these men. For the couple as a unit, the issue becomes not merely one of managing the actual division of household work, but also of managing the feelings the partners develop toward each other as a consequence. Once more, the issue is compounded due to the dearth of role models.

Similar issues also arise with respect to child care and parenting responsibilities, except insofaras most couples attach greater importance to the parent role and the strength of the stressor is intensified as a result. As mentioned earlier, parenting issues are the strongest stressors for women who are employed outside the home (Johnson and Johnson, 1977). Bryson et al. (1978) also reported that women in professional couples tend to bear a disproportionate share of the child-care responsibilities. Still, both men and women experience stress from this source. It is easier to delegate housework responsibilities to other people (or to neglect these responsibilities) than it is to delegate or neglect child-care issues. The stress potential is intensified further because child-care problems are typically long lasting.

Finally, the partner roles of members of dual-career couples cannot be overlooked. Many dual-career couples address their career conflicts by maintaining two households and commuting on weekends and holidays (Gross, 1980; Hall and Hall, 1979). This arrangement necessitates the generation, not only of alternative life styles, but of new techniques for managing interpersonal relationships as well. Titus (1980) noted that, in many marriages, at least one member of the couple made comparisons with others in terms of interaction patterns and the quality of relationship between the spouses. The availability of adequate reference groups and role models may provide guidance about the best ways to manage the relationships between the partners of a dual-career couple. In their absence the probability of uncertainty is much higher.

Most dual-career couples are quite committed to the decision to make their marriages "work" (Hall and Hall, 1979; Holmstrom, 1973; Rapoport and Rapoport, 1971, 1976; Shaevitz and Shaevitz, 1979). This, coupled with the fact that uncertainty is prevalent in the interindividual family roles of dual-career couples, and the fact that the issues are enduring rather than short term, can lead to severe stress in this domain of the lives of dual-career couples.

Cell 6: Interindividual Interrole Stressors

These stressors have been the subject of the largest amount of descriptive and empirical research about dual-career couples. These stressors arise from the interactions among the work and family roles of one partner and the work and family roles of the other partner. Figure 6-2 shows that these stressors are shared by dual-job and dual-career couples, but once more the specifics of these stressors are unique for dual-career couples, by and large. Several sources of stress from the interactions of the work and family roles of the partners can be delineated, not the least of which is the impact of the work role of one partner on the family role of the other. Coordination of the different roles during the different family and career stages of dual-career lives can also pose significant stressors.

That the career aspirations and commitments of one partner affect the family role of the other partner is well established in the research. Papanek (1973), in her exposition of the concept of "two-person career," discussed the ways in which occupational demands extend beyond organizational boundaries to include the family. Traditionally, the woman was expected, not only to handle domestic duties, but also to fulfill many obligations in furthering her husband's career. Entertaining colleagues, clients, and bosses, handling the trials and tribulations of transfers and promotions, and so on are among the traditional expectations for wives of upwardly mobile career-oriented men, that is, for "two-person careers." Even in conventional marriages meeting these expectations is often stressful for the woman (Tallman, 1969). In a dual-career marriage the woman is not always able (or willing) to perform the supportive duties and obligations. To compound the problem, the woman's career demands may also place similar expectations on the husband. Thus, the man must take over some domestic responsibilities, at least partly; he may also be expected to fulfill supportive functions that further the wife's career. In any case both partners of a dual-career marriage are unable to hold two-person careers, and their career aspirations and attainments are affected as a consequence.

Furthermore, dual-career couples are deviant from traditional sex-role dictates. This deviance often creates barriers to the social and organizational assimilation and acceptance of dual-career couples into more traditional social circles (Hunt and Hunt, 1977). Thus, the woman's work role can pose at least four kinds of problems for the male in a dual-career situation: (1) increased family demands; (2) limited auxiliary role of the wife; (3) barriers to professional advancement; (4) and constraints against assimilation into the social network.

Likewise, problems can ensue for the woman's family role from the man's career. Expectations from the husband's organizational colleagues and supervisors often pose demands in the woman's family role that are well beyond her time constraints; she also may not have the inclination to be the perfect "corporate wife" (Seidenberg, 1973). Some of the conflicts and ambiguities resulting from these expectations were discussed earlier. These conflicts and ambiguities may be intensified from feelings that the woman is not fulfilling her family role adequately. Burke and Weir (1976) found that husbands of employed women were in poorer health and less satisfied with their marriages than husbands of housewives. Although these findings were disputed in later research (Booth, 1977), the fact remains that the potentially marginal fulfillment of the spouse role can threaten the self-concepts of women in dual-career families (Holahan and Gilbert, 1979).

Many role coordination issues that arise among dual-career couples have been discussed previously. For instance, difficulties in dual-job searches are often detailed in the literature (e.g., Berger et al., 1978; Wallston et al., 1978). Although many couples begin by using egalitarian job-search strategies, they often revert to a more traditional approach later, largely as a result of institutional constraints. In the end it is generally the woman's career that suffers. Likewise, transfers and geographic movement are problematic for dual-career couples, not just in terms of the impact on the partner's career, but also in terms of the disruption of the family life that such relocations usually entail (Duncan and Perrucci, 1976; Flynn and Litzsinger, 1981; Frank, 1978; Long, 1974; Sussman and Cogswell, 1971). When synchronized moves are impossible, alternative life styles must be developed, such as living apart and commuting. These alternative strategies, however, also have problems (Gross, 1980), not the least of which are the limited social acceptance afforded by traditional couples and the dearth of role models and defined role behaviors.

Coordination issues also arise in terms of multiple role cycling (Rapoport and Rapoport, 1969, 1971). It may be easier to prioritize career and family demands when the partners are at different stages in their careers. For instance, if the husband has an established career and the wife is just beginning, it may be possible for him to take on many of the domestic chores (Hall and Hall, 1979). Such accommodations are harder to achieve when both spouses are at approximately the same stage in their careers. Under these circumstances it may become necessary to compress child-rearing activities into a relatively short time span (Rapoport and Rapoport, 1971) or to employ domestic help.

Coordination of different career and family roles takes time to accomplish, however, a commodity dual-career couples have in only short supply. Thus, they suffer severe overload (St. John-Parsons, 1978). Most issues must also be resolved in the absence of clear guidelines for action. Furthermore since many of the compromises and accommodations arrived at by dual-career couples are "deviant," these couples must deal with the societal and organizational sanctions that they accrue.

In short, given the unique career and family roles of dual-career couples, given the importance that dual-career couples tend to attach to these roles, and given the ongoing uncertainties and conflicts inherent in their enactment of these roles, interindividual interrole stressors are quite significant in the lives of these individuals.

Summary

Stressors are present in many life spheres of dual-career couples. These couples can experience stress in the execution of each work role, each family role, and in the joint execution of the work and family roles. In general, stressors arise in the lives of dual-career couples because of conflicts between personal and social/organizational expectations, because of ambiguities about effective role behaviors, and because of overload in terms of the sheer number of role expectations that they must fulfill.

As mentioned earlier, conflict, ambiguity, overload, and similar characteristics in the work and family environments of dual-career couples can lead to uncertainty with respect to expectations, methods, and outcomes. The dearth of role models and established behavior patterns, furthermore, minimizes the likelihood that uncertainty can be easily obliterated. The uncertainty that faces dual-career couples is usually an ongoing concern. Rather than characterizing a particular career or family stage, uncertainty tends to be an enduring characteristic of the dual-career relationship. Finally, it was emphasized that their career and family roles are important to members of dual-career couples. These individuals tend to have a strong investment, not only in the continued existence, but also in the effective performance, of their work and family roles. Given the presence of the major components of the experience of stress—uncertainty, importance, and duration—in the lives of dual-career couples, and given the magnitude with which these components proliferate among dual-career couples, it is not surprising that stress experiences are common among this group.

CONSEQUENCES OF DUAL—CAREER STRESS

In the previous section some causes of stress among dual-career couples were discussed. These stressors, and the resultant stress, can have deleterious consequences for the couple. At the same time, several benefits also derive for the couple from the dual-career status. In this section the positive and negative consequences of dual-career stress are discussed in terms of the work and family lives of the partners. Although little is known about the health consequences of dual-career stress, this matter is also addressed here. In addition, this section elaborates upon the consequences of dual-career stress for institutions employing one or both partners.

Work Role Consequences

To a large extent the work role consequences of dual-career stress have been examined in terms of the productivity of the partners. Some of this research deals with married professional women (rather than women in dual-career couples per se). But it is quite probable that samples of married professional women and women in dual-career couples are drawn from similar populations—professional women are likely to be married to professional men (Frank, 1978). In other words, findings from research on married professional women are generally applicable to women in dual-career couples.

Martin et al. (1975) noted that, compared with other women in the profession, wives in dual-career sociologist couples were much more successful at completing doctoral degrees, acheiving higher academic ranks, gaining promotions, avoiding demotions, and practicing longer professional careers. In a similar vein it was mentioned earlier that Bryson et al. (1976) found wives in professional psychologist pairs to be more productive than their counterpart women in the profession; these wives were, however, more likely to feel professionally discriminated against, and were less satisfied with their careers. The authors also found that husbands in professional psychologist couples were extremely productive and satisfied with their careers, and more so than their counterpart males, wives in professional psychologist couples, or other females. From further analyses of these data, Bryson et al. (1978) concluded that wives were less satisfied and productive than husbands in dual-career couples, but that a number of control variables (such as years since final degree, age, full-time employment) were also relevant in this context. On the other hand, Broschart

(1978), while finding no differences in the productivity and professional recognition of married women/women with children versus single or childless women, did report the former group to be holding lower-ranking occupational positions that the latter group. The author attributed the results to the differential pattern of labor force participation of married versus single women. Women in dual-career couples, like single women, are likely to display a pattern of relatively uninterrupted employment. It is not surprising, therefore, that productivity differentials between the two groups are rarely observed. By the same token, managerial attitudes and policies could well retard the career advancement of these women (Bowman et al., 1965; Madani and Cooper, 1977; Rosen et al., 1975), accounting for their lower occupational achievements.

Many other factors, some of which were discussed earlier, also impair the professional advancement of dual-career couples. For instance, constraints against mobility can prevent a dual-career partner from capitalizing on an excellent advancement opportunity. Likewise, the fact that the spouse cannot serve the auxiliary role to nearly the same extent as in a traditional couple, the fact that nonwork demands may place severe constraints on the work role enactment of dual-career couples, and so on all combine to hurt the career development of dual-career couples. In short, although their dual-career status may enhance their productivity and recognition, it also impedes the career growth of dual-career couples.

Issues of competitiveness and colleagueship with reference to the work roles of dual-career couples were discussed earlier. Competitiveness tends to be more prevalent among similar-occupation dual-career couples than among different-occupation dual-career couples. Likewise, a colleagial relationship is also much more likely to occur between a similar-occupation dual-career couple than between a different-occupation dual-career couple. Holmstrom (1973) reported that many couples had influenced each other's work roles in at least minor ways. Similar results were also reported by Martin et al. (1975). That working together is common among similar-occupation dual-career couples can also be inferred from another source, namely, the number of publications in the area by dual-career couples (e.g., Bryson and Bryson, Fruchter and Fruchter, Galbraith and Galbraith, Hall and Hall, Hunt and Hunt, Johnson and Johnson, Licht and Licht, Pahl and Pahl, Rapoport and Rapoport, Shaevitz and Shaevitz, a list that does not include those of us who maintain *different* last names). St. John-Parsons (1978), however, found little integration of the work roles of partners in dual-career couples. The author also reported that, in his sample of 20 dual-career couples, only one couple showed genuine enthusiasm about the other's work. But, taken together, the weight of the evidence indicates that colleagueship, rather than competitiveness, is characteristic of dual-career couples.

In short, the work roles of dual-career couples *are* affected by their special status. Performance and productivity can be enhanced, and mutual benefits from working together can accrue to the partners. Despite these gains, the career advancement of dual-career couples, and particularly of women in such couples, tends to be somewhat retarded.

Family Role Consequences

By far the vast majority of research in this area has focused on the effectiveness with which dual-career couples enact their family roles. Within the family role the effects of dual-career status on marital satisfaction and adjustment and on children have been the most frequent foci of research.

Comparing one-career and two-career families, Burke and Weir (1976) reported that women in two-career families were more satisfied and performed more effectively than women in one-career families, but that men in dual-career families were *less* satisfied and productive than men in single-career families. These findings were challenged by Booth (1977) on grounds of sampling, measurement, and analysis procedures. The author reported that husbands of employed women evidenced no greater signs of marital discord and stress than did husbands of housewives. Likewise, Ridley (1973) reported that married teachers and their husbands were reasonably successful in preventing work-related issues from interfering with their marital satisfaction. Hall and Gordon (1973) also found that married women who were working full-time tended to be more satisfied in general than did married women who were working part time or who were housewives. Other studies that have found the same or higher levels of satisfaction among dual-career than among single-career families include those of Arnott (1972, 1977), Blood (1965), Orden and Orden (1969), and Martin et al. (1975). Staines, Pleck, Shepard, and O'Connor (1978), analyzing data from two national surveys, reported that a wife's employment status had no significant effects on her husband's marital adjustment. The data also indicated that working wives whose husbands also worked reported wishing they had married someone else and thinking about divorce more often than did housewives. But the scores of working wives and housewives on marital happiness, marital satisfaction, and marital adjustment scales were not significantly different from each other. Parsons' (1954) early prediction—that the sex desegregation of work and family roles would lead to the disruption and dissolution of the traditional family—seems largely disconfirmed by subsequent empirical data. Dual-career couples are as happy as, if not happier than, traditional couples with their marriages.

Marital adjustment and satisfaction may be contingent on a number of factors other than dual-career status. Some moderator variables that may account for the differential levels of marital satisfaction among different dual-career couples have been proposed in the past. For instance, Bailyn's (1971) data supported the argument that the husband's mode of integrating work and family in his own life was critical for the marital satisfaction of women who were trying to combine career and family. More recently, Hornung and McCullough (1981) reported that status inconsistencies and status incompatibilities between the spouses were largely responsible for explaining variations in marital and life satisfaction in dual-employment marriages. The presence of children has also been found to be a moderator of the relationship between career status and satisfaction (Heckman et al., 1977; Holahan and Gilbert, 1979). Bryson et al. (1978) noted that family size could significantly affect domestic and other satisfactions experienced by dual-career couples. The relative availability of domestic help from relatives and others (Szinovacz, 1977), location of the partners at different career stages (Hall and Hall, 1979), husband's and wife's attitudes about wife's employment (Staines et al., 1978), are all considered moderators of the relationship between dual-career status and marital satisfaction/ adjustment. Thus, Wright (1978) remarked that both work outside the home and full-time homemaking have costs and benefits— the net result is that the relationship between employment and satisfaction is inconsistent.

In addition, of course, the impact of career status on marital satisfaction is partly dependent on the accommodations worked out by the partners. Huber and Spitze (1981) argued that the household division of labor is affected by the wife's employment status. But Szinovacz's (1977) results lent support to the assumption that female employment does not necessarily result in the development of egalitarian domestic role relations between the spouses. Weingarten (1978) found significant differences in the way couples allocated domestic tasks, depending on whether or not the wife had worked full time throughout her career. The impact of attitudes as moderators was also highlighted in another study. Houseknecht and Macke (1981) reported that the accommodations of family experiences to a wife's employment, rather than the wife's employment per se, was critical in determining marital adjustment among professional women.

Despite the cross-sectional nature of most of the foregoing research, and despite the varying definitions of "dual-career" used, it seems safe to conclude that their dual-career status affects marital adjustment and satisfaction among the couples. Whether the effects are positive or negative, however, depends largely on the willingness and ability of the partners to work out a satisfactory solution to the increased demands posed by their employment status.

Ultimately, if the partners cannot work through the issues, problems, and the tensions that often accompany the fact that they both have careers, the option of terminating the familial relationships gains viability. Few data are available on the proportion of dual-career relationships that have been terminated so far because the partners were unable to resolve their differences. The dearth of relevant statistics is largely attributable to the absence of longitudinal investigations in the area. Holmstrom (1973), however, reported divorce to be relatively rare in her sample. Furthermore, the reasons for divorce among dual-career and traditional women in her sample were remarkably similar, and largely centered on differences between the partners about how egalitarian their relationship should be. Hall and Hall (1979) also argued that career did not *cause* people to split up; rather, careers highlighted latent problems in the relationship. In short, although dual-career couples may have a slightly higher divorce rate than traditional couples, this fact may be attributed to the greater economic independence of the former (Hall and Hall, 1979); career conflicts are merely the catalysts that bring to the fore problems endemic to the relationships between single-career as well as dual-career couples.

Children of dual-career couples may be affected by their parents' special employment status. Although the impact *of* children on dual-career couples has often been studied, research is rare on the impact of dual-career parents *on* children. Extrapolating from maternal employment research, however, it may be concluded that the effects are positive rather than negative. Blood (1965) argued that maternal employment may result in daughters becoming more masculine and sons becoming more feminine than would otherwise be the case. But as Madani and Cooper (1977) noted, this trend is not necessarily undesirable; it stimulates greater role convergence and equality across sexes. The authors also cited evidence suggesting that children of dual-career couples are more independent than children of more traditional couples. These findings are consistent with those St. John-Parsons (1978) obtained in an intensive study of 20 dual-career couples—children of these couples were independent, resourceful, and self-confident, and there was no evidence to suggest that they would have fared better had their parents followed a more conventional employment pattern.

To recapitulate, dual-career couples may have higher levels of marital satisfaction and adjustment than other couples, particularly if the domestic relationship between the partners is egalitarian. The children of dual-career couples are more independent and flexible than are children of other couples.

Health Consequences

The impact of their employment status on the health of dual-career couples has rarely been examined systematically, but inferences about the health consequences of being a dual-career couple can be drawn from general organizational literature.

First, it was reported earlier that dual-career couples can experience higher levels of marital satisfaction than conventional couples, and that at least the male members of dual-career couples experience higher levels of satisfaction with their careers than their single-career counterparts. These variables—job satisfaction, life satisfaction, and so on—in turn have been related to various indicators of physical and mental health. For instance, Zimmerman et al. (1980) noted a significant negative relationship between job strain and job satisfaction among a sample of 79 married home economics teachers and their spouses. Gupta and Beehr (1981) reported that job satisfaction fell in the same factor as many indicators of mental health (including depression, self-esteem, and life satisfaction), but not physical health, among a sample of employees from five diverse organizations. These data suggest that, to the extent that dual-career couples are happier with their careers, lives, and jobs, they will be less likely to suffer from poor mental health.

Occasional empirical evidence also exists specifically about the health of working women and dual-career couples. A study of 135 two-job families by Keith and Schafer (1980) indicated that women in these families were more likely to be depressed than were men. The reasons for depression were also different across sex. Feelings of deprivation at work and at home and their involvement in traditionally female household chores were among the common correlates of depression among males; financial troubles were more likely to depress the females. Allen and Keavney (1979) reported that the health and well-being of working women were affected positively, if at all, by their combined work and family pressures. Supporting these data are statistics cited by Bird (1979) showing that working women and men are ill less often than full-time housewives. Finally, St. John-Parsons (1978) found that, in his sample of dual-career couples, most couples were noticeably energetic, active, and in good health, although most also reported experiencing periods of complete physical exhaustion but not mental depression. Physical exhaustion, in fact, has often been cited as a frequent complaint among dual-career couples.

In short, there is little evidence about how the health of dual-career couples fares, compared with other couples. The data that do exist suggest that if anything, dual career couples may enjoy better physical and mental health than others. It may well be that a curvilinear relationship exists between being a dual-career couple and health. Those couples who are able to cope effectively with their unique problems, pressures, and stressors enjoy remarkable physical and mental health, superior to that of single-career couples. Couples who cannot resolve these problems to their mutual satisfaction, on the other hand, may suffer poor health.

Consequences for Employers

Organizations that employ one or both members of dual-career couples can also experience some different consequences, particularly with respect to recruitment, retention, and performance.

Recruitment issues arise in terms of the employment of both male and female members of dual-career couples. Frank (1978) noted that the restriction that both members of a dual-career couple work in the same geographic location works against professional women more often than against professional men, since more of the former than the latter live in dual-career families. Because of constraints about the spouse's employment, dual-career wives limit the pool of qualified female applicants (or employees) available to an employing organization. The dearth of professional women is particularly problematic when affirmative action and equal employment opportunity pressures are strong. Thus, Hall and Hall (1978) reported the problems experienced by a bank when, in compliance with antinepotism rules, the female (rather than the male) member of a dual-career couple resigned at a time when affirmative action was a thrust for the organization. This type of recruitment problem can plague organizations located in small towns much more than organizations in large cities. The number of employment options available to (and, therefore, the availability of) the spouse are simply greater in large metropolitan areas. Thus, the roster of professional women candidates to which organizations in large cities have access is likely to be much larger than that to which organizations in small towns have access.

Other recruitment problems can also arise with dual-career couples. For instance, Weaver and Couchman (1980) noted that instead of accommodating to the needs of *one* individual, recruiters must now attend to *both* dual-career partners. Antinepotism policies must also often be revised to develop a satisfactory candidate pool (Hall and Hall, 1978). Likewise, conflict-of-interest policies restrict, not only the career opportunities of dual-career couples, but also the roster of candidates available for recruitment. These restrictions can be detrimental to effective organizational functioning, in that dual-career couples are often more productive than their same-sex, single-career counterparts (Bryson et al., 1976; Martin et al., 1975).

The *retention* of dual-career couples is also more difficult than that of single-career couples, particularly in occupations where geographic flexibility is important. Long (1974) reported that families in which the wife works are more likely to undertake short-distance moving and slightly less likely to undertake long-distance migration than families in which the wife does not work. Organizations that require frequent moves of their upper-level employees (employees who are likely to have careers) may experience higher levels of turnover among members of dual-career couples. Because of their unique family demands, dual-career partners may also be less prone to remaining with an organization that has rigid administrative policies (e.g., fixed hours, inflexible leave arrangements). The retention of dual-career members under these circumstances may be particularly problematic in large cities, where alternative career options are more easily available. Likewise, discriminatory managerial attitudes about women (Rosen et al., 1975) may trigger the departure of dual-career employees. Job stress has been found to affect the retention of organizational employees (Gupta and Beehr, 1979); it is reasonable to infer that it may also affect the turnover rates of dual-career couples. Again, since these couples tend to be productive and effective employees, their turnover has particularly serious consequences for the organization.

It was mentioned earlier that dual-career partners show somewhat better *productivity* than their same-sex, single-career counterparts. But because of their unique family situations, these dual-career partners may not be able to display the same level of day-to-day consistency in their organizational behaviors that other employees do. For organizations that require employees to be on their toes from 8 to 5 every day of the week, the employment of members of dual-career couples may not be the best option. For organizations where long-term results, rather than short-term consistency, is important, however, the employment of these individuals may be quite advantageous.

Thus, dual-career issues can lead to problems for the organization in recruiting qualified professional employees, in retaining them with the organization on a long-term basis, and in eliciting consistent short-term performance.

Summary

Their dual-career status enhances productivity, but retards the professional advancement of many couples. In addition, colleagial relationships tend to flourish, particularly among similar-occupation dual-career couples. Marital satisfaction and adjustment can be high, especially if egalitarian strategies are adopted in the division of household labor. Children of dual-career couples tend to develop less sex-role stereotypic traits, and exhibit greater independence. Although the evidence is scant, it points to equal, if not better, physical and mental health among dual-career couples, compared with single-career couples. Some employing organizations may also experience problems with the satisfactory recruitment, retention, and performance of dual-career couples.

STRATEGIES FOR HANDLING DUAL-CAREER STRESS

Dual-career couples do not appear to experience particularly deleterious consequences of the stress they undergo; in fact, on most conventional measures regarding work and family, these couples fare better than their traditional counterparts. These gains are achieved by dual-career couples through considerable compromise, concern, consideration, and cooperation. Dual-career couples, more often than others, are willing to work through issues and problems to their mutual satisfaction. Were it not for this accommodation, dual-career stress could be intolerable and take a severe toll on the organizational and personal lives of these couples. In this section, strategies used (and usable) by dual-career couples to minimize the adverse effects of stress are discussed. Strategies that employers and others can use to alleviate noxious effects of dual-career stress are also discussed here.

Coping Strategies for Couples

Many coping strategies and styles, ranging from employing domestic help to alternating career stages, are adopted by dual-career couples to handle their stress. Hall (1972) and Hall and Hall (1978) classified these strategies into three broad groups: *role redefinition* entails altering expectations of role senders regarding the work and family roles of each partner. Many strategies can be subsumed under this classification. For instance, one can limit the number of different activities that he or she commits to undertaking. Often, external resources (babysitters, domestic help) can be found to facilitate fulfilling the role expectations of relevant role senders. Another strategy is collaboration between the spouses in terms of careers, that is, "linking-up" the two careers (Bailyn, 1971). Thus, dual-career lawyers may set up a joint practice, minimizing some career coordination problems. All in all, role redefinition can help reduce overload problems experienced by dual-career couples; it may also be useful in eliminating some sources of uncertainty. *Personal reorientation* is similar to role redefinition in that it also entails the reorganization of role expectations; it is different in that *personal* values and priorities, rather than external demands, are reorganized. The most significant personal reorientation strategy available to members of dual-career couples is the establishment of priorities. A temporal ordering of role expectations can be constructed, for instance. Thus, overload problems may be avoided by concentrating exclusively on only some role expectations at a particular point in time, and by ignoring or neglecting other role expectations. Personal reorientation is often facilitated by a recognition that self-imposed expectations have as much legitimacy as do externally imposed expectations (Gilbert et al., 1981), and that the former must be prioritized along with the latter. *Reactive role behavior* involves searching for ways to meet all role expectations satisfactorily. Planning and organization, heightened effort, and sheer luck can often result in effective fulfillment of most (if not all) role expectations. Reactive role behaviors also encompass such strategies as time and energy management, career competence development, and so on, that is, strategies to reduce some of the burden that accepting multitudinous role expectations simultaneously can impose.

The foregoing strategies, suggested by Hall and Hall (1978), are primarily individual in nature. They entail each partner in a dual-career couple adopting them for effective stress management. Additionally, couples can generate *combined* strategies for averting the negative consequences of dual-career stress, strategies that require effort on the part of couples as units. Combined strategies can focus on household issues, career issues, and issues that cut across career and family.

Among the *household* issues, the two that have been addressed most often are domestic chores and child care. A fair division of household labor between the partners is often useful, particularly for the women, who otherwise are stuck with the major responsibility for these duties (Bernard, 1972; Bird, 1979; Holmstrom, 1973; Shaevitz and Shaevitz, 1979). Domestic responsibilities include many activities, such as house-cleaning, house maintenance, meals and food, clothing, yards and plants, automobiles, finances, health-related activities, family and social relationships and events, vacation-related activities, religious activities, family pets, and emergencies (Shaevitz and Shaevitz, 1979). With reference to these activities the authors suggest that two steps can be taken to ensure effective stress management, namely, deciding on standards (what chores must be done and how well they must be done) and deciding on task allocation (who will do what). Often, these decisions require hiring full-time or part-time help (Bird, 1979). Likewise, many couples compromise on standards, deciding, for instance, that a clean house is less important than effective job performance for both partners (Holmstrom, 1973). The author found that most couples in her sample used three techniques for coping with the house—increasing efficiency, lowering standards, and using money to save time and effort (by hiring external help, for example).

Child care is a more significant issue among dual-career couples (Levine, 1976). Holmstrom's (1973) study discovered that most couples solved child-care problems in three ways: (1) the husband routinely helped his wife with the children; (2) the wife modified her work schedule; (3) or the couple hired help. To this list can be added a few strategies suggested by Shaevitz and Shaevitz (1979). First, of course, is a joint decision by the couple about whether or not to have children. If the decision is positive, the couple must also decide when, how many, and how far apart. These decisions, when made jointly and rationally, can minimize future parenting problems. As with housework, furthermore, child care appears handled best through a combination of all three strategies suggested by Holmstrom (1973), that is, by the couple sharing the responsibility, modifying their work schedules, *and* using external help when necessary.

Career issues must also be addressed jointly by dual-career partners. Rapoport and Rapoport (1969, 1971, 1976) often addressed the multiple-role cycling dilemmas confronting members of dual-career couples. With these couples it is often the case that the husband is in a more advanced cycle of his career than the wife is in hers. Careful role cycling must be conducted, so that the wife's career is not jeopardized by the dual-career status of the couple. Arrangements that accommodate role-cycling dilemmas include job-sharing (Arkin & Dobrofsky, 1978), giving preferential treatment to the woman's career until relative equality in career status has been achieved (Rapoport and Rapoport, 1976), and maintaining homes in different cities to hold two geographically separated jobs (Douvan and Pleck, 1978). These and similar strategies may reduce stress experienced from the cycling of the career roles of the dual-career partners.

Role-cycling dilemmas can also characterize the interplay of *family and work roles* (Rapoport and Rapoport, 1976). The authors pointed out that in the past the women in dual-career couples bore the brunt of this dilemma. They were considered lucky if they managed to salvage any career at all after fulfilling the demands of full-time motherhood. Obviously, this is not an ideal strategy. Hall and Hall (1979) suggested that partners mutually agree that one partner consider the career role primary and the other partner consider the family role primary, and mutually agree on which partner does which. Insofar as this strategy may be considered withdrawal from the dual-career status, at least partly, it also remains suboptimal as a solution to role-cycling dilemmas. Thus, seeking flexible occupations and work hours, alternating the partner who gives primary emphasis to the work versus the family role, and careful timing of family role demands may be the few options available to dual-career couples. But for couples with mutual support, understanding, consideration, and cooperation, these strategies may alleviate the noxiousness of dual-career stress.

Strategies for Employers

The organizations that employ one or both dual-career partners can also do much to relieve the problems experienced by these couples. The strategies that employers can use include primarily the development of innovative policies and the provision of support and training services.

Innovative policies can be developed in a number of areas of organizational life. Hall and Hall (1978, 1979) suggest a variety of policies that organizations can generate or modify to help dual-career couples. First, special recruiting techniques must be used in hiring dual-career couples. Dual-recruiting, or at least helping the spouse to find suitable employment, can be quite useful in this context. Wallston et al. (1978) concluded that the traditional job decisions made by many dual-career couples were largely the result of institutional constraints. The removal of such constraints should be sought by "protean" employers (Hall and Hall, 1979). Transfer policies must likewise be revamped. An organization must explore whether career advancement for a dual-career partner can be achieved without geographic relocation. Travel plans and policies must, of course, also be updated in view of the growing numbers of dual-career partners. Nepotism policies are detrimental to dual-career recruitment (Pingree et al., 1978) and must be revised to remove this bias. Finally, leave and vacation policies can be adjusted to facilitate effective multiple-role cycling among dual-career couples.

Beyond the formal administrative policies of the organization, innovative norms and procedures could be useful. For instance, a flexible work environment, where rigid 8 to 5 schedules, dress, and work habit rules are not observed, can minimize many time and coordination difficulties experienced by dual-career couples. Informal norms that support dual-career partners during difficult times (e.g., child care is not available one day and the husband brings the child to work with him) could also assist dual-career couples in managing their lives better.

Employing organizations can provide various kinds of *support and training services* for dual-career couples. On-site day-care for children could ease the burden of these couples considerably, for instance. As alternatives to on-site day-care, Hall and Hall (1979) suggest the development of community programs such as lunch programs, after-school centers, sports programs, and facilities to take care of children during school holidays. They also highlight several other support/training services that companies can offer to mitigate dual-career stress. These include training supervisors in career counseling skills; providing marital counseling to dual-career couples to help them sort out priorities and resolve conflicts; and assisting couples in career management. Not only do these services help alleviate dual-career stress; they also emphasize to the employee that his or her welfare, retention, and advancement are important priorities for the organization.

Overall, an understanding, accommodating, and sympathetic approach to the management of dual-career stress can improve organizational effectiveness by fostering continued employment and maximum performance among dual-career couples.

Additional Remarks

In many ways the process of learning to handle dual-career stress is a matter of social learning (Bandura, 1977), a matter of reciprocal determination between couples and employing organizations. Organizations are influenced by their environments and constituents (Pfeffer and Salancik, 1978; Salancik and Pfeffer, 1978). The growing numbers of dual-career couples within and outside organizational boundaries must stimulate changes in the organization; increased interaction with organizational realities must also trigger changes among dual-career couples. In this way couples and organizations learn from one another, and become more and more mutually adaptive as a result. The strategies used by couples and organizations to handle dual-career stress must not be considered independent of one another. Rather, they must be viewed as processes of mutual influence. Only thus can dual-career stress continue to have minimum adverse effects on couples, organizations, and society.

SUMMARY AND CONCLUSIONS

Dual-career issues are critical, not only for dual-career couples themselves, but also for organizations that employ these couples. Stress can result from many sources for dual-career couples. The satisfactory resolution of this stress is imperative if dual-career partners are to maximize their human potential. So far, members of dual-career couples have combined their work and family roles effectively, with little or no impairment of organizational performance, marital satisfaction, and physical and mental health. Still, the unique problems of these couples must be recognized, and necessary corrective actions undertaken, if dual-career stress is to be prevented from undermining organizational effectiveness.

The issue of dual-career stress has been the subject of much speculation, introspection, and qualitative research. Carefully planned systematic examinations of the issue have been the exception rather than the rule. For instance, large-scale surveys of dual-career couples are remarkable by their absence. Consequently, few statistics are available about the magnitude of dual-career problems and the prevalence of dual-career couples in the country. Likewise, little has been done to establish the viability of the proposition that dual-career issues are qualitatively different from those experienced by other working couples. An empirical validation of the job-career continuum/dichotomy must be achieved if we are to continue emphasizing the uniqueness of dual-career couples. Longitudinal examinations of dual-career couples are rare too, and nonexistent when sample sizes of any magnitude (larger than 30) are considered. Such longitudinal examinations are essential to establish the applicability of dynamic conceptual frameworks of the nature, causes, and consequences of dual-career stress. Systematic examinations of dual-career issues have also omitted a simultaneous exploration of the problem from the perspectives of the couple and the employing organizations. Finally, little empirical examination has been directed at the children of dual-career couples.

The need to address these and similar problems is urgent. The number of dual-career couples in America is on the rise. If the problems and issues of these people are addressed in an effective and timely fashion, dual-career couples can contribute much to corporate and societal success. Effective solutions, however, require careful consideration and intensive information. Without systematic, comprehensive, and longitudinal examinations of stress and strain among dual-career couples, therefore, individual, organizational, and public welfare may be irreparably jeopardized.

REFERENCES

Allen, R. E. and Keavney, T. J. Does the work status of married women affect their attitudes toward family life? *Personnel Administrator*, 1979, **24**(6), 63–66.

Amatea, E. S. and Cross, E. G. Competing worlds, competing standards: Personal control for the professional career woman, wife, and mother. *Journal of the National Association of Women Deans, Administrators, and Counselors*, 1981, **44**(2), 3–10.

Arkin, W. and Dobrofsky, L. R. Job sharing. In R. Rapoport, R. N. Rapoport, and J. M. Bumstead (Eds.), *Working couples*. New York: Harper Colophon, 1978.

Arnott, C. C. Husbands' attitude and wives' commitment to employment. *Journal of Marriage and the Family*, 1972, **34**, 673–674.

Arnott, C. C. Married women and the pursuit of profit: An exchange theory perspective. *Journal of Marriage and the Family*, 1977, **39**, 122–131.

Bailyn, L. Career and family orientations of husbands and wives in relation to marital happiness. *Human Relations*, 1971, **23**, 97–113.

Bandura, A. *Social learning theory*. Englewood Cliffs, N. J.: Prentice-Hall, 1977.

Beehr, T. A. and Newman, J. E. Job stress, employee health, and organizational effectiveness: A facet analysis, model, and literature review. *Personnel Psychology*, 1978, **31**, 665–699.

Berger, M., Foster, M., Wallston, B. S., and Wright, L. You and me against the world: Dual-career couples and joint job-seeking. *Journal of Research and Development in Education*, 1977, **10**(4), 30–37.

Bernard, J. *The future of marriage*. New York: Bantam, 1972.

Bhagat, R. S. and Chassie, M. B. Determinants of organizational commitment among working women: Some implications for organizational integration. *Journal of Occupational Behaviour*, 1981, **2**, 17–30.

Bird, C. *The two-paycheck marriage*. New York: Rawson Wade, 1979.

Blood, R. O. Long-range causes and consequences of the employment of married women. *Journal of Marriage and the Family*, 1965, **27**, 43–47.

Booth, A. Wife's employment and husband's stress: A replication and refutation. *Journal of Marriage and the Family*, 1977, **39**, 645–650.

Bowman, G., Worthy, B. N., and Greyser, S. A. Are women executives people? *Harvard Business Review*, 1965, **43**(3), 14–17.

Broschart, K. R. Family status and professional achievement: A study of women doctorates. *Journal of Marriage and the Family*, 1978, **40**, 71–76.

Bryson, R. B., Bryson, J. B., and Johnson, M. F. Family size, satisfaction, and productivity in dual-career couples. *Psychology of Women Quarterly*, 1978, **3**, 67–77.

Bryson, R. B., Bryson, J. B., Licht, M. H., and Licht, B. G. The professional pair: Husband and wife psychologists. *American Psychologist*, 1976, **31**, 10–16.

Burke, R. J. and Weir, T. Relationship of wives' employment status to husband, wife, and pair satisfaction and performance. *Journal of Marriage and the Family*, 1976, **38**, 279–287.

Cobb, S. Social support as a moderator of life stress. *Psychosomatic Medicine*, 1976, **38**, 300–314.

Cooper, C. L. and Marshall, J. Occupational sources of stress: A review of the literature relating to coronary heart disease and mental health. *Journal of Occupational Psychology*, 1976, **49**, 11–28.

Cooper, C. L. and Marshall, J. Sources of managerial and white-collar stress. In C. L. Cooper and R. Payne (Eds.), *Stress at work*. New York: Wiley, 1978.

Curtis, J. *Working mothers*. New York: Doubleday, 1976.

Darley, S. A. Big-time career for the little woman: A dual-role dilemma. *Journal of Social Issues*, 1976, **32**, 85–98.

Douvan, E. and Pleck, J. Separation as support. In R. Rapoport, R. N. Rapoport, and J. M. Bumstead (Eds.), *Working couples*. New York: Harper Colophon, 1978.

Duncan, R. P. and Perrucci, C. C. Dual occupation families and migration. *American Socio-logical Review*, 1976, **41**, 252–261.

Epstein, C. F. *Women and professional careers: The case of the woman lawyer*. PhD dissertation, Columbia University, 1968.

Epstein, C. F. Law partners and marital partners: Strains and solutions in the dual-career family experience. *Human Relations*, 1971, **24**, 549–564.

Flynn, W. R. and Litzsinger, J. U. Careers without conflict. *Personnel Administrator*, 1981, **26**(7), 81–85.

Frank, R. H. Family location constraints and the geographic distribution of female professionals. *Journal of Political Economy*, 1978, **86**, 117–130.

Gilbert, L. A., Holahan, C. K., and Manning, L. Coping with conflict between professional and maternal roles. *Family Relations*, 1981, **30**, 419–426.

Gross, H. E. Dual-career couples who live apart: Two types. *Journal of Marriage and the Family*, 1980, **42**, 567–576.

Gupta, N. *The organizational antecedents and consequences of role stress among teachers*. Final report to the National Institute of Education, 1981.

Gupta, N. and Beehr, T. A. Job stress and employee behaviors. *Organizational Behavior and Human Performance*, 1979, **23**, 373–387.

Gupta, N. and Beehr, T. A. Relationships among employees' work and nonwork responses. *Journal of Occupational Behaviour*, 1981, **2**, 203–209.

Hall, D. T. A model of coping with role conflict: The role behavior of college educated women. *Administrative Science Quarterly*, 1972, **17**, 471–485.

Hall, D. T. and Gordon, F. E. Career choices among married women: Effects on conflict, role behavior, and satisfaction. *Journal of Applied Psychology*, 1973, **58**, 42–48.

Hall, F. S. and Hall, D. T. Dual-career couples—How do couples and companies cope with the problem? *Organizational Dynamics*, 1978, **7**, 57–77.

Hall, F. S. and Hall, D. T. *The two-career couple*. Reading, Mass.: Addison-Wesley, 1979.

Heckman, N. A., Bryson, R., and Bryson, J. B. Problems of professional couples: A content analysis. *Journal of Marriage and the Family*, 1977, **39**, 323–330.

Hoffman, L. W. and Nye, F. I. *Working mothers*. San Francisco, Calif.: Jossey-Bass, 1975.

Holahan, C. K. and Gilbert, L. A. Conflict between major life roles: Women and men in dual-career couples. *Human Relations*, 1979, **32**, 451–467.

Holmstrom, L. L. *The two-career family*. Cambridge, Mass.: Schenkman, 1973.

Hornung, C. A. and McCullough, B. C. Status relationships in dual-employment marriages: Consequences for psychological well-being. *Journal of Marriage and the Family*, 1981, **43**, 125–141.

House, J. S. *Work stress and social support*. Reading, Mass.: Addison-Wesley, 1981.

Houseknecht, S. K. and Macke, A. S. Combining marriage and careers: The marital adjustment of professional women. *Journal of Marriage and the Family*, 1981, **43**, 651–661.

Howell, M. C. Employed mothers and their families—I. *Pediatrics*, 1973a, **52**, 252–263.

Howell, M. C. Effects of maternal employment on the child—II. *Pediatrics*, 1973b, **52**, 327–343.

Huber, J. and Spitze, G. Wives' employment, household behaviors, and sex-role attitudes. *Social Forces*, 1981, **60**, 150–169.

Hunt, J. G. and Hunt, L. L. Dilemmas and contradictions of status: The case of the dual-career family. *Social Problems*, 1977, **24**, 407–416.

Johnson, C. L. and Johnson, F. A. Attitudes toward parenting in dual-career families. *American Journal of Psychiatry*, 1977, **134**, 391–395.

Kahn, R. L., Wolfe, D. M., Quinn, R. P., Snoek, J. D., and Rosenthal, R. A. *Organizational stress: Studies in role conflict and ambiguity.* New York: Wiley, 1964.

Kanter, R. M. *Men and women of the corporation.* New York: Basic Books, 1977.

Kassner, M. W. Will both spouses have careers? Predictors of preferred traditional marriage among university students. *Journal of Vocational Behavior,* 1981, **18**, 340–355.

Keith, P. M. and Schafer, R. B. Role strain and depression in two-job families. *Family Relations,* 1980, **29**, 483–488.

LaRocco, J. M., House, J. S., and French, J. R. P., Jr. Social support, occupational stress, and health. *Journal of Health and Social Behavior,* 1980, **21**, 202–218.

Levine, J. A. *Who will raise the children?* Philadelphia: Lippincott, 1976.

Long, L. H. Women's labor force participation and the residential mobility of families. *Social Forces,* 1974, **52**, 342–348.

Madani, H. and Cooper, C. L. The impact of dual career family development on organizational life. *Management Decision,* 1977, **15**, 487–493.

Marshall, J. and Cooper, C. L. The mobile manager and his wife. *Management Decision,* 1976, **14**, 179–225.

Martin, T. W., Berry, K. J., and Jacobsen, R. B. The impact of dual career marriages on female professional careers: An empirical test of a Parsonian hypothesis. *Journal of Marriage and the Family,* 1975, **37**, 734–742.

McGrath, J. E. Stress and behavior in organizations. In M. D. Dunnette (Ed.), *Handbook of industrial and organizational psychology.* Chicago: Rand McNally, 1976.

Orden, S. and Orden, B. Working wives and marriage happiness. *American Journal of Sociology,* 1969, **74**, 392–407.

Pahl, J. M. and Pahl, R. E. *Managers and their wives.* London: Allen Lane, 1971.

Papanek, H. Men, women, and work: Reflections on the two-person career. *American Journal of Sociology,* 1973, **78**, 852–872.

Parsons, T. The kinship system of the contemporary United States. In T. Parsons (Ed.), *Essays in sociological theory,* rev. ed. New York: Free Press, 1954.

Perrucci, C. C., Potter, H. R., and Rhoads, D. L. Determinants of male family role performance. *Psychology of Women Quarterly,* 1978, **3**, 22–29.

Pfeffer, J. and Salancik, G. R. *The external control of organizations.* New York: Harper & Row, 1978.

Pingree, S., Butler, M., Paisley, W., and Hawkins, W. Anti-nepotism's ghost: Attitudes of administrators toward hiring professional couples. *Psychology of Women Quarterly,* 1978, **3**, 53–66.

Pleck, J. The work-family role system. *Social Problems,* 1977, **24**, 417–427.

Rapoport, R. and Rapoport, R. N. The dual-career family: A variant pattern and social change. *Human Relations,* 1969, **22**, 3–29.

Rapoport, R. and Rapoport, R. N. *Dual-career families.* Harmondsworth, U.K.: Penguin, 1971.

Rapoport, R. and Rapoport, R. N. *Dual-career families re-examined: New integrations of work and family.* New York: Harper Colophon, 1976.

Rapoport, R., Rapoport, R. N. and Bumstead, J. M. (Eds.), *Working couples.* New York: Harper Colophon, 1978.

Rapoport, R. N. and Rapoport, R. Dual-career families: Progress and prospects. *Marriage and Family Review,* 1978, **1**(5), 1, 3–11.

Ridley, C. A. Exploring the impact of work satisfaction and involvement on marital interaction when both partners are employed. *Journal of Marriage and the Family,* 1973, **35**, 229–237.

Rosen, B., Jerdee, T. H., and Prestwich, T. L. Dual career marital adjustment: Potential effects of discriminatory managerial attitudes. *Journal of Marriage and the Family*, 1975, **37**, 565–572.

Rowe, M. P. That parents may work and children may thrive. In N. Talbot (Ed.). *Raising children in modern America: Problems and prospective solutions*. Boston: Little, Brown, 1976.

Rowe, M. P. Child care in the 1980's: Tradition or androgyny? In J. Chapman (Ed.), *Women into wives*. Beverly Hills, Calif.: Sage, 1977.

Salancik, G. R. and Pfeffer, J. A social information processing approach to job attitudes and task design. *Administrative Science Quarterly*, 1978, **23**, 224–253.

Schuler, R. S. Definition and conceptualization of stress in organizations. *Organizational Behavior and Human Performance*, 1980, **25**, 184–215.

Seidenberg, R. *Corporate wives—Corporate casualties?* New York: AMACOM, 1973.

Shaevitz, M. H. and Shaevitz, M. H. *Making it together as a two-career couple*. Boston: Houghton Mifflin, 1979.

Stafford, R., Backman, E., and Dibona, P. The division of labor among cohabiting and married couples. *Journal of Marriage and the Family*, 1977, **39**, 43–57.

Staines, G. L., Pleck, J. H., Shepard, L. J., and O'Connor, P. Wives' employment status and marital adjustment: Yet another look. *Psychology of Women Quarterly*, 1978, **3**, 90–120.

St. John-Parsons, D. Continuous dual-career families: A case study. *Psychology of Women Quarterly*, 1978, **3**, 30–42.

Sussman, M. B. and Cogswell, B. E. Family influences of job involvement. *Human Relations*, 1971, **24**, 477–487.

Szinovacz, M. E. Role allocation, family structure, and female employment. *Journal of Marriage and the Family*, 1977, **39**, 781–791.

Tallman, I. Working-class wives in suburbia: Fulfillment or crisis? *Journal of Marriage and the Family*, 1969, **31**, 65–72.

Titus, S. L. A function of friendship: Social comparisons as a frame of reference. *Human Relations*, 1980, **33**, 409–431.

Wallston, B. S., Foster, M. A., and Berger, M. I will follow him: Myth, reality, or forced choice—Job seeking experiences of dual-career couples. *Psychology of Women Quarterly*, 1978, **3**, 43–52.

Weaver, C. and Couchman, L. Dual career couples: A corporate personnel dilemma. *Texas Business Executive*, 1980, **6**(1), 28–31.

Weingarten, K. The employment pattern of professional couples and their distribution of involvement in the family. *Psychology of Women Quarterly*, 1978, **3**, 43–52.

Working Family Project. Parenting. In R. Rapoport, R. N. Rapoport, and J. M. Bumstead (Eds.), *Working couples*. New York: Harper Colophon, 1978.

Wright, J. D. Are working women *really* more satisfied? Evidence from several national surveys. *Journal of Marriage and the Family*, 1978, **40**, 301–313.

Zimmerman, K. W., Skinner, D. A., and Birner, R. Career involvement and job satisfaction as related to job strain and marital satisfaction of teachers and their spouses. *Home Economics Research Journal*, 1980, **8**, 421–427.

CHAPTER SEVEN

Stress at the Decline of One's Career
The Act of Retirement

ANN E. McGOLDRICK AND CARY L. COOPER

The attitudes and experiences of older workers in their later working years and their views on retirement vary enormously. For some, the stresses and pressures experienced in later years at work find relief in retirement. Others feel able to cope adequately with physical and mental changes that occur in later life, and see retirement as the greater stressor, preferring to continue in their work role as long as possible. Our own work with older employees and retirees in the U.K. clearly demonstrated the variety of viewpoints on retirement and responses to it. This can be seen from the comments of three men who had retired from similar manual work in the same department of their organization, but had vastly different views on the retirement experience:

> After being 60 years of age I knew more aches and pains than I ever thought existed. Now, in retirement I think there are too few hours in a day—so my aches and pains do not worry me.

> Every person is different. Several of my friends could not abide it and took part-time jobs. For a week or so they were happy, but then they began to complain that the boss was piling the chores on them. Others just watch the traffic till the pubs open, sit in the park or go to bingo. They say they are not bored, but their expression belies them. For me, life is full—my family, hobbies and social life. I should have retired 40 years ago. It's smashing!

In my case there was a real mental shock, after being in employment for 48 years, to become suddenly "unemployed" at the age of 62. It has left a void, a feeling of now being "unwanted," a bit of a "nuisance" or just a "pensioner."

In this chapter we consider the implications of growing old in the employment situation, and how this affects men and women at the end of their working lives. The stressors experienced in the later working years, in relation to psychological changes and coping abilities are outlined, as well as a consideration of the effects of work stress and mental strain from a wide variety of sources. The implications of these for the individual's view of and attitude toward work and retirement are presented, together with discussion of their effect on employees' reactions to the retirement decision. In the second part of the chapter we examine the evidence on physical and mental health after retirement and give consideration to the stresses and problems that are faced by many of the retired. The multiplicative function of uncertainty, importance, and duration, which forms the integrative model for the understanding of the role of stress developed in Chapter 1, will thus be related to the final stage of the work career and to the act of retirement. Throughout our review we refer to existing research, published mainly in the United States; with supportive evidence from our own enquiries in the United Kingdom, where retirement policy and practices have closely followed those in the United States.

GROWING OLD IN THE WORK ENVIRONMENT

First, we briefly consider in turn the major areas of potential stress that individuals must face in the final stage of their working careers, examining the elements in them in conformity to the components of our overall model. These stresses can arise from their psychological changes associated with aging, from the individual's perceptions of work and retirement, from the work environment and the individual's job, and from features of the individual's personal nonwork domain. Having so done, we can combine them into a meaningful framework for the understanding of approaches to the act of retirement.

Psychological Changes in Later Years and Retirement

One of the most basic sources of stress in the later years in employment originates in the aging process itself. Just growing old and feeling that you have not achieved all you would have liked is a problem faced by many people who are approaching the end of their lifelong careers. The self-reproaching questions that come up in one's mind are "What have I accomplished in my life?", "Have I left anything of significance?", "What was it all about?" Alexander had conquered the world and died before he was 35, while Julius Caesar wept because he was a mere commander in

Spain at around the same age. The yearnings and reflections about lost opportunities and lost youth are inevitable, even for the most apparently successful among us. Jung best summed up these internal struggles when he wrote:

> Often, indeed, a false ambition survives in that an old man wants to be a youth again or at least feels he must behave like one although in his heart he can no longer make believe.
>
> (Jung, 1960)

Commentators agree that in the later middle years of life an important turning point occurs, which requires the individual to restructure and reformulate perceptions of self, time, and death. It is a reflective period of self-evaluation, with a move from active to passive modes of perceiving and mastering the environment (Neugarten, 1968a,b). The age at which such changes occur varies widely. Chronological age is, of course, not a good measure of aging, since individuals vary considerably in their rates of physiological, psychological, and social aging (e.g., Heron and Chown, 1967; Atchley and George, 1973). Similarly, it is necessary to distinguish between "personal age" (or how a person seems to himself) and "interpersonal age" (how old he appears to be to others) (Kasterbaum et al., 1972). For most people, however, this reassessment occurs somewhere in the decade of the fifties, and is consequently intricately related to the final career stage and the approach of retirement.

This period of transition produces many potential stresses. The individual must accomodate to his or her changing physical, psychological, and social circumstances. An evaluation must be made of both work and nonwork domains, assessing what is of importance and considering likely adaptations and changes that will have to be made in the future. There will be many uncertainties requiring consideration: loss of work, future finances, family relationships, time and activities, personal identity, and so on. Individuals will, of course, differ considerably both in terms of the importance they attach to different facets of their lives, and their perception of their abilities to cope with the impending changes. These differences will determine their outlooks on retirement and their approaches to it.

For some, the very approach of retirement age may appear as a threat, symptomatic of advancing or "old" age and the end of the useful and active part of life—becoming a dependent rather than fulfilling a positive role in society. For others, it may bring the prospect of relief from the stresses experienced in these years, or may represent a time looked forward to as a new and challenging life-stage. It is, however, a major transition, which can only be successfully achieved if the individual can reassess what is important in his or her life and refocus the criteria that contribute to his or her psychological well-being, reestablishing in the nonwork domain an equivalent set of rewards to those previously obtained through employment—a set of rewards that are acceptable to and adequate for him or her as an individual. These will be discussed more fully below. At this point it is sufficient to note that throughout the final years at work, many employees will suffer stress through doubts and uncertainties about their future, which center on the act of retirement. While only in a minority of cases do these psychological changes result in severe emotional breakdown and clinical symptomology (e.g. Hildebrand, 1981), the effects are a reality for the majority of employees. The approach of retirement must be considered as a "stressful life event" (Dohrenwend and Dohrenwend, 1974), to which each individual must accommodate.

Changing Work Abilities with Age

A further potential source of stress for the older worker relates to changing mental and physical work abilities with age. At one time it was argued that this was a time of general decline, when an individual increasingly became less capable of coping with his or her work. Recent research has dispelled many such stereotypes regarding the effects of age on the abilities of older workers. Physiological changes occur very gradually and without much outwardly noticeable effect (e.g., Weg, 1975). Psychological changes similarly occur slowly. There appears to be no conclusive evidence, for example, that older people show marked deterioration in I.Q. levels until very late in the aging process, when they are still only slight (e.g., Schaie, 1958; Schaie and Labouvie-Vief, 1974). Moreover, older people's lower rates of adaptability in learning and memory processes (e.g., Fozard and Popkin, 1978) have been related to motivational factors rather than absolute decline (e.g., Walsh, 1975). There is, in fact, evidence that older workers do generally perform as well in their jobs as younger employees; sometimes also contributing greater experience to the work situation (e.g., Sonnerfeld, 1978). In heavy, manual production it appears that the performance does decline in the fifties and sixties, resulting also in higher absenteeism. This must be balanced, however, by the preference of employees in such industries for mandatory retirement policies and upper age limits rather than upward flexibility (Fleisher and Kaplan, 1980).

While such myths regarding age and work abilities have been dispelled in absolute terms, however, the potential dangers of discrimination based on such erroneous age-related stereotypes has now received due emphasis in aging research (e.g., Rosen and Jerdee, 1976a,b). There is no doubt of the effect that this has had in influencing employers in both the United States (Brousseau, 1981) and in Britain (Makeham, 1980) against older workers. Moreover, while the evidence suggests that changes relate more to individuals than as a universal aging process, it is necessary to consider the perspective of the older employees themselves. They are similarly influenced by the awareness of such stereotypes and the additional insecurity this gives to their position. The uncertainty of continuing to adequately perform their work role is increased; particularly in times of economic recession, with manpower cuts and technological change. Awareness of the likelihood of their being foremost to be pressurized out of their jobs, while alternative sources of employment are closed to older workers (e.g., Sheppard and Belitsky, 1966; Sheppard, 1971) increases this insecurity. Even for those who feel they are able to demonstrate their ability to completely cope with their jobs, the current industrial scene causes uncertainties regarding the future.

Importance of the Work Role and Its Loss on Retirement

There has been much controversy among researchers regarding the issue of the importance of the work role for the individual, and thus the impact of its loss at retirement. A provocative statement to this effect, for example, was made in the Work in America Report (1973):

> Without work all life goes rotten—but when work is souless, life stifles and dies.

The absence of work, or meaningless work, it is concluded, causes severe effects in alienation, mental and physical health decline, alcoholism, and drug addiction. From the time of the work of Friedman and Havighurst (1954), the values of work other than financial security have been much discussed. Work contributes to many important facets of life for the individual: social contacts, status, self-image, a place in the social system, identity, and "meaning" for the individual's life (e.g., Erikson, 1956; Miller, 1963; Morse and Weiss, 1955).

Recently these assumptions have been questioned (e.g., Gechman, 1974; Kahn, 1974; O'Toole, 1974) and other elements of the individual's life, such as health, family, and avocational interests have been held to be more important (e.g., Campbell et al., 1976; Quinn and Sheppard, 1974). The balance, it has been claimed, now falls on those other aspects of life (e.g., Dubin, 1956; Dubin and Goldman, 1972). While the results of this debate remain inconclusive, the importance of the many rewards that the individual can find in the work situation has been further demonstrated in recent studies of redundancy and withdrawal from employment. Hayes and Nutman (1981), for example, emphasize the pessimism, depression, and loss of purpose and identity following long-term unemployment, as well as the deleterious health consequences. Our own studies of retired employees have similarly shown that not all individuals can easily replace these important features of their working life, sinking pessimistically into an inactive and negative retirement existence (McGoldrick and Cooper, 1980).

It is suggested here, that work, like retirement, can have widely different meanings for different people. For those who see work only as a mechanism to earn a living, it can be speculated that the move out of the employment system will be comparatively easy, if financial circumstances permit. On the other hand, for those employees who rely on their work to provide other important rewards in their lives, the success of adaptation will be dependent on how well they can reestablish other sources for such outcomes in the nonwork domain. For the majority, therefore, there will be some need to accommodate to the approach of retirement and, to a greater or lesser degree, seek new mechanisms to obtain the extrinsic and intrinsic rewards and outcomes of their working life from their impending retirement status.

The "transition" to retirement or accommodation to this "stressful life event" is thus a personal act, and even more because of the nature of retirement itself. The question that must be asked about this transition is "transition to what?" While the work/employment situation is culturally determined and a socially defined role, the retirement role has been described as a "roleless role" (Burgess, 1960), with no predetermined role-set or specifications, lacking in cultural value. This vagueness and lack of structure in itself can provide problems for the ill-prepared. For some employees the lessened importance of their status and place in society, becoming "retirees", "pensioners" or "senior citizens" rather than being active within the social system, is a barrier that cannot be overcome. Their ability to obtain satisfactory outcomes and successfully adapt to the retirement situation will be inhibited, since they will suffer the potential uncertainties of how to achieve, in terms of this new status, the social rewards they value.

In the case of retirement, moreover, the loss of important outcomes through work will be anticipated for some time, especially for those leaving at statutory or expected retirement age. For many there will be a significant period of uncertainty regarding the nature of the experience ahead and the required coping abilities. While for some this will be a time for assessing and building upon resources, for others it will be one of gloom and despondency. Certainly it has been shown that, as a result of this impending status change, as retirement age approaches, it tends to be less positively perceived by many older employees (e.g., Ekerdt et al., 1976). The imminence of the event increases both the uncertainties of the change and the importance of successfully accomplishing the transition.

Work Stresses in Later Years

On the other hand, work does involve an increasing range of stresses for large numbers of individuals. Poor fit between stresses of the job and worker needs has been strongly associated with dissatisfaction with work (e.g., Caplan, 1975); the resultant strains can cause a variety of negative medical and behavioral effects (e.g., Beehr and Newman, 1980; Murrell, 1978). There is also little doubt that older workers are more prone to many of the stressors that exist within the work situation. The changes that occur in these years, as well as the complex processes of personal assessment and realization, may be assumed to be related to the problems faced in the work environment. These pressures and stresses can become intolerable for some employees, causing severe health problems, but to a lesser extent affect many more older workers.

Much research, for example, has been accomplished in relation to changes in technology and the consequences for older people (e.g., Adams et al., 1969). Similarly work in the United Kingdom has highlighted the job pressures and difficulties experienced by employees in their later years: ill health, enforced mobility, work strain, lack of promotion, need to retrain, attitudinal and personality difficulties, and discrimination (e.g., Nuffield Foundation, 1963; Medical Research Council, 1961; Le Gros Clark, 1959; Makenham, 1980). These difficulties have been enhanced by current employment problems, causing fears of redundancy and lack of alternative job opportunities.

Evidence from our own studies has shown a widespread awareness of these pressures and strains in the later years at work, which grow in importance with the age of the employee and are intensified over time. Of 1200 early retired men, the majority became less satisfied with their jobs in the years preceding retirement, and about half indicated changing attitudes toward work and found their jobs harder to cope with. Again, in a survey of 192 older employees (45 years +) from all job levels, well over half felt that the stresses and problems faced by older workers were already important for them and were good reasons for considering retiring earlier. The vast majority of workers in their later fifties and sixties were personally experiencing age-related stresses in the work environment, as well as coping difficulties. Over the years the pressures increased, as did the employees' growing uncertainty of being capable of maintaining their positions and performing adequately in their jobs. At the same time the importance of so doing was intensified by awareness of the lack of opportunity for occupational mobility and job change.

While a wide range of problems were discussed by the employees, perhaps the most frequently mentioned were those relating to rates of technological change: new production techniques, computerization, and the dreaded microchip. Obviously the older employees' insecurity in the work situation caused much anxiety, which increased over time and in relation to the manpower reductions now prevalent in many industries. While respondents were adamant about the need for progress and new ideas, their problem was to define their own position in this changing world. They were often acutely aware of current unemployment problems, particularly if there had been redundancies within their own organization. This could leave them with a high level of uncertainty as to their ability to perform their job satisfactorily; and even their right to remain in the employment situation at all, rather than to make way for younger workers—an attitude often reinforced by management, unions, and younger colleagues. Their greater propensity to experience tiredness and minor illnesses similarly increased their growing insecurity, as did the increased effort they sometimes felt they needed to put into their jobs to maintain standards. Where such pressures were felt, and earlier retirement terms were known to be available or even encouraged by management, the individual was often influenced toward them by his or her perception of possible inability to continue to adequately cope with this stressful job situation over time.

Stresses in the Personal/Nonwork Domain

Finally, the employee can experience a variety of pressures from his or her nonwork domain, which reflect back on his or her work and attitude toward retirement. The chief pressures in this respect relate to the marital relationship, home circumstances, employee's own health, health of spouse, financial security, dependents, and family. Seventeen percent of the workers studied in the U.K. 45+ age group, for example, already felt that their health might be affecting their work. Some 42% were experiencing definite tiredness as a result of their jobs, and indicated ways in which the tensions caused problems in their marital relationships, home and family lives.

Thus extraorganizational stresses can compound with the stress experienced in the work domain, putting severe demands on coping resources. The majority of those affected felt it necessary to put all their endeavors into maintaining work performance, valuing their good work record and not wishing to further endanger the security of the position. In turn, this could increase the strain in the nonwork domain: home tensions, marital problems, reduced social life, tiredness, and health decline. The results of such spillover were, of course, bound to increase with the duration of the problem and could force individuals to reassess priorities and face the decision concerning which facets of life were important for future well-being.

THE RETIREMENT DECISION

As is specified in Chapter 1, within any given culture there are shared norms among people in how they value various events and objects, but there is also variation from person to person according to his or her unique set of circumstances and experience. From the foregoing discussion it will have become clear that individuals will place different importance on the various facets of their lives later in life, and will be influenced in different ways and to different degrees by stresses inherent in their working situations. This will obviously affect their attitude toward retirement. Changes in retirement policy have given more employees the flexibility to retire earlier, and an examination of factors to be considered in deciding whether to do so provides further insight into the stresses of the later working years.

Changing Retirement Patterns and Attitudes

In both the United States and the United Kingdom, changes in the economic climate in the 1960s and 70s, with the need for manpower reduction in many industries, meant that older workers were encouraged toward earlier retirement. Public benefits were relaxed, special liberalized company benefits were offered, and existing pension schemes were adapted to permit retirement at the initiative of the employee (McGoldrick and Cooper, 1978). The figures of the U.S. Bureau of Census and Department of Labor clearly demonstrate the decline in the United States over these years of older age groups' participation in the labor force.

Such changes, it is maintained, occurred within a generally more positive climate of social opinion toward the idea of retirement time. Traditional associations with the end of the useful working life—inactivity, poverty, sickness, disability, and death—were breaking down for workers at all levels of employment. The better financial security provided by state and company pensions, as well as the increased savings capacity of a wealthier working population, combined with such factors as increases in life expectancy and medical advances, to change such views and permit larger numbers of employees to look forward to an active and secure retirement (e.g., Crawford and Matlow, 1974; Orbach et al., 1969). At the same time, it is argued that attitudes toward the value of work were changing and the so-called "Protestant Ethic" was in decline. Surveys carried out during these years showed that growing numbers of workers appeared to hold positive attitudes toward retirement and regarded a planned early retirement or mid-career job change as a goal (e.g., Parnes et al., 1974).

Thus, emphasis is placed on the positive features of earlier retirement and the opportunities it can provide for the retiree. Careful examination of the reasons why employees elect to retire early, however, reveals also a strategy to cope with the stressful factors and uncertainties in job and work environment under discussion here.

Reasons for Early Retirement

The most detailed study of intentions to retire early in the United States was undertaken by Barfield and Morgan (1969 and 1972), with a national sample and with a sample of automobile workers who had a specific early retirement offer. Their overriding conclusion was in the paramount importance of financial considerations as decision criteria. This has been confirmed in many other studies (e.g., Boskin, 1977; Orbach, 1969; Parnes,

1974; Quinn, 1977). The subjective assessment of health by the employee was also considered to be an influential variable, and the significance of the health factor has again been frequently demonstrated (e.g., Pollman, 1971; Quinn, 1977). Our own study in the United Kingdom of 1200 early retired men similarly highlighted the primary significance of financial factors, as well as the importance of health criteria.

Many other factors in the decision have been established, however, both in the Barfield and Morgan study and in other research. The importance of these factors must not be underestimated as part of this decision process. While financial adequacy would obviously be expected to be a prerequisite, once this is attained, individuals must consider the importance of the work role for their well-being and assess their ability to satisfactorily maintain their work performance, and must balance this against the outcomes they perceive for themselves in retirement. Health, as stated above, is one such factor. Other factors that have received the attention of researchers are the work ethic, job satisfaction and values (e.g. Davidson and Kunze, 1965); work dissatisfactions, strains, coping problems, job status, and skill levels (e.g., Jacobson, 1972a,b; Messer, 1964; Sheppard, 1976; Sheppard and Herrick, 1976); occupational level and status (e.g., Fillenbaum, 1971; Jaffe, 1972; Rowe, 1976); attitudes toward retirement, planned activities, further work (e.g., Orbach, 1969; Owen and Belzung, 1967; Streib and Schneider, 1971); and demographic correlates (e.g., Schmitt et al., 1979).

Respondents in our own survey clearly indicated the importance of a wide range of work stresses as factors in their decisions, with diminishing work satisfaction and increasing problems in coping in their later years at work. As we indicated in our discussion of such stress in the first part of this chapter, these factors applied to about half the retirees, with many more experiencing a decline in their overall satisfaction from their jobs. Similarly, health factors—actual health problems and more subjective health assessments, tiredness, and the desire to prevent or forestall future health decline—were frequently given as reasons for retiring. On the other hand, the retirees indicated many positive outcomes of their retirement option: rest and relaxation, increased leisure and free time, opportunities for hobbies and recreation, time with family and friends, voluntary work, new careers, part-time jobs, and so on.

Rather than seeing individual features of the early retirement decision in isolation, therefore, it seems more appropriate to consider the inter-relationship of all the potential factors that the individual must balance. Walker and Price (1976) and Walker and Lazer (1978) proposed a model of the process in a systems perspective, including the range of environmental, institutional, and individual variables within the employee's decision. In this way early retirement is not only viewed in terms of the positive outcomes it can provide, but also as a coping mechanism—a double-edged strategy (McGoldrick, 1982). For the individual who believes he or she has a basic financial security, adequate to retirement needs, it is an opportunity to review his or her situation and take stock. Awareness of the option may indeed place such individuals in a situation of further uncertainty while they make this assessment, particularly if they are unsure of the significance of their role as workers or of features of their potential situations after retirement. For some the answer is clear-cut, whether it is to remain at work or to retire. For others it is the resultant balance of the multiplicity of factors involved. As we indicated at the outset, however, while individuals will be influenced by current cultural norms, it is their own sets of circumstances and experiences that must dictate their decisions if those decisions are to be appropriate to their needs as individuals.

THE RETIREMENT EXPERIENCE

In this section we ask what we know from the research can be the expected outcomes of retirement for the individual. The earlier sections of this chapter have shown health factors and reactions to the effects of aging to be important criteria in the employee's prior assessment of retirement, and his or her experience of stress in the later working years. We have also viewed retirement itself as a stressful life event. Health problems are themselves a major outcome of stress and, as we will discuss later in this section, health is a major predictor of retirement satisfaction. Consequently, at this point we must examine the evidence relating to the effect of retirement on both physical and mental health, after which we focus on the principle components of retirement satisfaction/dissatisfaction, isolating as key factors the roles of finances, health, and psychological stresses.

Physical Health and Retirement

Perhaps one of the most widespread beliefs regarding retirement has been that it directly causes health decline. The individual, it is argued, should continue in the routine and interests of work for as long as he or she is physically able to cope, in order to maintain his or her physical and mental health. Failure to do so can result in health problems, but also in early death. This myth connecting retirement and the reduction of life expectancy has now been largely dispelled by the results of studies of mortality and longevity, examining data on employees from a wide range of industries and occupations (e.g., Haynes, 1975; McMahan and Ford, 1955; Palmore, 1971; Riley and Foner, 1968; Tyhurst et al., 1957). Many of these studies have been reviewed recently by Kasl (1981), who gives detailed attention to the methodological weaknesses in their design and the need for further research. He is forced to conclude, however, that the consistency of their outcomes is indisputable.

Again, research on physical health and retirement produced relatively consistent results: The transition from work to retirement does not generally appear to cause physical health problems. Most studies, in fact, have found no differences, or in some cases positive improvement, in health before and after retirement. Similarly, no differences have been found between the retired and nonretired. While Kasl (1981) again highlights the many methodological weaknesses inherent in individual studies, particularly in the use of indices of self-assessment of health, the combined strength of evidence they present is overwhelming. This is demonstrated in Table 7-1, which provides examples of such studies and briefly summarizes the procedures followed and their findings.

If retirement does not have any clearly demonstrable effect on mortality rates or physical health, however, what about the emotional or mental well-being of retirees?

Mental Health and Retirement

In viewing the mental health implications in the transition from the role of worker to that of retiree, earlier commentators emphasized the extreme negative effects of the ensuing identity crisis. Miller (1965), for example, saw retirement as a degrading loss of all legitimate identity, which would consequently have severe effects on the individual's mental status. As we indicated in our earlier discussions, however, this assumes that the individual can only acquire identity through the work role. While for some employees this may be true, it is by no means universal. Many retirees, in fact, find that sufficient positive values can be obtained through their new leisure roles to maintain their self-esteem and psychological well-being (e.g., Atchley, 1971).

While a large number of retirement studies have attempted to assess mental health implications, however, their comparability in terms of definition and measurement must be viewed as problematic. The weight of evidence and agreement between disparate studies, nonetheless, forces us to conclude that retirement cannot be associated directly with decline in mental well-being for the majority of retirees. This has been similarly shown in: (1) longitudinal analyses (e.g., Streib and Schneider, 1971; Thompson and Streib, 1958; Thompson, Streib, and Kosa, 1960); (2) studies of life quality for different age groups (e.g., Campbell et al., 1976); (3) studies of specific retired populations (e.g., Atchley, 1975; Barfield and Morgan, 1969; Barfield, 1970; Bell, 1974, 1975; Shanas et al., 1968); and (4) studies comparing the morale of the retired with that of the employed (e.g., Streib, 1956; Thompson, 1973). The most usual conclusion, in fact, is that between two-thirds and three-quarters of retirees are generally satisfied with the retirement experience and suffering no psychological ill effects once they have adapted to their transition. Where problems do occur, they can usually be related to specific aspects of the individual's situation rather than retirement itself. We therefore now turn to the most important studies in this field, which focus on the conditions that favorably or un-

Table 7-1 Examples of Studies Investigating the Association of Retirement and Physical Health

Study	Date	Country	Sample	Emphasis	Procedure	Major Findings
Tyhurst et al.	1957	Canada	Communications industry employees	Comparison of pre/post retirement	Company records of absence data/post retirement interviews	1. No change in health status 2. No difference between volunteers & compulsorily retired 3. No connection with pre-retirement attitudes
Cornell Study: Streib &) Thompson)	1957 & 1958	U.S.	Cornell study national sample, longitudinal analysis before and after retirement	Health status changes with age	Reports and self-assessments and doctors' rating of sub-sample	1. No change in health status with retirement 2. Change more frequently associated with health improvement 3. Similar for both sexes; and between occupational groups, although with slight improvement at manual level and slight decline in other groups.
Streib &) Schneider)	1971					
Emerson	1959	U.K.	124 men for 1 year after age 65 years	Comparison of retired and workers	Cornell Medical Index	No differences between retired and workers
Martin and Doran	1966	U.K.	604 men aged 55 years & over, retired and working	Comparison of retired and workers; exam-	Interview reports of serious illness	1. Comparison of retired/ workers showed no difference

(Continued)

Table 7-1 (Continued)

Study	Date	Country	Sample	Emphasis	Procedure	Major Findings
				ination of trends of serious illness over time, before and after retirement		2. Trends over time, before and after retirement, showed a distinct drop in two years after retirement with slower increase rate there-after (especially for blue-collar workers).
Ryser and Sheldon	1969	U.S.	500 retired men and women, aged 60–70 years	Health status in retirement	Interviews giving self-assessments and objective data on health	1. No difference reported by over two-thirds 2. Positive change reported more frequently than decline 3. Satisfaction increased with better socioeconomic conditions
Crawford	1975	U.K.	53 married couples, slightly over-representative of lower socioeconomic classes	Changes of health with retirement	Interviews before and after retirement, subjective health status and illness reports	1. No change for retirees 2. Little change for wives

favorably predispose a person to a satisfying (or otherwise) period of retirement.

Retirement Satisfaction

There is general agreement between studies on the two major sources of stress and dissatisfaction with retirement: poor health and inadequate finances. These will be discussed in turn below. Other determinants that, it has been suggested, are of relevant though lesser importance include age, education, occupational status, and involvement in leisure activities (e.g., Barfield and Morgan, 1969; Barfield, 1970; Campbell et al., 1976; Kimmel et al., 1978; McGoldrick and Cooper, 1980; Schmitt et al., 1979b). There is also evidence to be found in our own and other studies of the relevance of a set of psychological criteria that can also limit retirement satisfaction.

Health

In the above discussion we have dismissed the myths directly relating retirement to health decline and early death. Where retirees are in poor health, however, or where health problems hinder retirement plans, their dissatisfaction with the retirement experience has been shown to increase significantly. In these cases the intended outcomes of retirement may be unattainable, and thus the transition has not produced the anticipated and desired result. In our own study of retired men we found that some retirees with health problems had, in fact, still attained the desired outcomes of retirement, since they had the relief of no longer needing to cope while continuing to perform adequately in their jobs. Retirees with severe health problems, however, did tend, overall, to be among the least satisfied of the sample in their general assessment of retirement life. On the other hand, more than two-thirds of the retirees reported similar or improved health during retirement in terms of actual health or reduction of the stresses and strains of their later working years. Thus, for them, retirement had in this respect brought important outcomes and was, as a result positively perceived.

Finances

A major source of stressors in the retirement years relate to income and financial security. It is suggested widely in the research that low income in retirement, inadequate income to carry out retirement activities, imbalance of pre- to postretirement income, and so on produce a high propensity to dissatisfaction, with resultant stresses and coping problems. In some cases this problem can be severe, but the majority of current retirees have to face at least some financial restrictions. In a U.K. study for the Department of Health and Social Security (Parker, 1980), for example, the widespread influence of inflation on retirement finances, savings, and pension benefits was emphasized. The relevance of financial security to the individual's perception of his or her retirement outcomes is of paramount importance: It both determines his or her abilities to achieve desired retirement goals and significantly reduces the uncertainties relating to his or her retirement experience. Consequently, it is a major factor in his or her overall satisfaction.

In the case of earlier retirement, financial problems can be further exaggerated—with a longer time in retirement and increased effects of inflation on retirement finances. Retirees in our own study indicated this as their chief concern. For some, it brought an unwelcome return to work (McGoldrick and Cooper, 1981); while for many it had meant unplanned economies and the need to use savings ahead of time. This has caused James Morgan (1979) to ask: "What with inflation and unemployment . . . who can afford to retire?", although he concludes that, at least in its early stages, this has not had much apparent effect on people's retirement plans. It may be speculated that the wider availability of such options may be permitting current employees to plan ahead if the rewards and outcomes perceived are of sufficient importance to them. It has, however, tended to reduce rates of satisfaction among those who have been retired for some time (Barfield and Morgan, 1978).

Psychological Stresses

A further group of problems that influence satisfaction in retirement relate to the retiree's reaction to his or her entry into the nonwork domain, which we can only mention briefly here. In our own study about 12% of the retirees experienced guilt feelings in leaving work and their status as retirees, even though the vast majority did not miss work after an adjustment period. For U.K. early retirees, a significant problem in this respect was that of registering as required at the Unemployment Exchange, feeling it an "embarrassment" or "disgrace." Similarly, the effects of the negative attitudes of spouse or family toward retirement could cause problems: the spouse's disapproval; the indication of children reacting to the implication of the implied status change of the parent; as well as the practical problems in terms of stress on the marital relationship that could be caused by more time at home. Again, in a smaller number of cases, loneliness or boredom could cause regrets. In the case of bereavement of the spouse, for example, this could be severe. Finally, as has been found elsewhere (e.g., Streib and Schneider, 1971; Price et al., 1979), those who had been compulsorily retired tended to be less satisfied than volunteers, although this difference diminished over time in retirement.

SUMMARY AND CONCLUSIONS: THE EMPLOYEE AND RETIREMENT

As we stated at the outset of this chapter, retirement is a stressful life event and can also be a mechanism for coping with the stresses experienced in later working life. So far we have discussed the components of the decline stage of the career and the approach of retirement that can result in stress for the employee. We have also examined evidence relating to the experience of retirement and the major determinants of satisfaction/dissatisfaction. At this stage we bring our discussion together in terms of the model of stress presented in Chapter 1: the multiplicative function of uncertainty, importance, and duration, suggesting the most likely causes of stress for the employee. Again in line with the overall aims of this book, it is relevant here to briefly outline mechanisms by which these stresses can be coped with or reduced by the individual and organizational support.

Stress at the Decline of the Career: Theoretical Model

From the foregoing it will be apparent that retirement must be considered as a stressful life event of major significance. It can, in fact, be one of the most disruptive events that the individual must face in his or her life. It involves the complete disturbance of his or her normal routines (Lazarus, 1978); involving the individual in a reassessment of the important outcomes and rewards previously gained through employment and the need to reestablish a new nonwork domain. It is hardly surprising, therefore, that it can potentially involve feelings of lack of control, uncertainties, and anxieties (Singer, 1978), which some employees may feel they cannot adequately cope with. Let us firstly summarize the components of this experience, before considering the procedures of coping.

Importance.   The importance of the transition to retirement for the employee is dependent on his or her own assessment of important outcomes, both the intrinsic and extrinsic rewards for which he or she looks in life. The set of routines to which he or she is accustomed, it has been suggested, are important and valued because they provide for the acquisition of desired outcomes; they are predictable, and behavior-outcome contingencies are known; and they provide a sense of personal control (Brett, 1980). Consequently, change is disruptive and introduces uncertainties. In retirement the employee must exchange the work role for one of leisure. The work role has been valued because it has provided important outcomes or rewards—financial security, status, identity, companionship, sense of usefulness, involvement, and so on. It is a predictable role in which the employee has operated for the major part of his or her life, and he or she has learnt how to acquire from it those rewards that are most important to the maintenance of his or her personal well-being. The employee can therefore be expected to feel a sense of control in this known pattern of interaction with his or her environment.

Uncertainty.   The perceived onset of retirement, on the other hand, can be a time of uncertainties regarding the future. The role of retiree is new and contains many potential uncertainties regarding the acquisition of desired outcomes, as well as uncertainties about the individual's abilities to satisfactorily replace those associated with the working career. Similarly, it requires the employee to review his or her behavior-outcome contingencies, establishing new patterns of reactions to suit his or her changed situation. In some cases these appropriate behaviors will be clear, while others will again present the uncertainty of how to adapt learned behaviors to suit new circumstances. Our foregoing discussion presented areas in which individuals may perceive uncertainties in the experience of retirement: adequacy of future finances, health, social life, activities and timespending, identity, and status in the new lifestyle, reactions of spouse and family and so on.

Duration.   Again in the framework of stress proposed here, an important distinction is made on the basis of the perceived duration of the uncertainties of a given situation, since they require the mobilization of different resources and adaptive skills. The examples given here that examine work-related stressful events of longer duration are those of job loss and plant closure (Kasl, 1979) and studies of job transfer (reviewed by Brett, 1980). Retirement can similarly be considered as a stressful event that can require a longer period of time to fully resolve or to cope with adequately. The unpredictable nature of the role the employee is moving toward, with all its uncertainties, can cause the individual to experience feelings of lack of personal control—contrasting with the certainties and control he or she has learned to expect in his or her job environment.

Reactions to Retirement

In his or her reaction to the onset of retirement, the individual will be influenced by his or her personal situation, experiences, and needs. In this chapter we have outlined some of the major factors relevant to the final career stage: effects of aging and awareness of physical, psychological, and social changes, which become apparent for the majority of people sometime in their fifties; changes in attitudes toward and the significance of work; changing coping abilities at work; pressures and stresses in the work environment; the effects of technological change and unemployment changes in health; and demands in the personal/nonwork domain.

The stress experienced at retirement will be dependent on the importance the individual ascribes to different facets of his or her life at this stage in attaining his or her desired outcomes, together with his or her uncertainties of obtaining them. Stress will be low when employees can readily adapt their desired values and goals to those that retirement and the leisure domain offer; and where uncertainties of being able to obtain them are at a minimum. Stress will be high when the employee's values and important outcomes are those provided by the work environment and when he or she cannot perceive their replacement in retirement; and for those who perceive many uncertainties in being able to achieve desired retirement outcomes (through lack of adequate finances, poor health, fear of boredom and loneliness, etc.). It has been maintained that when a person experiences such stressful feelings, he or she will be motivated to reduce the uncertainty and to attempt to replace the valued outcomes (e.g., Lazarus and Launier, 1978). Thus, some employees who experience these long-term stresses can adapt to and cope with the retirement experience. For those, however, who cannot perceive the opportunity of replacing the valued outcomes of work and reducing the uncertainties associated with retirement, retirement will remain a dreaded event—either causing consistent anxiety, or being put out of mind as far as possible and thus causing maximum impact when the time comes that it can no longer be ignored.

Coping Mechanisms

Our own studies and recent research findings reviewed here would imply a generally more positive outlook on retirement. There is a growing body of evidence in the United States and in Europe that many people want to retire, once their finances are adequate. Some of the reasons for this have been discussed in this chapter—in terms of the more positive view of life in retirement, the negative effects of work in later life. Similarly, research has demonstrated that retirement can no longer be associated with physical and mental health decline; and can, in fact, result in improvement of health. The majority of people are satisfied with their retirement experience. The major dissatisfactions, it has been shown, arise not from retirement itself, but from factors more generally associated with aging, and with inadequate finances to carry out desired retirement activities. Nonetheless, retirement is not positively perceived by all older workers; and the transition can be a stressful one, involving many potential uncertainties to which each individual must personally accommodate.

There is substantial evidence that the employee's prior perceptions of likely retirement outcomes significantly relate to his or her satisfaction with the retirement experience. Those who expect a positive retirement experience in terms of anticipated financial status, friends, social activities, and level of preparedness tend to be more satisfied after retiring (e.g., Glamser, 1976; Jacobson, 1974; Thompson, 1958). Similarly, prior reassessment of goals, value orientations, and life appraisals before retirement—a decline in emphasis on material-instrumental values and an increase in ease-contentment and hedonistic values—has also been shown to significantly assist adjustment (e. g., Clark and Anderson, 1967; Ludwig and Eickhorn, 1967; Thurnher, 1974). The role of retirement preparation has therefore received recognition both in the United States, and somewhat later in the United Kingdom. The need to encourage personal reassessment of both practical and emotional retirement outcomes—encouraging the development of coping behaviors that reduce feelings of lack of control that may occur—is of extreme importance. On a wider scale we would advocate a flexible approach to retirement age, which gives the individual the opportunity to balance the factors in his or her own situation. The introduction of earlier retirement policies in the United States and Europe has been discusssed here. In the United States the Age Discrimination in Employment Act and its amendments (1967 and 1978) also introduced some degree of upward flexibility, further extending the individual's discretion. Similarly, the European Economic Community Commission (1980) has recently reviewed retirement practices and encouraged a move toward more flexible policies. Such an approach more adequately copes with the differences among individuals' mental, physical, financial, and social needs—permitting them to respond according to their own outlook on work and retirement.

REFERENCES

Adams, L. P., Axelbank, R. G., and Jaffe, A. J. *Employment of the Middle-Aged Worker.* National Institute of Gerontology, The National Council on the Ageing in cooperation with U. S. Department of Labor Manpower Administration, 1969.

Atchley, R. C. Retirement and leisure participation: continuity or crisis. *The Gerontologist,* 1971, **11**(1), 13–17.

Atchley, R. C. and George, L. K. Symptomatic measurement of age. *The Gerontologist,* 1973, **13**, 332–336.

Atchley, R. C. Adjustment to loss of job at retirement. *International Journal of Ageing and Human Development,* 1975, **6**, 17–27.

Barfield, R. F. *The automobile worker and retirement: A second look.* Ann Arbor: Institute for Social Research, University of Michigan, 1970.

Barfield, R. F. and Morgan, J. N. *Early Retirement: the Decision and the Experience.* Ann Arbor: Institute for Social Research, University of Michigan, 1969.

Barfield, R. Some observations on early retirement. In G. M. Shatto (Ed.), *Employment of the middle-aged.* Springfield, Ill.: Charles C. Thomas, 1972.

Barfield, R. F. and Morgan, J. N. Trends in satisfaction with retirement. *The Gerontologist,* 1978, **18**, 19–23.

Beehr, T. A. and Newman, J. E. Job stress, employee health, and organisational effectiveness: a facet analysis, model, and literature review. *Personnel Psychology,* 1978, **31**, 665–700.

Bell, B. D. Cognitive dissonance and the life satisfaction of older adults. *Journal of Gerontology,* 1974, **29**, 564–571.

Bell, B. D. "The limitations of crisis theory as an explanatory mechanism in social gerontology. *International Journal of Ageing & Human Development* 1975, **6**, 153–168.

Boskin, M. Social security and the retirement decision. *Economic Enquiry*, 1977, **January**, 1–25.

Brett, J. M. The effect of job transfer on employees and their families. In C. L. Cooper and R. Payne (Eds.), *Current concerns in occupational stress*. Chichester: Wiley, 1980.

Brousseau, K. R. After age forty: employment patterns & practices in the United States". In C. L. Cooper and D. P. Torrington (Eds.), *After forty*, Chichester: Wiley, 1981.

Burgess, E. W. Ageing in Western Culture. In E. W. Burgess (Ed.), *Ageing in western society: A comparative survey*. Chicago: University of Chicago Press, 1960.

Campbell, A., Converse, P. E., and Rogers, W. L. *The quality of American life,* New York: Russel Sage Foundation, 1976.

Caplan, R. D., et al. *Job demands and worker health: Main effects and occupational differences*. University of Michigan: Institute for Social Research, U.S. Department of Health, Education and Welfare, April 1975.

Clark, M. and Anderson, B. G. *Culture and ageing: An anthropological study of older Americans*. Springfield, Ill.: Charles C. Thomas, 1967.

Crawford, M. P. Retirement as a psychosocial crisis. *Journal of Psychosomatic Research*, 1972, **16**, 375–380.

Crawford, M. and Matlow, J. Some attitudes towards retirement among middle-aged employees. *Industrial Relations*, 1974, **24**, 616–631.

Davidson, W. R. and Kunze, K. R. Psychological, social and economic meanings of work in modern society. *The Gerontologist*, 1965, **5**, 3, 129–133.

Dohrenwend, B. S. and Dohrenwend, B. P. *Stressful life events: Their nature and effects*. New York: Wiley, 1974.

Dubin, R. Industrial workers' worlds: a study of the "central life interests" of industrial workers. *Social Problems*, 1956, **3**, 131–142.

Dubin, R. and Goldman, D. R. Central life interests of American middle managers and specialists. *Journal of Vocational Behaviour*, 1972, **2**, 133–141.

Eden, D. and Jacobson, D. Propensity to retire among older executives. *Journal of Vocational Behaviour*, 1976 **8**, 145–154.

Ekerdt, D. J. et al. Longitudinal changes in preferred age of retirement. *Journal of Occupational Psychology*, 1976, **49**, 161–169.

Emerson, A. R. The first year of retirement. *Occupational Psychology*, 1959, **33**, 197–208.

Erikson, E. H. The problem of ego identity. *Journal of the American Psychoanalytical Association*, 1956, **4**, 56–121.

European Economic Community Commission. *Community guidelines on flexible retirement*. COM (80), 393 (final), Brussels, July 14, 1980.

Fillenbaum, G. G. The working retired. *Journal of Gerontology*, 1971, **26**, 82–89.

Fleisher, D. and Kaplan, B. M. Characteristics of older workers: implications for restructuring work. In P. K. Ragan (Ed.), *Work and retirement: Policy issues*. Los Angeles: Andrus Gerontology Center, 1980.

Fozard, J. L. and Popkin, S. J. Optimizing adult development: ends and means of an applied psychology of ageing. *American psychologist*, 1978, **33**, 975–989.

Friedmann, E. A. and Havighurst, R. J. (Eds.). *The meaning of work and retirement*. Chicago: University of Chicago Press, 1954.

Friedmann, E. A. and Orbach, H. L. Adjustment to retirement. In S. Arieti (Ed.), *American handbook of psychiatry*. Vol. 1. New York: Basic Books, 1974.

Gechman, A. S. Without work, life goes . . . . *Journal of Occupational Medicine*, 1974, **16**, 749–751.

Glamser, F. D. Determinants of a positive attitude towards retirement. *Journal of Gerontology*,1976, **31**, 104–107.

Hayes, J. and Nutman, P. *Understanding the unemployed. The psychological effects of unemployment*. New York: Tavistock, 1981.

Haynes, S. G. *Mortality around Retirement and the Socio-Medical Correlates of Early Death among Retirees in the Rubber Industry*. Unpublished doctoral dissertation, Chapel Hill, University of North Carolina.

Heron, A. and Chown, S. *Age and function*, Boston: Little, Brown, 1967.

Hildebrand, P. Psychological problems of the over forties. In C. L. Cooper and D. Torrington (Eds.), *After forty: The time for achievement?* Chichester: Wiley, 1981.

Jacobson, D. Willingness to retire in relation to job strain and type of work. *Industrial Gerontology*, 1972A, **13**, 65–74.

Jacobson, D. Fatigue-producing factors in industrial work and pre-retirement attitudes. *Occupational Psychology*, 1972B, **46**, 193–200.

Jacobson, D. Planning for retirement and anticipatory attitudes toward withdrawal from work. *British Journal of Guidance & Counselling* 1974, **2**(1), 72–83.

Jaffe, A. J. The retirement dilemma. *Journal of Industrial Gerontology*, 1972, **14**, 1–89.

Jung, C. G. *Jung's collected works*, Vol. 8. London: Routledge & Kegan Paul, 1960.

Kahn, R. L. On the meaning of work. *Journal of Occupational Medicine*, 1974, **16**, 716–719.

Kasl, S. V. *The impact of retirement*. In C. L. Cooper and R. Payne (Eds.), Chichester: Wiley, 1980.

Kasterbaum, R., et al. The ages of me: Towards personal and interpersonal definitions of functional ageing. *Ageing and Human Development*, 1972, **3**, 197–211.

Kimmel, D. C., et al. Retirement choice and retirement satisfaction. *Journal of Gerontology*, 1978, **33**, 575–585.

Lazarus, R. H. Cognitive and coping processes on emotions. In A. Moviat and R. S. Lazarus (Eds.), *Stress and Coping*. New York: Columbia University Press, 1977.

Lazarus, R. H. and Launier, R. Stress related transactions between person and environment. In L. A. Pervin and M. Lewis (Eds.), *Internal and external determinants of behavior*. New York: Plenum, 1978.

Le Gros Clark, F. *Age and the working lives of men*. London: Nuffield Foundation, 1959.

Ludwig, E. G. and Eichorn, R. L. Age and disillusionment: a study of value change with ageing. *Journal of Gerontology*, 1967, **22**, 59–65.

McGoldrick, A. E. *Early retirement: A new leisure opportunity?* Paper presented at the conference of the Leisure Studies Association, London, April 1982.

McGoldrick, A. E. and Cooper, C. L. Early retirement for managers in the US and the U.K. *Management International Review*, International Business Information, 1978a, **3**, 35–43.

McGoldrick, A. E., and Cooper, C. L. Early retirement: the appeal and the reality. *Personnel Management*, 1978b, **July**, 25–28, 41.

McGoldrick, A. E., and Cooper, C. L. Voluntary early retirement—Taking the decision. *Employment Gazette*, 1980, *August*, 859–864.

McGoldrick, A. E. and Cooper, C. L. Retiring early—to start another job. *The Times*, November 10, 1981, 17.

McMahan, C. A. and Ford, T. A. Surviving the first five years after retirement. *Journal of Gerontology*, 1955, **10**, 212–215.

Makeham, P. *Economic aspects of the employment of older workers*. Research Paper No. 14. London: Department of Employment, 1980.

Martin, J. and Doran, A. Evidence concerning the relationships between health and retirement. *Sociological Review*, 1966, **14**, 329–343.

Medical Research Council. *Ageing and the semi-skilled: A survey in manufacturing industry on Merseyside*. MRC Memorandum No. 40, London: HMSO, 1961.

Messer, E. A. Thirty-eight years is a-plenty: Early retirement survey. *Civil Service Journal*, 1964, **5**(2), 6–24.

Miller, D. R. The study of Social Relationships: situations, identity and social interaction. In S. Koch (Ed.), *Psychology: A study of a science*, Vol. 5. New York: McGraw-Hill, 1963.

Miller, S. J. The social dilemma of the aging leisure participant. In A. M. Rose and W. A. Peterson (Eds.), *Older people and their social world*, Philadelphia: F. A. Davis, 1965.

Miller, S. J. *The dilemma of a social role for the ageing*. Papers in Social Welfare, No. 8, Meller Graduate School, Brandeis University, Waltham, Mass. 1965.

Morgan, J. What with inflation and unemployment, who can afford to retire? In M. W. Riley (Ed.), *Aging from birth to death—Interdisciplinary perspectives* AAAS Selected Symposium. Boulder, Colo.: Westview Press, 1979.

Morse, N. E. and Weiss, R. S. The function and meaning of work and the job. *American Sociological Review*, 1955, **20**, 191–198.

Murrell, H. *Work stress and mental strain: A review of some of the literature*. Work Research Unit Occasional Paper No. 6, London: Department of Employment, January 1978.

Neugarten, B. L. Adult personality: toward a psychology of the life cycle. In B. L. Neugarten (Ed.), *Middle age and aging*. Chicago: University of Chicago Press, 1968(a).

Neugarten, B. L. Age norms, age constraints and adult socialization. In B. L. Neugarten (Ed.), *Middle age and aging*. Chicago: University of Chicago Press, 1968(b).

Neugarten, B. L. and Datan, N. Sociological perspectives on the life cycle. In R. C. Atchley and M. M. Seltzer (Eds.), *The sociology of aging: Selected readings*, 1976. Belmont, Calif.: Wadsworth Publishing.

Nuffield Foundation, *Workers nearing retirement*. London: Nuffield Foundation, 1963.

O'Toole, J. Work in America and the great job satisfaction controversy. *Journal of Occupational Medicine*, 1974, **16**, 710–715.

H. L. Orbach, et al. (Eds.), *Trends in early retirement*. Michigan: Institute of Gerontology, University of Michigan, Wayne State University. Occasional Papers in Gerontology No. 4., 1969.

Owen, J. P. and Belzung, L. Consequences of voluntary early retirement: a case study of a new labor force phenomenon. *British Journal of Industrial Relations*, 1967, **5**, 162–189.

Palmore, E. The relative importance of social factors in predicting longevity. In E. Palmore and F. C. Jeffers (Eds.), *Prediction of the life span*. Lexington, Mass.: Heath Lexington Books, 1971.

Parker, S. *Older workers & retirement*. Office of Population censuses & Surveys, Social Survey Division (U.K.) for the Department of Health & Social Security. London: HMSO 1980.

Parnes, H. S. et al. *The pre-retirement years: Five years in the work lives of middle-aged men*, Vol. 4. Washington: U.S. Department of Commerce, 1974.

Pollman, A. W. Early retirement: a comparison of poor health to other retirement factors. *Journal of Gerontology*, 1971, **26**, 41–45.

Price, K. F., Walker, J. W., and Kimmel, D. C. Retirement timing and retirement satisfaction. *Aging and Work*, 1979, **2**, 235–245.

Quinn, J. Microeconomic determinants of early retirement: a cross-sectional view of white married men. *Journal of Human Resources*, 1977, **12**, 329–346.

Quinn, R. P. and Sheppard, L. J. *The 1972–73 quality of employment survey.* Ann Arbor: Institute for Social Research, University of Michigan, 1974.

Riley, M. W. and Foner, A. *Aging and society. An inventory of research findings.* Vol. 1. New York: Russel Sage Foundation, 1968.

Rosen, B. and Jerdee, T. H. The nature of job-related age stereotypes. *Journal of Applied Psychology,* 1976a, **61**, 180–183.

Rosen B. and Jerdee, T. H. Too old or not too old? *Harvard Business Review,* 1977b, **November-December**, 97–108.

Rowe, A. R. The retired scientist: the myth of the aging individual. In J. F. Gubrium (Ed.), *Time roles, and self in old age.* New York: Human Sciences Press, 1976.

Ryser, C. and Sheldon, A. Retirement and health. *Journal of the American Geriatrics Society,* 1969, **17**, 180–190.

Schaie, K. W. Rigidity-flexibility and intelligence: a cross-sectional study of the adult life span from 20–70. *Psychological Monographs,* 1958, **72**, No. 9.

Schaie, K. W. and Labouvie-Vief, G. Generational versus ontogentetic components of change in adult cognitive behaviour: A fourteen-year cross-sectional study. *Developmental Psychology,* 1974, **10**, 305–320.

Schmitt, N., et. al. Comparison of early retirees and non-retirees. *Personnel Psychology,* 1979, **32**, 327–340.

Schmitt, N., et. al. Retirement and life satisfaction. *Academy of Management Journal,* 1979, **22**(2), 282–291.

Schmitt, N., and McCune, J. T. The relationships between job attitudes and the decision to retire. *Academy of Management Journal,* 1981, **24**, 795–802.

Shanas, E., et al. *Old people in three industrial societies.* New York: Atherton Press, 1968.

Sheppard, H. L. A perspective on the status of older Americans in today's job market. In H. L. Sheppard (Ed.), *New perspectives on older workers,* Kalamazoo, Mich.: Upjohn Institute for Employment Research, 1971.

Sheppard, H. L. Work and retirement. In R. H. Binstock and E. Shanas (Eds.), *Handbook of aging and the social sciences.* New York: Van Nostrand Reinhold, 1976.

Sheppard, H. L. and Belitsky, H. A. *The job hunt.* Baltimore: Johns Hopkins Press, 1966.

Sheppard, H. L. and Herrick, N. Q. *Where have all the robots gone? Worker dissatisfaction in the 1970s.* New York: Free Press, 1972.

Singer, J. *Round table discussion: Current issues in stress research.* American Psychological Association Annual Convention (1978), 1979.

Streib, G. F. Morale of the retired. *Social Problems,* 1956, **3**, 270–276.

Streib, G. F., and Thompson, W. E. Personal and social adjustment in retirement. In W. Donahue and C. Tibbitts (Eds.), *The new frontiers of aging,* Ann Arbor: University of Michigan Press, 1957, 43.

Streib, G. F. and Schneider, C. J. *Retirement in American society: Impact and process.* Ithaca, N. Y.: Cornell University Press, 1971.

Thompson, G. B. Work versus leisure roles: an investigation of morale among employed and retired men. *Journal of Gerontology,* 1973, **29**(3), 339–344.

Thompson, W. E. Pre-retirement anticipation and adjustment in retirement. *Journal of Social Issues,* 1958, **14**, 35–45.

Thompson, W. E. and Streib, G. F. Situational determinants: health and economic deprivation in retirement. *Journal of Social Issues,* 1958, **14**, 18–34.

Thompson, W. E., Streib, G. F., and Kosa, J. The effect of retirement on personal adjustment. *Journal of Gerontology,* 1960, **15**(2), 165–169.

Thurnher, M. Goals, values and life evaluations at the pre-retirement stage. *Journal of Gerontology*, 1974, **29**, 85–96.

Tyhurst, Salk, L., and Kennedy, M. Mortality, morbidity, and retirement. *American Journal of Public Health* 1957, **47**, 1434–1444.

U.S. Bureau of Census. *Historical statistics of the United States*. Washington, D.C.: U.S. Government Printing Office, 1975.

U.S. Department of Labor. *Employment and Training Report to the President*. Washington, D.C.: U.S. Government Printing Office, 1978.

Walker, J. W. and Lazer, H. L. *The end of mandatory retirement. Implications for management*. New York: Wiley, 1978.

Walker, J. W. and Price, K. F. Retirement policy formulation: A systems perspective. *Personnel Review*, 1976, **5**(1), 39–43.

Walsh, D. A. Age differences in learning and memory. In D. S. Woodruff and J. E. Birren (Eds.), *Aging: Scientific perspectives and social issues*. New York: Van Nostrand, 1975.

Weg, R. B. Changing physiology in aging: normal and pathological. In D. S. Woodruff and J. E. Birren (Eds.), *Aging: Scientific perspectives and social issues*. New York: Van Nostrand, 1975.

Work in America: Report of a special task force to the Secretary of Health, Education and Welfare. Cambridge: MIT Press, 1973.

CAUSES AND CONSEQUENCES OF STRESS FROM THE DOMAIN OF NONWORK

Part Four expands the scope of the book by reporting the causes and consequences of stress in people's nonwork lives. In Chapter 8 Bhagat discusses the popular concept of personal life stress and describes its effects on people's work lives, crossing the boundary between the work and nonwork domains.

Segovis, Bhagat, and Coelho, in Chapter 9 describe further the stressful life events concept, proposing principles related to the way in which people become aware of and appraise these events.

CHAPTER EIGHT

The Role of Stressful Life Events in Organizational Behavior and Human Performance

RABI S. BHAGAT

The process of human stress and cognition in organizations can be conceptualized as comprising three major conceptual domains: the sources of stress, the mediators of stress, and the manifestations of stress. Each of these domains subsumes a variety of important constructs that have been studied in recent years. In our search for sources and mediators of stress, considerable interest has been directed to various job- and organization-specific sources of stress as well as various conditions capable of mediating the impact of stressful circumstances such as coping and social supports. A careful overview of the large literature that deals with these domains would reveal important achievements mixed with certain critical deficiencies. One of the major deficiencies is the lack of concern for the role of stressful life events in organizational behavior and human performance. It is especially striking given that the research on psychological effects of major life events has burgeoned in the past 20 years since the publication and popularization of the Holmes—Rahe scale of life-change events (Holmes and Rahe, 1967). This research on stressful life events has considerable potential for helping us gain a more complete understanding of how individuals in their work roles function when they are confronted with stressful experiences in their work as well as non-work lives.

The purpose of this chapter is to review some of the important findings on the etiology of stressful life events in causing psychological disturbance and to explore their significance in organizational behavior and human performance.

RESEARCH ON STRESSFUL LIFE EVENTS

The foundation of life events research can be traced to W. B. Cannon (Dohrenwend and Dohrenwend, 1974; Mason, 1975). Cannon (1929) proposed and demonstrated with animals that emotion-provoking stimuli can produce the physiological and bodily alterations necessary for flight or fight (e.g., increased blood sugar and adrenalin, circulatory changes, more red corpuscles, rapid clotting, etc.). Cannon argued that the existence of stimuli that evoke strong reactions leads to persistent derangement of bodily functions. In support for his propositions, Cannon based his arguments on clinical cases of pathology that appeared to follow directly severe emotional trauma in the lives of patients. Thus, Cannon's research and observations suggested that traumatic events are capable of producing physiological reactions that could indeed lead to illness if not properly discharged or eliminated. This argument was later extended by Meyer (1951) who trained physicians to utilize a life chart as a diagnostic device. Meyer suggested that life events might be important factors in the etiology of disease and that these events need not necessarily be *pathogenic* in order to produce physiological reactions and illness. That is, ordinary changes in the lives of people, such as births, deaths, and job changes, might play a part in the etiology of disease. Since World War II the relationship between stressful life events and psychological disturbance has been investigated in three major ways. First, there have been studies dealing with psychiatric effects of particular events such as soldiers' reactions to different degrees of combat (Grinker and Spiegal, 1945; Star, 1949) and psychiatric adjustments of concentration camp survivors (Eitinger, 1964). Second, there are studies of events–disorder relationships which examine the effects of multiple events in the lives of random samples of adults or children. The effectiveness of this approach was enhanced with the development of life event scales particularly the Holmes–Rahe Social Readjustment Rating Scale (SRRS) (Holmes and Rahe, 1967). These studies have focused on the cumulative impacts of various types of events, weighted or unweighted by their readjustment values, on respondents' reported levels of psychological disturbance and illness (Myers et al., 1971, 1974; Dohrenwend and Dohrenwend, 1974, 1981; Brown and Harris, 1978). Third, there have been several investigations that compared the number and severity of life events experienced by psychiatric patients prior to hospitalization to those experienced by non-patient control subjects (Birley and Brown, 1970; Paykel et al., 1975; Paykel, 1979). Findings of these studies enable the researchers to identify stressful

events that might precipitate serious psychiatric disorders such as schizophrenia, psychotic depression, and suicide attempts.

The existence of a causal relationship between stressful life events and
illness is clear from the well established studies conducted in the tradition
of clinical, social, and medical sciences. However, the fact that severe
stressful personal life events cause serious depression and illness is hardly
a new idea. Physicians, psychiatric social workers, religious leaders, and
individuals who are concerned with health and emotional well being have
long been aware of the etiological significance of stressful life events or
personal life stresses. Harold S. Kushner's best-selling *When Bad Things
Happen to Good People* is a good case in point. Confronted with the impending death of his 3-year-old son Aaron, Kushner began to seriously question
the theological significance of why bad things happen to good people. In his
preface to the book, he says that he ". . . wanted to write a book that could
be given to the person who has been hurt by life—by death, illness or
injury, rejection or disappointment . . . ." He wanted to highlight those
theological processes that confuse people during times of such severe
distresses and to show how people can find strength and hope during such
crises. No wonder then that since Holmes and Rahe's early attempts at
developing the Schedule of Recent Experiences (SRE), numerous investigations have focused on the predictive relationships between life stress
and various indices of mental health, psychosocial adjustments, and illness (Dohrenwend and Dohrenwend, 1974, 1981). Given the etiologic as
well as popular significance of stressful life events, it is therefore surprising to note the striking lack of concern among organizational researchers.
Earlier research by Kornhauser (1965) and Kahn and co-workers (1964)
have focused on some of the important antecedents of industrial mental
health, but the role of stressful life events on individual work behavior was
not considered. Only recently studies by Vicinio and Bass (1978), Kobasa
(1979), and Kobasa and associates (Kobasa et al., 1982; Kobasa and
Pucetti, 1983) which deal with stressful effects of life events on executive
performance and illness have suggested the need for a new area of inquiry
in human stress and cognition in organizations. In this chapter I discuss
some research themes that I believe have relevance for examining the role
of stressful life events in organizational behavior and human performance.

*Theme I: It Would Be Most Efficient to Focus on Those Dimensions of
Life Events Which Have Been Found to Be Most Predictive of Psychological Disturbance in Earlier Studies in the Field of Medical Sciences,
Clinical and Social Psychology.*   Holmes and Rahe and their associates
suggested and have continued to argue that the crucial quality of life
events that produces illness is change as measured by the total amount of
adjustments required by events (Holmes and Rahe, 1967; Masuda and
Holmes, 1967; Rahe, 1974; Holmes, 1979). However, there is another
school of thought suggesting that the crucial quality of life events is their
undesirability as opposed to the total amount of change or adaptations that

events may generate. At least 20 studies have examined the comparative predictive efficacies of the total amount of change and total undesirable change in the prediction of psychological disturbance. Events were classified on the basis of either researchers' or judges' evaluations of their cultural or social desirability or on the basis of each respondent's unique subjective ratings of each event on some ordinal scale (e.g., positive–negative, desirable–undesirable, etc.). The evidence is overwhelming: psychological disturbance is more highly correlated with total undesirable change than with the total amount of change *per se*. In a similar vein, a recent study by Bhagat et al. (in press) has found that negative total life stress is more predictive of organizational outcomes and withdrawal behaviors compared to positive total life stress. The consistency of findings of these studies also reveals that undesirable life event changes are superior predictors of psychological outcomes compared to total amount of changes *per se*. In addition, several of these studies demonstrate that when effects of undesirable events are controlled, total life event changes fail to predict psychological outcomes. I believe it is important for organizational researchers to focus on the cumulative effects of those undesirable events which have been found to be predictive of psychological distress. This line of research will be more useful compared to one focusing on the cumulative changes of all events experienced by the individual.

Theme 2: In Order for Organizational Research on the Role of Stressful Life Events to Have Theoretical as Well as Practical Implications, It Would Be Necessary to Focus on the Psychological Properties of the Events Themselves. This theme is related to the earlier theme. Social psychological theories of helplessness have demonstrated that the experience of undesirable, uncontrollable events often result in harmful psychological effects (Glass and Singer, 1972; Schmale, 1972; Seligman, 1975; Abramson et al., 1978). In more specific terms, research on these theories have shown that when aversive events which are also perceived to be *uncertain* occur in the people's lives, feelings of helplessness and hopelessness would result. These feelings in turn could generate psychological disturbance such as depressive symptoms. In addition, it has been found that existence of such events also lead to chronic disturbance (Silver and Wortman, 1980).

In terms of the components of the model of stress as proposed in Chapter 1, I suggest that events occurring fairly unexpectedly and leading to uncertain psychological outcomes (Bhagat, 1980) are quite stressful. Such stressful experiences get more intense when these uncertain outcomes are related to other important outcomes whose resolution take a fairly long period of time (i.e., when the duration of the existence of those uncertainties are extended over time). Thoits (1983) notes that a majority of the life events researchers have not made full use of the findings of the helplessness literature. I believe it is important in future research designs to explore the psychological properties of life events in terms of the postulates of learned helplessness theories and to examine the joint occurrence of undesirability and uncontrollability which affect subjective states of uncertainty, importance, and duration.

Theme 3: In Addition to Measuring and Estimating the Impact of Life Event Changes, It Would Be Important to Incorporate the Stressful Effects of Daily Hassles. Recently, Lazarus and associates (Kanner et al., 1981; DeLongis et al., 1982) have advanced an alternative approach to conceptualizing and measuring stress, one that brings in additional information concerning the irritating, frustrating, distressing demands and troubled relationships that affect individuals day in and day out. They suggest that some of these hassles are transient while others are chronic in nature. These hassles are distinguished from traumatic life event changes in the sense that hassles are more commonplace. The hassles scale which Lazarus and associates designed include stresses like misplacing or losing car keys, filling out routine forms, constant concern about dieting, and so on. Kanner et al. (1981) have found that this strategy of measuring stress seems to be more useful than that of life events in predicting psychological outcomes and somatic illness. They argue that hassles should have a stronger relationship to health outcomes compared to major events because they are more *proximal* measures of stress as opposed to life events which are *distal*. While it is tempting to think of hassles as being byproducts or outcomes of life events themselves, many hassles have little or almost no relationship to life events and the correlation between life events and daily hassles is relatively weak. Therefore, as DeLongis et al. (1982) have argued the construct of hassles makes an independent contribution to adaptational outcomes and experience of illness. I believe this line of research will have important implications for furthering our knowledge of how stressful life events might affect organizational behavior and human performance. Hassles such as having to clean up snow covered driveways, commuting to work in unreliable transit systems, fear of being robbed in the company parking lot, and having to cook meals for children alone after divorce are quite troublesome and do have significant consequences for organizational outcomes. It would be wise to supplement life events approach with "hassles" in order to gain a fuller understanding of how individuals react to and cope with stresses while performing in their organizational roles.

Theme 4: Organizational Researchers Should Focus on the Joint Influences of Both Stressful Life Events and Stressful Organizational Events. A recent study by Bhagat and his co-workers (in press) demonstrates that greater understanding of the effects of stress on organizationally valued outcomes and withdrawal behaviors is achieved when effects of life stresses are considered in addition to the effects of stresses that are already inherent in the job. Bhagat (1983) has proposed a conceptual model that incorporates the joint role of life-specific and organization-specific stresses. It would be important in future research to examine the additive, curvilinear, and interactive effects of these two kinds of stress. Most researchers assume that effects of life events are additive; that is, cumulative effects of three life events are more severe than two, and two more than one. These assumptions certainly seem to be supported by research as has already been mentioned. But as Brown and Harris (1978) have shown, these additivity assumptions have not been tested systematically. Thoits (1983) suggests that systematic comparisons might reveal functions other than an additive one. It is also possible as Bhagat (1983) has argued that individuals might attempt to compensate the effects of stressful life events by attempting to overperform in their work roles. Such attempts might have the effects of distorting the magnitude of the impacts of stressful organizational events on psychological distress and health status. The point is that researchers should not *necessarily* accept the validity of the additivity assumption while estimating the effects of both kinds of stresses on measures of employee behavior and performance in organizational contexts. It would be important to evaluate the full range of alternative ways of testing the interactive effects that might characterize the way job stresses and life stresses combine.

Theme 4: Moderating Influences of Various Individual Coping Skills, Social Support Mechanisms, and Relevant Organizational Factors Should Be Investigated.   Currently, there is considerable interest among researchers to explore the range of moderating influences that exist on stress–strain relationships in organizational contexts. It would be necessary to expand this list of moderating variables to include such factors as family-based social support, organizational control systems, employee career stage, and so on. The conceptual model proposed by Bhagat (1983) should aid in this process. Therefore, the full range as well as the significance of these moderating variables is not discussed. For details, the reader is referred to Bhagat (1983).

IMPLICATIONS OF FUTURE RESEARCH ON STRESSFUL LIFE EVENTS FOR ORGANIZATIONAL BEHAVIOR AND HUMAN PERFORMANCE

As research by Bhagat et al. (in press) and Cooke and Rousseau (1983) demonstrate, the impact of stresses that occur outside the employee's organizational role have important implications for both affective and behavioral outcomes. The process is also quite complex and the interactions are not necessarily linear as Bhagat (1980, 1983) has argued. The intent of this chapter is to encourage researchers to look beyond the immediate boundaries of the work organization and examine the significance of stress in the employee's life outside as well as within the work situation. The development of a research tradition that incorporates the joint influences of both work and non-work consideration in the prediction of organizational behavior and human performance should be an immediate concern for researchers in the field of human stress and cognition in organization.

REFERENCES

Abramson, L. Y., Seligman, M. E., and Teasdale, J. D. Learned helplessness in humans: Critique and reformulation. *Journal of Abnormal Psychology*, 1978, **87**, 49–74.

Bhagat, R. S., McQuaid, S. J., Lindholm, H., and Segovis, J. Total life stress: A multi-method validation of the construct and its effects on organizational outcomes and withdrawal behaviors. *Journal of Applied Psychology*, in press.

Bhagat, R. S. Effects of personal life stress upon individual performance effectiveness and work adjustment processes within organizational settings. James McKeen Cattell Invited Address delivered to the Division of Industrial and Organizational Psychology, American Psychological Association (J. R. Hackman, Chair), Montreal, 1980.

Bhagat, R. S. Effects of stressful life events on individual performance effectiveness and work adjustment processes within organizational settings: A research model. *Academy of Management Review*, 1983, **8** (4), 660–671.

Birley, J. L. T. and Brown, G. W. Crises and life changes preceding the onset of relapse of acute schizophrenia: clinical aspects. *British Journal of Psychiatry*, 1970, **116**, 327–333.

Brown, G. W. and Harris, T. O. *Social origins of depression: A study of psychiatric disorder in women*. New York: Free Press, 1978.

Cannon, W. B. *Bodily changes in pain, hunger, fear and rage*. New York: Appleton, 1929.

Cooke, R. A. and Rousseau, D. M. Relationship of life events and personal orientations to symptoms of strain. *Journal of Applied Psychology*, 1983, **3**, 446–458.

DeLongis, A., Coyne, J. C., Dakof, G., Folkman, S., and Lazarus, R. S. Relationship of daily hassles, uplifts and major life events to health status. *Health Psychology*, 1982, **1**, 119–136.

Dohrenwend, B. S. and Dohrenwend, B. P. (Eds.) *Stressful Life events: Their nature and effects*. New York: Wiley, 1974.

Dohrenwend, B. S. and Dohrenwend, B. P. (Eds.). *Stressful life events and their contexts*. New York: Prodist, 1981.

Eitinger, L. *Concentration camp survivors in Norway and Israel*. London: Allen and Unwin, 1964.

Glass, D. C. and Singer, J. E. *Urban stress: Experiments on noise and social stressors*. New York: Academic Press, 1972.

Grinker, R. R. and Spiegal, J. P. *Men under stress*. New York: McGraw-Hill, 1945.

Holmes, T. H. and Rahe, R. H. The social readjustment rating scale. *Journal of Psychosomatic Research*, 1967, **11**, 213–218.

Holmes, T. H. Development and application of a quantitative measure of life change magnitude. In J. E. Barrett (Ed.), *Stress and mental disorder*. New York: Raven Press, 1979.

Kahn, R. L., Wolfe, D. M., Quinn, R. P., Snoek, J. D., and Rosenthal, R. A. *Organizational stress: Studies in role conflict and ambiguity*. New York: Wiley, 1964.

Kanner, A. D., Coyne, J. C., Schaefer, C., and Lazarus, R. S. Comparison of two modes of stress measurement: Daily hassles and uplifts versus major life events. *Journal of Behavioral Medicine*, 1981, **4**, 1–39.

Kushner, H. S. *When bad things happen to good people.* New York: Schochen Books, 1981.

Kobasa, S. C. Stressful life events, personality and health: An inquiry into hardiness. *Journal of Personality and Social Psychology*, 1979, **37**, 1–11.

Kobasa, S. C., Maddi, S. R., and Pucetti, M. C. Personality and exercise as buffers in the stress–illness relationship. *Journal of Behavioral Medicine*, 1982, **5**, 391–404.

Kobasa, S. C. and Puccetti, M. C. Personality and social resources in stress resistance. *Personality and Social Psychology*, 1983, **45** (4), 839–850.

Kornhauser, A. *Mental health of the industrial worker.* New York: Wiley, 1965.

Masada, M. and Holmes, T. H. Magnitude estimations of social readjustments. *Journal of Psychosomatic Research*, 1967, **11**, 219–225.

Mason, J.W. A historical view of the stress field, Part I. *Journal of Human Stress*, March 1975, 6–12.

Meyer, Adolf. The life chart and the obligation of specifying positive data in psychopathological diagnosis. In E. E. Winters (Ed.) *The Collected papers of Adolf Meyer*, Vol III. Baltimore: Johns Hopkins Press, 1951, pp. 52–56.

Myers, J., Lindenthal, J. J., and Pepper, M. P. Life events and psychiatric impairment. *Journal of Nervous and Mental Disease*, 1971, **152**, 149–157.

Myers, J. K., Lindenthal, J. J., and Pepper, M. P. Social class, life events and psychiatric symptoms: A longitudinal study. In B. S. Dohrenwend and B. P. Dohrenwend (Eds.), *Stressful life events: Their nature and effects.* New York: Wiley, 1974.

Paykel, E. S. Causal relationships between clinical depression and life events. In J. E. Barrett, (Ed.), *Stress and mental disorder.* New York: Raven Press, 1979.

Paykel, E., Prusoff, B. A., and Myers, J. K. Suicide attempts and recent life events. *Archives of General Psychiatry*, 1975, **32**, 327–333.

Rahe, R. H. The pathway between subjects' recent life change and their near-future illness reports: Representative results and methodological issues. In B. S. Dohrenwend and B. P. Dohrenwend (Eds.), *Stressful life events: Their nature and effects.* New York: Wiley, 1974.

Schmale, A. H. Giving up a final common pathway to changes in health. *Advances in Psychosomatic Medicine*, 1972, **8**, 20–40.

Silver, R. L. and Wortman, C. B. Coping with undesirable life events. In J. Barber and M. E. P. Seligman (Eds.) *Human helplessness: Theory and its applications.* New York: Academic Press, 1980.

Star, S. A. The screening of psycho-neurotics in the army: Technical development of tests. In S. A. Stouffer et al. (Eds.), *Studies in social psychology in World War II*, Vol. 4. Princeton, N. J.: Princeton University Press, 1949.

Thoits, P. A. Dimension of life events that influence psychological distress: An evaluation and synthesis of the literature. In H. B. Kaplan (Ed.), *Psychosocial stress: Trends in theory and research.* New York: Academic Press, 1983.

Vicino, F. L. and Bass, B. M. Life space variables and managerial success. *Journal of Applied Psychology*, 1978, **63**, 81–88.

CHAPTER NINE

The Mediating Role of Cognitive Appraisal in the Experience of Stressful Events

A Reconceptualization

JAMES C. SEGOVIS, RABI S. BHAGAT, AND GEORGE V. COELHO

"Sticks and stones may break my bones, but names will never hurt me!" Children growing up in America who are exposed to this folklore intuitively understand that the impact of an event on their emotions (how they feel) depends on their perceptions of it (how they perceive it). People interpret the stresses from their jobs and their personal lives in different ways (Lazarus and Delongis, 1983; Sarason et al., 1978; Mueller et al., 1977; Vinokur and Selzer, 1975). Some individuals ignore the event; others may find it threatening; and still others may judge it as beneficial (Lazarus, 1966). They can also modify the impact of the event (a stressor) by downgrading its importance or focusing on its benefits. Selective perception, therefore, operates as a psychological process that determines the level of stressfulness of an event and the individual's response to it. How people perceive and evaluate events becomes crucial for their mental and physical well-being. This theme can be seen in the following examples:

1.   Gerhard Schramm, 58, was an apparent suicide victim. He bled to death of a shotgun wound to the chest. He was severely depressed after the

loss of his family hog business. An expanded successful farm quickly became a disaster as a result of high interest rates, increased feed costs, greatly decreased hog prices, and an outbreak of disease. He sold the family assets at a very large loss. According to his wife: "It immobilized him. He felt that he had failed. One of the first things my husband told me was that it didn't really matter what people thought. But it did." Mrs. Schramm, in spite of this failure, chose to live and find a new life typing and learning shorthand. Other farmers with similar problems found outlets for these tremendous pressures in racquetball, dancing, or religion (Waterloo, 1982).

2.   Two married professionals (one a lawyer and the other a professor) each had a crucial presentation due on the same day. Both were under considerable pressure from their employers and personal ambitions. When they awoke that morning, two of their three young children had chicken pox. They could not take them to the day-care center or find a babysitter. After an emotional discussion, the husband stayed home in order to support his wife's legal career. He decided that his children and marriage had higher priority than his career. Also, the couple determined that the consequences of his not doing the presentation had fewer costs. He began to create alternative strategies to still give the presentation and reduce the consequences. What was initially a highly stressful experience evolved into a manageable situation. What was first seen as crucial was then viewed as important. The date was no longer unalterable. Though this decision would create some negative impressions among his peers and superiors, he saw his decision as an opportunity to succeed in his personal life where others in his organization had failed.

3.   An engineer for a major electronic computer firm looked forward to his transfer and promotion into sales. He saw this as an opportunity in an area of the company that was growing. After a short period of time this "opportunity" was seen as a nightmare. The depressed economy prevented him from achieving his quota of sales. His superior demanded more of him, in spite of the fact that the key elements in the sales decision were beyond his control. The superior defined the problem in terms of the lack of ability on the part of this engineer. If only he had tried harder and he had the "right" attitude, everything could have worked out. After several months he was laid off, in spite of being a loyal and effective employee during his tenure of 10 years. He experienced considerable distress at this state of affairs. Fortunately, his friends in his previous community stayed in close contact. His friends not only offered helpful information pertaining to other jobs, but also helped in maintaining his self-esteem. They supported his appraisal of the events as to how he was "screwed to the wall" by the company.

These examples highlight the major themes of this chapter. In the case of the farmer a family business failure situation was interpreted differently by the spouses concerned. For the husband it signified despair with no future options. For the wife, though the loss was greatly stressful, it was judged to be temporary. She could visualize a future with different opportunities. In the second case of the professional couple, the appraisal of the event changed in a relatively short period of time. What was defined as "crucial" was redefined as being less "crucial." An "unalterable" picture of one's predicament became "alterable." Uncertainty about the future was reduced, and the problem became manageable. The third and final case shows that social information plays an important role in how one appraises a stressful event. The engineer's friends offered more than what is usually understood as social support—that is, emotional, informational, and structural resources (see Chapter 14). They helped sustain his sense of worth and competence. Their assessment played a key role in influencing the engineer's redefinition of the situation.

Cognitive appraisal, then, plays a powerful role in shaping the efficacy of individual coping behaviors in stressful situations. It is an emotionally toned and judgment-based process. Interpretations are made about the future importance of a situation for an individual's well-being (Lazarus, 1966). These redefinitions of the meaning of events are complex and dynamic. They mediate transactions occurring between the individual and the environment.

The purpose of this chapter is to elucidate the appraisal mechanisms that operate when an individual is confronted with stressful life events, including stressors on the job. Our literature review has identified several conceptualizations of this process, but they tend to be somewhat limited, focusing on one set of variables to the exclusion of other relevant ones. Also, there is a limited amount of empirical research dealing with earlier conceptualizations. Our discussion attempts to fill in these gaps by presenting an integrative framework of cognitive appraisal. In contrast to earlier formulations, we emphasize the need to view cognitive appraisal as having cognitive, social, and contextual determinants. According to our view this process consists of three phases: staging, judgment, and enactment. We explain each phase in terms of the interrelationships among the key variables within the phase as well as between the phases. Several propositions pertaining to these relationships are presented. Finally, we discuss the utility of this alternative conceptualization for researchers and practitioners in the field of organizational stress.

AN INTEGRATIVE FRAMEWORK FOR COGNITIVE APPRAISAL: AN OVERVIEW

Cognitive appraisal can be conceived as unfolding in three phases: staging, judgment, and enactment. The *staging phase* (Figure 9-1) entails the interplay among an individual's cognitive complexity, social contextual information, and the event's attributes. The outcome of this interaction leads to a redefinition of the event in subjective terms. The redefined event is further redefined at the *judgment phase* (Figure 9-2). There is an interaction among an individual's assessment processes, attributions, and belief patterns in determining whether the event is perceived as stressful and what to do about it if it is. At the end of the judgment phase the individual forms certain hypotheses relating to his or her hopes, expectancies, and coping strategies. The final phase, *enactment*, includes self-fulfilling prophecies (Figure 9-3). In this phase an individual has chosen one or more of the response alternatives based on the hypotheses formulated in the judgment phase. The responses help him or her cope with the redefined event with varying degrees of effectiveness. They also create a new situational perspective that affects future actions in the stressful environment. These behaviors confirm previous event redefinition and hypotheses and hence help recreate the environment the individual has constructed. From Figure 9-3 it may appear that coping precedes enactment. However, it is conceivable that there exist situations where coping and enactment are integral to each other and may occur simultaneously.

We suggest two caveats in understanding interrelationships among these phases. First, we should not view them as being composed of distinct and linear interactions. Stress exists in the form of a transaction between the individual and the environment (Lazarus and Delongis, 1983; Lazarus and Launier, 1977; Coyne and Lazarus, 1980). A dynamic interplay within as well as between the various phases characterizes this process. A unidirectional flow of events cannot adequately explain the cognitive, social, and situational exchanges that occur between the individual and the stressful environment. Thus, in our integrative framework a reciprocal interdependence is emphasized. Second, in contrast to some earlier views of appraisal as primarily a conscious, unemotional, and logical process, judgments concerning an event's stressfulness can be unintentional and unconscious (Lazarus, 1982). A person does not necessarily carefully weigh the time or temper the facts inherent in a given situation and reach a cool unhurried decision. There are definite cognitive limits to effective information processing, and in highly ambiguous situations, one could indeed be appraising an event without much intentional control (March, 1978; Weick, 1983). In addition, emotions are fused with cognitions (Folkman et al., 1977; Lazarus, 1982), and separation of the two may not occur in most situations. When a person appraises an event as a threat, an emotional response often accompanies it. The interpretation of the situation could indeed be associated immediately with fear, anger, anxiety, and other emotions. Besides being fused with emotions, cognitions may also distort reality through their association with irrational beliefs (Ellis, 1962; Meichenbaum, 1977). At times these irrational beliefs may be a source of stress, and at other times they may aid in short-term coping through illusions (Katz et al., 1977).

THE STAGING PHASE: EVENT REDEFINITION

Event Redefinition

Cognitive appraisal has been viewed as a redefinition process (Hackman, 1970). An objective event in a stressful situation or nonstressful situation is "redefined" by the individual to make it consistent with his or her needs, values, and goals before work activity begins (see Figure 9-1). The task is perceived and coded in order to make it fit a person's psychological needs. This redefinition process is also affected by the degree to which a person understands and accepts the task, as well as by how it matches his or her previous experiences in similar situations. Task-relevant ability also affects this redefinition process. A transaction between the task and the person begins. This transactional process is mediated by the social context and cognitive complexity of the individual. The objective event transforms into a psychological event. It fits into a set of existing schemata. In our

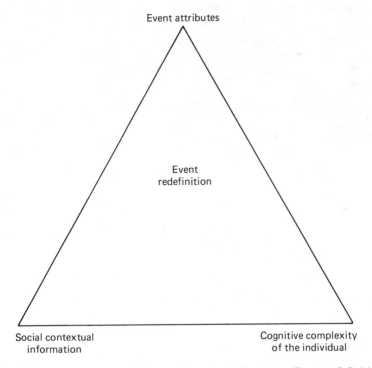

Figure 9-1 Staging phase of the cognitive appraisal process: Event redefinition.

conceptualization the staging phase of event redefinition initiates the cognitive appraisal process.

Cognitive Complexity

Cognitive complexity plays an important role in how an event is redefined. It affects the degree of fit of a given stressful event with a person's psychological makeup. To understand the importance of cognitive complexity in interpreting an event, we provide an overview of a typology of individual complexity in information processing and then discuss the implications of different types of complexities in terms of their roles in helping to redefine a stressful event.

Human information processing abilities may be conceptualized along a continuum of cognitive complexity within which individuals function with varying degrees (Brainerd, 1978; Inhelder and Piaget, 1958; Wadsworth, 1979). There are people who are relatively *concrete* in their cognitive styles, and there are some who think in more *abstract* terms. Two interdependent attributes have been identified in the way people process environmental information (Schroder et al., 1967). The first, differentiation, is concerned with one's ability to differentiate among various relevant dimensions of a stressful event. It usually results in being able to recognize and then process apparently incompatible informational cues concerning an event. Differentiation is characterized by (1) the number of dimensions that are perceived as being relevant, (2) the number of perspectives that can be generated about these dimensions, (3) the extent to which decisions concerning how to discern the differences among these dimensions are delayed, and (4) the openness to increasing incremental information. Another component of cognitive complexity that is relevant for redefining the event is the extent of integration that an individual employs after some amount of differentiation is accomplished (Scott et al., 1979). Integration is concerned with one's ability to organize and connect the relevant dimensions in multiple ways so as to generate new and contrasting views about the event. Integration is characterized by (1) how an individual uses the preexisting cognitive schemes to combine the various dimensions, (2) how many rules and procedures are used to combine the dimensions, and (3) how many interconnections among the rules and procedures are available to form alternative perspectives for comparing a variety of cognitive outcomes.

The two components of differentiation and integration combine in redefining a stressful event. Individuals who do not differentiate and integrate well have the following characteristics. Their view of the world is structurally simple. There is often little room for fine discrimination or internal conflict. What does not fit into a preexisting category is likely to be ignored or inappropriately categorized, leading to a premature closure that inhibits generation of alternative perspectives. Gross environmental features of the stressful event predominate in the redefinition process.

One shapes one's responses in a relatively undifferentiated fashion. On the other hand, individuals who are more complex differentiate and integrate more in the redefinition process and are more concerned with understanding the eventual significance of the event in terms of other preexisting schemata. Their cognitive structure allows for greater tolerance of dissonant information, including a capacity to invoke new ways to explain events and discover patterns in these events.

One would expect cognitively complex individuals to perform better under pressure than cognitively simple ones, given the focus of the earlier discussion. However, this may not be a straightforward process (Schroder et al., 1967). In situations characterized by extreme levels of environmental complexity and time pressures, there is little difference in the way the two types of individuals approach the event. In situations characterized by only moderate levels of environmental complexity and pressure, however, cognitively simple individuals filter out considerably more relevant information and cues, as compared with complex individuals. They therefore receive less information about various dimensions of the situation as environmental complexity increases. This may lead to several dysfunctional outcomes, including interpersonal hostility, poor communication styles, and reduced efficacy in coping. Integratively complex persons differentiate more aspects of the environment and seek a variety of informational cues, especially those aspects that may not be readily available. Integratively simple individuals, on the other hand, are likely to attend more to external authority figures and a few salient cues and to differentiate and integrate less information as uncertainty increases (Schroder et al., 1967). Cognitively complex individuals are more sensitive to a broader range of information, including those cues that are not necessarily specific to the given situation. Indeed, these individuals may desire increasingly uncertain and complex environments (Ungson et al., 1981). Such situations may be appraised as opportunities leading to eustress, that is, a kind of stress that is pleasant, curative, or energizing (Selye, 1976).

As one might surmise by now, it should not be assumed that cognitively complex individuals necessarily perform better than simple individuals in all situations. Two other contingencies could exist that would complicate interpreting the performance of these two groups. First, most of the research has focused on general responses of complex and simple individuals in a range of environmental complexity and time pressures. Yet it is possible that complex individuals may compartmentalize different parts of their lives, so as in certain situations they act as cognitively simple. On certain types of life tasks they may respond in a relatively rigid and simplistic fashion due to prior experiences that have created beliefs and social needs that have blocked their growth in these conceptual areas. For example, an executive may approach his or her pressured job with a highly proficient style. Yet when it comes to handling the life tasks of his or her marriage, children, and friendships, he or she may be found to be immature and inept (Maccoby, 1976). A second contingency would be that different tasks require different cognitive skills for success (Schroder et al., 1967; Staw et al., 1981). If a task is complex but the criterion for judging success is relatively simple, then cognitively simple individuals may perform better than cognitively complex individuals. An example would be a task requiring responses to salient information from one unchanging source. A production operator reacts to his or her superior's demand for higher production at *all* costs in a moment of crisis. He or she might push subordinate personnel for higher productivity, ignoring standards of quality, morale, and equipment maintenance. This operator would be considered successful since output is the only goal. A cognitively complex person, on the other hand, might analyze the production system and be more sensitive to the long-term implications of such behavior. However, this person might receive an inferior evaluation since the immediate, short-term output would be judged to be below expected levels. When the task criterion for performance increases in complexity (i.e., several aspects of performance, including aspects related to long-term effectiveness, are taken into consideration), then complex individuals are likely to be evaluated as performing in a superior manner. Such tasks usually involve discrepant information and flexible integration strategies. Stress-reducing strategies that emphasize simplifying one's life could well be dysfunctional unless one is likely to be evaluated by a simple criterion. This kind of emphasis on simplification would restrict integration of information concerning other relevant alternatives. In situations involving complex performance criteria, for example, in research and development and upper levels of management, one could indeed perform better by developing a perspective that is cognitively more complex than simple.

In perceiving the world in a more complex fashion, an individual matches the complexity of the task with his or her own levels of cognitive complexity. A perspective emphasizing cognitive complexity may offer an explanation of one's experienced stress that is theoretically more robust than a perspective that emphasizes the role of personality types (e.g., tolerance for ambiguity, locus of control, or Type A/B behaviors). For example, individuals with high tolerance for ambiguity may take into account relevant dimensions of the stressful events and possess more flexible adaptation patterns. Similarly, when people perceive themselves to be in control, it is probable that they may have conceptualized the situation more efficiently. It is conceivable that individuals with internal loci of control could indeed learn to increase their cognitive complexities as environmental complexity increases.

Proposition 1. In a stressful situation, cognitive complexity affects the nature of the transaction between the individual and the environment in redefining the event. Cognitively complex individuals assess relevant environmental attributes of the event in more detailed and variable terms than do cognitively simple ones.

Social Information

Few formulations of cognitive appraisal (Lazarus, 1966, 1982; Mechanic, 1977) have explored the significance of social cues or processes in the appraisal process. We suggest that a perspective that focuses on the role of social cues is valuable. Social cues and social information (Weick, 1975; Pfeffer and Salancik,1977) are useful because they interact with a person's cognitive complexity and situational attributes in the redefinition process. When encountering a relatively novel and stressful situation that provides fewer cues to help decide upon a course of action, social cues and norms become important. One's peers and socially significant others provide sources of information about how to label the situation in order to reduce uncertainty. They provide an interpretation of what the event means and how one should respond to it. This process is so significant that psychosomatic reactions often can be moderated by social cues and information (McGrath, 1977; Pfeffer and Salancik, 1978; Lazarus, 1982). This was demonstrated in an experiment by Schachter and Singer (1962) where participants were injected either with a drug which causes physiological arousal or witha placebo. The injections were described as a vitamin supplement. One group of subjects was forewarned about the symptoms of the drug, such as heart palpitations and shaking hands; others were not. Thus, one group had an explanation for their physical reactions, and the other did not. In experimental groups a confederate was to act in a euphoric manner in one situation and angry in another. When the physical reactions began, subjects experienced uncertainty. In situations where "appropriate" cues for labeling their unexpected and unknown emotions were available through the confederate's behavior, the majority of group members reacted either in a euphoric or an angry manner. In groups who were either forewarned or had received the placebo, the confederate's behavior had comparatively little effect. The meaning of the physiological reactions was less ambiguous. It was less necessary to have socially relevant others define the situation. When one's peers model or label certain behaviors as stressful, one may use these cues to redefine one's confused emotions. People act to confirm and provide social validation for interpreting environmental cues (Weick, 1975; Pfeffer and Salancik, 1973). This effect has been noticed in sensory deprivation experiments where outcomes depend upon whether a person has received prior information concerning how to react to and experience sensory deprivations (McGrath, 1977). Mechanic (1977, p. 246) found that in stressful situations, individuals often sought "comforting cognitions" by favorable comparisons with one's peers and then finding additional social cues that reinforce such a redefinition process. In a similar vein Kobasa et al. (1982) have provided evidence that lawyers are relatively unaffected by similár stressful episodes, compared with executives because of a relative nonsalience of social cues in appraising such episodes in their work environment. Their research indicates that in the managerial environment, a given stressful episode may be perceived as uncontrollable. Managers are often told by various stress management consultants, as well as by their peers, that work stress can severely affect their health and well-being. However, in the work environment of the lawyers such social cues are generally absent, and therefore such redefinition processes rarely take place. Social comparison processes provide reference norms about the level of stressfulness that is appropriate in a given work situation.

The importance of contextual information in redefining the social reality of a person under stress can be further evidenced in a study of two young men who became permanently crippled in accidents (Adams and Lindemann, 1974). One man persisted in maintaining an image of himself as being sick and disabled. Such an image was reinforced by his family and friends. They mirrored his disappointment and helped sustain his refusal to take responsibility for himself. They denied his physician's prognosis and corroborated his fears. The other young man, however, successfully adapted. His family and significant others played a different role. They maintained an early facade of hope but then quickly adjusted with minimal distress when it became apparent that he was a quadriplegic. His parents modified their home with ramps and wider doorways. A great amount of emotional support and information was given, which helped the young man master his emotional distress and develop a new role for himself. His family helped him appraise himself as an independent person instead of reinforcing a sense of dependency. They managed his fears of being crippled and reinforced the idea of being "permanently different" with positive expectations about future activities.

The impact of social information will vary with different levels of cognitive complexity. Since cognitively simple individuals are less sensitive to situational contexts, they would be significantly more threatened by incongruent information from their social peers. Even though these individuals might conform to similar beliefs held by others, effects of social information are likely to be minimal (Aronson, 1980). On the other hand, cognitively complex individuals are considerably more attuned to social cues and other relevant contextual features. Highly complex individuals usually utilize a "generalized other" (Mead, 1934) as their reference. Although these individuals might refer to the experiences of significant others in stressful situations, their redefinition processes are largely a product of past experiences with other perspectives (Schroder et al., 1967).

Many social cues as to whether an individual should feel or act stressed may be communicated by language metaphors. Weick (1970) labels this "stress rhetoric." Language provides a mechanism for sharing cultural assumptions about the situations in which we find ourselves (Sproull, 1982). We use them as commonly understood cues, especially in conditions of uncertainty. Words (such as, *hassle, pressure, beat, deadline, stress,* and recently, *burned out*) are rich in their symbolic persuasiveness to help redefine a situation as stressful under ambiguous circumstances. These metaphors help create a mind set that blocks alternative interpretations of the event. They evoke an interpretation of "stress" as a class of events that is different from interpretations that do not emphasize stressfulness of the event.

Proposition 2.   Social cues and information embedded in the context affect the redefinition process in the appraisal of stressful events. In addition, the influence of social information has its most pronounced effect in uncertain, equivocal, and ambiguous situations.

Proposition 3.   Individuals with moderate levels of cognitive complexity are likely to be most influenced by social cues and information.

Event Attributes

An event's characteristics vary on three dimensions: time sequencing, complexity, and consequences. All of these dimensions interact in helping to redefine the event. First, an event, whether it is work and, or, personal life oriented, has a certain time sequencing (Warburton, 1979; Hackman, 1970; Schroder et al., 1967). An event may be perceived as stressful when it has either a high or a low rate of presentation and requires either a fast or a slow response, as long as the response is important (see Chapter 1). Depending upon the rate of change of the information's presentation and demands, different levels of uncertainty can be created for the individual. There can be conditions of information proliferation or restriction (characterized respectively as overload and underload). A second attribute of the event is its inherent complexity (Hackman, 1970; Schroder et al., 1967; Ungson et al., 1981). A complex event is likely to elicit competing redefinitions. Information pertaining to the desired outcomes is not readily available. Such events would typically be characterized as being equivocal (Weick, 1979). The event has multiple determinants and messages that require extensive examination over a fairly long period of time in order to resolve inherent ambiguities and conflicts of interpretation. The complexity of the situation is sometimes increased by the uniqueness of the event and by discrepancies with previously understood causes perceived by the individual (Schroder et al., 1967). A third attribute that is also relevant in the redefinition process is the importance of physical and psychological consequences of the event (Schroder et al., 1967; Hackman, 1970). An event may consist of an inherent threat with adverse consequences. An event could be punishing, or full of interruptions. It may also provide a pleasurable way of reaching one's desired objectives. It may facilitate a eustress reaction (Selye, 1976). An example of this eustress reaction would be found in a person receiving a promotion resulting in an opportunity to work with stimulating colleagues on a challenging project.

Cognitive complexity will interact with the event's time sequencing and complexity. Depending on whether an individual is cognitively complex or not, the attributes of the event get defined accordingly. An array of issues or aspects could either be misinterpreted or ignored by a cognitively simple individual. This would be especially true if the situation is characterized by overload and complexity. It could then be so overwhelming that, in order to avoid a feeling of helplessness, the individual may resort to a simplifying strategy (e.g., attack) as the only alternative. On the other hand, in a situation characterized by information underload and with relatively low degrees of complexity, a cognitively complex individual could easily feel bored. It is conceivable that some individuals might like to create some turbulence in this type of situation in order to generate sufficient environmental complexity to match their cognitive styles. Such persons thrive on excitement as a form of eustress, sometimes perceiving imaginary problems and deadlines that create crises for themselves and others. The crises provide an opportunity to feel the rush of adrenalin the body produces to meet the new challenges.

Social cues play influential roles in shaping a person's redefinition of event attributes of time sequencing, complexity, and consequences. A person's peers could help him or her to perceive certain situations as "highly pressured" even though the actual rate of time sequencing may be low. This may usually be seen in projects where everyone defines the situation as a crisis and pushes to complete the task. Afterward, the finished report is still waiting for approval on a supervisor's or client's desk. The "emergency" seems to have disappeared. In other situations the social context can alter the perceived complexity of an event. The "groupthink" phenomenon strongly reflects these processes (Janis, 1972). In the Bay of Pigs fiasco during the Kennedy administration, a highly complex situation was, by this "groupthink" process, redefined as simple to fit the preconceived notions of the decision makers.

Proposition 4. An event's attributes redefine the significance of the event in the appraisal process.

Proposition 5. An individual's cognitive complexity interacts with the attributes of the event and with social contextual information in redefining the stressfulness of the event.

THE JUDGMENT PHASE: FORMATION OF HYPOTHESES

The staging phase initiates the appraisal process by redefining the event. The redefinition process now joins the judgment phase of cognitive appraisal (Figure 9-2). In this phase an individual appraises the redefined event through an interplay of assessment processes, attributions and belief patterns. The goal of the judgment phase is to develop hypotheses concerning the event that have implications for coping and adaptation.

Hypothesis Formation

After an event is redefined and judged for its potential stressfulness, an individual then forms certain hypotheses (Hackman, 1970). Three basic types of hypotheses may be created about the redefined event. First, people form hypotheses in terms of their probable affective response (Weiner, 1972). This response may include the emotions of hope, frustration, anger, joy, despair, or anxiety. Individuals could feel overwhelmed and, or, helpless in coping with a redefined event. In another situation they might experience stress and still be confident about adopting an appropriate coping strategy. Second, people anticipate the probabilities of their success on a given task by making a subjective estimate concerning how a desired level of performance might be attained and how a given outcome for reducing the distress of the event might be achieved (Beehr and Bhagat, Chapter 1 of this book). Finally, people form hypotheses as to what per-

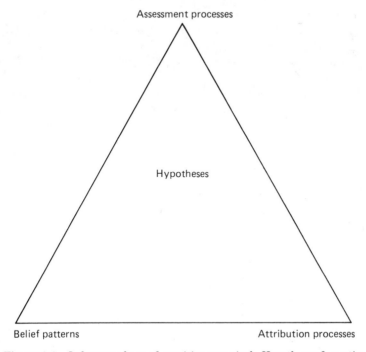

Figure 9-2 Judgment phase of cognitive appraisal: Hypotheses formation.

formance strategy is appropriate for accomplishing a given task (Hackman, 1970).

Cognitive complexity will influence the nature of the hypotheses that will be formed at this judgment stage. Cognitive complexity affects what range of environmental cues is distinguished, which ways they foster different types of affective responses, and what kinds of performance strategies are developed. For example, an abstract individual may have higher probabilities for success on an ambiguous task than a more concrete person. Also, in uncertain situations, social norms or situational constraints may encourage psychic withdrawal (Lazarus, 1966). Thoughts such as "I want to make a fool of him, but what will others think? Maybe I should wait for a while" might emerge as crucial concerns in these types of situations. Another example would be a situation where regulation of emotions becomes more crucial than performance of strategies that could lead to task accomplishment (Hackman, 1970; Lazarus and Launier, 1977). Thoughts such as "If I don't get a grip on myself, I will fall apart and really mess up!" would predominate in this situation.

Assessment Processes

In the past, cognitive appraisal has been conceptualized in terms of two evaluative themes (1) its significance for one's well-being, and (2) its effects on perceived and social resources for coping (Folkman, Schaeffer, and Lazarus, 1979; Lazarus and Launier, 1977; Lazarus, 1966). These two themes have been conceived as primary and secondary appraisals. In a recent statement Lazarus and Launier (1977) noted that such a distinction might be inappropriate. It creates the erroneous impression that these two processes are sequential and temporally spaced, as opposed to being interdependent and transactional in nature. An appraisal of an event's perceived stressfulness for one's well-being depends upon whether one judges whether he or she has the appropriate ability or resources to cope with the situation. The notion of this interdependence between the two processes is perhaps best illustrated in McGrath's (1976) definition of experienced stress.

In this conceptualization stressfulness of an event is a function of the anticipated consequences of a successful versus unsuccessful encounter with the event. First, an individual makes a decision concerning whether the consequences of the event are indeed important for one's welfare. Second, the severity of the favorableness or unfavorableness of the event is determined with respect to one's frame of reference. Third, one focuses on the uncertainty about being vulnerable. Uncertainty has been found to vary with the goodness of fit between an individual's perceived ability and the perceived demands of the stressful situation (McGrath, 1976). Experience of stress is highest when the consequences are perceived to be important and the probability of success is unknown—equivalent to the chance of a coin flip. If one judges the task to be too difficult for one's abilities or one's abilities to exceed the requirements of the task, then one would not likely experience this situation as highly stressful. However, as one perceives that (1) one's ability to gradually match the demands of the stressful event, and (2) the event has uncertainties pertaining to whether one's effort would lead to certain valued outcomes, then one is in a stressful situation (Beehr and Bhagat, Chapter 1). In McGrath's (1976) formulation the concept of uncertainty concerning a stressful event serves as an integrating mechanism between these two appraisal processes as conceived by Lazarus (1966). McGrath emphasizes that appraisals of well-being (primary appraisals) and of coping resources (secondary appraisals) are not sequentially independent and separable. What one appraises is indeed one's vulnerability in a given stressful situation.

Based on McGrath's definition, cognitive appraisal of a redefined event can be seen as a series of interrelated questions focusing on how an individual judges the event (Table 9-1). A person has to judge the relevance of these issues for his or her well-being. Successful resolution of these issues determines one's level of experienced stress.

First, the individual evaluates the significance of the event in terms of its consequences. Is it important and substantial? If not, could it be ignored (Coyne and Lazarus, 1980)? If it is important, what are some of the specific consequences that the event may trigger? The consequences of an event may exist separately or together in terms of opportunity, demand, and constraint stresses (Schuler, 1980). An event has the potential of leading to a desired opportunity, and such an opportunity could then lead to eustress. On the other hand, in a situation characterized by demand stress, one perceives a potential loss of a valued outcome. Constraint situations are characterized by a maintenance of the status quo. In demand and constraint situations, distress is likely to emerge. One feels thwarted, threatened, or pressed, and therefore has to struggle. It is possible for an event to be perceived and evaluated as having all three kinds of stresses. In writing

Table 9-1   Issues Encountered During Judgmental Processes

1. Are the anticipated consequences of the event important and substantial?
2. If yes, will the anticipated consequences be favorable or unfavorable?
   (a) Does the event present an opportunity?
   (b) Does the event present a demanding situation taxing to one's coping and adaptational resources?
   (c) Does the event prevent the accomplishment of what is desired, leading to a constraining situation?
3. If not, what are the outcomes of ignoring the event for the present and for the future?
4. How certain is one concerning one's ability to meet the opportunity, demand, or constraints that the event may present?

this chapter, for example, the authors looked forward to the challenge of finding a richer description of cognitive appraisal. At the same time, we also were concerned with working long hours, conflicts with family members, lost opportunities in other domains of life, and stringent deadlines.

When one considers uncertainty in determining the level of experienced stress, one should not consider it to be a straightforward process. The conventional wisdom treats uncertainty along a single dimension and then tends to use this term interchangeably with ambiguity. Only recently it has been postulated by Folkman et al. (1979) that this could be midleading. Judgments may vary, depending upon the nature of uncertainty that a given event may foster. Besides the probability of the occurrence of the event (event uncertainty), there are several other psychological dimensions that need consideration (Folkman et al., 1972). They are ambiguity (i.e., lack of clarity), equivocality (i.e., uncertainty of meaning due to the potential of multiple interpretations) (Weick, 1979), temporal uncertainty (i.e., timing of the event), process uncertainty (i.e., how the event unfolds over time), results uncertainty (i.e., the possible consequences of the event), and coping uncertainty (i.e, what strategies are likely to be more successful). Within an expectancy framework of stress (Chapter 1), for example, uncertainty about the probability of the event, process, and coping refers to the likelihood of how one's effort will be linked to one's performance in a given situation. Uncertainties related to both results and coping strategies reflect problems in one's ability to identify the link between one's performance and valued outcomes.

Proposition 6.   The efficacy of one's judgmental processes during hypothesis formation is governed by one's vulnerability and the types of uncertainties that the situation presents.

Attributional Processes

Individuals need to achieve cognitive mastery over their environment (Weiner, 1972). They seek to make sense of an otherwise uncertain and ambiguous world and to be cognitively consistent. They ascribe explanations for stressful events in their lives. Causal attributions could operate in different ways to influence a person's perceptions of a stressor's origins. When a person receives a threat in an uncertain environment, he or she is likely to search for ways to locate the agent of harm (Weick, 1970). Who might be responsible for the predicament? According to Lazarus' (1966) notion of cognitive appraisal, the location of the agent of harm is embedded in the secondary appraisal process. In our reconceptualization of the appraisal process, however, the mechanism surrounding the location of harm is, in essence, an attributional process.

While confronting a stressful event, an individual often asks two interrelated questions in evaluating the predicament: "Am I in power?" and

"Why did it happen?" (Weiner, 1972). These are questions about perceived control and causality. In the first instance, attributional processes serve a control function. People will tend to utilize the attribution that fosters the greatest amount of perceived control over the situation (Weick, 1970). In situations where people feel powerless, they may cope better if they externalize the threat (e.g., projection). However, if an internal attribution is made where the self is seen as the agent of harm, then it could result in guilt, depression, and defensiveness. An internal attribution may also encourage efforts toward adaptive instrumental behaviors in attempting to change the stressful situation. It has been found that individuals with a high need for achievement (n-Ach motive) are likely to make internal attributions (Weiner, 1972; Weiner and Sierad, 1975); they will ascribe their successes to ability and their failures to inadequate effort or bad luck. On the other hand, individuals with a low need for achievement will most likely make external attributions; they will attribute success to good luck and failure to task difficulty. Such causal attributions are responsible for different types of coping strategies and affective responses concerning the significance of potential stressors at the hypothesis formation stage. In stressful situations where mechanisms of feedback are considerably disrupted, high n-Ach individuals are more likely to engage in adaptive, instrumental, and coping behavior, whereas low n-Ach individuals might spend more time in regulating their emotions through projection and other defense mechanisms. High n-Ach individuals could moderate their perceptions of the event by adopting a position of "constructive worrying" (Janis, 1977) and then by culling relevant information in order to reduce uncertainty. For individuals with low achievement drives, a different scenario is likely. They initially experience lower levels of stress since they perceive themselves at the whim of fate and external causes. They are likely to withdraw from the situation since their attempts would have little effect. Another approach would be to employ beliefs characterized by one's faith and sense of stoicism. Adoption of these strategies maintains a sense of control by attributing it to forces beyond their control. It has been found that these strategies may reduce experienced stress, even though these beliefs could delay the act of dealing with the problem effectively (Katz et al., 1977). Low n-Ach individuals may create the circumstances for experiencing more stress and depression in the long term.

If one discovers favorable consequences as a result of an attribution, then that attribution is likely to be retained (Weiner, 1972). However, if the consequences are perceived as unfavorable, the search for an alternative attribution begins. Therefore, the favorableness of the consequences retrospectively and almost simultaneously monitors the attributional process. Since stressors might create more primitive appraisals and responses (Staw et al., 1981), this tendency is most likely to occur as a satisficing procedure. A person is likely to choose a reasonable attribution as opposed to a necessarily valid one (Gochman, 1979). Such an attribution is most likely in uncertain environments since many alternative interpretations are generally possible. There might be fewer externally valid indicators to judge the relevancy of one attribution as opposed to another.

Attributions concerning responsibility in stressful situations involve attempts to make an external agent accountable for the state of affairs. For example, during recessionary periods when organizations reduce personnel and increase the work load for remaining employees, a situation filled with attributional outcomes is often created. Supervisors' reactions to the problem of budget cuts and reduction of work force are "to get more organized and stop complaining" (Scott, 1983, p. 12). They attribute the stressfulness of the situation to poor ability on the part of the subordinate, while subordinates attribute their difficulties to the organizational situation created as a result of the budget cuts. A study by Beehr (1981) suggests that people experiencing stress are more likely to view their coworkers as causes of such stresses than to attribute causation to other aspects of the situation in which they find themselves. It is probable that an actor emphasizes situational issues while an outside observer might focus on personal characteristics. A tendency to perceive the most salient environmental features and distinctive individual disposition as causal (Lord and Smith, 1983; Gochman, 1979) is also present in the appraisal of a stressful event. These naive appraisals may hinder adaptive efforts. In a study of job transfers, for example, Brett (1980) explored the folklore that job transfers (salient feature) are stressful for the family. This naive attribution was not supported in her research.

The type of attributions that people use varies with their level of information processing (Lord and Smith, 1983). In perceiving relevant environmental information and in making judgments, there exist automatic and controlled attributional processes in attention, detection, and selection (Feldman, 1981). In situations where the need to process information is relatively low, automatic processes predominate (Lord and Smith, 1983). Individuals may follow scripts or mental programs, and these are well-learned behavior sequences. Individuals function with global impressions and with the most salient cues. Routine social events are handled in this fashion (Feldman, 1981). Controlled monitoring processes emerge when the incoming flow of information no longer fits the prototypes. A "threshold of discrepancy" makes the linkages between effort-performance and performance-outcomes too uncertain and triggers a search for new information to understand the situation (Feldman, 1981; Sproull, 1980).

Causal attributions foster self-fulfilling prophecies (Weick, 1970). Once an attribution is made, people take actions to confirm the conclusions and are reluctant to consider alternative scenarios. The causal attribution process enhances the threat-rigidity effects postulated by Staw, Sandelands, and Dutton (1981). As a person attempts to find attributions to control the situation, information may be restricted, and individual control could become more centralized, leading to more primitive responses.

This response confirms the individual's original appraisal, forming a self-fulfilling prophecy (Weick, 1970; Jones, 1977). This process will be further accelerated by individuals who are in a state of automatic attributional processing. An example would be the reaction of an untenured English professor at a small college to recent budget cutbacks. Seeing few employment prospects for English teachers in the country, the faculty member felt a great deal of uncertainty and, therefore, experienced severe distress. The faculty member immediately assumed that his job was in jeopardy. He suspected that the area chairman did not like him, and began to blame the chairman for failing to protect faculty in the political budget in-fighting. In spite of information to the contrary, he began to act with hostility toward the chairman, thus putting him on the counteroffensive. This only compounded the problem since it encouraged the chairman to react negatively. If the chairman had any doubts concerning the competence of the faculty member, they were further confirmed in a "self-fulfilling" vicious circle, and the chairman could then use the cutbacks as excuses to terminate him.

The self-fulfilling prophecy effect of causal attribution is further illustrated in Weick's work on ambiguity and its relationship to attributional processes. A situation of ambiguity makes locating the agent of harm more difficult. In an ambiguous situation fewer cues exist, and this allows a person to blame whatever agent he or she chooses and to create explanations that are the most reasonable. Under these circumstances ambiguity enhances the likelihood that the most characteristic cognitive style will emerge that will enable an individual to cope. The causal attribution is adapted to his or her idiosyncratic needs and transitory mood (Gochman, 1979). Therefore, this would compel a person to confirm this attribution. His or her self-concept may be at stake. A considerable amount of energy will be used in maintaining this causal attribution in highly ambiguous situations. This is consistent with recent theorizing about the reasons individuals use to escalate their commitment to a course of action (Staw, 1981).

Proposition 7.   Causal attributions will have a direct effect on the type of judgments made about the potential stressfulness of an event and the type of hypotheses generated.

Belief Patterns

In appraisal processes, categorization is essential in the selective retention of large amounts of information (Weick, 1977, 1979; Feldman, 1981). We have category prototypes that are "fuzzy sets" of relevant attributes (Feldman, 1981). These category prototypes are used to compare and contrast information. One makes judgments concerning people and situations based on what he or she perceives from a prototype. One possesses a package of fairly rigid and stereotyped cause-effect relationships to impose on a stream of experience (Norman and Rumelhart, 1975; Weick, 1977, 1979). One makes inferences and fills in details on what is perceived.

These prototypes are cognitive scripts that contain one's beliefs about how the world operates (George, 1974; Sproull, 1980; Ungson et al., 1981). They contain the norms, standards, and criteria for strategy selection. The cognitive scripts explain why individuals seem to maintain their original diagnoses and automatic attributions in spite of contrary evidence. In novel situations people continue to use common frameworks of reference (Goffman, 1974, 1959). Much of human behavior can be characterized by a process of tacit action with unintended consequences that individuals reflexively monitor (Giddens, 1979). People rationalize reasons for and make sense of their actions after having performed them (Weick, 1979). This process is further fostered by memories that amalgamate over time (Loftus and Loftus, 1976). Our memories of events are revised with the slow assimilation of information. In essence, we learn by analogy when we impose an old memory upon a new experience (Sternberg, 1977) in order to make decisions. Most social behavior, therefore, becomes a function of past experiences rather than of the present (Kuhn, 1974; Payne, 1978). People are governed by automatic processes based on habits (Ungson et al., 1981). Individuals create solutions and then search for appropriate problems that fit into them (Weick, 1979).

Category prototypes and cognitive scripts play a considerable role in hypothesis formation. Individuals maintain an internal dialogue with themselves, drawing upon cognitive scripts that entail stress-producing belief patterns (Meichenbaum, 1977). These belief patterns may contain statements such as "I must move, I must hurry.", "I can't make mistakes.", "This is too much for me.", or "I can't keep on top of things!" that promote different beliefs about the causal properties of their work processes versus their environments. With work processes workers believe they have control over multiple paths to a goal even when they do not. On the other hand, when these beliefs concern controlling the environment, they see few alternatives. In each of these examples of cognitive scripts, the belief patterns encourage people to react with firm expectations that will most likely elicit the expected, that is, a self-fulfilling prophecy (Snyder and Swann, 1978). A classic example of this problem may be Type A/B personalities (Friedman and Rosenman, 1974; Chesney and Rosenman, 1980). The Type A person possesses belief patterns that foster competitive, impatient behavior. The individual has built a cognitive prototype of the world that leads to the beliefs that one must hurry, struggle, possess, and push. In working with individuals with these characteristics, coworkers would most likely react negatively to the imposed deadlines, impatience, and aggressiveness. As people begin to act negatively and hesitate, this validates the Type A person's prototype of the world as a competitive and hostile place that needs structure. This imposes a relatively stronger need to control his or her environment and to increase the pace of his or her activities (Glass, 1977). On the other hand, a Type B personality's characteristics would suggest belief patterns that view the world as unhurried and less demanding. Therefore, they would generate hypotheses that foster a different reaction. If an environment is less malleable to a Type B's efforts to implement deeply ingrained cognitive scripts, the results would be costly. For example, Type B individuals have greater levels of hypertension than Type A individuals in air traffic control positions (Chesney and Rosenman, 1980).

Proposition 8. Belief patterns affect the nature of the hypotheses that are formed in the cognitive appraisal process. Belief patterns interact with judgmental and attributional processes in shaping the hypotheses.

The Enactment Phase

The third phase of the cognitive appraisal process centers on enactment processes. After an event is redefined and some hypotheses are formulated, an individual begins to cope with the situation. The mental health literature on coping is extensive, and clinical issues are not discussed here (Coelho and Irving, 1981). However, what is relevant for our understanding of cognitive appraisal is the notion of "enactment" (Weick, 1979) because enactments might affect the efficacy of future efforts that an individual might attempt in redefining stressful events. Enactment processes link the outcomes of coping with the two elements of the initial staging phase: social cues and event properties.

Enactment may be defined in terms of two basic forms of bracketing of experiences and retrospective actions (Weick, 1979). In the first form people bracket some portion of their stream of experiences for further monitoring. By this act of selective attention, individuals choose a selected portion of the environment for making sense of it. Aspects of stressful situations with which people could not cope are ignored because they might have the potential of altering one's redefinition of the stressful event created at the staging phase. Enactment helps create a simulated environment, which helps maintain cognitive consistency. What is accomplished is a creation of an internally consistent order in the mind of the focal person that may not be isomorphic with the objective situation as perceived by other actors. A scenario of interrelated cognitions is created, which is comforting for the individual in a highly subjective sense (see Figure 9-3).

In bracketing of experiences, people may ignore alternative redefinitions of a situation and might not be sensitive to other relevant hypotheses that could as well be generated. Individuals may experience something as threatening based on how they enact after coping with the event, when

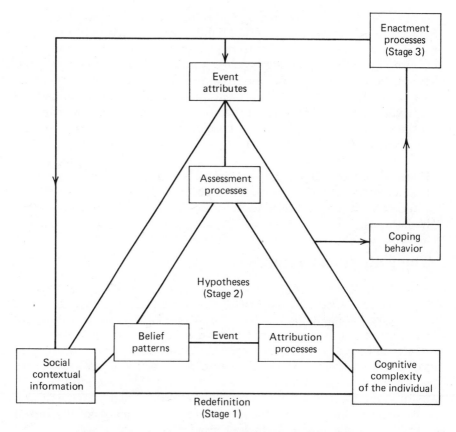

Figure 9-3   An integrative cognitive appraisal framework.

indeed benign, challenging, or other kinds of "bracketing" or "sense-making" would be equally valid. Weick (1975) illustrates this with an example of a professor who has experienced stress writing publishable manuscripts. He might have suffered family difficulties, physical discomfort, job-related conflicts, and rejection of some of his previous professional efforts. He perhaps perceives writing a paper under these circumstances as a dreadful event. However, if he is enacting this scenario, he could as well be ignoring other relevant environmental cues that might tell a different story. He could also make sense of this event by enacting it differently. For example, the professor could have interpreted his feelings as being irritable rather than stressful. He is irritable from uncomfortable summer weather, being oversensitive to everyday problems due to being older, or recognizing that all writers face temporary instead of unending pain at the start of a writing project. A person could also make sense of his feelings by accepting his ambivalent tendencies (Weick, 1975). The professor, in this case, would acknowledge his capacity to produce work filled with insights and mistakes. He could then interpret his feelings as a sign of the normal excitement of doing a worthwhile but difficult task. Since the task is complex, it will have many opportunities for errors. He could see a scenario of a quality product evolving in several smaller stages with a number of rewrites. This would "bracket" an experience as being manageable and energizing. The essence of all these possible examples lies in the fact that images of stressfulness can be superimposed when alternative interpretations are equally valid. In equivocal situations individuals can utilize the multiple images and meanings of an event to increase their sensitivity toward nuances, defuse their uncertainty from demands and constraints, and produce different coping patterns.

The second form of enactment occurs when an individual acts and then the results of the actions constrain future actions. The enacted environments begin to foster their distinctive meanings for the individual. The conditions that were imposed by actions based on previous redefinitions and hypotheses begin to be rediscovered. Cognitions may trail one's actions (Weick, 1979; Salancik and Pfeffer, 1978). The enacted behavior helps create an environment which is then used to reconstruct the meaning of one's social cues and properties of the event. The enacted behavior provides new information to help interpret what has occurred (Aronson, 1980). For example, if a person enacts the situation in a Type A fashion, then this behavior will be rediscovered in the individual's future appraisal of the stressful event. According to this interpretation, stress-related predispositions can easily be the result of one's enactment. Stress may well be reinvented and constructed as opposed to being assessed in a relatively static fashion. For example, in our earlier illustration of the job cutback situation in which the English teacher experienced a great deal of stress, it was also possible that he could have enacted a different scenario. He could have redefined the situation and perhaps enacted differently. The following options could have been visualized as well: (1) tutoring students in one's home; (2) writing technical manuals for electronics firms; or (3) undergoing career change. Such options might have helped in (1) appraising the "budget cut" situation in a rather unique way, and (2) reducing distress.

Proposition 9. Enactment intervenes between coping and the redefinition of a stressful event.

Proposition 10. Stress predispositions such as Type A/B behavior patterns are psychological outcomes of enactment processes based upon individuals' prior attributions and beliefs.

CONCLUSION

In reconceptualizing cognitive appraisal, our approach to an integrative framework has the following distinct advantages. First, the model integrates divergent thinking on this topic. Attribution and redefinition processes, for example, have been discussed earlier as being related to cognitive appraisal. Yet these processes were not conceptualized as being integral to cognitive appraisal, and having interactive relationships with each other. Second, the model recasts earlier descriptions of cognitive appraisal in a multidimensional framework. In determining the significance of an event for one's well-being and assessing one's reasons for coping, as originally conceived by Lazarus (1966), other cognitive processes occur that make it more than a simple straightforward process. For example, an event in one model cannot be taken for granted as unidimensional; as we have seen, the event's attributes interact with social cues and with an individual's cognitive complexity and are redefined in psychological terms for the individual. Lazarus's notion of primary and secondary appraisals can be enriched by picturing a redefined event becoming further redefined by an interaction among judgments of uncertainty, attributions, and beliefs. Third, the integrative model incorporates previous stress research on cognitive processes with cognitive appraisal. Cognitive complexity and belief patterns, for example, help researchers predict individual differences in appraising events as stressful. Finally, the model is designed to enhance one's understanding of cognitive appraisal by considering the effects of social information and enactment processes. The relevance of social cues has been briefly considered before in stress literature, but there has been little regard for its relationships with cognitive appraisal and coping. Similarly, enactment has not been thoroughly explored in the cognitive appraisal literature as an alternative explanation of the impact of coping in altering the significance of the environmental milieu. This is especially significant since appraisal must be considered as an ongoing process of interpreting the continuous flow of events in terms of one's self-esteem and adaptive behavior in problem solving.

The integrative model also offers some guidelines for future research on cognitive appraisal. One may not assume simple cause-effect relationships between the environmental stressor and the individual. Life event surveys, such as Holmes and Rahe's (1967), fail to capture a considerable amount of the variance in people's perceptions of life stressful events. Stress exists as a series of transactions between the individual and the environment, and cognitive appraisal unfolds as part of this transaction. In order to capture the complexity of the appraisal process, researchers should move away from static approaches to qualitative and longitudinal designs (Coyne and Lazarus, 1980). Multidimensional measures need to be utilized to measure the different phases of cognitive appraisal. The types of uncertainty an individual judges to be present need to be measured since they may reveal different qualities of experienced stress (Folkman et al., 1979). Also, instead of relying on measures of stress predispositions, researchers need to emphasize the relational process among attributions, beliefs, and enactments. Based on attributional effects, researchers should reconsider the use of role stress measures. Previous research on job stress has focused on expectations of coworkers on the focal person's work role as significant determinants of job stress. In a sense other people are attributed to be the locus of ambiguous and conflicting expectations. These attributions tap the salient cues perceived by the focal person, but may miss other situational cues and the person's personal characteristics in the redefinition process.

The integrative model also provides some guidelines to practitioners. Organizations need (1) to consider the significance of social and contextual cues as sources of stress, and (2) to focus on the psychological impact of situational properties. Do wall colors suggest warmth or aggressiveness? Managers might consider the labels and images and rhetoric that others use to describe stressful situations. It is important to avoid labels such as "sick," "crippled," or "bogged-down." If these words enact dysfunctional cognitive scripts, perhaps more constructive labels could be utilized to help individuals redefine the situation. Such words could be "different," "challenge," "opportunity," "overly-sensitive," "unique," or "creative." Cognitive restructuring therapies have provided supportive evidence for the effectiveness of these strategies (Meichenbaum, 1977). These techniques often go beyond the positive thinking approaches by considering the situation's attributes, social cues, attributions, belief scripts, and enactments. Individuals learn how to evaluate and cope with a stressful episode depending on the cultural rhetoric or imagery it evokes.

In situations of equivocality there might be a variety of interpretations available. What might be challenging to one could indeed be a situation of overload for another. Individuals might take advantage of these different plausible interpretations to reduce their stress by redefining their situations (Weick, 1975). Since behavior might be interpreted in a restrospective manner, people could be encouraged to choose from the variety of explanations. Beliefs and attributions can be modified by reinterpreting past events with newer perspectives. For example, instead of saying: "These phone calls are nothing but interruptions!", one could reinterpret the event as: "These phone calls are an essential part of my job." Childbirth classes reflect the significance of this approach by emphasizing the pain of childbirth as being manageable and indeed part of a natural process. Art has been used in transforming stressful images into more pleasurable ones. An individual describes his or her pain in pictures and then redraws himself or herself experiencing less pain. Pain reduction has been an outcome in several individuals where this technique was used (Langarten, 1981). These results may be due to attribution processes. The person no longer ascribes his or her pain to external forces but to self-induced efforts. Cognitive dissonance research has obtained similar results (Aronson, 1980).

A FINAL WORD

Our analysis suggests that as we are moving into an infinitely more complex world (Naisbitt, 1982), we ought to develop more complex mindsets to redefine and cope with these information-rich and sociotechnically complex organizations. It might be useful for management educators to emphasize the long-term significance of human cognitive abilities in the management of human resources. One ought to go beyond the conceptions of a "one minute manager" (Blanchard and Johnson, 1982) in understanding the effectiveness of the management process.

The integrative model of cognitive appraisal casts doubts on the efficacy of simplifying one's life in order to reduce stress. In order to deal with complicated situations, people need to utilize alternative responses and interpretations. Individuals might increase their cognitive abilities to discriminate and integrate information under these conditions (Weick, 1975). The more complex the event stressor, the more cognitively complex one should learn to be.

REFERENCES

Adams, J. E. and Lindemann, E. Coping with long-term disability. In G. V. Coelho, D. A. Hamburg, and J. E. Adams (Eds.), *Coping and adaptation.* New York: Basic Books, 1974.

Aronson, E. *The social animal*, 3rd ed. San Francisco: W. H. Freeman, 1980.

Beehr, T. A. Work-role stress and attitudes toward coworkers. *Group and Organization Studies*, 1981, **6**, 201–210.

Blanchard, K. and Johnson, S. *The one minute manager.* New York: William Morrow, 1982.

Brainerd, C. J. *Piaget's theory of intelligence.* Englewood Cliffs, N.J.: Prentice-Hall, 1978.

Brett, J. M. The effect of job transfer on employees and their families. In C. L. Cooper and R. Payne (Eds.), *Current concerns in occupational stress*, Vol. II. Chichester: Wiley, 1980.

Chesney, M. A. and Rosenman, R. Type A behavior in the work setting. In C. L. Cooper and R. Payne (Eds.), *Current concerns in occupational stress*, Vol. II. Chichester: Wiley, 1980.

Coelho, G. V. and Irving, R. I. *Coping and adaptation: An annotated bibliography and study guide.* Washington, D.C.: National Institute of Mental Health, DHHS Publication No. (ADM) 81, 863, 1981.

Coyne, J. C. and Lazarus, R. S. Cognitive style, stress perception and coping. In I. L. Kutash, L. B. Schlesinger, and Associates (Eds.), *Handbook on stress and anxiety.* San Francisco: Jossey-Bass, 1980.

Ellis, A. *Reason and emotion in psychotherapy.* New York: Lyle Stuart, 1962.

Feldman, J. M. Beyond attribution theory: Cognitive process in performance appraisal. *Journal of Applied Psychology*, 1981, **66**, 127–148.

Folkman, S., Schaefer, C., and Lazarus, R. S. Cognitive processes as mediators of stress and coping. In V. Hamilton and D. M. Warburton (Eds.), *Human stress and cognition: An information-processing approach.* London: Wiley, 1979.

Friedman, M. and Rosenman, R. H. *Type A behavior and your heart.* New York: Knopf, 1974.

George, A. L. Adaptation of stress in political decision making: The individual, small groups and organizational contexts. In G. V. Coelho, D. A. Hamburg, and J. E. Adams (Eds.), *Coping and Adaptation.* New York: Basic Books, 1974.

Giddens, A. *Central problems in social theory: Action, structure, and contradiction in social analysis.* Berkeley: The University of California Press, 1979.

Glass, D. C. *Behavior patterns, stress and coronary disease.* Hillsdale, N.J.: Lawrence Erlbaum, 1977.

Gochman, I. R. Arousal, attribution, and environmental stress. In I. G. Sarason and C. D. Spielberger (Eds.), *Stress and anxiety,* Vol. 6. Washington, D.C.: Hemisphere Publishing Corp., 1979.

Goffman, E. *The presentation of self in every day life.* Garden City, N.Y.: Doubleday, 1959.

Goffman, E. *Frame analysis.* New York: Harper & Row, 1974.

Hackman, J. R. Tasks and task performance in research on stress. In J. E. McGrath (Ed.), *Social and psychological factors in stress.* New York: Holt, Rinehart & Winston, 1970.

Holmes, T. H. and Rahe, R. H. The social readjustment rating scale. *Journal of Psychosomatic Research,* 1967, **11**, 213–218.

Inhelder, B. and Piaget, J. *The growth of logical thinking from childhood to adolescence: An essay on the construction of formal operational procedures.* New York: Basic Books, 1958.

Janis, I. L. *Victims of group think: A psychological study of foreign policy decisions and fiascoes.* Boston: Houghton-Mifflin, 1972.

Janis, I. L. Adaptive personality changes. In A. Monat and R. S. Lazarus (Eds.), *Stress and coping.* New York: Columbia University Press, 1977.

Johnson, J. H. and Sarason, I. G. Recent development in research on life stress. In V. Hamilton and D. Warburton (Eds.), *Human stress and cognition: An information processing approach..* Chichester: Wiley, 1979, pp. 205–233.

Jones, R. A. *Self-fulfilling prophecies: Social, psychological and physiological effects of expectancies.* New York: Wiley, 1977.

Katz, J. L., Weiner, H., Gallagher, T. F., and Hellman, L. Stress, distress and ego defenses: Psychoendocrine response to impending breast tumor biopsy. In A. Monat and R. S. Lazarus (Eds.), *Stress and coping.* New York: Columbia University Press, 1977.

Kobasa, S. C., Hilker, R. R. J., and Maddi, S. R. Who stays healthy under stress? *Journal of Occupational Medicine,* 1979, **21**, 595–598.

Kuhn, A. *The logic of social systems.* San Francisco: Jossey-Bass, 1974.

Langarten, H. *Clinical art therapy: A comprehensive guide.* New York: Brunner Mazel, 1981.

Lazarus, R. S. *Psychological stress and the coping process.* New York: McGraw-Hill, 1966.

Lazarus, R. S. A cognitively oriented psychologist looks at biofeedback. *American Psychologist,* 1975, **30**, 553–561.

Lazarus, R. S. Thoughts on the relations between emotion and cognition. *American Psychologist,* 1982, **37**, 1019–1024.

Lazarus, R. S. and DeLongis, A. Psychological stress and coping in aging. *American Psychologist,* 1983, **38**, 245–254.

Lazarus, R. S. and Launier, R. Stress-related transactions between person and environment. In L. A. Pervin and M. Lewis (Eds.), *Perspectives in interactional psychology.* New York: Plenum, 1977.

Loftus, G. R. and Loftus, E. F. *Human memory, the processing of information.* New York: Wiley, 1976.

Lord, R. G. and Smith, J. E. Theoretical information processing and situational factors affecting attribution theory models of organizational behavior. *The Academy of Management Review,* 1983, **8**, 50–60.

March, J. G. Bounded rationality, ambiguity, and the engineering of choice. *The Bell Journal of Economics,* 1978, **9**, 587–608.

Maccoby, M. *The gamesman.* New York: Bantam, 1976.

McGrath, J. E. Stress and behavior in organizations. In M. D. Dunnette (Ed.), *Handbook of industrial and organizational psychology.* Chicago: Rand McNally, 1976.

McGrath, J. E. Settings, measures and themes: An integrative review of some research on social-psychological factors in stress. In A. Monat and R. S. Lazarus (Eds.), *Stress and coping.* New York: Columbia University Press, 1977.

Mead, G. H. *Mind, self, and society.* Chicago: University of Chicago Press, 1934.

Mechanic, D. Some modes of adaptation: Defense. In A. Monat and R. S. Lazarus (Eds.), *Stress and coping.* New York: Columbia University Press, 1977.

Meichenbaum, D. *Cognitive behavior modification: An integrative approach.* New York: Plenum, 1977.

Mueller, D. P., Edwards, D. W., and Yarvis, R. M. Stressful life events and psychiatric symptomatology: Change or undesirability? *Journal of Health and Social Behavior,* 1977, **18,** 307–317.

Naisbitt, J. *Megatrends: Ten new directions transforming our lives.* New York: Warner Books, 1982.

Norman, D. A., Rumelhart, D. E., and The LNR Research Group. *Explorations in cognition.* San Francisco: W. H. Freeman, 1975.

Payne, R. L. Stress and cognition in organizations. In V. Hamilton and D. M. Warburton (Eds.), *Human stress and cognition: An information-processing approach.* London: Wiley, 1979.

Rotter, J. B. Generalized expectancies for internal vs. external control of reinforcement. *Psychological Monographs,* 1966, **80,** 1–28.

Sarason, I. G., Johnson, J. H., and Siegel, J. M. Assessing the impact of life changes: Development of the life experiences survey. *Journal of Consulting and Clinical Psychology,* 1978, **46,** 932–946.

Salancik, G. R. and Pfeffer, J. A social information processing approach to job attitudes and task design. *Administrative Science Quarterly,* 1978, **23,** 224–253.

Schachter, S. and Singer, J. Cognitive, social and physiological determinants of emotional state. *Psychological Review,* 1962, **69,** 379–399.

Schroder, H. M., Driver, M. J., and Streufert, S. *Human information processing: Individuals and group functioning in complex social situations.* New York: Holt, Rinehart & Winston, 1967.

Scott, N. Overworked employees are not good business. *Dallas Times Herald,* March 16, 1983, p. 12.

Scott, W. A., Osgood, D. W., and Peterson C. *Cognitive structure: Theory and measurement of individual differences.* Washington, D. C.: Winston, 1979.

Schuler, R. S. Definition and conceptualization of stress in organizations. *Organizational Behavior and Human Performance,* 1980, **25,** 184–215.

Selye, H. *The stress of life,* rev. ed. New York: McGraw-Hill, 1976.

Shalit, B. Structural ambiguity and limits to coping. *Journal of Human Stress,* 1977, **3,** 32–45.

Sproull, L. S. Beliefs in organizations. In P. C. Nystrom and W. H. Starbuck (Eds.), *Handbook of organizational design: Remolding organizations and their environments,* Vol. 2. New York: Oxford University Press, 1981.

Staw, B. M. The escalation of commitment to a course of action. *Academy of Management Review,* 1981, **6,** 577–587.

Staw, B. M., Sandelands, L. E., and Dutton, J. E. Threat-rigidity effects in organizational behavior: A multilevel analysis. *Administrative Science Quarterly,* 1981, **26,** 501–524.

Sternberg, R. J. *Intelligence, information processing, and analogical reasoning: The componential analysis of human abilities.* New York: Wiley, 1977.

Snyder, M. and Swann, W. B., Jr. Behavioral confirmation in social interaction: From social perception to social reality. *Journal of Experimental Social Psychology*, 1978, **14**, 148–162.

Ungson, G. R., Braunstein, D. N., and Hall, P. D. Managerial information processing: A research review. *Administrative Science Quarterly*, 1981, **26**, 116–134.

Vinokur, A. and Selzer, M. L. Desirable versus undesirable life events: Their relationship to stress and mental distress. *Journal of Personality and Social Psychology*, 1975, **32**, 329–337.

Wadsworth, B. J. *Piaget's theory of cognitive development: An introduction for students of psychology and education*, 2nd ed. New York: Longman, 1979.

Warburton, D. Stress and the processing of information. In V. Hamilton and D. Warburton (Eds.) *Human stress and cognition: An information processing approach*. Chichester: Wiley, 1979.

Waterloo, C. Farm life is changed as perilous economics undermine confidence. *Wall Street Journal*, April 9, 1982, pp. 1, 11.

Weick, K. E. The "ess" in stress: Some conceptual and methodological problems. In J. E. McGrath (Ed.), *Social and psychological factors in stress*. New York: Holt, Rinehart & Winston, 1970.

Weick, K. E. The management of stress. *MBA*, 1975, **October**.

Weick, K. E. Enactment processes in organizations. In B. M. Staw and G. R. Salancik (Eds.), *New directions in organizational behavior*. Chicago: St. Clair Press, 1977.

Weick, K. E. *The social psychology of organizing*, 2nd ed. Reading, Mass.: Addison-Wesley, 1979.

Weick, K. E. Small wins: Redefining the scale of social problems. *American Psychologist*, 1984, **39**, 40–49.

Weiner, B. *Theories of motivation: From mechanism to cognition*. Chicago: Markham, 1972.

Weiner, B. and Sierad, J. Misattribution for failure and enactment of achievement strivings. *Journal of Personality and Social Psychology*, 1975, **31**, 415–421.

PART FIVE

SOCIODEMOGRAPHIC AND CULTURAL ANTECEDENTS OF STRESS RELEVANT TO THE STUDY OF ORGANIZATIONAL BEHAVIOR

Part Five expands the scope further than Part Three by examining the way in which stress varies across sociodemographic groups. Chapter 10 recognizes the special problems of women employees, a group of workers who have been around for a long time but who have been neglected until recent years in much of the work-related literature. Uncertainty, importance, and duration may arise from different sources for women and men employees.

In a somewhat parallel vein, Chapter 11 examines the experience of stress among professionals who are part of minority racial or ethnic groups. As with the women workers, the minorities face some problems that are unique to them as a group—often in addition to the stressful uncertainties they share in common with other workers.

Finally in this section, Chapter 12 brings attention to a group of workers who have attracted far less notice even than working women and minorities: the immigrants. Delving into the previously almost unexplored area of stress among this group of employees, it is proposed that poorer cultural fits result in more stressful uncertainty than better fits do.

Thus, part five examines women's large scale entrance into the work force, minority group's recent entrance into the professions, and immigrants who are entering the work force of an adopted country. Each of these groups of workers experiences stressful new situations.

CHAPTER TEN

Working Women and Stress

JAMES R. TERBORG

The experienced civilian labor force in 1979 totaled over 102 million people (U.S. Department of Labor, 1980). Nearly 43 million of those people, or 42 percent, were adult women. This marked the first time that more than half of all adult women between the ages of 20 and 65 were employed outside the home.

This chapter explores issues surrounding working women and stress. Women who work outside the home are likely to experience stress from demands and challenges associated with work and nonwork responsibilities. But, because of problems stemming from sex-role stereotypes and occupational sex discrimination, there is reason to expect an even greater likelihood of stress for women who are employed in nontraditional jobs and careers (Brief et al., 1981). Although a considerable amount has been written about the topic of working women and about the topic of stress, surprisingly little attention has been directed toward the *joint* topic of *working women and stress*. Consequently, it quickly becomes apparent that there are large gaps in what we know and what we do not know about the connection between employment for women and stress.

This chapter is organized into seven parts. It will begin with discussion of the status of women employed outside the home. Next, attention will turn to whether or not women show different rates of stress-related outcomes than do men. Third, the literature on sex differences will be reviewed in the context of personality dimensions thought to be important for understanding individual reactions to stress. This will be followed with discussion of the interface between work and life and the implications of competing demands experienced by working women. The fifth section of the paper is concerned with organizational antecedents of stress for employed women. Having reviewed the relevant literature on working

245

women and stress, I will use the concepts of *importance, uncertainty,* and *duration* (see Chapter 1 of this book) to interpret existing data and suggest directions for future research.

STATUS OF WOMEN EMPLOYED OUTSIDE THE HOME

To better appreciate connections between work and stress for working women, it would be helpful to become familiar with the status of employed women. In this section I will discuss the sex segregation of occupations, labor market experiences of employed women, the marital status and family status of employed women, and the participation and earnings of women in various.

Sex Segregation of Occupations

Garbin and Stover (1980), in their recent review of the literature on vocational behavior and career development, noted that cultural prescriptions regarding appropriate jobs for men and women are still very evident in American society. These values reflect themselves in such ways as limited career alternatives, blocked career pathways, underutilization of abilities, and fewer or smaller rewards. A nationwide opinion survey conducted by the Gallup organization (Women in America, 1976) found that nearly 30 percent of those questioned disapproved of a woman working outside of the home if her husband were capable of supporting her. The proportion was virtually identical regardless of whether the person polled was a man or a woman. Other data from the same survey show that women and men believe women make better nurses, grade school teachers, and secretaries, and men make better police officers, automobile mechanics, airline pilots, and fire fighters. These data suggesting the existence of occupational sex stereotypes are especially interesting because Arvey and Begalla (1975) found the job of homemaker to be highly similar to the jobs of both police officer and fire fighter when the Position Analysis Questionnaire (McCormick et al., 1972) was used as the basis for the job analysis.

The primary determinant of occupational sex stereotypes is the existence of widespread sex segregation across different occupations. Occupations are segregated by sex when the proportion of one sex in the occupation is substantially higher than the proportion of that sex in the available labor market. To provide some examples, consider that 2 in 100 engineers are women, 4 in 100 top level administrators are women, 1 in 100 commodity brokers is a woman, yet 97 in 100 secretaries are women and 94 in 100 telephone operators are women. Approximately 75 percent of all employed women belong to only five occupational groups (Keyserling, 1976). Those groups are nurse, household worker, secretary/clerical, elementary school teacher, and service employee.

Occupational sex segregation takes on greater significance when characteristics of sex-typed jobs are examined. Brief et al. (1981) report that "women's" occupations tend to have low wages, limited opportunities for promotion, few on-the-job training programs, high job insecurity, and weak labor unions. On the other hand, "men's," occupations are positive on all these dimensions.

It is clear that women who work outside the home often find employment opportunities in jobs that pay low wages and offer little chance for improvement. Those women who seek employment in nontraditional areas face resistance associated with widely held views concerning the sex stereotyping of occupations.

Labor Market Experiences of Employed Women

Using aggregate statistics, the "typical" woman will work three or four years after completing her education. She will get married, have her first child, and leave the work force for a period of 5 to 10 years. After the last child enters school, the now 35 year old woman attempts to reenter the work force at least on a regular part-time basis. She will remain in the work force for another 20 to 30 years (Lemkau, 1980). Compared with similarly qualified men, women will experience greater problems in getting the job they want. Taken together these experiences often lead to lower expectations about ever obtaining desirable employment and reduced feelings of personal efficacy (Gurin, 1981).

Longitudinal studies of labor market experiences of men and women indicate that women are not as able to translate their potential for achievement into work-related achievement. Using a sample of 4035 participants in Project TALENT, Card et al. (1980) found that although achievement potential for 14 and 15 year old girls was greater than that of similar age boys, that is, better grades in school and higher scores on standardized ability tests, a follow-up 11 years after graduation from high school showed men being much higher on achievement measures of salary and education. One explanation for these differences is the conflict between career and family for many women. Sewell et al (1980) supported this view with data collected from a sample of high school seniors in the state of Wisconsin. Eighteen years after graduation from high school, the process of occupational attainment for women who remained childless was highly similar to that of men. Women who had children did not achieve similar levels of occupational prestige.

Although there has been considerable consciousness raising over women's rights, and legislation has been passed to prevent occupational sex discrimination, current evidence suggests that women are not being fully integrated into the work force. Women have been well represented in Federal Government sponsored training programs focused at the skilled trades. Participation of women in such programs has increased substantially over the past 15 years. But, even so, women are disproportionately concentrated in training programs that lead to low paying and low skill jobs within the skilled trades (Briggs, 1978). Further evidence of this lack of integration is the percentage of women who work on a part-time basis compared with men. Over 11 million women, or 26 percent of all employed women, work part-time while only 3 million men, or 5 percent of all employed men, work part-time (U.S. Department of Labor, 1980).

There are several reasons why women do not have the same labor market experiences as men. Many women probably place their family and children above a career and do not seek employment opportunities with the same conviction as do men. Although this may be true, some women undoubtedly have strong desires for full-time employment and for careers. In this regard, Warr and Parry (1982) found the inability to find work was particularly stressful for single women without children, a group Warr and Parry presumed to have high occupational involvement.

Labor statistics reflect aggregations of data. Therefore, it is possible that the comparatively negative labor market experiences of women do not accurately portray the experience of all women. Nevertheless, it is sobering to note that working women are less likely than men to translate achievement potential into achievement outcomes.

Marital and Family Status of Employed Women

It is not necessary to review the literature on working women to suspect a relationship between employment and both marital status and family status. In this section empirical verification of such relationships will be presented. It is important to recognize the connection because employment and family life can lead to incompatible or competing roles.

Over 24 million women who work are married. This converts to 56 percent of the total adult civilian female work force. Approximately 13 million married women who work have children under the age of 18 who are still living at home (U.S. Department of Labor, 1980). The incidence of mothers in the labor market who also have very young children is at an all time high (Mednick, 1982). Women constitute one out of eight heads of families. Single women with children at home are much more likely to be employed than are married women with children at home (Lemkau, 1980). Employed women have fewer children and expect to have fewer children than do women who are not in labor market (Beckman, 1978). Women with traditional sex-role values and attitudes are less likely to work, have fewer plans for future employment, and have more children than do women with nontraditional sex-role values and attitudes (Thornton and Cambrun, 1979). Finally, women in traditionally male occupations and professions are most likely to be childless or single. These women are very concerned about possible interference in their career resulting from marital and family responsibilities (Beckman, 1978; Greenfeld et al., 1980).

These statistics and empirical findings tell a great deal about working women. For some, marriage and a family are incompatible with pursuit of their career objectives. Consequently, they put off marriage and childbirth permanently or until their careers are established. But another group of women seem to have no choice. Single women with young children show particularly high levels of employment. For both groups of women, considerable stress might result.

Participation and Earnings in Various Occupations

Examination of Department of Labor statistics (U.S. Department of Labor, 1980) indicates an increasing rate of participation by women in the labor force. Participation does not imply equity, however, as a disproportionate demand for labor has been concentrated in occupations already identified as "female." This fact contributes to the lack of progress women have made in earnings. In 1939, the median income for women who worked full-time was 60.8 percent of the median income for men who worked full-time. In 1979, 40 years later, women earned 58.9 percent of the median income for men. Women are concentrated in low skill and low pay jobs within occupational groups. Deaux (1982) reports that metal workers are paid an average of $8.83 per hour while textile workers are paid an average of $4.52 per hour. The former is a male populated job and the latter is a female populated job.

One explanation for the earnings gap is that women tend to work in jobs that have low mental, physical, and social skill requirements. England and McLaughlin (1978) demonstrated support for this interpretation using data from the Dictionary of Occupational Titles (U.S. Department of Labor, 1965). The Dictionary of Occupational Titles contains information that can be used to represent the content of a job in terms of relationships to people, data, and things. Jobs and occupations with high proportions of women employees generally had the lowest requirements. But, these same authors also considered the possibility that regardless of job content, people in male populated jobs earn more than people in female populated jobs. When the effect of job content on salary was controlled, the results indicated a significant effect for percent male. In other words, sex segregation of occupations contributes to the persistent salary differential between men and women above and beyond any salary differential produced by differences in job content or requirements.

An additional perspective on the status of women can be seen when statistics on pay and participation are broken down by occupational grouping (U.S. Department of Labor, 1979, 1980). Women constitute approximately 25 percent of people employed in management and administrative jobs. They earn 54 percent of the median income for men, however. Approximately 43 percent of workers in professional and technical jobs are held by women, yet female accountants earn 64 percent of what male accountants earn and female computer specialists earn 80 percent of what male computer specialists earn when median incomes are compared. Even in the office/clerical category where women make up over 80 percent of all workers, the median income for women is 64 percent of the median income for men.

Summary

Many opportunities for stress seem to confront women who are employed outside the home. Cultural prescriptions leading to sex-role stereotypes and occupational sex stereotypes limit full expression of vocational choice and work-related achievement. Marital and family responsibilities impact on work and career options in ways not usually experienced by men. And, there is considerable evidence suggesting possible stress from economic burdens.

INCIDENCE OF STRESS-RELATED OUTCOMES: WOMEN COMPARED WITH MEN

One interpretation of the status of women employed outside the home would be the expectation of greater evidence of stress-related outcomes for women than men. Sex segregation of occupations should be examined to determine whether women are disproportionately employed in high stress occupations. Job outcomes commonly used to index quality of work life might provide some indication of stress. Finally, sex differences in rates of mental health and physical health problems merit review.

Occupational Sex Segregation and Job Stress

A report published by the National Institute for Occupational Safety and Health (see Steers, 1981, p. 347) identified seven high stress jobs and seven low stress jobs. The high stress jobs were manager, foreman, office manager, product inspector, secretary, waitress, and clinical laboratory technician. The low stress jobs were farm laborer, craft worker, warehouse stock handler, heavy equipment operator, college professor, personnel worker, and maid. If we use government statistics to identify male-populated jobs, female-populated jobs, and jobs populated nearly equally by both sexes (U.S. Department of Labor, 1977), it appears that women are slightly over represented in high stress jobs and under represented in low stress jobs. The jobs of secretary, waitress, and clinical laboratory technician are female sex-segregated jobs while the jobs of manager and foreman are male sex-segregated. Office manager and product inspector employ people of both sexes. In comparison, the jobs of farm laborer, craft worker, warehouse stock handler, heavy equipment operator and college professor, all low stress jobs according to this report, are male sex-segregated. Personnel work is mixed and the job of maid is clearly female sex-segregated.

Albrecht (1979) rated nonmanagerial jobs for stress on the basis of stress disorders for people in those jobs. Out of the ten most stressful jobs identified, five jobs are female sex-segregated: health technician, waitress, practical nurse, clinical laboratory technician, and nurses aide; four jobs are mixed: assembly line operator, musician, public relations official, and dishwasher; and only one job is male sex-segregated, the job of warehouse stock handler.

Colligan et al. (1977) examined mental health center admission rates for 1 year in a southeastern state. They found a disproportionately high incidence of mental health problems among people in the hospital and health care professions. With the exceptions of administrators and physicians, women are concentrated in these fields.

Stress-Related Job Outcomes

Beehr and Newman (1978), Schuler (1980), Ivancevich and Matteson (1980), and Brief et al. (1981) have all written extensively about job stress and employee reactions to stress. Turnover, absenteeism, sick days, and job satisfaction are thought to be effected by job stress. Do women who work outside the home, when compared with men, have greater turnover and absenteeism, take more sick days, and report lower job satisfaction?

A U.S. Government sponsored study of women in traditionally male jobs (U.S. Department of Labor, 1978) found little evidence of differential turnover rates for women in white-collar jobs. Turnover among women in blue-collar jobs was higher than that for men, but this seems to have been a function of lack of technical skills in basic tool usage. Companies that incorporated remedial training in this area did not show differential turnover rates. In a different study limited to college graduates using data from 1976 to 1979, Endicott (1979) found that although 30 percent of college graduates changed jobs within 3 years of graduation, the termination rates were virtually identical for women and men. Although some evidence can be found suggestive of higher turnover rates among women (Mathews et al., 1974), overall differences are not great and vary with occupation.

Similar results are found when absenteeism and illness are examined. A Department of Labor study disputed the myth that women are more likely to be absent and take sick days than are men (U.S. Department of Labor, 1974). Thus, whereas single studies can show sex differences with women often being absent more than men (Muchinsky, 1977), national labor statistics show no difference.

Job satisfaction primarily depends on the nature or content of work performed. Because women tend to be in jobs low in pay, promotion opportunities, power, autonomy, variety, and skill usage, we should expect to find differences between men and women on job satisfaction when job content is not controlled. Research evidence bears this out (Smith et al., 1969). But, it is incorrect to attribute differences to sex when differences in job content is the explanation. Smith et al. (1977), found no evidence of sex differences in job satisfaction based on responses from over 11,000 managers and professionals belonging to a single organization. Furthermore, the results were stable over a 3-year period. Weaver (1980) also found no evidence of job satisfaction differences based on a national sample of over 4,000 employees.

These results for job satisfaction might be surprising given the earlier discussion on the status of employed women. Weaver (1979) explains it by suggesting many women are not aware of the extent they are discriminated against. Gruenberg (1980) believes people in limited jobs accommodate their desires to limited opportunities.

Stress-Related Mental and Physical Health Outcomes

Few sex differences were found when job outcomes were examined. Unfortunately, there is considerable evidence that women in the general population experience more mental health problems than do men, that past differences in stress-related physical problems are disappearing, and that some of these findings can be attributed to work.

In an excellent review of stress and the mental health of women, Makosky (1980) concludes that in the general population women have higher depression scores and higher levels of psychophysiological symptoms than do men. Female heads of households have higher rates of utilization of outpatient psychological services than do male heads of households or females in households where the husband is present. The same relationship is found when admissions to mental health hospitals is examined (Belle, 1980). Although these statistics include women who do not work outside the home, recall that one of every eight families is headed by a woman and that this group of women has a high rate of labor participation. However, these data should be interpreted with the knowledge that our society discourages men from seeking psychological counseling.

Compared with men, women are more likely to be diagnosed as suffering from neuroses, functional psychoses, transient situation disturbances, and psychophysiological disorders (Gove and Tudor, 1973). Twice as many women than men are diagnosed as suffering from depression (Guttentag and Salasin, 1976). Depressive disorders peak during the ages of 25 to 44 and account for more than 40 percent of admissions to mental health institutions. Guttentag and Salasin (1976) believe women experience considerable life stress due to increased demands and conflicts in areas over which they have little control. Although alcoholism is more prevalent among men, women are more likely to turn to alcohol in response to feelings of inadequacy and a sense of futility (Beckman,1975). Women alcoholics have very low self-esteems, report confusion over sex roles, and lack feelings of "womanliness." Although some evidence suggests men are more dependent on drugs (Ivancevich and Matteson, 1980), there also is evidence that use of psychotropic drugs is higher among women (Stellman, 1977).

Research focusing on women who work outside the home suggests the impact of work on stress for women is significant, frequently harmful, but sometimes beneficial. Ivancevich and Matteson (1980) report a British study on work days lost due to mental health problems. Over a 15-year period, the number of days lost rose 152 percent in men and 302 percent in women. Unfortunately, mean levels of days lost and the nature of work women performed were not given. Ivancevich and Matteson (1980) go on to state that rates of heart disease and peptic ulcers are rapidly increasing among women under the age of 45. Cooper and Davidson (1982) similarly found that working women report more psychological maladies, for example, tiredness, irritation, and anxiety, than do people in general. One inference from these trends is that as women enter the work force they experience job-related stress and have similar reactions as do men. Another inference suggests women experience additional stress than do men. In their study of women managers, Cooper and Davidson (1982) noted that women in their sample smoked more frequently than either men managers or women nonmanagers, and they smoked in response to stress, whereas men smoked for enjoyment or out of habit. Women managers also reported greater reliance on tranquilizers, antidepressants, and sleeping pills than did men in similar job positions. It is sobering to note that although men are twice as likely to commit suicide than are women, among professionals, the trend is reversed (Ivancevich and Matteson, 1980).

But, we should not dwell on the negative aspects of work for women at the expense of losing sight of benefits work provides. Employment can lead to enhanced self-esteem, personal growth, and a better standard of living. Although positive versus negative reactions to work will depend on many factors including job level, job type, marital status, quality of working life, and quality of nonworking life, recent evidence indicates employment for women might have less of a negative impact than what could be assumed from the literature reviewed thus far. Warr and Parry (1982) concluded that paid employment contributes to the psychological well-being of women just as it contributes to the psychological well-being of men, and the effects of unemployment can be stress producing for women just as for men.

Summary

It would appear that women who work outside the home are more likely to work in jobs identified as high stress jobs than in jobs identified as low stress jobs. Research also shows that women experience greater mental and physical health problems than men experience. Problems are especially great among single women who work and are heads of households with small children. Finally, women who enter professional and managerial occupations seem to be susceptible to many of the same mental and physical health problems experienced by men in those occupations. But, in spite of these findings, working women as a group differ little from working men in rates of turnover, absenteeism, and illness, and both groups report similar levels of job satisfaction. One explanation for these findings would have to include the cognitive appraisal of the situation. Do women as a group perceive their job experiences differently than do men? Or, a second explanation might consider whether women are more likely than men to persevere.

SEX DIFFERENCES ON SELECTED PERSONALITY DIMENSIONS

There is growing evidence that personality is related to stress (Ivancevich and Matteson, 1980; Brief et al., 1981). First of all, people with certain characteristics might be more likely to seek situations that while stimulating might also be stressful. High need for achievement individuals, for example, might accept additional job responsibilities in their striving for success, yet this creates the potential for role overload. Low need for achievement individuals might be less likely to place themselves in such situations. Consequently, personality can be related to stress through the process of self-selection to potentially stressful situations. Second, personality can affect the perception and cognitive interpretation of events. People unable to tolerate ambiguity might be more likely to experience cognitive uncertainty, which could lead to stress. Finally, methods used to respond and cope will vary to some degree depending on personality. Internal locus of control individual might use more active coping strategies and thus experience less stress than external locus of control individuals. In this section sex differences on personality dimensions thought to be important for understanding stress are reviewed.

Type A and Type B

Men classified as Type A have a much higher incidence of heart disease than do men classified as Type B. The behavior pattern of Type A men includes a chronic sense of time urgency, tendency to do several things at once often underestimating the amount of effort involved, and a hard-driving competitive orientation (Chesney and Rosenman, 1980). Whereas Type B individuals also might have strong goal orientations, they seek satisfaction in less stress producing ways.

At the present time little research has been conducted comparing men with women on Type A personality styles. What research does exist suggests that in the general population, men are more likely than women to be Type A. But, the highest occurrence of Type A is found among working men and women between the ages of 26 and 35 (Brief et al., 1981). Type A is more pronounced in women who work than in women who do not work (Chesney and Rosenman, 1980). And, as with men, the Type A behavioral pattern is related to career success and marital failure for women (Waldron, 1978). Of interest, women classified as Type A also have relatively high scores on measures of masculine sex-role identification (De-Gregoria and Carver, 1980).

Locus of Control

People who believe they are primarily responsible for what happens to them and who believe in personal power and control are said to have an internal locus of control. In contrast, people who believe that their actions have little impact on what happens to them and who attribute outcomes to fate and luck are said to have external locus of control (Rotter, 1966).

Although internals might be expected to experience more stress than would externals, and research shows internals as having greater anxiety when first exposed to a stressful situation, this is not always true (Brief et al., 1981). An important difference between internals and externals can be found in the ways they respond to stress. Internals cope better with a stress event because they take action designed to remove or reduce the source of stress. Externals are less likely to take such action as they see little connection between their behavior and the consequences of their behavior (Anderson, 1977). Research also shows internals to be more resilient to stress induced physical illness (Kobasa, 1979).

Compared with men, there is a tendency for women to be more external (Johnson and Black, 1981). There seems to be a sense that things happen to them about which they have little or no control (Makosky, 1980). Women attribute events to luck more frequently than do men (Mednick, 1982).

Self-Esteem

People with good self-esteem possess positive self-images and see a match between their abilities and what is required of them. They have high performance expectancies and attach value to what they do. Bettelheim (1958) reports self-esteem as a key factor differentiating people who survived wartime prison camps and those who did not. Ivancevich and Matteson (1980) indicate a negative relationship is found between self-esteem and coronary heart disease risk factors. Self-esteem is thought to be important for stress because of consequences associated with mismatches of abilities and job demands. Overload and underutilization, which are two job stressors that result from such mismatches, can both lead to stress (French et al., 1974).

In their extensive review of sex differences, Maccoby and Jacklin (1974) found a consistent difference between the sexes on self-ratings of performance expectancies and self-evaluations. Lenney (1977) qualified this difference by concluding the effects are most pronounced when performance feedback is not available, the task is ambiguous, and women will be compared with men. Although these situational modifiers would seem descriptive of many management jobs, Morrison and Sebald (1974) found no difference in self-esteem between women and men managers when matched on age, education, work site, and location. Terborg et al. (1982), however, in a study of graduate student socialization did report evidence of lower perceived ability-task match among women. Furthermore, for both men and women, lower performance expectancies and self-evaluations were predictive of psychological and physical problems throughout the first year of graduate school.

Sex-Role Identity

Our society holds expectations regarding appropriate characteristics and behaviors for men and women (Terborg, 1977; Ruble and Ruble, 1980.) These expectations are shared across groups differing in age, religion, sex, marital status, and educational level. Characteristics ascribed to men are valued more highly than characteristics ascribed to women. Masculine traits form a cluster of behaviors that suggest competence, rationality, and assertion. Feminine traits form a cluster of behaviors that suggest warmth and expressiveness (Broverman et al., 1972). Males are expected and encouraged to be independent, competitive, adventurous, self-confident, and superior. Females, on the other hand, are expected and encouraged to be emotional, considerate, grateful, helpful, and kind (Spence et al., 1975). People who violate accepted sex-role norms are open to sanctions (Wallston and O'Leary, 1981). We find, for example, that women who display "womenly traits" and men who display "manly traits" are evaluated more favorably and judged more psychologically healthy than those who engage in sex-role reversals (Costrich et al., 1975). Sex roles are so strongly ingrained that even newborn infants are treated differently by adults depending on whether the newborn is wrapped in a blue, pink or white blanket (Ruble and Ruble, 1980). As early as three and four years of age, children develop sex-role stereotypes for activities, occupations, and toys (Ruble and Ruble, 1980). Indeed, Mussen (1969) believes that of all the social roles, the sex role exerts primary influence over behavior, emotions, cognitive functioning, attitudes, and general adjustment to life.

It is important to understand sex roles because, as was noted earlier, many jobs and occupations are sex-typed. Consequently, the possibility exists that women who seek employment in traditionally masculine jobs, whether professional or blue collar, might experience conflict and confusion with regard to sex-role identity. Do women in masculine sex-typed jobs have to sacrifice their femininity in order to be effective?

Horner (1972) proposed that women learn to fear success in achievement situations because of anticipated social rejection, loss of love, and loss of femininity. Although Horner's thesis has prompted considerable research not always supportive of her position, it does appear that some women have a tendency to avoid success because of anxiety produced over sex-role identity (Mednick, 1982). Women with strong achievement motives and nontraditional career objectives might be particularly prone to stress produced by fear of success because of high visibility (Kanter, 1977). This exacerbates any display of sex-role deviance. One consequence could be use of self-defeating strategies in crucial achievement settings. For example, Hoffman (1977) found that women with a high fear of success were more likely to become pregnant at times when they were about to experience a change that would have placed them in positions of higher status than their husbands. Similarly, Stewart (1977) demonstrated that women with high fear of success and traditional sex-role identities avoided making career commitments. Not all women with strong achievement motives experience anxiety over fear of success, however. Mednick (1982) reports a series of studies in which she found differences due to career orientation, sex-role identity, and perceived support from others. Nevertheless, anxiety and stress might be expected to occur for some women in situations where success would be perceived as out-of-role behavior and where that behavior would evoke unpleasant consequences (Deaux, 1976).

A growing body of research indicates a consistent relationship between sex-role identity and career decisions. Women with high scores on measures of masculinity show high academic achievement (Olds and Shaver, 1980), have vocational interest in nontraditional careers (Tipton, 1976), enroll in sex-inappropriate college majors (Wertheim et al., 1978), and value their career above other life options (Marshall and Wijting, 1980). Of interest, some data also suggest that these women report low anxiety, little depression, and few mental health symptoms (DeGregorio and Carver, 1980; Olds and Shaver, 1980). This is surprising because out-of-role behavior should evoke negative sanctions. It is possible, however, that these women do not experience conflict because they have unambiguously resolved their sex-role identities. They view themselves as competent, rational, and assertive. These are characteristics ascribed to the masculine sex-role stereotype and to perceptions of a mentally healthy person (Broverman et al., 1970). In contrast, women who view themselves as androgynous, which Bem (1975) envisions as a combination of positive attributes associated with masculinity and femininity and as a sex-role identity free from constraints, seem to report greater conflict. Kutner and Brogan (1981) found some evidence that women in medical school who were concerned about maintaining their femininity in this male dominated career field had a more difficult time coming to terms with their sex-role identity. Also, Kelly and Worell (1977) noted androgynous women seemed to be in greater conflict over whether to pursue a career or to seek a more traditional lifestyle. Drawing on the stress model presented in the first chapter of this book, perhaps women with masculine sex-role identities experience less conflict because little *importance* is attached to feminine stereotypes and because there is reduced *uncertainty* with regard to appropriate behavior.

Personal Efficacy

Personal efficacy refers to a belief or expectation that one can successfully bring about change. There would be overlap between this belief and previously discussed personality traits of self-esteem and locus of control in addition to sex-role identity. People with high expectations are more likely to take risks, set more difficult goals, persist longer at chosen activities, and be more involved in what they are doing (Mednick, 1982). Such individuals attribute success to ability or high effort and attribute failure to a lack of effort, or in some instances to external factors (Deaux, 1976). They expect to be successful in what they do and others expect them to be successful as well.

It is generally found that women have lower expectancies about their potential to bring about change and that women internalize failure and externalize success (Deaux, 1976; Mednick, 1982; O'Leary and Hansen, 1982). These attributional tendencies are learned through social interaction in achievement settings. Dweck et al., (1978), for example, demonstrated in a school setting that boys learn to attribute failure to lack of motivation whereas girls learn to attribute failure to lack of ability. This occurs as a result of differences in expectations, rewards, praise, and criticism given boys compared with girls. Some consequences for women are self-blame, low self-confidence, low expectancies, and low aspirations.

Personal efficacy should be closely related to stress because of the links between efficacy and both uncertainty and duration (see Chapter 1 in this book). Kahn (1974) states people who turn job problems inward experience greater tension than those who can evaluate problems more objectively. Makosky (1980) notes that women seem to be affected more negatively than men by life changes which women view as being beyond their control, for example, death of a relative, major illness, children leaving home. Finally, Seligman's (1975) work in the area of learned helplessness seems particularly relevant. People who learn it is futile to respond in attempts to avoid or escape unpleasant consequences show little involvement with life, become depressed, and often develop ulcers and other stress-related diseases. It should be noted, however, that little research on personal efficacy and stress has been conducted in field settings with employed men and women; and one recent study of accountants, a traditionally male occupation, found no difference between men and women on behavior-performance expectancies (Kaufman and Felters, 1980).

Summary

Women employed outside the home, and especially those women employed in nontraditional career fields, can expect to encounter resistance to equal and full participation. A review of selected personality dimensions suggests that women as a group compared with men as a group are less likely to respond effectively to demanding job situations. Women seem to have poor self-concepts, internalize failure, externalize success, and see little relationship between what they do and what happens to them. All of these characteristics could result from lifelong socialization pressures to conform with the stereotypic feminine sex role. Women who identify with the masculine sex role might encounter sanctions because of their failure to comply with prescribed behavior patterns. Also, those women displaying Type A behaviors can expect stress related problems even though such activities might be important for job and career success. Individual differences, however, are quite large and considerable overlap in these dimensions implies that group differences might infrequently characterize single individuals. Also, many situational factors should be considered as alternative explanations for atypical findings.

INTERFACE BETWEEN LIFE AND WORK

Fifty-six percent of women who work outside the home are married, and 54 percent of those have children under the age of 18 living at home. An important issue for many working wives and mothers concerns the interface between life and work. Women seem able to add the role of wage earner but often have considerable difficulty in dropping the roles of housewife and mother. Consequently, the full-time employed wife and mother might feel harassed, overburdened, and resentful about holding two jobs.

It is important to understand the connection between life stress and work stress for two reasons. First, research suggests a spillover effect. Stress at work can manifest itself at home where it creates new problems that further contribute to stress (Ivancevich and Matteson, 1980). Research is just beginning to address the question of stress "aftereffects" (Cohen, 1980). Similarly, stress produced by home and life events can impact on job behavior (Bhagat, 1983). Second, a supportive home life can moderate effects of a stressful job and a supportive job can moderate effects of a stressful home life. Because women who work outside the home often add this role to their other duties and responsibilities, examination of the interface between life and work would be especially relevant to any discussion of working women and stress (see Chapter 8 for a more in depth discussion of this topic).

Life Change and Stress

It has been repeatedly demonstrated that significant changes in one's life precipitates the onset of mental health and physical health problems (see Bhagat, 1983, for a review). Much of this research has used the Schedule of Recent Experiences (SRE) to assess life change. The SRE was developed by Holmes and Rahe (Holmes and Rahe, 1967) and includes 43 events such as death of spouse, marriage, pregnancy, change in residence, and minor violations of the law. Points are assigned to life event changes according to the severity of stress produced by that event as judged by people of different ages and social classes.

Little research has considered the possibility of sex differences on the SRE or other similar measures of life event changes. But, the work done so far suggests the possibility that women experience more life event changes than men, interpret the same changes as more stress producing, are affected more strongly by events they cannot control, and react differently (Makosky, 1980). The SRE includes many work related events but few events related to child care and responsibilities of maintaining a home. There also is evidence that certain events such as marriage, separation, divorce, and death of close friends and relatives are more stressful for women. Finally, although women tend to have better established social support networks, which may buffer the individual from stress (see Chapter 8 and Chapter 14), they also tend to be less active in coping with the source of the stress event. Selective ignoring, a method where the person attempts to block out the stress event from cognitive experience such as might occur when a woman acts as if she did not hear a sexist remark, is an ineffective coping strategy because it does not improve the situation by reducing the likelihood the event will happen in the future.

Women might experience greater life stress than men experience. This could spill over to the job situation with negative effects (Bhagat, 1983). To the extent that women experience considerable stress at work, the job is unable to mediate life stress and might even exacerbate life stress.

Family Responsibilities

Hall (1972) suggested women who work outside the home are more likely to face role conflicts than are men because the roles women have are salient simultaneously whereas the roles men have operate sequentially. This can produce person-role conflict when the woman must make decisions between marriage, family, spouse's career, and her job or career. It also can produce interrole conflict as women without support often maintain a home in addition to working full time outside the home. Finally, it can produce role-sender conflict when the spouse encourages his wife to work or pursue a career but resents her absence or career success.

There is considerable evidence to support the contention that working women with families face a dual role burden, and evidence is accumulating that points to negative effects of this burden. For example, working women with job and family role conflicts are more likely to be depressed than are working women without such conflicts (Warr and Parry, 1982). Even more striking is documentation of a positive relationship between coronary heart disease and the number of children at home for women who work while a negative relationship exists between coronary heart disease and number of children at home for housewives who do not work outside the home (Cooper and Davidson,1982). Nye (1976) found 70 percent of husbands surveyed believed keeping the children clean and fed was primarily their wife's responsibility. The wives responded even more strongly and it was determined that the actual involvement of women was even higher. Other responsibilities pertaining to school, day care, and recreation also were perceived as being the wife's role more than the husband's. Even when husbands help with child dressing and household chores, women spend more time on these activities than do their spouses (Cooper and Davidson, 1982). Pines and Kafry (1981) studied professionals. Men and women listed work demands as a reason to avoid housework. But, many women reported feeling guilty when housework was not done and consequently took responsibility for doing it. Men did not report the same guilt. Of interest, however, women did not cite greater work-home conflict even though they did more activities at home.

Conflict between work and home is a barrier for most working women. Time and energy demands and children are listed as reasons why women are less able than men to upgrade their job skills so they can be qualified for better jobs (U.S. Department of Health, Education, and Welfare, 1979). These same reasons are given by women seeking careers in professional, managerial, and technical fields (Rosen, 1982). Unfortunately, these conflicts can prevent women from working in addition to making work more difficult. Mathews et al. (1974) compared reasons for quitting given by men and women air traffic controllers. Family responsibilities were often mentioned as the primary reason for termination by women, but this was rarely mentioned as the reason by men. Finally, inability to meet home and work demands can reduce the woman's commitment to the organization (Bhagat and Chassie, 1981).

Interrole conflict among working women has been documented (Hall and Gordon, 1973; Gordon and Hall, 1974). The results are not always consistent, however. Herman and Gyllstrom (1977) found that interrole conflict was related to the number of different roles held by both working men and working women. But, because there were no differences in the number of roles held between sexes, women did not report greater role conflict. Married individuals reported more roles and more role conflict than did single individuals and those with families reported more roles and more role conflict than did those without families. Bhagat and Chassie (1981), however, found that the number of different roles held by working women was unrelated to role stress. Rather, the inability to meet role demands predicted role stress. Perhaps methods of coping are more important than the number of roles held. Holahan and Gilbert (1979) surveyed married women with careers and married women who worked but did not consider their job a career. Noncareer women reported greater role conflict than career women. But, the reason for this difference seems to be greater spouse support with family duties among career women. Methods of coping with conflict also could explain Herman and Gyllstrom's results because many of the women in their study were unmarried, or if married, they were childless.

The implications of the above research studies are obvious. Women who work outside the home must find effective methods of coping with the often conflicting demands of a job and a family. One method is to remain single or childless. Other methods require (1) a supportive and understanding spouse who is willing to take on additional responsibilities, (2) sufficient income to hire help with child care and home maintenance, and (3) access to company sponsored programs, for example, day care facilities.

Person-Role Conflict

Women who work are often forced to compromise and make personal sacrifices in areas never experienced or even considered by men. Women who work in nontraditional jobs and careers expose themselves to situations that foster dilemmas of identity. These factors contribute to life stress and work stress.

Yeager (1977) interviewed several successful career women in their thirties. Reading what these women said points to compromise and sacrifice. For some women, the choice was between a career or marriage. Another chose a career and paid the price of a divorce. Yet another accepted the reality that she will remain childless. We continue to see evidence that marital adjustment is worse for dual career wives than for nonworking wives (Cooper and Davidson, 1982). Marriage and raising children are important life experiences. How many men would have to be interviewed before even one mentioned having to make a choice between a career and marriage or a career and children?

Women today can more easily remain childless or single than they could twenty years ago. Birth control and changes in attitudes brought about by the feminist revolution give women a viable choice. But, forces in our society and culture still pressure women toward marriage and childbirth. Those who do not conform can experience self-doubts about one's chosen life-style. A man is capable of fathering a child throughout much of his adult life. A woman must face biological changes that limit the years she can give birth to a healthy child. Many successful career women have husbands and children. A child, however, is a critical decision for most career couples (Hall and Hall, 1980), and the consequences of the decision are almost always more severe for the woman than the man.

Studies of successful and satisfied executives indicate the importance of spouse support (Handy, 1978). Wives often play a crucial role in their husbands' careers. Women who work will face conflicts between their work demands and the demands of their husbands' careers. For women who are not career oriented themselves, these demands produce role overload. But, for women who are career oriented and are in the midst of establishing their own careers, the problems are more serious. Unless these women have strong identities and supportive and understanding spouses, they might experience considerable person-role conflict.

Women in nontraditional jobs face additional pressures, beside those associated with marriage and a family, that can contribute to self-doubt about sex-role identity. A government study of women in male populated white collar and blue collar jobs showed evidence of social pressure directed toward these women in their atypical roles (U.S. Department of Labor, 1978). For women in white collar positions, problems related to women friends with more traditional attitudes and to the wives of male coworkers. Women in male-populated blue-collar positions experienced negative pressures from husbands or boyfriends in addition to that from women friends. Women in nontraditional job fields experience discouragement and negative attitudes from friends and acquaintances. But, women in more traditional job fields seem to have few of these problems.

Economic and Financial Pressures

Earlier in the chapter it was noted that one out of eight households in the United States is headed by a woman, and that a high proportion of these women work outside the home. It also was noted that the median salary for women was 58.9 percent of the median salary for men. Single women with children have child care and medical expenses that require adequate salaries if debt is to be avoided. These women often are responsible for maintaining the home because domestic help is too expensive. Anxiety over lack of sufficient money and physical fatigue resulting from working full time and caring to the needs of a home and children will eventually produce stress-related outcomes. Mental health and physical health problems, however, are likely to have a negative impact on income, which of course will only make the situation more unbearable.

Summary

The interface between work and life has potential to be more stressful for women who work outside the home than for men. Although a good job can contribute to overall quality of life through increased income and more satisfying experiences than those available to a traditional housewife (Hoffman and Nye, 1974; Holahan and Gilbert, 1979; Warr and Parry, 1982), women who work outside the home are required to make many social readjustments that can contribute to stress. Wives and mothers who work rarely have any substantial reduction in responsibility for people, which is known to produce stress. Men, however, seem to feel entitled to reduced responsibilities. Women in nontraditional careers may experience conflict with sex-role identity. Inadequate social support from significant others can be both a source of stress and an unrealized method of coping with stress. Finally, discrimination in pay and access to high paying jobs can interact with life stress so that work increases potential for stress rather than reducing potential for stress.

Organizational Antecedents of Stress for Employed Women

Several writers have identified sources of job stress (Beehr and Newman, 1978; Cooper and Marshall, 1978; Ivancevich and Matteson, 1980; Brief et al., 1981). This section loosely follows the work of Cooper and Marshall (1978) and Ivancevich and Matteson (1980) as categories they associate with stress coincide with existing literature on working women. This section is divided into five parts. First, stress associated with career entry and development is discussed. This is followed with consideration of aspects intrinsic to the job that might cause stress. Role-based stress is the third topic, and interpersonal relations with superiors, peers, and subordinates is covered next. The section concludes with a brief discussion of organization structure and climate.

Career Entry and Development

When the literature on women and work is reviewed, it is not unreasonable to conclude that women more so than men will experience frustration, anxiety, and stress produced by barriers to career entry, underpromotion, overpromotion, mid-career obsolescence, status incongruity, and mismatches between career aspiration and career achievement. In addition, women who see their work as a central life interest and have career salience might be expected to have higher stress than women who view work and a career as secondary to other pursuits. Beehr and Bhagat note in Chapter 1 that importance is a key factor in determining whether stress will occur. Consequently, barriers to career entry and development probably are less relevant to women with traditional sex-role attitudes and values who also work in feminine sex-typed occupations. But, for women seeking work and careers in masculine sex-typed occupations, regardless of whether the job is in the skilled trades or in management and the technical professions, barriers to career entry and development might be an area of acute sensitivity. Recall that for many women a career often requires compromise and sacrifice whereas most men can better combine a career with other life roles.

Previous reviews of this literature noted considerable barriers faced women desiring jobs and careers in masculine sex-typed occupations. Some barriers pertained to attitudes women held about themselves (O'Leary, 1974), whereas other barriers dealt with family responsibilities and organizational sex discrimination (Terborg, 1977). Unfortunately, the current literature does not indicate much change since past reviews. Women have learned to use the law as leverage for gaining access to male-populated blue-collar and professional jobs and have successfully challenged unfair pay differentials for comparable or identical work. Many examples of discrimination, however, still exist.

Rosen (1982), reflecting on ten years of research conducted with his colleague Thomas Jerdee in the area of occupational sex discrimination, noted that sex-role stereotypes still are widely held and they depict women as better suited for clerical and light assembly work than for managerial/professional and skilled craft work. He listed several obstacles women face when attempting to make transitions from work to career and from entry level management to middle and upper management. Among the more commonly identified barriers as viewed by women were (1) exclusion or tokenism, (2) discrimination, (3) limited political skills, (4) conflicts between work and home, (5) competition from peers, (6) poorly articulated career goals, and (7) limited promotion opportunities (Rosen et al., 1982).

Research by others supports many of these problems to career entry and development. Heilman (1980) recently demonstrated the negative impact of tokenism on personnel hiring decisions. Ratings given to applicant resumés were most negative when the proportion of women in the applicant pool was low. This occurred even though only sex of applicant but not quality of applicant varied across raters. Women experience differential recruitment and placement such that even when they gain access to masculine sex-typed jobs they are disproportionately represented in low skill and low paying positions (Briggs, 1978), they are more likely found in particular jobs thought to require dependence, passivity, and concern for people (Acker and Van Houten, 1974), and they tend to be in specialties with limited career opportunities in their organization (Smith, 1979).

A recent survey of 600 top level executives conducted by *Business Week* magazine "How Executives See Women in Management," 1982) indicated the problem may have shifted from hiring to promotion. Men do not like taking orders from women and it has been more difficult promoting women than originally thought. Perhaps even more disturbing is the discovery that in some companies, middle management gave highest promotion evaluations to older, less aggressive women, while senior management was looking for young, aggressive people to fill those positions. Women who might have fit the pattern were not being promoted to levels where they could be recognized ("Study Shows How Women Face Hurdles," 1982).

Multinational corporations feel constrained in how they utilize women managers and professionals because executives in Western Europe do not view women as legitimate top level administrators (Izraeli et al., 1980). In the United States, some women are willing to do menial work for low pay in the hope they will learn skills and develop contacts for entry into their chosen field even though they realize that most men avoid such "dues paying" activities (Mackay-Smith, 1982). Women tend to be older, better educated, and in certain instances better qualified than their male management peers (Kanter, 1977). Women must demonstrate superior performance to obtain evaluations of "good" or "excellent" (U.S. Department of Labor, 1978), and often comparable levels of performance fail to merit comparable levels of reward and praise (O'Leary and Hansen, 1982). Evidence of overpromotion, without attention given to providing the women with necessary and basic skills and knowledge that experience normally provides, is also found (U.S. Department of Labor, 1978; Deaux and Ullman, 1982; Kanter, 1977). Presumably this occurs as a result of an organization's attempt to comply with legal demands, but the combination of high visibility and lack of background experience makes it very difficult for the token woman to succeed.

Women seeking jobs and careers in masculine sex-typed occupations face a variety of obstacles that collectively should produce anxiety, frustration, and stress above normally expected levels faced by men at similar career stages and in similar job circumstances. Because women seeking access to previously denied jobs and careers have made sacrifices and compromises in order to make their own opportunities, they might be especially susceptible to stress resulting from blocked career pathways. Unfortunately, natural expressions of indignation often are perceived as over reaction, which further exacerbates the problem (Rosen, 1982).

Stressors Intrinsic to the Job

Factors intrinsic to the job that contribute to stress include quantitative and qualitative role overload and underload, time pressures, responsibilities for people and things, insufficient power, and aversive characteristics of the job itself. The status of working women has been discussed earlier in the chapter and will not be repeated here even though many of the characteristics identified should contribute to stress. Attention will be focused in other areas.

Implicit throughout this chapter has been the categorization of work into three general areas (1) traditionally feminine sex-typed occupations, (2) blue-collar masculine sex-typed occupations, and (3) white-collar masculine sex-typed occupations. Each one will be discussed as they provide different stressors.

The most common traditionally feminine sex-typed job deals with clerical and secretarial duties. Nearly 15 million women, or 35 percent of all working women, are clerical workers or secretaries (U.S. Department of Labor, 1980). Brief et al. (1981) cite reports indicating this job is characterized by inadequate pay, boring and repetitive tasks, little opportunity for training and advancement, and little use of skills and abilities. They go on to note that a dead-end clerical or secretarial job combined with a demanding and unsupportive boss can lead to increased risk of coronary heart disease. Other traditionally feminine sex-segregated occupations involve hospital and health care (e.g., nurse, nurse's aide, clinical laboratory technician) and working with children in various capacities (e.g., grade school teacher, child care provider). These occupational groups have been associated with high stress (Colligan et al., 1977; Albrecht, 1979). In fact, work involving children has been singled out as being particularly stressful, with burnout mentioned as a hazard of the occupation (Freudenberger, 1977; Maslach and Pines, 1977). These largely white-collar jobs and occupations were described, not because they are examples of stressful forms of work, but because they are highly sex segregated and employ a majority of all working women.

At the present time not much published research on women in blue-collar masculine sex-typed occupations is available. Considerable agreement, however, is found on certain issues. In spite of technological advancements reducing the need for physical strength and stamina, women in some blue-collar jobs report minor problems associated with physical demands inherent in the work (U.S. Department of Labor, 1978; U.S. Department of Health, Education and Welfare, 1979; Deaux and Ullman, 1982). Supervisors also indicate a slight need to consider strength and stamina of women more so than men when giving job assignments (U.S. Department of Labor, 1978). Although physical demands of work can be a problem, it does not affect all women. Vocational guidance counselors must become aware of legitimate physical demands so as to avoid invalid discouragement to women seeking jobs in skilled trades, construction, mining, and steel.

A second problem area capable of producing stress has to do with technical and mechanical skills. Women hired to blue-collar positions sometimes lack familiarity with simple mechanical principles and tool identification and usage (U.S. Department of Labor, 1979; Deaux and Ullman, 1982). Unless remedial training programs are designed to correct shortcomings in women who need training, it is possible these women could experience both qualitative role overload and quantitative role overload.

A third stressor for women intrinsic to many masculine sex-typed blue collar jobs stems from the fact that work settings often were not designed to include women. Locker rooms, showers, bathrooms, and work areas accommodate the needs of men. Organizations sometimes are unwilling to make expensive modifications in order to satisfy a few women who choose to work there. As a result, daily activities may take new meanings, for example, having to walk one-half mile to use the bathroom is both uncomfortable and a continual sign of lower status and worth.

Women in many blue-collar jobs, however, have a distinct advantage compared with women in white-collar jobs when it comes to performance evaluation. Blue collar jobs often have objective performance measures and standards. In a short period of time the new woman employee as well as the men around her are able to determine probable success or failure. Among carpenters, there is little ambiguity over whether you can build a door frame and hang a door. Perceptual distortion and selective perception, which can bias subjective performance ratings given to women and adversely impact pay and promotion, are less likely to happen in blue collar occupations than in white collar and professional occupations.

Managerial and professional jobs are high on stress, and women in white-collar masculine sex-typed jobs will experience all of the stressors associated with those positions that men experience. Strength demands and inconveniences of the work setting, which are intrinsic to blue-collar jobs, are not likely to be particular problems for managerial and professional women. As just mentioned, however, lack of objective performance measures could contribute to uncertainty in self-evaluation. Perhaps the major stressor women face in masculine white collar jobs is lack of power and resources. Evidence suggests women are placed in peripheral functions (Smith, 1979). Resulting lack of control and inability to make an impact will lead to frustration and stress. Lack of control and the uncertainty that goes along with lack of control is especially evident when women travel. Women travelers report problems eating dinner, having a drink in the hotel lounge, and even resting quietly in their hotel room. It is not uncommon for a woman's room number to be given to a man who asks for it from the hotel clerk. Regardless of the intentions of the caller, it is not comforting to know that a stranger has your room number. In response to this very real problem, some hotels are attempting to provide better services to women business travelers, such as the availability of separate floors for women and training hotel staff how to accommodate the special needs of women. Although we might commend hotels for doing this, that the need exists at all for special treatment of women business travelers is a telling commentary on the status of women who work outside of the home.

Role Ambiguity and Role Conflict

Roles are expectations for attitudes and behaviors. A crucial task of new employees often involves learning what is expected of them in conducting the daily activities associated with their job. Prescriptions and proscriptions define that which is pivotal, relevant, or peripheral for success.

Role ambiguity and role conflict are major sources of job tension and stress (Beehr and Newman, 1978; Ivancevich and Matteson, 1980). Role ambiguity occurs when the person has insufficient information about the duties, objectives, and responsibilities of one's job. Lack of clarity often is temporary and is found among (1) new employees, (2) employees who get a new supervisor, and (3) employees who receive transfers or promotions. Role conflict is present whenever compliance with one set of role pressures makes compliance with another set of role pressures difficult, objectionable, or impossible.

Role ambiguity and role conflict are inherent in all jobs. But, women who work outside the home are especially likely to experience role induced stress. Conflict between job versus family responsibilities has already been discussed in the section on the interface between life and work. Attention now is on role induced stress produced in the work setting.

Role ambiguity is likely to be a greater problem for women than for men. Women in masculine sex-typed jobs might be expected to have lower tolerances for ambiguity than women in traditional jobs or men in masculine sex-typed jobs. Because of their uniqueness, these women have high visibility. Men in the organization are closely watching the behavior and performance of the first women entering their ranks. Women in such positions are acutely aware of this and report considerable self-pressure to live up to personal expectations and to perform well (Kanter, 1977). Emphasis is on demonstrating competence (Deaux and Ullman, 1982). Women in blue-collar jobs seem particularly concerned with avoiding trouble so they work hard, try to be cooperative to everyone, and ignore harassment. A feeling exists that this is their one chance and they do not want to make any mistakes or violate any social standards of conduct.

Role ambiguity is further exacerbated by lack of role models and an unwillingness among colleagues to offer assistance and advice (Kanter, 1977; Rosen, 1982). Holahan (1979) studied women doctoral students in masculine sex-typed areas of education. Stress was a function of need for support and support offered by students and faculty in the department. Women with high support needs in masculine departments received the least support and experienced the greatest stress. Mackay-Smith (1982) found that male commodity brokers not only failed to provide assistance, but they actually sabotaged the work of new and naive women brokers. For example, attempts would be made to run up a bid beyond the point where the woman broker wanted to buy and sometimes her bids would be ignored. Evidence suggests men are less likely to share job information with women than with other men, and this is seen to happen in blue-collar as well as white-collar jobs (Deaux and Ullman, 1982). Women in nontraditional jobs have an especially strong need for role clarity because of increased visibility and importance attached to their behavior. Unfortunately, it also seems that these women are less likely to be given job information often crucial for early job success.

Role conflict, in addition to role ambiguity, is a persistent problem faced by women in nontraditional jobs (Terborg and Zalesny, 1980). Out of role behavior generally is evaluated negatively (Mednick, 1982; O'Leary and Hansen, 1982; Rosen, 1982). If women try to act like "men," they run the risk of sanctions because they violated accepted sex-role stereotypes. If they try to act like "women," they might be out of role for the demands of the job. Not only are many of the women confused; their male colleagues also report some uneasiness. Can you still tell "dirty" jokes at the coffee break? Who picks up the check for a business lunch, the male client or the female sales representative? Is it proper for a 35-year-old woman to fire a colleague who has been with the company for 20 years?

Although research results are inconsistent, there is a tendency for women and men managers and women and men professionals to use leadership styles consistent with sex-role stereotypes (Adams, 1978; Brown, 1979; Donnell and Hall, 1980). Even though women on the whole manage "like men do," when faced with pressure, men are more likely to fall back on autocratic dictatorial methods while women are more likely to fall back on compromising conciliatory methods (Donnell and Hall, 1980).

Pressure to engage in "appropriate" sex role behavior is particularly strong when the proportion of women in the job category within the organization is small (Laws, 1975; Kanter, 1977). In a group meeting, for example, the only woman member might be asked to take notes of the meeting, get coffee, or comment on what the "woman's" view is likely to be on a given issue. Faced with these pressures, as a solo, she might readily comply with expectations of the male group members. This tendency to ascribe sex-stereotypes to a single individual and to engage in stereotypical behaviors becomes less frequent as the proportion of women increases. Once a critical mass is achieved, the limited evidence to data points to a reduction in stereotyping behaviors. Many women in nontraditional jobs are solos or members of a small minority. This situational factor can lead to continued conflict between sex-role and job-role pressures even though it might temporarily reduce ambiguity surrounding the immediate behavior setting.

A final source of role conflict that should be mentioned involves sex bias in attributions. This phenomenon is thoroughly covered in Deaux (1976) and O'Leary and Hansen (1982), so only a brief summary will be provided here. Research has established the existence of a male competency bias. Performance attributed to a man is evaluated more highly than if that same level of performance were attributed to a woman. Explanations for successful performance by men cite superior ability while women are thought to be successful because of luck or high effort. Although there are some instances where successful performance by women in masculine activities is judged worthy of extra merit, the attribution is usually based on high effort and not on superior ability. Most studies find, however, that successful performance by a woman in a sex-incongruent task results in lower rewards than equal performance by a man in the same task.

O'Leary and Hansen (1982) have proposed that while effort is a key factor in allocating rewards, the role of effort is interpreted differently depending on the sex of the performer and the nature of the task. Preliminary data collected by these authors support the contention that attributions of high effort given to men are diagnostic of men's ability, but attributions of high effort given to women in sex-incongruent tasks reflect the woman's need to compensate for her *lack* of ability. It seems many individuals are unwilling to accept female competence in masculine sex-typed jobs. Cognitive reinterpretation of performance takes place to justify low rewards and to reinforce biased beliefs. If a woman receives rapid promotions to positions of considerable responsibility it is almost inevitable that questions will be raised about her capability and that attributions for success will focus on other characteristics such as appearance, personal relationships, and sexuality. Women in masculine sex-typed occupations will experience role conflict when others in the organization communicate expectations of limited potential and limited merit.

Interpersonal Relations Within the Organization

Closely related to the topic of role conflict and ambiguity is the nature of interpersonal relations with superiors, peers, and subordinates. Interpersonal relationships of high quality include social support, trust, communication, involvement, participation, and appreciation of individual worth and dignity.

The limited research evidence currently available strongly indicates women in masculine sex-typed jobs have difficulty being integrated into the work group. Unfortunately, comparative data with women in feminine sex-typed jobs is not available, but it can reasonably be assumed that problems of establishing quality relationships would be considerably less for these working women.

Women in both blue-collar and white-collar masculine sex-typed jobs still report discouragement and negative attitudes on the part of many coworkers (U.S. Department of Labor 1978; U.S. Department of Health, Education and Welfare, 1979; Deaux and Ullman, 1982). When women are in the minority, they are less likely to receive social support and technical assistance (Holahan, 1979; Mackay-Smith, 1982). There even is some evidence that managers with traditional sex-role stereotypes engage in behaviors that knowingly or unknowingly create distance between the manager and the woman subordinate. Rosen (1982) notes, for example, that women are given routine assignments with little autonomy and rapid negative feedback in an attempt by the manager to minimize damage expected from an incompetent woman. A study conducted at the Wellesley College Center for Research on Women ("Study Shows How Women Face Hurdles," 1982) uncovered a different and more subtle form of discrimination. Rather than receiving rapid negative feedback, this research found a reluctance among male supervisors to confront low performing female subordinates with corrective feedback, thus denying those women the opportunity to improve their performance.

Women in masculine sex-typed jobs report less communication with colleagues. They seem to feel excluded from the informal social network (Rosen, 1982). They are less likely to share information with others and they are less likely to solicit information from others (Donnell and Hall, 1980). Resulting lack of involvement and participation will lead to problems of adjustment and experience of stress (Segovis and Bhagat, 1981). Perhaps this exclusion from daily activities and information flow helps explain the finding that successful women in management endorse McGregor's Theory X style of leadership, which is based on distrust and need for direction and control of subordinates, whereas successful men in management reject Theory X (Donnell and Hall, 1980).

Sexual harassment is a problem common to most working women. It is a continual reminder of second class status. Although differences exist in defining harrassment and in estimating the frequency and magnitude of occurrence, for example a recent survey showed 66 percent of men and 32 percent of women believe the amount of sexual harassment at work is greatly exaggerated (Collins and Blodgett, 1981), several studies indicate women believe harassment is a problem (U.S. Department of Labor, 1978; U.S. Department of Health, Education and Welfare, 1979; Renick, 1980; Collins and Blodgett, 1981; Deaux and Ullman, 1982; Rosen, 1982). One study found that husbands and boyfriends were against having their wives or friends work in blue-collar, masculine, sex-typed jobs because of concern over possible sexual abuse (U.S. Department of Labor, 1978). Although some men believe their actions show affection, only 15 percent of women answering a survey in *Redbook Magazine* perceived mild forms of harassment as flattering (Safran, 1976). The consequences of sexual harassment are serious. Women report feeling helpless, and because they worry that complaints might result in additional problems, the predominate coping strategy is to ignore sexual remarks and avoid future harassment situations. Such actions are examples of inactive coping because it fails to remove the source of stress. Inactive coping is generally thought to be one of the least effective strategies for dealing with stress. A study conducted by the Work Clinic at the University of California-Berkeley found women who complained of sexual harassment had chronic fatigue, loss of strength, aches, pains, depression, nervousness, hostility, and feelings of victimization. Unfortunately, most men, especially those in middle and upper management, do not seem to understand how much sexual harassment humiliates and frustrates women (Collins and Blodgett, 1981).

It would seem important to discern the difference between harassment and hazing, both of which happen to women who work outside the home. Harassment is intended to exclude the person from the group. It preserves group membership and maintains the status quo. Hazing, on the other hand, often is undertaken with the intention of admitting the person into the group. It is a ritual or rite of passage that newcomers must experience to show their desire for group membership and their inability to successfully handle work pressures. Consequently, the cognitive interpretation of the event becomes important for understanding how the person will react. I would suspect that men are better able than women to distinguish hazing from harassment. Those women who attach high importance to their job and career might be even more likely to misinterpret hazing for harassment and to experience greater stress as a result of this misinterpretation. This topic of harassment versus hazing would seem to be a particularly good area for research.

Establishing supportive relationships with superiors, peers, and subordinates is one of the most critical tasks facing women who work in nontraditional areas. Men and women must become aware of underlying issues preventing full integration.

Organization Structure and Climate

Research has not formally addressed structural and climate factors as they relate to working women. It would be valuable to learn whether decentralized organizations, which tend to have greater capacity for innovation, are structurally more equipped to absorb women into management and blue collar positions. Technology also should be considered as modern steel mills are vastly different from older mills. A final example of needed research might be an attempt to assess or create a "climate for sex integration" within the organization.

Research currently available does point to the importance of organizationally sponsored programs designed to place and utilize women effectively in nontraditional job areas. Support groups, hiring several women at a time, training supervisors on how to avoid unfair discrimination in dealing with women, remedial training programs to compensate for sex differences in life experiences that might impact on job performance (e.g., names of mechanical tools), and career development plans are some tactics that have shown success (U.S. Department of Labor, 1978).

Women and other members in the organization must become knowledgeable in structural determinants of power and in effects of different coordination and control mechanisms. The above suggestions will not be successful if women continue to be placed in dead-end jobs or subjected to differential control mechanisms that discourage risk taking and responsibility (Acker and Van Houten, 1974). Considerably more attention must be given to structural factors in attempts to reduce or remove sources of stress encountered by working women. Far too much has been written about differences between men and women while ignoring the impact of structure and environment on sex discrimination (Terborg, 1977).

Summary

Women who work outside the home in feminine sex-typed jobs are suscep-tible to stressors intrinsic to the nature of those occupations. These stressors include low pay, little opportunity for skill development, little variety and autonomy, and high responsibility for people. In addition, these women are likely to hold traditional sex-role attitudes, have several children, and be primarily responsible for maintaining the home.

Women who work in blue-collar masculine sex-typed jobs are more likely to be single heads of households with recurring financial needs. Resistance in the form of strongly held sex-role stereotypes is commonly found in blue-collar men. Physical demands and unfamiliarity with tools and equipment make high performance more difficult. Sexual harassment is a problem as is the fact that many work settings were not designed to accommodate women.

Those women who work in white-collar, masculine sex-typed jobs face barriers in career advancement. They might have high aspirations but assignment to low power positions and exclusion from informal communi-cation and influence networks perpetuates low status. Role conflict and ambiguity associated with equivocal standards of performance coupled with poor interpersonal relations contribute to frustration and futility. White-collar women also experience sexual harassment.

IMPORTANCE, UNCERTAINTY, AND DURATION: IMPLICATIONS FOR WORKING WOMEN AND STRESS

In Chapter 1, Beehr and Bhagat provided frameworks for understanding stress resulting from situations requiring problem solving and decision making, and stress resulting from situations requiring behavioral action. When faced with a problem-solving or decision-making task, the cognitive experience of stress will be greatest when high levels of uncertainty are associated with the attainment of important outcomes during periods of long duration. Situations requiring behavioral action will produce the cognition of stress when the individual perceives an inability or difficulty in meeting demands where failure to meet demands results in important consequences. The total amount of stress experienced by the person is proposed to be equal to the summation of work domain-related stress and nonwork domain-related stress. This section will examine working women and stress from the Beehr and Bhagat perspective.

Importance

Decisions concerning important outcomes are more likely to be stress producing than decisions where unimportant outcomes are involved.

Women who seek careers in masculine sex-typed white collar occupations make that decision knowing the outcomes are very important. Earlier in this chapter it was shown that women often view a professional career as incompatible with a family or children. They also seem aware of possible resistance by family, friends, and co workers. Finally, pursuit of a career requires a considerable commitment in time and money and plots a course of action that sometimes is irreversible. Women with nontraditional sex-role identities might still value marriage and childrearing, and this makes the decision extremely consequential. Those who do marry and have children might never be able to launch a serious career if they wait until their children are older or in school. Considerable satisfaction can be derived from watching a child grow, develop, and learn, but women with talent might always wonder how they would have done if they pursued a career.

Because of the importance associated with a managerial or professional career, women who make this decision are resolute. They are likely to interpret situations and events differently from other women and from most men. Not only are selected decisions more important but a greater number of decisions become important.

Women who seek jobs in sex-typed blue-collar occupations do not face the same issues because of differences between what constitutes a career and what constitutes a job. A career requires extensive training, progresses over a long period of time, and involves a willingness to put the organization above personal desires. Even in the skilled trades, women would be able to maintain a reasonable personal life that could include marriage and family.

In contrast with career oriented women and those in sex-typed blue collar jobs, women who work in traditional feminine sex-typed jobs often work to provide income. The job is instrumental to a better nonwork domain life-style. There is perhaps less commitment in time and training, less inclusion and involvement in the job, and less one has to give up.

To the extent that importance is related to stress, the Beehr and Bhagat framework would predict greatest opportunities for stress among women choosing masculine sex-typed white collar careers, fewer opportunities for stress among women choosing masculine sex-typed blue-collar jobs, and the fewest opportunities for stress among women with traditional sex-role identities who work in feminine sex-typed jobs. The concept of importance also points to women who were career oriented but chose a family instead. These women might be less resilient to pressures of raising a family than women with more traditional sex-role stereotypes.

Uncertainty

Uncertainty is a second factor Beehr and Bhagat associate with stress. Uncertainty can pertain to choice of methods used to obtain some outcome and choice of outcome one should try to obtain. One might add anticipated satisfaction or value one might experience after obtaining the outcome as a third source of uncertainty. People may understand how to acquire a particular outcome they want but still have some uncertainty over whether they really will like it or not. A couple may decide they want a child and understand what they must do to have a child, but be uncertain whether they will enjoy parenthood once they experience it.

Based on this review of the literature, it would appear women in masculine sex-typed white-collar careers have the greatest uncertainty associated with their decision. Success often is ambiguous and might not be determined for a period of several years. Outcomes vary and are the result of complex means-ends relationships. Failure to receive social support, failure to receive information about efficient work methods, and lack of sponsorhip by influential superiors all contribute to chronic role ambiguity and role conflict. Confusion also seems to cloud behavior expectations. Should the young and new woman professional try and act like "one of the boys" or should she look for opportunities to reinforce her femininity? Will attempts to meet with colleagues so that role expectations and responsibilities can be charted be viewed as a lack of competence? Is she in that job primarily because she is a woman and not because of her potential to make a contribution? Managerial and professional work are long-cycle jobs, with few tangible outputs, that require considerable amounts of social interaction in order to get things done. Stereotypes will not be broken down easily in such settings. Resistance might be a continual problem for women in minority positions. Even when they have been accepted by their own colleagues, interaction with others outside the immediate office might produce the need to demonstrate competence all over again. Women who have not attained unambiguous levels of success and who have delayed marriage or pregnancy might begin to have serious doubts about whether all the effort, compromise, and sacrifice was worthwhile.

In contrast to managerial and professional work, most blue-collar jobs are short-cycle jobs with tangible measures of success requiring limited social interaction. Although some women might experience considerable uncertainty in areas of physical strength and technical knowledge, after a short while on the job it will become clear whether success is likely or not. Similarly, women in feminine sex-typed jobs will not experience the same degree of role ambiguity and role conflict that results from sex-role incongruency. There are fewer areas where uncertainties exist and reduction of uncertainties is more easily and rapidly accomplished.

Duration

Duration of uncertainties also differentiates managerial and professional jobs from blue-collar jobs and feminine sex-typed occupations. Problems brought about by sex-role stereotypes will require more or less continuous monitoring and repeated coping. It is not likely that one or two successful women managers in a company will dramatically change attitudes and values that are the products of lifelong socialization. Rather than changing attitudes and values, male colleagues might find it easier to label those women as exceptions.

Characteristics of managerial and professional jobs that contribute to the existence of uncertainties also contribute to longer duration of those uncertainties for women seeking careers in masculine sex-typed fields. In blue-collar jobs, for example, effort or skill is more directly and immediately evidenced in better performance. People in those jobs learn that they can impact their environment. In contrast, feelings of job efficacy are subjective and open to interpretive bias when many white collar jobs are studied. To the extent women are unable to resolve uncertainties over long periods of time and develop the belief that actions are not likely to produce desired outcomes, feelings typical of learned helplessness can result. Learned helplessness only can increase stress and stress-related outcomes as it leads to ineffective coping. Both men and women can learn to be helpless. But because women are more likely than men to have low power and to experience male competency sex bias in attributions for performance, characteristics of learned helplessness might be observed more frequently among women than men. Recall that women tend to have lower expectancies about their potential to bring about change in their environment.

Stress and Behavior

The previous discussion focused on decision-making and problem-solving situations; what should I do rather than what can I do. Limitations to action also deserve some mention as stress can occur when the person perceives an inability to take action where failure to take action is thought to produce an undesirable outcome.

A major source of stress for working women seems to be associated with quantitative role overload produced by an inability to shed home and family responsibilities. Time constraints, incompatible demands, and physical limitations contribute to mental and physical exhaustion. Methods for reducing stress include removal of roles and responsibilities and cognitive reappraisal of the situation such that less importance is attached to particular aspects of work and nonwork domain. Women professionals are best equipped to remove role demands as there is some evidence of greater spouse support, and dual career families are likely to earn higher incomes (Herman and Gyllstrom, 1977; Holahan and Gilbert, 1979).

Women in feminine sex-typed occupations, however, are most likely to be married to husbands with traditional sex-role attitudes, which the women also subscribe to, making spouse support less likely for them. Thus, we might expect a high incidence of role based stress for these women. But, such families often have older children who can help, and, the occurrence of regular part-time work is highest for women in feminine sex-typed jobs. Also, these women might receive more pleasure from family duties than do women with nontraditional sex-role stereotypes.

Single mothers who are heads of households probably are most vulnerable to quantitative role overload. Those who work in masculine sex-typed blue collar jobs might also be the most physically tired when they return home. Overrepresentation of women in low paying craft and trade positions places additional financial burdens on working mothers who are heads of households. It has been noted that this group had exceptionally high rates of admittance to mental health hospitals and use of mental health services. It also should be noted that home and family responsibilities are of long duration. Thus, the cumulative effects of otherwise minor demands can produce stress-related physical and mental health problems.

Work and Life Stress

The combination of stress from the work domain is the final area to be considered. Women who work in masculine sex-typed professional and white collar jobs are likely to encounter the greatest job-related stress, but the potential for stress outside the work domain is reduced through more effective coping strategies. Career women are more likely to be single, or childless if married. Good incomes and spouse support further contribute to effective coping. The rewards of a successful career are considerable, and this incentive might encourage persistence in goal directed behavior and continued backing by the spouse.

In contrast, women who work in nontraditional blue-collar jobs probably do not experience the same high level of job-related stress as do women professionals because uncertainty and duration about job outcomes becomes less important. Considerable frustrations and adjustments are required, however, so stress should be greater for women in blue-collar jobs than for men in blue collar jobs. Potential for excessive nonwork domain related stress exists as these women attempt to accommodate job and family demands.

Finally, women who work in traditional feminine sex-typed occupations might be expected to experience the least life stress. First, they do not face sanctions for out-of-role behavior. Second, this group of working women includes many who work part time so job and family demands do not overlap as much as they might for women who work full time. And third, these women do not attach the same importance to their work domain as women in nontraditional fields. While objectively, women who work in feminine sex-typed jobs might experience low pay, low quality jobs, and responsibilities beyond given authority, and, while objectively they might assume primary responsibilities for taking care of a home and raising a family, they also might cognitively appraise the situation in a manner that minimizes felt stress. Past experiences, perceptions of available alternatives, and expectations provide anchors that working women with traditional sex-role attitudes and values might use to indicate things are not as bad as they might seem to others.

Beehr and Bhagat (see Chapter 1) view stress as a cognitive state in which the perception of stress is critical. Sex-role identity and views on appropriate and inappropriate sex-role behavior might be key factors in determining the cognitive experience of stress. Self-selection to particular situations, selective perception of particular cues in the environment, and cognitive evaluation of the impact of those cues could vary with sex-role identity. Unfortunately, cognitive appraisal cannot remove objective sources of stress. Nursing, for example, may be a stressful job regardless of cognitive appraisal. But, the cognitive aspect of stress might explain differences and lack of differences in stress experienced by working women beyond that attributable to objective job and family characteristics.

FUTURE RESEARCH NEEDS

This chapter reviewed an extensive literature on working women and stress. An analysis of the status of working women, characteristics of feminine sex-typed occupations, and occupational sex-discrimination suggests women who work outside the home are more likely to experience stress than are men. Of all the material reviewed, however, only a small proportion actually examined working women, working men, and stress in the same study. The existing literature can be divided into three categories: (1) those studies that examine work-related antecedents of stress, for example, blocked career pathways cause stress; (2) those studies that examine women in the work force, for example, women in masculine sex-typed white-collar jobs encountered barriers to career advancement; and (3) those studies that examine overall sex differences in physical and mental health, for example, women are twice as likely to be diagnosed as depressed as are men. Consequently, a great deal of research remains to be done in order to establish or disconfirm much of what has been said in this chapter about women, work, and stress.

Terborg et al. (1982) studied socialization experiences of men and women graduate students in male sex-typed, female sex-typed, and mixed-sex academic career fields. No sex differences were found on measures of role conflict or ambiguity, psychological or physical symptoms of stress, or satisfaction with work and life. Of interest, women reported lower self-confidence, but greater support from faculty, especially in male sex-typed fields such as chemistry and biology. These data were collected over a 2-year period. Tung (1980) did a comparative analysis of the occupational stress profiles of male and female educational administrators. She found that males reported greater stress than females even when controlling for position level and tenure. Unfortunately, she did not assess school district characteristics that might have produced these results if women were in smaller and less hostile community environments. Nevertheless, comparative studies like these are valuable.

What must be done? What should the research agenda for women, work, and stress look like? First, a desperate need exists for descriptive research on women in (1) masculine sex-typed, white-collar jobs, (2) masculine sex-typed, blue-collar jobs, (3) feminine sex-typed jobs, and (4) full-time homemaker positions. At the present time it is very difficult to make comparative statements because so little research has focused on women in blue-collar jobs or on women as full-time homemakers. To illustrate, it would be valuable to know if reliable differences exist across these four groups on any of the personality measures discussed earlier in this chapter. It also would be valuable at the same time to collect information on the physical and psychological well-being of women in the four groups and on perceptions of the levels of importance, uncertainty, and duration associated with major life decisions and everyday problem-solving activities. A broad based study designed to establish relationships among characteristics of the objective situation, personality dimensions of people in different objective situations, perceptions of importance, uncertainty, and duration, and measures of the physical and psychological well-being of people in the sample would help focus future research. If similar data could be collected on a sample of men, the findings would be of immense value. If such a study were conducted, it most certainly would raise more questions than it would answer. But, the important first step of basic descriptive research would be completed.

Although I would probably favor descriptive research at the current level of understanding, there are some rather intriguing questions that merit attention. The literature is not clear on the function sex-role identity plays in mediating work and stress. For example, Bem (1975) believes androgeny leads to a positive and healthy life-style, yet evidence is just beginning to surface that suggests greater deference be placed on "masculine" characteristics (Olds and Shaver, 1980). Therefore, one research question would focus on relationships between sex-role identity, perceptions of importance and uncertainty, and stress. Do androgenous women experience greater uncertainty with regard to how they should behave and what the consequences of their behaviors are likely to be?

The entire question of cognitive appraisal is a second area that offers interesting possibilities. Traditionally feminine sex-typed jobs were found to be classified as stressful. Women with traditional sex-role stereotypes who also work full time should have the greatest quantitative role overload. Yet it is not clear that women who work full time in feminine sex-typed jobs experience the greatest amount of stress.

A third question I will propose for study brings in the topic of learned helplessness. I find fascinating the results of studies like that conducted by Dweck, Davidson, Nelson, and Enna (1978) in which they discovered girls were given subtle cues and reinforcements that fostered self-blame, low self-confidence, low expectancies, and low aspirations. What could be more stressful than facing a situation where you perceive considerable uncertainty about your ability to change the occurrence of an unpleasant outcome especially when the outcome is important? Bandura's (1977) social learning theory concepts of self-efficacy and modeling would be relevant for understanding whether sex-role stereotypes prevalent in our society cultivate learned helplessness among girls and women.

In conclusion, the current explosion of research on stress must continue. In an earlier review on women in management (Terborg, 1977) I suggested that we perhaps could learn more about women in management if we studied management in general rather than focusing all of our attention on women in management. I similarly believe that we will learn a lot about working women and stress if we study what it is about work that causes stress. But, in contrast to my earlier remarks, I believe attention also should be directed specifically to women, work, and stress. Adoption of a common framework to guide research and to facilitate accumulation to knowledge would be beneficial. This chapter and the others in the book represent one approach that deserves attention.

ACKNOWLEDGMENTS

I would like to thank Carol Arian, Angie McArthur, and Shirlynn Spacapan for many helpful comments.

REFERENCES

Acker, J. and Van Houten, D. R. Differential recruitment and control: The sex structuring of organizations. *Administrative Science Quarterly*, 1974, **19**, 152–163.

Adams, E. F. A multivariate study of subordinate perceptions of and attitudes toward minority and majority managers. *Journal of Applied Psychology*, 1978, **63**, 277–288.

Albrecht, K. *Stress and the manager.* Englewood Cliffs, N.J.: Prentice-Hall, 1979.

Anderson, C. R. Locus of control, coping behaviors, and performance in a stress setting: A longitudinal study. *Journal of Applied Psychology*, 1977, **62**, 446–451.

Arvey, R. D. and Begalla, M. E. Analyzing the homemaker job using the Position Analysis Questionnaire (PAQ). *Journal of Applied Psychology*, 1975, **60**, 513–517.

Bandura, A. *Social learning theory.* Englewood Cliffs, N.J.: Prentice-Hall, 1977.

Beehr, T. A. and Newman, J. E. Job stress, employee health, and organizational effectiveness: A facet analysis, model, and literature review. *Personnel Psychology*, 1978, **31**, 665–700.

Beckman, L. J. Women alcoholics: A review of social and psychological studies. *Journal of Studies on Alcohol*, 1975, **36**, 797–824.

Beckman, L. J. The relative rewards and costs of parenthood and employment for employed women. *Psychology of Women Quarterly*, 1978, **2**, 215–234.

Belle, D. Mothers and their children. In C. L. Heckerman (Ed.), *The evolving female.* New York: Human Sciences Press, 1980.

Bem, S. L. Sex role adaptability: One consequence of psychological androgyny. *Journal of Personality and Social Psychology*, 1975, **31**, 634–643.

Bettelheim, B. Individual and mass behavior in extreme situations. In E. E. Maccoby (Ed.), *Readings in social psychology.* New York: Holt, Rinehart & Winston, 1958.

Bhagat, R. S. Effects of stressful life events upon individual performance effectiveness and work adjustment processes within organizational settings. *Academy of Management Review,* 1983, **8**, 660–671.

Bhagat, R. S. and Chassie, M. B. Determinants of organizational commitment in working women: Some implications for organizational behavior. *Journal of Occupational Behavior,* 1981, **2**, 17–30.

Brief, A. P., Schuler, R. S., and Van Sell, M. *Managing job stress.* Boston: Little, Brown, 1981.

Briggs, N. L. *Adult women in the skilled trades.* Columbus: Ohio State University, 1978. (ERIC Document Reproduction Service No. ED 164975)

Broverman, I. K., Broverman, D. M., Clarkson, F. E., Rosenkrantz, P. S., and Vogel, S. Sex-role stereotypes and clinical judgments of mental health. *Journal of Consulting and Clinical Psychology,* 1970, **34**, 1–7.

Broverman, I. K., Vogel, S. R., Broverman, D. M., Clarkson, F. E., and Rosenkrantz, P. S. Sex-role stereotypes: A current appraisal. *Journal of Social Issues,* 1972, **28**, 59–79.

Brown, S. M. Males versus female leaders: A comparison of empirical studies. *Sex Roles,* 1979, **5**, 595–611.

Card, J. J., Steel, L., and Abeles, R. P. Sex differences in realization of individual potential for achievement. *Journal of Vocational Behavior,* 1980, **17**, 1–21.

Chesney, M. A. and Rosenman, R. H. Type A behavior in the work setting. In C.L. Cooper and R. Payne (Eds.), *Current concerns in occupational stress.* New York: Wiley, 1980.

Cohen, S. Aftereffects of stress on human performance and social behavior: A review of research and theory. *Psychological Bulletin,* 1980, **88**, 82–108.

Colligan, M. J., Smith, M., and Hurrell, J. Occupational incidence rates of mental health disorders. *Journal of Human Stress,* 1977, **3**, 34–39.

Collins, E. G. and Blodgett, T. B. Sexual harassment: Some get it; some don't. *Harvard Business Review,* 1981, **59**, 77–94.

Cooper, C. L. and Davidson, M. J. The high cost of stress on women managers. *Organizational Dynamics,* 1982, **10**, 44–53.

Cooper, C. L. and Marshall, J. Sources of managerial and white-collar stress. In C. L. Cooper and R. Payne (Eds.), *Stress at work.* New York: Wiley, 1978.

Costrich, N., Feinstein, J., Kidder, L., Marecek, J., and Pascale, L. When stereotypes hurt: Three studies of penalties for sex-role reversals. *Journal of Experimental Social Psychology,* 1975, **11**, 520–530.

Deaux, K. *The behavior of women and men.* Monterey, Calif.: Brooks/Cole, 1976.

Deaux, K. and Ullman, J. C. Hard-hatted women: Reflections on blue collar employment. In J. Sgro and H. J. Bernardin (Eds.), *Women in the work force.* New York: Praeger, 1982.

DeGregorio, E. and Carver, C. S. Type A behavior pattern, sex role orientation, and psychological adjustment. *Journal of Personality and Social Psychology,* 1980, **39**, 286–293.

Donnell, S. M. and Hall, J. Men and women as managers: A significant case of no significant differences. *Organizational Dynamics,* 1980, **8**, 60–77.

Dweck, C. S., Davidson, W., Nelson, S., and Enna, B. Sex differences in learned helplessness. *Developmental Psychology,* 1978, **14**, 268–276.

Endicott, F. S. *Employment trends for college graduates: The Endicott Report, 1980.* Chicago: Northwestern University, 1979.

England, P. and McLaughlin, S. D. *The sex segregation of jobs and the male-female income differential.* Paper presented at the Annual Meeting of the Southwest Academy of Management, Dallas, March 1978.

French, J. R. P., Rogers, W., and Cobb, S. Adjustment as a person-environment fit. In G. U. Coelho, D. A. Hamburg, and J. E. Adams (Eds.), *Coping and adaptation*. New York: Basic Books, 1974.

Freudenberger, H. J. Burn-out: Occupational hazard of the child care worker. *Child Care Quarterly*, 1977, **6**, 90–99.

Garbin, A. P. and Stover, R. G. Vocational behavior and career development 1979: A review. *Journal of Vocational Behavior*, 1980, **17**, 125–170.

Gordon, F. E. and Hall, D. T. Self-image and stereotypes of femininity: Their relationship to women's role conflicts and coping. *Journal of Applied Psychology*, 1974, **59**, 241–243.

Gove, W. R. and Tudor, J. F. Adult sex roles and mental illness. In J. Huber (Ed.), *Changing women in a changing society*. Chicago: University of Chicago Press, 1973.

Greenfeld, S., Greiner, L., and Wood, M. M. The "feminine mystique" in male-dominated jobs: A comparison of attitudes and background factors of women in male-dominated vs. female-dominated jobs. *Journal of Vocational Behavior*, 1980, **17**, 291–309.

Gruenberg, B. The happy worker: An analysis of educational and occupational differences in determinants of job satisfaction. *American Journal of Sociology*, 1980, **86**, 247–271.

Gurin, P. Labor market experiences and expectancies. *Sex Roles*, 1981, **7**, 1079–1092.

Guttentag, M. and Salasin, S. Women, men and mental health. In L. Cater and A. Scott (Eds.), *Changing roles of men and women*. Aspen. Colo.: Aspen Press, 1976.

Hall, D. T. A model of coping with role conflict: The role behavior of college educated women. *Administrative Science Quarterly*, 1972, **17**, 471–486.

Hall, D. T. and Gordon, F. E. Career choices of married women: Effects on conflict, role behavior, and satisfaction. *Journal of Applied Psychology*, 1973, **58**, 42–48.

Hall, D. T. and Hall, F. S. Stress and the two-career couple. In C. L. Cooper and R. Payne (Eds.), *Current concerns in occupational stress*. New York: Wiley, 1980.

Handy, C. The family: Help or hindrance? In C. L. Cooper and R. Payne (Eds.), *Stress at Work*. New York: Wiley, 1978.

Heilman, M. E. The impact of situational factors on personnel decisions concerning women: Varying the sex composition of the applicant pool. *Organizational Behavior and Human Performance*, 1980, **26**, 383–395.

Herman, J. B. and Gyllstrom, K. K. Working men and women: Inter and intrarole conflict. *Psychology of Women Quarterly*, 1977, **1**, 319–333.

Hoffman, L. W. Fear of success—1965 and 1974: A follow-up study. *Journal of Consulting and Clinical Psychology*, 1977, **45**, 310–321.

Hoffman, L. W. and Nye, R. I. *Working mothers*. San Francisco: Jossey-Bass, 1974.

Holahan, C. K. Stress experienced by women doctoral students, need for support, and occupational sex typing: An interactional view. *Sex Roles*, 1979, **5**, 425–536.

Holahan, C. K. and Gilbert, L. A. Interrole conflict for working women: Careers vs. jobs. *Journal of Applied Psychology*, 1979, **64**, 86–90.

Holmes, T. H. and Rahe, R. H. The social readjustment rating scale. *Journal of Psychosomatic Research*, 1967, **11**, 213–218.

Horner, M. S. Toward an understanding of achievement related conflict in women. *Journal of Social Issues*, 1972, **28**, 157–175.

How Executives See Women in Management. *Business Week*, June 28, 1982, p. 10.

Ivancevich, J. M. and Matteson, M. T. *Stress and work: A managerial perspective*. Glenview, Ill.: Scott, Foresman, 1980.

Izraeli, D. N., Banai, M., and Zeira, Y. Women executives in MNC subsidiaries. *California Management Review*, 1980, **23**, 53–63.

Johnson, S. J. and Black, N. The relationship between sex-role identity and beliefs in personal control. *Sex Roles*, 1981, **8**, 425–431.

Kahn, R. Conflict, ambiguity, and overload: Three elements in job stress. In A. Mclean (Ed.), *Occupational stress*. Springfield, Ill.: Thomas, 1974.

Kanter, R. M. *Men and women of the corporation*. New York: Basic Books, 1977.

Kaufman, D. and Felters, M. L. Work motivation and job values among professional men and women: A new accounting. *Journal of Vocational Behavior*, 1980, **17**, 251–261.

Kelly, J. A.and Worell, J. New formulations of sex roles and androgyny: A critical review. *Journal of Consulting and Clinical Psychology*, 1977, **45**, 1101–1115.

Keyserling, M. D. The economic status of women in the United States. *American Economic Review*, 1976, **66**, 205–212.

Kobasa, S. C. Stressful life events, personality, and health: An inquiry into hardiness. *Journal of Personality and Social Psychology*, 1979, **37**, 1–12.

Kutner, N. G. and Brogan, D. R. Problems of colleagueship for women entering the medical profession. *Sex Roles*, 1981, **7**, 739–746.

Laws, J. L. The psychology of tokenism: An analysis. *Sex Roles*, 1975, **1**, 51–67.

Lemkau, J. P. Women and employment. In C. L. Heckerman (Ed.), *The evolving female*. New York: Human Sciences Press, 1980.

Lenney, E. Women's self-confidence in achievement settings. *Psychological Bulletin*, 1977, **84**, 1–13.

Lyle, J. R. and Ross, J. L. *Women in industry*. Lexington, Mass.: Heath, 1973.

Maccoby, E. E. and Jacklin, C. N. *The psychology of sex differences*. Stanford, Calif.: Stanford University Press, 1974.

Mackay-Smith, A. Women are facing hostility and hazing as few break into commodity trading. *Wall Street Journal*, January 22, 1982, pp. 29, 43.

Makosky, V. P. Stress and the mental health of women: A discussion of research and issues. In M. Guttentag, S. Salasin, and D. Belle (Eds.), *The mental health of women*. New York: Academic Press, 1980.

Marshall, S. J. and Wijting, J. P. Relationships of achievement motivation and sex-role identity to college women's career orientation. *Journal of Vocational Behavior*, 1980, **16**, 299–311.

Maslach, C. and Pines, A. The burn-out syndrome in the day care setting. *Child Care Quarterly*, 1977, **6**, 100–113.

Mathews, J. J., Collins, W. E., and Cobb, B. B. A sex comparison of reasons for attrition in a male dominated occupation. *Personnel Psychology*, 1974, **27**, 535–541.

McCormick, E. J., Jeanneret, P. R., and Mecham, R. C. A study of job characteristics and job dimensions based on the Position Analysis Questionnaire. *Journal of Applied Psychology*, 1972, **56**, 347–368.

Mednick, M. T. Women and the psychology of achievement: Implication for personal and social change. In J. Sgro and H. J. Bernardin (Eds.), *Women in the work force*. New York: Praeger, 1982.

Morrison, R. F. and Sebald, M. Personal characteristics differentiating female executive from female non-executive personnel. *Journal of Applied Psychology*, 1974, **59**, 656–659.

Muchinsky, P. M. Employee absenteeism: A review of the literature. *Journal of Vocational Behavior*, 1977, **10**, 316–340.

Mussen, P. H. Early sex-role development. In D. A. Goslin (Ed.), *Handbook of socialization theory and research*. Chicago: Rand McNally, 1969.

Nye, R.I. *Role structure and analysis of the family*. Beverly Hills, Calif.: Sage, 1976.

Olds, D. E. and Shaver, P. Masculinity, femininity, academic performance and health: Further evidence concerning the androgyny controversy. *Journal of Personality*, 1980, **48**, 323–341.

O'Leary, V. E. Some attitudinal barriers to occupational aspirations in women. *Psychological Bulletin*, 1974, **81**, 809–826.

O'Leary, V. E. and Hansen, R. D. Trying hurts women, helps men: The meaning of effort. In J. Sgro and H. J. Bernardin (Eds.), *Women in the work force*. New York: Praeger, 1982.

Pines, A. and Kafry, D. Tedium in the life and work of professional women as compared with men. *Sex Roles*, 1981, **7**, 963–977.

Renick, J. C. Sexual harassment at work: Why it happens, what to do about it. *Personnel Journal*, 1980, **59**, 660–663.

Rosen, B. Career progress of women: Getting in and staying in. In J. Sgro and H. J. Bernardin (Eds.), *Women in the work force*. New York: Praeger, 1982.

Rosen, B., Templeton, M. E., and Kichline, K. The first few years on the job: Women in management. *Business Horizons*, 1981, **24**, 26–29.

Rotter, J. B. Generalized expectancies for internal vs. external control of reinforcement. *Psychological Monographs*, 1966, **80**, 1–28.

Ruble, D. N., and Ruble, T. L. Sex stereotypes. In A. G. Miller (Ed.), *In the eye of the beholder: Contemporary issues in stereotyping*. New York: Holt, Rinehart & Winston, 1980.

Safran, C. What men do to women on the job—A shocking look at sexual harassment. *Redbook Magazine*, 1976, **148**, pp. 149, 217–224.

Schuler, R. Definition and conceptualization of stress in organizations. *Organizational Behavior and Human Performance*, 1980, **25**, 184–215.

Segovis, J. C. and Bhagat, R. S. Participation revisited: Implications for organizational stress and performance. *Small Group Behavior*, 1981, **12**, 299–328.

Seligman, M. E. P. *Helplessness: On depression, development and death*. San Francisco: W. H. Freeman, 1975.

Sewell, W. H., Hauser, R. M. and Wolf, W. C. Sex, schooling, and occupational status. *American Journal of Sociology*, 1980, **86**, 551–583.

Smith, F. J., Scott, K. D., and Hulin, C. L. Trends in job-related attitudes of managerial and professional employees. *Academy of Management Journal*, 1977, **20**, 454–460.

Smith, P. C., Kendall, L.M., and Hulin, C. L. *The measurement of satisfaction in work and retirement*. Chicago: Rand McNally, 1969.

Spence, J. T., Helreich, R., and Stapp, J. Ratings of self and peers on sex role attributes and their relation to self-esteem and conceptions of masculinity and femininity. *Journal of Personality and Social Psychology*, 1975, **32**, 29–39.

Steers, R. M. *Introduction to organizational behavior*. Santa Monica, Calif.: Goodyear, 1981.

Stellman, J. M. *Women's work, women's health: Myths and realities*. New York: Random House, 1977.

Stewart, A. J. *Fear of success and achievement behavior in adult females*. Paper presented at the Annual Meeting of the Eastern Psychological Association, Philadelphia, March 1977.

Study Shows How Women Face Hurdles. *Eugene Register-Guard*, June 1, 1982, p. 11B.

Terborg, J. R. Women in management: A research review. *Journal of Applied Psychology*, 1977, **62**, 647–664.

Terborg, J. R. and Zalensky, M. D. Women as managers: A review of research on occupational sex discrimination. In K. M. Rowland, M. London, G. R. Ferris, and J. L Sherman (Eds.), *Current issues in personnel management*. Boston: Allyn & Bacon, 1980.

Terborg, J. R., Zalesny, M. D., and Tubbs, M. E. Socialization experiences of women and men graduate students in male sex-typed career fields: A longitudinal field survey investigation. In J. Sgro and H. J. Bernardin (Eds.), *Women in the work force*. New York: Praeger, 1982.

Terborg, J. R. and Shingledecker, P. S. Employee reactions to supervision and work evaluation as a function of subordinate and manager sex. *Sex Roles*, 1983, **9**, 813–824.

Thornton, A. and Cambrun, D. Fertility, sex role attitudes, and labor force participation. *Psychology of Women Quarterly*, 1979, 4, 61–80.

Tipton, R. M. Attitudes towards women's roles in society and vocational interests. *Journal of Vocational Behavior*, 1976, **8**, 155–165.

Tung, R. L. Comparative analysis of the occupational stress profiles of male versus female administrators. *Journal of Vocational Behavior*, 1980, **17**, 344–355.

U.S. Department of Health, Education, and Welfare. *Working women speak*. Washington D.C.: U.S. Government Printing Office, 1979.

U.S. Department of Labor. *Dictionary of occupational titles*. Washington, D.C.: U.S. Government Printing Office, 1965.

U.S. Department of Labor. *Women's Bureau Bulletin: The myth and the reality*. Washington, D. C.: U.S. Government Printing Office, 1974.

U.S. Department of Labor. *Employment and earnings*. Washington, D.C.: U.S. Government Printing Office, 1977.

U.S. Department of Labor. *Women in traditionally male jobs: The experiences of ten public utility companies*. Washington, D.C: U.S. Government Printing Office, 1978.

U.S. Department of Labor. *The earnings gap between women and men*. Washington, D.C.: U.S. Government Printing Office, 1979.

U.S. Department of Labor. *Handbook of labor statistics*. Washington, D.C.: U.S. Government Printing Office, 1980.

Waldron, I. The coronary-prone behavior pattern, blood pressure, employment and socioeconomic status in women. *Journal of Psychosomatic Research*, 1978, **22**, 79–87,

Wallston, B. S. and O'Leary, V. E. Sex and gender make a difference: The differential perceptions of women and men. In L. Wheeler (Ed.), *Review of personality and social psychology*, Vol. 2. Beverly Hills, Calif.: Sage, 1981.

Warr, P. and Parry, G. Paid employment and women's psychological well-being. *Psychological Bulletin*, 1982, **91**, 498–516.

Weaver, C. N. The irony of the job satisfaction of females. *The Personnel Administrator*, 1979, **24**, 70–74.

Weaver, C. N. Job satisfaction in the U. S. *Journal of Applied Psychology*, 1980, **65**, 364–367.

Wertheim, E. G., Widom, C. S., and Wortzel, L. H. Multivariate analysis of male and female professional career choice correlates. *Journal of Applied Psychology*, 1978, **63**, 234–242.

Women in America. The Gallup opinion index, March 1976. Report No. 128.

Yeager, D. S. The balancing act: No tea, no sympathy. *MBA Magazine*, February 1977, pp. 23–24; 39.

CHAPTER ELEVEN

Job-Related Stress of the Minority Professional

An Exploratory Analysis and Suggestions for Future Research

DAVID L. FORD, JR.

The volume of research on the causes and consequences of stress experienced by workers in organizations has grown in recent years, and a number of publications have dealt with the topic of job-related stress (see, e.g., Ivancevich and Matteson, 1980; McLean, 1980; Cooper and Payne, 1978, 1980; Schuler, 1980; Brief et al., 1981). A related body of literature encompassing a broader range of topics dealing with the "quality of work life" has also mushroomed in recent years (see, e.g., Hackman and Suttle, 1977; Lawler et al., 1980; Greenberger, 1981a). If one reviewed what would be considered the major works in each of these bodies of literature, it would become readily apparent that a large segment of the working population—that is, blacks and other ethnic minorities—has been ignored in these works, especially in studies of job-related stress. The quality of work life literature has not been quite so negligent in its considerations of working minorities, but even here the available literature is limited.

Several recent literature reviews and theoretical model developments have attempted an integrative approach to the study of job stress (see, e.g., Matteson and Ivancevich, 1979; Beehr and Newman, 1978; Newman and Beehr, 1979; Schuler, 1980). In each of these conceptualizations of a stress research model, individual difference variables or characteristics are a component of the model. The most comprehensive delineation of individual characteristics considered in a model is provided by Beehr and Newman (1978), who explicitly included the variable of race in their model. All other models previously cited omit the variable of race as a specific variable of importance in the study of job stress. Beehr and Newman (1978) further noted that race had not been studied empirically within the context of job stress—employee health relationships. In the more than three years since the publication of their review, little has changed with respect to the availability of studies of job stress that incorporated samples of ethnic minorities. Most of the studies reported to date have involved only anglo samples from mainstream American populations or samples in which data on minorities were not analyzed separately.

One could certainly speculate as to why there have been so few publications in the job stress area that have dealt with ethnic minorities. This author believes that this state of affairs is largely due to the fact that most of the researchers do not belong to minority groups, and there are very few minority researchers engaged in job stress research projects. This latter fact became readily apparent at a recent conference (Conference on Black Stress/Distress and Coping Strategies, Oct. 21–23, 1981, University of Alabama, Tuscaloosa, Alabama), in which some 55 presentations were made on a variety of topics. While a good deal of information was imparted at the conference, the overwhelming majority of the presentations were not empirically based or derived from ongoing or completed research studies, notwithstanding the fact that practically all of the presenters were black. That is, very little research data on black stress was reported, but rather, the presentations were based on impressionistic, anecdotal evidence and reviews of past literature. Perhaps this is not so much a statement of the lack of interest on the part of black researchers in empirically based research, but more a reflection of the difficulty minority researchers have historically had in securing funds for research purposes (Brazziel, 1973; Friedlander, 1970).

My own research interests in recent years have focused on the work experiences of black and other minority professionals in predominantly white work environments (cf. Brown and Ford, 1977; Ford and Gatewood, 1976; Ford, 1976, 1978a, 1979) and, more recently, on job stress experienced by minorities at work (cf. Ford and Bagot, 1978; Ford, 1980, 1981).

The following sections of this chapter I (1) briefly review and summarize several studies, including this author's own, that deal with job-related stress in minority professionals (several of which are unpublished), and, where possible, discuss issues related to minorities other than blacks, (2) discuss this author's own approach to the study of job stress vis-a-vis the present editors' framework, and finally (3) offer some suggestions for future research. My discussion is limited to minority *professionals*, that is, persons employed as executives, managers, supervisors, clerks, and professional/technical personnel such as engineers, salespersons, scientists, and so on in a nonsupervisory capacity, or otherwise white-collar workers in major organizations. Minority workers employed as operatives, trade workers, craftspersons, and otherwise blue-collar workers are not considered explicitly, although some of the discussion might be relevant and applicable to these groups of workers. For a review of some of the issues facing them at work see Bhagat (1979). Additionally, our use of the term *minority* or *ethnic minority* is generally meant to apply to "people of color" (and includes such groups as blacks, hispanics, Asian Americans, American Indians, and so on). Other anglo/European ethnic persons residing in the United States—though they might consider themselves a minority—are not meant to be covered by this discussion.

MINORITY PROFESSIONALS AND JOB-RELATED STRESS

The editors of this volume have defined stress as a cognitive state that exists when an individual confronts a decision-making and problem-solving situation that exhibits high levels of *uncertainty* associated with obtaining *important* (i.e., valent) outcomes for the person, and when the existence of such uncertainties is long in its *duration*. Elements of this definition are similar to the definition of stress offered by Schuler (1980), in which stress is defined as a dynamic condition in which an individual is confronted with an opportunity, a constraint, or a demand on being/having/ doing what he or she desires and for which the resolution is perceived to have *uncertainty* but which will lead (upon resolution) to *important* outcomes.

On the other hand, other researchers and scholars have conceptualized stress in different terms. Recent work in the area of job-related stress has conceptualized stress in terms of a relationship between the person and the environment. Where either an environmental demand exceeds a person's response capability (overload), or the person's capabilities exceed the environmental demand (underload), the resulting misfit represents stress. Person-environment $(P-E)$ fit formulations of job stress have been incorporated in the studies by French (1974), Coburn (1975), and Blau (1981). Although Schuler (1980) criticizes $P-E$ formulations of stress as being inadequate (e.g., the assumption that when a person is in a situation of "fit" he or she is without stress—a condition that may or may not be true), this author believes the $P-E$ fit is useful for examining issues of stress as they relate to minority professionals working in predominantly white organizational settings.

Therefore, this chapter will incorporate both the present editors' definition of stress and the $P-E$ fit formulation of stress in the discussions. I believe both conceptualizations are useful and complementary approaches for understanding stress of minority professionals. Additionally, even the present editors of this volume recognize the person-environment transaction as a feature of their framework (see Chapter 1 of this volume).

Race-related stress is an unavoidable reality for minority professionals working in large, complex, predominantly white work organizations (Brown, 1977). The rigors of work and leadership make job stress a common phenomenon for many managers and other professionals, regardless of their ethnicity. Minority professionals, on the other hand, in addition to the usual stresses, must confront a set of personalized social strains that grow out of their ethnicity. In the almost exclusively white upper echelons of many large, complex organizations, many black executives, managers, and professionals especially have been known to experience certain role strains which, in ethnic parlance, are referred to as the "Black Tax" (Brown, 1975). Taxes are compulsory levies by authorities on persons and property for general governmental purposes. As evidenced by Proposition 13 in California and Proposition 2½ in Massachusetts in recent years, people are beginning to revolt against taxes in increasing numbers. Of the several categories of levies, it is the progressive tax that most parallels the "Black Tax." That is, the greater the income, the heavier the tax to be paid. Similarly, as blacks have moved into the management ranks in organizations, approaching greater power and control, the ratio of stress related to blackness has increased. Brown (1977, p. 351) has noted some of the manifestations of the Black Tax as being:

1. Conspicuous powerlessness or the "spook-who-sat-by-the door" syndrome.
2. A mutual distrust between black executives and their peers, which often places the black executives in paranoid isolation.
3. The double bind of being labeled an "Uncle Tom" and a sellout by blacks, and a racial militant by whites.
4. Participating in and rationalizing organizational policies while knowing they do not serve the interests of blacks.
5. Attempting to prove competence through "workaholism."

Matteson and Ivancevich (1979) and Schuler (1980) have delineated several antecedents or stressors associated with organizational life which, though they affect all organizational actors, are indicative of the types of "Black Tax" exacted from black workers. For example, Matteson and Ivancevich's (1979) notions of role overload, career goal discrepancy, lack of cohesiveness, intergroup conflict, and job characteristics reflect the taxes associated with types (5), (4), (2), (3), and (1) above, respectively, while Schuler's (1980) notion of leader processes, organizational structure, and interpersonal conditions are indicative of tax types (2), (1) and (4), and (2) and (3), respectively.

In recent years we have seen the revolt of black professionals against the "Black Tax." Many of the above taxing transactions, Brown (1977) believes, derive from the omnipresence of racism in organizational life.

Such transactions are demeaning to both blacks and whites because racism is a social pathology with heavy personal and social consequences.

Moreover, two recent reports concerning racial dynamics in organizations raised some unexplored theoretical questions regarding minority professionals' capacity to achieve a level of parity and fair treatment without enduring excessive psychological costs. The award-winning article by Alderfer, Alderfer, Tucker, and Tucker (1980) was based on an action-research study and vividly illustrated the wide discrepancies in perceptions of organizational phenomena by blacks and whites in the various divisions of the research organization. Space precludes an in-depth summary of this study. However, several of their observations and findings are worth mentioning (Alderfer et al., 1980):

1. On the subject of advancement, blacks in the organization tended to mention items relating to how the promotional system was structurally biased against them, while whites mentioned items that indicated how undeserving blacks were receiving accelerated promotions to the detriment of qualified whites.

2. Whites were less likely to believe that black managers were hired on the basis of competence and more likely to believe that they were hired just to fill racial quotas.

3. Black managers perceived that blacks were frequently given assignments by white managers who could not deal with competent blacks and who had the expectation that they would fail. However, few white managers felt they behaved this way or that they were unable to deal with competent blacks.

4. Both blacks and whites felt that if a black fails at a job, *all* blacks suffer in the eyes of management, but if a white fails at a job, it is an individual issue.

5. Two-thirds of the black managers and a small proportion of whites believed that blacks are almost never fairly evaluated by white supervisors.

6. White managers reported sharing relevant career information with black managers at more than twice the rate that black managers reported receiving such information.

The above findings represent some of the results of the Alderfer et al. (1980) study. A report of data gathered from several thousand interviews with black managers and professionals from a number of major corporations tends to corroborate the findings reported above. Dr. Price Cobbs, a noted black psychiatrist and partner in the consulting firm, Pacific Management Systems, Inc., which provides professional and management development seminars for black managers, addressed the Black Alumni Association of the Harvard Graduate School of Business and made the following observations, based on interviews with many of his clients (Cobbs, 1981):

1. The reality of blacks in corporations in 1981 is that they continue to be viewed from a deficit model, that is, a black is considered incompetent until he or she proves otherwise.

2. Blacks are overscrutinized and given less margin for error, even though most whites feel they get away with almost everything. The implication is that blacks are not given an *equal opportunity to fail*!

3. Blacks are still excluded from informal lines of communication—where *real* information is exchanged.

4. Blacks are faced with a promotion/earnings ceiling and a lack of role models.

5. Fast-tracking and mentorship decisions are not impacted by the credentials of blacks.

As can be seen from the above observations, there are many similarities to the Alderfer et al. (1980) findings. Additionally, the above findings have been illustrated even further in the recent works by America and Anderson (1978) and Fernandez (1981). However, these latter works failed to address the issue of job stress per se. Fernandez (1981) did not focus on the topic specifically at all and America and Anderson (1978) devoted 2½ pages out of a total of 208 to the topic of stress. Thus, all of these works could be considered related more to the general topic of quality of work life rather than job stress specifically.

However, if we examined the above findings of Alderfer et al. (1980) and Cobbs (1981), as well as the Black Tax notions of Brown (1977), within the context of the framework presented in Chapter 1, it would be readily seen that many, if not all, of the outcomes noted above would fall into a very high stress category. For example, consider the diagram in Figure 11-1 that illustrates eight cell categories of possible stress resulting from various combinations of levels of uncertainty, importance, and duration associated with a decision-making/problem-solving situation that confronts an individual.

Most of the outcomes discussed above that are difficult for black professionals to achieve in organizations—namely, advancement, being considered competent, being given assignments for which the expectation for success is high, having failure by a black viewed as an individual case rather than a group issue, fair evaluations by superiors, access to relevant career information, being given credit for credentials and access to mentor relationships—are all very *important* to the individuals concerned, but the *uncertainties* associated with achieving them is likely to be very high, and the length of time to receipt of the outcomes is likely to be long rather than short, especially in light of prior organizational history regarding access and treatment discrimination against blacks and other minorities (cf.

Duration

		Long		Short	
		Uncertainty		Uncertainty	
		High	Low	High	Low
Importance	High	Maximum Stress 1	Moderate Stress 2	High Stress 3	Moderate Stress 4
	Low	High Stress 5	Low Stress 6	Moderate Stress 7	Minimum Stress 8

Figure 11-1 Possible stress conditions resulting from uncertainty, importance, and duration associated with decision-making/problem-solving situations.

Brown and Ford, 1977; Terborg and Ilgen, 1975). Therefore, the outcomes noted by Cobbs (1981), Alderfer et al. (1980), and Brown (1977) would all fall into cell 1 of Figure 11-1, which is a very stressful situation for the individual. We would speculate that few opportunities exist in which the outcomes noted above would be expected to fall into cells 6 or 8. Therefore, the implication is that where important outcomes are involved, most minority professionals would continually experience at least a moderate level of stress in many organizational contexts due to the fact that they would encounter more uncertainties because rarely is the organization clear as to what is expected of them.

Support for this conclusion can be inferred from the work of Van Maanen and Schein (1979), who discuss a theory of organizational socialization based on three dimensions: (1) a functional dimension that refers to the tasks performed by organizational members; (2) a hierarchical dimension that concerns the distribution of rank within an organization; and (3) an inclusion dimension that concerns the interpersonal domain of organizational life and relates to the degree to which an organizational member is fully "accepted." Each of these three dimensions are discussed by Van Maanen and Schein in terms of "boundaries" that have to be crossed by an organizational member who moves from being an outsider, on the organizational periphery, to being an insider with all the rights and privileges of position. For minority professionals transgressing all three types of boundaries is difficult and most likely stressful. The outcomes noted above all have elements associated with the crossing of hierarchical, inclusionary, and functional boundaries.

Van Maanen and Schein (1979) also provide several propositions that offer additional insight into the job stresses likely to be experienced by minority professionals. For example, these authors noted that "socialization . . . is no doubt more intense and problematic for a member just before and just after a particular boundary passage" (p. 224). That is, stress and anxiety are highest during the anticipatory and initiation phases of an organizational boundary passage. Additionally, the more boundaries that are crossed at any one time, the more profound the experience (more stress) for the person. They further noted that, " . . . socialization along the inclusionary dimension is likely to be more critical to lower-placed members than higher-placed members since . . . to move up in the organization indicates that some movement has already occurred inward" (p. 225). The implication of this latter proposition by Van Maanen and Schein (1979) for minority professionals is that if inclusionary movement hasn't occurred, upward movement is less likely to occur. This is certainly evident in the conclusions of Alderfer et al. (1980) and Cobbs (1981).

The works by America and Anderson (1978) and Fernandez (1981) further illustrate in detail how perceptions related to the above proposition are held by many minority professionals employed in predominantly white organizations.

At this point we will shift our focus somewhat to discuss briefly several studies of a more empirical nature, and will return to the issues raised by the framework in Chapter 1 as well as the theoretical work of Van Maanen and Schein as they apply to minority professionals and job-related stress in a later section of this chapter. However, before proceeding with this discussion, it is worth noting an issue raised by Korchin (1980) with which I, as a black researcher and scholar, am in agreement. Korchin makes the observation that many studies of minority people are based on the deeply ingrained assumption that the "proper" approach to the study of minorities is to compare them to whites. However, Korchin questions the validity of this orthodox assumption and offers an alternative approach in this area, which incorporates a cross-cultural perspective that does not necessarily include white comparison groups. Bhagat (1979) also advocated the need for a sound cross-cultural perspective on ethnic group experiences. While the "proper" method of studying minorities is a debatable question, I feel that there are benefits to be gained from the study of minority groups in isolation as well as in comparison to whites. A good deal of research in the job stress area has been based on white anglo-saxon samples. We know very little about minorities and their experiences of job-related stress. Those experiences have theoretical significance and indeed offer us insights into the unique sources of stresses and strains in minority groups when comparisons with whites are made.

While some of the issues discussed herein as applied to blacks can be generalized to other ethnic minorities or people of color, we also recognize the uniqueness of responses of different ethnic minorities to the same or similar organizational stimuli, and indeed such differences have been demonstrated empirically (see, e.g., Ford, 1980; Triana, 1981). Unfortunately, few empirical research findings, especially of a developmental nature, are available that would further our understanding of the relative similarities and differences in the responses of different minority groups to organizational phenomena.

The five studies that are now briefly reviewed included studies that had samples of black, Mexican American, and American Indian participants, as well as white participants in one instance. With one exception these studies reflect the experiences of minority professionals relative to one another, without comparison to a similar group of white professionals. The studies were not designed to test specific research models of job stress per se, but were designed in most instances to examine the relationships between the experience of job-related stress and other organizationally valued outcomes. Table 11-1 summarizes the major findings of each study, and additional background information on each study is provided below.

Ramos' (1975) study of 202 physical and social scientists and engineers employed at a large aerospace firm on the West Coast sought to determine if minority (male ethnic minority and female) research and development (R&D) professionals experienced more job-related stress than nonminority (white male) professionals. The R&D setting was such that the scientists' and engineers' tasks were aggravated by technological advances and by the need to be creative and innovative. These pressures occurred in addition to the stresses associated with being a minority. Ramos' hypotheses were based on the assumption that the combination of sociocultural, psychological, and somatic factors would be potentially predictive of stress for the minority professional compared with the nonminority professional. The study participants included white male and female, black male, and American Indian male subjects. The Job-Related Tension Index was used as the primary dependent measure in the study. Generally, the results indicated that minority professionals experienced more job-related stress than nonminority professionals, thus confirming most of the study's hypotheses. However, white female professionals' experience of job-related stress was not different from that of white males. This result is at variance with other studies which report that white females experience significantly more stress than their white male counterparts (cf. Zappert and Weinstein, 1980; Chapter 10 in this volume).

In contrast, Edwards' (1980) research focused solely on black females and their work experiences. The purpose of the study was not to determine whether minorities in organizations are under more stress than other groups. Rather, the study examined (1) the extent to which black females perceived their work environment to be supportive of their development and career advancement, (2) the nature of this support, and (3) the influence of job support on perceived job stress and job satisfaction. A measure called work environment support, based on the work of Kanter (1977) and the conceptual scheme of Cobb (1976), was developed, which included three facets: emotional support, informational support, and structural support. Emotional support focuses on the affective and interpersonal

Table 11-1 Summary of Research Studies of Job-Related Stress in Minority Professionals

Author(s)	Subject Groups	Variables Examined	Measurement Procedures	Results
Ramos (1975)	American Indian males Black American males White females White males $N = 202$	Job related tension	Job-related tension index	Minority professionals' job-related stress was greater than that of nonminority professionals. Male ethnic minority professionals' job-related stress was greater than that of nonminority professional. Female professionals' stress levels were not different from nonminority professionals' stress levels. Black male professionals experienced the highest mean tension, and experienced greater stress only when compared with white males and American Indian professionals.
Ford and Bagot (1978)	Black professionals Mexican American professionals $N = 22$	Job-related stress Job satisfaction Instrumental leader behavior Supportive leader behavior	State-trait anxiety inventory (Speilberger et al., 1970) Job descriptive index (Smith et al., 1969) House and Dessler (1974)	Job satisfaction was significantly positively correlated with both leader behavior dimensions. Job stress was significantly negatively correlated with supervisor supportive behavior as a whole. The job stress-supervisor

Study	Sample	Variables	Instruments	Findings
				instrumental behavior relationship was negative and nonsignificant for both blacks and Mexican Americans.
				For Mexican Americans the supervisor supportive behavior-job stress relationship was significant and positive, while for blacks it was negative and nonsignificant.
Edwards (1980)	Black female professionals $N = 66$	Work environment support Job stress Job satisfaction	Author-developed instruments State-trait anxiety inventory (Speilberger et al., 1970) Job descriptive index (Smith et al., 1969)	Women in both line and staff positions were equally found to report relatively low to moderate job stress and high satisfaction.
				Women reported receiving higher emotional and informational support than structural support.
				Job stress was significantly and negatively correlated with structural support, satisfaction with work, and satisfaction with supervision.
Ford (1980)	Black professionals Mexican American professionals $N = 57$	Job-related stress Job satisfaction Role clarity Overall job complexity	State-trait anxiety inventory (Speilberger et al., 1970) Job descriptive index (Smith et al., 1969) Rizzo et al. (1970) Turner and Lawrence (1965)	Mexican American females expressed significantly more job stress than Mexican American males.
				Black and Mexican American females' affective responses were generally less positive than their male counterparts.

(Continued)

297

Table 11-1 (Continued)

Author(s)	Subject Groups	Variables Examined	Measurement Procedures	Results
				Black subordinates of black supervisors expressed significantly lower levels of job stress than black or Mexican American subordinates of white supervisors.
				Black subordinates of black supervisors expressed significantly higher levels of satisfaction with their supervisors than did blacks supervised by whites.
Ford (1981)	Black professionals $N = 150$	Episodic job stress Chronic job stress Frustration Burnout Job satisfaction Work environment support	Organizational readjustment Adams (1980) Peters et al. (1980) Murphy (1981) Job descriptive index (Smith et al., 1969) Edwards (1980)	Chronic job stress, burnout, and frustration were significantly and negatively related to all facets of work support. Chronic job stress, burnout, and frustration were more strongly related to emotional support and informational support than to structural support. Chronic job stress was significantly and positively related to role ambiguity. Emotional support was more important than other facets of support in the prediction of work outcomes.

relationships that help to sustain someone in his or her job through trust, encouragement, dependability, and concern (similar to Cobb's (1976) notion of esteem support). Informational support focuses on gaining system knowledge or knowledge about one's work environment; for example, policies, rules, decisions, and norms (similar to what Cobb (1976) calls belonging to a network of mutual obligation). Structural support focuses on the advocacy and manipulation of a system by one person for the purpose of career advancement and upward mobility of another person (similar to Kanter's (1977) notion of sponsored mobility).

Sixty-six managerial and professional women employed in private manufacturing firms in three midwestern cities participated in the Edwards (1980) study. Three hypotheses were examined in the study. The first two hypotheses suggested that persons employed in staff, as opposed to line, positions would perceive different amounts and facets of job support available to them and different amounts of job stress experienced. The third hypothesis suggested that job support, as opposed to management function, would be a major factor influencing both attitudes toward job satisfaction and work and perceived job stress. The results of a study indicated that management function (line versus staff) made little difference in the subjects' perceptions of job stress and reported job satisfaction. Job support, however, accounted for more variance in perceived stress and facets of satisfaction than did management function. Other results are reported in Table 11-1. I have provided a somewhat detailed background description of the Edwards (1980) study because my own recent research efforts, to be discussed later in this chapter, build on the work of Edwards.

Initially, however, my focus on and interest in job stress experiences of minority professionals followed an exploratory and developmental approach in a series of studies involving (1) an examination of relationships between personal and organizational factors and job stress and satisfaction in an exploratory study (cf. Ford and Bagot, 1978), followed by (2) a test of specific research hypotheses designed to answer specific research questions (cf. Ford, 1980). In the Ford and Bagot (1978) study, the personal factors of race, Type-A personality, and growth need strength (GNS) and the organizational factors of instrumental and supportive leader behaviors, task structure, role clarity, and organizational level were correlated with the outcome variables of job stress and job satisfaction. The sample included 13 black and 9 Mexican American professionals employed by a large, decentralized manufacturing and sales organization. Job satisfaction was significantly related to more organizational factors than was job stress. Race moderated the relationships between supportive leader behavior and job stress, and organizational level and job stress, wherein these relationships were positive for Mexican Americans but negative for blacks. The relationship between role clarity and job satisfaction was nonsignificant for persons with high GNS but significant and negative for low GNS persons, thus producing a moderating effect for GNS. Additionally, this same relationship was significant and negative for persons classified as Type-A personality types but was nonsignificant for persons classified as Type-B personality types. Unfortunately, many of the anticipated significant relationships did not occur in this study, due perhaps to the small sample size.

A follow-up to the Ford and Bagot (1978) study was undertaken, which incorporated a larger sample of Mexican American ($N=24$) and black ($N=53$) professionals from the same work organization as that of the Ford and Bagot study participants (cf. Ford, 1980). Unlike the exploratory and pilot nature of the previous study, this latter study sought to answer specific research questions by testing several research hypotheses. In particular, the study sought to examine (1) the effects of job stress as a moderator of the relationship between supervisory behavior and subordinate satisfaction, in an attempt to replicate the results of Schriesheim and Murphy (1976), and (2) the effects of supervisor race on the work outcomes experienced by minority professionals. The pattern of correlations for job stress as a moderator of leader behavior–subordinate job satisfaction relationships did not replicate Schriesheim and Murphy. However, some interesting findings did emerge relative to differential experiences of male versus female professionals and black versus Mexican American professionals as a function of supervisor race. It was hypothesized that the work outcomes for female professionals would be less gratifying than those for their male counterparts. While the differences in affective responses were in the predicted direction for the black participants, none of the differences were significant. However, Mexican American females expressed significantly higher job stress and significantly lower growth need strength, and worked on jobs significantly lower in scope or complexity than did Mexican American males. Other work outcome differences involving job satisfaction, though not significant, were in the predicted direction.

Another hypothesis examined in the Ford (1980) study suggested that subordinates of white supervisors would exhibit less positive affective responses and work outcomes than would subordinates of black supervisors. The pattern of response scores were as predicted, but only a few of the differences were significant. Black subordinates of black supervisors expressed significantly lower levels of job stress than did black or Mexican American subordinates of white supervisors. Additionally, black subordinates of black supervisors expressed significantly higher levels of satisfaction with their supervisors than did blacks supervised by whites. These results were consistent with the findings of E. Adams (1978), who reported that black subordinates of white female and male managers generally had lower mean affective responses than black subordinates of black managers.

In the Ford and Bagot (1978), Ford (1980), and Edwards (1980) studies, the authors used Spielberger's (Spielberger et al., 1970) State-Trait Anxiety Inventory as the measure of job-related stress, and each study reported less than satisfactory results with this measure. Other research studies have often used measures based on role theory (e.g., role conflict and role ambiguity) as measures of job stress (Beehr and Love, 1980). None of these measures appear to adequately capture the meaning of job stress as promulgated in recent publications on the topic. Schuler's (1980) notions of opportunity stress, constraint stress, and demand stress—which represent potential gains, maintaining the status quo, or potential losses, respectively, for an individual—appear to be reflected somewhat in Naismith's (1975) Organizational Changes Rating Scale, an instrument similar to the Holmes and Rahe (1967) Social Readjustment Rating Inventory. However, the uncertainty and importance dimensions of each type of stress as discussed by Schuler are not tapped by the Naismith measure.

The Naismith scale represents a measure of what J. Adams (1978, 1980) calls *episodic* stress, which centers around recent but infrequent events occurring on the job that require a certain amount of readjustment for one to feel "back to normal" following the change event. This notion of stress, coupled with Adams's (1980) measure of *chronic* stress, that is, the ongoing, day-to-day job conditions and pressures a person faces in the workplace, offer an alternative approach in operationalizing job-stress constructs that are intuitively appealing. Also, they reflect Love and Beehr's (1981) suggestions that future research approaches on job stress should be based on notions other than role theory. As such, the chronic/episodic job-stress notions have been incorporated in our current research endeavors (see, e.g., Ford, 1981).

Several prior studies of job stress, particularly those which sought to examine the stress-buffering hypothesis (see, e.g., House and Wells, 1977; Pinneau, 1976a; LaRocca and Jones, 1978; Blau, 1981), incorporated measures of social support that only reflected a general socioemotional nature, without any attention being given to other kinds of support. That is, prior research results have not been established as to the relative importance of facets of work support in the prediction of organizationally valued work outcomes. The more general finding seems to be that a strong relationship exists between social support (defined in terms of general socioemotional measures) and the experience of job stress. Therefore, our third study in the series of studies incorporated Edwards' (1980) measures of work environment support and the measures of episodic and chronic stress previously mentioned, in an effort to determine the relative contribution of each facet of work support in the prediction of each type of job stress as well as other negative work outcomes, including job burnout and frustration (cf. Ford, 1981).

One hundred and fifty black clerical, supervisory, technical, and managerial personnel who worked for geographically dispersed organizational units in the southern region of a large decentralized manufacturing and sales organization were subjects in this latter study. There were 84 men and 66 women, ranging in age from 24 to 53 years of age (average around

30 years). The average job tenure was 27 months. The dependent measures included episodic and chronic stress, job burnout, and job frustration, along with measures of work environment support.

Burnout was measured using a scale developed by Murphy (1981) in collaboration with the present author. The scale items captured the essence of the burnout syndrome as defined by several authors (cf. Freudenberger, 1977; Maslach, 1976, 1978; Daley, 1979) and reflected (1) emotional exhaustion and cynicism, (2) demoralized, frustrated feelings and reduced efficiency, and (3) excessive demands on energy, strength, and resources resulting in exhaustion, among other things. Frustration was measured by a 12-item instrument developed from one used previously by Peters et al. (1980) and reflected negative affective responses resulting from a mismatch of an individual's personal characteristics and the requirements of the work setting.

The results of multiple regression analyses used to determine the relative contribution of each facet of social support in predicting the work outcomes revealed that emotional support entered each regression equation first for the negative outcomes of chronic stress, episodic stress, and job burnout, and accounted for between 4 and 22 percent of the variance in these variables. In the case of frustration, structural support entered the equation, first accounting for 12 percent of the total 14 percent in explained variance, followed by emotional support, which contributed an additional 2 percent in explained variance. Thus, relatively speaking, emotional support appears to be more critical in the prediction of negative work outcomes, followed by structural support. Additionally, zero order correlations of support facets with work outcomes indicated that all three facets of work support correlated negatively and significantly with job burnout, frustration, and chronic job stress. Episodic job stress and emotional support correlated significantly and negatively, while episodic stress was unrelated to structural and emotional support.

The studies discussed above provide additional evidence to corroborate the folklore and general discussions reported in a number of nonempirical works (see, e.g., Woodard, 1978; Brown, 1977). A variety of findings were highlighted above, including: (1) the limited amount of structural support, as opposed to emotional and informational support, received by black female professionals (Edwards, 1980); (2) the greater stress experienced by minority professionals relative to nonminority professionals (Ramos, 1975); (3) the role that supportive leader behaviors play in increasing stress in Mexican Americans while they apparently have little negative or even positive effects for blacks (Ford and Bagot, 1978); (4) the greater amount of stress and lower job satisfaction of minority females relative to minority males (Ford, 1980); (5) the greater amount of stress and lower affective responses of minority professionals supervised by whites versus those supervised by blacks (Ford, 1980); and (6) the relative importance of emotional support vis-a-vis other facets of support in the prediction of negative work outcomes (Ford, 1981).

One theme that begins to emerge from the above findings is the impact of the work supervisor's behavior and race on the experience of job stress and positive versus negative work outcomes for minority professionals. I believe this is one avenue of research that should be pursued in light of the implications of House and Wells' (1977) suggestions the work supervisor should be especially targeted as the focus of providing social support in the work setting for subordinates as an aid in reducing occupational stress or its impact on health. As seen from the reports of E. Adams (1978), Ford (1980), and Kaufman (1980), incorporation of these suggestions does not appear to be occurring, especially when cross-race relationships are involved for minority subordinates with white supervisors.

The suggestions of House and Wells (1977) mentioned previously are helpful guidelines in our current investigations of job-related stress experiences of minority professionals. In particular, the notion of sources and types of social support as a primary "buffer" or moderator of stress-strain relationships is a key component of our research investigations. In the next two sections we briefly elaborate on our present approach to the study of job stress vis-a-vis the present editors' framework and discuss these with a review of some current research findings.

ORGANIZATIONAL STRESS AND SUPPORTIVE SOCIAL RELATIONSHIPS AT WORK

Several research studies in the quality of work life literature have pointed out wide disparities between the career success and work experiences of minority professionals and their white counterparts in terms of job levels and salaries attained, occupational prestige attained, job isolation experienced, and job satisfaction differences (see, e.g., Brown and Ford, 1977; Moch, 1980; Vecchio, 1980; Norman, 1981; Barclay et al., 1981).

Other anthologies and collections of edited works have also dealt with the plight of minorities in organizational life (see, e.g., Epstein and Hampton, 1971; Purcell and Cavanagh, 1972; Fromkin and Sherwood, 1974; Ford, 1976). These works, some of which are more than a decade old, have focused more on the access and treatment discrimination experienced by minorities in organizations as well as other problems associated with integrating work organizations, rather than on job stress, per se. However, as noted previously in our discussion of the studies by Brown (1977), Alderfer et al. (1980), and Cobbs (1981), these problems are still very much in existence today and represent considerable sources of stress for minorities in organizations.

Recent work in the area of job stress has demonstrated the beneficial effects of a supportive work environment. In particular, Pinneau (1976a) has suggested that social support processes have three potential effects: (1) directly on the sources of stress (prevention); (2) directly on measures of strain or well-being (therapeutic); and (3) a moderating effect on the stress-strain relationship (buffering). In other words, those individuals with a high level of social support at work would be less likely to have stressful transactions with the work environment resulting in the experience of strain and ill-health (Beehr, 1976), as illustrated in Figure 11-2. In fact, in situation (2) above, low social support is proposed as being a stressor in itself.

While evidence exists for the direct effects of social support on job stress, the evidence of the "buffering" effect of social support is mixed (Payne, 1980). Some researchers have concluded that social support buffers the individual from job stress and strain (Caplan, 1971; Cobb, 1976; House and Wells, 1977; LaRocco et al., 1980), while other researchers have only found direct effects of social support and failed to find evidence for a buffering effect (Pinneau, 1976b; LaRocco and Jones, 1978; Blau, 1981).

I believe this state of affairs is due largely to (1) a lack of an adequate conceptual framework of social support on the part of various researchers,

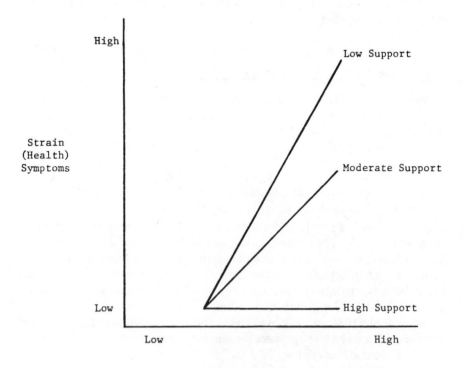

Figure 11-2   Buffering effect of social support on the stress-strain relationship.

(2) inconsistent use of different measures of job stress by various research-ers (e.g., job dissatisfaction, work overload, role conflict, role ambiguity, etc.), and (3) inconsistent use of different measures of social support by various researchers (e.g., supervisor support, coworker support, socio-emotional support, instrumental support, etc.).

The problems identified with demonstrating the buffering effect might be overcome by incorporating an adequate conceptual framework and alternative approaches to the measurement of job stress and strain in one's research efforts. House (1981) has provided a review of the social support literature and presents a four-part typology of social support including (1) emotional support (esteem, affect, trust, etc.), (2) appraisal support (feed-back, social comparison, etc.), (3) informational support (advice, direc-tives, information, etc.), and (4) instrumental support (aid in kind, modi-fying environment, etc.). There are many similarities between the House (1981) and Edwards (1980) formulations of social support. However, one critical difference, I believe, which is crucial to minority professionals, is the structural support dimension incorporated in the Edwards (1980) framework. (See Chapter 14 which provides an updated discussion of the social support literature.)

Therefore, in my own current research efforts, I have incorporated measures of social support or work environment support developed by Edwards (1980) in order to further examine its effects in combating stress. Additionally, I have incorporated measures of episodic job stress and chronic job stress discussed earlier. This latter concept of job stress has a temporal tone associated with it. This implied time dimension is somewhat analogous to the duration dimension stress uncertainties in the present editor's framework discussed in Chapter 1. However, the nature of chronic versus episodic stress events are more a reflection of the demands (or constraints or opportunities) that confront the individual at work than desired outcomes and uncertainties associated with obtaining these out-comes. The framework of stress provided in Chapter 1, along with its mathematical formulation in equation 1, represents a bold and interesting approach to the conceptualization and study of stress. Unfortunately, the framework and subsequent discussion in Chapter 1 deal only with problem-solving and decision-making situations. However, not all stress experi-ences eminate from problem-solving and decision-making situations, and this fact is recognized by the editors. I believe the conceptualization of experienced stress that results from non−decision-making/problem-solving situations and that is operationalized as being a function of the demands confronting the individual, the resources available for meeting the demands, and the perceived consequences for not meeting the de-mands, is more representative of my own current research approach to the topic. Beehr and Bhagat do not provide much discussion of this portion of their framework in Chapter 1.

Finally, I recognize the fact that people experience stress resulting from extraorganizational and nonwork sources, and this latter stress could ultimately affect one's performance and experiences on the job (see Chapter 7 by Bhagat in this volume). My framework is consistent with Beehr and Bhagat's notion of the degree of total stress encompassing work and nonwork domains. However, since my data focus primarily on the work domain in my current research efforts, the following discussion will deal with the effects of job-related stress only.

JOB STRESS AND MINORITY PROFESSIONALS: ADDITIONAL CONSIDERATIONS

A supplementary analysis of data conducted as part of our ongoing series of studies of minority professionals and job-related stress revealed some interesting results. Recall from the description of the Ford (1981) study that the sample included 150 black professionals employed by a large, decentralized manufacturing and sales organization. In addition to the measures described previously (i.e., episodic stress, chronic stress, job burnout, and job frustration), measures of role conflict and role ambiguity (Rizzo et al., 1970) and facet satisfaction (Smith et al., 1969) were also obtained from the participants in the study. Of interest in this supplementary analysis was the question of the independent and joint contributions of episodic and chronic stressful events in the prediction of organizationally valued outcomes. That is, which type of stress is more critical in the prediction of both positive and negative work outcomes.

The analysis consisted of entering the episodic and chronic stress scores simultaneously as independent predictors in a regression equation such that the predictor accounting for the greatest amount of variance entered the equation first. The cross product of the two stress variables was finally entered into the regression equation last.

The results of this analysis revealed that chronic job stress was more strongly related to both positive (i.e., facet satisfaction) and negative (i.e., role stress, frustration, burnout) work outcomes than was episodic job stress. In every case, chronic stress entered the regression equation first and accounted for between 2 to 43 percent of the variance in the dependent outcomes out of a total of 45 percent in explained variance. For all practical purposes, episodic job stress did not contribute to any additionally explained variance in the dependent outcomes nor did the cross product of the two stress measures. With respect to the positive work outcomes, chronic job stress was most strongly related to satisfaction with supervision $(r = -.57, p<.001)$, followed by satisfaction with coworkers $(r = -.39, p<.001)$, satisfaction with work and promotion opportunities $(r = -.38, p<.001$ each), and satisfaction with pay $(r = -.16, p<.05)$. For the negative work outcomes, chronic job stress correlated positively and significantly $(p<.001$ in each case) with frustration $(r = .66)$, burnout $(r = .65)$, role conflict $(r = .55)$, and role ambiguity $(r = .42)$, respectively.

The findings of most interest to us from the above analysis is the strength of the relationships between chronic job stress and the work outcomes of satisfaction with supervision, burnout, and frustration. For the positive work outcomes, the strongest relationship was for satisfaction with supervision. This result, coupled with the very strong correlations between chronic job stress and frustration and job burnout would seem to support the earlier observations of Brown (1977) regarding the "Black Tax," that is, attempting to prove competence through workaholism (thus perhaps contributing to a feeling of being burned out), a mutual feeling of distrust between black executives and their peers and superiors (contributing to lack of satisfaction with supervision), and participating in organizational policies not in the best interests of blacks (contributing to a sense of frustration). Perhaps these extrapolations and interpretations of the data do not appear to be warranted initially, but corroborating evidence provided by the study's participants would seem to indicate so.

Additional data collected from participants involved a subjective assessment of the most stressful chronic or day-to-day conditions experienced at work. The participants were asked to rank-order several conditions that prevail in their job situations that are possible sources of stress. A summary of the top ranked items based on the percentage of participants ranking each item revealed that the continuing conditions that were most stressful for the participants included (in decreasing order of importance) (1) a lack of participation in crucial decisions affecting them, (2) feelings of underutilization of skills, (3) considerable time spent handling little difficulties as opposed to a planned and organized approach to work, (4) receipt of negative feedback only, and (5) lack of confidence in their superiors. The first condition ranked as the most stressful chronic condition is important in the light of recent theoretical analyses provided by Segovis and Bhagat (1981) which suggest that lack of participation could lead to strong feelings of experienced job stress. Other items that were ranked as stressful also point toward interpersonal problems relating to boss-subordinate relationships and the nature of supervisory behavior by the participants' supervisors.

Kram (1980) has indicated the delicate nature of certain issues involved in cross-sex mentoring relationships (i.e., male mentor–female protege) and Cunningham (1981) has provided additional insight related to this issue. I suspect that equally delicate issues are involved in cross-race mentoring, coaching, or helping relationships at work in the provision of structural support (for career advancement) and informational support (for career development) to minority professionals by white supervisors who, in turn, also must contend with possible charges of reverse discrimination from their white subordinates. Edwards' (1980) data revealed that structural support was the least received of the three types examined for her sample of black female managers.

A recent study by Dovidio and Gaertner (1981) also sheds additional light on the issue raised here. This study attempted to determine whether or not the reversal of the traditional status relationship between whites and blacks contributed to whites' resistance to affirmative action programs. More specifically, their contention was that the reversal of the traditional role relationship between blacks and whites wherein the latter were subordinate to the former represented a primary threat to whites. The white male subjects in their study were presented with opportunities to provide help to a white or black partner in need of help. However, the status and intellectual ability of the black partner was manipulated to be either above or below that of the white subject. The results of the study clearly indicated that status, rather than ability, influenced the frequency with which whites helped blacks, whereas ability rather than status primarily influenced whites' helping behavior toward other whites. Subsequent ratings revealed that subjects evaluated even high-ability blacks as less competent than themselves, while they acknowledged the greater competence of high-ability whites. Thus, high ability among whites was regarded as desirable, while among blacks it was not fully appreciated.

These results of the Dovidio and Gaertner (1981) study seem to provide some interesting insights with regard to helping or supportive behaviors of whites towards blacks and other minorities. Needs for self-esteem and superior status are frequently hypothesized to be among the major causes and perpetrators of prejudice and racial discrimination (Ashmore and DelBoca, 1976). Additionally, rigid stereotypic thinking of many whites often results in misperceptions of the behavior of blacks (Hamilton, 1979). Therefore, in the Dovidio and Gaertner (1981) study, systematic bias in perceiving the intellectual competence of blacks due to traditional stereotypes resulted in the failure of whites to differentiate meaningfully between high and low ability black partners regardless of their role status. Black subordinates were helped more frequently than black supervisors by the white subjects and, in fact, were helped significantly more than white subordinates. The implications of these results are that black subordinates of white supervisors who are high in competence and ability may not get the structural support they need for career advancement if their supervisors' perceptions of them are threatening to their own self-esteem.

Of course, it is not possible to know the extent to which the findings of the Dovidio and Gaertner (1981) study can be applied to the empirical results discussed herein. The results do raise issues which need to be examined in future research endeavors. I believe that, by and large, the work experiences of the present study's participants and participants of the studies reviewed are a reflection somewhat of the typical state of affairs of race relations in organizations today which, as noted earlier in the discussions of the Alderfer et al. (1980) study, could still stand a great deal of improvement. With this thought in mind, we suggest in the section below an approach for examining the issue of cross-race boss-subordinate relationships in the work setting.

COMPLEX ORGANIZATIONS AND THE MINORITY MEMBER INTERFACE

Several authors have suggested that minorities (ethnic and female) do not fit into the conventional organizational mold and as a result experience less than desirable work outcomes (cf. Taylor, 1972; Kanter, 1977; Kanter and Stein, 1980; Ford, 1978a). The person-environment (P-E) fit formulation of job stress was discussed earlier. However, I believe that a particular aspect of the person-environment match in organizations should be examined. This aspect includes the point at which the individual interfaces with the organization—the boss-subordinate interface. There are, however, other interfaces of importance as noted by Nadler and Tushman (1980) in their congruence principle. But according to several authors, the organization lives and breathes in the boss-subordinate dyad (Graen, 1976; Graen and Cashman, 1975; Dansereau et al., 1975) and an understanding of this role-making process might prove useful in understanding the differential experiences of minority and majority professionals.

Large complex organizations in the United States might accurately be characterized as white male clubs (WMC) (Terry, 1974). As such, they are also the purveyors of inauthenticity in our society as well. An authentic society is one characterized by (1) equitable distribution of resources (by race and sex for purpose of this paper), (2) shared power, (3) cultural pluralism, and (4) flexible and responsive institutions (Gibb and Terry, 1979). Not everyone will agree with these requirements for an authentic society. However, it is reasonable to assume that the denial of authenticity creates alienations and/or inauthenticity. Alienation occurs when a person is unaware or vaguely aware of the exclusions, dependency, and manipulation by a hostile social system and unable to participate authentically in that system. Inauthenticity exists when there is the appearance of authenicity but the underlying reality is alienating (Etzioni, 1968). Increasingly today, organizations are inauthentic, making it more difficult to uncover the underlying alienating forces at play within them.

The WMC image captures many alienating and inauthentic dimensions of large organizations today. Organizational *resources* are disproportionately distributed to white males; *power* is held by white males; organizational *climate* and *ethos* legitimizes selected white male values and behavior; and *institutional policies*, *practices*, and *programs* support and reinforce white male ascendency. To protect itself, club members, drawing on club traditions, often unintentionally or even intentionally rationalize their behavior with rhetoric about nondiscrimination, equal opportunity, and victim help programs. What escapes challenge is the club itself.

An example of manifestations of the alienating forces at work against black victims of the WMC is the "Black Tax" (Brown, 1977) which is extracted from the victims of the club. These taxing transactions, Brown believes, derive from the omnipresence of racism in organizational life. To some extent these issues as they apply to blacks can be generalized to other ethnic minorities and possibly even women. Indeed, there are similarities between racism and sexism, both of which have their genesis in the WMC, in terms of their impact on the victims. In particular, Gibb and Terry (1979, p. 3) note the similarities between the two in the following definition:

> Racism and sexism exist when one race or sex group, intentionally or unintentionally, inequitably distributes *resources*, refuses to share *power*, maintains closed, unresponsive and inflexible *policies, practices,* and *programs* and imposes ethnocentric and gendercentric *culture* on another race or sex group, for its supposed benefit and justifies these actions by blaming the other race or sex group.

In light of Nadler and Tushman's congruence hypothesis which states that "the congruence between two components is defined as the degree to which the needs, demands, goals, objectives and/or structures of one component are consistent with the needs, demands, goals, objectives, and/or structures of another component" (Nadler and Tushman, 1980, p. 224), and the notion of lack of *P-E* fit as stress producing experiences of organizational members, it seems reasonable to conclude that most large, complex organizations which employ minorities and/or women are potential sources of stress for these groups, especially if the organizations fit the image of the white male club. That is, anyone who is not white and male will encounter difficulty in the work environment. Indeed, there are accounts of "nonclub" members who are relegated to positions that lack upward mobility or opportunity for advancement (Taylor, 1973) or who are shunted into sex-segregated positions with noticeable wage differentials (England and McLaughlin, 1979). These findings seem to suggest that oftentimes minorities and women are relegated to an "out-group" status, with members of the WMC being the "in-group."

AN APPROACH TO UNDERSTANDING MINORITY STRESSES IN ORGANIZATIONS

Differentiation of organizational members into in-group and out-group categories is a part of the role-making process that occurs in the vertical dyadic linkage (VDL) model of leadership. This model of leader behavior suggests that superiors relate differently and differentially toward individual subordinates and that subordinates' reports about leaders vary relative to the quality of leaders' relationships with them. The quality of exchange between leaders and subordinates is posited to be an important predictor of subordinates' organizational commitment and performance as well as a determinant of the quality of subordinates' work life (Taber et al.,

1979). Research studies involving the VDL model attempted to classify leader-subordinate relationships on the basis of an index of leader-member exchange quality, wherein those with leader-subordinate relationships characterized by a low degree of individualized leader assistance were classified as outgroup members and those with high degrees of individualized leader assistance as ingroup members (Dansereau et al., 1975; Cashman et al., 1976). Individuals classified as in-group members consistently received greater amounts of assessed resources such as greater latitude in role definition, more inside information, and greater influence in decision making, as well as more supportive and sensitive treatment from their superiors. This was not the case with out-group members.

To date, the research on the VDL model has not been exceptionally clear as to how subordinates are differentiated into various subgroups. The research indicates that in-group members are not basically different from out-group members. Demographics explored across work groups in VDL research have not systematically varied with leader-subordinate exchange quality. This finding suggests that if leaders use demographics to discriminate between in-group and out-group subordinates, they use different information or the same information differently in their sub-group selection process (Chassie, 1982). Regardless of what the research has shown, I believe that demographics do play a key role in determining in-group and out-group status. Thus, race and sex are critical variables to be examined in future VDL research, especially if we accept the earlier characterization of complex organizations as essentially white male clubs. Moreover, I believe that a leader's initial assignment of subordinates to the in-group and out-group is related to categorical data which is easily accessed and assessed, that is, biodata profile similarity with the leader (demographics), similarity in attitudes, and physical attractiveness.

Therefore, it seems that several questions of importance are posed by the above discussion which deserve in-depth study in order to further understand the job stress experiences of minority professionals in organizations. Such study should involve the examination of boss-subordinate relationships in organizations from the perspective of the vertical dyadic linkage model. Secondly, such study should focus on cross-race and cross-sex boss-subordinate relationships. For example, what proportion of cross-race and cross-sex boss-subordinate relationships are in-group versus out-group relationships? What are the configurations of in-group versus out-group exchanges in cross-race boss-subordinate relationships? How do these differ from same-race and same-sex boss-subordinate relationships?

If a significant portion of cross-race boss-subordinate relations are exemplified by in-group types of exchange relationships, then perhaps factors other than *race* per se account for the stressful experiences of subordinates. If so, what are the similarities in these relationships to other same-race boss-subordinate relationships in which the subordinates feel highly stressed?

A vehicle is needed for isolating the unique sources of stress in organizations attributable to race. It seems plausible that a study designed around the model shown in Figure 11-3 which incorporated the vertical dyadic linkage leadership model as a framework for examining boss-subordinate relationships would begin to allow us to isolate the race-related sources of stress.

Three main components or dimensions are reflected in the model in Figure 11-3: (1) the type of support provided at work; (2) the source of each type of support; and (3) the nature of the boss-subordinate relationship. Assuming that no new additional types or sources of support were added, the model in Figure 11-3 represents a $4 \times 4 \times 4 = 64$ cell design—a complex research undertaking at the very least. Primary dependent variables of interest for such a study might include the variables discussed previously (job stress, frustration, satisfaction, etc.) along with additional variables designed to reflect the self-esteem of the supervisors and subordinates, perceived threats to self-esteem, and other variables related to health and

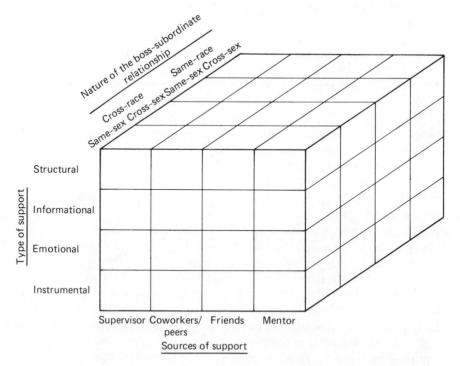

Figure 11-3 Research design for examining organizational experiences of minority professionals in terms of sources and types of work environment support provided them.

well-being, including physiological measures of health when possible (e.g., blood pressure readings, blood analyses for cholesterol content, etc.).

Certainly one may not wish to attempt to undertake the complete research design illustrated in Figure 11-3 all at once. However, the above-mentioned trends in research findings which pointed toward a need to examine boss-subordinate relationships suggest a starting point for future research efforts relative to the research design. This starting point could be the 16-cell portion of Figure 11-3 involving the supervisor as primary source of social support in the work setting. Moreover, this portion of the model is especially suited for incorporating a vertical dyadic linkage perspective of supervisory behavior. Such a starting point for future research would provide a means for examining the questions raised above along with other unanswered questions about the dynamics of cross-race boss-subordinate relationships (cf. Bartol et al., 1978; Bass, 1981; Parker, 1976). As such, the design for the research perspective can be represented as shown in Figure 11-4.

As seen from Figure 11-4, the critical cells of the design appear on the diagonal (cells, 4, 7, 10, 13) since these are the most ticklish situations for understanding the boss-subordinate relationship. That is, these four cells involve both cross-race and cross-sex relationships, which will make even

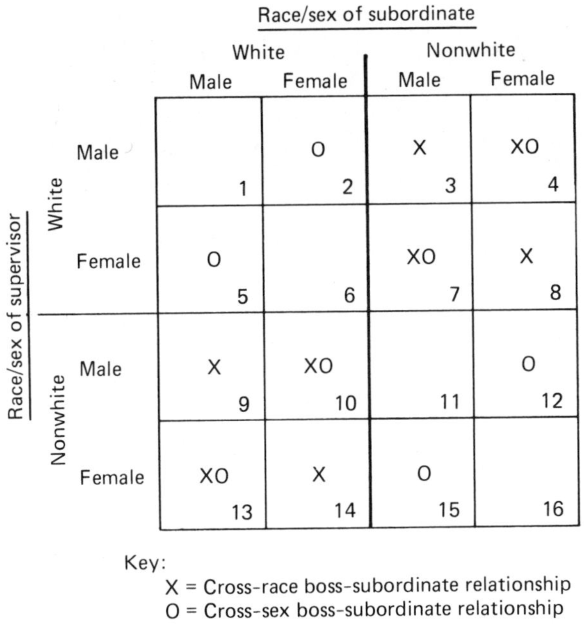

Key:
X = Cross-race boss-subordinate relationship
O = Cross-sex boss-subordinate relationship

Figure 11-4   Research design for examining the independent and joint effects of race and sex in boss-subordinate relationships.

more difficult the task of sorting out the dynamics of the boss-subordinate relationship than would be the case for only cross-race or cross-sex situations.

Since available research studies relating to minority female professionals, especially those which systematically examine their work experiences in the context of racism and sexism, are vastly unexplored as yet, research efforts should be directed in accordance with Figure 11-4. It would be a step in the direction of providing answers for some of the unanswered questions.

A decade ago King and Bass (1974) addressed the issue of race and leader-subordinate relations. Their discussion, however, was not in the context of attempting to understand how the boss-subordinate relationship impacts the experience of stress in the workplace. I would urge organizational researchers, managers, and other practitioners interested in understanding the effects of stress on work outcomes of minorities to explore research based on the suggested design in Figure 11-4. Once these relationships are explored, the path of inquiry might proceed to look at other sources of work support (e.g., coworkers, peers, or friends, etc.) and their contributions to positive organizational experiences vis-a-vis the supervisor's support. Although Woodard and Harris (1978) would leave the job of illuminating some of the unique sources of stress and strain on minority professionals to minority scholars and researchers, I believe that more would be gained from the diversity of perspectives if researchers and scholars of all ethnic backgrounds would undertake some portions of the program of research outlined here.

As the white male clubs become bombarded from all sides by minorities and women, the encroachment of this turf is bound to be resented. As such, it seems plausible that club members would relegate the invaders to out-group status more likely than not or, if unable to do so, scream charges of reverse discrimination. By the same token, those invaders who are welcomed into the in group might gain admission at great psychological costs, for example, loss of racial identity or feminine characteristics resulting in increased levels of stress in order to be successful. Additionally, those invaders who do obtain a quasi in-group status by virtue of their position, for example, instances where minorities are in supervisory and management positions (thus implying movement across hierarchical boundaries) might act in ways that are perceived by their peer and subordinate WMC members as not being in their best interests. Such perceptions might be due to threats to the WMC members' self-esteem (Dovidio and Gaertner, 1981) and might result in behaviors on their part designed to undermine the effectiveness of the minority supervisor. Research evidence exists that indicates that minority supervisory effectiveness is impeded by white subordinates' behavior (see Richards and Jaffee, 1972). These are nontrivial issues which heretofore have not received sufficient attention in the job stress literature, especially with respect to the cross-race issue. Another aspect of the issues raised here involves the nature of peer-peer relationships in work groups. Kanter's work has shown that these coworker relationships can be very stressful, particularly for a "O" isolated in an "X" environment (e.g., a black in an all-white work group or a female in an all-male work group) (see Kanter and Stein, 1980). Therefore, like it or not, the implication of this is that organizations may need to pay much closer attention to the racial configuration of work groups (see Parker, 1976) as well as the gender configuration in order to minimize undue stress of potential outgroup members. Perhaps a logical extension of the VDL model would be the development of the H/PDL—horizontal/peer dyadic linkage perspective of work relationships.

In summary, the invasion of the white male clubs will continue. If the process is to be humane rather than bloody, then increased efforts on the part of all involved is needed to improve the status of race relations in organizations which, as noted previously, are less than satisfactory. However, some victims of the WMC are optimistic (Greenberger, 1981b). And WMC club members should be willing to assist the "enemy" in invading their turf because it is in their best interest.

For example, Bergmann (1971) has estimated that at least a 6 percent increase in the gross national product would result from the elimination of race and sex discrimination. Additionally, Thurow (1969) has estimated that the potential return on investment directed toward reducing discrimination through both public and private sector efforts would exceed 65 percent per year. In an age of shrinking resources, organizations can ill afford to squander its most valuable resource—human capital. According to Nadler and Tushman's (1980) congruence hypothesis, organizational effectiveness is greater when there exists a fit or congruence between *all* its components. Thus, if everyone became in-group members in terms of fit, presumably the organization would function more effectively and efficiently. And that has to be good for everybody concerned.

SUGGESTED PROPOSITIONS FOR RESEARCH EXPLORATION

I have said a lot in the preceeding pages. To close out this chapter, I offer a few suggested propositions derivable from the models presented in Figures 11-1 and 11-4. The first set of propositions related to Figure 11-1 are an attempt to integrate the research perspective of the editors with a focus of my own research endeavors. The propositions related to Figure 11-4 are concerned more with the issues raised in the latter portions of this chapter. In both cases the propositions suggest how social support might interact with the person-environment situation in predicting organizationally valued outcomes, and, as such, suggest a contingency perspective to the prediction of certain work outcomes. The reader is invited to derive additional propositions for possible research explorations.

PROPOSITIONS RELATED TO FIGURE 11-1

1.   Structural social support will interact with environmental complexity (where environmental complexity is a function of the uncertainty, importance, and duration of uncertainties associated with possible outcomes) in the prediction of the dependent variables of stress and health symptoms (or job satisfaction and performance). More specifically, the relationship between structural support and the dependent variables will be significant and negative (positive for satisfaction and performance) and will conform to the following significantly different categories:

Cells 1,2 <3,4 <5,6 <7,8.

Additionally, the strength of the correlation between structural support and the dependent variables will be significantly greater than the strength of the correlations between these same dependent variables and informational support or emotional support in cells 3, and 4.

2.   Informational social support will interact with environmental complexity (where complexity is a function of the uncertainty, importance, and duration of uncertainties associated with possible outcomes) in the prediction of the dependent variables of stress and health symptoms (or job satisfaction and performance). More specifically, the relationship between informational support and the dependent variables will be significant and negative (positive for satisfaction and performance) and will conform to the following significantly different categories:

Cells 1,3 <5,7 <2,4,6,8.

Additionally, the strength of the correlation between informational support and the dependent variables will be significantly greater than the strength of the correlation between these same dependent variables and structural support or emotional support in cells 3, and 7.

3.   Emotional social support will interact with environmental complexity (where complexity is a function of the uncertainty, importance, and duration of uncertainties associated with possible outcomes) in the prediction of the dependent variables of stress and health symptoms (or job satisfaction and performance). More specifically, the relationship between emotional support and the dependent variables will be significant and negative (positive for satisfaction and performance) and will conform to the following significantly different categories:

Cells 1,2 <5,6 <3,4,7,8.

Additionally, the strength of the correlation between emotional support and the dependent variables will be significantly greater than the strength of the correlation between these same dependent variables and structural support or informational support in cells 1,2,5, and 6.

The rationale for the above propositions is based on the following assumptions. Structural support would have its greatest impact on the importance dimension of environmental complexity as defined (thus facilitating the crossing of hierarchical and inclusionary boundaries in the organization through the development of mentor relationships with senior organizational officials) and thus impact more heavily in cells 1, 2, 3, and 4. Informational support would have its greatest impact on the uncertainty dimension (thus facilitating the crossing of inclusionary boundaries in the organization through having access to heretofore unavailable information, being plugged into the grapevine, and so on) and thus impact more heavily in cells, 1, 3, 5, and 7. Emotional support would have its greatest impact on the duration dimension of environmental complexity (also facilitating the crossing of inclusionary boundaries through the development of warm, trusting, and supportive relationships, enabling the person to endure stressful situations the resolution of which would be long in duration), and thus impact more heavily in cells 1, 2, 5, and 6. However, there is some overlap in terms of which support facets would have greater impact in which cells of the model. Because the results of the Ford (1981) study, as discussed previously, indicated that emotional support was more critical in the prediction of negative work outcomes (recall that emotional support entered the regression equations first when all three facets were entered simultaneously), it was decided to give the weight of impact to emotional support in the propositions where overlap occurred. This is reflected in the latter portion of each of the above propositions.

PROPOSITIONS RELATED TO FIGURE 11-4

1. Emotional social support will interact with boss-subordinate congruence (where congruence is a function of same race for both boss and subordinate) in the prediction of the dependent variables of job satisfaction and work performance. More specifically, the relationship between emotional support and the dependent variables will be significant and positive and conform to the following significantly different categories:

Cell 1 >4,7,8,10,13,14 >9,3.

2. Emotional social support will interact with boss-subordinate congruence (where congruence is a function of same race for both boss and subordinate) in the prediction of the dependent variables of job stress, burnout, and health symptoms. More specifically, the relationship between emotional support and the dependent variables will be significant

and negative and conform to the following significantly different categories:

$$\text{Cells } 9,13,3 < 10,14,4,7,8 < 1.$$

The rationale for the above propositions is based on the assumptions that the critical cells in Figure 11-4 are those involving cross-race and, or, cross-sex relationships. However, the above propositions relate only to cross-race relationships as reflected in the cells identified in the propositions with the exception of cell 1. This latter cell represents a boss-subordinate relationship between members of the WMC and is included for comparative purposes on the assumption that the strength of relationship between support and work outcomes would be strongest in this cell relative to the others.

As presented here, the reader might infer that I am recommending a cross-sectional research perspective. However, I do recognize the persistent problems of determining causality in behavioral science research and am aware of the need to make allowances, where possible, for determining the causal nature of observed relationships. Therefore, I further suggest that future research efforts should also be directed at longitudinal research undertakings in which repeated measures of the study variables are taken over time.

It is hoped that the discussion provided in this chapter has kindled some interest on the part of researchers and practitioners in the issues related to stress of minority professionals at work. In future years the issues that are salient for black-white relationships in organizations will require more multicultural and, or, cultural pluralism perspectives (cf. Ford, 1978b; Harris and Moren 1979), especially given the increasing numbers of undocumented Mexican aliens, Haitian, Cuban, Indo-Chinese, and other third-world immigrants who are seeking employment and the pursuit of happiness in America. Fortunately, the present editors have chosen to address some of these issues with the inclusion of the next chapter on acculturative stress in immigrants. The task ahead is arduous but the potential rewards are well worth the effort.

REFERENCES

Adams, E. F. A multivariate study of subordinate perceptions of and attitudes toward minority and majority managers. *Journal of Applied Psychology*, 1978, **63**, 277–288.

Adams, J. D. Improving stress management: An action-research based OD intervention. In. W. W. Burke, (Ed.), *The cutting edge.* San Diego, Calif.: University Associates, 1978.

Adams, J. D. *Understanding and managing stress: A workbook in changing life styles.* San Diego, Calif.: University Associates, 1980.

Alderfer, C. P., Alderfer, C. J., Tucker, L., and Tucker, R. Diagnosing race relations in management. *Journal of Applied Behavioral Science*, 1980, **16**, 135–166.

America, R. F. and Anderson, B. E. *Moving ahead: Black managers in American business.* New York: McGraw-Hill, 1978.

Ashmore, R. D. and DelBoca, F. K. Psychological approaches to understanding conflict. In P. Katz (Ed.), *Toward the elimination of racism.* New York: Pergamon Press, 1976, 73–123.

Barclay, L. A., Fields, M. W., and Halpert, J. A. Perceived differences in job isolation and related satisfaction in different racial groups. Paper presented at the 24th Annual Meeting of the Midwest Academy of Management, Chicago, Ill., 1981.

Bartol, K. M., Evans, C. L., and Stith, M. T. Black versus white leaders: A comparative review of the literature. *Academy of Management Review,* 1978, **3**, 293–304.

Bass, B. M. Blacks and leadership. In B. M. Bass (Ed.), *Stogdill's handbook of leadership.* Riverside, N.J.: The Free Press, 1981.

Beehr, T. A. Perceived situational moderators of the relationship between role ambiguity and role strain. *Journal of Applied Psychology,* 1976, **61**, 35–40.

Beehr, T. A. and Love, K. E. Social stressors on the job. Paper presented at the annual meeting of the Academy of Management, Detroit, August 1980.

Beehr, T. A. and Newman, J. E. Job stress, employee health, and organizational effectiveness: A facet analysis, model, and literature review. *Personnel Psychology,* 1978, **31**, 665–699.

Bergmann, B. R. The effect of white incomes on discrimination in employment. *Journal of Political Economy,* 1971, **79**, 294–313.

Bhagat, R. S. Black-white ethnic differences in identification with the work ethic: Some implications for organizational integration. *Academy of Management Review,* 1979, **4**, 381–391.

Blau, G. An empirical investigation of job stress, social support, service length, and job strain. *Organizational Behavior and Human Performance,* 1981, **27**, 279–302.

Brazziel, W. F. White research in black communities: When solutions become part of the problem. *Journal of Social Issues,* 1973, **29**, 41–44.

Brief, A. P., Schuler, R. S., and Sell, M. V. *Managing job stress.* Boston: Little, Brown, 1981.

Brown, H. A. and Ford, D. L. An exploratory analysis of discrimination in the employment of black MBA graduates. *Journal of Applied Psychology,* 1977, **62**, 50–56.

Brown, R. W. The black tax: Stresses confronting black federal executives. *Journal of Afro-American Issues,* 1975, **3**, 207–218.

Brown, R. W. Stress and the black executive: A coping strategy. In L. Howard, L. Henderson, and D. Hunt (Eds.), *Public administration and public policy: A minority perspective.* Pittsburgh: Public Policy Press, 1977, 361–362.

Caplan, R. D. Organizational stress and individual strain: A social-psychological study of risk factors in coronary heart disease among administrators, engineers and scientists. PhD dissertation, University of Michigan, 1971.

Cashman, J., Dansereau, F., Graen, G., and Haga, W. J. Organizational understructure and leadership: A longitudinal investigation of the managerial role-making process. *Organizational Behavior and Human Performance,* 1976, **15**, 278–296.

Chassie, M. B. Vertical dyadic linkage formation: Predictors and processes determining quality superior-subordinate relationships. Unpublished manuscript, The University of Texas at Dallas, Richardson, Texas, March 1982.

Cobb, S. Social support as a moderator of life stress. *Psychosomatic Medicine,* 1976, **38**, 300–314.

Cobbs, P. Challenge of the 80's: Corporations, credentials, and race. Invited address presented at the Black Alumni Conference, Harvard Graduate School of Business, Boston, February 27–28, 1981.

Coburn, D. Job-worker incongruence: Consequences for health. *Journal of Health and Social Behavior*, 1975, **16**, 198–212.

Cooper, C. L. and Payne, R. (Eds.), *Stress at work*. New York: Wiley, 1978.

Cooper, C. L. and Payne, R. (Eds.), *Current concerns in occupational stress*. New York: Wiley, 1980.

Cunningham, M. Mary Cunningham on: Corporate ethics and sexual prejudice. *Working Woman*, 1981 (July), 53–56.

Daley, M. R. Burnout: Smoldering problem in protective services. *Social Work*, 1979, **24**, 375–379.

Dansereau, F., Graen, G., and Haga, W. J. A vertical dyad linkage approach to leadership within formal organizations: A longitudinal investigation of the role making process. *Organizational Behavior and Human Performance*, 1975, **13**, 46–78.

Dovidio, J. F. and Gaertner, S. L. The effects of race, status, and ability on helping behavior. *Social Psychology Quarterly*, 1981, **44**, 192–203.

Edwards, K. L. The influence of management function and perceived environmental support on perceived stress and job satisfaction of black females in managerial and professional positions in industry. PhD dissertation, University of Cincinnati, 1980.

England, P. and McLaughlin, S. "Sex segregation of jobs and male-female income differentials." In R. Albarez, K. Lutterman, and Associates (Eds.), *Discrimination in organizations*. San Francisco: Jossey-Bass, 1979, 189–213.

Epstein, E. M. and Hampton, D. R. (Eds.), *Black Americans and white business*. Encino, Calif.: Dickenson Publishing Company, 1971.

Etzioni, A. *The active society*. New York: Free Press, 1968.

Fernandez, J. L. *Racism and sexism in corporate life: Changing values in American business*. Lexington, Mass.: Lexington Books, 1981.

Ford, D. L. *Readings in minority group relations*. San Diego, Calif.: University Associates, 1976.

Ford, D. L. The black adult and the world of work. In L. Gary (Ed.), *Mental health: A challenge to the black community*. Philadelphia: Dorrance and Company, 1978a.

Ford, D. L. Cultural influences on organizational behavior: Can the *Fortune* 500 learn from the *Black Enterprise* 100? *Social Change* 1978b, **8**, 1–8.

Ford, D. L. On being culturally disadvantaged: Its impact on the development of job expectancies and valences for job rewards among three ethnic groups. *Journal of Social and Behavioral Sciences*, 1979, **25**, 26–37.

Ford, D. L. Work, job satisfaction, and employee well being: An exploratory study of minority professionals. *Journal of Social and Behavioral Sciences*, 1980, **26**(3), 70–75.

Ford, D. L. The relative contributions of facets of work support in the prediction of stress-related work outcomes for black professionals. Presented at the Conference on Black Stress/Distress and Coping Strategies, University of Alabama, Tuscaloosa, October 21–23, 1981.

Ford, D. L. and Bagot, D. Correlates of job stress and job satisfaction for minority professionals in organizations: An examination of personal and organizational factors. *Group and Organization Studies*, 1978, **3**, 30–41.

Ford, D. L. and Gatewood, L. B. Uncle Tom in the executive suite. *Working*, 1976, **1**, 18–21.

French, J. R. P. Person-role fit. In A. McLean (Ed.), *Occupational stress*. Springfield, Ill.: Thomas, 1974.

Freudenberger, H. J. Burnout: The organizational menace. *Training and Development Journal*, 1977, **31**, 26–27.

Friedlander, F. Emerging blackness in a white research world. *Human Organization*, 1970, **29**, 239–250.

Fromkin, H. L. and Sherwood, J. J. (Eds.) *Integrating the organization*. New York: The Free Press, 1974.

Gibb, B. and Terry, R. Advocating change in the white male club. Unpublished manuscript, Neely, Campbell, Gibb, Terry and Associates, Ann Arbor, Mich., 1979.

Graen, G. Role making processes within complex organizations. In M.D. Dunnette (Ed.), *Handbook of industrial and organizational psychology*. Chicago: Rand McNally, 1976.

Graen, G. and Cashman, J. A rolemaking model of leadership in formal organizations: A developmental approach. *Organization and Administrative Sciences*, 1975, **6**, 143–165.

Greenberger, R. S. How "burnout" affects corporate managers and their performance. *Wall Street Journal*, April 23, 1981a, p. 1.

Greenberger, R. S. Many black managers hope to enter ranks of top management. *Wall Street Journal*, June 17, 1981b, p. 1.

Hackman, J. R. and Suttle, J. L. *Improving life at work*. Santa Monica, Calif.: Goodyear, 1977.

Hamilton, D. L. A cognitive-attributional analysis of stereotyping. In L. Berkowitz (Ed.), *Advances in experimental social psychology*, New York: Academic Press, 1979, 53–85.

Harris, P. R. and Moren, R. T. *Managing cultural differences*. Houston: Gulf Publishing Company, 1979.

Holmes, T. H. and Rahe, R. H. The social readjustment rating scale. *Journal of Psychosomatic Research*, 1967, **11**, 213–218.

House, J. S. *Work stress and social support*. Reading, Mass.: Addison-Wesley, 1981.

House, J. S. and Wells, J. A. Occupational stress, social support, and health. Paper presented at the Conference on Reducing Occupational Stress, White Plains, N.Y., May 1977.

Ivancevich, J. M. and Matteson, M. T. *Stress and work: A managerial perspective*. Glenview, Ill.: Scott, Foresman, 1980.

Kanter, R. M. *Men and women of the corporation*. New York: Basic Books, 1977.

Kanter, R. M. and Stein, B. A. *A tale of "O": On being different in an organization*. New York: Harper and Row, 1980.

Kaufman, J. Black executives say prejudice still impedes their path to the top. *Wall Street Journal*, July 9, 1980, p. 1.

King, D. C. and Bass, B. B. Leadership, power, and influence. In H. L. Fromkin and J. J. Sherwood (Eds.), *Integrating the organization*. New York: The Free Press, 1974, 247–268.

Korchin, S. J. Clinical psychology and minority problems. *American Psychologist*, 1980, **35**, 262–269.

Kram, K. E. Mentoring processes at work: Developmental relationships in managerial careers. PhD dissertation, Yale University, 1980.

LaRocco, J. M., House, J. S., and French, J. R. P. Social support, occupational stress, and health. *Journal of Health and Social Behavior*, 1980, **21**, 201–218.

LaRocco, J. M. and Jones, A. P. Co-worker and leader support as moderators of stress-strain relationships in work situations. *Journal of Applied Psychology*, 1978, **63**, 629–634.

Lawler, L. L., Nadler, D., and Cammann, L. *Assessing the quality of work life in organizations*. New York: Wiley, 1981.

Love, K. G. and Beehr, T. A. Social stressors on the job: Recomendations for a broadened perspective. *Group and Organization Studies*, 1981, **6**, 190–200.

Maslach, C. Burned-out. *Human Behavior*, 1976, **5**, 16–18.

Maslach, C. Job burnout: How people cope. *Public Welfare*, 1978, **36**, 56–58.

Matteson, M. T. and Ivancevich, J. M. Organizational stresses and heart disease: A research model. *Academy of Management Review*, 1979, 4, 347–357.

McLean, A. A. *Work stress*. Reading, Mass.: Addison-Wesley, 1980.

Moch, M. K. Racial differences in job satisfaction: Testing four common explanations. *Organizational Behavior and Human Performance*, 1980, **65**, 299–306.

Murphy, C. J. An exploratory development and validation of a perceptual job burnout inventory. Paper presented at the 46th Annual Meeting of the Association of Social and Behavioral Scientists, Atlanta, March 1981.

Nadler, D. A. and Tushman, M. L. A congruence model for organizational assessment. In E. E. Lawler, D. A. Nadler, and C. Cammann (Eds.), *Organizational Assessment*. New York: Wiley, 1980, pp. 260–278.

Naismith, D. Stress among managers as a function of organizational change. PhD dissertation, George Washington University, 1975.

Newman, J. E. and Beehr, T. A. Personal and organizational strategies for handling job stress: A review of research and opinion. *Personnel Psychology*, 1979, **32**, 1–43.

Norman, B. Career burnout. *Black Enterprise Magazine*, July 1981, 45–48.

Parker, W. S. Black-white differences in leader behavior related to subordinates' reactions. *Journal of Applied Psychology*, 1976, **61**, 140–147.

Payne, R. Organizational stress and social support. In C. L. Cooper and R. Payne (Eds.), *Current concerns in occupational stress*. New York: Wiley, 1980.

Peters, L. H., O'Connor, E. J., and Rudolf, C. J. The behavioral and affective consequences of performance-relevant situational variables. *Organizational Behavior and Human Performance*, 1980, **25**, 79–96.

Pinneau, S. R. Effects of social support on psychological and physiological strains. *Dissertation Abstracts International*, 1976a, **10**, 5359B.

Pinneau, S. R. Effects of social support on occupational stresses and strains. Paper presented at the 84th Annual Convention of the American Psychological Association, Washington, D.C., September 1976b.

Purcell, T. V. and Cavanagh, G. F. *Blacks in the industrial world*. New York: The Free Press, 1972.

Ramos, A. A. The relationship of sex and ethnic background to job related stress of research and development professionals. *Dissertation Abstracts International*, 1975, **9**, 1862A.

Richards, A. S. and Jaffe, C. L. Blacks supervising whites: A study of interracial difficulties in working together in a simulated organization. *Journal of Applied Psychology*, 1972, **56**, 234–240.

Rizzo, J. R., House, R. J., and Lirtzman, S. I. Role conflict and ambiguity in complex organizations. *Administrative Science Quarterly*. 1970, **15**, 150–163.

Schriesheim, C. A. and Murphy, C. J. Relationships between leader behavior and subordinate satisfaction and performance: A test of some situational moderators. *Journal of Applied Psychology*, 1976, **61**, 634–641.

Schuler, R. S. Definition and conceptualization of stress in organizations. *Organizational Behavior and Human Performance*, 1980, **25**, 184–215.

Segovis, J. C. and Bhagat, R. S. Participation revisited: Implications for organizational stress and performance. *Small Group Behavior*, 1981, **12**, 299–328.

Smith, P. C., Kendall, L. M. , and Hulin, C. L. *The measurement of satisfaction in work and retirement*. Chicago: Rand McNally, 1969.

Spielberger, C. D., Gorsuch, R. L., and Lushene, R. E. *Manual for the state-trait anxiety inventory*. Palo Alto, Calif.: Consulting Psychologist Press, 1970.

Taber, T. D., Green, S. G., and Verderber, K. S. Differential behavior of a leader toward work group members: A partial test of heterogeneous dyads model of leadership. In J. Hair (Ed.), *Proceedings of the American Institute for Decision Sciences*, 1979.

Taylor, S. A. The black executive and the corporation: A difficult fit. *MBA Magazine*, 1972, **8**, 91–102.

Taylor, S. A. Room at the top? Not for blacks. *New York Times*, January 14, 1973, Section F, p. 14.

Terborg, J. R. and Ilgen, D. R. A theoretical approach to sex discrimination in traditionally masculine occupations. *Organizational Behavior and Human Performance*, 1975, **13**, 352–376.

Terry, R. White male club: Biology and power. *Civil Rights Digest*, 1974, **6**, 66–77.

Thurow, L. *Poverty and discrimination*. Washington, D. C.: The Brookings Institute, 1969.

Triana, A. R. A cross-cultural model of supervision: An empirical study of Hispanic Americans. Presented at the Twenty-fourth Annual Meeting of the Midwest Academy of Management, Chicago, April 9–11, 1981.

Van Maanen, J. and Schein, E. H. Toward a theory of organizational socialization. In B. Staw and L. L. Cummings (Eds.), *Research in Organizational Behavior*, 1975, **1**, 209–264.

Vecchio, R. P. Worker alienation as a moderator of the quality–job satisfaction relationship: The case of racial differences. *Academy of Management Journal* 1980, **23**, 479–486.

Woodard, J. C. and Harris, C. W. Administrative stress: Viewed from the perspective of the black administrator. In S. L. Woodard (Ed.), *Reducing stress on the black administrator*. New York: Vantage Press, 1978, 13–35.

Woodard, S. L. (Ed.) *Reducing stress on black administrators*. New York: Vantage Press, 1978.

Zappert, L. T. and Weinstein, H. M. Sex differences in adaptation to work: Physical and psychological consequences. Paper presented at the Annual Meeting of the American Psychological Association, Montreal, Canada, 1980.

CHAPTER TWELVE

Acculturative Stress in Immigrants
A Developmental Perspective

RABI S. BHAGAT

During the last two decades the liberalization of U.S. immigration laws, along with other political developments in the world, have produced a stream of immigrants in this country. The vast majority of these immigrants have been from the continents of Asia and Latin America, in marked contrast to the predominantly European origins of the immigrants before 1920. Census data and other demographic analyses of the new immigrants show that they are similar to the mainstream U. S. population in terms of socioeconomic characteristics and geographical dispersion (Massey, 1981). However, as early as between 1952 and 1965, the U. S. immigration policy, in the words of Newsweek magazine "treated the American national character like a prized recipe, to be preserved in perpetuity in its exact ethnic composition." The tendency was to put new immigrants through a rigorous process of assimilation until they become "Americans" with relatively little remaining of their ethnic identities. However, during the 1970s an average of one-half million immigrants entered the United States legally each year, and the process of rapid assimilation that was observed during the earlier era slowed. Consider the following:

1. Census data collected in 1980 show that while the percentage of white population rose only by 6.0 percent from 1970 to 1980 (a rate slightly greater than half of the 11.5 percent increase for the country as a whole), the number of Koreans underwent a fivefold in-

crease, registering a total gain of 412.8 percent. The number of Filipinos increased by 125.8 percent, and the number of persons of Chinese origin increased by 85.3 percent.

2. Among Japanese-Americans the most acculturated group had a coronary heart disease (CHD) rate that is 3 to 5 times that of the least acculturated. The rate for the least acculturated approximated the low rate for the country of Japan itself. The differential rate of the CHD could not be explained by differences in the usual major coronary risk factors such as diet, smoking, blood pressure, and so on (Marmot and Syme, 1976).

3. Portuguese females are more sensitive than males in terms of their responses to stressful life events, as indicated by high levels of psychoneurotic symptom scores (Roskies et al., 1978).

4. Among the Mexican-Americans, women who are more acculturated to Anglo-American society remain in psychotherapy longer (five or more sessions), as compared with those who are less acculturated (one or two sessions) (Miranda and Castro, 1977).

5. In New York the Puerto Ricans who are geographically most mobile, and who thus tend to be more isolated from their own ethnic culture, also have the highest rate of psychiatric breakdown (Srole et al., 1962).

6. The rate of growth of Indian-born scientists is such that if the current trend of immigration continues, the number of Indian scientists in the United States will be about 63 percent of those in India and only about half of Indian scientists will be in their native land by the early 1980s (Inhaber, 1975). A survey by the National Science Foundation placed the Indian scientists with doctorates and publications above other immigrants, noting that their research activities and scholarly contributions to their professions have been more significant than other similar immigrant groups (Datta, 1975).

7. Taken as a whole, the rate of fertility of the post-1970 immigrants is lower than that of the native U. S. population. Groups with high fertility rates—for example, Mexicans and Puerto Ricans—are effectively held in check by groups with very low fertility, such as the Japanese, Chinese, Cubans, and South and Central Americans. Fertility rate tends to decline even among Mexicans and Puerto Ricans with acculturation and rising socioeconomic status. Thus, new immigration is not expected to lead to a long-term increase in the overall fertility rate in the United States (Massey, 1981).

These examples illustrate the growing importance of studying the psychological adaptations of immigrants from the perspective of social and behavioral sciences. This chapter provides a conceptual rationale for examining the stress reactions of immigrants in the context of their work settings. Massey (1981) concluded that the new immigrants appear to be well prepared in their tendencies to assimilate with the mainstream values of American life. With increasing exposure to the U. S. society over the generations and socioeconomic advancement, traditional values of the home country culture change to accommodate life in an urban industrial society. Sex roles tend to become less rigid, and the importance of nuclear family increases. Unlike stresses that accompany social changes within a given culture, stresses of acculturation typically involve changes in the underlying structure of cultural values, which take generations to resolve.

ACCULTURATION AND ACCULTURATIVE STRESS

Acculturation is a complex process and has been conceptualized at the individual, ethnic, or cultural level. Given the diversity of definitions on acculturation, it often becomes difficult to integrate findings from earlier studies. Controversy surrounding the definition dates back to 1935. Campici (1947) noted that the confusion surrounding the term was so overwhelming that the Social Science Research Council appointed a task force consisting of Ralf Linton, Robert Redfield, and Melville Herskovitz to provide a suitable definition. This committee defined acculturation as

> " . . . Those phenomena which result when groups of individuals having different cultures come into continuous first-hand contact with subsequent changes in the original cultural patterns of either or both groups." (page 7)

In more recent studies it has been defined as a process by which minorities learn to perform the roles that are valued by the dominant majority (Smither, 1982). The idea that the immigrant groups slowly learn to change some of their cultural values during the course of adapting to a new culture is reflected in the definitions given by Szapocznik, Scopetta, Kurtines, and Arnahde (1978) and Berry (1980). In brief, acculturation may be defined as a process of accommodation and adaptation, on the part of members of a minority or ethnic culture, to the dominant cultural values of a majority culture. For the majority of the members of an ethnic group such a process of culture change is not an easy one, and considerable difficulties often arise. Acculturative stress is a product of these difficulties associated with culture change. It may be defined to include those experiences and behaviors that are generated during acculturation and that are mildly pathological and disruptive to the individual and to his or her cultural group (Berry, 1980). Various kinds of psychosomatic symptoms, feelings of alienation, and marginality are often results of experiencing acculturative stress.

Causes and consequences of both acculturation and acculturative stress have been studied in social, clinical, and cross-cultural psychology, but its importance has not yet been realized in the growing literature on organizational stress. Our review of the literature revealed the existence of three empirical studies that deal with work-related consequences of acculturation and acculturative stresses. Adler (1977) examined the nature of work satisfaction in a group of immigrants to Israel, using Maslow's need hierarchy framework. Krau (1981) examined the significance of status incongruence between present occupation in the host country and the past occupation in the home country in fostering cognitive dissonance in a group of immigrants in Israel, and found that a change in the immigrant's career was not necessarily a preplanned or desired event and that some preparation for career change did indeed take place after arrival in the new country. Both psychological dissonance reduction strategies (i.e., denying the existence of status incongruence) and behavioral strategies (i.e., increased vocational involvement) are important in managing the transitional difficulties associated with career changes. Berman (1981) found that adjustment to life was a function of work satisfaction in a sample of North American immigrants to Israel. His results clearly showed that, in the absence of alternative commitments such as religious activities to offset the importance of work, job satisfaction affects the general life adjustment patterns of immigrants. The literature on social and cultural change that deals with various aspects of acculturation is vast, and several important themes have emerged in the recent reviews. It would be useful to review these themes before we delineate a model of acculturative stress in organizational contexts.

Theme I. Acculturation and acculturative stress are a function of prevailing patterns of cultural differences that exist between the two countries involved. Specifically, if the differences in cultural values are substantial, the necessary shifts accompanying acculturation and acculturative stresses are also substantial.

Theme II. Immigration policies of the host country (i.e., the degree to which the official government policy encourages assimilation versus pluralism), as well as some dominant characteristics of the home country (i.e., familism), strongly influence acculturation and acculturative stresses among immigrants.

Theme III. Attempts to acculturate a given immigrant group may take relatively distinct forms. The first form is known as *assimilation*, in which the immigrants relinquish cultural identity of their home country. Assimilation can also be achieved by merging many distinct ethnic immigrant groups to form a new societal culture (the "melting pot" notion) in which the original distinctive patterns of ethnic cultures slowly give way in favor of a mainstream cultural pattern. The second form of acculturation is known as *integration* which, in contrast to assimilation, implies the maintenance of ethnic cultural integrity as well as the movement to become an integral part of a larger societal framework. Countries favoring the integrative mode of acculturation typically result in "mosaic" of cultures where there is some degree of "structural assimilation" to signify that the ethnic groups actively participate in the socioeconomic systems of the larger society but do not necessarily favor a mainstream of model culture in lieu of their own (Berry 1980).

Theme IV.   Acculturation and acculturative stress may be understood and examined at the individual level, at the interpersonal level, or at the level of the ethnic immigrant group itself.

Given these themes, one can see the relevance of examining the nature and consequences of acculturative stress in organizations. Research on this topic is important for the following reasons:

1. It will help organizational researchers understand the role of cultural differences in fostering stress reactions and coping behaviors in organizations.

2. It will increase our insights into the moderating role of social support in stress-outcome relationships. The pattern of social support mechanisms seems to be relatively distinctive for immigrants, as compared with those of the local born (Nair, 1980).

3. From an organizational perspective research information on this topic will assist organizations in designing suitable intervention programs for immigrant employees that take the cultural perspective into account. Since the number of immigrants has been continuously on the rise and their contributions are important for various organizations, it is important to understand the special nature of their integration within the organization.

A MODEL OF ACCULTURATIVE STRESS IN A DEVELOPMENTAL PERSPECTIVE

The conceptual model depicted in Figure 12-1 focuses on the nature of various environmental as well as organization factors that might precipitate stress and stress reactions in the immigrant worker. As discussed earlier, the author adopts the essence of Berry's (1980) definition and further suggests that an immigrant employee experiences acculturative stress in the context of his or her work role when he or she is confronted with an environmental situation or a series of situations that present a *demand*, an *opportunity* or a *constraint* (McGrath, 1976; Schuler, 1980) and that possess considerable potential for long-term emotional and physical well-being. Demand stresses are those dynamic organizational situations

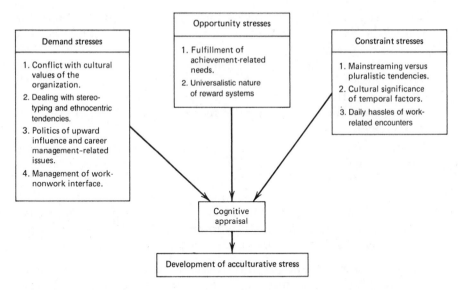

Figure 12-1 Three aspects of ethnic immigrant experience and development of acculturative stress in organization. (Solid lines, presumed causal effects.)

that prevent an individual to be, to have, or to do what he or she desires. Opportunity stresses are those dynamic organizational situations that present the individual with opportunities to be, to have, or to do what he or she desires. Constraint stresses are those dynamic organizational situations that put some restrictions on the individual to be, to have, or to do what he or she desires (Schuler, 1980). Furthermore, the total amount of acculturative stress experienced by an individual is a function of all these three stresses (Figure 12-1). However, as the model shows, for any of these interpersonal or organizational factors to have stressful implications, it must be perceived and appraised as being "stressful" by the immigrant employee. Furthermore, the greater the importance of the organizational outcomes associated with such stressful situations, the stronger the uncertainties, and the longer the duration of such uncertainties, the greater the amount of stress (Chapter 1).

DEMAND STRESSES

According to the model, there are four different types of demanding stressful experiences that an immigrant employee is likely to encounter. First of these concerns the conflict with cultural values of the workplace. Since an immigrant's subjective culture is different from the subjective culture of the host country's work organizations, such differences may often be significant sources of stress. Subjective culture is a group's characteristic way of perceiving its social environment (Triandis et al., 1972). When individuals from one culture interact with individuals from another culture, the differences in norms, values, roles, and attitudinal orientations that separate the two cultures tend to become salient (Bochner and Ohsako, 1977; Bochner and Perks, 1971; Hartley and Thompson, 1967; Triandis, 1967). Physical appearances, skin color, and accent in the language spoken provide definitive clues about ethnic origin and, by implications, to the status of the immigrants as members of a different cultural group. Such differences in cultures, both in perceptual and in real terms, are likely to be stressful for the immigrant. They are stressful because they induce social and cultural readjustments on the part of the immigrants in order to accommodate the role of cultural differences in his or her organizational life. Some authors (Coelho and Ahmad, 1980) have noted that maintenance of self-esteem becomes problematic during various phases of acculturation. Consider the following example. An immigrant from Venezuela, a country that emphasizes familism and collectivism, working in an organization in Texas, U.S.A., a state within a country that strongly emphasizes individualism, is likely to experience stress and conflict in dealing with this culture-specific difference in his or her work role in the organization. It might be necessary for him or her to reconstruct his or her self-esteem and other related attitudinal orientations in individualistic as opposed to collectivistic terms. There are also other aspects of conflict of cultural values. Based on Hofstede's (1980) recent extensive work in 40 countries, one might examine the relevance of cultural differences in power distance, uncertainty avoidance, and masculinity/femininity between the work values fostered in the immigrant's native home culture and the work values of the host culture in creating stress and conflicts. Hofstede's (1980) constructs for understanding cultural differences in values were individualism versus collectivism, power distance, uncertainty avoidance, and masculinity versus femininity. Individualism in the context of work organizations is concerned with strong emphasis on self-directed motivations for personal achievement and self-sufficiency, whereas collectivism emphasizes greater emotional dependence of members on their organizations and on each other. Societies that emphasize the value of collectivism would stress ideological involvement of the individual with the organization, whereas those societies that emphasize the value of individualism would encourage calculative involvement. The concept of power distance in the context of work organizations refers to the uneven distribution of power and status among members of the organization. Hofstede (1980) noted that societies characterized by high power distance accept and legitimize societal inequalities that exist between various social and occupational classes. In such societies a latent conflict is presumed to exist between the powerful and powerless. As the powerful attempt to increase power, the powerless attempt to reduce such tendencies through various kinds of organized activities such as strikes, unionism, sabotage, and so on. Uncertainty avoidance, the third dimension of cultural difference in Hofstede's framework, is concerned with the extent to which the members of a culture are concerned with excessive emphasis on rules and procedures, employment stability, and reduced propensities toward risk taking. Work organizations in high uncertainty-avoidance cultures are often characterized by strict rules and regulations, formalism, and bureaucratic rigidity. Hofstede's (1980) data indicate that individuals in these cultures tend to experience high levels of anxiety and attempt to cope with such anxieties by making their organizations more bureaucratic and inflexible. The rationale is that as organizations become more inflexible in the way they are organized, they also become more predictable. Masculinity versus femininity, the final dimension of cultural difference in Hofstede's framework, refers to the extent to which the members of a cultural group are preoccupied with such concrete objectives as personal earnings, recognition, advancement, and other performance-oriented outcomes, as opposed to quality of work life, friendly atmosphere, and expression of aesthetically oriented attributes. Masculinity is characterized by high degrees of assertiveness, and acquisition of tangible objects such as money and material possessions, whereas femininity is expressed through one's concern for more intangible aspects such as quality of life, people, and natural surroundings. Cultures that are highly masculine tend to emphasize performance-related criterion. Based on the above discussion, we are led to believe that the greater the discrepancies between an immigrant employee's home culture and his or her host culture in terms of individualism, power distance, uncertainty avoidance, and masculinity, the greater would be the amount of acculturative stress experienced by the employee.

The second demanding aspect of immigrant experience is concerned with the nature of cultural stereotypes that are often generated in the context of his or her organizational life. Studies dealing with contacts among members from different cultural groups have shown that even relatively small differences become quite noticeable, and that these differences are exaggerated and often distorted to create a stereotype of that culture (Allport, 1954; Campbell, 1967; Triandis and Vassiliou, 1967). These stereotypes, while they may contain a grain of truth (Allport, 1954) often are incorrect (e.g., see the classic study of Armenians in California by La Piere, 1936). Ethnic stereotyping reflected in such notions as the formality of the Englishman, the pugnacity of the Irish, and the simple-mindedness and the naiveté of the Portuguese generally shape the attributional processes of the members of the dominant culture, and examples that disconfirm such stereotypes may be dismissed as deviation from the norm (Klineberg, 1982). Immigrants encountering such stereotyping tendencies often experience stress. Furthermore, such tendencies may adversely affect employee evaluations and other processes that are often crucial for success in organizational roles.

Persistent stereotyping and other related evaluative processes in organizations of the ethnic immigrant's home culture often constitute a demand stress for the immigrant and could lead to rejection of appropriate behaviors in the work role. The longer the duration of these stereotyping tendencies, and especially concerning those important cultural attributes that are likely to cause success, the more intense is the experience of stress. It is possible that many immigrants simply learn to live with such stressful experiences, with the result that their mental health is adversely affected.

The third source of demand stress for the immigrant employee is concerned with the politics of upward influence and the processes related to career management. Social influence processes are important in organizational life and one often has to learn the political norms of an organization in order to succeed (Porter et al., 1981). There is ample evidence that informal "political" norms exist in various types of organizations. Real-life reports of organizational life (e.g., Frost et al., 1978; Kanter, 1977) provide anecdotal evidence of political processes at work. Schein (1977) argued that political processes are almost as central to organizational life as planning, organizing, directing, and controlling. Tushman (1977) also suggested that conflict, bargaining, and other commonly occurring political behaviors could be viewed as essential for organizational functioning. Madison et al. (1980) found that more than 90% of managers in their study reported decisions influenced by organizational politics, at upper and middle levels of management. Learning of political norms, as Porter et al., (1981) claim, is particularly difficult for the newcomer in the organization. The stimuli are often ambiguous, and it is quite likely that informal political norms probably exist in certain situational contexts and in localized forms. That is, there is a great deal of situational influence in the generation and exercise of upward organizational politics. Furthermore, since formal organization neither prescribes nor forbids political behaviors, political norms are not easily understood in the formal context of the organization. Therefore, as Porter et al. (1981) suggest, learning of political norms may require considerable sensitivity on the part of the newcomer. Past experience in similar organizational contexts might help, but it is important for the incumbent to ensure that significant learning attempts are not attributed by others to his or her (i.e., the immigrant's) self-serving tendencies. Obviously it is a difficult process, and this author suggests that for immigrants who do not often possess similar experiences and who are already experiencing culture shock and other value-related conflicts, it becomes very difficult to learn the appropriate political cues, strategies, and behaviors. Lack of such knowledge is likely to cause difficulty in the management of one's career.

Successful managers often have a powerful mentor—one who helps the protegé understand the intricate and complex social processes surrounding such issues as performance appraisal, managerial succession, and so on (Clawson, 1980; Dalton et al., 1977; Kram, 1983). It is quite likely that immigrants might have some difficulty in establishing fruitful mentor-protegé relationships because of their slow rate of learning and understanding of prevailing organizational political norms.

The fourth type of demand stress that may often confront the immigrant employee is concerned with his or her ability to manage the work-nonwork interface in the context of an increasingly complex modern society. Cohen (1980) suggested that an overwhelming majority of immigrants "self-sacrifice" (p. 355) in order to commit themselves to their work roles. Latinos, for example, cope with ambiguous aspects of their jobs by engaging in self-sacrifice. One of the most important aspects of working conditions for them is their congenial relations with their supervisors, colleagues, and other important members of the organizations. *Buen trato* (proper and fair treatment by employers includes getting *respeto* (respect) (a core value of the traditional Latin American society) and being treated with *dignidad* (dignity). *Mal trato* (poor treatment or lack of genuine consideration) by employers diminishes the *dignidad* of persons and therefore ought to be avoided at all costs. In their attempts to achieve *dignidad*, some immigrants might work even harder and maintain their self-esteem by performing at a considerably higher rate than would otherwise be necessary or called for. Such propensities often cause work-nonwork role conflicts in the lives of immigrants. Kahn et al. (1964) defined role conflict as the simultaneous occurrence of two or more sets of demands, such that compliance or fulfillment of one would make compliance or fulfillment of the other difficult. Based on limited available evidence (Cohen, 1980; Coelho and Ahmed, 1980), it would appear that such role conflicts pertaining to the management of the work-nonwork interface often constitute stressful experiences for immigrants. Korman, et al. (1981) found that contradictory role demands are significant factors in personal and social alienation. Margolis (1979), in her study of managers of one large organization, found that the managers themselves had been so socialized into an acceptance of organizational expectations that they were often unaware of what might be their appropriate nonwork and family-role-related behaviors. Such tendencies of being overinvolved in the domain of work might be even stronger in immigrants who, as suggested earlier, might use successful work role performance as a means of coping with conflicts between different cultural values in the workplace, stereotyping tendencies, the politics of upward influence, and other related difficulties. Furthermore, persistence of such tendencies over long periods of time might become quite stressful for the employee and his or her family as well.

OPPORTUNITY STRESSES

As shown in the model (Figure 12-1), stresses pertaining to the opportunity-related aspects of the immigrant work experience are also important in the development of acculturative stress. It has been argued that work contexts of Western society such as the United States provide better opportunities for fulfillment of achievement-related needs and motives of immigrants originating from the developing nations than do work contexts in their home countries. DeVos (1968), for example, observed that Indians and Chinese achieve considerable economic success outside their native cultures even though their cultures have traditionally been characterized by low achievement orientation. Maher's (1974, 1977) analyses of the influence of socioeconomic conditions in fostering achievement motivation also indicate the usefulness of the contextual influences in the fulfillment of achievement-related needs. Since a majority of the immigrants migrate from developing countries, where work organizations often do not provide adequate opportunities for fulfillment of achievement-related needs, immigrants generally view the enriched working conditions of their jobs as appropriate contexts for satisfying their achievement-related needs. The universalistic nature of reward systems in the context of work organizations of the developed countries constitute yet another important aspect of opportunity stress for the immigrant employee. The Parsons and Shils (1951) conceptualization of universalism (applying general standards) versus particularism (taking particular relationships into account) is used in this analysis of opportunity stress. Parsons (1977) suggests that as societies evolve, an emphasis on particularism and ascription is replaced by an emphasis on universalism and achievement. Since most immigrants originate from developing countries where familism (Massey, 1981) and particularism (Triandis and Vissiliou, 1972) are important values, they might experience the universalistic mode of reward distributions of more developed countries as sources of personal growth, and such situations could be characterized as being filled with opportunity stress (Schuler, 1980).

CONSTRAINT STRESSES

In addition to the above two major classes of stresses there are three kinds of constraining influences on the immigrant in the context of his or her work life. First, immigrants often have to manage the dilemma of merging with the mainstream values of the society versus keeping the distinctiveness of their ethnic cultural heritages in their occupational lives. This stressful experience also involves the extent to which ethnic immigrants confront the notion that the culture of their host country might be "superior" when compared with their own native cultures. Even though many individuals have now rejected the idea that the Anglo-Saxon culture is intrinsically superior, in the context of ethnic assimilation practices in the United States, the assimilation or mainstream tendencies do surface with great regularity in the mass media, as well as within the subcultures of the immigrants.

On the one hand, advocates of the mainstreaming tendencies among the immigrants agree that it is functional to orient one's cultural value systems with that of the dominant cultural group in the organization. On the other hand, those who favor pluralism feel that under the rubric of functionalism, distinctive patterns of ethnic cultural traditions may be eliminated, and the immigrants might therefore lose some of the important sources of historical information that are relevant for coping with value-related difficulties and conflicts in the workplace.

At any rate, the argument is far from resolved (see Sue, 1983 for details), and it is indeed a source of stress that constrains the occupational as well as personal lives of immigrants.

Second, immigrants often have to undergo a significant attitudinal orientation pertaining to the significance of time and temporal factors in the context of their occupational lives. McGrath and Rotchford (1983) suggest that various cultures determine the significance of time and time-utilization processes quite differently, and such differences become even more noticeable in work organizations. Time is a valuable commodity in the industrial cultures (particularly in Japan) and it is put to use in the most economically sound and rational way (Jul Kunen, 1977). This implies a strong concern, not only with temporal coordination of activities of various members of the organization, but also with the scheduling of those activities with respect to an outside "clock" and "calendar" so that the total amount of wasted time in the context of working hours is minimized (McGrath and Rotchford, 1983). Time is viewed as linear-separable and therefore as segmented into various distinct units, in order to make the best possible use of it. In contrast, the conception of time in some of the developing countries is procedural-traditional (Graham, 1981). What is important is that an activity be done according to some established and culturally appropriate pattern, not that it be done on time. Immigrants originating from cultures that emphasize such procedural-traditional ways of conceptualizing and utilizing time might indeed experience the linear-separable conception of time in their host cultures as a significant factor in constraining their work lives. Existence of such subjective and culturally determined differences in the significance of time and time-utilization processes may also cause misunderstandings and nonisomorphic attributions between the members of the mainstream culture and the immigrants in the organization. Nonisomorphic attributions take place when a member of the mainstream culture makes attributions that are dissimilar to those made by the members of the immigrant group's ethnic culture. This author views such conflicts as constraint stresses because they often pose problems inhibiting a more complete utilization of the abilities and talents of the immigrant worker.

Third, the immigrant also has to cope with the daily hassles of work-related encounters that are often present in a culturally heterogeneous organization. Daily hassles, a term coined by Kanner et al. (1981), is designed to capture the irritating, frustrating, distressing, and troubled relationships and expectations that confront us day in and day out. Some of the hassles are chronic while others may be transient. Kanner et al. (1981) and DeLongis et al. (1982) have found that these hassles are more useful than life events in predicting adaptational outcomes such as depressed mood and various kinds of psychological symptoms. They argue that hassles are more proximal measures of stress and, therefore, are better predictors of psychological and health-related outcomes. Following Lazarus and his associates' approach (Kanner et al., 1981), this author suggests that some significant sources of hassles exist in the work lives of immigrants and that these hassles often constitute a major form of constraint stress. Various communication-related difficulties that arise due to differences in accent or manners of speech (Bochner, 1982) are some of the examples of daily hassles that could constitute constraints in the work lives of immigrants.

THE ROLE OF COGNITIVE APPRAISAL IN THE DEVELOPMENT OF ACCULTURATIVE STRESS

The model shows that environmental events that are classified as demand, opportunity, and constraint stresses lead to the development of acculturative stress in immigrants. However, for these events to have stressful implications for the immigrant, they must be accurately perceived and interpreted by the individual. Cognitive appraisal mediates the effects of these stressful environmental events in the process of development of acculturative stress. Psychological processes surrounding the role of cognitive appraisal are already discussed by Segovis, Bhagat, and Coehlo in Chapter 9 and therefore will not be presented here. It is important to note, however, that many individual differences exist in the way immigrants learn to appraise and interpret these stressful experiences in the context of their work roles in the organization.

Figure 12-2 presents the consequences of acculturative stress for the individual immigrant as well as for the organization. This author has suggested that acculturative stress leads to acculturative strain, which has consequences for the organization as well as for the individual. The moderating effects of intercultural effectiveness and social support on this stress-strain are discussed in a later section. Organizationally valued outcomes that are likely to be affected by acculturative strain are organizational commitment, job satisfaction, and job performance. It is also conceivable that turnover among the immigrants might increase with increasing levels of strain associated with acculturation. At the individual level it is likely that acculturative stresses would affect mental health, self-esteem, and feelings of self-efficacy (Fried, 1980).

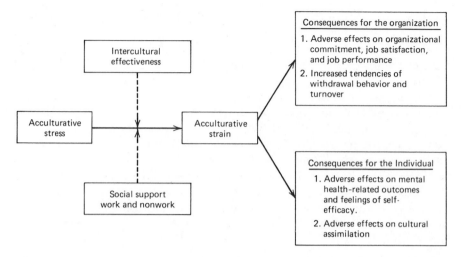

Figure 12-2 Consequences of acculturative stress in terms of organizationally and individually valued outcomes. (Solid lines, presumed causal effect; dotted lines, presumed moderating influence.)

Immigrants might also experience adverse effects in their tendencies toward assimilation with the mainstream culture. While empirical evidence on this proposed link, as depicted in the model, is not available at the present time, research data reported by Sue, Ito, and Bradshaw (1982) indicates that conflicts and constraints experienced during the acculturation process are primarily responsible for creating adverse effects on cultural assimilation.

MODERATING EFFECTS OF INTERCULTURAL SENSITIVITY AND SOCIAL SUPPORT

As shown in the model, the causal impact of acculturative stress in creating acculturative strain is moderated by intercultural effectiveness and social support. Following the work of Hammer et al. (1978) on dimensions of intercultural effectiveness, I propose that those immigrants who possess the ability (1) to communicate effectively at the interpersonal level, (2) to establish interpersonal relationships, and (3) to cope with ambiguities in one's social environment would be quite effective in handling their acculturative stresses. They would also experience significantly less strain, with the result that their role effectiveness both at the organizational and at the individual level would not be greatly affected. On the other hand, immigrants who are less able to communicate effectively, establish interpersonal relationships, and cope with ambiguities in their social worlds experience more acculturative strain. Consequently their work and individually valued outcomes suffer more.

Recent studies by Abe and Wiseman (1983), comparing Japanese and Americans, have shown the utility of the construct of intercultural effectiveness. This author believes that some cultures foster higher levels of intercultural effectiveness as compared with others, and that immigrants originating from cultures that are similar to the host culture in terms of the Hofstede's (1980) value dimensions are likely to be able to handle the stresses that are present during acculturation.

Social support is also of crucial importance in moderating the relationship between acculturative stress and acculturative strain. Since the moderating role of social support is already discussed in this book in Chapter 14, it will not be discussed in detail here. However, it might be useful to mention that social support systems are particularly useful to new immigrants (Nair, 1980). It might also be appropriate to add that without adequate social supports many immigrants would be rather ineffective in coping with the stresses associated with acculturation. Nair's (1980) investigation with new immigrants supports this argument. He found that the process of searching for correct information is most difficult for the immigrants, and it is commonly the members of their own native cultural group who are likely to be helpful in this regard. Social support in the form of providing appropriate cultural information and emotional support is most useful for immigrants in reducing the effects of acculturative stress on the experience of strain.

CONCLUSIONS AND DIRECTIONS FOR FUTURE RESEARCH

As has already been mentioned, the issues surrounding immigrant assimilation in the United States and other developed countries are of growing importance. As more and more immigrants seek occupations in cultures that are dissimilar from their own, research on acculturative stress in organizational contexts is likely to become an important area of investigation. The satisfactory resolution of acculturative stress is essential if immigrant professionals are to maximize their contributions to their work organizations. I suggest that future research on acculturative stress within organizational contexts focus on the following.

First, there is need for adequate operationalization of the constructs of acculturative stress, strain, and intercultural effectiveness. While the definitional issues surrounding these constructs have been dealt with in this chapter as well as in other edited volumes (e.g., Berry, 1980; Coelho and Ahmed, 1980), we do not yet have good operational measures of these and other related constructs. It is essential to make some progress in this area.

Second, the process of acculturation and the development of acculturative stress should be analyzed from a longitudinal perspective. The conceptual model described in this chapter is meant to focus on the longitudinal processes surrounding acculturation, and we need empirical evidence on links, as proposed in the model, from a dynamic and adaptational perspective. Immigrants generally learn to cope (Coelho and Ahmed, 1980) with the cultural ambiguities associated with living in a host culture, and this process of culture learning (Brislin et al., 1975) is best viewed from a longitudinal perspective.

Third, as Sue (1983) has so aptly argued, researchers need to be aware of the pervasiveness of cultural bias and ethnocentricism that have largely undermined the validity of most studies dealing with ethnic minority issues. Recognition of cultural bias should be combined with the motivation to learn the distinctiveness of various cognitive appraisal schemes and social support mechanisms that are often present in the immigrant culture. Research on causes and consequences of acculturative stress among immigrants should be viewed in a cross-cultural perspective, and the methodological problems associated with cross-cultural research (Bhagat and McQuaid, 1982) should be adequately analyzed before valid conclusions are drawn. Obviously, not all investigators can have easy access to immigrant populations in order to gain the necessary familiarity into the dynamics of the immigrant cultures. However, there exist immigrant professionals working in the field of behavioral sciences who could provide assistance, not only in collecting the necessary research information, but also in examining the pervasiveness of cultural biases in the formative stages of the research endeavor. At any rate, it is clear that we need a much larger number of empirical studies dealing with the causes and consequences of acculturative stress in organizations. It is hoped that the conceptual model described in this chapter will stimulate future research in this important yet unexplained phenomenon.

REFERENCES

Abe, H. and Wiseman, R. L. A cross-cultural combination of the dimensions of intercultural effectiveness. *International Journal of Intercultural Relations*, 1983, **7** (1), 53–68.

Adler, S. Maslow's need hierarchy and the adjustment of immigrants. *International Migration Review*, 1977, **11**, 444–451.

Allport, G. W. *The nature of prejudice*. Garden City, N.Y.: Doubleday Anchor, 1954.

Berman, G. S. Work satisfaction and general adjustment of migrants. *Sociology of Work and Occupations*, 1981 **8**, 417–438.

Berry, J. W. Social and cultural change. In Triandis, H. C. and Brishin, R. W. (Eds), *Handbook of cross-cultural psychology*, Vol. 5 Boston: Allyn and Bacon, 1980, 211–279.

Bhagat, R. S. and McQuaid, S. J. The role of subjective culture in organizations: A review and directions for future research. *Journal of Applied Psychology Monograph*, 1982, **67**, 5, 653–685.

Bochner, S. The social psychology of cross-cultural relations. *Cultures in contact: Studies in cross-cultural interaction*. New York: Pergamon Press, 1982.

Bochner, S. and Ohsako, T. Ethnic role salience in racially homogeneous and heterogeneous societies. *Journal of Cross-Cultural Psychology*, 1977, **8**, 477–492.

Bochner, S. and Perks, R. W. National role evocation as a function of cross-national interaction. *Journal of Cross-Cultural Psychology*, 1971, **2**, 157–164.

Brislin, R. W., Bochner, S., and Lonner, W. J. *Cross-cultural perspectives on learning.* New York: Halsted/Wiley, 1975.

Campbell, D. T. Stereotypes and the perception of group differences. *American Psychologist,* 1967, **22**, 817–829.

Campici, P. J. A scale for the measurement of acculturation. PhD dissertation, University of Chicago, 1947.

Clawson, J. Mentoring in managerial careers. In C. B. Derr (Ed.), *Work, family and the career.* New York: Praeger, 1980.

Coelho, G. V. and Ahmed, P. I. *Uprooting and development: Dilemmas of coping with modernization.* New York: Plenum, 1980.

Cohen, L. M. Stress and coping among Latin American women immigrants.In G. V. Coelho and P. I. Ahmed (Eds.), *Uprooting and development,* New York: Plenum, 1980, 345–374.

Dalton, G., Thompson, P., and Price, R. The four stages of professional careers—A new look at performance by professionals. *Organizational Dynamics,* 1977, **6**, 19–42.

Datta, R. K. Characteristics and attitudes of immigrant Indian scientists and engineers in U.S.A. *Journal of Scientific and Industrial Research,* 1975, **34** (2), 74–79.

DeLongis, A., Coyne, J. C., Dokof, G., Folkman, S., and Lazarus, R. S. Relationship of daily hassles, uplifts, and major life events to health status. *Health Psychology,* 1982, **1**, 119–136.

DeVos, G. A. Achievement and innovation in culture and personality. In E. Norbeck, D. Price-Williams, and W. M. McCord (Eds.), *The study of personality: An interdisciplinary approach.* New York: Holt, Rinehart & Winston, 1968.

Fried, M. Stress, strain and role adaptation: Conceptual issues. In G. V. Coelho and P. I. Ahmed, *Uprooting and development.* New York: Plenum, 1980.

Frost, P. J., Mitchell, V. F., and Nord, W. J. *Organizational reality. Reports from the firing line.* Santa Monica, Calif.: Goodyear, 1978.

Graham, R. J. The role of perception of time in consumer research. *Journal of Consumer Research,* 1981, **7**, 335–342.

Hammer, M. R. Gudykunst, W. B., and Wiseman, R. L. Dimensions of intercultural effectiveness: An exploratory study. *International Journal of Intercultural Relations,* 1978, **2**, 382–393.

Hartley, E. L. and Thompson, R. Racial integration and role differentiation. *Journal of the Polynesian Society,* 1967, **76**, 427–443.

Hofstede, G. *Cultures consequences: International differences in work related values.* Beverly Hills, Calif.: Sage Publications, 1980.

Inhaber, H. The brain drain from India. *Social Biology,* 1975, **22**, (3), 250–254.

Jul Kunen, R. A. A contribution to the categories of social time and the economy of time. *Acta Sociologica,* 1977, **20**, 5–24.

Kahn, R. L., Wolfe, D. M., Quinn, R. P., and Snoek, J. D. *Organizational stress: Studies in role conflict and ambiguity.* New York: Wiley, 1964.

Kanner, A. D., Coyne, J. C., Schaefer, C., and Lazarus, R. S. Comparison of two modes of stress measurement: Daily hassles and uplifts versus major life events. *Journal of Behavioral Medicine,* 1981, **4**, 1–39.

Kanter, R. M. *Men and women of the corporation.* New York: Basic Books, 1977.

Klineberg, O. Contact between ethnic groups: A historical perspective of some apsects of theory and research. In S. Bochner (Ed.), *Cultures in contact: Studies in cross-cultural interaction,* New York: Pergamon Press, 1982, 45–55.

Korman, A. K., Wittig-Berman, U., and Lang, D. Career success and personal failure: Alienation in professionals and managers. *Academy of Management Journal*, 1981, **24** (2), 342–360.

Kram, K. E. Phases of the mentor relationship. *Academy of Management Journal*, 1983, **26** (4), 608–625.

Krau, E. Immigrants preparing for their second career: The behavioral strategies adapted. *Journal of Vocational Behavior*, 1981, **18**, 289–303.

La Piere, R. T. Type-rationalizations of group antipathy. *Social Forces*, 1936, **15**, 232–237.

McGrath, J. E. Stress and behavior in organizations. In M.D. Dunnette (Ed.), *Handbook of industrial and organizational psychology*, Chicago: Rand McNally, pp. 1351–1395.

McGrath, J. E. and Rotchford, N. L. Time and behavior in organizations. In L. L. Cummings and B. M. Staw (Eds.), *Research in Organizational Behavior*, Vol. 5. Greenwich, Conn.: Jai Press, 1983, 57–102.

Madison, D. L., Allen, R. W., Porter, L. W., Renwick, P. A., and Mayes, B. T. Organizational politics: An exploration of manager's perceptions. *Human Relations*, 1980, **33**, 79–100.

Maher, M. L. *Socio cultural origins of achievement*. Monterey, Calif.: Brooks Cole, 1974.

Maher, M. L. Socio cultural origins of achievement motivation. *International Journal of Intercultural Relations*, 1977, **I**, 81–104.

Margolis, D. R. *The managers: Corporate life in America*. New York: William Morrow, 1979.

Marmot, M. G. and Syme, S. L. Acculturation and coronary heart disease in Japanese-Americans. *American Journal of Epidemiology*, 1976, **104**, 225–247.

Massey, D. S. Dimensions of the new immigration to the United States and the prospects for assimilation. In R. H. Turner and J. S. Short (Eds.), *Annual Review of Sociology*, 1981, **7**, 57–85.

Miranda, M. R. and Castro, E. G. Culture distance and success in psychotherapy with Spanish speaking clients. In J. L. Martinez, Jr. (Ed.), *Chicano psychology*. New York: Academic Press, 1977.

Nair, M. New immigrants and social support systems: Information seeking patterns in a metropolis. In G.A. Coelho and I. P. Ahmed (Eds.), *Uprooting and development: Dilemmas of coping with modernization*. New York: Plenum, 1980.

The new immigrants *Newsweek*, 1980, **July 7**, 26–31.

Parsons, T. *The evolution of societies*. Englewood Cliffs, N. J.: Prentice-Hall, 1977.

Parsons, T. and Shils, E. A. (Eds.), *Toward a general theory of action*. Cambridge: Harvard University Press, 1950.

Porter, L. W., Allen, R. W., and Angel, H. L. The politics of upward influence in organizations. In L. L. Cummings and B. M. Staw (Eds.), *Research in organizational behavior*, Vol. 3. Greenwich Conn.: JAI Press, 109–149.

Roskies, E., Iida-Miranda, M. L., and Strobel, M. G. The applicability of life events approach to problems of immigration. *Journal of Psychosomatic Research*, 1978, **19**, 235–240.

Schein, V. Individual power and political behavior in organizations: An inadequately explored reality. *Academy of Management Review*, 1977, **2**, 64–72.

Schuler, R. S. Definitions and conceptualization of stress in organizations. *Organizational Behavior and Human Performance*, 1980, **25**, 184–215.

Smither, R. Human migration and acculturation of minorities. *Human Relations*, 1982, **35**, 57–68.

Srole, L., Langer, T., and Michael, S. *Mental health in the metropolis: The midtown study*, Vol. I. New York: McGraw-Hill, 1962.

Sue, S. Ethnic minority issues in psychology: A reexamination. *American Psychologist*, 1983, **38** (5), 583–592.

Sue S., Ito, J., and Bradshaw, C. Ethnic minority research: Trends and directions. In E. E. Jones and S. J. Korchin (Eds.), *Minority mental health*. New York: Praeger, 1982.

Szapocznik, J., Scopetta, M. A., Kurtines, W., and Arnahde, M. D. Acculturation: Theory and measurement. *Interamerican Journal of Psychology*, 1978, **12**, 113–130.

Triandis, H. C. Intercultural relations in international organizations. *Organizational Behavior and Human Performance*, 1967, **2**, 26–55.

Triandis, H. C., and Vassiliou, V. Frequency of contact and stereotyping. *Journal of Personality and Social Psychology*, 1967, **7**, 316–328.

Triandis, H. C. and Vassiliou, V. Interpersonal influence and employee selection in two cultures. *Journal of Applied Psychology*, 1972, **56**, 140–145.

Triandis, H. C., Vassiliou, V., Vassiliou, G., Tanaka, Y., and Shanmugam, A. *The analysis of subjective culture*. New York: Wiley, 1972.

Tushman, M. E. A political approach to organizations: A review and rationale. *Academy of Management Review*, 1977, **2**, 206–216.

MANAGING THE DYSFUNCTIONAL ASPECTS OF STRESS: THE ROLE OF COPING AND ADAPTATION

In Part Six, two ways of coping with stress are proposed. Chapter 13 proposes a transactional process model of coping with work-related stress. This model consists of processes composed of reciprocal relationships among the factors involved in occupational stress. Employees cognitively appraise situations and choose a particular set of coping techniques. After the application of the techniques, a reappraisal occurs, and the cycle may start again. Uncertainty, importance, and duration may enter at a number of points in this ongoing process.

Chapter 14 reviews the literature on the role of social support in coping, a frequently recommended technique for alleviating the negative effects of stress. When this coping technique is successful, it is unclear from the empirical literature whether it is through a moderating or a direct causal process. Its relative effectiveness may be due to its success at affecting uncertainty, importance, or their duration.

CHAPTER THIRTEEN

Integrative Transactional Process Model of Coping with Stress in Organizations

RANDALL S. SCHULER

All of the deleterious effects of stress suggest that there is a need for academics and practitioners to focus their efforts on dealing with stress, that is, affecting potential stressors in organizations and promulgating coping strategies by which individuals can most effectively manage to reduce their stress. This chapter is not an easy one, particularly since almost every aspect of an organization is labelled as stressful or a stressor. The task, however, can be facilitated by developing a model of stress in organizations based upon the general definition of stress presented by Beehr and Bhagat in Chapter 1, that is,

$$S = Uc \times I \times D$$

where S = experienced stress.
Uc = perceived uncertainty of obtaining outcomes where uncertainty is associated with the effort-performance and/or performance-outcome relationship.
I = perceived importance of those outcomes.
D = perceived duration of the uncertainties.

Based upon this definition and the model of stress in organizations, a model of coping can be developed to help understand coping. This will enable more individuals and organizations to effectively deal with stress and its deleterious outcomes.

Thus the purposes of this chapter are to (1) offer a model of stress in organizations, (2) present a definition and integrative transactional process model of coping, (3) develop a typology of potential individual and organizational coping strategies, (4) offer several research hypotheses, and (5) discuss several methodological issues involved in testing hypotheses.

INTEGRATIVE TRANSACTIONAL PROCESS MODEL OF STRESS IN ORGANIZATIONS

The integrative transactional process model, detailed elsewhere (Schuler, 1982), is a useful heuristic device for examining stress processes.

Transactional indicates that the relationships shown in the model are not linear but rather reciprocal. Thus it is important to treat the components of the stress model as having multidirectional causation between them so that all components can be viewed as both causes and effects (Lazarus, 1978).

Process refers to what happens over time or across stressors. It contains two elements: (1) the actual interchange between the person and the environment (full of potential stressors) and (2) the person's responses over time to the stress experienced. Thus stress is not just a dynamic situation of importance involving uncertainty and duration, but one which evokes different kinds of individual responses which may occur over time. In addition an individual experiences stress from his or her perception of the environment with his or her own set of unique skills, needs, and characteristics. Thus, what is a stressor for one person may not be one for another. Furthermore, an individual's response to the stress may alleviate the stress or provoke even more stress.

It is an *integrative* model since it has been developed from the stress literature and research in several, diverse areas and because it incorporates not only what stress is, but also with what it is associated.

The components of the transactional process model are the environmental stressors, individual characteristics, and individual responses. An illustration of these components is shown in Figure 13-1. The first set of individual characteristics include those that influence the primary appraisal process an individual makes of the environment to determine if there are stressors. The individual characteristics II and III shown in Figure 13-1 influence the magnitude, direction, duration, and intensity of an individual's short, intermediate, and long-term physiological, psychological, and behavioral responses to stress. These characteristics, discussed in detail elsewhere (Beehr and Schuler, 1982), include age, experience, ability, physical condition, life stages, and needs and values.

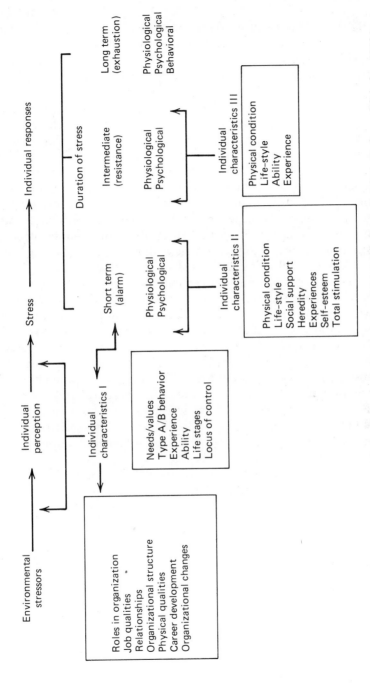

Figure 13-1 Integrative transactional process model of stress in organizations. (Adapted from Beehr and Schuler, 1982.)

Although these three sets of characteristics may be relatively stable or fixed in the short term, some of them can be altered over the long term to help deal with stress. Indeed these characteristics are often altered incrementally based upon an individual's continuous analysis of stress situations he or she encounters. Not all stress situations, however, require an individual to alter these characteristics. Sometimes the situation can be changed. Nevertheless to make this decision to alter the individual or alter the situation requires continuous analysis of situations which produce stress symptoms for an individual. In addition to the skills necessary in monitoring, analyzing, and interpreting the situation, effective coping is also dependent on an individual's qualities in problem solving and deciding (decision making) how to resolve these situations, developing and implementing strategies to cope, and evaluating the success of these strategies. This analysis, interpretation of stress situations, and the attendant decision making, problem solving, implementing, and evaluating are dependent on the individual's *cognitive skills* in coping with stress. These skills are critical here for they help shape the *process of coping* and help determine the *extent of success in coping*. It should be emphasized here that coping with stress is a process, that is, it is a complement of activities including appraising, problem solving, decision making, developing, implementing, and evaluating. Underlying these activities are the respective cognitive skills of the individual. Since there are rather large individual differences in these cognitive skills, for example, in problem-solving and decision-making abilities (Driver and Streufert, 1969), the extent of success individuals are likely to have in coping with stress across situations is likely to vary considerably. Specific hypotheses with respect to these variations are presented after the integrative transactional process model is considered.

The integrative transactional process model of coping offered here is based upon these cognitive skills and recognition of individual differences. As such, they are discussed in detail with the model of coping. This approach is the approach to stress taken in the rest of this book. Before presenting the model of coping, however, it is necessary to offer a definition of coping and to examine the critical issues associated with a definition and model of coping.

WHAT IS COPING?

According to Lazarus and Launier (1978), coping is defined as "efforts, both action-oriented and intraphysic, to manage (i.e., to master, tolerate, reduce, and minimize) environmental and internal demands and conflicts among them which tax or exceed a person's resources." Based on this definition Lazarus and his associates (e.g., Folkman, Schaefer, and Lazarus, 1979) describe four strategies of coping (all essentially process-oriented, cognitive strategies): (1) *information search*; (2) *direct action*; (3)

intraphysic modes; and (4) *inhibition of action*. These strategies are used either to mediate person-environment relationships and, or, to control selectively individual stress responses in a pallative mode. For example, an individual may take direct action and talk with his or her supervisor who is sending ambiguous messages. Or the individual may decide not to take direct action with the supervisor and avoid seeing him or her as much as possible. Which strategy is selected and how it is used may be a function of individual differences such as cognitive complexity, problem-solving and decision-making skills, experience, personality, and total stress.

Pearlin and Schooler (1978) state that coping refers to "behavior that protects people from being psychologically harmed by problematic social experience: Coping protects by (1) eliminating or modifying stressors; (2) perceptually controlling the meaning of the stress experience thus neutralizing its problematic character; or (3) keeping emotional consequences within manageable bounds. McGrath (1970) defines coping as an array of covert and overt behavior patterns by which the organism can actively prevent, alleviate, or respond to stress-inducing circumstances.

Drawing upon these other definitions of coping, *coping* is defined here as *a process of analysis and evaluation to decide how to protect oneself against the adverse effects of any stressor and its associated negative outcomes yet to take advantage of its positive outcomes*. This definition is closely aligned with Beehr and Bhagat's definition of stress presented in Chapter 1 and the model of stress presented at the start of the chapter. In addition, this definition has several important aspects:

1. Coping is an intentional, cognitive act of analyzing the perceived qualities or conditions in the environment that are associated with the experienced stress. In essence, this is Lazarus' primary appraisal process where the individual asks, "What is it?" "Does it offer harm, threat or benefit?" "Is it important?" Thus an individual may experience stress without really having thoroughly *evaluated or analyzed* the stressor, that is, its associated uncertainty and importance. In coping, however, it is necessary that the individual begins to explicitly do this analysis and evaluation or what amounts to analysis, problem-solving and decision making.

2. The challenge and effort involved in this process of analysis and evaluation are determined in part by the *structural ambiguity* of the situation, that is, the degree of ease identifying the stressor, its uncertainty (of obtaining outcomes), and its importance (Shalit, 1977). Clearly and correctly identifying these characteristics becomes important in determining how effective a selected coping strategy will be. As structural ambiguity increases, coping effectiveness is influenced by the level of an individual's *cognitive complexity* in dealing with complex situations (Driver and Streufert, 1969; Hamburg and Adams, 1967; and Lazarus, 1966 provide a fuller discussion of this relationship). The greater an

individual's cognitive complexity, the easier it is for the individual to differentiate a complex situation and then to integrate the appropriate information for effective coping. Increased cognitive complexity facilitates effective analysis, problem solving, and decision making (more specific hypotheses are offered later in this chapter).

3.   Stress can be associated with uncertain positive as well as negative outcomes as long as they are important to the individual. It is in regard to the *negative outcomes* that an individual copes in order to *protect*. It is with the stress situations having *positive outcomes* that an individual engages in coping *to take advantage*. The process of coping applies in either case however.

4.   Coping strategies are those actions taken on the basis of the analysis and evaluation of the stressor, especially its importance and associated uncertainty. In addition, the strategy selected should be influenced by an analysis and evaluation of the personal and situational resources and constraints as well as personal values and needs. Strategy selection should reflect the costs and benefits in the long run as well as the short run. For example some types of coping strategies may reduce negative physiological consequences. (See Gal and Lazarus, 1975 for a review of these studies indicating these findings.) As a second example, an individual may find leaving a stressful or demanding job more costly than the potential benefits associated with taking a new job.

An important aspect of this strategy selection process is the evaluation of the probabilities of success of the various strategies that can be used. Only with the incorporation of these probabilities can the true costs and benefits of strategies be estimated.

5.   Costs and benefits of coping strategies imply criteria upon which to evaluate the effectiveness of strategies. Criteria may include (1) physiological and psychological well being (Pearlin and Schooler, 1978); (2) success in altering the source of stress; (3) success in attaining the opportunity associated with a stress condition; (4) success in removing the condition associated with a constraint, that is, gaining ability to anticipate stress conditions so as to reduce their potential adverse effects; (5) gaining skills and ability to analyze and evaluate stress situations and develop appropriate strategies more quickly; (6) the time it takes to develop an effective strategy; (7) the number of iterations it takes in developing, implementing, and evaluating strategies to find one that is acceptable; (8) the impact of a current strategy selection on future coping strategy selections; and (9) the extent to which valid information is obtained and processed in the analysis and evaluation of a stressful condition (for a thorough review of possible strategy analysis and evaluation based on the functions of coping see Haan, 1977; Menninger, 1963; Vaillant, 1977; Janis and Mann, 1977; Cohen and Lazarus, 1979; White, 1974; Mechanic, 1974; Burke and Weir, 1980; and Folkman and Lazarus, 1980).

6.   A sixth aspect of this definition of coping is the provision for a typology of coping strategies. Since developing a typology is integral to coping strategy development and selection, this aspect of coping is discussed more extensively after the presentation of the coping model.

7.   Another aspect of this definition is that coping, just as stress, is highly dependent on the perception of the environment and what it means to the individual. Coping involves a transaction with the environment as does stress itself. *Thus coping is a process of gathering information, evaluating information, generating alternatives, weighting* (through cost-benefit analysis) *alternatives, selecting alternatives, implementing alternatives* (strategies), *evaluating the effectiveness of the strategy selected*, and then *considering additional strategies.* Coping thus involves a self-analysis of needs and values as well as an analysis of the situation. In this transaction between the person and environment both may change, perceptually if not objectively.

8.   A final aspect of this definition is that coping is integrative, that is, the definition is tied closely to (integrated with) the definition and model of stress. It is also integrative in that it is based upon the work of several diverse areas of research and writing such as medicine, psychology, nutrition, and organizational behavior. It is through its integrative nature that the coping process may be better understood and effective coping strategies prescribed (Burke and Weir, 1980).

INTEGRATIVE TRANSACTIONAL PROCESS MODEL OF COPING IN ORGANIZATIONS

Based upon the above definition of coping and the definition and model of stress in organizations, the following model of coping is presented. As shown in Figure 13-2, there are several aspects of coping in organizations: (1) *the coping trigger*, (2) *primary appraisal*, (3) *secondary appraisal*, (4) *strategy development and selection*, (5) *strategy implementation*, (6) *strategy evaluation*, and (7) *feedback*. Together these seven aspects constitute the process of coping in organizations. Although this refers to coping in organizations, the model can also be applied to nonorganizational settings. Indeed, many writers suggest the importance of considering both nonjob and job stress and coping since they are so highly interrelated (Holmes and Rahe, 1974; Pearlin, 1979; Bhagat, 1982, 1983). Due to space limitations, however, only stress coping strategies within organizations are considered here.

Coping Trigger

An individual begins to engage in coping upon the advent of the perception of stress and its felt response. The advent of this perception and response is

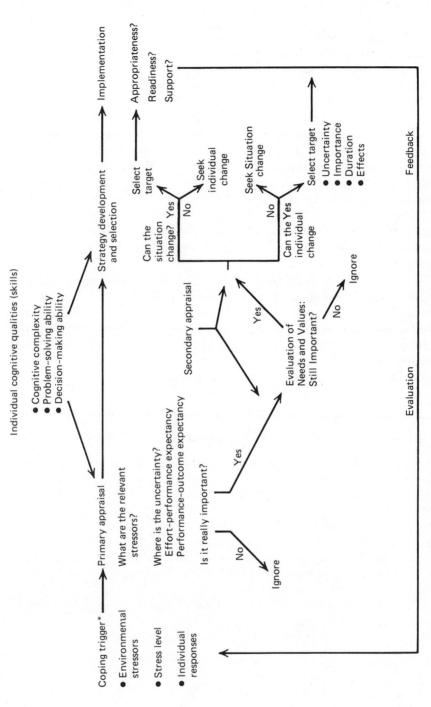

Figure 13-2 Integrative transactional process model of coping in organizations.

the trigger that starts the coping process. This requires that a stressor has entered the individual's environment and is interpreted as stressful, that is, as a dynamic situation of uncertainty with something of importance at stake (Schuler, 1980, 1982). Almost instantaneously as stress is perceived, the individual experiences a short-term physiological response (for discussion see Mason, 1972 and Selye, 1956). Although the individual may not have conspicuously and methodically interpreted the environment stressors in terms of uncertainty and importance, the short-term physiological response is experienced nonetheless. It is because of the discomfort associated with this physiological response that the body/person desires to return to a state of homeostasis (Cannon, 1929). Thus this discomfort triggers the individual to find a solution to the stressful condition. The search for resolution of this condition begins with the primary appraisal (Figure 13-2).

Primary Appraisal

This aspect involves generating answers to three questions: (1) What is the relevant stressor? (2) Where is the uncertainty? and (3) Is it really important? These questions are essentially those which are part of Lazarus's primary appraisal process and fit with Beehr and Bhagat's definition of stress. For Lazarus this process initiates the coping process. For the model of coping presented here, this aspect of coping initiates a systematic evaluation of a stress event that has already occurred and for which the individual has experienced a short-term physiological or psychological response as shown in Figure 13-1.

These three questions of the primary appraisal process directly link coping with the definition of stress presented above. To answer the first question, the individual seeks to locate which of the seven potential stressors identified in Figure 13-1 might be associated with the individual's discomfort. The degree of uncertainty associated with the stressor is then determined. The individual tries to determine if the uncertainty is associated with the effort-performance relationship or with the performance-outcome relationship. An individual's success in accurately perceiving and determining the degree as well as the type of uncertainty can be critical in the development of coping strategies. Thus an individual's ability to perceive the relevant information in the environment and process it is an important individual quality in the coping model. Also the individual cognitive qualities of cognitive complexity, problem-solving ability and decision-making ability are important in this coping process.

The final question in this primary appraisal is, "Is it really important?" Is what is causing discomfort really important? If the answer is "no," the coping process is terminated. If the answer is "yes," then the secondary appraisal process begins.

Secondary Appraisal

This appraisal begins with an analysis of why the stressful situation is really important. This requires the individual to analyze his or her needs and values having been identified as being associated with stress (Schuler, 1980). This analysis is critical because it not only attempts to determine *if* a situation is really important, but also *why* it is important, that is, with what needs and values is this situation associated? Such an identification is important in the development of coping strategies and their relative appropriateness.

After the question of why has been addressed, the question of "Is it still important?" must be addressed. It is possible that after this second query regarding importance that the answer may be negative. If it is, the coping process is terminated. If the response is still affirmative, the final question in the secondary appraisal process is "What can (should) be changed, the situation or the individual?" The answer to this question initiates the strategy development process. It should be noted that during the primary and secondary appraisal processes the individual may wish to involve other individuals in the analysis of the environment and of his or her needs and values. For example, an individual may perceive that the supervisor is sending ambiguous messages and have to decide what strategy to take to deal with this situation. Although a direct action strategy of talking with the supervisor may appear reasonable, colleagues with previous experience may know that the supervisor would perceive this action as a direct threat on his or her ability to communicate. Consequently, if the individual asked his or her colleagues for their advice on what to do, the path of direct action may not be selected. Others can be useful in providing much needed information to make coping as effective as possible.

Strategy Development and Selection

This aspect of coping is what Lazarus refers to as secondary appraisal. His secondary appraisal is essentially answering the question, "What should I do now?" The answer to this is critical in developing ways to deal with the stressful situation. As shown in Table 13-1, many responses to this question have already been identified. The purpose here is to offer a typology of the strategies that can be considered in attempts to reduce the stressfulness of situations for individuals. This typology is presented after discussing strategy implementation, strategy evaluation, and feedback.

Strategy Implementation

Strategy implementation should consider the cost/benefit of alternative strategies, readiness for change, and support. The analysis of the cost versus benefits of alternative coping strategies should include the specification of what is needed to implement each strategy and what is to be

Table 13-1   Coping Strategies Proposed in the Popular Literature[a]

1. Talk with sympathetic other person.
2. Build work-group norms of cooperation not competition.
3. Delegate, seek help of others.
4. Build satisfactory relationship with supervisor.
5. Plan instead of responding to pressure.
6. Make time for fun, solitude, tranquillity.
7. Divert attention from stressul situation.
8. Self-awareness—what causes your stress, how do you respond to stress?
9. Problem-solving, planning, pacing of one's working day.
10. Professional counselling and therapy, group therapy, encounter groups.
11. Hobbies, leisure activities, recreation.
12. Leave job for another.
13. Tranquillizers, drugs.
14. Change to tasks that allow mind to wander.
15. Change to leisure task guaranteeing immediate satisfactions.
16. Proper nutrition and diet.
17. Short or long breaks.
18. Devote yourself fully to what you are doing.
19. Pamper your body—sleep, for example.
20. Erhard Seminar Training (EST).
21. Learn to do one thing at a time.
22. Do not rely too heavily on one person.
23. Behavior modification.
24. Develop perspective—recognize the inevitable.
25. Promise yourself a reward when situation is over.
26. Develop interests in other people.
27. Have yearly medical examination.
28. Develop peer support.
29. Biofeedback.
30. Transcendental meditation.
31. Relaxation.
32. Take vacation and holiday time.
33. Rotation of authority.
34. Physical exercise.
35. Compartmentalize work and home life.
36. Remove petty annoyances in physical environment.
37. Develop growth, interpersonal skills, consideration for others.
38. Company-developed diagnostic and remedial programmes (health, rest, education, exercise, etc.).
39. Maintain life change events within tolerable limits.
40. Work smarter not harder.

[a]Adapted from Burke and Weir, pp. 302–303, 1980.

gained from each strategy. Essentially this is a utility analysis as suggested by Landy et al. (1982). Implementation must include an analysis of the readiness for change and what it will take for the appropriate level of readiness to transpire. For example, an individual may decide that the best way to deal with the stress of being unemployed is by getting a job and that this requires further education, for example, a degree in accounting. Yet the individual also realizes that he or she is not ready to go back to school. Thus deciding to go back to school at this time, though potentially most effective over the long term, may prove to be ineffective as long as the individual is not ready and motivated to learn. If the individual believes that getting a degree in accounting is the best thing to do but that now is not the time, he or she may determine what things are necessary before readiness is established. For example, he or she may determine to begin an independent reading program in accounting to see how it feels to read and study again.

In addition to readiness, support conditions must be established. If group support is necessary to implement a strategy for an individual, the group must be available and ready. If an individual decides to lose weight as a way of dealing with social rejection, it may be much easier to be successful in losing weight by joining a weight reducing club. The organization can be generally helpful in assisting its employees cope with stress by building and maintaining social support groups (House, 1981). These social support groups can provide advice on what the individual can do to cope and can provide unconditional support. Unconditional support serves to increase an individual's self-esteem and self-confidence, both of which can reduce the stressfulness of situations and increase the effectiveness of the individual's coping efforts.

Just as an organization can assist individuals in coping with stress, so it can prove to be a roadblock. An organization may prevent the formation of social support groups. It may also prohibit its employees from taking continuing education courses on company time or it may not provide tuition reimbursement assistance.

Strategy Evaluation

After the chosen strategy has been implemented, its effects must be evaluated. This can be done at the organizational, group, and individual levels. Currently evaluation of coping strategies is rare at best (Newman and Beehr, 1979; Beehr, 1980). Evaluation, however, is critical in order to determine if opportunities have been utilized and, or, if constraints have been successfully removed.

Criteria for evaluation of coping strategies include the three classes of outcomes of stress shown in Figure 13-1: physiological, psychological, and behavioral. Since these three classes of outcomes are so diverse, using them necessitates evaluating coping effectiveness using several methodologies (see McGrath, 1976 and Burke and Wier, 1980). In particular, physiological outcomes require medical methodologies such as measures of heart rate, blood pressure, catecholamines and cholesterol. Psychological outcomes require methodologies such as interviews and questionnaires while behavioral outcomes require industrial engineering and personnel methodologies in order to measure employee performance, safety, absenteeism, and turnover. Consequently, extensive evaluation would require the efforts of a team of researchers. Many individuals and organizations, however, are likely to use fewer than all three classes of outcomes. Individuals, for example, may evaluate the success of their coping effort with how well they feel (psychologically). Organizations may attempt to evaluate their efforts to help employees cope by the rate of absenteeism in the organization. Although there is nothing inherently wrong with this restricted evaluation, it may understate the real effects of a coping strategy or result in a strategy being evaluated as unsuccessful. Since such results would likely have a serious impact on the future use of a coping strategy, evaluation using all three sets of outcomes should be done whenever possible.

A final consideration in strategy evaluation is determining the appropriate time to gather the three classes of outcomes. As illustrated in Figure 13-1, it is probable that the effects of a coping strategy will occur over time with some physiological and psychological effects occurring before some behavioral effects. Employees are likely to become dissatisfied with their jobs before deciding to quit. Although these and other relationships seem plausible, little evidence exists as to their order of occurrence. However, because an understanding of their relationships appears critical to an evaluation of any coping strategy, extensive research in this area is warranted.

Feedback

The results of the strategy evaluation stage are feedback to the individual, group, and, or, organization. Since evaluation occurs over time so will the feedback of the results. Although for purposes of rigorously evaluating the effectiveness of coping strategies, evaluation, and feedback should be done formally by the individual, and, or, the organization, individuals can provide their own informal evaluation.

Individuals are perhaps best able to make informal judgments about whether they have coped successfully, especially when using psychological criteria such as satisfaction, esteem, and involvement. Individuals, however, may be less able to make informal judgments on physiological criteria such as blood pressure, or may be inappropriate sources of judgments on criteria such as the performance level of a unit in the organization or even their own performance. Consequently, formal evaluations by others are appropriate and necessary. This formal outside evaluation can then be made available to the individual or the organization.

Feedback serves the individual (and organization) by providing information (especially over time) about the effectiveness and efficiency of various coping strategies. This, of course, is useful for dealing with future stress episodes. This can be useful in assisting the individual or organization in determining the utility of alternative coping strategies. When feedback is provided, it is important that facts such as who was involved, what strategy was used, who was in charge, under what conditions was the strategy implemented, and what was the history of coping, be provided. This feedback information is critical in enhancing the future coping strategies undertaken by the individual alone or conducted by the organization for its employees.

Feedback to the individual, whether based upon informal or formal evaluation can be critical to an individual's self-esteem. To the extent the strategy selected was effective and efficient, the individual's self-esteem will be positively influenced. This, in turn, may serve to enhance the individual's problem-solving and decision-making skills, which may enable the individual to be even more effective in dealing with stress in the future.

Now that the transactional process coping model has been considered, it is important to develop a typology of the strategies that can be used to cope with stress.

TYPOLOGY OF COPING STRATEGIES

The typology begins with an analysis and consideration of the situation and the individual. The critical questions here are: (1) Will the situation be changed or modified, and if so, how? and (2) How can the individual manage or change? As a consequence of these questions, a four-category typology can be used to classify coping strategies. These categories are shown in Figure 13-3 and discussed below.

Since we are addressing coping strategies for stress in organizations, the typology is based upon either the organization or aspects of the organization changing or the individual managing or changing. Since stress is a perception of uncertainty about something important lasting over some time period, only a few individuals in an organization may be perceiving stress (perhaps due to their unique on-the-job conditions, their hereditary characteristics and/or their off-the-job stress conditions) (Bhagat, 1983). This being the case, organizationally based coping strategies may be inappropriate; therefore, it is likely the organization (or aspects) will not be changed. Thus the strategies to deal with the stress in this example, must be focused on the individual managing or changing. Note, however,

Situational (Organizational)	Individual		
Targets	Reduce Uncertainty	Reduce Importance	Reduce Effects
Roles in organization	Experience	Denial	Dietary
Job qualities	Training	Avoidance	Exercise
Relationships	Education	Withdrawal	Meditation
Organizational structure	Colleague	Projection	Social support
Physical qualities	interaction		groups
Career development	Confrontation		
Organizational change			

Figure 13-3 Typology of coping strategies and targets.

that the individual strategies need not be developed solely by the individuals. The organization, through the personnel department, may assist the individuals in developing *their* strategies to cope (Beehr and Schuler, 1982).

In circumstances where many individuals are experiencing stress and exhibiting its symptoms, changing the organization is appropriate. It is also likely to be much more effective for the organization to change (and reduce the negative symptoms of stress such as absenteeism or low performance) than to rely upon individuals to each develop effective coping strategies. Based upon the major consideration of how many people are experiencing stress in the organization, either the organization or the individual will be the major focus of implementing coping strategies. If it is decided that many individuals are experiencing stress, the organization should change; if only a few individuals are experiencing stress, the individual should change.

The Organization

If the organization is to be changed, one must ascertain the most effective strategy. What's most effective will depend upon the particular stressor. As Hall (1972) indicated, several strategies may be taken to deal with just one stressor, but some are likely to be more effective than others. Thus information is needed on both the stressor and the availability and efficacy (utility) of strategies related to that stressor.

There are several strategies that can be used if the organization is to be changed. There are seven major aspects of organizations, previously identified as potential environmental stressors, that may be changed: organizational structure, relationships, roles, change processes, physical environment, career development, and intrinsic job qualities. (See Cooper and Marshall, 1976; Brief, et al., 1981; and Beehr and Schuler, 1982 for a fuller discussion of all of these.)

Within each of these seven aspects there are several specific conditions generally associated with stress. Space prohibits a full elaboration of each aspect, but a discussion of one will illustrate the complexity of that process. In that one, organizational structure, there are six conditions typically associated with stress:

1. Lack of participation.
2. No sense of belonging.
3. Poor communications.
4. Restrictions on behavior.
5. Lack of opportunity for advancement.
6. Inequity in pay and performance evaluation.

For discussions of these conditions see Cooper and Marshall (1976), Harvey (1970), Coch and French (1948), French and Caplan (1970), Cameron (1971), Katz and Kahn (1978), McLean (1979), Drabek and Hass (1969), Jacobson (1972), and Galbraith (1977). Based on these six conditions, one or several coping strategies could be used to reduce or eliminate the stress associated with them. These strategies include:

1. Clarification of policies regarding transfer and promotions.
2. Decentralization and increased participation.
3. Change in the selection and placement policies.
4. Change in the communication procedures and networks in the organization.
5. Change in the reward systems.
6. Utilization of training and development programs.
7. Statement of the performance evaluation system.
8. Development and utilization of permanent and temporary work groups.
9. Change in shift patterns and job rotation policies.

Each of these strategies and how they are each related to the six organizational structure conditions are extensively explicated in Brief et al. (1981). The same level of detail for the other six organization aspects is provided in the same source. The reason for the potential efficacy of the strategies is that they (1) reduce the uncertainty perceived by individuals in the organization resulting from the organizational stressors, and (2) are the most appropriate strategy for the stress identified in the organization. The appropriateness of these strategies initially depends on the correctness of the answer to the first questions in the primary appraisal, "What is the relevant stressor? and where is the uncertainty?" If this appraisal indicates that organizational structure is really the stressor, further analysis should be done to determine which specific structure condition is the stressor. The choice may then be made among the possible alternative strategies listed above (1 to 9).

This discussion appears to suggest that there is a one best strategy, just find the source of the stress and pick the coping strategy that fits that source. This, however, would be premature to do for several reasons. In actuality, individuals often experience stress from several stressors. These several stressors are generally highly interdependent—dealing successfully with one is almost impossible. Several need to be dealt with concurrently. Furthermore, for each stressor there are probably several strategies, not just one per condition of each stressor as implied in the above discussion of organization structure and structure strategies. In addition, each of these several strategies is potentially effective. The contingencies to determining effectiveness, however, remain to be identified.

The Individual

If a rather limited number of individuals are identified as being under stress, having the individual change or manage the stress may be more appropriate.

If the individual is to change or manage the stress, there are three major sets of strategies. One set is aimed at uncertainty associated with the stressful condition. Strategies to reduce uncertainties associated include additional experience, training, and education. Associating with individuals who have information related to the stressful condition can also be an effective strategy to reduce the uncertainty. In essence these strategies represent ways to gain control over the situation that in turn can result in less uncertain situations (Thompson, 1981). For example, if an individual is experiencing stress because of the uncertainty of not knowing how to perform a task, appropriate training can eliminate this uncertainty. Or if an individual is uncertain about the appropriate behavior in an organization, collegial interaction can provide the information to enable the individual to define an appropriate role behavior. By taking this action sooner rather than later, the duration of the experienced stress and its effects are also reduced. The duration of the stressfulness of a situation can also be reduced by minimizing the importance of the situation.

When it is not feasible or appropriate for the individual to change in order to reduce the uncertainty of the situation, he or she can engage in strategies to reduce the importance of the situation and/or those to diminish the impact of the effects of stress. Strategies to reduce the importance or the impact of stress are also referred to as palliative strategies (Lazarus, 1978).

Strategies to reduce the importance of stress can involve denial, avoidance, withdrawal and projection (Folkman, et al., 1979). Strategies to reduce the effects can include taking advantage of the main or buffering effects of social support groups (House and Wells, 1978; Beehr, Chapter 14 in this book), dietary changes, physical exercise,meditation,feedback and muscle relaxation exercises (Benson, 1974; Sethi and Schuler, 1983).

With so many strategies individuals can use to cope with stress, the question becomes, which strategy will be selected? Which strategy an individual will select depends upon several factors: (1) the potential (and perceived) costs and benefits of each strategy; (2) environmental constraints and, or, support; (3) individual experience; and (4) individual attributes. The potential costs and benefits of a strategy can be determined by an individual in many ways. The appropriateness depends upon the situation. If the individual is experiencing stress from being uncertain about how to perform a job (which, if performed well, can lead to a promotion) he or she can determine the costs (in dollars and time) of getting the training to perform the job and the benefits (in dollars and self-satisfaction) of knowing how to do the job and getting the promotion. The environment (the organization) may help determine which strategy is chosen by the support, or lack of it, that it provides. If the organization provides tuition reimbursement to individuals for taking training or education classes, individuals may find (by cost/benefit analysis) training an attractive strategy to cope.

Individual experiences are also likely to influence strategy selection. If an individual has previously and successfully coped with role ambiguity by talking to his or her supervisor, he or she is likely to do the same thing when experiencing stress again from role ambiguity. If an individual has experienced failure with a particular strategy, it is likely that he or she will avoid using the strategy in the future.

Individual attributes likely to influence strategy selection include problem solving and decision making skills, cognitive complexity, self-esteem, Type A personality, and an individual's total level of skills. There are individual differences in problem-solving and decision-making skills. Furthermore these differences are influenced by an individual's level of cognitive complexity (Driver and Streufert, 1969; Hamburg and Adams, 1967; Milburn, 1981). In addition, individuals high on these skills will be more likely to diagnose and analyze stressful conditions more effectively than individuals low on these skills. Subsequently, individuals who are high on these skills will also be more likely to select effective coping strategies than individuals low on these skills.

Individuals with high self-esteem are likely to be more confident and willing to engage in direct confrontation to seek information to reduce uncertainty than individuals with low self-esteem. Those with low self-esteem are also likely to have a low sense of personal efficacy and consequently withdraw from stressful situations. They may do this even after correctly diagnosing the situation and realizing that direct confrontation may be better.

An individual's current level of stress may also have an impact on the selection of strategies. As shown by Anderson (1976), problem-solving activities (those which seek to incorporate more information and decision making) are more likely to be involved at low and moderate levels of stress. At higher levels of stress, emotional activities displace problem-solving activities. In addition, it is important to keep in mind that cognitive processes pertaining to coping with stress with long-term duration are different from those pertaining to coping with stress with short-term duration (Weick, 1979; Doob, 1971). The Abramson et al. (1978) theory about learned helplessness can be tied with our notion of duration associated with some stressful events. Stressful events requiring long-term and repeated coping and adaptive resources may induce the person to experience lack of control (because success seems to be elusive) over the event and his or her environment, and such lack of control over important outcomes could lead to depression (Abramson et al., 1978). In turn, this depression is likely to result in a withdrawal from active coping and a reduced sense of personal efficacy. This phenomenon of learned helplessness seems to be more likely to occur for those who seek control and quick solutions to problems such as Type A personality and behavior people (Sanders and Milkus, 1982).

Thus, and this is a key point, some individuals may not implement the appropriate coping strategy either because they cannot diagnose the situation or because they are not able to implement the most appropriate strategy. Of course, another reason for not using the appropriate strategy could also be due to a lack of correct information. Whatever the specifics, however, there is evidence to suggest that not everyone always selects the best strategy to cope. For example, Lazarus and his colleagues

> observed that one of the most common ways women coped with the threat of having discovered a breast lump was a pattern of avoidance-denial which resulted in delay in seeking medical evaluation. If the growth were malignant, excessive delay could result in metastasis and a much poorer medical outlook. Similarly, Hackett and Cassem (1975) observed men who, during symptoms of a heart attack, did vigorous pushups or ran up and down some flights of stairs, on the reasoning that they could not be having a heart attack since the exercise didn't kill them. These men were trying to feel better psychologically (palliation) at the expense of taking the adaptive action of getting medical attention. As it turned out, they were, indeed, having a heart attack and they did survive but the coping process clearly endangered their lives (Lazarus, 1978).

RESEARCH HYPOTHESES

In the following section, some research hypotheses on the transactional process model of coping are presented. Developing research hypotheses may not only be desirable but be a real necessity if an understanding of coping as well as stress is to emerge. Hypotheses can suggest a research focus, thereby potentially stimulating research in the area. But even with several hypotheses and a definition and model of coping, research on coping strategies is still "fraught with difficulties" (Burke and Weir, 1980). This is because coping is a complex and dynamic process, which may evolve slowly over time as does stress itself. In addition, coping involves multiple decision points which may be difficult to capture (Folkman et al., 1979). Nevertheless, such research efforts are underway in an attempt to capture this richness and complexity in the coping process (Folkman and Lazarus, 1980).

> **Hypothesis 1.** Individuals who engage in the process of gathering information, generating alternatives, selecting and implementing an alternative and finally evaluating the implemented strategy will be more effective and efficient at coping with stress than individuals who do not take this methodological approach to coping.

Partial support for this hypothesis is based on the work of Howard et al. (1975), Antonovsky (1979), Lazarus (1978), and Gal and Lazarus (1975) which suggests that when individuals are methodical in their analysis of a stressful situation they are more likely to produce a wide range of potentially effective coping strategies than if they do not. Also supportive are Anderson's (1976) findings suggesting that individuals should try to avoid situations in which they are facing too much stress since this may preclude engaging in problem-solving activities.

> **Hypothesis 2.** Individuals who have a higher self-esteem, higher cognitive complexity, better problem-solving and decision-making skills and who have a high sense of personal efficacy are likely to be more methodical than individuals without these attributes.

> **Hypothesis 3.** A specific coping strategy is more likely to be effective when it is selected after a thorough analysis and consideration of the feasability of organizational coping strategies and individual coping strategies.

Obviously, a strategy to change the organization when it *is not* likely to change will be less successful than if it *is* likely to change. Furthermore, it is likely that more stress will result if the inappropriate strategy is chosen than if none is chosen. Thus it is important to be able to analyze stress situations and successfully identify the realistic constraints. In addition to the identification, it is necessary to develop a repertoire of strategies, applicable to changing the organization or the individual, which can be matched and evaluated in comparison with different stressful situations. A consequence of this matching and testing may be a contingency for situational approach to coping. Some current research suggests that a broad, general contingency approach may not only be an effective and efficient way of coping but, in fact, describe what individuals do, at least those who are successful. (See, for example, the work by Folkman and Lazarus, 1980, and Jackson and Maslach, 1982.)

These first three hypotheses imply that for an individual to engage in effective coping he or she must be not only perceptive, but adaptable as well. Thus making individuals aware of this cognitive-diagnostic approach to coping strategies will not ensure that they will actually select or implement the most effective strategy. But even if individuals are completely adaptable, it is possible that individuals will not maximize or select the most effective strategy. Because of time and information-processing capabilities it is more probable to suspect that individuals will satisfy or select a coping strategy that at best produces a satisfactory resolution (Simon, 1976). Some individuals, however, will be more capable of developing coping strategies which produce more satisfactory solutions than others.

Hypothesis 4. Only when organizations perceive that a sufficiently large number of its employees are experiencing stress, will they implement, or strongly support the implementation of coping strategies that involve organizational change.

It is likely to be inappropriate and dysfunctional for organizations to make organizational changes to improve conditions for a relatively small group of employees. The stress experiences of a limited number of employees could largely reflect conditions associated with the individual more than the organization. Thus, although our organizational change could prove to be a successful coping strategy for a few employees, it may prove detrimental to those who were previously not in need of coping.

Hypothesis 5. Individuals under similar conditions are likely to adopt very dissimilar coping strategies.

This hypothesis suggests that there are likely to be very substantial individual differences (due to attributes, experiences, cognitive abilities, and behaviors) that influence what coping strategy individuals prefer and will use. These individual differences may also influence how individuals perceive the same situation thus explaining some of the differential in strategy selection.

Hypothesis 6. Coping strategies can be effective to the extent that they (a) reduce the uncertainty associated with a situation, (b) reduce the importance of the situation, or (c) reduce the duration of the stress. The less effective strategy reduces only the effects of stress on the individual.

This final hypothesis is critical. Upon this hypothesis rests the usefulness of the entire model of coping presented in this chapter. Some individuals are hypothesized to be more effective in their coping with stress than others because of their personal characteristics to deal with the essence of stress: uncertainty, importance, and duration. Not only is it hypothesized here that some individuals will be more effective than others in dealing with stress, but also that those individuals who deal with stress by addressing uncertainty, importance and/or duration will be more effective than those who only deal with the results of stress.

METHODOLOGICAL ISSUES
Measuring the Process

According to Lazarus (1978), the assessment of coping processes requires strategies of measurement and research that are quite different from those employed by personality assessors to measure coping styles or traits. One must develop means of describing what the person is doing and thinking in specific encounters (p. 38).

Fortunately, individuals are generally able to reconstruct their cognitions and attitudes associated with coping with stressful conditions. As Lazarus (1978, 1979) suggests and Lazarus and Launier (1978) and Folkman and Lazarus (1980) have shown, individuals can describe how they have dealt with stressful conditions in the past, how they are dealing with them in the present, and how they would deal with future stressful conditions. In fact, if individuals were not able to do this, it would be much more difficult to study coping strategies. It would preclude the use of ipsative studies, which at this time appear to be so fruitful a method of studying coping (Folkman and Lazarus, 1980).

The assessment of coping processes can be very appropriately conducted in a naturalistic setting using an ipsative-normative design if one is to capture the richness, complexity, and process of coping (Lazarus, 1978; Lazarus and Launier, 1978; Burke and Weir, 1980; and Hamburg and Adams, 1967). Lazarus (1978) provides five reasons utilizing a naturalistic setting: (1) the laboratory cannot begin to tell us about the daily hassles individuals face nor; (2) the full range of behaviors individuals use to cope with these daily hassles; (3) many outcomes of stress occur over a long period of time; (4) it is difficult (for ethical and practical reasons) in the laboratory to subject individuals to the same severe stressors that may occur in real life; and (5) the rigor and precision of the laboratory are more apparent than real.

The assessment can also be done very appropriately in laboratory settings, although there may be some limits on the questions that can be addressed (Lazarus, 1978). Nevertheless the laboratory setting may prove fruitful in identifying individual attributes that prevent or facilitate a methodical search for coping strategies. It may also be useful in identifying the conditions under which individuals are likely to be more problem-solving oriented or emotion oriented in their approach to stress coping.

Measuring what individuals do to cope in the real world, however, is not without major difficulties (Lazarus, 1978; Folkman, 1980; Folkman and Lazarus, 1980; Latack et al., 1980). It is necessary to follow individuals through past or present stressful events and have them describe what they thought or felt. This process requires that the researcher be able to relate and translate what individuals are describing since it is unlikely individuals are capable of introspection and verbalization in classic psychological terms. As reported by Folkman (1980), however, this translation can be done with data that are gathered through interview and questionnaire media.

Another aspect of measuring the process is gathering the data for evaluation. Although interviews and questionnaires can capture the problem-solving and decision-making phases for qualitative and ideographic data, quantitative data and hard measures (both from the individuals and the organization) are also necessary. These hard measures (e.g., physiological measures of heart rate, catecholamines, blood pressure, performance, and absenteeism) can be combined with the interview and questionnaire data measuring an individual's subjective reactions such as satisfaction and job involvement. Because of the nature of these different measures, there is a need for an interdisciplinary team of researchers who are competent to employ a variety of measuring instruments (Schuler, 1980; Beehr and Newman, 1978.)

Evaluating the Process

As indicated earlier, there are many potential criteria against which to determine the effectiveness of a selected stress coping strategy. Thus the criteria chosen may reflect, more than anything else, the values of the individuals and, or, organizations involved in the evaluation. Less dependent on these values in the evaluation are the research or statistical methodologies used to analyze the data. The selection of the statistical methodology is dependent on the nature of the research design.

In order to make some inference about causality, that is, whether the coping strategy caused the improved conditions, cross-lagged panel correlation designs can be used when no control group is available. In contrast to this rather passive design are the experimental and quasi-experimental designs (Cook and Campbell, 1976). Within the quasi-experimental design are three that can be useful in the study of coping strategies: (1) nonequivalent control group; (2) regression-discontinuity; and (3) interrupted time series (See Beehr and Schuler, 1982 for a more complete description of these methodologies). Implied in these designs and in the discussion of the measuring of the coping process is the requirement that coping be studied over time.

SUMMARY

Stress in organizations is becoming an important concern for individuals and organizations because of its severe deleterious effects. By reducing or managing stress these effects may be significantly reduced, benefiting both individuals and organizations. Since reducing or managing stress is the essence of coping, an understanding of coping can aid in attaining the benefits of dealing with stress successfully.

It is proposed here that effective coping depends upon an individual's cognitive skills. These skills enable an individual to analyze a stress situation, develop and select a coping strategy, implement the strategy, and then get feedback on its effects in order to evaluate it. The transactional process model of coping presented here described each of these steps in detail so individuals can take a methodical approach in coping with stress. This model can also assist organizations in helping their employees cope with stress. Basically, however, effective coping with stress depends on reducing the uncertainty or importance associated with a situation, reducing the length of the stress situation or reducing the effects on the individuals experiencing the stress.

Since effective coping depends upon utilizing the appropriate strategy, a discussion of possible strategies and situations for potential application was presented. These strategies and situations were framed in a typology to suggest a starting point for strategy development and selection. Critical to our understanding of coping is the evaluation of the typology of coping strategies. This evaluation, however, is complex. Nevertheless the evaluation can be done. Since the criteria for evaluation are so diverse, an interdisciplinary team of researchers may be necessary to conduct effective evaluation of coping strategies.

REFERENCES

Abramson, L. Y., Seligman, M. E. P., and Teasdale, J. D. Learned helplessness in humans: Critique and reformulation. *Journal of Abnormal Psychology*, 1978, **87**, 49–74.

Albrecht, K. *Stress and the manager*. Englewood Cliffs, N. J.: Prentice-Hall, 1979.

Anderson, D. R. Coping behaviors and intervening mechanisms in the inverted-U-stress performance relationship. *Journal of Applied Psychology*, 1976, **61**, 30–34.

Antonovsky, A. *Health, stress and coping*. San Francisco: Jossey-Bass, 1979.

Beehr, T. A. *Organizational strategies for managing job stress*. Paper presented at the Midwest Academy of Management, Cincinnati, 1980.

Beehr, T. A. and Newman, J. E. Job stress, employee health, and organizational effectiveness: A facet analysis, model and literature review. *Personnel Psychology*, 1978, **31**, 665–699.

Beehr, T. A. and Schuler, R. S. Current and future perspectives on stress in organizations. In Rowland and Ferris (Eds.), *Personnel management: New perspectives*. Boston: Allyn and Bacon, 1982.

Benson, H., Beary, J. F., and Carol, M. P. The relaxation response. *Psychiatry*, 1974, **37**, 37–46.

Bhagat, R. S. Effects of stressful life events upon individual performance effectiveness and work adjustment processes within organizational settings: A research model. *Academy of Management Review*, 1983, **8**, 660–671.

Brief, A. P., Schuler, R. S., and Van Sell, M. *Managing stress*. Boston: Little, Brown, 1981.

Burke R. J. and Weir, T. Coping with the stress of managerial occupations. In C. L. Cooper and R. L. Payne (Eds.) *Current concerns in occupational stress*. London: Wiley, 1980, 299–335.

Cameron, C. Fatigue Problems in Modern Industry. *Ergonomics*, 1971, **14**, 713–718.

Cannon, W. B. Organization for physiological homeostasis. *Physiological Review*, 1929, **9**, 339–430.

Caplan, R. D. and Jones, K. W. Effects of workload, role ambiguity and Type A personality on anxiety, depression and heart rate. *Journal of Applied Psychology*, 1975, **60**, 713–719.

Coch, L. and French, J. R. P. Overcoming resistance to change. *Human Relations*, 1948, **11**, 512–532.

Cohen, F. and Lazarus, R. S. Active coping processes, coping dispositions and recovery from surgery. *Psychosomatic Medicine*, 1973, **35**, 375–389.

Colligan, M. and Smith, M. A methodological approach for evaluating outbreaks of mass psychogenic illness in industry. *Journal of Occupational Medicine*, 1978, **20**, 6–15.

Cook, T. D. and Campbell, D. T. The design and conduct of quasi-experiments and true experiments in field settings. In M. D. Dunnette (Ed.), *The handbook of industrial and organizational psychology*. Chicago: Rand McNally, 1976.

Cooper, C. L. and Marshall, J. Occupational sources of stress: A review of the literature relating to coronary heart disease and mental ill health. *Journal of Occupational Psychology*, 1976, **49**, 11–28.

Cooper, C. L. and Payne, R. L. (Eds.). *Stress at work*. London: Wiley, 1979.

Cooper, C. L. and Payne, R. L. (Eds.). *Current concerns in occupational stress*. London: Wiley, 1980.

Cox, T. *Stress*. Baltimore: University Park Press, 1978.

Dohrenwand, B. S. and Dohrenwand, B. P. (Eds.). *Stressful life events*. New York: Wiley, 1974.

Doob, L. *Patterning of time*. New Haven: Yale University Press, 1971.

Drabek, T. E. and Haas, J. E. Laboratory simulation of organizational stress. *American Sociological Review*, 1969, **34**, 223–238.

Driver, M. and Streufert, S. Integrative Complexity: An approach to individuals and groups as information-processing systems. *Administrative Science Quarterly*, 1969, **14**, 272–285.

Folkman, S. *An approach to the measurement of coping*. Paper presented at the research conference on Current Issues in Occupational Stress: Theory, Research and Intervention, York University, 1980.

Folkman, S. and Lazarus, R. S. An analysis of coping in a middle-aged community sample. *Journal of Health and Social Behavior*, 1980, **21**, 12–26.

Folkman, S., Schaefer, C., and Lazarus, R. S. Cognitive processes as mediators of stress and coping. In V. Hamilton and D. M. Warburton (Eds.) *Human stress and cognition*, Chichester: Wiley, 1979.

Frankenhaeuser, M. and Gardell, B. Underload and overload in working life: Outline of a multidisciplinary approach. *Journal of Human Stress*, 1976, **2**, 35–45.

French, J. R. P. Person role fit. In McLean, A. (Ed.), *Occupational stress*. Springfield, Ill.: Charles C. Thomas, 1974.

Friedman, M. and Rosenman, R. H. Association of a specific overt behavior pattern with blood and cardiovascular findings. *Journal of American Medical Association*, 1959, **169**, 1286–1296.

Friedman, M. and Rosenman, R. H. *Type A behavior and your heart*. New York: Alfred A. Knopf, 1974.

Galbraith, J. *Organization design*. Reading, Mass.: Addison-Wesley, 1977.

Gastorf, J. W., Suls, J., and Sanders, G. S. Type A coronary-prone behavior pattern and social facilitation. *Journal of Personality and Social Psychology*, 1980, **38**, 773–780.

Gal, R. and Lazarus, R. S. The role of activity in anticipating and confronting stressful situations. *Journal of Human Stress*, 1975, **2**, 4–20.

Greenwood, J. W. *Management stressors*. In reducing occupational stress. Cincinatti: NIOSH Research Report, 1978.

Haan, N. *Coping and defending*. New York: Acamedic Press, 1977.

Hackett, T. P. and Cassem, H. Psychological management of the myocardial infarction patient. *Journal of Human Stress*, 1975, **1**, 25–38.

Hackett, T. P., and Weisman, A. D. Reactions to the imminence of death. In G. H. Grosser, H. Wechsler, and M. Greenblatt (Eds.), *The threat of impending disaster*. Cambridge: MIT Press, 1964, pp. 300–311.

Hall, D. T. A model of coping with role conflict: The role behavior of college educated women. *Administrative Science Quarterly*, 1972, **17**, 471–486.

Hamburg, D. A. and Adams, J. E. A perspective on coping: Seeking and utilizing information in major transactions. *Archives of General Psychiatry*, 1967, **17**, 277–284.

Harvey, D. F. Cross-Cultural Stress and Adaptation in Global Organizations. Doctoral dissertation, Case Western Reserve University, 1969. *Dissertation Abstracts International*, 1970, **31**, 2958B. (University Microfilms, No. 70–4931)

Holmes, T. H. and Rahe, R. H. Social readjustment rating scale. *Journal of Psychosomatic Research*, 1967, **11**, 213–218.

House, J. S. *Social support and stress*. Reading, Mass.: Addison-Wesley, 1981.

House, J. S. and Wells, J. A. Occupational stress and health. In *Reducing occupational stress*. Cincinnati: NIOSH Research Report, 1978.

Howard, J. H., Rechnitzer, P. A., and Cunningham, D. A. Coping with job tensions—effective and ineffective methods. *Public Personnel Management*, 1975, **1**, 317–326.

Jackson, S. E. and Maslach, C. After-effects of job related stress: Families as victims. *Journal of Occupational Behavior*, 1982, **3**, 63–77.

Jacobson, D. Fatigue-producing factors in industrial work and preretirement attitude. *Occupational Psychology*, 1972, **46**, 193–200.

Janis, I., and Mann, L. *Decision making*. New York: The Free Press, 1977.

Jick, T. D. and Payne, R. Stress at work. *Exchange*, 1980, **3**, 50–56.

Kahn, R. L., Wolfe, D. M., Quinn, R. P. Snoek, J. D. and Rosenthal, R. A. *Organizational stress: Studies in role conflict and ambiguity*. New York: Wiley, 1964.

Katz, D. and Kahn, R. L. *The social psychology of organizations*, 2nd ed. New York: Wiley, 1978.

Landy, F. J., Farr, J. L. and Jacobs, R. R. Utility concepts in performance measurements. *Organizational Behavior and Human Performance*, 1982, **30**, 15–40.

Latack, J., Van Sell, M., and Schuler, R. S. *Measurement of coping with stress.* Paper presented at the Midwest Academy of Management, Cincinatti, 1980.

Lazarus, R. S. Positive denial: The case for not facing reality. *Psychology Today,* November 1979, 44, 47, 48, 51, 52, 57, 60.

Lazarus, R. S. *Psychological stress and the coping process.* New York: McGraw-Hill, 1966.

Lazarus, R. S. *The stress and coping paradigm.* Paper presented at conference entitled The Critical Evaluation of Behavioral Paradigms for Psychiatric Science at Glendon Beach, Oregon, November 3–6, 1978.

Lazarus, R. S. and Launier, R. Stress-related transaction between person and environment. In Pervin and Lewis (Eds.), *Perspectives in interactional psychology.* New York: Plenum, 1978, 287–327.

Lesser, P. J. The legal viewpoint. In A. McLean (Ed.), *To work is human.* New York: Macmillan, 1967.

Levi, T. *Stress and distress in response to psychosocial stimuli.* Elmsford, N.Y.: Pergamon Press, 1972.

Locke, E. A. The nature and causes of job satisfaction. In M. D. Dunnette (Ed.), *Handbook of industrial and organizational psychology.* Chicago: Rand McNally, 1976.

Mason, J. W. A historical view of the stress field. Part I. *Journal of Human Stress,* 1975, 1, 6–12.

McGrath, J. E. (Ed.) *Social and psychological factors in stress.* New York: Holt, Rinehart & Winston, 1970.

McGrath, J. E. Stress and behavior in organizations. In M. D. Dunnette (Ed.), *Handbook of industrial and organizational psychology.* Chicago: Rand McNally, 1976.

McLean, A. A. *Work stress.* Reading, Mass.: Addison-Wesley, 1979.

Mechanic, D. *Students under stress.* New York: The Free Press of Glencoe, 1962.

Menninger, K. *The vital balance: The life process in mental health and illness.* New York: Viking, 1963.

Milburn, T. W. *Maximizing degrees of freedom over time as a principal of rational behavior.* Working paper, The Ohio State University, 1981.

Newman, J. F. and Beehr, T. A. Personal and organizational strategies for handling job stress: A review of research and opinion. *Personnel Psychology,* 1979, 32, 1–43.

Payne, R. L. Demands, supports, constraints and psychological health. In C. J. McKay and T. Cox (Eds.), *Response to stress: Occupational aspects.* London: International Publishing Corporation, 1979.

Payne, R. L. Organizational stress and social support. In C. L. Cooper and R. L. Payne (Eds.), *Current concerns in occupational stress,* London: Wiley, 1980.

Pearlin, K. I. and Schooler, C. The structure of coping. *Journal of Health and Social Behavior,* 1978, 19, 1–21.

Pearlin, L. I. *The life cycle and life strains.* Paper presented at the American Sociological Meetings, Boston, 1979.

Plaut, S. M., and Friedman, S. B. Psychosocial factors in infectious disease. In R. Ader (Ed.), *Psychoneuroimmunology.* New York: Academic Press, 1981.

Sanders, G. S. and Milkus, F. S. Type A behavior; Need for control, and reactions to group participation. *Organizational Behavior and Human Performance,* 1982, 24, 194–216.

Schuler, R. S. Definition and conceptualization of stress in organizations. *Organizational Behavior and Human Performance,* 1980, 24, 115–130.

Schuler, R. S. An integrative transactional process model of stress in organizations. *Journal of Occupational Behavior,* 1982, 3, 5–19.

Selye, H. *The stress of life*. New York: McGraw-Hill, 1956.

Sethi, A. S. and Schuler, R. S. (Eds.). *Handbook of stress coping strategies and techniques*. Cambridge, Mass.: Ballinger Publishing Company, 1983.

Shalit, B. Structural ambiguity and limits to coping. *Journal of Human Stress*, 1977, **3**, 32–45.

Shostak, A. B. *Blue collar stress*. Reading, Mass.: Addison-Wesley, 1980.

Simon, H. A. *Administrative behavior*, 3rd ed. New York: The Free Press, 1976.

Smith, M. J., Colligan, M. J., and Harnell, J. J. *A review of psychological stress research of the national institute for occupational safety and health, 1971 to 1976*. Cincinnati: NIOSH Research Report, 1978.

Steers, R. M. *Organizational effectiveness*. Santa Monica, Calif.: Goodyear, 1977.

Theorell, T. Workload, life change and myocardial infarction. In *Reducing occupational stress*. Cincinnati: NIOSH Research Report, 1978.

Thompson, S. C. Will it hurt less if I can control it? A complex answer to a simple question. *Psychological Bulletin*, 1981, **90**, 89–101.

Vaillant, G. Theoretical hierarchy of adaptive ego mechanisms. *Archives of General Psychiatry*, 1971, **24**, 107–18.

Warshaw, L. J. *Stress management*. Reading, Mass.: Addison-Wesley, 1979.

Weick, K. *Social psychology of organizing*, 2nd ed. Reading, Mass.: Addison-Wesley, 1979.

White, R. Strategies of adaptation: an attempt at systematic description. In G. Coelho, D. A. Hamburg, and J. E. Adams (Eds.), *Coping and adaptation*. New York: Basic Books, 1974.

CHAPTER FOURTEEN

The Role of Social Support in Coping with Organizational Stress

TERRY A. BEEHR

Many researchers and practitioners in organizational behavior and psychology have expounded upon the belief that the influence of people on each other's lives is strong indeed. Since the Hawthorne studies, it has almost been accepted as axiomatic that productivity and satisfaction in organizations can be strongly influenced by the words and activities of coworkers, experimenters, supervisors, or almost anyone who is somehow important to the individual employee. It should come as no surprise, then, that social influence is proclaimed important in the etiology of mental and physical illnesses thought to be caused or made more severe by stress. In fact, since some forms of stress may be caused in part by actions of other people, it would be remarkable if this were not true. There are, however, several problems in explaining the influence of social support on stress and health. These problems include conceptual and operational definitions of social support, the precise effects of social support in the context of stressor-strain relationships, and how to implement what is known or believed about social support in attempting to alleviate the aversive effects of stress. In exploring these problems, it will be proposed that the concepts of uncertainty, importance, and duration are explanatory and meaningful in understanding the effects of social support on worker health.

DEFINING SOCIAL SUPPORT

Kaplan et al. (1977) have noted that conceptualization and operationalization of social support have been very inconsistent among different writers, perhaps due to the frequent usage of posthoc analyses and explanations in research on stress. Similarly, House (1981) has concluded that the definitions of social support offered by the experts are often contradictory or vague. Thus, social support might be offered as the explanation for the better health of married people in comparison with unmarried people, in which case being married is considered an operational definition, albeit a very specific and narrow one, of social support. In other attempts to explain the effects of stressful events, very general operationalizations comprised of such diverse elements as job satisfaction and satisfaction with one's neighborhood have been labeled social support by investigators. Often there is little evidence that the experience of supportive activities by other people has occurred for the focal person in such research. Many of the operational definitions of social support, therefore, are puzzling. Beehr (1976) has argued that "it cannot be said that a subordinate is given true psychological support unless the subordinate *feels* supported" (p. 36). Yet many of the studies that have claimed social support as an explanatory factor in their results have not even had very convincing face validity for their measures of this kind of support.

Three expert definitions of social support come from well-known reviews on the effects of support on occupational stress. House (1981) has defined social support as "emotional concern, instrumental aid, information, and/or appraisal" (p. 26) given to people by each other. Cobb (1976) focuses on information passing between or among individuals, information that an individual is (1) loved, (2) esteemed or valued, or (3) part of a group, the members of which share information and mutual obligations. Payne (1980) settled on Gerald Caplan's (1976) list of the eight support functions that are offered by the family to its members: (1) giving information about the world; (2) giving feedback and guidance; (3) providing ideology; (4) acting as mediator for problem-solving activities; (5) providing instrumental help and aid; (6) allowing a sanctuary for rest; (7) acting as a social control on the person's behavior; and (8) helping the person to master his or her emotions, especially negative ones. Although Caplan had proposed these as primary functions of the family, it may be possible for others to provide these functions to some extent also. One of the commonalities in these definitions is the concept of informing or directing, which will be further discussed later in this chapter.

Sources of Social Support

A broad definition of social support would imply that it does not much matter who provides the social support to the individual in the stressful situation. In fact, House (1981) cites studies in which social support is provided by goats, rats, and mice to others of their own species and by humans to rabbits! Extrapolating from such research, one might conclude that support from any source might be as good and as effective in reducing mental or physical illness as support from any other source. Intuitively, this seems unlikely, however.

Primary Versus Secondary Sources of Support.   Primary sources of social support are those people who have an intimate association with the person and who provide social support as a part of their friendship with him or her. The most typical examples of such sources of social support in the presence of stress are family and friends. Secondary sources are those people with whom the person has a less intimate relationship. The easiest examples of secondary support sources would be people who one has to go to a special place to see and who receive a fee for providing social support (or other services), for example psychotherapists, physicians, and counselors (e.g., Lindenthal et al., 1971). The primary-secondary distinction of the sources of social support is a continuum rather than a dichotomy, however, partially varying according to the degree of intimacy that the person has with the sources. Acquaintances, for example, are people with whom one is only somewhat or only occasionally intimate. These people may provide social support less frequently or less deeply than more intimate friends. For our purposes, the extreme of the secondary sources of support (those to whom a fee is paid) will be ignored—this chapter is concerned with primary or relatively primary sources social support.

Sources of Social Support in the Workplace.   Since occupational stress occurs in the workplace, one could logically argue that the remedial actions would be most effective if they occurred in the workplace also. Using an analogy, when one receives a physical wound, it is prudent to get it treated immediately, instead of waiting until the end of the workday. People who could serve as supporters at work include supervisors, coworkers (peers in the organizational hierarchy), subordinates, and customers or other nonorganizational members with whom the employee might have contact during his or her working hours. Most of the theorizing and empirical research on the problem has centered on either supervisor support, coworker support, or both.

Supervisor support has a history of being studied intensely by social scientists in organizations, although not usually in conjunction with occupational stress. Likert's (1961) principle of supportive relationships, for example, contends that supervisor support is good management, that is, it will help subordinates to be more effective and satisfied with their jobs. Similarly, leader consideration is one of the two most important leader behaviors in the Ohio State leadership theories and research (Stogdill, 1974), presumably because it helps subordinates to be more effective. The idea that supervisor support may also help reduce the incidence of mental and physical health of subordinates has come to organizational behavior researchers only recently, however. This is probably due to the fact that most organizational researchers did not have much knowledge of occupational stress until about the last fifteen years or less. Since the supervisor is higher in the organizational hierarchy than the subordinate, it stands to reason that support from this source will be relatively important for the subordinate. After all, such support may be interpreted as meaning that powerful others are sympathetic to the person experiencing stress. Thus, supervisor support may carry with it the implicit promise that the organization's sanctions and rewards will be favorable for the employee.

Coworker support is the second major type of support in the workplace thought to relieve the pressures of occupational stress. Variants of coworker support have also been discussed and studied in organizational behavior for some time before the idea was introduced that they may relieve the harmful effects of stress. As examples, the Hawthorne studies (Roethlisberger and Dickson, 1964) are often cited as evidence that coworkers have important influences on productivity and morale. Seashore's (1954) study of cohesiveness of the industrial work group concluded, in part, that coworkers develop production norms that are enforced by social reinforcement. And even Zajonc's (1965) discussion of social facilitation has found its way into organizational behavior text books (e.g., Scott and Cummings, 1973), presumably on the grounds that the mere presence of coworkers (and others) can influence worker productivity (Ferris et al., 1978). Bowers and Seashore (1966), in their four-factor theory of leadership, proposed that peer (coworker) support as well as supervisor support was essential to good leadership, and found that coworker support was related to some types of satisfaction in a study of life insurance agencies.

Thus, the two sources of social support in the workplace that are most frequently proposed by stress researchers as potentially helpful in alleviating the harmful effects of occupational stress have historically been of interest to organizational behavior researchers, albeit for other reasons. Simple logic argues that sources outside of the workplace also must be considered, and this has been done in some previous empirical work (e.g., Caplan et al., 1975) and conceptual work (e.g., Bhagat, 1983; House, 1981). These could be divided into categories such as family versus friends or spouse versus other family and friends, but the literature seldom makes such fine distinctions among the extraorganizational sources of support.

Types of Social Support

In defining social support, it was noted that some writers have listed several types of support (e.g., see the definitions by Cobb and Caplan presented earlier in this chapter). Others have also provided definitions in which more than one specific type of social support were delineated. After reviewing many studies of social support, House (1981) concluded four types of social support encompass the entire spectrum offered by the literature. These are emotional support (providing esteem, affect, trust, and listening), appraisal support (providing affirmation, feedback, and social comparison), informational support (providing advice, suggestion, directives, and information), and instrumental support (providing aid in kind, money, labor, time, or modification of the environment). Although there are a large number of specific types of social support presented in the literature, there is actually little evidence upon which to base many of the distinctions. Pinneau (1976) reported that the questionnaire items intended to measure tangible and emotional supports separately were so intercorrelated that it was decided to combine these two types of support measures in to a single index for analyzing the effects of support on occupational stress. Similarly, LaRocco et al. (1980) combined questionnaire items regarding psychological and tangible supports into a single index for each source of support.

Apparently, those two studies come from the same set of data (i.e., the data set described by Caplan et al., 1975), and it is therefore not surprising that the types of social support were combined in each study. In a separate study using similar measures of social support, it was found that measures of the two different types of support, emotional and tangible, from a single source (i.e., supervisor, coworker, *or* extraorganizational) correlated very highly with each other. The median correlation among a sample of police was .65 (Kaufmann, 1981) and among a sample of nurses was .67 (Kaufmann and Beehr, 1982). In contrast, the median correlations of similar types of support from different sources with each other (i.e., supervisor, coworker, and extraorganizational tangible supports with each other, and supervisor, coworker, and extraorganizational emotional supports with each other) were much lower—.25 for police and .175 for nurses (Tables 14-1 and 14-2). It appears that when people perceive one type of support coming from a given source, they tend to believe that other types are also available from that source. Overall, therefore, some empirical evidence

Table 14-1   Correlation Among Two Types and Three Sources of Support in a Sample of Police $(N = 121)^a$

Source and Type of Support	1	2	3	4	5
1. Supervisor tangible support					
2. Coworker tangible support	$.27^b$				
3. Extraorganizational tangible support	.04	$.26^c$			
4. Supervisor emotional support	$.65^c$	$.29^c$	.11		
5. Coworker emotional support	$.17^c$	$.64^c$	$.15^b$	$.50^b$	
6. Extraorganizational emotional support	.02	.14	$.73^c$	$.20^c$	$.24^c$

^{a} This is part of Table 20 from Kaufmann (1981).
$^b p < .05.$
$^c p < .01.$

Table 14-2   Correlations Among Two Types and Three Sources of Support in a Sample of Nurses $(N = 102)^a$

Source and Type of Support	1	2	3	4	5
1. Supervisor tangible support					
2. Coworker tangible support	$.21^b$				
3. Extraorganizational tangible support	.07	.14			
4. Supervisor emotional support	$.74^b$	.14	.03		
5. Coworker emotional support	$.21^b$	$.52^b$	$.19^b$	$.45^b$	
6. Extraorganizational emotional support	.03	.07	$.67^b$	.09	$.34^b$

^{a} This is part of Table 19 from Kaufmann (1981).
$^b p < .01$.

indicates that there are not as many operationally identifiable types of social support as the current theorizing suggests.

This lack of empirical definition of types of social support is somewhat surprising, since a long line of both laboratory and field research on leadership has employed two types of leadership variables that resemble emotional and tangible support. As noted by Blau (1981), these two types of support appear to parallel the results of the early Ohio State (e.g., Fleishman, 1957; Halpin and Winer, 1957) and Michigan (e.g., Katz et al., 1950) studies on leadership in organizations. The Ohio State terminology for these leader behaviors is the better known—consideration (a parallel of emotional support) and initiating structure (a parallel of tangible support). Although it has been common in the leadership literature (e.g., Bowers and Seashore, 1966) to think only of consideration as support, the occupational stress literature (e.g., House, 1981) has defined social support broadly enough to encompass initiating structure as a form of support.

While the Ohio State measures of these two leader behaviors are widely used and were developed empirically via factor analyses, they often do intercorrelate with each other, and in fact it is usually recommended that an effective leader do both of these types of support behaviors. Thus they are by no means totally separate. Given these warnings, it is only with caution that even two different types of social support are suggested here. In spite of the history of belief in two such leader behaviors, it remains to be proven convincingly that emotional and tangible supports are separate types of support. To offer more than two types, as many of the authors reviewed do, would be even less justifiable at present.

In this chapter the two types of support will be labeled instrumental and emotional. Instrumental social support is help from others in getting the work done or indirectly altering the stressors in the person's job. Emotional social support is characterized by intimacy, caring, and sympathetic listening.

Table 14-3   Six Social Supports for Potential Help in Alleviating
Occupational Stress

Types of Social Support	Source of Social Support		
	Supervisor	Coworker	Extraorganizational
Emotional			
Instrumental			

The Six Social Supports: Three Sources × Two Types of Support

Table 14-3 outlines the six typical social supports that an organizational member may encounter when faced with occupational stress. For both the practitioner and the researcher, it would be helpful if the body of this table could be completed by entering information regarding the degree to which each of these supports are sought by people experiencing stress, the degree to which each support is successful in alleviating the harmful effects of stress, and the techniques for using such information (i.e., if one of the six supports is especially effective in treating occupational stress, what are the steps that can be used to implement that support as a treatment for stress?). These issues are not yet answered by the existing research on occupational stress and social support, however. These questions represent areas in need of systematic and rigorous research.

RESEARCH EVIDENCE FOR THE EFFECTS OF SOCIAL SUPPORT IN STRESSOR—STRAIN RELATIONSHIPS

House and Wells (1978) have noted that the effects of social support on stress and health have been the target of study for less than a decade, although the roots of this work date back to the early 1900s. A variety of reasons may exist for the inconsistent or nonexistent research results regarding the effects of social support in the stressor-strain relationships. The studies aiming directly at discovering the effects of social support in the context of work-related stress are still few in number, tempting writers to rely upon older research that is only partially related to the topic. Thus some of the claims regarding social support come from research that varies greatly in design, measurement, and context. There may be a tendency for many of us to believe that social support is beneficial in the context of occupational stress because (1) such past research seems to imply that support is generally beneficial, and (2) it seems to be a common sense notion that people can help others in almost any situation.

A Classic Example

An older, but well-known research effort will help to illustrate the effects of some of the classic literature in sociology and social psychology on the thinking about social support and stress. Schachter (1959) did a set of experiments in which college students awaiting an experiment in which they expected to receive electrical shocks were allowed some choices regarding the conditions under which they would await the experiment. The general conclusion is that they preferred to await the stressful experiment in the presence of others, especially if those others were also awaiting the experiment in which they would be shocked. This is often interpreted as meaning that people under stress might expect to have the anxiety associated with stress reduced by associating with others, that is, misery loves company. It should be noted that this example, while a classic in social support and stress, seems to have little in common with the concept of occupational stress. The subjects of the experiment were not experiencing *work-related* stress. In addition, they preferred the company of others who were experiencing the same stress—a condition not usually considered important by modern writers in occupational stress. In addition, there was not strong evidence in the studies that the potential experience of such support did in fact reduce the stress very greatly. Nevertheless, Schachter's work, along with other related pieces, has had a strong influence on much of the modern day thinking about occupational stress.

Other Related Evidence

In a very general sense many studies have linked social support with health outcomes. These results are general because the operationalization of social support is varied and sometimes questionable for our purposes, and because it is often unclear *why* social support is linked with health. Kaplan et al. (1977) have summarized much of this approach. They report that such studies have found that the highest rates of tuberculosis occur among ethnic minority groups (even controlling for socioeconomic class), people who are single, and people who change residences frequently. This mirrors the incidence of many other types of illnesses, including schizophrenia, multiple accidents occurring to people, suicide, and respiratory diseases other than tuberculosis. Following the Kaplan et al. review, but consistent with it, Pearlin and Johnson (1977) and Eaton (1978) have found marital status to be a moderator of the life stress-strain relationship. In addition, Kaplan et al. (1977) cite evidence that social support (broadly defined) helps people through difficulties associated with unemployment, bereavement of the death of a spouse, and battle stress (among soldiers). In relation to this last type of stress, it is considered common knowledge in the military that infantrymen under fire tend to cluster together (reminiscent of Schachter's subjects preferring to be with others in a stressful situation), even though this tendency could have deleterious consequences.

Bovard (1959) has reviewed several studies suggesting the usefulness of small groups for reducing battle-induced stress. In general, there is an apparent association between affiliation and welfare or happiness.

This evidence leads to the belief that social support is good for people—whether they are experiencing stress or not. As can be seen in these examples, the operational definition of social support is so varied between studies and at times so obtuse within a single study that it is of questionable validity to generalize these results to imply that social support will alleviate harmful effects of work-related stress. The numbers of studies of this nature, however, far exceed the numbers of studies aimed directly at the more specific topic at hand.

Direct Attempts to Study Social Support in Relation to Work-Related Stress

Most relevant of all are those handful of studies that have measured social support in terms of the psychological closeness of relationships available to the focal person while investigating employee experiences of work-related stress. There are several types of effects of social support that can conceivably be found in such studies. Of special interest here are main effects of social support on stressors, main effects of social support on strains, and interaction effects of social support on the relationships between stressors and strains. In this last effect the interaction would be between stressors and support in predicting strains. House (1981) has described the mechanics of computing these effects statistically via multiple regression, but a short conceptual description of each will be offered here.

Main effects indicate that social support is directly affecting an element in the job stress process by itself, aside from any effect that it might have in combination with other characteristics of the environment or the person. A simple example, consistent with Handy's (1978) comments about a "thrusting" male executive and his "caring" wife, would occur when a sympathetic spouse offers support in the form of a listening ear and a shoulder to lean on after a hard day's work. If this support eases strains such as tension, fatigue, or even blood pressure, we would conclude that there is a main effect of this support on strain. Specifically, this would be an example of extraorganizational emotional support affecting strain (Table 14-3). A main effect of support on a stressor would be illustrated in the situation where a supervisor offers social support in the form of helping a subordinate who is working under a tight deadline by giving him or her the necessary information or instruction to solve a work-related problem. The employee was experiencing a stressor, overload (too much work to do in the time available), and the supervisor eased that stressor by helping him or her to get the job done within the necessary time by indicating a means for solving the problem quickly. This example illustrates a form of instrumental support emanating from the supervisor.

In the literature on social support and occupational stress an interaction effect has often been labeled a "buffering" effect (e.g., House, 1981). The idea is that social support acts as a buffer in the relationship between stressors and strains. When an employee is in a situation with many strong stressors, he or she would ordinarily experience a great deal of strain, but when social support is also available, the employee would not experience as much strain. Thus, social support in this buffering example would not reduce the stressors, but it would protect the employee by breaking the link between the stressors and strains. This is a description of an interaction between social support and stressors in predicting strains.

Evidence for Main Effects of Social Support on Job Stressors. Seldom has research focused on the question of whether support has main effects on stressors, but some tentative conclusions can be offered by reexamining the previous literature in this light. Whenever there is a significant relationship between social support and a stressor, there is the possibility of a main effect, even though such a relationship is hardly proof that social support is affecting stressors.

Some studies have found virtually no relationship between support and job stressors. In a sample of Navy personnel, LaRocco and Jones found virtually no relationship between the stressors, conflict and ambiguity, and supervisor and coworker support. House and Wells (1977), in a study of hourly workers in a large rubber and chemical plant, found virtually no relationships between social support and several stressors.

On the other hand, some studies have found a moderate relationship (i.e., correlations between .30 and .50) between social support and occupational stressors. Caplan et al. (1975), in a study of employees in 23 occupations, found moderate negative correlations between supervisor support and some role stressors. Blau (1980) found that supervisor support was negatively correlated with stressors related to time pressures among a sample of 166 urban bus drivers. Beehr (1976) reported moderate negative correlations between supervisor support and a stressor, role ambiguity. Kaufmann (1981) found moderate negative correlations between supervisor emotional support and the stressors job future ambiguity, role overload, and underutilization of skills among nurses and police officers. Each of these investigators had measured support from sources other than the supervisor (especially from the coworkers), but these other sources were generally not related very strongly to any of the stressors.

Overall, therefore, the evidence is mixed regarding the potential main effects of social support on stressors, but if such an effect does exist, it is probably a function of support from the supervisor only. This makes sense, since the supervisor has more formal control over the objective work environment and the expectations of work required from the employee than any other single person has. He or she may be able to provide meaningful tangible support to a subordinate experiencing stress by altering the job in a way that reduces the strength of the stressors. In fact, emotional support from a person in a position of power (e.g., a supervisor) may carry with it the implicit promise that the person would use his or her power in some tangible way to reduce the subordinate's problem. This alone might serve to reduce somewhat the employee's subjective experience of stressors.

Kaufmann (1981) provided an interesting test of a moderating or buffering effect of social support on subjective stressors among his sample of nurses. He proposed that self-reported life events (e.g., Holmes and Rahe, 1967) would be somewhat more objective that the self-reported stressors usually used in organizational research, and he computed moderator analyses to determine whether social support might moderate the relationship between objective and subjective stressors. This was only a crude attempt to answer this question, since the objective life events were still measured via self-report questionnaire (Holmes and Rahe, 1967) and since the life events were not necessarily events that would automatically lead to the experience of subjective *job* stress. He found that there were no moderating effects of social support on the relationship between life event stressors and the subjective job stressors. This attempt, however, points to an area in which there has been no research on social support. Investigations are needed in which objectively measured job stressors are tested for interactions with social supports in leading to the identical job stressors, subjectively measured.

This relationship between objective and subjective stressors has been a concern since the very beginning of research on job stress. Kahn et al. (1964), for example, showed that the stressor level reported by job incumbents was related to the stressor levels on those job incumbents that were reported by their supervisors and coworkers. Jenkins et al. (1975), however, found that trained outsider observers (not members of the organization) could not identify two stressors (role conflict and role ambiguity) reported by job incumbents. It may be that social support could help to explain why two people in the same objective situation do not always experience stressors to the same degree.

Salancik and Pfeffer's (1978) proposed social information processing model suggests that social information guides employees in developing their perceptions of their job situations. As noted previously, writers (e.g., Cobb, 1976; House, 1981; Payne, 1980) have usually included such information as part of the definition of one or more types of social support. It has been suggested above that these types of social support may play a role in determining employees' perceptions of the job characteristics called stressors. This model needs testing, however.

Evidence for Main Effects of Social Support on Strains.   Most of the research on social support in conjunction with job stress has focused on either its main or interaction effects on strain. This is probably because employee strain is the main concern of stress workers. Without strain, there would be no reason to be concerned about job stress. If social supports have main effects on strain, that means that they would work to decrease the frequency or severity of psychological or physical ill health. Most of the research on social support and its effects on strain in the context of occupational stress are non-experimental field studies and can only show that social support and strain are *related*. The idea that the relationship is causal, that is, that social support *causes* decreased strain is based purely on logic and inference, not upon proof. This is true of the examples that follow. This section reports studies finding main effects of social support on strain. Those finding interaction effects between social support and stressors on strains are discussed in the following section.

Beehr (1976) reported negative correlations between supervisor support and a set of psychological strains (viz., dissatisfaction with work, low self-esteem, high depression, and life dissatisfaction) among a sample of employees from five different work organizations, indicating possible main effects for supervisor emotional support. Coworker support (a group cohesiveness measure in this study) had no main effects, however. Among Blau's (1981) sample of bus drivers, supervisor and coworker support had main effects on overall job satisfaction but extraorganizational support did not. Among a sample of Navy enlisted men, LaRocco and Jones (1978) found main effects for supervisor support on job satisfaction and Navy satisfaction and for coworker support on job satisfaction, Navy satisfaction, and self-esteem. Some studies (e.g., Gore, 1978), while showing that social support probably has some effect on strain among employees, cannot be classified as evidence for either main or interaction effects because the stressor was treated as a constant rather than a variable. That is, only data from a group who all experienced the same stress were reported. In such studies it is impossible to ascertain whether social support interacts with the stressor. They found no important effect on physical illness, however. Kaufmann (1981), among his sample of police, reported main effects for coworker, supervisor, and extraorganizational support on psychological strain (a measure consisting of several strain indices, i.e., job dissatisfaction, workload dissatisfaction, boredom, and depression).

In general, it is concluded that there is some evidence that social support has main effects on strains among employees experiencing job stress, but it primarily has main effects on job satisfaction and psychological strains. This is consistent with House's (1981) observation that social support tends to have main effects on psychological strains and job attitudes such as job satisfaction.

Evidence for Buffering Effects of Social Support on Job Stressor-Strain Relationships. Buffering effects of social support on the relationship between stressors and strains are indicated when social support interacts with a stressor in predicting strain. In order to be an instance of buffering, there must be a specific type of interaction, however. It must be an interaction in which people who receive high levels of support have a weaker relationship between stressors and strains than people who receive low levels of social support do. Some studies have found this type of buffering effect in studies of job stress.

Beehr (1976) reported a buffering effect of coworker support on the relationship between one stressor (role ambiguity) and one psychological strain (low self-esteem). House and Wells (1978), in a study of white male workers in a rubber and chemicals plant, found that supervisor support buffered the relationship between several job stressors and several physiological symptoms of strain and between one job stressor (role conflict) and psychological strain, that is, neurosis. Extraorganizational support (viz., wife support) moderated the relationship between several job stressors and psychological strain. Coworker support had relatively little effect in buffering the stressor-strain relationship. LaRocco et al. (1980), in a sample of males from 23 occupations, found several buffering effects of social support on stressor-strain relationships. In particular, support buffered the effects of stressors on psychological strains such as depression, irritation, and anxiety, and on the physiological strain, somatic complaints. Regarding the effects of the various sources of support, they concluded that "coworker support has a somewhat more pervasive buffering effect than supervisor or home support" (p. 210). House (1981), in graphing data from the Cobb and Kasl (1977) study of unemployment, has shown that there tends to be a buffering effect of extraorganizational social support on the relationship between degrees of unemployment (expressed as the relative amount of time unemployed) and psychological strain and to a lesser extent that there tends to be a buffering effect of extraorganizational support on the relationship between unemployment and physiological strain indicators.

These studies all showed that the experience of social support may serve to decrease the severity of strains during the experience of job stressors. Consistent with House's (1981) observation, it appears that the strains that are more health oriented (psychological or physiological health) and less attitude oriented (e.g., job satisfaction) are more likely to be affected by social support interacting with stressors.

There are occasionally some disturbing interaction results that question the whole notion of social supports' buffering (or for that matter main) effects on strains, however. Some studies have reported the effect of "reverse" buffering, that is, and interactions in which high levels of social support lead to stronger rather than weaker relationships between job stressors and strains. If this were to occur, it would mean that employees experiencing high levels of stressors at work would actually be worse for the wear (experience more strain) if they received social support than if they received no support!

LaRocco et al. (1980) found a few instances of reverse buffering in the sample of males in 23 occupations, especially in the case of supervisor support buffering the relationship between two person-environment fit stressors (work-load fit and role-ambiguity fit) and psychological strains that were attitudinal in character (job dissatisfaction, boredom, and work-load dissatisfaction). Kaufmann and Beehr (1982) found instances of reverse buffering among their sample of nurses. Supervisor support, co-worker support, and extraorganizational support all had reverse buffering effects on the relationship between a combined stressor index of job future ambiguity and role overload, and psychosomatic strain. In addition, supervisor tangible support and instrumental support (an index of support determining whether there was tangible support available to help get one's job done, but without reference to any particular source of such support) were reverse buffers of the job-future ambiguity-overload stressor and nurse's absenteeism (which may act as a surrogate measure of psychological and physiological health). Among the police sample Kaufmann (1981) reported that instrumental support interacted with stressors in predicting psychological strain, and this was also an example of reverse buffering. In neither sample did Kaufmann find a single example of social support buffering the stressor-strain relationship in the expected direction. Beehr (1976) found a reverse buffering effect of coworker support on the relationship between role ambiguity and an attitudinal strain, job dissatisfaction. Finally, in a result regarding job performance among Blau's (1981) sample of bus drivers, there was an instance of reverse buffering of supervisor social support on the relationship between a work-role stressor and driver performance. This last finding is offered tentatively, since job performance is not a strain in the typical definition of the term.

The existence of reverse buffering is quite unexpected, given the intuitive position that being nice (supportive) to people ought to be helpful rather than harmful, and given the findings from studies of stressors other than job stressors which indicate that social support is an all-purpose remedy for psychological and physiological illnesses. Therefore, researchers who have discovered these effects have felt obligated to explain them. Taking their explanations chronologically, Beehr (1976) focused on intragroup communication to explain the reverse buffering effect of coworker support on job dissatisfaction. He argued that people experiencing the stressor, role ambiguity, would communicate with each other in ways that would reduce self-blame. They blame the ambiguity on the job rather than on themselves, thereby resulting in dissatisfaction with the job. Such social support allows and encourages the work group member to place the blame for a bad situation externally, thereby defending the member's ego. LaRocco et al. (1980) take a similar approach, noting that social support may take on different faces. Our coworkers, supervisors, friends, and family can attempt to be supportive and comfort us while telling us a variety of quite different things. For example, they might either "convince us that job conditions are not as bad as they seem, . . . (or) that they are as bad as or even worse than, we thought" (p. 214). In the second instance, LaRocco et al. argue that reverse buffering occurs. Blau (1981) speculated that the source of social support, in interaction with the source of the stress, may be crucial in determining whether it can buffer the effects of job stress positively or negatively. There is no particular reason to expect that social support and stress will always be totally independent from each other. The same people who are available to provide the employee with social support can also be partially responsible for the strength of any of stressors present in the employee's job. If so, any association with the source of the stress, while ostensibly supporting the employee, might also exacerbate the employee's stress. If through no other means, the presence of the other person might do this simply by reminding the employee of the stressful condition.

Kaufmann (1981) reviewed all of these explanations and called for research to determine the validity of each. In order to do this, more variables would have to be measured, for example, (1) the amount and type of communication between the job incumbent and his or her supervisor, coworkers, friends, and family, and (2) the source of the stressors (i.e., supervisor, coworkers, family, and friends). This is work that still needs to be done, and it could be fruitful for practitioners and researchers alike if it helps to clarify the instances of reverse buffering. Beehr's (1981) recent research has shown that employee stressors may at times be more strongly related to dissatisfaction with other people at work than to dissatisfaction with nonsocial facets of the workplace. This might be expected to happen in instances where the employee's stressor levels are in part caused by the other people at work.

CONCLUSIONS, HYPOTHESES, AND A MODEL TO GUIDE RESEARCH

While the evidence regarding the effects of social support on the experience of occupational stress is still somewhat limited, enough has accumulated to offer some tentative conclusions and hypotheses. The model in Figure 14-1 illustrates the three effects of social support. Future research on each of these topics would be useful.

In the model, the arrows from one variable to another indicate proposed causal relationships, and the plus (+) or minus (−) sign next to the arrow indicates whether an increase in the first variable is proposed to cause an increase in the strength of the next variable (+), or a decrease in the next variable (−). Briefly, the model proposes (1) that instrumental social support can decrease the strength of job stressors, (2) that job stressors can increase the uncertainty of $E \rightarrow P$ expectancies or $P \rightarrow O$ expectancies, (3) that these expectancies are multiplied by the importance of relevant

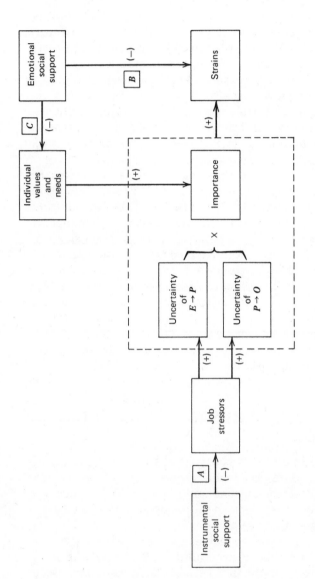

Figure 14-1 Effects of instrumental and emotional social support in the context of job stress.

A Main effect of instrumental social support on job stressors.

B Main effect of emotional social support on strains.

C Buffering effect of emotional social support on the relationship between job stressors and strains.

(+) or (−)
Indicates the direction of the effect, i.e., increasing (+) or decreasing (−) the strength of the variable.

outcomes in the situation to result in strains (as suggested by the model in Chapter 1 of this book), (4) that increases in relevant individual needs and values can increase the strength of importance, (5) that emotional social support can decrease the strength of the strains, and (6) that emotional social support can decrease the strength of the relevant individual needs and values. The model's proposals regarding the effects of the two types of social support are discussed in more detail below.

Effects of Social Support on Stressors

The studies reporting main effects of social support on stressors, a topic of relatively little discussion in this area of job stress, led to the conclusions that support probably can affect levels of stressors and that the supervisor is the source most likely to be effective in reducing stressors. Admittedly going well beyond the evidence, it is hypothesized here and illustrated by arrow A in the model in Figure 14-1 that instrumental support will have this effect rather than emotional support. This is surmised based on the inference that the supervisor has an effect because of his or her real or perceived ability to alter the tangible aspects of the focal person's job. That is, the supervisor often has more power in the work situation than other sources typically investigated in studies of support and job stress. Compared with coworkers and extraorganizational sources of support, the supervisor is in a much better position to affect the levels of stressors in the employee's work environment. Still needed are studies that determine whether social support moderates the relationship between objectively stressful situations and the subjective experience of stressors. A strong attempt to examine this question has never been made, even though Kahn et al. proposed this as early as 1964. According to the well-known model they presented, social support (interpersonal relations) would moderate the relationship between potentially stressful elements of the objective environment (pressures from role senders) and the subjective experience of the stressors by the focal person. Instead, most of the work on social support has focused on its potential for moderating the relationship between subjective stressors and strains (the buffering effect discussed in this chapter).

Effects of Social Support on Strain

There also appear to be main effects of social supports on employee strain. It is hypothesized here and illustrated by arrow B in the model that emotional social support is the type of support most likely to have this effect. The comfort offered by sympathetic others in the environment is proposed to have a direct calming effect on the individual employee.

This effect on strains appears strongest when one considers attitudinal strains such as job satisfaction and psychological strains. Main effects for social support on physiological strain have not been reported as often. It must be acknowledged, however, that more studies have been undertaken of the effects of social support on psychological strains than of the effects of social support on physiological strains within the context of job stress. Therefore, it is offered primarily as a hypothesis that social support affects psychological strains more than it affects physiological strains. An alternative hypothesis is that the apparent main effect of social support on job attitudes and psychological strain is spurious. This hypothesis would claim that the association of the support variables and the psychological strain variables are due to the use of common methods of measurement of these sets variables. Both sets of variables are most often measured via a self-report technique (e.g., a questionnaire or set of questionnaires). Common response biases, for example, a halo effect, may be operating to cause an association between two variables measured with this method. For example, people who are generally happy with some important areas of their lives or their work may give positive responses to all types of questions about themselves and their work, while people who are generally unhappy with some important areas of their lives or their work may give negative answers to all types of questions about themselves and their work. This would be true of questions about social support and about psychological and attitudinal strains, among others. Further research utilizing more than one method of measurement is necessary in order to shed light on this issue.

The Buffering Hypothesis

The evidence on the buffering hypothesis regarding social support is mixed. There are investigations indicating that people experiencing high levels of job stress are protected from strain by having social support available, but there is now enough evidence of a reverse buffering effect that the entire concept of social support generally being able to buffer this relationship between stressors and strains is in doubt. If reverse buffering effects continue to come to light, this would very seriously damage the concept of social support as being beneficial for those experiencing job stress. Three hypotheses can be offered to explain the discovery of buffering in some situations and reverse buffering in others.

First, based upon only the small amount of evidence available it is hypothesized that reverse buffering is more likely with psychological health and attitudinal strains than with physiological strains. There is some suggestion in the evidence that this may be true, although there are not enough studies to make a firm conclusion. Thus, depending upon the particular strains investigated, researchers are more likely to discover either buffering or reverse buffering. Second, reverse buffering may occur more frequently when the source of the support is also the source of the stressor. Thus, for example, if the supervisor is partially responsible for the job being stressful, further association with the supervisor (attempted supervisor support) may aggravate the situation rather than alleviate it. Third, buffering and reverse buffering may be the results of different types of communications involved between the focal person and the supportive person. The supportive person may only lend a listening ear, but it is more likely that he or she will engage in two-way communication with the stressed employee. The supportive person, for example may suggest or reinforce suggestions by the employee that the situation is indeed stressful; alternatively, the supportive person may attempt to comfort the employee by suggesting that there is a silver lining behind every cloud (the situation is not so bad). These variations in types of communication have not been addressed in studies of social support in the context of job stress. In general, more work needs to be done, (1) to determine whether buffering and reverse buffering effects are widespread, and (2) to determine when and why these effects occur.

Arrow C in the model in Figure 14-1 can be used to illustrate the hypotheses regarding the proposed buffering effects of social support on the relationship between job stressors and strains. In Chapter 1 it was proposed that uncertainty and importance combine multiplicatively to result in strains. Arrow A in the model in Figure 14-1 proposes that instrumental social support has its effect on the uncertainty of $E \rightarrow P$ and $P \rightarrow O$, via its effects on changing the job characteristics that are stress-producing (job stressors). Emotional social support has direct effects on strains (arrow B), but it also has the potential to buffer the relationship between job stressors and strains (arrow C) by affecting the other variable from the multiplicative equation: importance. It does this through its effects on individuals' needs or values. This assumes that the importance an employee places on the outcomes expected from his or her work is a function of his or her work-related needs and values.

The Salancik and Pfeffer (1978) social information processing model proposes that individuals' needs are in part a function of the social information they receive. Since so many researchers (e.g., Cobb, 1976; House, 1981; Payne, 1980) in the job stress and social support literature have concluded that the passing of information is one of the most important functions of social support, it is proposed in the model here that emotional social support provides information that helps the employee to know what needs and values are appropriate in the particular job stress situation. Specifically, in job stress situations supportive others may help to reduce the strength of needs that would make work-related outcomes important to the employee. Previous research suggests that social support sometimes does and sometimes does not buffer the relationship between job stressors and strains, and the model explains why this has occurred. It is hypothesized, therefore, that: (1) if social support is successful in reducing the importance that employees place on relevant job outcomes, buffering will occur; (2) if the support does not reduce importance, it will not buffer the stressor-strain relationship; and (3) if the information offered to the employee suggests that it is appropriate to place great importance on the outcomes, reverse buffering will occur.

The Sources of Social Support

Two comments are also in order now about the elements of Table 14-3, sources of social support and types of social support. Regarding sources of social support, House (1981) has concluded that one source of support may be enough to alleviate or buffer the effects of stressors. He makes this conclusion relying primarily on the House and Wells (1978) data. The other studies reviewed here do not analyze their data in a way that addresses this issue adequately, but House's observation makes sense. It suggests that the most crucial difference is between having no source of support and having some (even if only one) source of support. This de-scribes a "threshold effect," in which strains due to job stress are alleviated after receiving support from at least one person and are not alleviated further by receiving support from additional sources. Figure 14-2 illus-trates this hypothesized threshold effect.

In Figure 14-2 the vertical axis indicates the strength of correlations or the relationships between stressors and strains. A correlation of 1.0 indi-cates that there is a perfect relationship between stressors and strains, while a correlation of 0 indicates that there is no relationship between stressors and strains. When there are zero sources of social support, there is a moderate correlation between stressors and strains, but when there is even one source of social support available for the employee, the relation-ship between stressors and strains is reduced substantially, to near zero in fact. This means that even though stressors are still present in the person's job, the strain has disappeared due to the social support of one person. If two, three, or more people are available for additional social support for the person, there is no further reduction in the strength of the relationship between stressors and strains. Fortunately, the relationship is reduced so

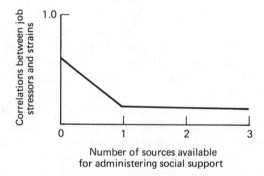

Figure 14-2 Threshold effect of social support in buffering the relationship job stressors and strains.

sharply by the social support of one person that no further reduction may be necessary. When House and Wells (1978) found a buffering effect for social support, this is what appeared to be happening, and this is the best estimate of the working of social support when it has a buffering effect.

House (1981) has further concluded that the two sources of social support originating from the workplace are the most important or effective sources of social support in alleviating the effects of job stress. "Work-related sources of support (work supervisors and coworkers) are most effective in both reducing occupational stress and buffering the impact of such stress on health, although support from spouses is also important in buffering the impact of work stress, especially on general affective and psychological states" (p. 85). This makes sense since people who are familiar with the workplace and are likely to be present when work stress is experienced are in the best position to alleviate job stress. In fact, in making the distinction between the two types of support in Table 14-3, extraorganizational sources of support are at an almost insurmountable disadvantage in administering one of the two—instrumental social support.

As was suggested earlier in the chapter, it would be logical to determine whether the source of support is also a source of the stressors in the focal person's work life. This combination of characteristics within a single source needs to be studied to untangle the inconsistent results emanating from previous research on job stress and social support.

The Types of Social Support

With regard to the two types of social support, emotional and instrumental, House (1981) concluded that emotional support seems to be the more important or effective of the two. "*Emotional support*, which involves providing empathy, caring, love, and trust, seems to be the most important" (p. 24). While emotional support is more often included in definitions of social support than instrumental support is, and while more studies include measures of emotional support than of instrumental support, the few pieces of literature attempting to assess the effects of both types of support within the context of job stress do not lead very strongly to the conclusion that emotional support is the more important type of support. In the first place when researchers have attempted to assess both types of support within a single study, they have often found that the two are difficult to distinguish empirically. To whatever extent this is true, it would be meaningless to try to compare the effects of the two. Neither can be judged better than the other if they always occur together. Secondly, in studies that did separately analyze the effects of both types of social support, instrumental support did often have as much effect as emotional support (e.g., Kaufmann, 1981). There is too little evidence at present to conclude that one type of social support is more effective than the other in alleviating the effects of job stress. Emotional support, to be sure, has a longer history of involvement in research and practice in the psychological and mental health areas and is somewhat a favorite explanation among many behavioral scientists, but the results are not yet available that would allow a legitimate comparison of the effectiveness of the two types of support. If the model and hypotheses in this chapter are correct, each may have an effect, but on a different part of the job stress process.

Finally, it may be better for researchers to start anew in classifying types of social support. It has been suggested in this chapter that future research investigate the specific types of communication between focal people and their supporters. Classification of the content of communication may prove to be more powerful in explaining the effects of support on stressors or strains than the present emotional/instrumental dichotomy is.

Research Design Issues

A final word is necessary regarding the research evidence on the usefulness of social support in alleviating the harmful effects of job stress. All of the research reviewed in this section has utilized the same design, that is, the nonexperimental field design. In these designs the researcher studies issues in the field, in this case the workplace where job stress occurs. This is a strength in the sense that the results of such research are probably more relevant to the real world than they would be if the same phenomena were studied in an experimental laboratory. The fact that the designs are nonexperimental, however, poses some problems in interpreting the meaning of the results. In nonexperimental designs the researcher cannot make very strong inferences regarding causality. Thus, we cannot be certain from the design that stressors are causing strain, for example. This inference must be based upon complementary experimental studies and upon reasoning. The primary issue for the present discussion is whether the administration of social support to someone experiencing job stress and strain causes the reduction of stress, strain, or both. We usually infer that this is true, but there is nothing in the design of the research that gives strong evidence for the validity of this inference. The inference that social support *causes* improvements in stressful job situations, therefore, is far from proven. Experimental or quasi-experimental research is needed to allow a stronger inference.

REFERENCES

Beehr, T. A. Perceived situational moderators of the relationship between subjective role ambiguity and role strain. *Journal of Applied Psychology*, 1976, **61**, 35–40.

Beehr, T. A. Work-role stress and attitudes toward co-workers. *Group and Organization Studies*, 1981, **6**, 201–210.

Bhagat, R. S. Effects of stressful life events upon individual performance effectiveness and work adjustment processes within organizational settings: A research model. *Academy of Management Review*, 1983, **8**, 660–671.

Blau, G. An empirical investigation of job stress, social support, service length, and job strain. *Organizational Behavior and Human Performance*, 1981, **27**, 279–302.

Bovard, E. W. The effects of social stimuli on the response to stress. *The Psychological Review*, 1959, **66**, 267–277.

Bowers, D. G., and Seashore, S. E. Predicting organizational effectiveness with a four-factor theory of leadership. *Administrative Science Quarterly*, 1966, **11**, 238–263.

Caplan, G. The family as a support system. In G. Caplan and M. Killilea (Eds.), *Support systems and mutual help*. New York: Grune and Stratton, 1976.

Caplan, R. D., Cobb, S., French, J. R. P. Jr., Van Harrison, R., and Pinneau, S. R. Jr., *Job Demands and Worker Health*. Washington, D.C.: U.S. Department of Health, Education and Welfare (NIOSH), 1975.

Cobb, S. Social support as a moderator of life stress. *Psychosomatic Medicine*, 1976, **38**, 300–314.

Cobb, S. and Kasl, S. V. *Termination: The consequences of job loss*. Washington, D. C.: U.S. Department of Health, Education and Welfare (NIOSH), Publication No. 77-224, 1977.

Eaton, W. W. Life events, social supports and psychiatric symptoms: A reanalysis of the New Haven data. *Journal of Health and Social Behavior*, 1978, **19**, 230–234.

Ferris, G. R., Beehr, T. A., and Gilmore, D. C. Social Facilitation: A review and alternative conceptual model. *Academy of Management Review*, 1978, **3**, 338–347.

Fleishman, E. A. The Leader Opinion Questionnaire. In R. W. Stogdill and A. E. Coons (Eds.), *Leader behavior: Its description and measurement*. Ohio State University Research Monograph No. 88, 1957.

Gore, S. The effect of social support in moderating the health consequences of unemployment. *Journal of Health and Social Behavior*, 1978, **19**, 157–165.

Halpin, A. and Winer, B. J. A factorial study of leaders' behavior description. In R. M. Stogdill and A. E. Coons (Eds.), *Leaders' behavior: Its description and measurement*. Ohio State University Research Monograph No. 88, 1957.

Handy, C. The family: Help or hindrance? In C. L. Cooper and R. Payne (Eds.), *Stress at work*. New York: Wiley, 1978, 107–123.

Holmes, T. H. and Rahe R. H. The social readjustment scale. *Journal of Psychosomatic Research*, 1967, **11**, 213–218.

House, J. S. *Work stress and social support*. Reading, Mass.: Addison-Wesley, 1981.

House, J. S. and Wells, J. A. Occupational stress, social support, and health. In A. McLean, G. Black, and M. Colligan (Eds.), *Reducing occupational stress: Proceedings of a conference*. Department of Health, Education, and Welfare (NIOSH), Publication No. 78-140, 1978, 8–29.

Jenkins, G. D. Jr., Nadler, D. A., Lawler, E. E.III, and Cammann, C. Standardized observations: An approach to measuring the nature of jobs. *Journal of Applied Psychology*, 1975, **60**, 171–181.

Kahn, R. L., Wolfe, D. M., Quinn, R. P., Snoek, J. D., and Rosenthal, R. A. *Organizational stress: Studies in role conflict and ambiguity*. New York: Wiley, 1964.

Kaplan, B. H., Cassel, J. C., and Gore, S. Social Support and health. *Medical Care*, 1977, **15**, 47–58.

Katz, D., Maccoby, N., and Morse, N. C. *Productivity, supervision, and morale in an office situation*. Ann Arbor, Mich.: Institute for Social Research, 1950.

Kaufmann, G. M. *The effects of social supports on job stressors and strains in police and nurses*. Doctoral project, Central Michigan University, 1981.

Kaufmann, G. M. and Beehr, T. A. *Social support, job stressors and employee strains among hospital nurses*. Paper presented at the meeting of the American Psychological Association, Washington, August 1982.

LaRocco, J. M., House, J. S., and French, J. R. P. Jr. Social support, occupational stress, and health. *Journal of Health and Social Behavior*, 1980, **21**, 202–218.

LaRocco, J. M. and Jones, A. P. Coworker and leader support as moderators of stress-strain relationships in work situations. *Journal of Applied Psychology*, 1978, **63**, 629–634.

Likert, R. *New patterns of management*. New York: McGraw-Hill, 1961.

Lindenthal, J. J., Thomas, C. S., and Myers, J. K. Psychological status and perception of primary and secondary support from the social milieu in time of crisis. *The Journal of Nervous and Mental Disease*, 1971, **153**, 92–98.

Payne, R. Organizational stress and social support. In C. L. Cooper and R. Payne (Eds.), *Current concerns in occupational stress*. New York: Wiley, 1980.

Pearlin, L. I. and Johnson, J. S. Marital status, life strains, and depression. *American Sociological Review*, 1977, **42**, 704–715.

Pinneau, S. R., Jr. *Effects of social support on occupational stress and strain*. Paper presented at the 84th Annual Convention of the American Psychological Association, Washington, D.C., 1976.

Roethlisberger, F. J. and Dickson, W. J. *Management and the worker*. Cambridge, Mass.: Harvard University Press, 1964.

Salancik, G. R. and Pfeffer, J. A social information processing approach to job attitudes and task design. *Administrative Science Quarterly*, 1978, **23**, 224–253.

Schachter, S. *The psychology of affiliation: Experimental studies of the sources of gregariousness*. Stanford, Calif.: Stanford University Press, 1959.

Scott, W. E. and Cummings, L. L. (Ed.) *Readings in organizational behavior and human performance*, rev. ed. Homewood, Ill.: Irwin, 1973.

Seashore, S. E. *Group cohesiveness in the industrial work group*. Ann Arbor, Mich.: Survey Research Center, Institute for Social Research, 1954.

Stogdill, R. M. *Handbook of leadership*. New York: Free Press, 1974.

Zajonc, R. B. Social facilitation. *Science*, 1965, **149**, 269–274.

PART SEVEN

CONCLUSION

This final section consists of two summary chapters in which the contents of the previous chapters are used to suggest directions for future research and to derive implications for managers and organization development practitioners. The complexity of making applied use of scientific knowledge is also examined.

CHAPTER FIFTEEN

An Evaluative Summary and Recommendations for Future Research

RABI S. BHAGAT AND TERRY A. BEEHR

One important aim of this book is to identify some of the systematic programs for long-range issues in organizational research on human stress and cognition. In Chapter 1 we began with a theoretical framework for understanding the concept of stress with the three components of uncertainty, importance, and duration. We have argued that these concepts are important in helping us understand the phenomenon of human stress with more rigor, and that the outcomes of stress reactions would also be interpreted more appropriately within such a theoretical framework.

The authors of the various chapters have applied this framework in the development of their arguments as well. In contrast to research on organizational effectiveness where researchers have generally aimed at replacing previous theoretical perspectives rather than adding to them (Cameron & Whetton, 1983), research on organizational stress has fortunately been cumulative. During the last few years empirical studies on job stress and outcome relations have followed some systematic theoretical models (e.g., the Kahn et al. (1964) role stress model; the French et al. (1974) (P-E) fit model, etc.) and we have some reliable sources of information based on research conducted within this social psychological mode. In this chapter we seek to identify some of the important themes of research on human stress and cognition within the theoretical framework developed in Chapter 1, derive some conclusions, and offer some guidelines for future research on organizational stress. Our conclusions are not, of course, meant to be a comprehensive summary of all the major points made in the previous chapters. Our main intent is to clarify the concept of stress and to encourage research along more fruitful avenues; the conclusions and guidelines proposed in this chapter reflect this intent. Two major sections follow. First we specify in theoretical terms some of the directions that we believe research in this area ought to take. In the second, "Guidelines for Enhancing Methodological Robustness," we propose four guidelines for enhancing the quality of research in this domain of organizational inquiry.

NEW DIRECTIONS FOR DEVELOPING THEORY IN HUMAN STRESS AND COGNITION IN ORGANIZATIONS

In articulating some of the strategic themes in the domain of research on stress, McGrath (1970) urged the researchers to approach the problem of stress systematically, with a set of concepts that depict the sequence of events (e.g., objective demand, subjective demands, response, and consequences) and their interrelationships. Research conducted by the Michigan group, especially by those working within the theoretical tradition of person-environment fit models have been useful in this regard. In particular, theoretical frameworks developed by French et al. (1974), McGrath (1976), Schuler (1980), and Payne (1980) have been effective in resolving some of the definitional issues pertinent to the construct of stress in organizations. Our own review of the empirical literature suggests that recent research on organizational stress has been rather explicit in dealing with the definitional issues (e.g., Jamal, 1984; Blau, 1981; Gupta and Beehr, 1979), and investigators have been able to build on the strength of findings of earlier studies. We urge the researchers to focus still more widely on other relevant issues and at the same time to integrate research findings in the area of stress in organizations with other more general psychological theories on human functioning. We propose the following new directions for theoretical research on human stress and cognition.

1. *Subjective Significance of Uncertainty, Importance, and Duration.* First, we recommend that future research endeavors should focus on the subjective meaning of the three basic components of stress as proposed in Chapter 1. Research is also needed on how individual difference−based variables (i.e., demographic and psychological) may aid in our attempts to understand the subjective significance of these three components. The way an individual appraises the subjective significance of these three components is of crucial importance in determining reaction to the event. Segovis, Bhagat, and Coelho (Chapter 9) provide some propositions that are likely to be helpful in future attempts at developing systematic research programs surrounding these issues.

2. *Cultural Significance of Stressful Events and Coping and Adaptational Mechanisms.* Second, the role of societal culture as well as organizational culture in determining the appropriateness of stress reactions and the effectiveness of coping mechanisms needs to be understood in greater depth. The literature on organizational stress has focused primarily on outcomes of stressful experiences. We know relatively little regarding how various stressful events are redefined in accordance with the schemes and scripts of a given organizational culture as well as with the culture of the society in which it is embedded. The September 1983 issue of the *Administrative Science Quarterly* on organizational culture has provided some new conceptual insights into this area. It would be useful for organizational researchers on human stress and cognition to incorporate these new developments in order to broaden the interpretation of their empirical results with reference to the relevant issues of both organizational and societal culture. Moreover, we need to know more about the structure of coping (Pearlin and Schooler, 1978) as well as the mechanism of coping and adaptation with reference to relevant contextual issues of these two cultures, that is, organizational as well as societal. Coping is best understood as a transactional process, as noted in Chapter 13, which unfolds over time as a constellation of many acts. There are undoubtedly styles or patterns of coping that are more or less characteristic of an individual in a given stressful encounter, but such styles often involve a combination of many acts and thoughts rather than a single one. Such acts or thoughts are likely to be governed by the values, norms, and role expectations embedded in a culture or a subculture within a given society. The observation that coping and adaptative technique of women, blacks, and ethnic minorities are different from those who occupy the important roles in a traditionally white Anglo Saxon organization needs to be examined more thoroughly with reference to the significance of cultural factors. Chapters in part V dealing with these issues provided important guidelines, but we need more empirical and replicated research guided by appropriate theoretical considerations.

3. *Relevance of Both Chronic as Well as Episodic Sources of Stress.* Careful examination of the literature on organizational stress suggests that researchers are primarily concerned with episodic events that have stressful consequences for an employee. Relatively little attention is paid to the role of chronic or ongoing events that might plague an individual employee day in and day out. Some of these events are transient, while others are of a recurring nature. For example, an abrasive supervisor who demands perfection in trivial tasks, a subordinate who always complains of inadequate supplies necessary to complete an assignment, or a persistently sick child at home could produce stressful effects on an employee which indeed have important adaptive consequences (Kanner et al., 1981; DeLongis et al., 1982). These chronic events—termed *daily hassles* by Lazarus and his associates—have been found to be better predictors of

health outcomes, compared with life events, which are more episodic or acute in nature. DeLongis and others (1982) have suggested that "hassles," or these chronic events, are more *proximal* measures of stress, whereas the episodic events reflect *distal* measures. As Bhagat argued in Chapter 8, one can make a strong case for the argument based on evidence found in recent clinical literature that chronic events are more powerful predictors of important stress-related outcomes. In addition to these chronic sources of stress, their counterpart—termed *daily uplifts* by Lazarus and his associates—have also been found to be effective in predicting stress outcomes. For example, a complimentary remark from one's colleagues, an inbasket free from unnecessary and troublesome paperwork, a smile from one's spouse, and so on have a hedonic quality and contribute to one's overall sense of emotional well-being on a daily basis. Klinger (1975, 1977) has noted that hassles and uplifts are likely to be associated with an individual's current concerns and commitments. In addition, since these concerns tend to shift across one's life span (Ryff and Baltes, 1976), the variability and the meaningfulness of these hassles and uplifts also change in the course of one's life span. We believe that it is important for researchers working with causes and consequences of stress in organizations to focus attention on this emergent trend in the social and clinical psychology. It would be useful to develop a taxonomy of work-related hassles and uplifts for various occupational groups and also to examine how the relevance of these factors changes in the working population with aging and during critical life event changes (Lazarus and DeLongis, 1983). As Bhagat has argued in Chapter 8, we are likely to benefit from a closer scrutiny of this area. In the conceptual model of stress (Chapter 1), the inclusion of duration suggests the relevance of chronic or persistent stresses that affect employees. In Chapter 4 Jick has also noted that multiple budget cuts have stronger effects than single cuts in generating chronic or persistent stress among those who experience such budget cuts.

4. *Broader Range of Dependent Variables.*   Recent research on organizational stress has focused on organizationally valued outcomes such as job satisfaction, absenteeism, turnover, and performance. This line of work reflects the established tradition of research in industrial and organizational psychology, whose primary concern has been to predict outcomes that affect productivity of work organizations. While research emphasis along these lines is unlikely to discontinue in the near future, we recommend focusing attention on other relevant outcomes of stressful experiences in organizations. For example, do capacities for creativity and innovativeness suffer from role overload and underutilization of skills? What are some of the health-related consequences of stress that result from, say, budget cuts, experience of discrimination, and failure to cope with an abrasive superior? Are organizational politics and strategies for upward influences results of persistent role ambiguities experienced during various organizational transitions or during changes in organizational

culture and leadership? Does underutilization of skills over an extended period affect the self-esteem and mental health of women and other minority professionals of the organization? What are some of the individual and organizational consequences of coping with stressful life events? Why do some individuals choose to cope with the dilemmas of their life changes both in work situations (for example, during organzational transitions) as well as in nonwork situations (for example, the delinquency of one's children) by attempting to overperform in their organizational roles? How do stress-performance relationships change over time, especially during the course of one's career and life? We have little doubt that simple bivariate relationships between stress and individual performance effectiveness masks most of the inherent complexity of this intriguing phenomenon. It is not clear that the widely held beliefs about an "inverted-U" relationship between stress (arousal level) and performance are necessarily true. In fact, one of the difficulties with the arousal explanation is that it can rather readily "explain" almost any combination of results dealing with stress and performance. Earlier research by Broadbent (1971), Näätänen (1973), and more recently Jamal (1984) have cast doubt on the existence of this rather straightforward explanation. We believe it would be useful to examine the role of potential moderators of this relationship both in terms of individual cognitive characteristics and organizational control–related characteristics. Bhagat (1983) has provided a comprehensive research model demonstrating the relevance of several such moderating influences on stress-performance effectiveness links. It would also be of considerable interest to know which aspect of individual performance (quantity, quality, or creativity, etc.) is most affected by stress and under what kind of situational influences?

All in all, we favor broadening the range of dependent variables normally investigated in organizational research on human stress and cognition. The experience of stress affects several different and important aspects of human functioning (Hogan and Hogan, 1982; Lazarus and Launier, 1978). It is important that organizational psychologists increase their theoretical contributions to the growing field.

5. *Problems of Temporal Considerations and Generalizability.*   McGrath (1970), in his recommendations for improving the rigor of stress research, noted that temporal dynamics of task-and role-related demands, temporal variations in human responses, temporal artifacts in measuring instruments, and most importantly, temporal variations of the coping and adaptation skills are crucial. He noted that research dealing with these issues should also focus on interactive effects of various settings such as physical, social, psychological, technological, or temporal aspects of stress-related adjustments and coping effectiveness. Looking back at the empirical evidence collected during the past 14 years,we find that this important recommendation has largely been ignored. Eden's (1982) analysis of multiple interrupted time-series data on critical job events is a notable exception.

We need more such studies in order to further enhance our understanding of the role of temporal factors in employee responses to organizationally induced stress. One important area that would benefit if such a recommendation is taken seriously is the role of moderator variables in stress research. Clearly there are other ways to analyze the 'stress-buffering' interactions besides the traditional interaction term in typical ANOVA designs or the interactive term in moderated regression formulations. Especially when we distinguish between environmental and personal aspects of coping resources, it becomes evident that certain environmentally based coping resources, such as social support from family, friends, and coworkers, are obtained from the individual's participation in these social groups. As noted by Beehr Chapter 14, employees may respond differently to various kinds of social support systems. It would be useful for researchers to follow the recommendations made by Terborg (1981) and Schneider (1983) in dealing with some of the complexities concerning the role of moderators in studies that explicitly deal with temporal dynamics of stress. In particular, we recommend investigation of the notion of reciprocal influence between the person and the situation over time (Terborg, 1981). Individuals appraise stressful events and react to them in a rather complex manner (Lazarus and Launier, 1978; Segovis, Bhagat, and Coelho, Chapter 9), which is best understood as a reciprocal process. Lazarus and Launier (1978), emphatically note that the continuous flow of person-environment relationships in stress, emotion, and coping has not been properly assessed in the traditional S-O-R linear causation models or in either traditional experimental or nonexperimental research.

Consider the stressful effects of job loss. The nature of stress changes over time, as do the coping tasks that the employee must perform. Continued unemployment might even reduce the level of social support one would otherwise experience because of the rearrangement of family roles that often take place in such situations. At any rate we need to be more concerned with such reciprocal influences between the person and his or her environment than we are at present.

Mohr (1982), in a fascinating chapter (Chapter 2) dealing with approaches to explanation in organizational sciences, distinguishes between variance and process theories. Process theories, as Mohr (1982) argues, are of great significance for developing theories in science, but the variance-theory outlook has generally dominated research traditions within social and behavioral sciences. Process theories deal with discrete states and events. Time-ordering among the contributing events is generally critical for the final outcome that is being explained. Process theories appear to be uniquely suited for explaining reciprocal relationships between the person and the environment that unfold over time. For detailed discussion of the utility of process theories in organizational theorizing, we recommend Mohr's 1982 book on *Explaining Organizational Behavior*.

In a related vein, Pearlin et al, (1981) articulate the need for conceptualizing life events, chronic life strains, self-concepts, coping, and social support within the framework of a longitudinal process model. Research on organizational stress has focused on various components of stress and their influence on outcome variables, with some selective attention to moderating influences (see Beehr, 1976; Jamal,1984 as examples), but the role of intricate linkages that connect these events are not adequately understood. As early as 1970, Mechanic, reflecting on the problems of developing a social psychology of adaptation of stress, commented that current social psychological theories share a common deficit in dealing with some of the central paradigmatic concerns of stress theories. Most of the theories are characterized by an extremely passive view of people, and some social psychological investigations are so structured that they do not allow the subject ample opportunities—even in real life organizational contexts—to select alternatives, to manage critical environmental contingencies, and in general to construe the situation so that the coping and adaptation is achieved. Mechanic also noted that the study of social stress, and we believe organizational stress, developed largely within the psychodynamic context and has been influenced by its assumptions. Such an orientation easily lends itself to a psychobiological and developmental orientation. While this orientation has resulted in some useful findings, there are others that merit attention as well. The processing of an individual's manipulation of the social environment and symbolic constructions that redefine environmental threat and stressful situations and assist in enactment (Weick, 1979) have received little attention from the researchers. The assumption of "passivity" that developed in much social psychological thinking, particularly among behaviorists, Mechanic (1970) argued, had some methodological advantages, enabling precise measurement of changes in human responses in the laboratory contexts. This approach, however, has not been particularly helpful in incorporating the role of symbolic processes, especially symbolic interactionisms in theoretical frameworks for research on stress.

Symbolic interaction views such as those of Mead (1934), Cooley (1956), Thomas (as quoted in Volkart, 1951), and Goffman (1959) developed about the same time as psychodynamic approaches and laboratory experimentation. In contrast to the psychodynamic framework, this view emphasizes the concept of "self" as derived from the interaction of symbolic communications and the individual's inherent potential to make meaningful responses to stressful events in ways that are as varied as the nature of symbolic environments that they create in a sociohistorical sense. The symbolic-interaction view, in contrast to the psychodynamic paradigm, regards man as an active participant in social processes and emphasizes the need to consider the influence of culture and social structure in shaping human responses for dealing with environmentally induced crises and stressful events. Such a perspective focuses on the nature of social psychological and symbolic processes in a dynamic sense. Generalizability

of the results in this theoretical tradition are made only with reference
to these processes that unfold over time. The implications of this perspective still need to be understood. If we accept this idea, it would generate a series of fresh insights in the current organizational research on
stress and cognition.

6. *Greater Emphasis on Interdisciplinary Frameworks.* As several
authors (Jick, Chapter 4; Cooper and McGoldrick, Chapter 7; Bhagat,
Chapter 8) have shown, the need for interdisciplinary frameworks to
explain the entire stress process is growing in importance. In the past we
have seen relatively little in the way of developing such frameworks to
grapple with the complexity of stress-related phenomena in work organizations. Dominant traditions of social psychological research on stress and
cognition have influenced the approaches to the problem, and the potential
contributions of other social science disciplines have not been recognized.
A closer examination of the major academic journals of the organizational
sciences such as *Administrative Science Quarterly, Journal of Applied
Psychology, Organizational Behavior and Human Performance, Academy
of Management Journal, and Human Relations* would reveal that sociological and health science – based research are hardly referred to, either in the
design of the studies or in the interpretation of the results.

We find that such a state of affairs poses a major problem in developing
directions within the field. An interesting analysis of the causes of such
divergence and how they have affected the paradigmatic status of organizational psychology has been offered by Kahn (1979) in his invited address
to the division of social psychology of the American Psychological Association. Kahn noted that the separation of the social psychological researchers into two camps, that is psychological social psychology and sociological
social psychology, has been particularly detrimental for organizational
psychology. According to him mainstream sociological thought has been
ideologically skeptical of social psychology, and sociological social psychology has retained its strong identification with sociology rather than
orienting itself toward interdisciplinary alliances. The emphasis has been
on macrosocial variables—social class, urban residence, occupational mobility, industrialization, and other supraorganizational and societal characteristics. These macro-level variables have been studied in relation to
stress experiences and stress outcomes, but without significant attention
to the role of interpersonal and psychological processes that produce these
outcomes. Researchers focusing on organizational antecedents of stress
and stress reactions have largely been unaware of these developments,
even though the potential for enriching the research process is considerable. Roberts et al. (1978) contrasted the theoretical and methodological
advantages and disadvantages of several social science disciplines and
also provided some blueprints for developing an interdisciplinary organizational science. It would be indeed very useful for future organizational

research on human stress and cognition to have a strong interdisciplinary focus along the lines suggested by Roberts et al. (1978). Research on budget cuts and their stressful consequences, as an example, is best understood by a team of investigators that includes economists, clinical psychologists, and organizational researchers. A multidisciplinary research team would aid in the identification of sources of variance that are presently being given unidisciplinary and incomplete interpretations. It has been said that if a problem is presented to an economist, an economic solution will be observed. The same problem presented to a psychologist will yield a psychological solution. The same problem presented still again to a political scientist will be approached through the avenues of politics. Yet the optimal solution might depend on a combination of all three perspectives. A recent handbook on stress and anxiety by Kutash et al. (1980) provides multidisciplinary theoretical perspectives and should be a valuable source in this area. So it is with organizational research on human stress and cognition. An interdisciplinary research orientation would yield benefits that would have far-reaching consequences for the state of theory development in this important domain.

GUIDELINES FOR ENHANCING METHODOLOGICAL ROBUSTNESS

Four major systematic guidelines are presented in this section. They are framed in the form of questions that researchers on organizational stress and cognitions ought to confront in the formative stages of their methodological designs. We believe that these guides can help remove some of the persistent methodological problems that are currently present in organizational research on human stress and cognition. These guides are proposed to be comprehensive and interrelated. If possible, we need to pay attention to all of them.

Guide 1: What are the Perspectives and Constraints in Applying the Multimethod, Multi trait (MM-MT) Paradigm in Construct Validation Efforts?

Stress must be defined and assessed from someone's viewpoint, and it is important to understand the nature of convergence or divergence that exists among several possible operationalizations of a stress-related construct. McGrath (1976) voiced a similar concern in that if multiple measures of the stress construct do not converge, how are we to interpret such information? No agreed upon decision rule is yet available to identify the appropriateness of this construct validity issue, and the solution depends on the nature of the questions being asked and the personal biases of the researcher. Nevertheless, it is important to specify the theoretical rationale for favoring one particular operational formulation over another so that what appears to be a low pattern of convergence in the MM-MT matrix could be interpreted within a meaningful framework.

Guide 2: What Are the Possibilities in the Various Assessment Phases of Stress Process for Triangulation of Research Methods?

As has been argued by the authors in various chapters of this book, perceptions of stress lie in the eyes of the beholder. Subjective appraisal of the stressful event plays the most crucial role in determining both the selection of the response modalities and the effectiveness of the coping techniques. It may help, therefore, to look for more vivid and enriched descriptions of such processes in qualitative as well as quantitative terms. Unfortunately, the predominance of quantitative methodologies in organizational psychology has led to the myopic view that research in a more qualitative mode either is not rigorous enough to meet the publication-related criteria in scientific journals or, at best, is impossible to conduct. However, as we have recently seen, the critical aspects of some of quantitative techniques favored by organizational psychologists have come under increasing scrutiny. *Administrative Science Quarterly*'s December, 1979, issue has established the legitimate role of qualitative methodologies in organizational sciences. Since then a number of important publications dealing with the philosophy and the technology of qualitative methodologies have appeared in the academic literature (Morgan and Smircich, 1980; Calder, 1980; Morgan, 1983). A recent symposium chaired by Bhagat (1983) also focused on issues related to the relevance of unobtrusive and contextual information in research on organizational stress and cognition. Jick (1979) discussed the process and strategy of triangulation of both types of methodologies in an innovative manner. We believe that these developments have important implications for future organizational research related to stress. We would recommend Lawler, Nadler, and Cammann's (1980) book on *Organizational Assessment* and Folger and Belew's forthcoming chapter on unobtrusive measures in *Research on Organizational Behavior* as useful sources of references. Bhagat's (1983) unobtrusive study of stressful effects of organizational transitions is an example of how one may arrive at meaningful research findings without necessarily sacrificing scientific rigor, understood even in a traditional sense of the term. To reiterate, we need studies that are designed to capture the emic aspects (Morey and Luthans, 1984) of the experience of stress and the accompanying processes. Organizational research on stress offers unique potential as a fertile ground for attempting triangulation techniques. It is hoped that this trend would reduce what Kasl (1978) called "a self-serving methodological trap which has tended to trivialize a good deal of research on stress" (p. 13).

Guide 3: What Are the Major Measurement-Related Issues?

Measurement-related issues in organizational stress and cognition vary considerably. There might be some difficulty in developing appropriate measures of uncertainty, importance, and duration. Uncertainty, especially, might be difficult to measure because of our use of two expectancies, that is, expectancy relating effort to performance and that relating performance to outcomes.

An overwhelming majority of studies are considerably weak in that both independent and dependent variables are measured with same method, usually self-reports by the subjects. The problem of confoundedness with dependent variables is serious. It increases the size of the correlation between measures of stress and the outcome variables, thereby overestimating the magnitude of the true relationships. In addition, the problems of priming, response consistency, and other related social desirability phenomena continue to affect the quality of data that is collected using primarily self-report techniques. One important way would be to put less reliance on self-report measures and to continue searching for other meaningful ways to assess dependent variables in a nomological network. Trace measures of outcome variables (Bhagat, 1983) would be quite helpful, but those measures presuppose that the researcher is as concerned with the notion of *mean* as with the notion of *variance* (Webb and Weick, 1979). Archival records in organizational settings are also useful, even though they may not be free from errors (Folger and Belew, in press). As already noted, the solution to the problem of confoundedness in stress research is best solved with the help of an imaginative mind in contrast to overemphasis on a given technique per se or enhanced quantitative sophistication. Lazarus and DeLongis (1983) discuss some crucial problems of measurement of stressful life events, which we need to consider in our research designs.

Guide 4: What Are the Advantages of Longitudinal versus Cross-Sectional Studies?

Much of the empirical literature on organizational stress and coping uses predominantly cross-sectional designs. There are obvious weaknesses to this kind of a design, as noted in several chapters of this book. It is quite likely that measurement of various stress-related constructs, including such moderating influences as social support and coping effectiveness, change over one's life span and in response to organizational role demands. Such systematic changes are impossible to assess in cross-sectional designs. Pearlin and Lieberman (1977) found, for example, that younger workers are more likely than older ones to experience disruptions with formation and dissolution of marriages and familial obligations. Older workers, on the other hand, are more apt to be confronted with illness and mortality. Longitudinal studies (Birren, Butler, Greenhouse, Sokolaff, and Yarrow, 1971; Granick and Patterson,1971) suggest that systematic variations in various age cohorts, as opposed to central tendencies, is the most prevalent pattern. We need to know how people change their coping techniques when they are unable to change the conditions of their jobs easily, and they must live with a job that is either too demanding or not demanding enough. Research on social support also reveals some interesting insights that would otherwise be absent in cross-sectional studies. It seems as though access to social support mechanisms is, at least in part, a function of an individual's social skills that enable him or her to develop and maintain close relationships. The social skills in their turn are affected by socioeconomic status, membership in certain disadvantaged groups, and so on. Complex patterns of bidirectional relationships, which unfold over time, may be present. Longitudinal research on social support that enables researchers to focus on these interactive issues is most appropriate for studies dealing with the moderating role of social supports (Thoits, 1982). Longitudinal research would also enable us to identify other relevant issues. For example, what is the nature of relationship between work stress and, say, intellectual functioning (Kohn and Schooler, 1983) and between stress and illness (Kobosa and Puccetti, 1983)? It would enable us to examine the effects of work-related stress on the family members or coworkers of the individual experiencing it. This area of study, heretofore almost totally unexplored, can contribute much to research on stress.

CONCLUSION

Our purpose in this chapter has been to go beyond the scope of each of the previous chapters and offer some guidelines for improving the theoretical rigor and methodological robustness of research on organizational stress. We have highlighted several interrelated themes underlying this mission. The history of research on stress in social, clinical, and medical sciences shows that each has followed its distinctive traditions and themes. We should be able to integrate these themes in organizational sciences (Payne et al., 1982). At the same time, we have a unique role to play in organizational science in order to understand the role of organizational factors and their symbolic significance in the experience of human stress. The time has come for organizational psychology based research on stress to contribute to knowledge of stress in other disciplines. The need to avoid a continuation of fragmented empirical studies typical in the past literature and to merge perspectives into an interdisciplinary mode is critical at this point of theory development. It seems clear that we need to work toward restructuring this view as a first step.

REFERENCES

Beehr, T. A. Perceived situational moderators of the relationship between subjective role ambiguity and role strain. *Journal of Applied Psychology*, 1976, **61**, 35–40.

Bhagat, R. S. Innovative uses of unobtrusive and contextual information in research on human stress and cognition in organizations. Paper presented at the Academy of Management joint symposium on qualitative versus quantitative measures, Dallas, Texas, (1984).

Birren, J. E., Butler, R. N., Greenhouse, S. W., Sokoloff, L., and Yarrow, M. R. (Eds.) *Human aging: A biological and behavioral study.* Washington, D.C.: U.S. Government Printing Office, 1971.

Blau, G. An empirical investigation of job stress, social support, service length and job strain. *Organizational Behavior and Human Performance*, 1981, **27**, 279–302.

Broadbent, D. E. *Decision and stress.* New York: Academic Press, 1971.

Calder, B. J. Focus group interviews and qualitative research in organizations. In E. E. Lawler, D. A. Nadler, and C. Cammann (Eds.), *Organizational assessment.* New York: Wiley, 1980, 399–417.

Cameron, K. S. and Whetten, D. A. *Organizational effectiveness: A comparison of multiple models.* New York: Academic Press, 1983.

Cooley, C. H. *Social organization and human nature and the social order.* New York: Free Press, 1956.

DeLongis, A., Coyne, J. C., Dakof, G., Folkman, S., and Lazarus, R. S. Relationship of daily hassles, uplifts and major life events to health status. *Health Psychology*, 1982, **I**, 119–136.

Daft, R. L. Learning the graft of organizational research. *Academy of Management Review*, 1983, **8** (4), 539–596.

Dohrenwend, B. S. and Dohrenwend, B. P. Overview and prospects for research on stressful life events. In B. S. Dohrenwend and B. P. Dohrenwend (Eds.), *Stressful life events. Their nature and effects.* New York: Wiley, 1979.

Eden, D. Critical job events, acute stress and strain: A multiple interrupted time series. *Organizational Behavior and Human Performance*, 1982, **30** (3), 312–329.

Folger, R. and Belew, J. Nonreactive measures in organizational settings with particular attention to absenteeism and occupational stress. In B. M. Staw and L. L. Cummings (Eds.) *Research in organizational behavior*, Greenwich, Conn.: JAI Press (in press).

French, J. R., Rodgers, R., and Cobb, S. Person-environment fit. In G. A. Coelho, H. Hamburg, and J. Adams (Eds.), *Coping and adaptation.* New York: Basic Books, 1974.

Granick, S. and Patterson, R. D. *Human aging II: An 11-year follow-up biomedical and behavioral study.* Washington, D.C.: U.S. Government Printing Office, 1971.

Goffman, E. *Presentation of self in everyday life.* New York: Doubleday, 1959.

Gupta, N. and Beehr, T. A. Job stress and employee behaviors. *Organizational Behavior and Human Performance*, 1979, **23**, 373–387.

Hogan, R. and Hogan, J. C. Subjective correlates of stress and human performance. In E. A. Alluisi and E. A. Fleishman (Eds.) *Human performance and productivity: Stress and performance effectiveness.* Hillsdale, N. J.: LEA Associates Publishing, 1982.

Jamal, M. Job stress and job performance controversy. An empirical assessment. *Organizational Behavior and Human Performance*, 1984, **33**(1), 1–21.

Jick, T. D. Mixing qualitative and quantitative methods: Triangulation in action. *Administrative Science Quarterly*, 1979, **24**(4), 602–611.

Kahn, R. L. Promise and postponement: The convergence of social and organizational psychology. Invited address, social psychology division, American Psychological Association, New York, 1979.

Kahn, R. L., Wolfe, D. M. Quinn, R. P., Snoek, J. D., and Rosenthal, R. A. *Organizational stress: Studies in role conflict and ambiguity.* New York: Wiley, 1964.

Kanner, A. D., Coyne, J. C., Schaefer, C., and Lazarus, R. S. Comparison of two modes of stress measurement: Daily hassles and uplifts versus major life events. *Journal of Behavioral Medicine,* 1981, **4**, 1–39.

Kasl, S. V. Epidemiological contributions to the study of work stress. In C. L. Cooper and R. Payne (Eds.), *Stress at work.* Chichester: Wiley, 1980, 3–48.

Klinger, E. Consequences of commitment to and disengagement from incentives. *Psychological Review,* 1975, **82**, 1–25.

Klinger, E. *Meaning and void.* Minneapolis: University of Minnesota Press, 1977.

Kobasa, S. C. O. and Puccetti, M. C. Personality and social resources in stress resistance. *Personality and Social Psychology,* 1983, **45**(4), 839–850.

Kohn, M. L. and Schooler, C. *Work and personality: An inquiry into the impact of social stratification.* Norwood, N. J.: Ablex Publishing, 1983.

Kutash, I. L., Schlesinger, L. B., and Associates. *Handbook of stress and anxiety,* San Francisco: Jossey-Bass, 1980.

Lawler, E. E., Nadler, D. A., and Cammann, C. *Organizational Assessment: Perspectives on the measurement of organizational behavior and the quality of work life,* New York: Wiley-Interscience, 1980.

Lazarus, R. S. and DeLongis, A. Psychological stress and coping in aging. *American Psychologist,* 1983, **38** (3), 4, 245–254.

Lazarus, R. S and Launier, R. Stress-related transactions between person and environment. In L. A. Pervin and M. Lewis (Eds.) *Perspectives in interactional psychology.* New York: Plenum, 1978, 287–327.

McGrath, J. E. Stress and behavior in organizations. In M. D. Dunnette (Ed.), *Handbook of industrial and organizational psychology.* Chicago: Rand McNally, 1976, 1351–1395.

McGrath, J. D. Some strategic considerations for future research on social psychological stress. In J. E. McGrath (Ed.), *Social Psychological factors in stress.* New York: Holt, Rinehart & Winston, 1970.

Mead, G. H. *Mind, self and society.* Chicago: University of Chicago Press, 1934.

Mechanic, D. Some problems in developing a social psychology of adaptation to stress. In J. E. McGrath (Ed.), *Social psychological factors in stress.* New York: Holt, Rinehart & Winston, 1970.

Mitroff, Ian I. and Kilmann, Ralph, H. *Methodological approaches to social science.* San Francisco: Jossey-Bass, 1978.

Mohr, M. *Explaining organizational behavior.* San Francisco: Jossey-Bass, 1982.

Morey, N. C. and Luthans, F. An ethnic perspective and ethnoscience methods for organizational research. *Academy of Management Review,* **9**(1), 27–36.

Morgan, G. and Smircich, L. The case for qualitative research. *Academy of Management Review,* 1980, **5**, 491–500.

Morgan, G. (Ed.). *Beyond method.* Beverly Hills, Calif.: Sage, 1983.

Näätänen, R. The inverted -U relationship between activation and performance: A critical review. In S. Kornblum (Ed.), *Attention and performance,* Vol. 4. New York: Academic Press, 1973.

Payne, R., Jick, T. D., and Burke, R. J. Whither stress research: An agenda for the 1980's. *Journal of Occupational Behavior,* 1982, **3**, 131–145.

Payne, R. Organizational stress and social support. In C. L. Cooper and R. Payne (Eds.), *Current concerns in occupational stress.* New York: Wiley, 1980.

Pearlin, L. I. and Lieberman, M. A. Social sources of emotional distress. In R. Simmons (Ed.), *Research in community mental health*. Greenwich, Conn.: JAI Press, 1977.

Pearlin, L. I., Menaghan, E. G., Lieberman, M. A., and Mullan, J. T. The stress process. *Journal of Health and Social Behavior*, 1981, **22**, 337–356.

Pearlin, L. I. and Schooler, C. The structure of coping. *Journal of Health and Social Behavior*, 1978, **19**, 2–21.

Roberts, K. H., Hulin, C. L., and Rousseau, D. M. *Developing an interdisciplinary science on organizations*. San Francisco: Jossey-Bass, 1978.

Ryff, C. D. and Baltes, P. B. Value transition and adult development of women: The instrumentality terminality sequence hypothesis. *Developmental Psychology*, 1976, **12**, 567–568.

Schneider, B. Interactional psychology and organizational behavior. In L. L. Cummings and B. M. Staw (Eds.), *Research in organizational behavior*, Vol. 5. Greenwich, Conn.: JAI Press, 1983, 1–32.

Schuler, R. S. Definition and conceptualization of stress in organizations. *Organizational Behavior and Human Performance*, 1980, **25**, 184–215.

Tausig, M. Measuring life events. *Journal of Health and Social Behavior*, 1982, **23**(1), 52–64.

Terborg, J. R. Interactional psychology and research on human behavior in organizations. *Academy of Management Review*, 1981, **6**, 569–576.

Thoits, P. A. Conceptual, methodological and theoretical problems in studying social support as a buffer against life stress. *Journal of Health and Social Behavior*, 1982, **23** (2), 145–158.

Volkart, E. H. (Ed.) *Social behavior and personality*. New York: Social Science Research Council, 1951.

Webb, E. and Weick, K. E. Unobtrusive measures in organizational theory: A reminder. *Administrative Science Quarterly*, 1979, **24** (4), 750–760.

Weick, K. E. Cognitive processes in organizations. In B. M. Staw (Ed.) *Research in Organizational Behavior*, Vol. 1. Greenwich, Conn.: JAI Press, 1977, 41–74.

CHAPTER SIXTEEN

Utilization and Diffusion of Knowledge on Human Stress and Cognition in Organizations

Constraints and Perspectives

RABI S. BHAGAT AND TERRY A. BEEHR

As we discussed in the earlier chapter, our goal in this book has been to identify some of the systematic research programs for long-range issues in organizational stress and the effects of stress on both organizationally as well as personally valued outcomes. In this chapter, we raise the issue of utilization and diffusion of knowledge on human stress and cognition in organizations and focus on some of the factors that might act as constraints in the process of effective utilization of such knowledge. We also discuss the nature of some of the strategies that facilitate this process. The importance of stress and stress-related disorders for organizations is easily accepted if the volume of publications in professional as well as popular literature is considered. There are also systematic attempts to calculate the costs of various kinds of stress in both psychological as well as monetary terms.

1.   Medical experts in the United States and Britain estimate that up to 70 percent of all patients currently being treated by doctors in general practice suffer from environmental conditions that could be considered stressful (Blythe, 1973).

2.   Approximately 3.932 billion dollars are lost in the United States in terms of gross national product due to executive work days lost when these losses are either directly or indirectly attributed to stressful experiences at work (Greenwood and Greenwood, 1979).

3.   The national cost of executive stress measured in terms of dollar values of days lost, hospitalization and outpatient visits, and mortality is approximately 10 billion dollars. Using 1970 census figures, the national cost of executive stress in 1970 is exceeded by the revenue of only three industrial corporations in that year (Greenwood and Greenwood, 1979).

4.   In intangible terms, the cost of employee stress to organizations is quite high. One stressed individual in an organization can serve as a potential stressor for many others with whom interaction takes place. In fact, the human and organizational costs of having abrasive personalities work in supervisory roles are almost incalculable (Levinson, 1978).

5.   Studies by occupational epidemiologists reveal significant differences in suicide rates among various occupational groups which could be attributed to stress-related factors in the work situation. For example, police officers, sheriffs, and marshals have at least twice as high suicide rates as do teachers, lawyers, and judges (Guralwick, 1963). Among professional groups such as physicians and psychologists, women have higher suicide rates than men, even though the reverse is true in the general population (Mausher and Steppacher, 1973). Also, among physicians, occupational demands of specialities like dentistry, psychiatry, ophthalmology, and anesthesiology are at least partially responsible for above average suicide rates in these groups compared to physicians in specialties like pediatrics, pathology, and surgery. The suicide rate among optometrists tends to be about one-tenth the rate of opthalmologists (Daubs, 1973).

6.   Syme and his associates (Syme et al., 1964, 1965) report that individuals with coronary heart disease (CHD) had experienced more occupational changes and had been in their principal occupation for fewer years than matched controls. Their findings indicate that stressful effects of occupational mobility might be at least partially responsible for such health-related effects.

These and similar accounts demonstrate the importance of the effects of stress and its consequences for employees and organizations. No one really knows if there is more stress now than in the past, but many experts believe that it has become more pervasive. Concern over the "stress epidemic" has encouraged the development of new fields of specialities: for example, *behavioral medicine* to battle stress-related illness and *psychoneuro-immunology* to explore the way emotional states affect the body's defenses. Major corporations such as the Kimberly-Clark Corporation, Tenneco, Inc., Hospital Corporation of America, Texas Instruments,

Electronics Data Systems, and others have established fairly elaborate stress-management programs to help harried and stressed employees to cope. And in the popular press, we are given vivid accounts of how individuals—famous as well as not so famous—engage in various kinds of health-related programs such as aerobic exercises, jogging, transcendental meditation, and even hot-tubbing to reduce stress and strain in their lives.

Despite all these trends, there is still widespread agreement that scientific research-based findings on organizational processes that are the causes and consequences of stress have done relatively little to solve organizational and human problems of the type mentioned earlier. Common to these findings is the assumption that knowledge of human stress and cognition—however useful it may be in scientific terms—is not being appropriately utilized by policymakers in various organizations. Comments to this effect are being heard more frequently at professional conventions such as the Academy of Management and the American Psychological Association, where researchers have an opportunity to discuss the ultimate purpose of their work—especially relevant issues concerning utilization and diffusion of knowledge on the causes and consequences of stress in organizations. Thomas and Kilmann (1983) capture this sentiment well by noting that "the simple fact that practitioners are unlikely to read and take note of the articles in our most prestigious journals leaves one wondering if academics are just writing to one another to maintain their existence" (p. 69). The basic debate seems to focus on the question of scientific rigor versus practical relevance of the findings.

Those who are satisfied with the present state of utilization of organizational research-based knowledge in contemporary organizations seem to focus more on the issues surrounding validity and robustness of organizational research. According to this group, research ought to be even more rigorous and journals should use higher standards of scientific precision in evaluating articles for publication. The fact that practitioners are unlikely to read and understand some of these rigorous articles is not of much importance to this group.

In contrast to this view, there is another perspective emerging from a group of scholars who would like to see increased emphasis on relevance in organizational research. This group argues that the validity criterion has been overemphasized to the exclusion of a relevance criterion. This group of researchers is concerned about the utility of the scientifically based rigorous knowledge if it is not conceived and communicated to practitioners in a manner relevant to their problems and contexts. Relevance is defined as the usefulness of a study's findings for a practitioner's decisions and actions. In a survey of 561 members of the Academy of Management, Thomas and Kilmann (1983) found the widely shared view that while the standards of rigor of current organizational research are high, the relevance or practical usefulness of such rigorous research is less than acceptable. Seventy six percent responded noting that the research findings appearing in the academic journals were products of carefully designed rigorous research investigations. In contrast 67 percent noted that the research findings were of some but insufficient relevance and 12 percent responded that the findings were of no value or irrelevant from the perspective of the practitioner. The notion that organizational researchers ought to carefully consider the criterion of usefulness of their findings while designing their research investigations has become an important issue. The special issues of *Administrative Science Quarterly* on utilization of organizational research (Beyer, 1982, 1983) and the University of Pittsburgh conference on producing useful knowledge (Kilmann et al., 1983) evaluate the usefulness of existing theories in organizational sciences and offer guidelines for improving the utilization of research findings. In this chapter, we examine some of the constraints to effective utilization of knowledge on human stress and cognition in organizations and offer some suggestions for improving such a state of affairs.

CONSTRAINT 1: SIGNIFICANCE OF USEFULNESS AS A RESEARCH CRITERION

For most managers, the value of a theoretical framework lies in its immediate utility in understanding, explaining, motivating, and communicating the need for some programmatic changes within their specific organizational settings. Peter Mathias, a senior manager of the General Foods Corporation, illustrates the differences in the way usefulness is perceived between researchers and practitioners by noting the following:

1. Managers usually approach problems by thinking through various analogies, whereas researchers are prone to specification, quantification, and model building.

2. Managers are likely to accept the test of the marketplace [i.e., *Theory Z* by William Ouchi (1981) is a best-seller among senior managers], whereas researchers are more concerned with acceptability of findings in the current research literature.

3. Managers are likely to find particularly useful those results that are easily *implemented*, enhance their group's effectiveness, and also have potential for advancing their careers in the organization. In contrast, the researchers are more concerned with *application* and *fine-tuning*, their favorite concepts and theories. It is the lack of fit between reality *mapped* and reality *captured* and especially the causes and consequences of such fits and misfits that interest academic researchers. On the other hand, managers are more concerned with grappling with an identifiable portion

of their organizational reality in terms of generating programs, policies, and future strategies. Whether the particular theory that worked conforms neatly to a given theoretical framework is of little significance for the practicing manager.

4. As a rule, managers are concerned with (1) improvement in performances of their subunits and their total organizational system and (2) management of system-wide changes in programs and policies that meet with the least resistance in their organizational cultures. Researchers, however, are more concerned with (1) theoretical implications of successes and failures of various programs and (2) communicating with scholars in the field about the significance of such implications in line with the expectations of their academic cultures.

We agree with Mathias that these differences are indeed real and pose significant problems in creating useful knowledge. In fact, Dunbar (1983) in an attempt to determine the extent to which an applied administrative science has developed, found that articles published in the *Administrative Science Quarterly* (a prestigious academic journal) emphasize a relatively objective view of organizations and are relatively unconcerned about relating findings to practice. On the other hand, *Harvard Business Review*, a practitioner-oriented journal, uses examples to illustrate rationalization about organizational phenomena, particular meanings proposed by the authors' analogies are accepted as data, and the scientific bases of the articles are not as apparent as their concern for relating the findings to practice. We believe that sharply different conceptions of usefulness currently exist and will continue to exist in the field. Beres (1983) proposes that usefulness as a research criterion is a function of (1) the user, (2) the time at which the findings are discovered, and (3) those in positions of power. She notes that while strong cooperation (and perhaps co-optation) between practitioners and organizational researchers might make it easier to produce useful knowledge from the perspective of the practitioner, it might also have the adverse effect of producing knowledge that serves the immediate vested interests of the managerial elite. The temporal perspective would therefore be lost and the status of a value-free organizational science would be severely undermined in the eyes of society. In a similar vein, Bhagat (1983) argued that in order to facilitate intellectual performance and utilization of current organizational science, it might be useful to recognize the existence of two contrasting paradigms—paradigms I and II. In the paradigm II view of organizational science, the researcher tends to be more aware of his or her unique sociocultural and sociohistorical position and accepts that scientific knowledge generated through particularistic and intrasubjective encounters is valid as well. There are other views of usefulness and the debate is far from over. The point is that issues concerning usefulness as a research criterion are not resolved as yet.

Researchers must achieve a more concrete understanding of the significance of usefulness—not only in terms of the philosophy and sociology of science but also in terms of its impact in the reward structure of the discipline and the universities in which they work (for further details see Bhagat, 1983; Thomas and Kilmann, 1983).

CONSTRAINT 2: CHOICE OF THE RESEARCH PROBLEM

What is the process by which researchers engage in significant research? How does a researcher identify innovative research projects that result in substantial increments in knowledge? Campbell, Daft, and Hulin (1982), in a monograph designed to provide better guidelines for organizational researchers in choosing "what to study," note that

> . . . . the selection of innovative research questions is not a single act or decision. Significant research is a process, an attitude, a way of thinking. Significant research is accomplished by people who are motivated to do significant research, who are willing to pay the cost in time and effort. (p. 109).

We suggest that the graduate training in organizational sciences in the departments of psychology and sociology and in business schools prepare researchers to think of significant research problems primarily in an academic mode. Pion and Lipsey (1984) found that graduates who took jobs outside of academia reported that it was not their first choice, for the most part, and that they would have preferred an academic job. Furthermore, they felt that the academic training did not seem to prepare them well for jobs in the practitioner-oriented service and/or organizational settings and they did not value such jobs much either. This is disappointing, considering that the growth rate of employment in the academic sector is slackening whereas nonacademic (business, federal, state, and local government agencies) employment has been increasing at a steady rate (Pion and Lipsey, 1984). We believe that the most important factor responsible for this state of affairs is the selection of content areas for research in the universities. As the choice of the problem becomes narrowly defined to make it amenable to rigorous research, the content of the study itself becomes devoid of practical issues of ultimate usefulness. Webb (1961), in his careful analysis of the issues surrounding choice of the problem, advised us that "it is likely that we can not all become geniuses. We can at least try to be less trivial. Learn as much as we can, believe in new ways, seek as great extensity in our variables as we can." (p. 227). Our analysis of the present trend of research in human stress and cognition suggests that choice of the problem is the second major constraint that affects usefulness.

CONSTRAINT 3: IGNORANCE OF ORGANIZATIONAL CULTURE AND POLICY VACUUMS IN THE IMPLEMENTATION PROCESS

Roy Serpa (1983), in his analysis of why some important research findings do not get appropriately utilized in organizations, noted that many researchers are acutely unaware of the various cultural forces that affect the utilization process. He warns researchers not to automatically expect that if there is need for change, new models and methods will be "warmly received and implemented with dedication" (p. 130). There is a culture of the organizations and the findings must be examined and interpreted in light of the values and culture of the dominant coalitions of the organization before they are implemented. The process, as Serpa has aptly noted, is not necessarily a rational one and the researchers must experience some frustration before they can create an environment in their client setting that will facilitate the process of implementation. The significance of this constraint became clear to one of the authors (Bhagat) when he made several presentations of his findings relating the effects of life stress on work outcomes in various academic as well as corporate settings. While the academic researchers expressed their interest and suggested various steps for increasing their relevance to organizations, the corporate managers were more keen in finding the results which could be immediately incorporated within some of their programs of well being and aerobics exercises that they were sponsoring. In their specific organizational cultures, those programs that focused primarily on moderating physiological antecedents and consequences of the stress resilience process had been implemented. As a result, findings from other research programs had to be evaluated for their usefulness in terms of the criterion variables of the established programs regardless of whether such an emphasis was meaningful. Corwin and Louis (1982) note that a key reason why research findings do not have discernible influence on administrative practice is due to the existence of what they call "policy vacuums". Policy vacuums are said to exist when a condition characterized by the absence of the following exist:

1. An *organized* constituency of policy-makers to whom the research is directed.
2. *Agreement* among significant constituents and dominant coalitions on clear policy issues and identifiable research questions that need to be addressed.
3. *Consistent policies* pertaining to research findings in several areas of applications.

4. *Coordination* among independent agencies responsible for developing policies in various areas.

5. *Concrete, ongoing operational programs* targeted to use research findings.

Louis and Corwin (1982) note that these conditions are overlapping and mutually reinforcing and could be present in organizations in varying degrees. The notion of a policy vacuum is a particularly important one when we consider the utilization of findings in the area of organizational stress. We believe that important policy issues which need to be formulated are either not attended to or are attended to by the wrong person (i.e, someone who might have the least inclination to formulate such policies). Issues that need to be translated into programs often fail to make it on to important agendas. Often an absence of clear-cut guidelines and procedures pertaining to evaluation of research findings makes it exceedingly difficult for the findings to be readily implemented into policies that matter. One gets the impression that administrators probably do not really want the information that they almost ritualistically commission (Downs, 1965; Knorr, 1977).

It is difficult to understand, let alone deal effectively with such issues pertaining to different mixes of organizational culture and policy vacuums existing in contemporary organizations. Identifying organizational variables that must either be manipulated or circumvented or order to achieve better implementation of research findings is an important first step. It requires knowledge of political processes surrounding organizational interventions (Pettigrew, 1982) in addition to expert knowledge in a given area of specialization in the growing body of literature on human stress and cognition. In a similar vein, Hakel, Sorcher, Beer and Moses (1982) note that research with implementation in mind requires a very different orientation on the part of the organizational researcher compared to research where such objectives are not of crucial importance. The researcher must examine the motivation of the client system, the research subjects, and the senior administrators to provide valid data and to act on the conclusions of the research. Unless genuine involvement on the part of ultimate users of such knowledge is either present to begin with or created through various persuasive meetings, chances are that policy vacuums will prevent utilization. They also note that perceived relevance of the research questions and instruments is sometimes as important and maybe even more important than "scientific rigor." The observation that researchers and users belong to separate communities with different values and ideologies and that these differences impede utilization has been made by several authors (Dunnette and Brown, 1968; Duncan, 1974a, 1974b; Dunn, 1980; Rothman, 1980; Serpa, 1983). Some writers on the utilization process (Archibald, 1970; Van de Vall et al., 1976) even suggest that such cultural gaps become more crucial and difficult to manage when researchers are academics.

IMPLICATIONS FOR THE UTILIZATION OF RESEARCH ON STRESS AND COGNITION

Our analysis of the above mentioned constraints suggests that the processes surrounding utilization of knowledge are complex. Intervention techniques reported in the current literature on organizational change and development are examples of useful research based on some assumptions and concerns of practitioners (Argyris, 1970; French and Bell, 1973; Mason and Mitroff, 1981). Srivastava and Mitroff (1984) observe that these approaches explicitly acknowledge the fact that substantial differences in assumptions and frames of reference between organizational researchers and practitioners do indeed exist and that it is important to bridge such gaps. We suggest the following guidelines which we hope would lead to better utilization of research findings on human stress and cognition.

Guide I: Generating More Situation-Specific Theories to Facilitate Utilizations

The existing theories of stress and cognition need to be evaluated for their usefulness in specific organizational contexts. The various frameworks presented in this book are not necessarily universal in applicability: they can be adapted only selectively to facilitate better fits to organizational situations.It might also be useful to design some elements of the theoretical framework which are consistent with the frame of reference of the user systems (Thomas and Tyman, 1982; Weiss and Bucuvales, 1980; Srivastava and Mitroff, 1984). In line with the suggestion made by Srivastava and Mitroff (1984) we believe the following steps are particularly useful to consider.

1. How well do the research findings reflect the organization's particular reality? Are the findings adequate in purely descriptive terms?
2. Do the recommendations of the research programs have the potential to overcome some of the organizational barriers (such as policy vacuums) to effective utilization?
3. To what extent is the theoretical framework consistent with the frame of reference of the user systems (such as the dominant coalitions) of the organization?

Guide 2: Recognizing that the Act of Producing Useful Knowledge May Differ from that of Building a Science

Lindblom and Cohen (1979) describe the typical researcher as wanting to produce "authoritative knowledge." Such knowledge tends to be derived from a research base so thoroughly researched that no administrator should fail to use it. They present a set of convincing reasons why such knowledge is not likely to be produced. Bray (1983) suggests that it could indeed be effective for researchers to attempt to have their findings utilized even though such knowledge might not seem rigorous enough by scientific standards. He argues that organizations do no necessarily conduct their business with scientific principles, but rather with informed judgment on the part of key decision-makers. For example, when managers raise capital and decide between selling stocks and issuing bonds, they may have enough financial data and projections of staff economists but there is no way to tell if they would use the scientific data completely. The same situation exists when marketing managers are confronted with decisions pertaining to effectiveness of various advertising techniques. One method may be preferred over another even though the former may be regarded as being less effective based on scientific projections. Bray advises organizational researchers that, in spite of such a state of affairs, managers are better off using scientific findings in their decisions rather than acting with no valid scientific data at all. Informed judgment could indeed become more effective when it is guided appropriately by scientific considerations.

It is also true that not all findings from ambitious research programs, even the truly useful ones, could necessarily be implemented by organizations. There are, as we have already noted, policy vacuums in organizations which when coupled with resource considerations might make it difficult for organizations to apply scientific knowledge in creating strategic changes in policies and programs. Given these considerations we believe that it is wise for researchers not to get discouraged when their scientific findings are not appropriately utilized. A more realistic picture is that the contribution of research on stress and cognition in improving organizational practice is complex. The process of utilization of knowledge in organizations is not sufficiently understood. The scientific bases of utilization processes remain to be explored further and until such knowledge becomes available, the best that we could hope for is a trial and error method of utilization of knowledge during which the researcher has to be patient.

Guide 3: Using Principles of Small Wins to Redefine Organizational Issues of Stress and Cognition

Our third guide is derived from Weick's (1984) analysis of the technique of small wins to redefine the scale of social problems. Weick argues that despite the widespread assumption that social science is best suited to generate solutions to problems, it may indeed be more effective in addressing the redefinitions of the problems in the first place. A focus away from attempting to provide solutions, that is, the outcomes of the programs, to redefinition of the problems is rather significant, Weick argues, because the content of appropriate solutions is often implied by the definition of what the problem is to begin with. If organizational researchers succeed in redefining the scale of the problem (e.g., how to manage employee stress during times of economic downturns or preventing stress from sex discrimination practices, etc.) as minor and manageable rather than serious and overwhelming then they also succeed in lowering arousal on the part of practitioners. A state of low arousal is very appropriate if people don't know what to do or are unable to do it. Weick suggests that since most people tend to pay little attention to detailed features of the problems and to think in terms of a force or an undifferentiated dominant response which was well learned in the past (Nettler, 1980), they also might ignore strategic advantages of minor leverage points from which the problem might be more effectively tackled. This leads to a state of increased arousal which interferes with the diagnostic and decision-making abilities and therefore further reduces the effectiveness of past knowledge in bringing about a solution. At relatively high levels of arousal, coping responses become more primitive (Staw et al., 1981) and people find it increasingly difficult to learn a novel response, to brainstorm, to focus on the problem with increased cognitive complexity and differentiation, to perform complex responses, or to delegate and to resist information that supports positions they have taken (Holsti, 1978).

If organizational researchers lend their expertise in redefining the scale of organizational situations (i.e., using the techniques of small wins) which are stress producing in terms of the components of uncertainty, importance, and duration as proposed in Chapter 1, they will succeed in overcoming a major block to utilization of knowledge. In light of Weick's insightful analyses of the effectiveness of small wins in psychological and political terms, we feel compelled to recommend this strategy as the way to "open the door" for more effective utilization in the future. Repeatedly, social scientists have demonstrated that small changes are easier to implement than large ones. For instance, successive small requests are more likely to induce compliance (Freedman and Fraser, 1966). Theories are judged interesting when they tend to challenge assumptions with moderate intensity (Davis, 1971). When theories of scientists challenge the deep-rooted assumptions of the managers' model of organizational realities or when research findings disconfirm the social constructions of such realities, chances are that such theories and findings will not be well received. Because they produce major disruptions in the operating principles of the organization, they also might evoke similar countermeasures and severely alter expectations on the part of key policy-makers. This kind of reaction has the potential to render any attempts at utilization of knowledge rather fruitless. We feel that it is indeed wise for researchers to reconstruct their scientific findings in the light of the situational context of the client organization and to disseminate such findings with the principle of small wins in mind.

Guide 4: Cultivating Managerial Skills to Sustain Effective Implementation

By managerial skills we mean skills relating to administering of research efforts and effective presentation of the results of those efforts to the key participants of the organization. For example, when a principal investigator has a team of junior scientists working on a project, the efforts of each member of the team must be coordinated so as to contribute toward the successful completion of the project. Bray (1983) noted that several research groups have had less impact than they could have had because staff members followed their own particular research interests which were often unrelated to each other. Such diverse tendencies conflict with the data-collection efforts of the major investigation by creating resistance and reactivity on the part of the respondents. The communication of the findings, the second important managerial skill of the academic researcher, tends to be at variance with the expectation of the managers who are products of a different kind of organizational culture. Managers prefer brief reports that use analogies and provide guidelines for action. To put it more concisely in Bray's (1983) words: "managers do not usually take action because they have read a complete technical report nor on the basis of a simple statement of conclusions. It may be a bit mundane after flying high in the realms of science, but a well-conceptualized condensation of the research accompanied by legible visual aids can do wonders" (p. 430). We too have found this assertation to be an extremely valid one. In dealing with eventual users of their scientific findings, the researchers must cultivate the necessary skills that most good managers have. Once again, Douglas Bray's (1983) advice may be useful: one should be assertive but deferential, persistent but flexible, respectful but sociable. These skills might enable them to flourish more effectively in the complex culture of client organizations that affect the process of knowledge use. It might also be useful to practice the art of a reflective practitioner as Schon (1983) has recently recommended.

CONCLUSION

Our purpose in this chapter has been to go beyond the usual disappointments of researchers concerning utilization of knowledge on human stress and cognition in organizations and offer some guidelines for improving such a process. We discussed three major constraints that currently exist and offered some guidelines for solving some of the dilemmas associated with these constraints. In particular, we highlighted the usefulness of the technique of small wins as elaborated by Weick (1984) in coping with these issues in an intelligent manner. We agree with some of the conclusions of Carolyn Payton who suggests that the researchers must do "these hard things" (1984, p. 391) in order to enhance the status of their discipline both as a science and as a profession. She also suggests ways by which researchers might become more active as social advocates and bring about strategic changes. One of her recommendations is that those who can should get involved in the process of tackling the "hard" stuff of putting knowledge to use. As we take genuine interest in confronting these issues, we should be able to integrate scientific concerns with issues of application. Such an orientation will enable us to further validate the usefulness of theories of stress and cognition in an emerging organizational science.

REFERENCES

Archibald, K. A. Alternative orientations to social science utilization. *Social Science Information*, 1970 **9**, 7–34.

Argyris, C. *Intervention theory and method*, Reading, MA: Addison-Wesley, 1970.

Beres, M. B. Usefulness a research criterion: Reflections of a critical advocate. In R. H. Kilmann, K. W. Thomas, D. P. Slevin, R. Nath, and S. L. Jerrell (Eds.), *Producing useful knowledge for organizations*. New York: Praeger Publishers, 1983, pp. 351–376.

Beyer, J. M. (Ed.). The utilization of organizational research. *Administrative Science Quarterly*, 1982, **27**, 4.

Beyer, J. M. (Ed.). The utilization of organizational research. *Administrative Science Quarterly*, 1983, **28**, 1.

Bhagat, R. S. Intellectual performance and utilization in a two paradigm administrative and organizational science. In R .H. Kilman, K. W. Thomas, D. P. Slevin, R. Nath, and S. L. Jerrell (Eds.), *Producing useful knowledge for organizations*. New York: Praeger Publishers, 1983, pp. 196–220.

Blythe, P. *Stress disease: The emotional plague*. New York: St. Martin's Press, 1973.

Bray, D. W. Psychology and organizations: Are science and utility compatible. In R. H. Kilmann, K. W. Thomas, D. P. Slevin, R. Nath, and S. L. Jerrell (Eds.), *Producing useful knowledge for organizations* New York: Praeger Publishing, 1983, pp. 416–432.

Campbell, J. P., Daft, R. L., and Hulin, C. L. *What to study: Generating and developing research questions*. Beverly Hills, CA: Sage Publications, 1982.

Daubs, J. The mental health crisis in opthalmology. *American Journal of Opthalmology and Archives of American Academy of Opthalmology*, 1973, **50**, 816–822.

Davis, M. S. That's interesting: Towards a phenomenology of sociology and a sociology of phenomenology. *Philosophy of Social Science*, 1971, **1**, 309–344.

Downs, A. Some thoughts on giving people economic advice. *American Behavioral Scientist*, 1965, **9**, 30–32.

Dunbar, R. L. M. Toward an applied administrative science. *Administrative Science Quarterly*, 1983, **28**, 1, 129–144.

Duncan, W. J. Transferring management theory to practice. *Academy of Management Journal*, 1974a, **17**, 724–738.

Duncan, W. J. The researcher and the manager: A comparative view of the need for mutual understanding. *Management Science*, 1974b, **20**, 1157–1163.

Dunn, W. N. The two communities metaphor and models of knowledge use. *Knowledge: Creation, diffusion utilization*, 1980, **1**, 515–536.

Dunnette, M. D. and Brown, Z. M. Behavioral science research and the conduct of business. *Academy of Management Journal*, 1968, **11**, 177–187.

Freedman, J. L. and Fraser, S. C. Compliance without pressure: The foot-in-the-door technique. *Journal of Personality and Social Psychology*, 1966, **4**, 195–202.

French, W. L. and Bell, C. H. *Organizational development*. Englewood Cliffs, NJ: Prentice-Hall, 1973.

Greenwood III, J. W. and Greenwood, Jr., J. W. *Managing executive stress: A systems approach*. New York: Wiley-Interscience, 1979.

Guralwick, L. *Mortaility by occupation and cause of death (No. 3), Mortality by industry and cause of death (No. 4), Mortality by occupational level and cause of death (No. 5), Among men 20 to 64 years of age U. S. 1950*. U.S. Department of Health, Education and Welfare, Public Health Services, Vital Statistics, Special Reports, Vol. 53, 1963.

Hakel, M. D., Sorcher, M., Beer, M., and Moses, J. L. *Making it happen: Designing research with implementation in mind*. Beverly Hills, CA: Sage Publications, 1982.

Holsti, O. R. Limitations of cognitive abilities in the face of crisis. In C. F. Smart and W. T. Stanbury (Eds.), *Studies on crisis management*. Toronto: Butterworth, 1978, pp. 35–55.

Kilmann, R. H., Thomas, K. W., Slevin, D. P., Nath, R., and Jerrell, S. Z. *Producing useful knowledge for organizations*. New York: Praeger Publishers, 1983.

Knorr, K. D. Policy makers' use of social science knowledge: Symbolic or instrumental. In C. Weiss (Ed.), *Using social research in federal policy making*. Lexington, MA: Lexington Books, 1977, pp. 165–182.

Levinson, H. The abrasive personality. *Harvard Business Review*, 1978, **56**, 3, 86–94.

Lindblom, C. D. and Cohen, D. K. *Usable knowledge: Social science and social problem solving*. New Haven: Yale University Press, 1979.

Louis, K. S. and Corwin, R. G. Organizational barriers to utilization of research. *Administrative Science Quarterly*, 1982, **27**, 4, 623–640.

Mason, R. O. and Mitroff, I. I. *Challenging strategic planning assumptions*. New York: Wiley, 1981.

Mathias, P. F. Introducing change in organizations: Moving from general theories of content to specific theories of context. In R. H. Kilmann, K. W. Thomas, D. P. Slevin, R. Nath, and S. Z. Jerrell (Eds.), *Producing useful knowledge for organizations*. New York: Praeger Publishers, 1983, pp. 133–144.

Mausher, J. S. and Steppacher, R. C. Suicide in professionals: A study of male and female psychologists. *American Journal of Epidemiology*, 1973, **98**, 436–445.

Nettler, G. Notes on society; sociologist as advocate. *Canadian Journal of Sociology*, 1980, **5**, 31–53.

Ouchi, W. G. *Theory Z: How American business can meet the Japanese challenge*. Reading, MA: Addison-Wesley, 1981.

Payton, C. R. Who must do the hard things. *American Psychologist*, 1984, **39**, 4, 391–397.

Pettigrew, A. M. Towards a political theory of organizational intervention. In M. D. Hakel, M. Sorcher, M. Beer, and J. L. Moses (Eds.), *Making it happen: Designing research with implementation in mind*. Beverly Hills, CA: Sage Publications, 1982, pp. 41–60.

Pion, G. M. and Lipsey, M. W. Psychology and society: The challenge of change. *American Psychologist*, 1984, **39**, 7, 739–754.

Rothman, J. *Using research in organizations: A guide to successful application*. Beverly Hills, CA: Sage Publications, 1980.

Schon, D. A. *The reflective practitioners: How professionals think in action.* New York: Basic Books, 1983.

Serpa, R. Culture: The often ignored factor in knowledge utilization. In R. H. Kilmann, K. W. Thomas, D. P. Slevin, R. Nath, and S. Z. Jerrell (Eds.), *Producing useful knowledge for organizations.* New York: Praeger Publishers, 1983, pp. 121–132.

Srivastava, P. and Mitroff, I. I. Enhancing organizational research utilization: The role of decision makers' assumptions. *Academy of Management Review*, 1984, **9**, I, 18–26.

Staw, B. M., Sandelands, L. E., and Dutton, J. E. Threat-rigidity effects in organizational behavior: A multi-level analysis. *Administrative Science Quarterly*, 1981, **26**, 501–524.

Syme, S. L., Human, N. M., and Enterline, P. E. Some social and cultural factors associated with the occurrence of coronary heart disease. *Journal of Chronic Diseases*, 1964, **17**, 277–289.

Syme, S. L., Borhani, N. O., and Buechley, R. W. Cultural mobility and coronary heart disease in an urban area. *American Journal of Epidemiology*, 1965, **82**, 334–346.

Thomas, K. W. and Kilmann, R. H. Where have the organizational sciences gone? A survey of the Academy of Management membership. In R. H. Kilmann, K. W. Thomas, D. P. Slevin, R. Nath, and S. Z. Jerrell (Eds.), *Producing useful knowledge for organizations.* New York: Praeger Publishers, 1983, pp. 69–81.

Thomas, K. W. and Tyman, Jr., W. G. Necessary properties of relevant research: Lessons from recent criticisms of the organizational sciences. *Academy of Management Review*, 1982, **7**, 3, 345–352.

Van de Vall, M., Bolas, C., and Kang, T. S. Applied social research in industrial organizations: An evaluation of functions, theory, and methods. *Journal of Applied Behavioral Science*, 1976, **12**, 158–177.

Webb, W. B. The choice of the problem. *American Psychologist*, 1961, **16**, 5, 223–227.

Weiss, C. H. and Bucuvales, M. J. Truth tests and utility tests: Decision-makers frames of reference for social science research. *American Sociological Review*, 1980, **45**, 302–314.

Weick, K. E. Small wins: Redefining the scale of social problems. *American Psychologist*, 1984, **39**, 40–49.

Biographies

Terry A. Beehr is Professor of Psychology and Director of Doctoral Training in Industrial/Organizational Psychology at Central Michigan University. He obtained his Ph.D. in Psychology (Organizational) from The University of Michigan. He has previously held positions in the Institute for Social Research Organizational Behavior Program and the psychology departments at The University of Michigan and Illinois State University. During the 1984–1985 academic year he served as Visiting Professor in the management department at Oregon State University. He has published widely on the topic of job stress and its relationship to individual and organizational consequences. In 1984, his proposal on retirement and stress received the honorable mention in the Edwin L. Ghiselli award for research design from the Society for Industrial and Organizational Psychology of the American Psychological Association. He is also on the editorial board of *Personnel Psychology*.

Rabi S. Bhagat is an Associate Professor of Organizational Behavior and International Management in the School of Management at The University of Texas at Dallas. He is also the head of the Organizational Behavior program in the School. He received his Ph.D. from the University of Illinois at Urbana-Champaign in 1977. He has published numerous articles in the areas of job design, organizational stress, cross cultural management, and related topics. He won the James McKeen Cattell Award from the Division of Industrial and Organizational Psychology of the American Psychological Association in 1979, and his research on stress and cognition has been funded by the National Science Foundation. Currently, he is working on a book entitled *Management Across Cultures* (Scott-Foresman Publishers) with Harry C. Triandis of the University of Illinois. He is also on the editorial boards of the *Journal of Management* and the *Academy of Management Review*.

George V. Coelho is Chief of the Research Development Review Branch at the National Institute of Mental Health, Rockville, Maryland. He received his Ph.D. in Social Psychology from Harvard University in 1956.

433

His research publications include journal articles on coping behavior in stressful situations; foreign students in America; intergroup contact; and cross-cultural research on college youth. He has authored and edited several books: *Social Change and Human Behavior* (with E. A. Rubinstein), NIMH, 1972; *Coping and Adaptation,* (with D. A. Hamburg and J. E. Adams, Basic Books, New York, 1974); *Uprooting and Development* (with P. I. Ahmed, Plenum, New York, 1980).

He has served as international education and health science consultant to the World Health Organization, UNESCO, International Institute for Environment and Development, Indian Science Congress Association, Indian Council for Social Science Research.

His current professional interests focus on health and behavior; stress management and executive health; dynamics of organizational behavior; comparative organizational climates; and managerial styles of coping.

Cary L. Cooper received his B.S. and M.B.A. degrees from the University of California, Los Angeles, his Ph.D. from the University of Leeds (U.K.) and an honorary M.Sc. from the University of Manchester (U.K.). He is the only American to have held a chair in a British university in the field of management and organization behavior. He is currently Professor of Organizational Psychology and immediate past Chairman of the Department of Management Sciences, University of Manchester Institute of Science and Technology. Professor Cooper is past Chairman of the Management Education and Development Division of the American Academy of Management (the first time a U.K.-based academic has been elected to this post). In addition, he was elected as a Fellow of the British Psychological Society and is an adviser to two United Nations agencies: the World Health Organization on Psychosocial Factors in Occupational Health and the International Labor Office on Automation, Work Intensity, and Occupational Stress.

Professor Cooper is currently editor of the international quarterly journal, the *Journal of Occupational Behaviour,* published by John Wiley and Sons, New York and London. He is also on the Editorial Board or has been special issue Editor of a number of other international scholarly journals, (e.g., Portuguese Journal of Psychology *Analise Psicologica,* Leadership and Organisation Development Journal, Small Group Behaviour, etc). He has published more than 30 books (e.g., *The Stress Check* and *Executive Families Under Stress*). He is also the author of more than 200 scholarly articles in academic journals.

David L. Ford, Jr. is Professor of Organizational Behavior in the School of Management at The University of Texas at Dallas. He obtained his Ph.D. in Organizational Analysis from the University of Wisconsin-Madison in 1972. Professor Ford has taught at Purdue University (1972–1975) and served as a Visting Professor at Michigan State University (1975) and Yale University (1980–81). He is a member of the Board of

Directors of NTL Institute for Applied Behavioral Science and will assume the Chairmanship of the Board in 1985. He has served on the Editorial Board of the *Academy of Management Review*, and has published a number of articles dealing with individual and group decision processes, job design issues, and minority group relations in organizations, including his book, *Readings in Minority Group Relations* (San Diego, Calif.: University Associates, 1976).

Nina Gupta is Assistant Professor of Management at the University of Arkansas. She received her Ph.D. in Organizational Psychology from the University of Michigan in 1975. Since then, she has worked as a Research Investigator at the Institute for Social Research (1975–1977), and as a Project Director at the Southwest Educational Development Laboratory (1978–1983), studying various aspects of employee stress, among other issues. She has published numerous journal articles on stress, withdrawal, financial incentives, and so on, and is currently preparing a book about "new design" organizations (with G. Douglas Jenkins, Jr.). She is part of a dual-career couple and, therefore, has both personal and professional interest in the stresses of dual-career couples.

G. Douglas Jenkins, Jr. is Associate Professor of Management at the University of Arkansas. After receiving his degree in Organizational Psychology at the University of Michigan in 1977, he joined the Department of Management at The University of Texas. In addition to his personal and professional interests in the problems faced by dual-career couples, he has researched and published in the areas of job design, employee compensation, employee participation, and employee withdrawal. He has a book in preparation on "new design" organizations (with Nina Gupta), and is engaged in a large sample study of the precursors and correlates of productivity among academic psychologists.

Todd D. Jick is Associate Professor of Organizational Behavior at the Faculty of Administrative Studies, York University (Toronto). He obtained his Ph.D. in Organizational Behaviour at Cornell University in 1978. Professor Jick has held visiting appointments at Columbia University Graduate School of Business (1981–1982) and at Harvard University Graduate School of Business (1984–1985).

Professor Jick has published several articles dealing with organizational change and crisis. He continues to do writing and research on the stress of hard times in organization and the management of recovery.

Ralph Katz is a Professor in the Mangement of Technology and Organizational Behavior areas at the College of Business Administration, Northeastern University. He received his Ph.D. in Management from the Wharton Graduate School, University of Pennsylvania. Prior to joining Northeastern University, Professor Katz taught for ten years at the Sloan School of Management, MIT, (1973–1983).

Professor Katz has published extensively in leading professional journals, including *The Academy of Management Journal, Management Science, R&D Management,* and the *Administrative Science Quarterly.* He was recently awarded the 1981 "New Concept Award" by the organizational behavior division of the National Academy of Management. Professor Katz's current research, education, and consulting activities are in the area of Research, Development, and Technology-Based Innovation with particular interests in the management of technical professionals and project teams.

Ann E. McGoldrick has been Research Fellow at the University of Manchester since 1973 and is now Research Fellow and Consultant working within the Department of Management Sciences at the University of Manchester Institute of Science and Technology in the areas of organizational psychology and personnel management. Two major studies she has undertaken for the Economic and Social Research Council concern the social and psychological effects of early retirement and older employees' attitudes toward work and retirement. She participated in the 1981–1982 House of Commons' enquiry into *The Age of Retirement* and has published many articles and conference papers on aspects of aging in industry and retirement.

Ann McGoldrick is currently serving as a Consultant to the Equal Opportunities Commission and will shortly be publishing a report for them entitled *Discrimination in Occupational Pension Schemes,* and she is working on another book for John Wiley with Cary L. Cooper: *Experiencing Early Retirement: The Economic, Social and Psychological Effects.*

Randall S. Schuler is Associate Professor, Graduate School of Business, New York University. Dr. Schuler's interests are stress and time management, organizational uncertainty, personnel and human resource management, and the interface of business strategy and human resource management. He has authored and edited several books including *Personnel and Human Resource Management, 2nd. ed., Case Problems in Management, 2nd. ed., Effective Personnel Management, Book of Readings in Personnel and Human Resource Management, 2nd ed., Human Resources Management in the 1980s,* and *Managing Job Stress.* In addition, he has contributed numerous chapters to reading books and has published extensively in professional journals. Currently he is serving as President-Elect of the Eastern Academy of Management and is on the Editorial Board of the *Academy of Management Journal, Journal of Management,* and *Group and Organizational Studies.* Since obtaining his Ph.D. from Michigan State University in 1973, he has taught at Cleveland State University, Penn State University, Ohio State University, and the University of Maryland as well as at New York University.

James C. Segovis is the program manager for the office of education for the Federal Home Loan Bank System. He was an Assistant Professor of Business Administration at Austin College, Sherman, Texas. He is currently completing the doctoral program at the University of Texas at Dallas in organizational behavior. He has coauthored several articles and book reviews that have appeared in the *Journal of Applied Psychology*, *Journal of Small Group Behavior*, *Administrative Science Quarterly*, the *Academy of Management Proceedings*, and *Personnel Selection and Training Bulletin*. His research interests have focused on cognitive appraisal, coping, and the effects of life stress and job stress in organizations.

James R. Terborg is Associate Professor and Head of the Department of Management at the University of Oregon. He obtained his Ph.D. in Organizational Psychology from Purdue University. Professor Terborg has taught at the University of Illinois-Urbana (1975–1978), the University of Houston (1978–1980), and the University of Oregon (1980–present).

Dr. Terborg has served on the Editorial Board of the *Journal of Applied Psychology* since 1982. In 1983 he was elected to the status of Fellow in the American Psychological Association. He has published more than 20 articles on topics of motivation, work groups, absenteeism, turnover, organizational effectiveness, and women in organizations.

R. Van Harrison is an Assistant Research Scientist at the Institute for Social Research, Assistant Professor in the Department of Postgraduate Medicine and Health Professions Education, and Director of the Office of Continuing Medical Education, University of Michigan. He received his Ph.D. in Social Psychology from the University of Michigan in 1976. Dr. Harrison's initial research activities focused on job stress, including coauthorship of the monograph *Job Demands and Worker Health* (Ann Arbor, Mich.: Institute for Social Research, 1980) and coauthorship of its sequel *The Mechanisms of Job Stress and Strain* (New York: Wiley, 1982). His research interests have broadened into other areas of health psychology and organizational behavior, including motivational factors affecting performance in the delivery of health care. While expanding his interests, he has continued to pursue the area of job stress. His current research activities include a study of the relationship of Type A behavior to fit between individuals and their jobs, relationships between individuals and their spouses, and job strain.

Author Index

439

Subject Index